Computers

Tools for an Information Age

Fifth Edition

H. L. CAPRON

Addison-Wesley

An Imprint of Addison Wesley Longman, Inc.

Reading, Massachusetts
Menlo Park, California
New York
Harlow, England
Don Mills, Ontario
Sydney
Mexico City
Madrid
Amsterdam

Sponsoring Editor	Carol Crowell
Production Management	Jean Lake
Project Manager	Bess Deck
Editorial Assistant	Kerry Connor
Senior Marketing Manager	Michelle Hudson
Marketing Coordinator	Deanna Storey
Market Specialist	David Noyes
Art Direction	Karen Rappaport, Gina Hagen
Text Design/Composition	Mark Ong, Susan Riley
Cover and Part Opener Concept Development	Joseph Maas, with Mark Ong and Karen Rappaport
Cover and Part Opener Illustrations	Joseph Maas
Cover Typography Design	Mark Ong
Text Illustrations	Illustrious, Inc.
Photo Editor and Researcher	Kelli d'Angona
Copy Editor	Rebecca Pepper
Prepress Services Buyer	Caroline Fell
Manufacturing Supervisor	Hugh Crawford

© Copyright 1998 by Addison Wesley Longman
Publishing Company, Inc.

Library of Congress Cataloging-in-Publication Data

Capron, H. L.
    Computers : tools for an information age / H. L. Capron. — 5th ed.
      p.   cm.
    Includes index.
    ISBN 0–201–30558–5 (Student)
    ISBN 0–201–33613–8 (AIE)
    1. Computers.   I. Title.
QA76.5.C363   1997
004- -dc21

97-18142
CIP

1 2 3 4 5 6 7 8 9 10   DOW   01 00 99 98 97

Dedicated to

> **Gretchen Schumacher**

Computers

Tools for an Information Age, Fifth Edition

➤ Complete Instructional Support System

The ancillary package for the Fifth Edition has been completely revised and expanded to meet the needs of a modern introduction to computer courses. The following ancillaries are free to qualified adopters.

Student CD-ROM. Included free with every new copy of the student text, this digital companion to the main text offers state-of-the-art 3-D animation, thought-provoking video clips, interactive tutorials, an off-line web simulator and tutorial, and sample software programs. The student CD is an expansion of the content in the main text and serves as a complementary learning tool.

Off-line Web Simulator and Tutorial provides students practice in navigating, understanding, and evaluating Internet content in a completely self-contained environment that does not require an online connection. The Web Simulator is included on both the student CD-ROM and on the Instructor's Resource Disk. Web browser software is included. Requires Windows 95.

World Wide Web Site (http://hepg.awl.com/capron/). Completely expanded and updated for the new edition, the Capron web site provides current updates to text and instructor support materials, links to external web sites for the Planet Internet exercises in the text, and expansions and updates to Pocket Internet.

Capron's *Pocket Internet: 2001 Sites.* This pocket reference guide is free with every new copy of the student text. The author personally selected 2001 Internet sites with content relevant and interesting to students' lives. Sites are grouped by topic. There are approximately 100 topics, some serious, some less so. A sample of topics includes Animation, Architecture, Arts, Best-Hot-Cool, Finance and Investing, Career/Jobs, Computer Science, Cool Companies, Education, Entertainment, Entrepreneurs, Financial Aid, Fitness and Health, Free Stuff, Home Page Advice, Internet Directories, Java, Multimedia, Research, Résumé Services, Robotics, Search Engines, Sports, and Virtual Community. Introductory sections are: Pocket Start, Pocket FAQs, Pocket Tips, and Pocket Dictionary.

Instructor's Edition with Annotations. This special edition contains annotations (by Jerry Reed) for lecture preparation and includes supplementary material not found in the Instructor's Resource Manual. The annotations include *Group Work* notes, *Critical Thinking* questions, *Infobits*, *Global Perspective* notes, *Learn By Doing* notes, and alphabetized key terms.

Instructor's Resource Disk. Packaged with the printed Instructor's Resource Manual, this CD-ROM provides the complete contents of the printed Instructor's Manual and Test Bank. Also included are Addison-Wesley's TestGen EQ and Quiz Master EQ networkable testing program, all the art from the main text, specially authored classroom presentation materials, and the Off-line Web Simulator and Tutorial.

Instructor's Manual and Test Bank, by H. L. Capron. Written by the author, this comprehensive manual provides the printed support you need for easier class preparation. Teaching notes from the author include learning objectives for each chapter, a chapter overview, a detailed lecture outline, and a list of key words for each chapter.

A printout of the complete electronic test bank is included. Question formats include multiple choice, true/false, matching, and completion exercises. Answer keys and page references for test questions are provided. Also includes Instructor's Resource CD-ROM.

Computerized Test Bank and Network Testing. The test generation software is fully networkable. TestGen EQ's graphical interface lets instructors view, edit, and add questions; transfer questions to tests; and print tests in various fonts and forms. Search and sort features let the instructor quickly locate questions and arrange them in a preferred order. Four question formats are available: multiple choice, true/false, matching, and short answer. Grading is done automatically, and analysis for each test is included.

Videotapes. Addison Wesley Longman makes available to qualified adopters free videotapes from our library of commercially produced tapes. Use this resource to enhance your lectures on concepts presented in the text. Your Addison Wesley Longman sales representative has details about this offer. Special restrictions sometimes apply.

Software. Addison Wesley Longman is aware of the need to have the most current software application programs available to students in introductory computer courses. We are pleased to partner with colleges and universities to achieve this goal through our Software Donation Program.

By adopting Addison Wesley Longman Information Systems textbooks, your school can qualify for free software programs and site licenses to be used by your students in your school's computer lab.

Brief Contents

Detailed Contents

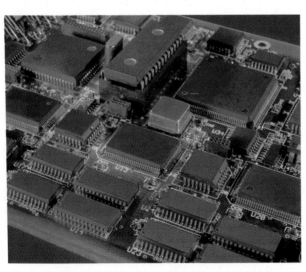

CHAPTER 8
Security and Privacy: Computers and the Internet   223

Part Five

Software Tools   317

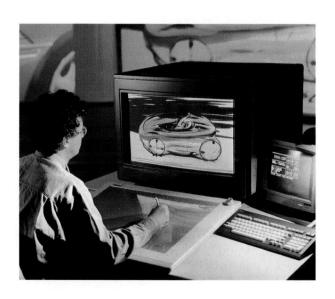

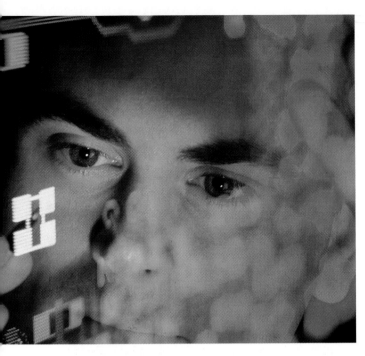

The Buyer's Guide and Galleries

Buyer's Guide
(follows page 32)

This eight-page section presents issues and questions to consider before buying a personal computer and software.

GALLERY 1
Making Microchips
(follows page 96)

This gallery describes how silicon chips are made, from the design stage through manufacturing, testing, and packaging the final product.

GALLERY 2
The Visual Internet
(follows page 192)

The Internet and the World Wide Web have added a new visual dimension to how we interact with computers. This gallery features World Wide Web sites with a strong visual impact and innovative multimedia aspects.

GALLERY 3
Computer Graphics
(follows page 288)

Rather than using paintbrushes or chalk, some artists use the computer to create their artworks. This gallery features both pure art and commercial applications.

GALLERY 4
Computers at Work
(follows page 416)

The computer has become an essential tool in the world of everyday workers. This gallery examines computers in a variety of workplace settings.

Preface

Computer technology, particularly the Internet, is changing so quickly that we decided to publish this edition a year early. *Computers: Tools for an Information Age,* fifth edition, is up-to-date in every respect, from DVDs to MMX chips to cookies to push technology. The connectivity theme is integrated into several aspects of the book. In particular, we make it easy for students to explore the Internet.

▶ New in the Fifth Edition: Focus on the Internet

The Internet is close to center stage in this edition. Notable additions and changes are as follows:

- **Quick start in Chapter 1.** The Internet is introduced in Chapter 1, in a section that gives basic information about the Web, browsers, servers, and Internet protocol.
- **New Internet chapter.** Chapter 7, "The Internet: A Resource for All of Us," focuses on the important aspects of Internet technology, from URLs to links to search engines. This chapter may be used independently of other chapters if students want information early on. Chapter 7 begins on page 195.
- **Planet Internet.** In this edition, Planet Internet has been expanded to a two-page spread at the end of each chapter. Without being technically oriented, each one introduces students to some aspect of the World Wide Web. Topics include places to start, global aspects of the Internet, FAQs, business, entrepreneurs, shopping, careers, entertainment, and resources. Each Planet Internet suggests hands-on Internet exercises and is supported through the Planet Internet pages on the Capron web site. To see Planet Internet examples, please turn to pages 64, 92, and 220, and visit the Planet Internet pages at:
  http://hepg.awl.com/capron/planet/
- **Web site.** The Capron web site provides links to all sites mentioned in the Planet Internet features and in the Visual Internet gallery, and to hundreds of other sites:
  http://hepg.awl.com/capron/

- **HTML Primer.** Appendix B provides HTML instruction for beginners. After studying the HTML tags and the corresponding examples, a student should be able to use HTML to write a simple home page.
- **Internet Gallery.** The Visual Internet gallery features World Wide Web sites that have a visual impact. In particular, a two-page spread in the gallery displays and describes sites that offer innovative multimedia features.
- **Java.** The use of Java applets on web sites is described in Chapter 7.
- **Internet service providers and rating the Internet.** Some boxed features about the Internet are "Should You Choose an Online Service or an Internet Service Provider?" (Chapter 6, page 185), "Choosing an Internet Service Provider" (Chapter 7, page 203), and "Internet Rating Systems" (Chapter 7, page 208).
- **Internet security and history.** Internet security issues, including cookies and government intervention, are examined in Chapter 8. The history of the Internet is described briefly in Chapter 7. As appropriate, the Internet is mentioned in several other chapters.

▶ Also New in This Edition

In addition to increased coverage of the Internet, we have added and re-emphasized several topics and have created new features.

- **Multimedia.** Whether on CD-ROMs or on the Internet, multimedia continues to be a major newsmaker in the computer industry. Underlying CD-ROM technology and multimedia applications are described in Chapter 5 on storage. See Figure 5-11 on page 137. A Planet Internet discussion focuses on multimedia on the Internet (Chapter 9, page 274).
- **Ethics.** Three major categories are included in the chapters: Ethics and Software (Chapter 2, page 47), Ethics and Data (Chapter 4, page 116), and Ethics and Privacy (Chapter 8, page 241). In addition, a two-page Planet Internet is devoted to Internet-related ethics (Chapter 12, page 344).

- **Office 97.** All screens for hands-on applications have been redone using Microsoft Office 97.
- **Getting Practical.** This boxed feature, one in each chapter, covers various topics of practical interest to students, such as getting pictures into the computer (Chapter 4, page 109), or even whether to build your own computer (Chapter 3, page 81).
- **New Directions.** This feature examines computer-related trends as they may affect people today and in the future. Examples include the computerized home (Chapter 2, page 46), future chips (Chapter 3, page 85), and a library without books (Chapter 5, page 127).
- **Quick Poll.** Some instructors find gathering student opinions to be a useful springboard for discussion. In each chapter, three possibilities are suggested on a topic from the chapter. See examples of Quick Polls on pages 89 and 188.

▶ Organization of the Text

The text is divided into an introductory photo essay and five parts, followed by four appendices:

- The opening Photo Essay gives students a feeling for the exciting world of computers and shows the diverse ways that people use them.
- Part 1, "An Overview of Computers," has two chapters, one to introduce hardware and another to introduce software, including home and business applications and brief coverage of operating systems.
- Part 2, "Hardware Tools," explores computer hardware, including coverage of the central processing unit, input/output, and storage.
- Part 3, "Internet Tools," begins with networking, moves forward to a separate Internet chapter, and concludes with security and privacy issues, especially as they relate to the Internet.
- Part 4, "Applications Tools," presents the basics of word processing and desktop publishing, spreadsheets and business graphics, and database management systems. These applications are presented in a generic manner to introduce students to the concepts of these applications without teaching commands specific to software packages.
- Part 5, "Software Tools," looks at software, including programming and languages, operating systems, and systems analysis and design. Subsequent chapters examine how computers are used in management of information systems and in cutting edge topics such as artificial intelligence, expert systems, robotics, and virtual reality.
- Appendices are offered on the history of computing, how to write your own web page using HTML, the programming process, and number systems.

▶ Special Features

We have already described the new features called Getting Practical and New Directions, the expanded two-page Planet Internet, and the Visual Internet gallery. In addition, the book offers:

- **Making the Right Connections.** Each chapter includes a feature article on linking people to computers. Topics range from the connectivity of workers in remote regions of Alaska (Chapter 2, page 56) to computers that can notify police if they are stolen (Chapter 4, page 96).
- **Margin notes.** To further engage the student, margin notes are placed throughout the text. The margin notes extend the text material by providing additional information and highlighting interesting applications of computers. Topics range from computerized student ID cards (Chapter 4, page 102) to shorthand favored by newsgroup users (Chapter 7, page 209).
- **Buyer's Guide gallery.** Students and their families are making important economic decisions about the purchase of a computer for their educational, personal, and business needs. This concise eight-page guide offers students information to aid hardware and software purchases.
- **Making Microchips gallery.** The gallery text, supplemented by color photos, describes how microprocessors are made.
- **Computer Graphics gallery.** The color photographs in this gallery vividly show the sophistication of computer graphics.
- **Computers at Work gallery.** This gallery of color photographs shows how computers are commonly and not-so-commonly used in the workplace.
- **Appealing writing style.** The author's writing style is known to be student friendly. More critical, however, is that the material is written in context. That is, material is presented with real-life examples, as opposed to the style of a hardware catalog. Each chapter begins with a real-world story that leads the student into the material; further examples are sprinkled throughout the chapter.

▶ In-Text Learning Aids

Each chapter includes the following pedagogical support:

- At the beginning of each chapter, **learning objectives** provide key concepts for students.
- **Key terms** are boldfaced throughout the text.
- A **Chapter Review** offers a summary of core concepts and boldfaced key terms.
- A **Quick Poll** offers ideas to generate class discussion.
- **Discussion Questions** encourage students to take what has been presented in the chapter and discuss it more thoroughly.
- The **Student Study Guide** offers objective questions that students can answer to check their comprehension of essential concepts.

A complete **Glossary** and comprehensive **Index** are included at the end of the text.

▶ Service

Addison Wesley Longman is committed to providing you with service that is second to none. We would like to thank you for your interest in this textbook, and encourage you to contact us with your questions and comments. Please write to:

is@awl.com if the Information Systems team can be of assistance. We welcome any and all feedback about our company and products.

capron@awl.com if you have questions for the author about the material in this book.

Capron's Proven Pedagogy

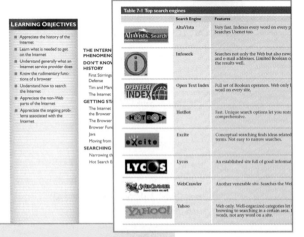

In Capron's fifth edition, the new **Chapter 7**, "The Internet: A Resource for All of Us," covers important aspects of Internet technology, from the Internet's origins to choosing a search engine.

Each chapter of the text features a two-page spread devoted to helping students appreciate the variety of information available on the Internet. Explanations are written in nontechnical terms. Hands-on Planet Internet exercises include links to web pages where students can continue their exploration.

I n each chap-
ter, a Getting
Practical box
describes how
students can
enhance their
experiences with
computers inside
or outside the
classroom.

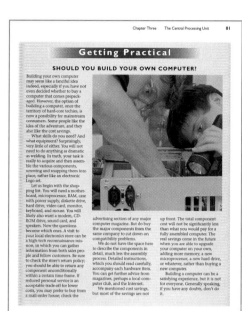

The Check Is Not in the Mail

As of January 1, 1999, all payments from the federal government, including Social Security
checks, are made directly to bank
accounts, using electronic funds
transfers.

Since it costs approximately
42¢ to issue and mail a paper
check but only 2¢ to process an
electronic payment, the government saves many millions of dollars every year. There are advantages to recipients too: the
payments arrive exactly on time
and, unlike paper checks, cannot
be lost in the mail.

M argin notes provide
interesting information
about computers that
motivates, entertains, and expands
on chapter content.

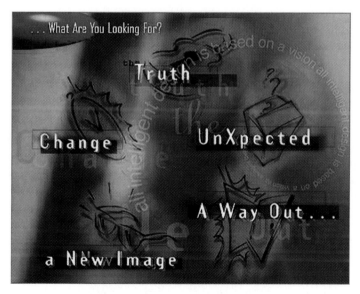

N ew Directions boxes
appear in each chapter to
highlight how technology
may affect our future.

B ringing the Internet alive, the new Visual Internet gallery features sites that
showcase the emerging visual and multimedia capabilities of the Internet.

Acknowledgments

Many people contributed to the success of this project. Although a single sentence hardly suffices, we would like to thank some of the key people. Jean Lake, as production manager, skillfully coordinated the efforts of many people, keeping the book on the accelerated schedule that contributes to its currency. Kelli d'Angona was a creative and tenacious photo researcher who tracked down outstanding pictures. Designer Mark Ong presented superb design solutions to endlessly changing thorny problems. Joseph Maas used his special talents to create the colorful and innovative cover and part openers. Project manager Bess Deck provided able assistance, on matters large and small, on a daily basis. Marketing manager Michelle Hudson raised marketing to a new level, so we could ascertain and respond to customer needs. Editorial assistant Kerry Connor's hard work and enthusiasm made a major contribution to the project, particularly Pocket Internet. Sponsoring editor Carol Crowell brought significant experience to the project, skillfully balancing creative and practical needs.

Reviewers and consultants have provided valuable contributions that improved the quality of the book. Their names are listed here, and we wish to express our sincere gratitude to them.

Ann Allen, Mid Michigan Community College, MI

William Allen, University of Central Florida, FL

GiGi Beaton, Tyler Junior College, TX

Linda Boyer, University of Phoenix, NM

Stuart Brown, Wichita State University, KS

Ken Craver, Tyler Junior College, TX

Peter Drexel, Plymouth State College, NH

Linda Ericksen, Lane Community College, OR

Carl Freitag, Florida A & M, FL

Burt Greene, Purchase College, State University of New York, NY

Elaine Haight, Foothill College, CA

Sally Hanson, Mercer County Community College, PA

Dan Heighton, Clark State Community College, OH

Lee Hunt, Collin County Community College, TX

Shelley Kersh, Tyler Junior College, TX

Emily Kim

Dan Leavitt, Queens College, City University of New York, NY

William Lupton, Morgan State University, MD

Donna Madsen, Kirkwood Community College, IA

Dan Marrs, Rose State College, OK

Dan Matthews, Tri-State University, IN

Lester McCann, University of Central Oklahoma, OK

John McClellan

Domingo Molina, University of Texas at Brownsville, TX

Pat Ormond, Utah Valley State College, UT

Mary Penick, Cameron University, OK

Richard Plant, Maritime Institute, MD

Patricia Riden, Western Illinois University, IL

Raymond Yu, Douglas College, British Columbia, Canada

Lynda VanVleet, Heidelberg College, OH

Survey Respondents

Ann Allen, Mid Michigan Community College, MI

Karen Rapp Anderson, Normandale Community College, MN

Don Bergman, Olympic College, WA

Janie Blum, Jefferson College, MO

Jim Broos, Davidson Community College, NC

Sherman Cold, Utah Valley State College, UT

Ken Crosslin, Yakima Valley Community College, WA

Sergio Davalos, University of Portland, OR

Bill Daley, University of Oregon, OR

Don Distler, Belleville Area College, IL

Allen Dooley, Pasadena City College, CA

Barbara Ellestad, Montana State University, MT

Michael Forgerson, Santa Clarita, CA

James Frost, Idaho State University, ID

Minnie Ghent, Indian River Community College, FL

Randolph Gibson, Indian River Community College, FL

Frank Green, University of Maryland, MD

Burt Greene, Purchase College, State University of New York, NY

John Gumaer, Utah Valley State College, UT

James Hammond, Winthrop University, SC

Dan Heighton, Clark State Community College, OH

Todd Herring, IUPUI, IN

George Hickman, Utah Valley State College, UT

Jon Huhtala, Ferris State University, MI

Connie Jensen

Jim Kasum, University of Wisconsin, WI

Gordon Kimbell, Everett Community College, WA

Gary Klotz, Milwaukee Area Tech College, WI

Taowen Le, Southern Utah University, UT

Deborah Ludford, Glendale Community College, CA

Donna Madsen, Kirkwood Community College, IA

Dan Marrs, Rose State College, OK

Barbara Mason, Wichita State University, KS

Dan Matthews, Tri-State University, IN

Lester McCann, University of Central Oklahoma, OK

Karen Meyer, Wright State University, OH

David Middleton, Indiana Institute of Technology, IN

James Moore, Indiana University–Purdue University Fort Wayne, IN

Denise Norris, Evergreen Valley College, CA

George Novotny, Ferris State University, MI

Pat Ormond, Utah Valley State College, UT

George Petrovay, University of Southern California, CA

Son Pham, California State University at Northridge, CA

Carol Pollard, University of Colorado, CO

Kristan Presnell, Anne Arundel Community College, MD

Susan Reeder, Seattle University, WA

Harold Sentman, Crafton Hills, CA

Michelle Setzer, Blue Ridge Community College, NC

Emily Stephens

Lesia Strong, Oklahoma State University, OK

Thomas Turner, University of Central Oklahoma, OK

Jack Van Deventer, Washington State University, WA

Roger VanHolzen, Northwest Missouri State University, MO

Teaching Software Applications?

Addison Wesley Longman offers two market-leading software lab series to choose from. It's easy to create a custom package designed specifically for your course by packaging any combination of lab manuals with Capron's *Computers: Tools for an Information Age.* Contact your local sales representative for details, or write to us at **is@awl.com.**

▶ The SELECT Lab Series

SELECT features a highly visual, project-based approach that includes running case studies based on real-world situations. Numerous full-color screen shots help students follow the projects step by step. End-of-project review questions, assignments, and Internet exercises help reinforce the material and encourage critical thinking.

Office 97 lab manuals are supported by an Instructor's Resource CD-ROM that includes test bank software, LAN-based testing, all art files from the books, a PowerPoint lecture show, solutions files, student data files, the Instructor's Manual, and more. Visit the SELECT web site at **http://hepg.awl.com/select/.**

SELECT Labs Available

Internet/WWW

Internet
HTML
Netscape Communicator
Internet Explorer

Office Suites

Microsoft Office 97 Professional
Microsoft Office Professional for Windows 95
Microsoft Office Professional

Integrated Packages

Works 4.0
Works 3.0

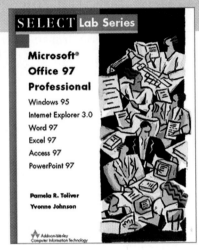

Operating Systems

Windows 95
Windows 3.1

Word Processing

Word 97
Word 7.0
Word 6.0
WordPerfect 7.0
WordPerfect 6.1

Spreadsheets

Excel 97
Excel 7.0
Excel 5.0
Quattro Pro 7
Quattro Pro 6
Lotus 1-2-3 release 5

Database

Access 97
Access 7.0
Access 2.0
Paradox 7

Presentation Graphics/Desktop Publishing

PowerPoint 97
PowerPoint 7.0
PowerPoint 4.0
PageMaker 6.5 for Windows 95

Programming

Visual Basic 5.0
Visual Basic 4.0

➤ Tim Duffy Lab Series for Office 97

Written by a highly successful author and experienced instructor, the *Tim Duffy Lab Series* features a visual and conceptual approach to learning Office 97. In full color and beautifully illustrated, Duffy's lab manuals begin by exploring what the software is and why it is important, then show how to use the software. Features throughout each project that help students master the software include a running case study, *Timely Tips, Own Your Own, Reinforcing the Exercise*, and Internet exercises.

Office 97 lab manuals are supported by an Instructor's Resource CD-ROM that includes test bank software, LAN-based testing, all art files from the books, a PowerPoint lecture show, solutions files, student data files, the Instructor's Manual, and more. Visit the *Tim Duffy Lab Series* web site at

http://www.awl.com/office97/

Recent Duffy releases:

Microsoft Office 97 Professional

Windows 95

Word 97

Excel 97

Access 97

PowerPoint 97

Common Features of Office 97

Internet Explorer

INTRODUCTION

Photo Essay

The Age of Information

The dawn of a new age—the Information Age—glows before us with the promise of new ways of thinking, living, and working. The amount of information in the world is said to be doubling every six to seven years. Can we keep up? We can, but not without an understanding of how computers work and the ability to control them for our own purposes.

STEPPING OUT
Forging a Computer-Based Society
A Computer in Your Future
Computer Literacy for All
THE NATURE OF COMPUTERS
WHERE COMPUTERS ARE USED

➤ Stepping Out

Your first steps toward joining the Information Age include understanding how we got to where we are today. Perhaps you recall from history books how the Industrial Age took its place in our world. In just a few years, society accepted the dizzying introduction of electricity, telephones, radio, automobiles, and airplanes. Compared to the Industrial Age, the Information Age is evolving even more rapidly. It is likely to continue to evolve well into the twenty-first century.

Forging a Computer-Based Society

Traditional economics courses define the cornerstones of an economy as land, labor, and capital. Today we can add a fourth key economic element: information. As we evolve from an industrial to an information society, our jobs are changing from physical to mental labor. Just as people moved physically from farms to factories in the Industrial Age, so today people are shifting muscle power to brain power in a new, computer-based society.

You are making your move, too, taking your first steps by signing up for this computer class and reading this book. But should you go further and get your own computer? We look next at some of the reasons why you might.

Workers and their computers.
Whether in the office or on the road, these workers all use computers to help get the work done.

A Computer in Your Future

Computers have moved into every nook and cranny of our daily lives. Whether or not you personally know anything about it, you invoke computers when you make a bank withdrawal, buy groceries at the supermarket, and even when you drive your car. But will you have a computer at your personal disposal? The answer today is "probably." Although only a third of Americans have personal computers in their homes, a much higher percentage use computers on the job. Almost any career in your future will involve a computer in some way.

In their homes people use various forms of computer technology not only as playthings but also for keeping track of bank accounts; communicating with friends and associates; monitoring inside temperature and humidity; and teaching math, reading, and other skills to children.

Computer Literacy for All

Why are you studying about computers? In addition to curiosity (and perhaps a course requirement), you probably recognize that it will not be easy to get through the rest of your life without knowing about computers. We offer a three-pronged definition of computer literacy:

- **Awareness.** As you study about computers, you will become aware of their importance, their versatility, and their pervasiveness in our society.
- **Knowledge.** You will learn what computers are and how they work. This requires learning some technical jargon, but do not worry—no one expects you to become a computer expert.
- **Interaction.** There is no better way to understand computers than through interacting with one. So being computer literate also means being able to use a computer for some simple applications.

Note that no part of this definition suggests that you must be able to create the instructions that tell a computer what to do. That would be akin to saying that anyone who plans to drive a car must first become an auto mechanic. Someone else can write the instructions for the computer; you simply use the instructions to get your work done. For example, an accountant might use a computer to prepare a report, a teenager to play a video game, a ranch hand to record data from the field.

➤ The Nature of Computers

Every computer has three fundamental characteristics. Each characteristic has by-products that are just as important. The three fundamental characteristics are

- **Speed.** Computers provide the processing speed essential to our fast-paced society. The quick service we have come to expect—for bank withdrawals, stock quotes, telephone calls, and travel reservations, to name a few—is made possible by computers. Businesses depend on the speedy processing provided by computers for everything from balancing ledgers to designing products.

- **Reliability.** Computers are extremely reliable. Of course, you might not think this from some of the stories you may have seen in the press about "computer errors." However, most errors supposedly made by computers are really human errors.

Computers in the office. Decision makers rely on the computer to analyze high-volume data.

- **Storage capability.** Computer systems can store tremendous amounts of data, which can be located and retrieved efficiently. The capability to store volumes of data is especially important in an information age.

These three characteristics—speed, reliability, and storage capability—have the following by-products:

- **Productivity.** When computers move into business offices, managers expect increased productivity as workers learn to use computers to do their jobs better and faster. Furthermore, jobs like punching holes in metal or monitoring water levels can be more efficiently controlled by computers.

- **Decision making.** To make decisions, managers need to take into account financial, geographical, and logistical factors. The computer helps decision makers sort things out and make better choices.

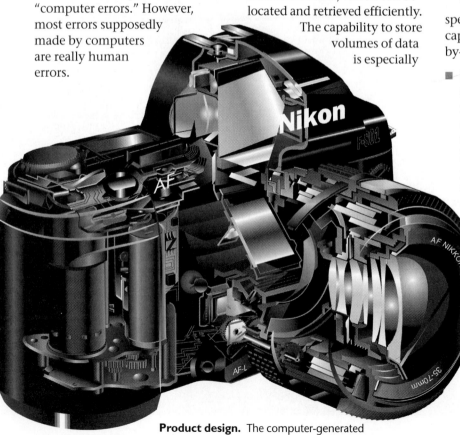

Product design. The computer-generated image shows every working part of the camera.

■ **Cost reduction.**
Finally, because it improves
productivity and aids decision
making, the computer helps us
hold down the costs of labor,
energy, and paperwork. As a
result, computers help reduce
the costs of goods and services
in our economy.

Next we look at some of the
ways we use computers to make
the workday more productive and
our personal lives more rewarding.

▶ Where Computers Are Used

Computers can do just about anything imaginable, but they really
excel in certain areas. This section
lists some of the principal areas of
computer use.

■ **Graphics.** Business people
make bar graphs and pie charts

from
tedious
figures to
convey
information
with far more
impact than
numbers
alone.
Architects use
computer-
animated
graphics to
experiment with possible
exteriors and to give clients a
visual walk-through of
proposed buildings. Finally, a
new kind of artist has emerged
who uses computers to express
his or her creativity.

Retailing. Products from meats to magazines are packaged with zebra-striped bar codes that can be read by computer scanners at supermarket checkout stands to determine prices and help manage inventory. Computers operate behind the scenes, too; for example, this book was tracked from printer to ware-house to bookstore with the help of computers and the bar code on the back cover. Computers can even be used to plan the perfect-fitting pair of jeans.

Retailing. This woman is being measured for her own personal pair of jeans. The order and the jeans are tracked by computer from the store to the Levi Strauss factory and back to the customer.

- **Energy.** Energy companies use computers to locate oil, coal, natural gas, and uranium. Electric companies use computers to monitor vast power networks. In addition, meter readers use handheld computers to record how much energy is used each month in homes and businesses.

- **Paperwork.** In some ways the computer contributes to paper use by adding to the amount of junk mail you find in your mailbox. However, in many ways it cuts down on paper handling. Using a

computer, for example, you might type several drafts of a term paper before printing anything. Computerized record keeping and ordering have also made paperwork more efficient.

- **Transportation.** Computers are used to help run rapid transit systems, load container-

ships, track railroad cars across the country, safeguard airport takeoffs and landings, monitor air traffic, and schedule travel. They are also used in cars to monitor fluid levels, temperatures, and electrical systems.

- **Law enforcement.** Recent innovations in computerized law enforcement include national fingerprint files, a national file on the mode of operation of serial killers, and the computer modeling of DNA, which can be used to match traces from an alleged criminal's body, such as blood at a crime scene.

- **Money.** Computers speed up record keeping and allow banks to offer same-day services and even do-it-yourself banking over the phone. Computers have helped fuel the cashless economy, enabling the widespread use of credit cards and instantaneous credit checks by banks and retailers.

- **Agriculture.** Farmers use small computers to help with billing,

crop information, cost per acre, feed combinations, and market price checks. Cattle ranchers can also use computers for information about livestock breeding and performance.

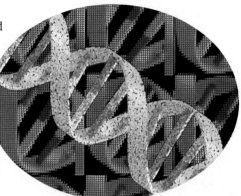

DNA Model

- **Government.** Among other tasks, the federal government uses computers to forecast weather, to manage parks, to process immigrants, to produce Social Security benefit checks, and—of course—to collect taxes. State and local governments also use computers routinely.

The approaching hurricane. When will the storm get here? First captured by a satellite, this photo of Hurricane Fran pinwheeling toward Florida was computer enhanced to provide color distinctions and a 3-D pop.

■ **Education.** Most schools in the United States have computers available for use in the classroom, and some colleges require entering freshmen to bring their own. Many educators prefer learning by doing—an approach uniquely suited to the computer.

■ **The home.** Many people have a computer in the home, often justifying it as an educational tool for their children. But that is only the beginning. Personal computers are being used at home to keep records, write letters, prepare budgets, draw pictures, publish newsletters, and connect with others. Most users also play games such as Time-lapse, a search via Easter Island for the lost city of Atlantis.

Sophisticated game playing. Games have gone far beyond tic-tac-toe and crude shoot-'em-ups. A click of the mouse on the scene on the screen, hopefully in the right place, propels a player along a route through Easter Island and other venues, in search of the lost city of Atlantis.

■ **Health and medicine.** Computers help monitor the gravely ill in intensive care units and provide cross-sectional views of the body. Physicians can also use computers to assist in diagnoses; in fact, computers have been shown to diagnose heart attacks correctly more frequently than physicians. If you are one of the thousands who suffer one miserable cold after another, you will be happy to know that computers have been able to map, in exquisite

■ **Robotics.** Computers have paved the way for robots to take over many of the jobs that are too unpleasant or too dangerous for humans, such as opening packages believed to contain bombs. Robots are best known for their work in factories, but they can do many other

things, not the least of which is finding their way through the bloodstream.

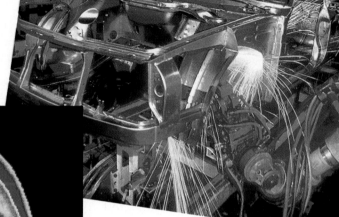

Robots. (above) This factory robot welds a new car under the direction of the computer. (below) In the not-so-distant future, nanorobots, as shown here, will be able to destroy diseased tissues inside a human blood vessel.

Medicine. A magnetic resonance image of a head section of a normal 42-year-old woman.

atomic detail, the structure of the human cold virus—the first step toward a cure for the common cold.

Cold virus. This computer-produced model of the cold virus named HRV 14 raises hopes that a cure for the common cold may be possible after all. With the aid of a computer, the final set of calculations for the model took one month to complete. Researchers estimate that without the computer the calculations might have required ten years of manual effort.

■ **The sciences.** Scientific researchers have long benefited from the high-speed capabilities of computers. Computers can simulate environments, emulate physical characteristics, and allow scientists to provide proofs in a cost-effective manner. Also, many mice—and other animals—have been spared since computers have taken over their research roles.

■ **Connectivity.** One of the most popular uses of computers today is communicating with other people who have computers, whether for business or personal reasons. In addition, computers can give people the option of working at their homes instead of in city offices.

■ **Training.** It is much cheaper to teach aspiring pilots to fly in computerized training "cockpits," or simulators, than in real airplanes. Novice railroad engineers can also be given the experience of running a train with the help of a computerized device. Training simulations are relatively inexpensive and always available on a one-to-one basis, making for very personal learning.

The environment via computer. Computers can model any landscape for environmental scrutiny. Shown here is a city that has been color-coded to show various land uses.

■ **The human connection.** Are computers cold and impersonal? The disabled do not think so; children, in particular, consider the computer their main education tool. Can the disabled walk again? Some can, with the help of computers. Can dancers and athletes improve their performance? Maybe they can, by using computers to monitor their movements. Can we learn more about our ethnic backgrounds and our cultural history with the aid of computers? Indeed we can.

★ ★ ★ ★

Computers and kids. These children have an expanded world via the computer.

Computers are all around us. You have been exposed to computer hype, computer advertisements, and computer headlines. You have interacted with computers in your everyday life—at the grocery store, your school, the library, and more. You know more than you think you do. The beginnings of computer literacy are already apparent.

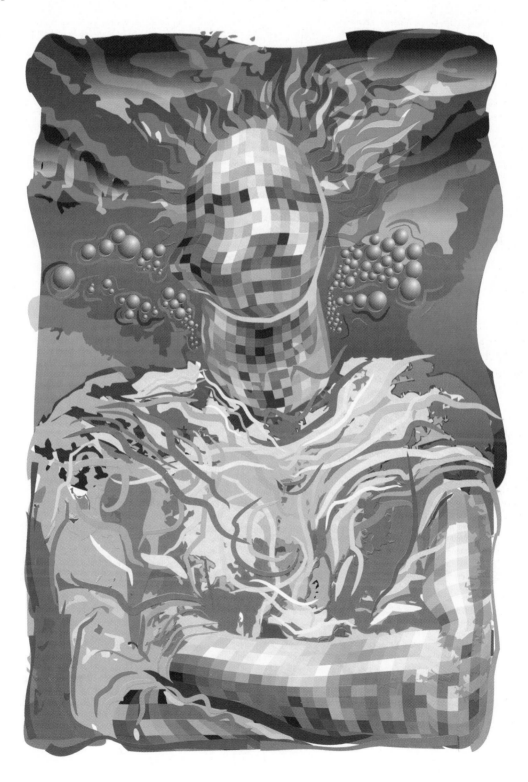

An Overview

of Computers

Ron Duce, a graduate assistant in chemistry, had never been anywhere near a computer. He did not plan to change that fact any time soon. But then he received an interesting note in his campus mailbox. The note was from a colleague in the Computer Science department, offering two hours of free one-on-one tutoring for any instructor who was interested. Now, what was that all about?

The instructor making the offer, Althea Burgess, had noticed that the computers in the science faculty room, placed there for the convenience of all science personnel, were used exclusively by the Computer Science faculty. She wondered if there was really such a lack of interest or if there were other factors, such as lack of time to take a course. On a whim, she put the offer note in each of 27 mailboxes, hoping that not everyone took her up on it.

Six people responded. One was Ron. On a late winter afternoon, Ron, with Althea standing at his shoulder, made his first stab at computer literacy. He moved along nicely and, after their second meeting, was thrilled to create his first computer-produced memo. He suddenly turned to Althea and said, "I never would have taken a class. I was too embarrassed that I didn't know anything about computers."

This is a true story. The memo was just the beginning. Ron now uses a computer to prepare his lectures and requires several computer-related exercises from his chemistry students.

Computer Hardware

Meeting the Machine

C H A P T E R

1

- Identify the basic components of a computer system: input, processing, output, and storage
- List some common input, output, and storage media
- Distinguish data from information
- Appreciate the significance of networking and data communications
- Understand the significance of the Internet
- Become familiar with the various classifications of computers

HARDWARE: THE BASIC COMPONENTS OF A COMPUTER

Your Personal Computer Hardware

Input: What Goes In

The Processor and Memory: Data Manipulation

Output: What Comes Out

Secondary Storage

The Complete Hardware System

DATA COMMUNICATIONS: NO NEED TO BE THERE

THE INTERNET

Getting Connected

Getting Around

CLASSIFICATION OF COMPUTERS

Supercomputers

Mainframes

Minicomputers

Personal Computers

Notebook Computers

Smaller Still: Personal Digital Assistants

Nothing but 'Net: The Network Computer

▶ The Big Picture

A computer system has three main components: hardware, software, and people. The equipment associated with a computer system is called **hardware**. A set of instructions called **software** tells the hardware what to do. People, however, are the most important component of a computer system—people use the power of the computer for some purpose.

Software is also referred to as programs. To be more specific, a **program** is a set of step-by-step instructions, created by people, that directs the computer to do the tasks you want it to do and produce the desired results. A **computer programmer** is a person who writes programs. **Users** are people who purchase and use computer software. In business, users are often called **end-users** because they are at the end of the "computer line," actually making use of the computer's capabilities.

This chapter examines hardware; software and people will be the subject of the next chapter. As the title of this chapter indicates, what follows is an overview, a look at the "big picture." Thus, many of the terms introduced in this chapter are discussed only briefly here. Subsequent chapters will define the various parts of a computer system in greater detail.

▶ Hardware: The Basic Components of a Computer

What is a computer? A six-year-old called a computer "radio, movies, and television combined!" A ten-year-old described a computer as "a television set you can talk to." The ten-year-old's definition is closer but still does not recognize the computer as a machine that has the power to make changes. A **computer** is a machine that can be programmed to accept data *(input)*, process it into useful information *(output)*, and store it away (in a *secondary storage* device) for safekeeping or later reuse. The *processing* of input to output is directed by the software but performed by the hardware, the subject of this section.

Figure 1-1 Four primary components of a computer system. To function, a computer system requires input, processing, output, and storage.

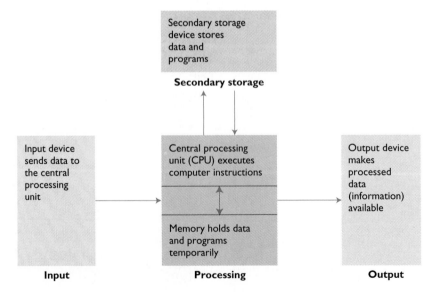

To function, a computer system requires four main aspects of data handling: input, processing, output, and storage (Figure 1-1). The hardware responsible for these four areas is as follows:

- *Input devices* accept data or commands in a form that the computer can use; they send the data or commands to the processing unit.
- The *processor,* more formally known as the *central processing unit (CPU),* has electronic circuitry that manipulates input data into the information people want. The central processing unit actually executes computer instructions.
- *Output devices* show people the processed data—information—in understandable and usable form.
- *Storage* usually means *secondary storage,* which consists of secondary storage devices such as disk—hard disk or diskettes—that can store data and programs outside the computer itself. These devices supplement *memory* or *primary storage,* which can hold data and programs only temporarily.

Before looking at each of these hardware aspects, consider them in terms of what you would find on a personal computer.

Your Personal Computer Hardware

Let us look at the hardware of a personal computer. Suppose you want to do word processing on a personal computer, using the hardware shown in Figure 1-2. Word processing software allows you to input data such as an essay, save it, revise and re-save it, and print it whenever you wish.

The Computer Is Watching
Since this spherical gadget looks unsettlingly like an eyeball, you may indeed get the feeling that your computer is watching you. And in a sense it is. The gadget is, in fact, another type of input device. Connected to your computer by a long cord, this video camera takes images of you and sends them directly to the computer, where they can be seen on the screen. Although the quality is not quite as good as that of the average handheld video recorder, it is a quick and easy way of getting your face on your computer screen. Accompanying software lets you fine-tune the results.

Figure 1-2 A personal computer system. In this personal computer system, the input device is a keyboard or a mouse. The input device feeds data to the central processing unit, which is inside the computer housing, the vertical box to the left of the screen. The output devices in this example are the screen, the printer, and the speakers. The secondary storage devices are hard drive, a 3½-inch disk drive, and a CD-ROM drive, all within the computer housing. This popular configuration, with the housing standing on end, is called a minitower.

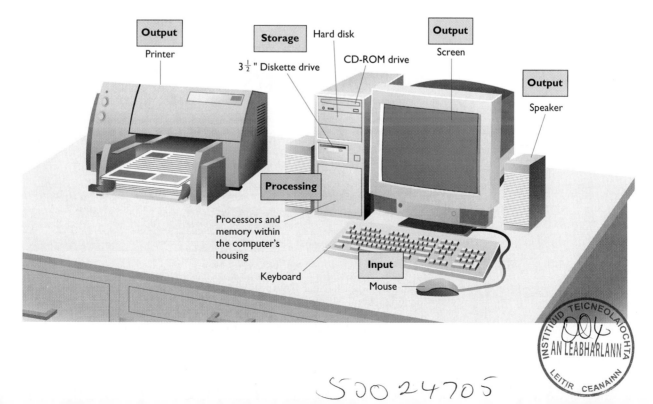

The *input* device, in this case, is a keyboard, which you use to key—type—the original essay and any subsequent changes to it. You will also probably use the mouse as an input device. All computers, large and small, must have a *central processing unit*, so yours does, too—it is within the personal computer housing. The central processing unit uses the word processing software to accept the data you input through the keyboard. Processed data from your personal computer is usually *output* in two forms: on a screen and by a printer. As you key in the essay on the keyboard, it appears on the screen in front of you. After you have examined the essay on the screen, made changes, and determined that it is acceptable, you can print the essay on the printer. Your *secondary storage device*, as shown in Figure 1-2, which stores the essay until it is needed again, will probably be a hard disk or diskette. For reasons of convenience and speed, you are probably more likely to store your data—the essay—on a hard disk than on a diskette. Incidentally, although Figure 1-2 shows CD-ROM disk storage, a CD-ROM is usually only for prestored information that can be purchased for use, not a medium to keep a document created by the user.

Next is a general tour of the hardware needed for input, processing, output, and storage. These same components make up all computer systems, whether small, medium, or large. These topics will be covered in detail in Chapters 3, 4, and 5.

Input: What Goes In

Input is the data that you put into the computer system for processing. Here are some common ways of feeding input data into the system:

- *Typing* on a **keyboard** (Figure 1-3a). The keys on a computer keyboard are arranged in much the same way as those on a typewriter. The computer responds to what you enter; that is, it "echoes" what you type by displaying it on the screen in front of you.
- *Pointing* with a **mouse** (Figure 1-3a). A mouse is a device that is moved by hand over a flat surface. As the ball on its underside rotates, the mouse movement causes corresponding movement of a pointer on the computer screen. Pressing buttons on the mouse lets you invoke commands.

(a)   (b)

Figure 1-3 Input devices. (a) The keyboard is the most widely used input device, though the mouse has become increasingly popular. Movement of the mouse on a flat surface causes corresponding movement of a pointer on the screen. (b) The bar code on this package of green beans is scanned into the computer.

■ *Scanning* with a **wand reader** or **bar code reader** (Figure 1-3b). These devices, which you have seen used by clerks in retail stores, use laser beams to read special letters, numbers, or symbols such as the zebra-striped bar codes found on many products.

An input device may be part of a terminal. A **terminal** includes an input device, a television-like screen display, and some connection to a large computer. For example, operators taking orders over the phone for a mail-order house would probably use terminals to input the order and send it to be processed by a large computer. You can input data to a computer in many other interesting ways, including by writing, speaking, pointing, or even just looking at the data. Input is examined in detail in Chapter 4.

The Processor and Memory: Data Manipulation

In a computer the **processor** is the center of activity. The processor, as already noted, is also called the **central processing unit (CPU)**. The central processing unit consists of electronic circuits that interpret and execute program instructions as well as communicating with the input, output, and storage devices.

It is the central processing unit that actually transforms data into information. **Data** is the raw material to be processed by a computer, such as grades in a class, baseball batting averages, or light and dark areas in a photograph. Processed data becomes **information**—data that is organized, meaningful, and useful. In school, for instance, an instructor could enter various student grades (data), which can be processed to produce final grades and perhaps a class average (information). Data that is perhaps uninteresting on its own may become very interesting once it is converted to information. The raw facts (data) about your finances, such as a paycheck or a donation to charity or a medical bill may not be captivating individually, but together these and other acts can be processed to produce the refund or amount you owe on your income tax return (information).

Computer **memory**, also known as **primary storage**, is closely connected to the central processing unit but separate from it. Memory holds the data after it is input to the system and before it is processed; also, memory holds the data after it has been processed but before it has been released to the output device. In addition, memory holds the programs (computer instructions) needed by the central processing unit. Memory can hold data only temporarily because it requires a continuous flow of electric current; if the current is interrupted, the data is lost.

Output: What Comes Out

Output—the result produced by the central processing unit—is, of course, a computer's whole reason for being. Output is usable information—that is, raw input data that has been processed by the computer into information. Common forms of output are text, numbers, graphics, and even sounds. Text output, for example, may be the letters and memos prepared by office workers using word processing software. Other workers may be more interested in numbers, such as those found in formulas, schedules, and budgets. In many cases numbers can be understood more easily when output is in the form of graphics.

A 2¢ Car

Countless articles have been written about the remarkable speed increase of the computer at the same time that its cost has been reduced. A telling comparison can be made between the computer and the magnificent Rolls Royce automobile. Start with the base year 1946. If a Rolls Royce had increased its speed in parallel to the computer's increase in speed, the car would now travel at the speed of light. Even more astonishing, if a Rolls Royce had dropped in price in parallel to the price of a computer, a Rolls Royce would now cost 2¢.

(a)

(b)

Figure 1-4 Output devices. Screens and printers are two types of output devices. (a) This screen can display text or the colorful graphics shown here. (b) This laser printer is used to produce high-quality output.

The most common output devices are computer screens and printers. A **screen**, the visible part of the **monitor**, can vary in its form of display, producing text, numbers, symbols, art, photographs, and even video, in full color (Figure 1-4a). **Printers** produce printed reports as instructed by a computer program (Figure 1-4b). Many printers, particularly those associated with personal computers, can print in color.

You can produce output from a computer in other ways, including film, voice output, and music. Output methods are examined in detail in Chapter 4.

Secondary Storage

Secondary storage provides additional storage separate from memory. Recall that memory holds data and programs only temporarily; thus there is a need for secondary storage. The two most common secondary storage media are magnetic disk and magnetic tape. A **magnetic disk** can be a diskette or a hard disk. A **diskette** usually consists of a magnetic disk 3½ inches in diameter, enclosed in a plastic case (Figure 1-5a). **Hard disks** usually have more storage capacity than diskettes and also offer faster access to the data they hold. With large computer systems, hard disks are often contained in disk packs (Figure 1-5c). Disk data is read by **disk drives**. Personal computer disk drives read diskettes; most personal computers have hard disk drives also. **Optical disks**, such as **CD-ROMs**, use a laser beam to store large volumes of data relatively inexpensively (Figure 1-5b).

Magnetic tape, which usually comes on a cartridge, is similar to tape that is played on a tape recorder. Magnetic tape reels are mounted on **tape drives** when the data on them needs to be read by the computer system or when new data is to be written on the tape. Magnetic tape is usually used for backup purposes—for "data insurance"—because tape is inexpensive.

Chapter 5 presents more detailed information about storage media.

The Complete Hardware System

The hardware devices attached to the computer are called peripheral equipment. **Peripheral equipment** includes all input, output, and sec-

(a)

(b)

Figure 1-5 Secondary storage devices. (a) A 3½-inch diskette is being inserted into a disk drive. (b) Optical disks can hold enormous amounts of data: text, music, graphics—even video and movies.

Getting Practical

ADDING ON

Just like people who have boats or cameras, computer owners are tempted to buy the latest gadget. There are many from which to choose, some more useful than others.

For greater comfort and flexibility, consider a wireless keyboard, which works just fine as long as it is in within direct line of sight of the computer. If you prefer to say what you think instead of writing it, you can

purchase a microphone and accompanying software to accept your voice input. A ring mouse, shown here, is comfortable and

easy to click, but aiming it at the right place on the screen requires some agility.

If you want to be more fanciful, you can purchase cardboard cutouts called Screenies that affix to the front of a monitor like a picture frame. Among the choices are a rain forest scene, a real corkboard, and a memo board you can wipe off.

ondary storage devices. In most personal computers, the CPU and disk drives are all contained in the same housing, a metal case; the keyboard, mouse, and screen are separate.

In larger computer systems, however, the input, processing, output, and storage functions may be in separate rooms, separate buildings, or even separate countries. For example, data may be input on terminals at a branch bank and then transmitted to the central processing unit at the bank's headquarters. The information produced by the central processing unit may then be transmitted to the international offices, where it is printed out. Meanwhile, disks with stored data may be kept at the bank headquarters, and duplicate data may be kept on disk or tape in a warehouse across town for safekeeping.

Although the equipment may vary widely from the simplest computer to the most powerful, by and large the four elements of a computer system remain the same: input, processing, output, and storage. These basic components are supplemented by hardware that can make computers much more useful, giving them the ability to connect to one another.

▶ Data Communications: No Need to Be There

Originally, before the advent of personal computers, hardware for the big computer was kept in one place; that is, it was **centralized** in one room. Anyone wanting computer access had to go to where the computer was located. Today most large computer systems are **decentralized.** That is, the computer itself and some storage devices may be in one place, but the devices to access the computer—terminals or even other computers—are distributed among the users. These devices are usually connected to the computer by telephone lines. For instance, the computer and storage that has the information about your checking account may be located in the bank headquarters, but the terminals are located in branch banks all over town, so a teller at any branch can find out what your balance is. The subject of decentralization is intimately tied to **data communications,** the process of exchanging data over communications facilities, such as telephone lines.

In many systems processing is decentralized as well—the computers and storage devices are in dispersed locations. This arrangement is known as **distributed data processing** because the processing is distributed among the different locations. There are several ways to configure the hardware; one common arrangement is to place smaller computers in local offices but still do some processing on a larger computer at the headquarters office. For example, an insurance company headquartered in Denver with branches throughout the country might process payments and claims through smaller computers in local offices. However, summary data could be sent regularly by each office for processing by the large computer in Denver (Figure 1-6).

Many organizations find that their needs are best served by a **network,** a computer system that uses communications equipment to connect computers and their resources. Resources include printers and hard

Figure I-6 A distributed data processing system. Branch offices of an insurance company have their own computers for local processing, but they can tie into the computer in the headquarters office in Denver.

MAKING THE RIGHT CONNECTIONS

THE HOTEL THAT HAS IT ALL

Many fine hotels offer the standard amenities—crisp sheets, fluffy towels, and tiny bottles of shampoo. Some, looking out for the business traveler, offer hookups for notebook computers and fax machines. But the Century Plaza hotel in Los Angeles has gone a step further: It offers the CyberSuite.

The key offering of the Cyber-Suite is access to the Internet, using a large-screen network computer. Input is via a wireless keyboard and a wireless mouse. A CD-ROM drive is included for multimedia.

In addition to Internet access, the suite has a voice-activated system called Butler in a Box that can be invoked to control the room's lighting, draperies, temperature, and appliances. If pampering is in order, you can call the Butler from a remote hotel telephone and order it to draw a bath, to be waiting upon your return to the room.

disks and even software and data. In one type of network, a **local area network (LAN)**, personal computers in an office are connected together so that users can communicate with one another. Users can operate their personal computers independently or in cooperation with other computers to exchange data and share resources.

Individual users have joined the trend to "connectivity" by hooking up their personal computers, usually via telephone lines, to other computers. Users who connect their computers to other computers via the phone lines must use a hardware device called a **modem** as a go-between to reconcile the inherent differences between computers and the phone system; this device will be described in more detail in Chapter 6. From their own homes, users can connect to all sorts of computer-based services, performing such tasks as getting stock quotes, making airline reservations, and shopping for videotapes. An important service for individuals is **electronic mail**, or **e-mail**, which lets people send and receive messages via computer.

Whether the user is operating in a business capacity or simply exploring the options, one possible conduit for connectivity is the Internet.

▶ The Internet

The **Internet**, sometimes called simply "the 'Net," is the largest and most far-flung network system of them all, connecting users worldwide. Surprisingly, the Internet is not really a network at all but a loosely organized collection of about 25,000 networks. Many people are astonished to discover that no one owns the Internet; it is run by volunteers. It has no central headquarters, no centrally offered services, and no comprehensive index to tell you what information is available.

Originally developed and still subsidized by the United States government, the Internet connects libraries, college campuses, research labs, businesses, and any other organization or individual who has the capacity to hook up.

Getting Connected

How are all kinds of different computers able to communicate with one another? To access the Internet, a user's computer must connect to a computer called a **server.** Each server uses the same special software called **TCP/IP** (for **Transmission Control Protocol/Internet Protocol**); it is this consistency that that allows different types of computers to communicate (Figure 1-7). The supplier of the server computer, often called an **Internet service provider (ISP)**, charges a fee, usually monthly, based on the amount of service provided. Once a user has chosen a service provider, he or she will be furnished with the information needed to connect to the server and, from there, to the Internet.

Getting Around

Since the Internet did not begin as a commercial customer-pleasing package, it did not initially offer attractive options for finding information. The arcane commands were invoked only by a hardy and determined few. Furthermore, the vast sea of information, including news and trivia, can seem an overwhelming challenge to navigate. As both the Internet user population and the available information grew, new ways were developed to tour the Internet.

The most attractive method used to move around the Internet is called browsing. Using a program called a **browser,** you can use a mouse to point and click on screen icons to explore the Internet, particularly the **World Wide Web** (**WWW** or **the Web**), an Internet subset of text, images, and sounds linked together to allow users to peruse related topics. Each different location on the Web is called a **web site** or, more commonly, just a **site.** You may have heard the term **home page**; this is just the first page of a web site.

The Internet is an important and complex topic. Although it is easy to use once you know how, there is much to learn about its use and its place in the world of

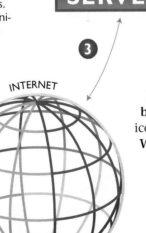

Figure I-7. The Internet. ① At his or her own computer, a user accesses the server computer, ② probably over the phone lines. ③ The server computer communicates with the Internet, perhaps passing on e-mail messages or requests for certain web sites, and picking up responses. ④ Incoming messages, e-mail or requested Internet information, are returned to the original requesting computer. This back-and-forth communication goes on as long as the user wishes to remain connected to the Internet.

computers. This opening chapter merely scratches the surface. In addition to a chapter devoted to the Internet, this book has a two-page feature at the end of every chapter called *Planet Internet.* You will also find a gallery of glossy pages, called *The Visual Internet,* that shows off some of the more attractive Web pages. Further, the more generic topic of connectivity is discussed in the feature *Making the Right Connections,* offered in each chapter of the book.

▶ Classification of Computers

Computers come in sizes from tiny to monstrous, in both appearance and power. The size of a computer that a person or an organization needs depends on the computing requirements. Clearly, the National Weather Service, keeping watch on the weather fronts of many continents, has requirements different from those of a car dealer's service department that is trying to keep track of its parts inventory. And the requirements of both of them are different from the needs of a salesperson using a small notebook computer to record client orders or of a student writing a paper.

Supercomputers

The mightiest computers—and, of course, the most expensive—are known as supercomputers (Figure 1-8a). **Supercomputers** process *trillions* of instructions per second. Most people do not have a direct need for the speed and power of a supercomputer. In fact, for many years supercomputer customers were an exclusive group: agencies of the federal government. The federal government uses supercomputers for tasks that require mammoth data manipulation, such as worldwide weather forecasting and weapons research. But now supercomputers are moving toward the mainstream, for activities as varied as stock analysis, automobile design, special effects for movies, and even sophisticated artwork (Figure 1-9).

Mainframes

In the jargon of the computer trade, large computers are called mainframes (Figure 1-8b). **Mainframes** are capable of processing data at very high speeds—millions of instructions per second—and have access to billions of characters of data. The price of these large systems can vary from several hundred thousand to many millions of dollars. With that kind of price tag, you will not buy a mainframe for just any purpose. Their principal use is for processing vast amounts of data quickly, so some of the obvious customers are banks, insurance companies, and manufacturers. But this list is not all-inclusive; other types of customers are large mail-order houses, airlines with sophisticated reservation systems, government accounting services, aerospace companies doing complex aircraft design, and the like. As you can tell from these examples of mainframe applications, a key characteristic of large computers is that they are designed for multiple users. For example, many reservations clerks could be accessing the same computer at the same time to make reservations for waiting customers.

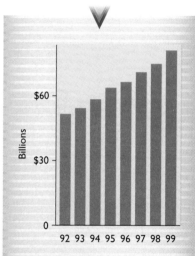

Skip the Clothes

Analysts who study market trends have made an interesting discovery: Consumers have stopped spending money on clothes. Well, not entirely. People still buy essential clothing, mostly casual, but have largely abandoned the notion of a full and frequently updated wardrobe.

So where are people spending the money that they used to spend on clothes? You guessed it—on electronics, especially personal computers with all the trimmings. Projections into the next century, based on records from the Consumer Electronics Manufacturers Association, show the trend only increasing.

Figure 1-8 Computer classifications. Here are some examples of computers by their informal classifications. (a) This Cray supercomputer has been nicknamed Bubbles because of its bubbling, shimmering coolant liquids. Cray computers have 75 percent of the supercomputer market. (b) Mainframe computers are usually shown in multiple units, looking like a group of sterile refrigerators. IBM has chosen to add a little flair to its presentation of the IBM 9672. (c) Individuals use personal computers in both the home and the office. (d) People who work in various locations favor portable notebook computers.

(a)

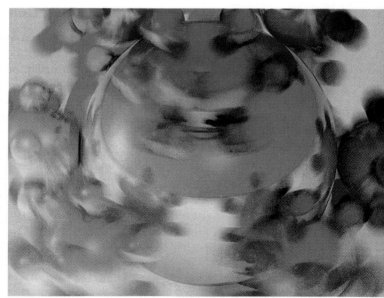

(b)

Figure 1-9 Supercomputer graphics.
These graphic images, called fractals, are formed by using the computer to repeat geometric shapes with color, size, and angle variations. (a) Note the basic triangle and circle elements on which the fractals are built. (b) Here, the artist makes slight adjustments to make the fractals appear to be in motion.

As computer users have marched inexorably toward personal computers and networking, pundits have predicted the demise of mainframes. But "big iron," the affectionate nickname for these computers, is proving to be hardy and versatile. More recent uses include helping large businesses carry out critical applications such as running automated teller machines and delivering e-mail. Thus, the mainframe has taken on the coloration of and even the name *server*. On the Internet, where computers of all stripes can coexist and even work in concert, vast data stores are being kept on the "large servers." The large server—the mainframe—is still the most reliable way to manage vast seas of data. As an example, national retailer L. L. Bean is using an IBM mainframe system to offer its entire catalog on the Internet.

Minicomputers

The next step down from mainframe computers, in terms of speed and storage capacity, are minicomputers. When **minicomputers** first appeared on the market, their lower price fell within the range of many small businesses, greatly expanding the potential computer market. Minicomputers are used by retail businesses, colleges, and state and city agencies. However, the minicomputer market has diminished in recent years, squeezed at the high end by multifunction mainframes and at the low end by less expensive but increasingly powerful personal computers.

Personal Computers

Most often called **personal computers**, or just **PCs**, these desktop computers are also known as **microcomputers** or sometimes home computers (Figure 1-8c). Today, for a few hundred dollars, anyone can own a personal computer. (Most people, however, are more likely to choose a computer that costs a few *thousand* dollars.) **Workstations**, the upper-end machines used by workers such as engineers, financial traders, and graphic designers, are small enough to fit on a desktop but approach the power of a mainframe.

Notebook Computers

A computer that fits in a briefcase? A computer that weighs less than a newborn baby? A computer you do not have to plug in? A computer to use on your lap on an airplane? Yes to all these questions. **Notebook computers** are wonderfully portable and functional, and they are popular with travelers who need a computer that can go with them (Figure 1-8d). Somewhat larger, heavier versions of these computers are known as **laptop computers.**

The memory and storage capacity of notebook computers today can compete with those of desktop computers. Notebooks have a hard disk drive, and most accept diskettes, so it is easy to move data from one computer to another. Some even offer a CD-ROM drive. Furthermore, notebooks can run any software available. Notebooks are not as inexpensive as their size might suggest; many carry a price tag greater than that of a full-size personal computer. However, like other technology, notebook computers are getting faster, lighter, and more feature-rich (Figure 1-10).

Smaller Still: Personal Digital Assistants

A handheld computer called a **personal digital assistant (PDA)** can be used to keep track of appointments and other business information,

Figure 1-10 Notebook computers. All these users, whether working in the office or in the field, find it convenient to use notebook computers.

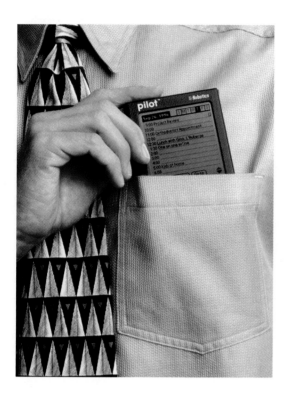

such as customer names and orders. PDAs are also called **pen-based computers** because, through a pen-like stylus, they can accept handwritten input directly on a touch-sensitive screen. Early PDAs faced criticism because the highly touted handwriting recognition simply did not work very well. Although this is still a problem area, many users limit the handwriting aspect to checking boxes or recording signatures for such items as package delivery acceptance.

Many PDAs offer multiple functions, including wireless e-mail and fax capabilities. However, recent versions have become more streamlined in size and operation and now stick to data to keep travelers organized (Figure 1-11).

Users of PDAs are mainly clipboard-carrying workers, such as parcel delivery drivers and meter readers. Other potential users are workers who cannot easily use a notebook computer because they are on their feet all day: nurses, sales representatives, real estate agents, and insurance adjusters.

Figure 1-11 Pen-based computers. The popular Pilot, which weighs just over 5 ounces and fits in a shirt pocket, is a handheld organizer that keeps track of a calendar, address book, and electronic notepad. The Pilot can exchange data with a personal computer with the press of a single button; that is, any appropriate data you have entered into your personal computer is sent to the Pilot and vice versa.

Nothing but 'Net: The Network Computer

It was bound to happen. With all the interest in the Internet, computer developers saw a need for a machine that could access the Internet, and perhaps send and receive e-mail, but not do much else. Such a machine, called a **network computer (NC)** or simply a **net computer** or **net box**, would plug into a television jack and sit on top of the set like a cable box. People who would not pay for a full-featured personal computer, it is thought, would be willing to part with a few hundred dollars for the privilege of surfing the net from their easy chairs. (Commercially, televisions sold with this setup are hawked as Web TVs.)

NEW DIRECTIONS

A BRIDGE TO THE FUTURE

We have heard a lot about bridges to the next century. Computer people talk the same way; they want to build bridges to technology that users will not be afraid to cross. In fact, a recurring theme is that computers will be more accessible if they disappear. Not disappear altogether, of course, just be transformed from today's clunky, putty-colored boxes into computers so unobtrusive that they are not noticed. An example from today's technology is the computer that manages a car's antilock braking system. Without even knowing that a computer is part of the action, a user jams on the brake pedal and a computer makes a series of decisions that could save a life.

The future is already in sight. Soon workers will wonder how today's mute, passive boxes were ever called computers. Already some personal computers, or terminals hooked up to bigger

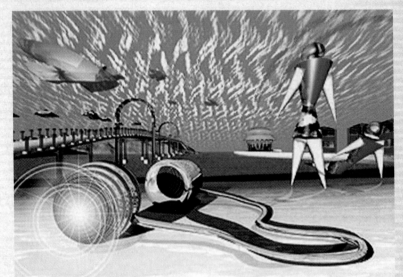

machines, can talk, listen, and display live images. No computer is an island: They can call one another and send faxes, mail, and messages. People who cannot leave their computers at home are taking them along—they may even wear them one day. Some

computers are disappearing altogether, into the walls and into the furniture to become part of the desk, the cabinet, the blackboard. It seems to be the fate of the computer to move into the background—and to be everywhere.

A net computer is, by definition, a limited piece of hardware. It does, of course, have a central processing unit, but its memory is minimal. The screen is the TV screen, which, by the way, is significantly less clear than a computer screen. Most net computers have no storage at all. The net computer hooks up to the Internet via the telephone lines. For sending e-mail, some net boxes offer the option of clicking letters on the screen. However, a user who wants to send anything more than a short note has to purchase a wireless keyboard.

Some users say the net box is easier to set up and use than a VCR. In fact, some people think of the net computer as less a computer than a new kind of television.

★ ★ ★ ★

This chapter has taken a rather expansive look at computer hardware. However, hardware by itself is just an empty shell. Before moving to hardware details, this book next considers the ingredient that gives value to the computer—software.

Buyer's Guide

How to Buy Your Own Personal Computer

We cannot choose your new computer system for you any more than we can select a new car for you. But we can tell you to look for or avoid various features. We will not be able to lead you to a particular brand and model—so many new products are introduced every month that doing so would be impossible. If you are just starting out, however, we can help you define your needs and ask the right questions.

Where Do You Start?

Maybe you have already done some thinking and have decided that owning your own personal computer offers advantages. Now what? You can start by talking to other personal computer owners about how they got started and how to avoid pitfalls. Or you can read some computer magazines, especially ones with evaluations and ratings, to get a feel for what is available. Next find several dealers. Most dealers are listed in the Yellow Pages of the phone book, and many advertise in your local newspaper. Visit several. Don't be afraid to ask questions. You are considering a major purchase, so plan to shop around.

Finally, you may consider buying a computer system by direct mail. You can find advertisements in any computer magazine. Call the listed toll-free number and ask them to send you a free brochure.

What to Look For in Hardware

The basic personal computer system consists of a central processing unit (CPU) and memory, a monitor (screen), a keyboard and a mouse, and assorted storage devices—probably a 3½-inch diskette drive, a CD-ROM drive, and a hard disk drive. Most people also want a printer, and many dealers offer package deals that include a printer. Unless you know someone who can help you out with technical expertise, the best advice is to look for a packaged system—that is, one in which the above components (with the exception of the printer) are assembled and packaged by the same manufacturer. This gives you some assurance that the various components will work together. Perhaps even more important, if something should go wrong, you will not have

to deal with multiple manufacturers pointing fingers at one another.

Computer Housing

Sometimes called the computer case or simply "the box," the housing holds the electronic circuitry and has external receptors called ports to which the monitor, printer, and other devices are connected. It also has the bays that hold the various disk drives. Traditionally, the monitor sits on top of the computer housing. More common today is the minitower, in which the case sits on end. The minitower was originally designed to be placed on the floor, conveniently out of the way. But the floor location turned out to be rather inconvenient, so many users keep their minitowers on the desk next to the monitor.

Central Processing Unit

If you plan to purchase a PC-standard machine, you will find that most software packages run most efficiently on computers using a Pentium Pro microprocessor. Any lesser version of the Pentium should carry a bargain-basement price. A microprocessor's speed is expressed in megahertz (MHz), and it is usually 100 MHz and up. The higher the number, the faster—and more expensive—the microprocessor.

Memory

Memory, or RAM, is measured in bytes, with each byte representing a character of data. The amount of memory you need in your computer is determined by the amount of memory required by the applications programs (like word processing or spread-

sheets) that you want to use. The minimum memory threshold keeps rising, as software makers produce sophisticated products that run efficiently only with ever-larger amounts of memory. The minimum for today's software is 16 megabytes (16MB) of memory, but we suggest 32MB. Most machines have expandable memory, so you can add even more later if you need it.

Monitor

Sometimes called a video display screen, the monitor is a very important part of your computer system—you will spend all your computer time looking at it. You can expect a color monitor as standard equipment.

Screen Size

Monitors usually have a screen display of between 12 and 17 inches, measured diagonally. Generally, a larger screen provides a display that is easier to read, so most monitors sold today have at least 14- or 15-inch

screens. However, the 17-inch screen reduces eyestrain and it is well suited for displaying Internet web pages, graphics, and large photos and illustrations.

Screen Readability

You may wish to compare the readability of different monitors. First, make certain that the screen is bright and has minimum flicker. Glare is another major consideration. Harsh lighting nearby can cause glare to bounce off the screen, and some screens seem more susceptible to glare than others.

A key factor affecting screen quality is resolution, a measure of the number of dots, or pixels, that can appear on the screen. The higher the resolution—that is, the more dots there are—the more solid the text characters appear. For graphics, more pixels means sharper images. Color monitors most commonly available are Video Graphics Array (VGA) and Super VGA (SVGA), with SVGA offering the highest resolution.

Ergonomic Considerations

Can the monitor swivel and tilt? If so, this will eliminate your need to sit in one position for a long period. The ability to adjust the position of the monitor becomes an important consideration when several users share the same computer, particularly people of different sizes, such as parents and children. Furthermore, if you expect to type for long periods of time, you would be wise to buy a wrist pad to support your hands and wrists.

THE MAJOR CHOICES

The PC Standard?
Although computers are sold under many brand names, most offer the "PC standard," also referred to as the business standard. The PC standard is a computer that uses the Microsoft Windows operating system and an Intel microprocessor, a combination sometimes called "Wintel." If you will be using your computer for business applications and, in particular, if you need to exchange files with others in a business environment, consider sticking with the standard. However, the Apple Macintosh, noted for its ease of use, is an attractive alternative, especially for beginners.

Family Computer or Business Computer?
Although the basic machine is probably the same, many dealers offer a

computer labeled a "family computer." The package typically comes with a good modem and sound system, a joystick, and plenty of educational, financial, and entertainment software. A "business computer" will have a modest sound system and, most likely, one good suite of business software for such tasks as word processing and spreadsheets.

Desktop or Notebook?
Do you plan to use your computer in one place, or will you be moving it around? Notebook computers—also called laptop computers—have found a significant niche in the market, mainly because they are packaged to travel easily. A notebook computer is lightweight (usually under 7 pounds) and small enough to fit in a briefcase. Notebooks are also a favorite of college students.

Today's notebook computers offer power and functionality that are equiv-

alent to that of a desktop computer. They also carry a similar price tag and are sometimes even more expensive.

Mail Order or In-Store?
Several reputable manufacturers sell reliable hardware at good prices. However, they tend to be patronized by experienced users who are on their second or third computer and who know what they want. These buyers peruse a catalog, place an order over the phone (or possibly through a web site), and have the new machine delivered to the door. Since there is no retail middleman, they save money and also get the latest technology fast.

A first-time buyer, however, usually wants to kick the tires. You will probably be more comfortable looking over the machines, tapping the keyboard, and clicking the mouse. An in-store visit also gives you the opportunity to ask questions.

Input Devices

There are many input devices. We will mention only the two critical ones here: a keyboard and a mouse.

Keyboard

Keyboards vary in quality. To find what suits you best, sit down in the store and type. You may be surprised by the real differences in the feel of keyboards.

Make sure the keys are not cramped together; you will find that your typing is error prone if your fingers are constantly overlapping more than one key. Assess the color and layout of the keyboard. Ideally, keys should be gray with a matte finish. The dull finish reduces glare.

Most keyboards follow the standard QWERTY layout of typewriter keyboards. Many have a separate numeric keypad. In addition, most keyboards have separate function keys, which simplify applications software commands.

Should you consider a wireless keyboard? A wireless keyboard uses infrared technology rather than wires to communicate with the computer. Thus, you could use the keyboard at the far end of a conference table or on the kitchen table—any place within 50 feet of the computer. Furthermore, a touchpad—a mouse substitute—that can be used to drag the cursor or click on screen objects is built into the keyboard.

Mouse

A mouse is a device that you roll on a tabletop to move the cursor on the screen to make selections. A mouse was originally considered merely a convenient option, but now most software is designed to be used with a mouse, making it a necessity. If you do not like the feel of the mouse that comes with a computer system you are buying, consider investing in a separately packaged mouse.

Secondary Storage

You will need disk drives to read software into your computer and to store software and data that you wish to keep.

Diskette Drive

Some personal computer software today comes on diskettes, so you need a diskette drive to accept the

software. Diskettes are also the common medium for exchange of data among computer users. Furthermore, many users keep backup copies of their software and data files on diskette. Most computer systems today come with a 3½-inch diskette drive.

CD-ROM Drive

Most personal computer software comes on CD-ROM disks, far handier than multiple diskettes. But the main attraction is the use of high-capacity CD-ROMs for holding byte-rich images, sounds, and videos—the stuff of multimedia. The smoothness of a CD-ROM video presentation is indicated by the "X factor"—8X, 12X, 16X, 24X—the higher the better. However, it is just a matter of

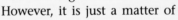

time before CD-ROM is supplanted by even higher-capacity DVD-ROMs.

Hard Disk Drive

A hard disk drive is a standard requirement. A hard disk is fast and reliable and holds large amounts of data. Software comes on a set of several diskettes or on optical disk; it

MULTIMEDIA? YOU BET

Multimedia refers to sophisticated software that offers text, sound, photos, graphics, and even movie clips. To take advantage of multimedia, which is presented on optical disks, you need a CD-ROM drive. Furthermore, you will need a sound card, which is installed inside the computer, and a set of speakers. Most computers today come equipped with these standard items.

However, if a computer is tagged as a "multimedia computer," this usually means that its processor is an MMX chip, which means that many of the functions that let the computer produce graphics, video, and sound are included right on the microprocessor, making the whole multimedia experience faster and more reliable.

would be unwieldy to load these each time the software is used. Instead, the software is stored on the hard drive, where it is conveniently accessed from that point forward.

Most computer systems offer a built-in hard disk drive, with variable storage capacity—the more storage, the higher the price. Storage capacity is measured in terms of bytes—characters—of data. Keep in mind that software, as well as your data files, will be stored on the hard disk; even a word processing program can fill up 20 million bytes. Hard disk capacity may be offered in megabytes—millions of bytes—but it is more likely to come with a few gigabytes—billions of bytes. The more the better.

Printers

A printer is probably the most expensive peripheral equipment you will buy. Although some inexpensive models are available, you will find that those costing $400 and up are the most useful. When choosing a printer, consider speed, quality, and cost.

Ink-jet printers, in which ink is propelled onto the paper by a battery of tiny nozzles, can produce excellent text and graphics. In fact, the quality of ink-jet printers approaches that of laser printers. The further attractions of low cost and quiet operation have made the ink-jet printer a current favorite among buyers, especially those who want color output.

Laser printers, which use technology similar to copying machines, are the top-of-the-line printers for quality and speed. The price of a low-end laser printer is within the budget of most users. Laser printers are particularly favored by desktop publishers to produce text and graphics on the same page. Affordable laser printers can produce output at 600 dots per inch (dpi), giving graphic images a sharpness that rivals that of photographs. At the high end, more expensive laser printers offer 1200 dpi. However, this rich resolution may be of little value to a buyer who plans to produce mostly text.

Affordable color printers are available for less than $500, although some are priced much higher. Even at a high price, color printers are not perfect. The rich color seen on the computer screen is not necessarily the color that will appear on the printed output. Furthermore, note that color printers often have fairly high operating costs for staples such as special coated paper and color ink cartridges. Still, color printers, once prohibitively expensive, are both attractive and affordable. The images shown on the next page, as well as the opening image of clocks, were all produced on a color laser printer.

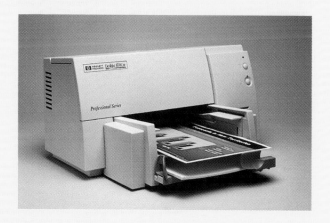

Portability: What to Look For in a Notebook Computer

Generally, you should look for the same hardware components in a notebook computer as you would in a desktop computer: a fast microprocessor, plenty of memory, a clear screen, and diskette and hard drives. You can also get a CD-ROM drive, although it will probably need to share a bay with the 3½-inch drive; that is, only one can be used at a time.

If you need to communicate from the road, you can buy a PC card modem that fits in a slot on the notebook. The PC modem has its own jack; you merely run a cord from the modem jack to the phone jack in the wall. Thus, from your hotel room or from anyplace else that has a phone jack, you can be connected to online services, e-mail, and the Internet.

You will have to make some compromises on input devices. The keyboard will be attached and the keys more cramped than those on a standard keyboard. Also, traveling users often do not have a handy surface for rolling a mouse, so the notebook will probably come with a built-in trackball or a touchpad. If you prefer a mouse, you can purchase it separately.

Other Hardware Options

There are a great many hardware variations; we will mention a few here. Note that, although we are describing the hardware, these devices may come with accompanying software, which must be installed according to directions before the hardware can be used.

Communications Connections

If you want to connect your computer via telephone lines to the office computer, or to an online service such as America Online, or to the Internet, or if you want to send and receive electronic mail, you need a modem. This device converts outgoing computer data into signals that can be transmitted over telephone lines, and does the reverse for incoming data.

Most buyers get an internal modem that fits inside the computer. Furthermore, most people choose a fax modem, which serves the dual purpose of modem and fax. Using a fax modem, you can receive a fax and then print it out, or send a fax if it originated in your computer (using, for example, word processing software) or was scanned into your computer. Most new computers come equipped with a fax modem.

Other Input Devices

If you are interested in action games, you may wish to acquire a joystick, which looks similar to the stick shift on a car. A joystick allows you to manipulate a cursor on the screen. A scanner is useful if you need to store pictures and typed documents in your computer. Scanners are often purchased by people who want to use their computers for desktop publishing. Finally, you can purchase voice input hardware, which is basically a microphone.

Surge Protectors

These devices protect against the electrical ups and downs that can affect the operation of your computer. In addition, a surge protector provides a receptacle for all power plugs and a handy switch to turn everything on or off at once. Some of the more expensive models, really uninterruptible power supply systems, provide up to ten minutes of full power to your computer if the electric power in your home or office is knocked out. This gives you time to save your work on disk (so that the work will not be lost if the power fails) or to print out a report you need immediately.

What to Look For in Software

The first software decision is made by the choice of the PC-standard or Macintosh computer: You will use software that was written for the operating system software of that machine. Almost all new PC-standard computers come with Microsoft Windows pre-installed; Windows users will want applications software written for the Windows environment.

Hardware Requirements for Software

Identify the type of hardware required before you buy software. Under the heading *System Requirements* (sometimes called *specifications*) right on the software package, a list will typically include a particular kind of computer and operating system and a certain amount of memory and hard disk space.

Brand Names

In general, publishers of well-known software offer better support than lesser-known companies. Support may be in the form of tutorials, classes by the vendor or others, and the all-important hotline assistance. In addition, makers of brand-name software usually offer superior documentation and upgrades to new and better versions of the product.

Where to Buy Software

Not very long ago, computer users bought their software at small specialty stores, where they hoped they could understand the esoteric language of the sales staff. In contrast, in enormous stores, buyers now pile software packages into their shopping carts like so many cans of soup. The choice of software vendors has expanded considerably.

Computer Superstores

The superstores, such as CompUSA, sell a broad variety of computer hardware and software. Although their primary advantage is a vast inventory, they also offer on-site technical support.

Warehouse Stores

Often billed as clubs, such as Wal-Mart's SAM's, these giant stores sell all manner of merchandise, including computer software.

Mass Merchandisers

Stores such as Sears sell software along with their other various merchandise.

Software-Only Stores

These stores, such as Egghead Software, offer a wide selection of software. Furthermore, in marked contrast to the larger stores, these stores are staffed by people who are familiar with the software.

Computer Dealers

Some small retail stores sell hardware systems and the software that runs on them. Such a store usually has a well-informed staff and may be your best bet for in-depth consulting.

Mail Order

Users who know what they want can get it conveniently and reasonably through the mail. Once an initial contact is made, probably from a magazine advertisement, the mail-order house will send catalogs of software regularly.

Over the Internet

Users who connect to the Internet often find it convenient to purchase software online. Each major software vendor has its own web site and, among other things, offers its wares for sale. A buyer usually is given the choice of receiving typical packaging—disks and documentation—through the mail or of downloading the software directly from the vendor's site to the buyer's computer.

Now That You Have It, Can You Use It?

Once the proud moment has come and your computer system is at home or in the office with you, what do you do with it?

Documentation

Computer systems today come with extensive documentation, the written manuals and disk files that accompany the hardware. Usually, a simple brochure

with detailed drawings will help you plug everything together. The installation procedure, however, is often largely (and conveniently) on disk. The same brochure that helps you assemble the hardware will guide you to the software on the diskette or CD-ROM. Using the software, the computer configures itself, mostly without any assistance from you.

Software documentation usually includes a user's guide, a reference manual for the various commands available with the software. Many software packages also include a workbook of some sort to help you train yourself. Software tutorials are also common and are useful for the novice and experienced user alike. Software tutorials usually come on a separate diskette or CD-ROM, and they guide you as you work through sample problems using the software.

Training

Can you teach yourself? In addition to the documentation supplied with your computer, numerous books and magazines offer help and answer readers' questions. Consult these sources. Other sources are classes offered by computer stores and local colleges. These hands-on sessions may be the most effective learning method of all.

Maintenance Contract

Finally, when purchasing a computer, you may wish to consider a maintenance contract, which should cover labor and parts and possibly advice on a telephone hotline. Such contracts vary in comprehensiveness. Some cover on-site repairs; others require you to pack up the computer and mail it in. Another option is that the replacement part, say a new monitor, is sent to you and you then return the old monitor in the same packaging.

CHAPTER REVIEW

Summary and Key Terms

- The equipment associated with a computer system is called **hardware.** The **programs,** or step-by-step instructions that run the machines, are called **software. Computer programmers** write programs for **users,** or **end-users**—people who purchase and use computer software.
- A **computer** is a machine that can be programmed to process data (input) into useful information (output). A computer system requires four main aspects of data handling—input, processing, output, and storage.
- **Input** is data to be accepted into the computer. Common input devices are the **keyboard;** a **mouse,** which translates movements of a ball on a flat surface to actions on the screen; and a **wand reader** or **bar code reader,** which uses laser beams to read special letters, numbers, or symbols such as the zebra-striped bar codes on products.
- A **terminal** includes an input device, such as a keyboard or wand reader; an output device, usually a television-like screen; and a connection to the main computer.
- The **processor,** or **central processing unit (CPU),** processes raw **data** into meaningful, useful **information.** The CPU interprets and executes program instructions and communicates with the input, output, and storage devices. **Memory,** or **primary storage,** is connected with the central processing unit but is separate from it. Memory holds the input data before processing and also holds the processed data after processing, until the data is released to the output device.
- **Output,** which is raw data processed into usable information, is usually in the form of words, numbers, and graphics. Users can see output displayed on a screen, part of the **monitor,** and use **printers** to display output on paper.
- **Secondary storage** provides additional storage space separate from memory. The most common secondary storage devices are **magnetic disks,** but **magnetic tape** also provides secondary storage. Magnetic disks are **diskettes,** usually 3½ inches in diameter, or **hard disks.** Hard disks on large systems are contained in a disk pack. Hard disks hold more data and offer faster access than diskettes do. Some hard disks come in removable cartridge form. Disk data is read by **disk drives. Optical disks,** such as **CD-ROMs,** use a laser beam to store large volumes of data. Magnetic tape comes on reels or in cassettes and is mainly used for backup purposes. Magnetic tape reels are mounted on **tape drives.**
- **Peripheral equipment** includes all the input, output, and secondary storage devices attached to a computer. Peripheral equipment may be built into one physical unit, as in many personal computers, or contained in separate units, as in many large computer systems.
- A **centralized** computer system does all processing in one location. In a **decentralized** computer system, the computer itself and some storage devices are in one place, but the devices to access the computer are somewhere else. Such a system requires **data communications**—the exchange of data over communications facilities. In a **distributed data processing** system, a local office usually uses its own small computer for processing local data but is connected to a central headquarters computer for other purposes.
- Often organizations use a **network** of personal computers, which allows users to operate independently or in cooperation with other computers, exchanging data and sharing resources. Such a setup is called a **local area network (LAN).**
- Users who connect their computers via the phone lines must use a hardware device called a **modem** to reconcile the inherent differences between computers and the phone system.

- Individuals use networking for a variety of purposes, especially **electronic mail**, or **e-mail.**
- The **Internet**, sometimes called simply "the 'Net," connects users worldwide. To access the Internet, a user's computer must connect to a computer called a **server**, which has special software called **TCP/IP** (for **Transmission Control Protocol/Internet Protocol**) that allows different types of computers to communicate with one another. The supplier of the server computer, often called an **Internet service provider (ISP)**, charges a fee based on the amount of service provided.
- Using software called a **browser**, a user can use a mouse to point and click on screen icons to explore the Internet, particularly the **World Wide Web (the Web)**, an Internet subset of text, images, and sounds linked together to allow users to peruse related topics. Each different location on the Web is called a **web site** or, more commonly, just a **site**. A **home page** is the first page of a web site.
- The most powerful and expensive computers are called **supercomputers.** Large computers called **mainframes** are used by large businesses such as banks, airlines, and large manufacturers to process very large amounts of data quickly. **Minicomputers** are the next step down from mainframes in terms of power and capacity but are being squeezed between mainframes and powerful personal computers.
- Desktop computers are called **personal computers (PCs)**, **microcomputers**, or sometimes home computers. **Workstations** combine the compactness of a desktop computer with power that almost equals that of a mainframe. **Notebook computers** are small portable computers; somewhat larger, heavier versions are called **laptop computers.**
- **Personal digital assistants (PDAs)**, also called **pen-based computers**, are handheld computers that accept handwritten input directly on a screen.
- A **network computer (NC)**, sometimes called simply a **net computer** or **net box**, operates in concert with a television set to access the Internet and send and receive e-mail.

Quick Poll

Compare your answers to those of your colleagues or classmates.
1. Do you prefer one of these statements over the others:
   ❑ a. A personal computer is a worthwhile investment.
   ❑ b. A personal computer probably costs more than it would return in benefits.
   ❑ c. A personal computer is an expensive and difficult undertaking.
2. For my personal use I would prefer
   ❑ a. A desktop computer
   ❑ b. A notebook computer
   ❑ c. A network computer

Discussion Questions

1. Consider the hardware used for input, processing, output, and storage for personal computers. If money were no object, how (generally) would you configure the hardware for your own personal computer? Some considerations:
   a. Input. Would a keyboard be sufficient, or would you want or need a mouse?
   b. Output: You would, of course, have a screen. After the computer itself, the biggest expense is the printer. Can you imagine getting along without a printer?
   c. Is a 3½-inch diskette drive sufficient? Why might you want a hard disk? Why might you want a CD-ROM drive?
2. Why do you think many companies prefer decentralized computer systems? Why might you, as an employee, prefer such a system?

3. Are you considering a particular career? Discuss how computers are used, or could be used, in that field.

Student Study Guide

Multiple Choice

1. The processor is an example of
   a. software
   b. hardware
   c. a program
   d. an output unit
2. Additional data and programs not being used by the processor are stored in
   a. secondary storage
   b. output units
   c. input units
   d. the CPU
3. Step-by-step instructions that run the computer are
   a. hardware
   b. CPUs
   c. documents
   d. software
4. A computer that accepts handwritten input on a screen:
   a. minicomputer
   b. mainframe
   c. desktop computer
   d. pen-based computer
5. Desktop and personal computers are also known as
   a. microcomputers
   b. mainframes
   c. minicomputers
   d. peripheral equipment
6. The raw material to be processed by a computer is called
   a. a program
   b. software
   c. data
   d. information
7. A home page is part of a(n)
   a. terminal
   b. web site
   c. NC
   d. LAN
8. A bar code reader is an example of a(n)
   a. processing device
   b. input device
   c. storage device
   d. output device
9. The computer to which a user's computer connects to access the Internet:
   a. server
   b. supercomputer
   c. notebook
   d. PDA
10. Printers and screens are common forms of
    a. input units
    b. storage units
    c. output units
    d. processing units
11. The unit that transforms data into information:
    a. CPU
    b. disk drive
    c. bar code reader
    d. wand reader
12. The device that reconciles the differences between computers and phones:
    a. TCP/IP
    b. LAN
    c. wand reader
    d. modem
13. A system whereby computers and data storage are placed in dispersed locations is known as
    a. centralized processing
    b. packaged software
    c. summarizing
    d. distributed data processing
14. An example of peripheral equipment:
    a. CPU
    b. printer
    c. spreadsheet
    d. microcomputer
15. A computer that interacts with a television set:
    a. desktop computer
    b. net computer
    c. supercomputer
    d. PDA
16. Software used to access the Internet:
    a. browser
    b. web
    c. server
    d. e-mail
17. A device that inputs data by scanning letters and numbers:
    a. keyboard
    b. mouse
    c. wand reader
    d. diskette
18. Another name for memory is
    a. secondary storage
    b. primary storage
    c. disk storage
    d. tape storage
19. Which is *not* a computer classification?
    a. maxicomputer
    b. microcomputer
    c. minicomputer
    d. mainframe
20. When all access and processing occurs in one location, a computer system is said to be
    a. networked
    b. centralized
    c. distributed
    d. linked
21. An input device that translates the motions of a ball rolled on a flat surface to the screen is a
    a. wand reader
    b. bar code reader
    c. keyboard
    d. mouse
22. Computer users who are not computer professionals are sometimes called
    a. librarians
    b. information officers
    c. peripheral users
    d. end-users
23. The most powerful computers are
    a. superminis
    b. supermainframes
    c. workstations
    d. supercomputers
24. Raw data is processed by the computer into
    a. number sheets
    b. paragraphs
    c. updates
    d. information
25. Laser beam technology is used for
    a. terminals
    b. keyboards
    c. optical disks
    d. magnetic tape

True/False

T F 1. The processor is also called the central processing unit, or CPU.

T F 2. Secondary storage units contain the instructions and data to be used immediately by the processor.

T F 3. A home page is the first page of a web site.

T F 4. Two secondary storage media are magnetic disk and magnetic tape.

T F 5. A diskette holds more data than a hard disk.

T F 6. PDAs accept handwritten data on a screen.

T F 7. The most powerful personal computers are known as supercomputers.

T F 8. A supplier of access to a server is called an Internet service provider.

T F 9. Processed data is called information.

T F 10. The Internet is a subset of the World Wide Web.

T F 11. A modem is the hardware device that is the go-between for computers and telephones.

T F 12. Secondary storage is another name for memory.

T F 13. Most computer systems today are decentralized.

T F 14. Computer hardware is always kept in one large room.

T F 15. These computers are arranged from least powerful to most powerful: microcomputer, mainframe, supercomputer.

T F 16. The Internet is an example of a peripheral device.

T F 17. A distributed data system is centralized in one location.

T F 18. A LAN is usually set up between two cities.

T F 19. Magnetic tape is most often used for backup purposes.

T F 20. Another name for memory is secondary storage.

T F 21. Most users use supercomputers to access the Internet.

T F 22. A modem is used to accept handwritten input on a pen-based computer.

T F 23. A notebook computer is a small, portable computer.

T F 24. A location on the World Wide Web is called a site.

T F 25. Another name for workstation is personal digital assistant.

Fill-In

1. The four general hardware units of a computer are

   a. _____

   b. _____

   c. _____

   d. _____

2. The part of the Internet noted for images and sound: _____

3. Where data is held after it is input to the system but before it is processed: _____

4. What are magnetic tape reels mounted on when their data is to be read by the computer system?

   _____

5. The input, output, and secondary storage devices attached to a computer are known as

   _____

6. Large computers in the computer industry are called _____

7. The term describing a system whereby computers and data storage are placed in geographically separate locations is _____

8. The word for raw material that is given to a computer for processing: _____

9. The exchange of data over communication facilities is called: _____

10. A hardware device that is the intermediary between a computer and the phone system:

    _____

11. The computer that must be accessed to reach the Internet: _____

12. The software used to access the Internet:

    _____

13. CPU stands for _____

14. Three types of input methods mentioned in the chapter:

    a. _____

    b. _____

    c. _____

15. Another name for a microcomputer:

    _____

16. The kind of system that does all its processing in one location: _____

17. Messages sent via a data communications system:

    _____

18. The supplier of the server: _____

19. The opening screen on a web site:

    _____

20. LAN stands for _____

21. PDA stand for _____

22. Another name for Web TV: _____

23. A computer that is as compact as a desktop but has power almost equal to that of a mainframe: _____

24. The software that makes it possible for different kinds of computers to communicate on the Internet: _____

25. The most powerful computers are called _____

26. A computer and its associated equipment are called _____

27. The CPU processes data into: _____

28. The step-by-step instructions that run the computer: _____

29. A particular location on the Web: _____

30. Similar to a laptop computer, but somewhat smaller: _____

Answers

Multiple Choice

1. b	6. c	11. a	16. a	21. d
2. a	7. b	12. d	17. c	22. d
3. d	8. b	13. d	18. b	23. d
4. d	9. a	14. b	19. a	24. d
5. a	10. c	15. b	20. b	25. c

True/False

1. T	6. T	11. T	16. F	21. F
2. F	7. F	12. F	17. F	22. F
3. T	8. T	13. T	18. F	23. T
4. T	9. T	14. F	19. T	24. T
5. F	10. F	15. T	20. F	25. F

Fill-In
1. a. input unit
   b. processor
   c. output unit
   d. storage unit
2. World Wide Web (or just the Web)
3. memory (or primary storage)
4. tape drives
5. peripheral equipment
6. mainframes
7. distributed data processing
8. data
9. data communications
10. modem
11. server
12. browser
13. central processing unit
14. keyboard, mouse, wand reader, or bar code reader
15. personal computer
16. centralized
17. electronic mail (or e-mail)
18. Internet service provider
19. home page
20. local area network
21. personal digital assistant
22. network computer, or net computer, or net box
23. workstation
24. TCP/IP (Transmission Control Protocol/Internet Protocol)
25. supercomputers
26. hardware
27. information
28. software (or programs)
29. web site (or just site)
30. notebook

PLANET INTERNET

OK, let's assume that it's easy enough even for me. Why should I jump in? The one answer that fits everyone is that you dare not risk being left behind. Futurists predict that networking of some kind will be as necessary to work and to living as technologies such as the telephone or computers.

After that, the answer to this question depends a lot on the individual. Are you curious? Would you like to connect with people around the world? Would you like an amazing library at your fingertips? Would you like the convenience of finding out just about anything current—the weather in London, the score of your team's ball game, the verdict of a court case—by typing at the keyboard? Would it amuse you just to see what other folks are up to?

Give me some more for-instances. OK. Do you plan a job search in the near future? The Internet offers job boards and online help. Looking for advice on backpacking? There are many sites with comprehensive information. Consider some screens that could show up during your Internet travels. The White House image shown here signals your ability to ask questions of the president or even take a picture tour inside the White House. You can also see Model T Fords at the Henry Ford Museum, see photos of the Titanic, order oranges from Florida, or even see the periodic table of the elements.

WHAT IS IT ALL ABOUT?

First, just what is the Internet? The Internet, sometimes called simply "the 'Net," is a loosely organized global collection of thousands of networks. It can be accessed by anyone who has a computer, appropriate software, and a connection to a computer called a server.

Why has it become so popular? The main reason is that the Internet offers so much information in a convenient way. The information is both high in volume and extremely varied in content. The Internet is also quite easy to use, at least compared to other technologies. A person with relatively minimal knowledge can access the 'Net from the nearest connected computer, even from home.

Is this going to cost money? *Maybe.* Free Internet access is common in schools and libraries and other government organizations. Your employer may offer free access. If you want to hook up from your own personal computer, the required software is probably free, but you will have to pay some sort of monthly charge to the company providing the physical connection.

Speaking of usage, I have heard that people spend hours and hours on the Internet. *This is not uncommon.* The Internet has so much to offer that a user can easily drift from one thing to another without realizing how the time passes by. But a specific task can often be done in a reasonable amount of time.

What's coming up later in the Internet discussions? For the most part, we'll examine various offerings on the Internet, some serious, some less so. Information about using the Internet will be tucked in here and there, so your knowledge will grow. In the next discussion of *Planet Internet* we'll start traveling on the most popular part of the Internet, the World Wide Web.

Somewhere along the way, you may wish to look over the Internet sites featured in the gallery called *The Visual Internet.* If you want detailed information right away, check out Chapter 7, *The Internet: A Resource for All of Us.*

Periodic Table of the Elements

IA																	0
1 H	IIA											IIIA	IVA	VA	VIA	VIIA	2 He
3 Li	4 Be											5 B	6 C	7 N	8 O	9 F	10 Ne
11 Na	12 Mg	IIIB	IVB	VB	VIB	VIIB	── VII ──		IB	IB		13 Al	14 Si	15 P	16 S	17 Cl	18 Ar
19 K	20 Ca	21 Sc	22 Ti	23 V	24 Cr	25 Mn	26 Fe	27 Co	28 Ni	29 Cu	30 Zn	31 Ga	32 Ge	33 As	34 Se	35 Br	36 Kr
37 Rb	38 Sr	39 Y	40 Zr	41 Nb	42 Mo	43 Tc	44 Ru	45 Rh	46 Pd	47 Ag	48 Cd	49 In	50 Sn	51 Sb	52 Te	53 I	54 Xe
55 Cs	56 Ba	57 *La	72 Hf	73 Ta	74 W	75 Re	76 Os	77 Ir	78 Pt	79 Au	80 Hg	81 Tl	82 Pb	83 Bi	84 Po	85 At	86 Rn
87 Fr	88 Ra	89 +Ac	104 Rf	105 Ha	106	107	108	109	110								

	58 Ce	59 Pr	60 Nd	61 Pm	62 Sm	63 Eu	64 Gd	65 Tb	66 Dy	67 Ho	68 Er	69 Tm	70 Yb	71 Lu
* Lanthanide Series	58 Ce	59 Pr	60 Nd	61 Pm	62 Sm	63 Eu	64 Gd	65 Tb	66 Dy	67 Ho	68 Er	69 Tm	70 Yb	71 Lu
+ Actinide Series	90 Th	91 Pa	92 U	93 Np	94 Pu	95 Am	96 Cm	97 Bk	98 Cf	99 Es	100 Fm	101 Md	102 No	103 Lr

After her first year in college, Anita Jefferson got a summer job in the resort town of Friday Harbor. She waited tables for both the noon and evening shifts. Her wages were supplemented nicely by generous tips from carefree tourists. An accounting major, Anita would have preferred a job in a business office, but at least her summer income would make a significant dent in her upcoming tuition.

As it turned out, Anita's summer was more valuable than she expected. On her second day on the job, she learned that a colleague had signed up for a morning computer class at the local branch of a community college. Since it was a beginning class and did not interfere with her work schedule, Anita signed up too.

Anita's previous computer experiences were limited to math drills in elementary school and playing games on her mother's home computer. She knew that, as an accountant, she would certainly use a computer. In fact, two of her fall classes, according to the schedule, required computer lab time. Although somewhat apprehensive, Anita was hoping to get a head start on computers.

The course included both lectures on the fundamentals of computer hardware and software and hands-on computer experience. By the end of the summer, Anita had a good grasp of computer basics and could perform such tasks as preparing memos on the computer. But her greatest reward was learning how to use spreadsheets, which let her enter, revise, and print numerical data in rows and columns. She recognized that budgets, ledgers, inventories, and other keystones of accounting would all be maintained using spreadsheets on a computer. She definitely got a head start.

Computer Software

Productivity and Systems Software

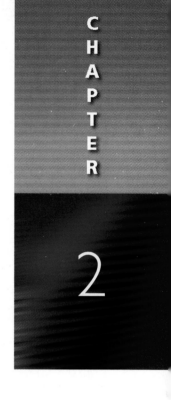

▶ Software: Telling the Machine What to Do

When people think about computers, they usually think about machines. The tapping on the keyboard, the rumble of whirling disk drives, the changing flashes of color on a computer screen—these are the attention getters. However, it is really the **software**—the planned, step-by-step set of instructions required to turn data into information—that makes a computer useful.

Generally speaking, software can be categorized as *systems software* or *applications software*. However, people rarely speak of systems software; it is more common to discuss a subset of systems software known as the **operating system**, the underlying software found on all computers. **Applications software** is *applied* to a real-world task. It can be used to solve a particular problem or to perform a particular task—to keep track of store inventory or design a car engine or draft the minutes of the PTA meeting or play a game of solitaire. Let us contrast these two categories of software.

Operating Systems

When a brand new computer comes off the factory assembly line, it can do nothing. The hardware needs software to make it work. But applications software cannot communicate directly with the hardware, so the operating system serves as intermediary software between the applications software and the hardware. Some important tasks of an operating system are managing the computer's resources—the central processing unit, memory, disk drives, and printers—and running applications software.

Operating systems for mainframe and other large computers are complex indeed, since they must keep track of several programs from several users all running in the same time frame. Although some personal computer operating systems—most often found in business or learning environments—can support multiple users, most are concerned only with a single user at a time. A common operating system for personal computers is Windows (Figure 2-1). Although the operating system is important and necessary software, users spend most of their time interacting with the kind of software highlighted in this chapter—applications software.

Applications Software

Applications software may be either custom or packaged. Many large organizations pay **computer programmers**—people who design, write, test, and implement software—to write **custom software**, software that is specifically tailored to their needs. Custom software for the tasks of a large organization may be extremely complex and take a lot of time—possibly years—to write.

The average person is most likely to deal with software for personal computers, called **packaged software** or **commercial software**. This software is literally packaged in a container of some sort, usually a box or folder, and is sold in stores or catalogs. Packaged software for personal computers often comes in a box that is as colorful as that of a board game. Inside the box you will find one or more disks holding the software and, usually, an instruction manual, also referred to as **documenta-**

Figure 2-1 Windows screen. The screen on this user's computer shows an icon for each of several software packages available on the computer. A double-click of the mouse on the icon invokes the desired program. Note the task bar at the bottom of the screen: it shows a button for each program currently in use. Note that the names of the programs on the buttons are abbreviated; the names become shorter and shorter as added buttons crowd the early arrivals.

tion (Figure 2-2). Note, however, that some packaged software has little written documentation; the information about the software is mostly on disk with the software for handy future reference.

To use personal computer software, you begin by inserting the disk in the disk drive. Then, depending on the hardware and software, you either type specified instructions on the keyboard or give a command with the click of a mouse; the software begins to run—that is, the computer follows the software instructions. Note, however, that complex software comes on either several diskettes or a CD-ROM, and usually requires a setup—installation—process before use. Furthermore, for future convenience, most users copy new software to their hard disk drive before they use it.

A great assortment of software is available to help you with a variety of tasks—writing papers, preparing budgets, storing and retrieving infor-

Figure 2-2 Packaged software. Each of the colorful software packages shown here includes one or more disks containing the software needed to run the program and at least a minimal instruction manual, or documentation, describing how to use the software.

Never Too Old

Computers in business? Of course. Computers for youngsters? Certainly. But the fastest-growing group of computer users is senior citizens. Many seniors, in fact, have more discretionary income and more time on their hands than teenagers.

The majority of seniors say they were drawn to computers because they did not want to be left behind. They flock to classes, both private and public. Many senior students use their new word processing skills to write memoirs for their grandchildren. Others monitor their investments, create greeting cards, or even begin post-retirement businesses.

One 72-year-old hauled her laptop on an eight-month journey by boat, bus, and bicycle around the world. She sent back periodic reports that were published in her local newspaper. Now, she says, she answers her grandchildren's questions about the world—and about computers.

mation, drawing graphs, playing games, and much more. This wonderful array of software is what makes computers so useful.

Most personal computer software is designed to be user friendly. The term **user friendly** has become a cliché, but it still conveys meaning: It usually means that the software is supposed to be easy—perhaps even intuitive—for a beginner to use or that the software can be used with a minimum of training.

But What Would I Use It For?

New computer owners soon discover a little secret: the box is only the beginning. Although they may have agonized for months over their hardware choice, they are often uncertain as to how to proceed when purchasing software. The most common pattern for a new user is to start out with some standard software packages, such as word processing and other basic applications, but then to expand the software universe as he or she becomes aware of what is available. The needs of different people will be met with different software. Here are two real-life scenarios.

Kristin Bjornson is a private detective who, using a computer, runs her business from her home. Her computer came with word processing software, plus some CD-ROMs holding an encyclopedia, a family doctor reference program, and several games. Her primary interest was business information and certain public files on the Internet. She selected an Internet service provider and used software supplied by the provider. She also prepared her income taxes using a question-and-answer tax preparation program. Over the next year, Kristin purchased other software unrelated to business applications: software to draw maps of highways for planned trips, a program to help her son study for the Scholastic Assessment Test, and a three-dimensional game called Knowledge Adventureland for her six-year-old (Figure 2-3).

As a second example, consider Max Prentiss, whose first job as an apprentice carpenter did not involve computers. But Max made a computer one of his first acquisitions. He subsequently purchased various software: software containing an atlas and quotations, an on-screen version of The Far Side calendar, and an all-in-one package that included software for a personal phone book, home budget planning, and home repair. But he eventually focused on the beautiful nature images available on CD-ROMs and acquired quite a collection (Figure 2-4).

The point of these stories is that different people want different software applications. You have only to stroll through a few aisles of software racks to appreciate the variety of software available. Whether you

Figure 2-3 Knowledge Adventureland software. This program offers children a sense of moving around a three-dimensional scene. Represented by the software's cartoon characters, children can explore on-screen communities, including libraries and museums.

(a)

(b)

Figure 2-4 Images from CD-ROM software. (a) This whale image is one of many from the CD-ROM called In the Company of Whales, which features whale sights, sounds, and habitats. (b) Although they look benign, polar bears are considered Dangerous Creatures on the CD-ROM of the same name.

want to learn to type or tour a museum or build a deck, or perhaps try such crazy-but-real titles as *Internet for Cats* or the sci-fi thriller called *I Have No Mouth and I Must Scream*, someone offers the software.

Acquiring Software

Sometimes software is free. Software is considered to be in the **public domain** if its author chooses to provide it free to all. Software in the public domain is sometimes called **freeware.** Such software might be offered by an individual at home or perhaps by an educator or student. Sometimes software is offered free from vendors as part of a marketing campaign. Software is often provided as part of a computer purchase, although it may be a stretch to call it free.

Software called **shareware** is also given away free; the maker hopes for voluntary payment—that is, he or she hopes that you like it well enough to send a contribution. Both public domain software and shareware may be copied freely and given to other people. But the software that people use most often, packaged software such as word processing or spreadsheet software, is **copyrighted software.** This kind of software costs money and must not be copied without permission from the manufacturer. In fact, software manufacturers call making illegal copies of copyrighted software **software piracy** and pursue miscreants to the full extent of the law.

Generally speaking, copyrighted software is vastly superior to freeware and shareware. Since the manufacturer is anxious to please many users, copyrighted software is likely to have many desirable features. Furthermore, it has been extensively tested by the manufacturer, so it is likely to be dependable. Finally, copyrighted software is fully documented and is updated at regular intervals.

What is the best way to purchase copyrighted software? The legendary small retail software store is disappearing fast because the price of software has declined too much to provide an acceptable profit margin. So software has moved to the warehouse stores and to mail-order houses, each with thousands of software titles. The high sales volume takes up the slack for slim per-unit profits. From the individual con-

NEW DIRECTIONS

THIS OLD HOUSE

The future is in sight. "This old house" will eventually become the intelligent networked home. This artist's depiction shows household computers and most appliances hooked to and under the control of an in-home central computer. That central computer is linked to the outside world, providing access to information networks and to community services such as the fire department.

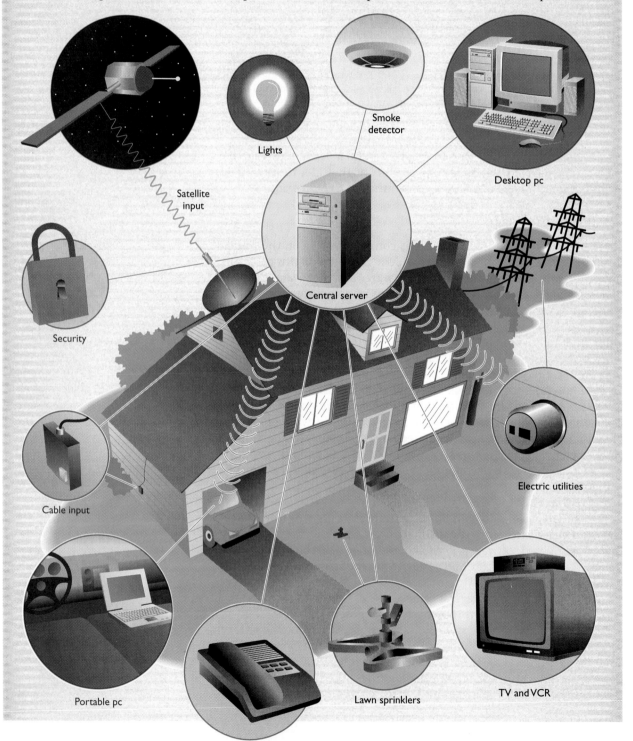

Satellite input

Lights

Smoke detector

Desktop pc

Security

Central server

Electric utilities

Cable input

Portable pc

Lawn sprinklers

TV and VCR

sumer's point of view, the lower prices and convenient one-stop shopping are significant advantages.

The organization, as opposed to individual users, must take a different approach. Most organizations—businesses, government, nonprofit agencies—have computers, and their users, of course, need software. The most widespread solution is obtaining vendor permission to copy software legally, an approach called site licensing. Typically, a **site license** permits an organization, for a fee, to make a limited number of copies of a software product. The customer agrees to keep track of who uses it, and takes responsibility for copying and distributing manuals to its own personnel. Incidentally, if you work for a large corporation, check with your employer before you buy a copy of the expensive software you use at the office. Under some license agreements, employees are allowed to use the same software at home.

Organizations with local area networks usually install widely used software such as word processing on the network's server computer. Thus, the software is available to users connected to the network without the necessity of installing the software on each user's computer.

Another software movement is afoot: **electronic software distribution.** Never mind the trip to the store. A user can simply pay to **download** the software—move it from another computer to the user's computer over data communications links. In fact, in the not-so-distant future, users will not need to purchase software, but will be able merely to download it temporarily from a vendor via the Internet for a per-use rental fee. Downloading software from the Internet is already a reality; many users get both freeware and shareware from the Internet.

▶ Ethics and Software

The most sizzling ethics issue related to software is the issuing of illegal software copies, the software piracy we mentioned earlier. Lamentations by both business and the computer industry are so persistent and so loud that we are devoting a separate section to this issue.

Have you ever copied a friend's music CD or tape onto your own blank tape? Many people do so without much thought. It is also possible to photocopy a book. Both acts are clearly illegal, but there is much more fuss over illegal software copying than over copying music or books. Why is this? Well, to begin with, few of us are likely to undertake the laborious task of reproducing *War and Peace* on a copy machine. Another difference is that a copied tape or book is never quite as good as the original; copied software, on the other hand, is identical to the original and works just as well. The other part of the issue is money. A pirated copy of a top-20 CD will set the recording company—and the artist—back just a few dollars. But pirated software may be valued at hundreds of dollars. The problem of stolen software has grown right along with the personal computer industry.

OK If I Copy That Software?

Consider this incident. Bill Huston got his computer education at a local community college. One of his courses taught him how to use software on personal computers. He had access to a great variety of copyrighted software in the college computer lab. After graduating, he got a job at a

The Entertainer

New users sometimes worry that a computer will be used mostly for games. Surveys show that about 70 percent of personal computer users happily admit that they play games—at least a little—almost daily. In fact, entertainment is a perfectly valid use of a personal computer in the home. But the entertainment need not be limited to games. Here is one sample of an entertainment package.

Snoopy's Campfire Stories. This software lets young children have fun interacting with the old Peanuts gang—and learn a bit at the same time. For example, when Snoopy recites a story, he is seen typing it on his laptop computer. The same words show up on the child's screen, making an association between the spoken and written word. This activity and a set of games offer a nice introduction to computers.

local museum, where he used database software on a personal computer to catalog museum wares. He also had his own computer at home.

One day Bill stopped back at the college and ran into a former instructor. After greetings were exchanged, she asked him why he happened to drop by. "Oh," he said, "I just came by to make some copies of software." He wasn't kidding. Neither was the instructor, who, after she caught her breath, replied, "You can't do that. It's illegal." Bill was miffed, saying, "But I can't afford it!" The instructor immediately alerted the computer lab. As a result of this encounter, the staff strengthened policies on software use and increased the vigilance of lab personnel. In effect, schools must protect themselves from people who lack ethics or are unaware of the law.

There are many people like Bill. He did not think in terms of stealing anything; he just wanted to make copies for himself. But, as the software industry is quick to point out, unauthorized copying *is* stealing because the software makers do not get the revenues to which they are entitled. Furthermore, if software developers are not properly compensated, they may eventually find it not worthwhile to develop new software for our use.

Why Those Extra Copies?

Copying software is not always a dirty trick—there are lots of legitimate reasons for copying. To begin with, after paying several hundred dollars for a piece of software, you will definitely want to make a backup copy in case of disk failure or accident. You might want to copy the program onto a hard disk and use it, more conveniently, from there. Software publishers have no trouble with these types of copying. But thousands of computer users copy software for another reason: to get the program without paying for it. This is clearly unethical and illegal.

▶ Some Task-Oriented Software

Most users, whether at home or in business, are drawn to task-oriented software, sometimes called productivity software, that can make their work faster and their lives easier. The major categories of task-oriented software are word processing (including desktop publishing), spreadsheets, database management, graphics, and communications. Further, software designated as office suites offers some combination of these categories in a single package. A brief description of each category follows.

Word Processing/Desktop Publishing

The most widely used personal computer software is **word processing** software. Business people use word processing for memos, reports, correspondence, minutes of meetings, and anything else that someone can think of to type. Users in a home environment type term papers, letters, journals, movie logs, and much more. Word processing software lets you create, edit, format, store, and print text and graphics in one document. In this definition it is the three words in the middle—*edit*, *format*, and *store*—that reveal the difference between word processing and plain typing. Since you can store on disk the memo or document you typed, you can retrieve it another time, change it, reprint it, or do whatever you like with it. You can see what a great time-saver word processing can be.

STUMPED? ASK YOUR SOFTWARE

For those who hesitate to pester their friends and colleagues with yet another software question, there is good news: Now you can ask the software itself. To help computer users help themselves, several software makers have equipped their programs with the ability to solicit and respond to questions in plain English. In a word processing program, for example, you could type the question "How do I insert a picture?" When using a spreadsheet, you might type "Show me how to add up the numbers in this column."

The software responds with a screen that is appropriate to the subject matter and proceeds to coach you through the procedure.

The software even "humanizes" the process by giving the coach a name, such as the Expert or the Wizard.

Unchanged parts of the stored document do not need to be retyped; the whole revised document can be reprinted as if new.

As the number of features in word processing packages has grown, word processing has crossed the border into desktop publishing territory. **Desktop publishing** packages are usually better than word processing packages at meeting high-level publishing needs, especially when it comes to typesetting and color reproduction. Many magazines and newspapers today rely heavily on desktop publishing software (Figure 2-5). Businesses use it to produce professional-looking newsletters, reports, and brochures—both to improve internal communication and to make a better impression on the outside world.

Electronic Spreadsheets

Spreadsheets, made up of columns and rows of numbers, have been used as business tools for centuries (Figure 2-6). A manual spreadsheet can be tedious to prepare, and when there are changes, a considerable amount of calculation may need to be redone. An **electronic spreadsheet** is still a spreadsheet, but the computer does the work. In particular, spreadsheet software automatically recalculates the results when a number is changed. If, for example, one chore of a spreadsheet is to calculate distance based on rate and time, a change in the rate would automatically cause a new calculation so that the distance would change too. This capability lets business people try different combinations of numbers and obtain the results quickly. The ability to ask "What if . . . ?" and then see the results on the computer before actually committing resources helps business people make better, faster decisions.

What about spreadsheet software for the user at home? The ability to enter combinations of numbers in a meaningful way—such as different combinations of down payments and interest rates for the purchase of a home—gives users financial vision that they could not readily produce on their own. Users at home use spreadsheets for everything from preparing budgets to figuring out whether to take a new job to tracking their progress at the gym.

Database Management

Software used for **database management**—the management of a collection of interrelated facts—handles data in several ways. The software can

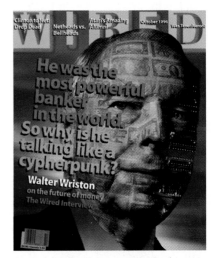

Figure 2-5 Desktop publishing. Many novice computer users produce attractive newsletters and brochures with desktop publishing, but professional publications, such as this cover for Wired Magazine, are also produced with desktop publishing. This magazine cover was produced with computer software. The art was created with graphics software. The photo was digitized with imaging software. The type and layout were produced with desktop publishing software, which was also used to combine the text and art. The completed cover was then printed to film, which a printer used to produce the finished product.

EXPENSES	JANUARY	FEBRUARY	MARCH	APRIL	TOTAL
RENT	425.00	425.00	425.00	425.00	1700.00
PHONE	22.50	31.25	17.00	35.75	106.50
CLOTHES	110.00	135.00	156.00	91.00	492.00
FOOD	280.00	250.00	250.00	300.00	1080.00
HEAT	80.00	50.00	24.00	95.00	249.00
ELECTRICITY	35.75	40.50	45.00	36.50	157.75
WATER	10.00	11.00	11.00	10.50	42.50
CAR INSURANCE	75.00	75.00	75.00	75.00	300.00
ENTERTAINMENT	150.00	125.00	140.00	175.00	590.00
TOTAL	1188.25	1142.75	1143.00	1243.75	4717.75

(a)

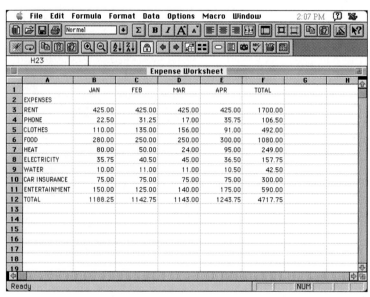

(b)

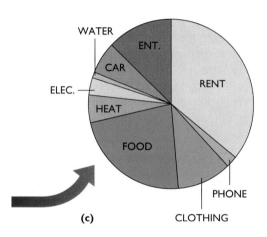

(c)

Figure 2-6 A simple expense spreadsheet. (a) This paper-and-pencil expense sheet is a typical spreadsheet of rows and columns. You have to do the calculations to fill in the totals. (b) This screen shows the same information on a computer spreadsheet program, which does the calculations for you. (c) The spreadsheet program can also present the expenses graphically in the form of a pie chart.

store data, update it, manipulate it, retrieve it, report it in a variety of views, and print it in as many forms. By the time the data is in the reporting stage—given to a user in a useful form—it has become information. A concert promoter, for example, can store and change data about upcoming concert dates, seating, ticket prices, and sales. After this is done, the promoter can use the software to retrieve information, such as the number of tickets sold in each price range or the percentage of tickets sold the day before the concert.

Database software can be useful for anyone who must keep track of a large number of related facts. Consider crime detection, which involves a process of elimination—a tedious task. Tedious work, however, is often the kind the computer does best. Once data is entered into a database, searching by computer is possible. Examples: Which criminals use a particular mode of operation? Which criminals are associates of this suspect? Does license number AXB221 refer to a stolen car? And so on. One particularly successful crime-detection database application is a fingerprint-matching system, which can match crime-scene fingerprints with computer-stored fingerprints.

Home users apply database software to any situation in which they want to retrieve stored data in a variety of ways. For example, one hobbyist stores data about her coin collection. She can retrieve information from the coin database by country, date, value, or size. Another user, a volunteer who helps find blood donors for the American Red Cross, maintains a file of all donors in his area so that he can retrieve names and phone numbers by querying on blood type, zip code, or the last date blood was donated.

Graphics

It might seem wasteful to show **graphics** to business people when standard computer printouts of numbers are readily available. However, graphs, maps, and charts can help people compare data, spot trends more easily, and make decisions more quickly (Figure 2-7a). In addition, visual information is usually more compelling than a page of numbers. Besides dressing up facts and figures, graphics are often used by business people, or anyone with a message to deliver, as part of a presentation.

The most pleasing use of graphics software is the work produced by **graphic artists,** people who have both artistic ability and the skills to use sophisticated graphics software to express their ideas. Artists use software as a tool of their craft to produce stunning computer art (Figure 2-7b).

Communications

Chapter 1 described communications in a general way. From the viewpoint of an individual with a personal computer at home, **communications** means—in simple terms—that he or she can hook a phone up to the computer and communicate with the computer at the office or access data stored in another computer in another location. The most likely way for such a user to connect to others is via the Internet. As noted in Chapter 1, a user needs software called a **browser** to access the Internet. A browser may be a single software package or it may be included as part of other software offerings. Internet access is described more completely in Chapter 7. Meanwhile, you can pick up the flavor of the Internet from the home page screens shown in Figure 2-8.

Although the Internet is heavily used by both individuals and businesses, organizations—mostly business and government—were major users of communications software long before the Internet was in the mainstream. Consider weather forecasting. Some businesses, such as

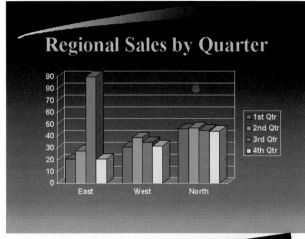

(a)

(b)

Figure 2-7 Graphics. (a) Colorful computer-generated graphics can help people compare data and spot trends. (b) This artwork was generated on the computer with graphics software. The artist has titled this piece Fantasy Diver.

(a)

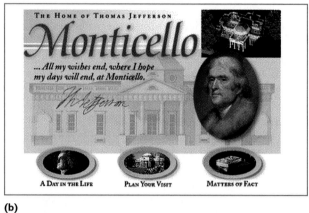

(b)

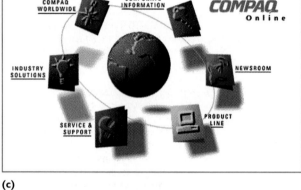

(c)

(d)

Figure 2-8 A sample of home pages from the Internet. These screens give some indication of the variety of home pages that can be found on the Internet: (a) Bicycle Masterpieces, featuring "the most beautiful bicycles in the world," (b) an historical view of Thomas Jefferson's Monticello home, (c) Compaq Computer's product line, and (d) car dealer Perkins's Internet showroom.

agriculture, amusement parks, and ski areas, are so dependent on the weather that they need constantly updated information. Various services offer analysis of live weather data, including air pressure, fog, rain, and wind direction and speed.

For a totally different type of communications application, consider the stock exchange. Stock portfolios can be managed by software that takes quotations over communication lines directly from established market monitors such as Dow Jones. The software keeps records and offers quick and accurate investment advice. And, of course, the stock exchange itself is a veritable beehive of computers, all communicating with one another and with remote computers that can provide current information.

Office Suites

Since most people need to use the kinds of task-oriented software just described, some choose to buy a **suite**—a bundle of basic software designed to work together. The phrase *work together* is the key. If you buy word processing software from one manufacturer and a spreadsheet package from another, they may be incompatible. Using suite software, however, means that you could easily build a spreadsheet and then move it into a report you are preparing using word processing.

Most personal computers come with simple suites that feature word processing, spreadsheet, and graphics programs. But even moderately sophisticated users may quickly outgrow such programs. The next step up, whether you are a professional working from home, a small business owner, or just a hobbyist, includes more sophisticated versions of these applications and additional software types, such as database management. In fact, one of the most common office application of suites is **mail merge**, in which certain names and addresses from a database are used on letters prepared using a word processor. Three or four software makers have dominated the suite market for years and continue to offer software upgrades—newer and better versions.

Software makers have long tried to outdo one another by offering software with myriad seldom-used features. However, they have recently begun to take a different approach. Vendors now focus on ease of use and on throwing in nifty programs such as personal time organizers, to-do list makers, e-mail programs, and—best of all—access to the Internet.

The do-everything programs, of course, need significant amounts of memory and also hog a lot of disk space, so be sure that the requirements listed on the software box fit your hardware. The good news, however, is that competition continues to heat up the price wars, causing the prices of these packages to fall.

▶ This Is Serious Business

We have already mentioned that many large organizations often hire their own programmers to write custom software. The Boeing Company, for example, will not find software to plan the electrical wiring of an airplane among off-the-rack packages. However, not all of a company's software need be custom-made. Many companies use standard packages for standard tasks such as payroll and accounts receivable. Furthermore, some software vendors specialize in a certain "vertical" slice of the business community, serving similar customers such as plumbers or accountants.

Vertical Market Software

Software written especially for a particular group of like customers, such as dentists or plumbers, is called **vertical market software**. This user-oriented software usually presents options with a series of easy-to-follow menus that minimize the training needed.

An auto repair shop is a good example of a business that can make use of vertical market software. Designed in conjunction with people who understand the auto repair business, the comprehensive software for an auto shop can prepare work orders, process sales transactions, produce invoices, evaluate sales and profits, track parts inventory, print reorder reports, and update the customer mailing list.

Another example is software designed for beauty salon operators. Does your hairdresser really remember exactly how to do your hair and that you like to talk about yardwork and movies? Maybe. But it is more likely that a card is on file somewhere, listing your preferences. In some shops that "card" is stored in the computer. Before you arrive, this data can be pulled up on a screen. After you leave, the hairdresser immediately updates your customer history. In addition, the software credits the stylist for providing the service and uses this data to calculate the stylist's commission. The computer can also produce reports, include sales summaries by period, product inventories, appointment reminder cards, thank-you cards, and promotional letters.

The Cost of Meetings
Many workers consider meetings boring and unproductive. Furthermore, studies have shown that as much as 30 percent of corporate overhead is burned up in traditional meetings. A software package called Meeting Meter dramatically refutes any lingering doubts about the cost of meetings.

Using a laptop computer, a manager can input "guesstimates" of the salaries of each attendee. The meter program then acts as a money clock, displaying the running salary cost of the meeting for all to see. For example, for a meeting of two managers (each earning approximately $35 per hour), seven professionals ($30), two assistants ($20), and one secretary ($10), the clock would display $495 after 1½ hours. The clock encourages attendees to focus on the subject at hand and to become more active participants.

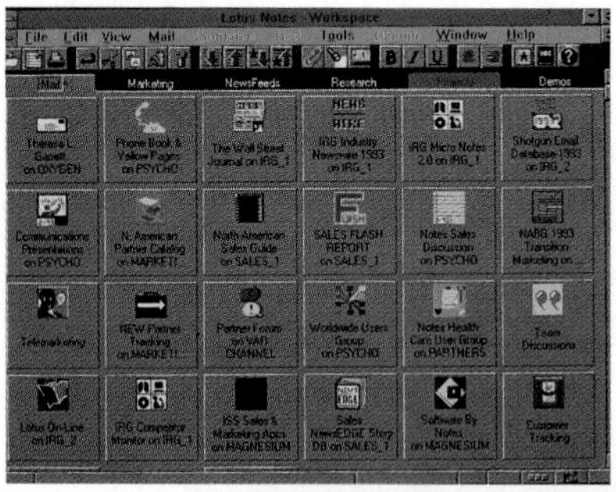

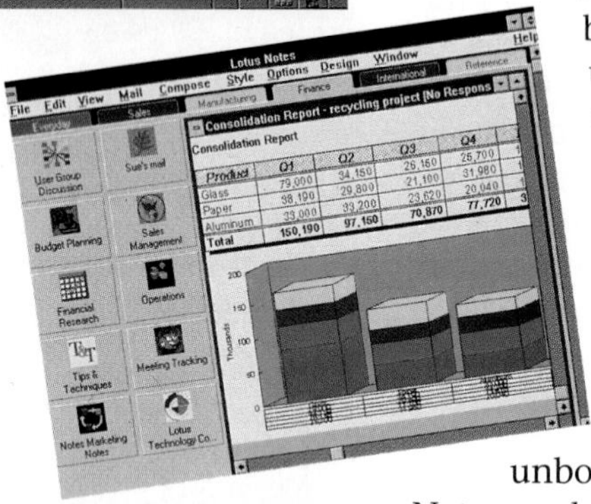

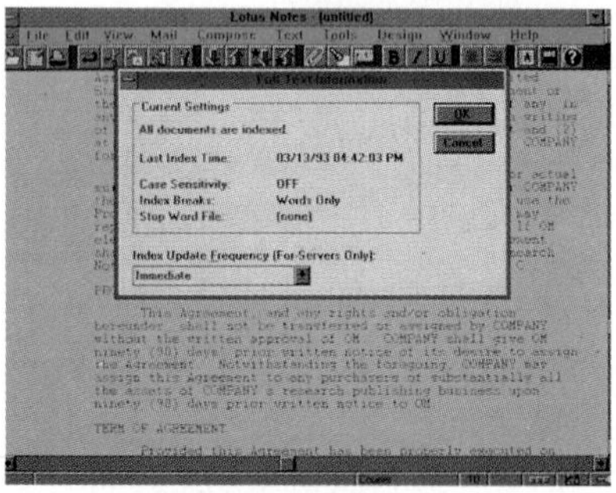

Figure 2-9 Notes. These three screens are from a groupware package called Notes. Groupware lets workers use the computer to collaborate on a project.

Software for Workgroups

If you work on a project with a group of people, it is likely that you will use software especially made for that scenario. **Groupware**, also called **collaborative software**, can be defined generally as any kind of software that lets a group of people share information or track information together. Using that general definition, some people might say that electronic mail is a form of groupware. But simply sending data back and forth by e-mail has inherent limitations for collaboration, the most obvious being confusion if there are more than two group members. To work together effectively on a project, the data being used must be in a central place that can be accessed and changed by anyone working on the project. That central place is a database, or databases, on disk. Having the data in just one place eliminates the old problem of separate and possibly different versions of the same project.

A popular groupware package called Notes combines electronic mail, networking, and database technology (Figure 2-9). Using such groupware, business people can work with one another and share knowledge or expertise unbounded by factors such as distance or time zone differences. Notes can be installed on all computers on the network.

Groupware is most often used by a team for a specific project. A classic example is a bid prepared by Price Waterhouse, an accounting firm, for a consulting contract. They had just a few days to put together a complex proposal, and the four people who needed to write it were in three different states. They were able to work together using their computers and Notes, which permitted a four-way dialogue on-screen. They also extracted key components of the proposal from existing company databases, including the résumés of company experts, and borrowed passages from similar successful proposals.

Getting Software Help at Work: The Information Center

More often than not, a worker in an office has a computer on his or her desk. It is just a matter of time until that user needs help. If personal computer users compared notes, they would probably find that their experiences are similar. The experience of budget analyst Manuela Lopez is typical. She was given her own personal computer so that she could analyze financial data. She learned to use a popular spreadsheet program. She soon thought about branching out with other software products. She wanted a statistics software package but was not sure which one was appropriate or how to get it. She saw that a colleague was using a database management program but had no idea how to use it herself. Most of all, Manuela felt her productivity would increase significantly if she knew how to use the software to access certain data in the corporate data files.

The company **information center** is the solution to these kinds of needs. Although no two centers are alike, all information centers are devoted exclusively to giving users service. Information centers usually offer help with software selection, software training, and, if appropriate, access to corporate computer systems.

▶ Software for a Small Business

Suppose that, as a fledgling entrepreneur with some computer savvy, your ambition is to be as competitive as one personal computer will let you be. You are not alone. Two interesting statistics are that more than half of American workers would like to own their own businesses and that the number of home-office workers is increasing by 5 percent a year. Savvy entrepreneurs realize that a computer is a major asset in running the business, even at the very start (Figure 2-10). The software industry has responded to this need with various packages that come under the generic heading **small office, home office,** or **SOHO** for short.

You know you cannot afford expensive software, but you also know that there is an abundance of moderately priced software that can enhance all aspects of your business. A look through any store display of software packages will reveal several aimed at small businesses, from marketing strategy software to software for handling mailing lists.

The following basic list is presented according to business functions— things you will want to be able to do. The computer can help.

■ **Accounting.** Totaling the bottom line must be the number one priority for any business. If you are truly on your own, or have just one or two employees, you may be able to get by with simple spreadsheet software to work up a ledger and balance sheet and generate basic invoices and payroll worksheets. Larger operations can consider a complete accounting package, which produces profit-and-loss statements, balance sheets, cash flow reports, and tax summaries. Most packages will also write and print checks and some have payroll capability.

Figure 2-10 A small business. Better make that plural—entrepreneur Bill Kimberlin owns several small businesses. When he heard that a large clothing manufacturer had 70,000 pairs of irregular jeans sitting in its factory, he called and asked if he could sell them. Calling mom and pop stores, he sold them all in three months. Bill uses his computer in a variety of ways. On one occasion, for example, when he had a chance to buy some property containing coal, he turned to the Internet to learn everything he could about the coal business, becoming something of an instant expert.

MAKING THE RIGHT CONNECTIONS

WE MEAN REALLY REMOTE

Need to send immediate reports from the Alaska hinterlands? No problem. As you can see, this troubleshooter carries a laptop computer to check out glitches along the Alaska pipeline. He can connect his computer's modem up to a conventional phone hookup or a cellular phone.

But what if a far-flung user needs to access files located elsewhere? Again, no problem. Remote control software lets a remote user, whether in a snowbank in Alaska or a home office in Albuquerque, access a network, transfer files, or even run a program. We hasten to add that not just anyone can pop into a network; proper authorization is required, even at long distance.

■ **Writing and advertising.** Word processing is an obvious choice because you will need to write memos and the like. Desktop publishing can be a real boon to a small business, letting you design and produce advertisements, flyers, and even your own letterhead stationery, business forms, and business cards. A big advantage of publishing your own advertisements or flyers is that you can print small quantities and start anew when your business or address or service changes. Finally, you may think it is worthwhile to publish your own newsletter for customers.

■ **Customer service.** Customer service is a byword throughout the business world, but the personal touch is especially important in a small business. Database software can be useful here. Suppose, for example, that you run a pet grooming service. You surely want to keep track of each customer by address, and so forth, for billing and advertising purposes. But this is just the beginning. Why not store data about each pet, too? Think how impressed the customer on the phone will be when you recall that Sadie is a standard poodle, seven years old, and that it is time for her to have her booster shots.

■ **Keeping up and making contacts.** Even if you have only one computer, you can still be networked to the outside world. Business connections are available in many forms from dozens of sites on the Internet.

■ **Making sales pitches.** If your business depends on pitching your product or service in some formal way, presentation software can help you create colorful demonstrations that are the equivalent of an electronic slide show. Presentation software is designed for regular people, not artists, so putting together a slick sequence of text and graphics is remarkably simple (Figure 2-11a and b).

Finally, consider an all-in-one software package specifically designed to help you get your home office organized. This is a variation on the suites described earlier, but geared specifically to the small business. If

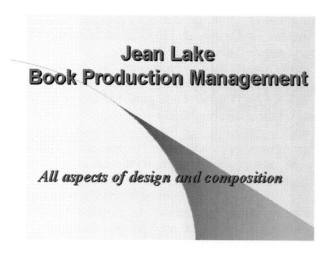
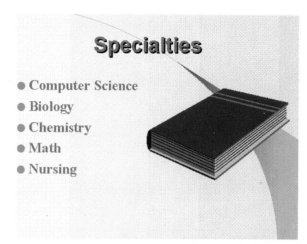

Figure 2-11 A computer-produced presentation. Shown here are just two of the screens that Jean Lake uses when making a presentation about her business. She was able to prepare them quickly using graphics software. She can show the screens directly with a projector connected to a computer or have them converted to conventional slides.

you are on your own, you need the organizational skills of a secretary, the research skills of a librarian, the accounting skills of a bookkeeper, and the experience of someone who has done it before. Comprehensive SOHO packages address all these needs, providing a searchable library of resources, a legal guide, and a tax guide. The packages also include collections of business documents for every situation, from asset depreciation to press release announcements. Such packages also typically offer links to useful business and government sites on the Internet.

Computers and People

These first two chapters have described hardware, software, and data, but the most important element in a computer system is people. Anyone nervous about a takeover by computers will be relieved to know that computers will never amount to much without people—the people who help make the system work and the people for whom the work is done.

Computers and You, the User

As noted earlier, computer users have come to be called just *users*, a nickname that has persisted for years. Whereas once computer users were an elite breed—high-powered scientists, research-and-development engineers, government planners—today the population of users has broadened considerably. This expansion is due partly to user-friendly software for both work and personal use and partly to the availability of small, low-cost, personal computers. There is every likelihood that all of us will be computer users, even if our levels of sophistication vary.

Computer People

Many organizations have a department called **Management Information Systems (MIS)** or **Computer Information Systems (CIS)**, **Computing Services**, or **Information Services.** This department is made up of people responsible for the computer resources of an organization. Large organizations, such as universities, government agencies, and corporations, keep much of the institution's data in computer files: research data, engineering drawings, marketing strategy, accounts receivable, accounts payable, sales facts, manufacturing specifications, transportation plans, and so forth. The people who maintain the data are the same people who provide service to the users: the computer professionals. Let us touch on the essential personnel required to run large computer systems.

Data entry operators prepare data for processing, usually by keying it in a machine-readable format. **Computer operators** monitor the computer, review procedures, keep peripheral equipment running, and make backup copies of data. **Librarians** catalog the processed disks and tapes and keep them secure.

Computer programmers, as noted earlier, design, write, test, and implement the programs that process data on the computer system; they also maintain and update the programs. **Systems analysts** are knowledgeable in the programming area but have broader responsibilities. They plan and design not just individual programs but entire computer systems. Systems analysts maintain a working relationship with both programmers and the users in the organization. The analysts work closely with the users to plan new systems that will meet the users' needs. A professional called a **network manager** implements and maintains the organization's network(s). The department manager, often called the **chief information officer (CIO)**, must understand more than just computer technology. This person must understand the goals and operations of the entire organization and be able to make strategic decisions.

These are some standard jobs and standard titles. There are many others, most specific to the organization.

★ ★ ★ ★

These opening chapters have painted a picture with a broad brush. Now it is time to get down to details. The next three chapters describe the central processing unit, input and output, and storage in more detail.

CHAPTER REVIEW

Summary and Key Terms

- **Software** is the planned, step-by-step set of instructions required to turn data into information.

- A subset of systems software is known as an **operating system**, the underlying software found on all computers. The operating system serves as an intermediary between the applications software and the hardware. Some important tasks of an operating system are managing the computer's resources and running applications software.

- **Applications software** can be used to solve a particular problem or to perform a particular task. Applications software may be either custom or packaged.

- **Computer programmers** are people who design, write, test, and implement software. Organizations may pay computer programmers to write **custom software**, software that is specifically tailored to their needs.

- **Packaged software**, also called **commercial software**, is packaged in a container of some sort, usually a box or folder, and is sold in stores or catalogs. Inside the box are one or more disks holding the software and perhaps an instruction manual, also referred to as **documentation.** Complex software comes on either several diskettes or a CD-ROM, and usually requires a setup process before use. Most users copy new software to their hard disk drive.

- The term **user friendly** means that the software is supposed to be easy for a beginner to use or that the software can be used with a minimum of training.

- Software is considered to be in the **public domain** if it is free to all; software in the public domain is sometimes called **freeware.**

- Software called **shareware** is also given away free; the maker hopes for voluntary payment.

- **Copyrighted software** costs money and must not be copied without permission from the manufacturer. Making illegal copies of copyrighted software is called **software piracy** and is punishable under the law.

- Software has moved to the warehouse stores and to mail-order houses, producing the advantages of lower prices and convenient one-stop shopping.

- A **site license** permits an organization, for a fee, to make a limited number of copies of a software product. Organizations with local area networks usually install software on the network's server computer, making it available to users connected to the network.

- **Electronic software distribution** means a user can pay to **download** the software—move it from another computer to the user's computer.

- **Word processing** software lets you create, edit, format, store, and print text and graphics in one document. It is the three words in the middle—*edit*, *format*, and *store*—that reveal the difference between word processing and plain typing.

- **Desktop publishing** packages meet high-level publishing needs to produce professional-looking newsletters, reports, and brochures.

- An **electronic spreadsheet,** made up of columns and rows of numbers, automatically recalculates the results when a number is changed. This capability lets business people try different combinations of "what if..." numbers and obtain the results quickly.

- **Database management** software manages a collection of interrelated facts. The software can store data, update it, manipulate it, retrieve it, report it in a variety of views, and print it in as many forms.

- **Graphics** software can produce graphs, maps, and charts and can help people compare data, spot trends more easily, and make decisions more quickly.

- **Graphic artists** use graphics software to express their ideas visually.

■ **Communications** software lets a user hook a phone up to the computer and communicate with the computer at the office or access data stored in another computer in another location.

■ A **browser** is software used to access the Internet.

■ A **suite** is a bundle of basic software designed to work together. A typical suite application is **mail merge**, in which certain names and addresses from a database are used on letters prepared using word processing.

■ Software written especially for a particular group of like customers is called **vertical market software.**

■ **Groupware**, also called **collaborative software**, is any kind of software that lets a group of people share information or track information together. To work together effectively on a project, the data being used must be in a central place, a database on disk, that can be accessed and changed by anyone working on the project.

■ The company **information center** is devoted to giving users help with software selection, software training, and, if appropriate, access to corporate computer systems.

■ Software designed for small businesses is termed **SOHO**, for **small office, home office.**

■ Many organizations have a department called **Management Information Systems (MIS)** or **Computer Information Systems (CIS)**, **Computing Services**, or **Information Services.** This department is made up of people responsible for the computer resources of an organization.

■ Large organizations, such as universities, government agencies, and corporations, keep much of the institution's data in computer files. The people who maintain the data are the same people who provide service to the users: the computer professionals.

■ **Data entry operators** prepare data for processing, usually by keying it in a machine-readable format. **Computer operators** monitor the computer, review procedures, and keep peripheral equipment running. **Librarians** catalog the processed disks and tapes and keep them secure. **Computer programmers** design, write, test, and implement the programs that process data on the computer system; they also maintain and update the programs. **Systems analysts** are knowledgeable in the programming area but have broader responsibilities; they plan and design not just individual programs but entire computer systems. A professional called a **network manager** implements and maintains the organization's network(s). The department manager, often called the **chief information officer (CIO)**, must understand more than just computer technology; this person must understand the goals and operations of the entire organization and be able to make strategic decisions.

Quick Poll

Compare your answers to those of your colleagues or classmates.

1. Of these, which software would probably be the most useful to you and why:
   ❏ a. Word processing
   ❏ b. Spreadsheet
   ❏ c. Database management
   ❏ d. Graphics
2. Preferred types of entertainment software:
   ❏ a. Action games
   ❏ b. Skill/thinking games
   ❏ c. Software for cruising the Internet
3. My own preference would be:
   ❏ a. Individual programs
   ❏ b. A suite of programs

Discussion Questions

1. Consider the task-oriented software for word processing/desktop publishing, electronic spreadsheets, database management, graphics, and communications. Which type of software (possibly more than one) would you use for each of the following tasks?
   a. Preparing an annual club report showing a comparison of the budget for last year and this year, and including that report in an attractive monthly letter sent to members
   b. Preparing a comparison report of sales of six different products in three sales regions and then showing the result to a group of 50 people at a sales meeting
   c. Gathering employee attendance data from managers in franchise stores in 17 locations and then writing a memo to your boss summarizing the results
   d. Storing data as it becomes available about hotel room use—customer name, date of arrival, expected date of departure, and so forth—and later retrieving the room number for a certain customer by name or retrieving the numbers of all rooms currently available

2. Consider these firms. What uses would each have for computer software? Mention as many possibilities as you can.
   a. Security Southwestern Bank, a major regional bank with several branches
   b. Azure Design, a small graphic design company that produces posters, covers, and other artwork
   c. Checkerboard Taxi Service, whose central office manages a fleet of 160 cabs that operate in an urban area
   d. Gillick College, a private college that has automated all student services, such as registration, financial aid, and testing
   e. Dayton Realty, a realty firm with multiple listings and 27 agents

3. Consider these businesses, with a solo owner, perhaps occasional temporary employees, and one personal computer. What business needs might be filled using the computer, and what type of software might fill each need? Incidentally, some of these, such as psychologist, may not seem much like businesses; do they still have business needs?

a. Plumbing contractor
b. Writer of children's stories
c. Photographer
d. Caterer
e. Freelance bookkeeper
f. Wedding planner
g. Importer
h. Nail artist
i. Independent truck driver
j. Investment planner
k. Jewelry maker
l. Roofer
m. Karate instructor
n. Psychologist
o. Window washer

Student Study Guide

Multiple Choice

1. Moving software from another computer to your own is called
   a. downloading   c. word processing
   b. documenting   d. marketing
2. A computer professional who writes and tests software is called a(n)
   a. programmer   c. librarian
   b. systems analyst   d. operator
3. Step-by-step instructions that run the computer are
   a. hardware   c. documents
   b. CPUs   d. programs
4. CIS stands for
   a. Computer Internet System   c. Collaborative Information Systems
   b. Commercial Internet System   d. Computer Information Systems
5. The actions that separate word processing from typing are
   a. format, store, print   c. create, edit, format
   b. edit, format, store   d. create, store, print
6. A term that means software is easy to use:
   a. custom   c. user friendly
   b. copyrighted   d. groupware
7. The underlying software:
   a. applications   c. groupware
   b. operating system   d. shareware
8. Which is *not* a description of certain software?
   a. custom   c. download
   b. freeware   d. collaborative
9. The department within an organization that is designed to help users with software:
   a. browser   c. information center
   b. SOHO   d. network
10. Software written especially for a group of like customers is called
    a. freeware   c. shareware
    b. word processing   d. vertical
11. Making illegal copies of copyrighted software is called
    a. software piracy   c. collaboration
    b. browsing   d. electronic distribution

12. Software considered to be in the public domain:
    a. commercial   c. freeware
    b. packaged   d. shareware
13. Software that allows the production of professional newsletters and reports:
    a. database management   c. spreadsheets
    b. groupware   d. desktop publishing
14. The type of software that can store, update, manipulate, and retrieve data:
    a. desktop publishing   c. database management
    b. spreadsheet   d. graphics
15. Another name for available-for-purchase software is
    a. secondary software   c. systems software
    b. packaged software   d. peripheral software
16. Permission for an organization to make copies of certain software:
    a. application   c. site license
    b. documentation   d. copyright
17. A bundle of basic software designed to work together:
    a. user friendly   c. suite
    b. operating system   d. browser
18. Another name for collaborative software:
    a. groupware   c. freeware
    b. browser   d. shareware
19. Another name for packaged software:
    a. commercial   c. freeware
    b. groupware   d. shareware
20. A computer professional who works with users to plan entire computer systems:
    a. programmer   c. operator
    b. systems analyst   d. CIO
21. Software used to access the Internet:
    a. browser   c. packaged
    b. spreadsheet   d. public domain
22. Software written to fulfill the specific needs of a user:
    a. freeware   c. suite
    b. browser   d. custom
23. A worker who catalogs and keeps secure disks and tapes:
    a. programmer   c. CIO
    b. librarian   d. operator
24. Software that can manipulate numbers in rows and columns:
    a. groupware   c. word processing
    b. spreadsheet   d. database management
25. Software designed specifically for a small business:
    a. public domain   c. SOHO
    b. shareware   d. custom

True/False

T F 1. A browser is software used to access the Internet.
T F 2. Word processing differs from typing in that it can print the results.
T F 3. Making illegal copies of copyrighted software is called software piracy.
T F 4. Vertical market software is designed for a group of like customers.
T F 5. Workers using groupware must be physically in the same office.
T F 6. Software documentation may be written or included as part of the software.
T F 7. The operating system is an example of applications software.
T F 8. Operating systems are a subset of systems software.
T F 9. Spreadsheet software can update the spreadsheet automatically if a change is made.
T F 10. User friendly refers to a special kind of computer.
T F 11. Custom software is specifically tailored to user needs.
T F 12. Complex software usually requires a setup process before use.
T F 13. Word processing is a type of task-oriented software.
T F 14. Desktop publishing software is used to manage numbers in columns and rows.
T F 15. CIO stands for chief information officer.
T F 16. The person who plans new systems is the network manager.
T F 17. Another name for groupware is SOHO.
T F 18. Copyrighted software is in the public domain.
T F 19. An advantage of groupware is collaboration.
T F 20. A site license entitles an individual to freeware.
T F 21. People can usually spot trends more quickly from numbers than from graphics.
T F 22. Desktop publishing is not useful for home business.
T F 23. A spreadsheet is made up of columns and rows.
T F 24. Applications software may be either custom or packaged.
T F 25. The software designed to let users collaborate on a project is called database management software.

Fill-In

1. A bundle of basic software designed to work together: _____
2. What kind of software presents numbers in columns and rows?_____
3. SOHO stands for _____

4. The name for collaborative software:

   _____

5. The general name for software that can be used to solve a problem or perform a task:

   _____

6. Software written for a group of like customers:

   _____

7. Software that is considered to be in the public domain: _____

8. The underlying software found on all computers:

   _____

9. The department within an organization that is dedicated to giving software help: _____

10. Software that is given away free but with a requested payment: _____

11. Software that is easy to use is said to be

    _____

12. MIS stands for _____

13. An agreement that permits an organization to make a limited number of copies of a software product:

    _____

14. CIS stands for _____

15. Another name for commercial software:

    _____

16. Making illegal copies of copyrighted software:

    _____

17. Software used to access the Internet:

    _____

18. The people who plan and design systems of programs: _____

19. The planned step-by-step set of instructions required to turn data into information:

    _____

20. The person who implements and maintains the organization's network: _____

Answers

Multiple Choice

1. a	6. c	11. a	16. c	21. a
2. a	7. b	12. c	17. c	22. d
3. d	8. c	13. d	18. a	23. b
4. d	9. c	14. c	19. a	24. b
5. b	10. d	15. b	20. b	25. c

True/False

1. T	6. T	11. T	16. F	21. F
2. F	7. F	12. T	17. F	22. F
3. T	8. T	13. T	18. F	23. T
4. T	9. T	14. F	19. T	24. T
5. F	10. F	15. T	20. F	25. F

Fill-In

1. suite
2. spreadsheet
3. small office, home office
4. groupware
5. applications software
6. vertical market software
7. freeware
8. operating system
9. information center
10. shareware
11. user friendly
12. Management Information Systems
13. site license
14. Computer Information Systems
15. packaged software
16. software piracy
17. browser
18. systems analysts
19. software (or program)
20. network manager

PLANET INTERNET

The publisher of this book, Addison Wesley Longman, has set up this URL for readers:

http://hepg.awl.com/capron/planet/

Once you use the URL to reach the publisher's site, you will find links to all other sites mentioned in this and other chapters. Simply click the desired link. Since everything on the 'Net, including URLs, is subject to change, we supply only the Addison Wesley Longman URL, which will not change, in the text.

What other starting points are there? Keep in mind that, unlike a commercial product, the Internet is not owned or managed by anyone. One consequence of this is that there is no master table of contents or index for the Internet. However, several organizations have produced ordered lists that can be used as a helpful starting place. Users often favor these as comprehensive starting places: Yahoo, Infospace, Starting Point, NetGuide, Yanoff's Internet Services, and LookSmart.

Each site has a set of major categories, and each major category has links of its own, as do the topics at the next level, and so on. Major categories typically include careers, computers, business, politics, education, society, kids, shopping, travel, magazines, recreation, government, events, science, sports, health, reference, and family. Most major starting sites also include special lists of new and "hot" sites. You could hang around for literally days, burrowing deeper and deeper, just from a starting point like Yahoo.

Of particular interest to college students is the All Campus directory, which

JUMPING-OFF POINTS

How do I start? Briefly, to get started, you need an URL for the Web. Translation: You need a starting address (*URL*, for *Uniform Resource Locator*) to find a site on the subset of the Internet called the *World Wide Web*, also called *WWW* or just *"the Web."* You can read more detailed information about URLs and the Web and, most importantly, *links*, in Chapter 7.

Where do I find an URL? As noted in Chapter 7, an URL is often pretty messy—a long string of letters and symbols. No one likes to type URLs and, what's more, there is a good chance of making an error. Fortunately, you rarely have to type an URL because, once started, you can click your mouse on links—icons or highlighted text—to move from site to site on the Internet.

has standard major categories but tends to focus on college-related sites. Another favorite site, deliberately unorganized but full of surprises, is BigEye, which accompanies its offerings with cheerful music. Remember that the links for all of these sites can be found at the Addison Wesley Longman site. Just point and click and go any-where on the Web.

But I need to get to the Web first. Yes. To use the Web you need a *browser*, special software devoted to managing access to the Web. You can get general information about browsers in Chapter 7, but you will need to ask your instructor, lab personnel, or a designated employee how to use

a *structured exercise* because once you are on the Addison Wesley Longman web site we can make sure that the sites you visit remain current. Use the URL supplied here to get started. If you are feeling adventurous, try the *freeform exercise*. We make suggestions but no guarantees.

1. **Structured exercise.** Go to the Addison Wesley Longman site using URL http://hepg.awl.com/capron/planet/. Link to the Yahoo site, and then link to the list of new sites. From there, choose two places to link to.
2. **Freeform exercise.** At the AWL site, link to Netizens, a changing list of individuals who maintain their own sites.

the web browser at your location. If you are using a browser pur-chased for your personal computer or have access to the Internet via some online ser-vice, then these suppli-ers will provide instruc-tions.

Internet Exercises

In each chapter, beginning in Chapter 2, two exercises are suggested. The first exercise is called

Hardware

Tools

Mark Ong, who hoped to be a scriptwriter, planned a double major in creative writing and drama. After his first year of college, he took a summer job as an editorial assistant, where he first used word processing. He decided that it would be helpful to have a personal computer of his own when he went back to college in the fall. But he felt unsure of how to make a purchase. In fact, he felt that he did not even know what questions to ask. He discussed this with an office colleague, who casually noted that any computer setup comes with the "standard stuff"—processor, keyboard, mouse, screen, disk drives—and that all he had to do was go to a computer store and pick one that fit his price range. Mark was not satisfied with this approach, especially in light of the advertisements he had seen in the local newspaper and in computer magazines.

Most advertisements displayed photos of personal computers, accompanied by cryptic descriptions of the total hardware package.

A typical ad was worded this way: *Pentium, 166MHz, 16MB RAM, 256K cache, 1.44MB diskette drive, 2GB hard drive*. The price for this particular machine was pretty hefty—over $2000. Mark noticed that the ads for machines with lower numbers, for example, only 133MHz, also had lower price tags. Similarly, higher numbers meant higher price tags. Although he did recognize the disk drives, he had no idea what the other items were or why the numbers mattered. Clearly, there was more to a purchasing decision than selecting a system with the "standard stuff."

Mark tore out some of the ads and marched to a nearby computer store. After asking a lot of questions, he learned that *Pentium* is a type of microprocessor, that *MHz* stands for megahertz and is a measurement of the microprocessor's speed, that *RAM* is the computer's memory, that *cache* is a kind of handy storage place for frequently used data and software instructions, and that *GB* is an abbreviation for gigabytes, a

measurement of storage size. Most importantly, Mark learned that the number variations mattered because they were factors in determining the computer's capacity and speed.

Many buyers do select their personal computer system merely on the basis of a sales pitch and price range. Those people could argue, with some success, that they do not need to know all the computer buzzwords any more than they need to know the technical details of their television sets or sound systems. They know that they do not have to understand a computer's innards to put it to work.

But there are rewards for those who want to dig a little deeper, learn a little more. Although this chapter is not designed to help you purchase a computer (see the *Buyer's Guide* for that), it does provide some background information and gives you the foundation on which future computer knowledge can be built.

C
H
A
P
T
E
R

3

The Central Processing Unit

What Goes on Inside the Computer

▶ The Central Processing Unit

The computer does its primary work in a part of the machine we cannot see, a control center that converts data input to information output. This control center, called the **central processing unit (CPU)**, is a highly complex, extensive set of electronic circuitry that executes stored program instructions. All computers, large and small, must have at least one central processing unit. As Figure 3-1 shows, the central processing unit consists of two parts: the *control unit* and the *arithmetic/logic unit*. Each part has a specific function.

Before examining the control unit and the arithmetic/logic unit in detail, consider data storage and its relationship to the central processing unit. Computers use two types of storage: primary storage and secondary storage. The CPU interacts closely with primary storage, or memory, referring to it for both instructions and data. For this reason this chapter will discuss memory in the context of the central processing unit. Technically, however, memory is not part of the CPU.

As noted in Chapter 1, memory holds data only temporarily, at the time the computer is executing a program. Secondary storage holds permanent or semipermanent data on some external medium, such as a disk, until it is needed for processing by the computer. Since the physical attributes of secondary storage devices determine the way data is organized on them, secondary storage and data organization will be discussed together in Chapter 5.

Now let us consider the components of the central processing unit.

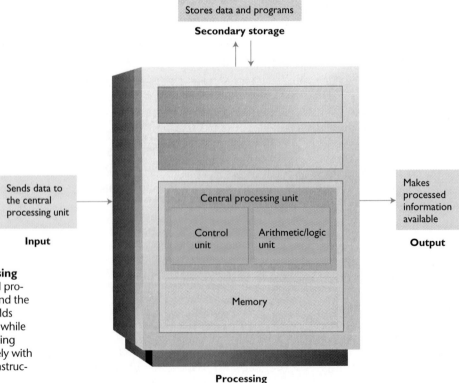

Figure 3-1 The central processing unit. The two parts of the central processing unit are the control unit and the arithmetic/logic unit. Memory holds data and instructions temporarily while the program they are part of is being executed. The CPU interacts closely with memory, referring to it for both instructions and data.

The Control Unit

The **control unit** contains circuitry that uses electrical signals to direct the entire computer system to carry out, or execute, stored program instructions. Like an orchestra leader, the control unit does not execute program instructions; rather, it directs other parts of the system to do so. The control unit must communicate with both the arithmetic/logic unit and memory.

The Arithmetic/Logic Unit

The **arithmetic/logic unit (ALU)** contains the electronic circuitry that executes all arithmetic and logical operations.

The arithmetic/logic unit can perform four kinds of **arithmetic operations**, or mathematical calculations: addition, subtraction, multiplication, and division. As its name implies, the arithmetic/logic unit also performs logical operations. A **logical operation** is usually a comparison. The unit can compare numbers, letters, or special characters. The computer can then take action based on the result of the comparison. This is a very important capability. It is by comparing that a computer is able to tell, for instance, whether there are unfilled seats on airplanes, whether charge-card customers have exceeded their credit limits, and whether one candidate for Congress has more votes than another.

Logical operations can test for three conditions:

- **Equal-to condition.** In a test for this condition, the arithmetic/logic unit compares two values to determine if they are equal. For example: If the number of tickets sold *equals* the number of seats in the auditorium, then the concert is declared sold out.
- **Less-than condition.** To test for this condition, the computer compares values to determine if one is less than another. For example: If the number of speeding tickets on a driver's record is *less than* three, then insurance rates are $425; otherwise, the rates are $500.
- **Greater-than condition.** In this type of comparison, the computer determines if one value is greater than another. For example: If the hours a person worked this week are *greater than* 40, then the program should multiply every extra hour by 1½ times the usual hourly wage to compute overtime pay.

A computer can test for more than one condition. In fact, a logic unit can usually discern six logical relationships: equal to, less than, greater than, less than or equal to, greater than or equal to, and less than or greater than. Note that less than or greater than is the same as not equal to.

The symbols that let you define the type of comparison you want the computer to perform are called **relational operators.** The most common relational operators are the equal sign (=), the less-than symbol (<), and the greater-than symbol (>).

Registers: Temporary Storage Areas

Registers are temporary storage areas for instructions or data. They are not a part of memory; rather they are special additional storage locations that offer the advantage of speed. Registers work under the direction of the control unit to accept, hold, and transfer instructions or data and

I Hate Standing in Line

Perhaps you have played the which-line-is-shortest game at the supermarket—and lost. Instead, how would you like to skip the checkout line altogether? Due to new computer chips with special functions, this is a real possibility.

Here is how it works. You choose a jar of peanut butter, swipe it across a reader on your chip-equipped cart, and its price is charged to your credit card. When you are done filling your cart, there is no need to stop by the checkstand; just pass through a gate that automatically checks whether everything in your cart has been charged.

More is afoot than can be described in this simple scenario. For example, you must, at some point, divulge your credit card number. And some of the chips control high-speed wireless communications. But the essence of the story is that consumers have more conveniences on the way.

perform arithmetic or logical comparisons at high speed. The control unit uses a data storage register the way a store owner uses a cash register—as a temporary, convenient place to store what is used in transactions.

Computers usually assign special roles to certain registers, including

- An **accumulator**, which collects the result of computations.
- An **address register**, which keeps track of where a given instruction or piece of data is stored in memory. Each storage location in memory is identified by an address, just as each house on a street has an address.
- A **storage register**, which temporarily holds data taken from or about to be sent to memory.
- A **general-purpose register**, which is used for several functions— arithmetic operations, for example.

Consider registers in the context of all the means of storage discussed so far. Registers hold data *immediately* related to the operation being executed. Memory is used to store data that will be used in the *near future*. Secondary storage holds data that may be needed *later* in the same program execution or perhaps at some more remote time in the future.

Now let us look at how a payroll program, for example, uses all three types of storage. Suppose the program calculates the salary of one employee. The data representing the hours worked and the data for the rate of pay are ready in their respective registers. Other data related to the salary calculation—overtime hours, bonuses, deductions, and so forth—is waiting nearby in memory. The data for other employees is available in secondary storage. As the computer finishes calculations for one employee, the data for the next employee is brought from secondary storage into memory and eventually into the registers.

▶ Memory

Memory is also known as **primary storage**, **primary memory**, **main storage**, **internal storage**, and **main memory;** all these terms are used interchangeably by people in computer circles. Manufacturers often use the term **RAM**, which stands for *random-access memory*. Memory is the part of the computer that holds data and instructions for processing. Although closely associated with the central processing unit, memory is separate from it. Memory stores program instructions or data only as long as the program they pertain to is in operation. Keeping these items in memory when the program is not running is not feasible for four reasons:

- Most types of memory store items only while the computer is turned on; data is destroyed when the machine is turned off.
- If more than one program is running at once (usually the case on large computers and sometimes on small computers), a single program cannot lay exclusive claim to memory.
- There may not be room in memory to hold the processed data.
- Secondary storage is more cost-effective than memory for storing large amounts of data.

The CPU cannot process data from an input device or disk directly; the data must first be available in memory. How do data and instructions get from an input or storage device into memory? The control unit sends them. Likewise, when the time is right, the control unit sends

MAKING THE RIGHT CONNECTIONS

THE COMPUTER SENDS FOR HELP

General Motors has incorporated technology in its cars to gain competitive advantage in the luxury car market. You may have heard of microprocessors controlling fuel injection and all kinds of other things under the hood, but that is old news. On the new models, computers can detect a problem for the passenger and, literally, send for help.

For example, a signal sent automatically from the in-car cellular phone via a satellite can notify emergency medical services when the vehicle's air bag inflates. Additional services include roadside assistance, routing and location assistance, theft detection and notification, and stolen vehicle tracking.

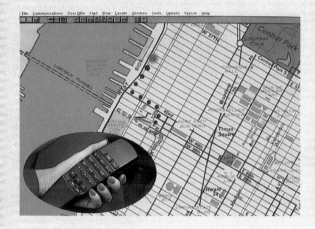

these items from memory to the arithmetic/logic unit, where an arithmetic operation or logical operation is performed. After being processed, the result is sent to memory, where it is held until it is ready to be released—sent—to an output or storage device.

The chief characteristic of memory is that it allows very fast access to instructions and data, no matter where the items are within it. A discussion of the physical components of memory—memory chips—appears later in this chapter.

▶ How the CPU Executes Program Instructions

Let us examine the way the central processing unit, in association with memory, executes a computer program. We will be looking at how just one instruction in the program is executed. In fact, most computers today can execute only one instruction at a time, though they execute it very quickly. Many personal computers can execute instructions in less than one-*millionth* of a second, whereas those speed demons known as supercomputers can execute instructions in less than one-*trillionth* of a second.

Before an instruction can be executed, program instructions and data must be placed into memory from an input device or a secondary stor-

Figure 3-2 The machine cycle. Program instructions and data are brought into memory from an external source, either an input device or a secondary storage medium. The machine cycle executes instructions one at a time, as described in the text.

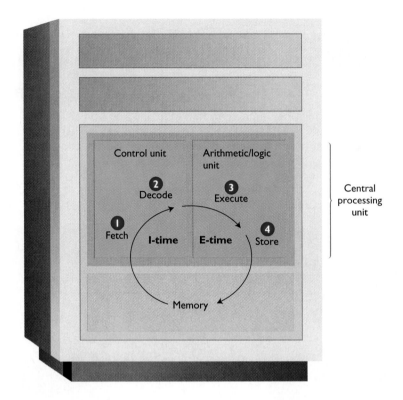

age device (the process is further complicated by the fact that, as noted earlier, the data will probably make a temporary stop in a register). As Figure 3-2 shows, once the necessary data and instruction are in memory, the central processing unit performs the following four steps for each instruction:

1. The control unit *fetches* (gets) the instruction from memory.
2. The control unit *decodes* the instruction (decides what it means) and directs that the necessary data be moved from memory to the arithmetic/logic unit. These first two steps together are called instruction time, or **I-time.**
3. The arithmetic/logic unit *executes* the arithmetic or logical instruction. That is, the ALU is given control and performs the actual operation on the data.
4. The arithmetic/logic unit *stores* the result of this operation in memory or in a register. Steps 3 and 4 together are called execution time, or **E-time.**

The control unit eventually directs memory to send the result to an output device or a secondary storage device. The combination of I-time and E-time is called the **machine cycle.** Figure 3-3 shows an instruction going through the machine cycle.

Each central processing unit has an internal **clock** that produces pulses at a fixed rate to synchronize all computer operations. A single machine-cycle instruction may be made up of a substantial number of subinstructions, each of which must take at least one clock cycle. Each type of central processing unit is designed to understand a specific group of instructions—such as ADD or MOVE—called the **instruction set.** Just as there are many different languages that people understand, so too are there many different instruction sets that different types of CPUs understand.

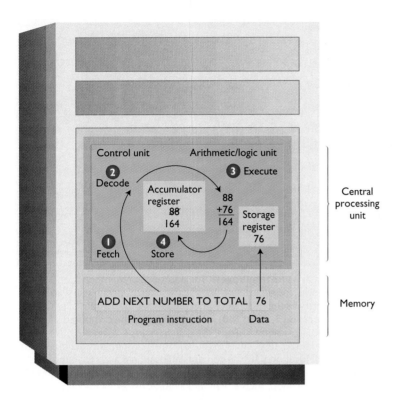

Figure 3-3 The machine cycle in action. Suppose a program must find the average of five test scores. To do this, it must total the five scores and then divide the result by 5. The program would begin by setting the total to 0; it then would add each of the five numbers, one at a time, to the total. Suppose the scores are 88, 76, 91, 83, and 87. In this figure the total has been set to 0, and then 88, the first test score, has been added to it. Now examine the machine cycle as it adds the next number, 76, to the total. Follow the four steps in the machine cycle. ① *Fetch:* The control unit fetches the instruction from memory. ② *Decode:* The control unit decodes the instruction. It determines that addition must take place and gives instructions for the next number (76) to be placed in a storage register for this purpose. The total so far (88) is already in an accumulator register. ③ *Execute:* The ALU does the addition, increasing the total to 164. ④ *Store:* In this case the ALU stores the new total in the accumulator register instead of in memory, since more numbers still need to be added to it. When the new total (164) is placed in the accumulator register, it displaces the old total (88).

Storage Locations and Addresses: How the Control Unit Finds Instructions and Data

It is one thing to have instructions and data somewhere in memory and quite another for the control unit to be able to find them. How does it do this?

The location in memory for each instruction and each piece of data is identified by an **address.** That is, each location has an address number, like the mailboxes in front of an apartment house. And, like the mailboxes, the address numbers of the locations remain the same, but the contents (instructions and data) of the locations may change. That is, new instructions or new data may be placed in the locations when the old contents no longer need to be stored in memory. Unlike a mailbox, however, a memory location can hold only a fixed amount of data; an address can hold only one number or one word.

Figure 3-4 shows how a program manipulates data in memory. A payroll program, for example, may give instructions to put the rate of pay in location 3 and the number of hours worked in location 6. To compute the employee's salary, then, instructions tell the computer to multiply the data in location 3 by the data in location 6 and move the result to location 8. The choice of locations is arbitrary—any locations that are not already spoken for can be used. Programmers using programming languages, however, do not have to worry about the actual address numbers, because each data address is referred to by a name. The name is called a **symbolic address.** In this example, the symbolic address names are Rate, Hours, and Salary.

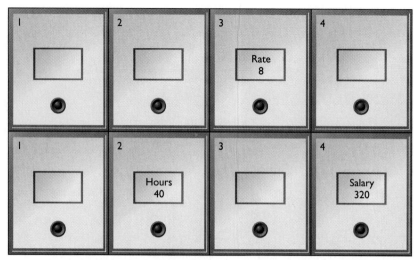

Figure 3-4 Addresses are like mailboxes. The addresses of memory locations are like the identifying numbers on apartment-house mailboxes. Suppose you want to compute someone's salary as the number of hours multiplied by the rate of pay. Rate ($8) goes in memory location 3, hours (40) in location 6, and the computed salary ($8 x 40 hours, or $320) in location 8. Thus, the *addresses* are 3, 6, and 8, but the *contents* are $8, 40, and $320, respectively. Note that the program instructions are to multiply the contents of location 3 by the contents of location 6 and move the result to location 8. (A computer language used by a programmer would use some kind of symbolic name for each location, such as Rate or Pay-Rate instead of the number 3.) The data items are the actual contents—what is stored in each location.

➤ Data Representation: On/Off

We are accustomed to thinking of computers as complex mechanisms, but the fact is that these machines basically know only two things: on and off. This two-state on/off system is called a **binary system.** Using the two states—which can be represented by electricity turned on or off—the computer can construct sophisticated ways of representing data.

Let us look at one way the two states can be used to represent data. Whereas the decimal number system has a base of 10 (with the ten digits 0, 1, 2, 3, 4, 5, 6, 7, 8, and 9), the binary system has a base of 2. This means it contains only two digits, 0 and 1, which correspond to the two states off and on. Combinations of 0s and 1s represent larger numbers (Figure 3-5).

Bits, Bytes, and Words

Each 0 or 1 in the binary system is called a **bit** (for *bi*nary digi*t*). The bit is the basic unit for storing data in computer memory—0 means off, 1 means on. Notice that since a bit is always either on or off, a bit in computer memory is always storing some kind of data.

Since single bits by themselves cannot store all the numbers, letters, and special characters (such as $ and ?) that a computer must process, the bits are put together in a group called a **byte** (pronounced "bite"). There are usually 8 bits in a byte (Figure 3-6). Each byte usually represents one **character** of data—a letter, digit, or special character.

Computer manufacturers express the capacity of memory and storage in terms of the number of bytes they can hold. The number of bytes can be expressed as **kilobytes.** *Kilo* represents 2 to the tenth power (2^{10}), or 1024. *Kilobyte* is abbreviated **KB,** or simply **K.** (Sometimes K is used casually to mean 1000, as in "I earned $30K last year.") A kilobyte is 1024 bytes. In an older computer, a memory of 640K means the computer can store 640x1024, or 655,360 bytes. Memory capacity may also be expressed in terms of **megabytes** (1024x1024 bytes). One megabyte, abbreviated **MB,** means roughly one million bytes. With storage devices, manufacturers sometimes express capacity in terms of **gigabytes** (abbreviated **GB**)—billions of bytes. In newer personal computers, memory may hold anywhere from 16MB to 32MB and more. Mainframe memories can hold gigabytes.

A computer **word,** typically the size of a register, is defined as the number of bits that constitute a common unit of data, as defined by the computer system. The length of a word varies by computer. Generally, the larger the word, the more powerful the computer. There was a time when word size alone could classify a computer. Word lengths have varied from 8 bits for very early personal computers to 64 bits, a number once reserved for supercomputers but now available in some personal computers. Note that an 8-bit machine could handle only 1 byte (character) at a time, whereas a 64-bit machine handles 8 bytes at a time, making its processing speed eight times faster.

Coding Schemes

As noted, a byte—a collection of bits—can represent a character of data. But just what particular set of bits is equivalent to which character? In theory we could each make up our own definitions, declaring certain bit patterns to represent certain characters. Needless to say, this would be about as practical as each person speaking his or her own special language. Since we need to communicate with the computer and with each other, it is appropriate that we use a common scheme for data representation. That is, there must be agreement on which groups of bits represent which characters.

The code called **ASCII** (pronounced "AS-key"), which stands for American Standard Code for Information Interchange, uses 7 bits for each character. Since there are exactly 128 unique combinations of 7 bits, this 7-bit code can represent only 128 characters. A more common version is ASCII-8, also called extended ASCII, which uses 8 bits per character and can represent 256 different characters. For example, the letter

BINARY EQUIVALENT OF DECIMAL NUMBERS 0–15	
Decimal	Binary
0	0000
1	0001
2	0010
3	0011
4	0100
5	0101
6	0110
7	0111
8	1000
9	1001
10	1010
11	1011
12	1100
13	1101
14	1110
15	1111

Figure 3-5 Decimal and binary equivalents. Seeing numbers from different systems side by side clarifies the patterns of progression.

Figure 3-6 Bit as light bulb. In this illustration each light bulb represents a binary digit (bit), with off representing 0 and on representing 1. The group of eight bulbs, each of which can be on or off, represents 1 byte. Light bulbs, of course, are not used in computers.

Character	ASCII–8
A	0100 0001
B	0100 0010
C	0100 0011
D	0100 0100
E	0100 0101
F	0100 0110
G	0100 0111
H	0100 1000
I	0100 1001
J	0100 1010
K	0100 1011
L	0100 1100
M	0100 1101
N	0100 1110
O	0100 1111
P	0101 0000
Q	0101 0001
R	0101 0010
S	0101 0011
T	0101 0100
U	0101 0101
V	0101 0110
W	0101 0111
X	0101 1000
Y	0101 1001
Z	0101 1010
0	0011 0000
1	0011 0001
2	0011 0010
3	0011 0011
4	0011 0100
5	0011 0101
6	0011 0110
7	0011 0111
8	0011 1000
9	0011 1001

(a)

Letter	ASCII–8
K	0100 1011
I	0100 1001
L	0100 1100
O	0100 1111
B	0100 0010
Y	0101 1001
T	0101 0100
E	0100 0101

(b)

Figure 3-7 The ASCII-8 code.
(a) Shown are the ASCII-8 binary representations for letters and digits. This is not the complete code; there are many characters missing, such as lowercase letters and punctuation marks. The binary representation is in two columns to improve readability. (b) The ASCII-8 representation for the word *KILOBYTE*.

A is represented by 01000001. The ASCII representation has been adopted as a standard by the U.S. government and is found in a variety of computers, particularly minicomputers and personal computers. Figure 3-7 shows part of the ASCII-8 code.

▶ Personal Computer Chips

The chips discussed here would be attached to the **motherboard,** the flat board within the personal computer housing that holds the computer circuitry (Figure 3-8). The motherboard, also called the main circuit board, is a mass of chips and connections that organize the computer's activities. The motherboard also holds **expansion slots** into which other circuit boards can be inserted to link peripheral devices to the processor. It is the central processing unit, the microprocessor, that is the most important component of the motherboard.

Microprocessors

A miniaturized central processing unit can be etched on a chip, a tiny square of silicon; hence the term *computer on a chip.* A central processing unit, or processor, on a chip is a **microprocessor** (Figure 3-9), or **microchip** for short. A microprocessor may be called a **logic chip** when it is used to control specialized devices (such as the fuel system of a car). Microprocessors contain tiny **transistors,** electronic switches that may or may not allow current to pass through. If current passes through, the switch is on, representing the 1 bit. If current does not pass through, the switch is off, representing a 0 bit. Thus, combinations of transistors can stand for combinations of bits, which, as noted earlier, represent digits, letters, and special characters.

The transistor is the basic building block of the microprocessor. Today's popular Pentium microprocessor contains more than three million transistors. Microprocessors usually include these key components: a control unit and an arithmetic/logic unit (the central processing unit), registers, and a clock. (Clocks are often on a separate chip in personal computers.) Notably missing is memory, which usually comes on its own chips.

How much smaller? How much cheaper? How much faster? Three decades of extraordinary advances in technology have packed increasingly greater power onto increasingly smaller chips. Engineers can now imprint as much circuitry on a single chip as filled room-size computers in the early days of computing. But are engineers approaching the limits of smallness? Current development efforts focus on a three-dimensional chip built in layers. Chip capacities in the future do seem almost limitless.

In addition to factors such as increased speed, microprocessors have historically increased their power by swallowing up functions previously accomplished by other hardware. For example, in the 1980s, chipmaker Intel incorporated a math coprocessor, a separate chip favored by engineers, into its microprocessor. Currently, Intel's **MMX** (for **multimedia extensions**) chip boosts a computer's ability to produce graphics, video, and sound. The more functions that are combined on a microprocessor, the faster the computer runs, the cheaper it is to make, and the more reliable it is.

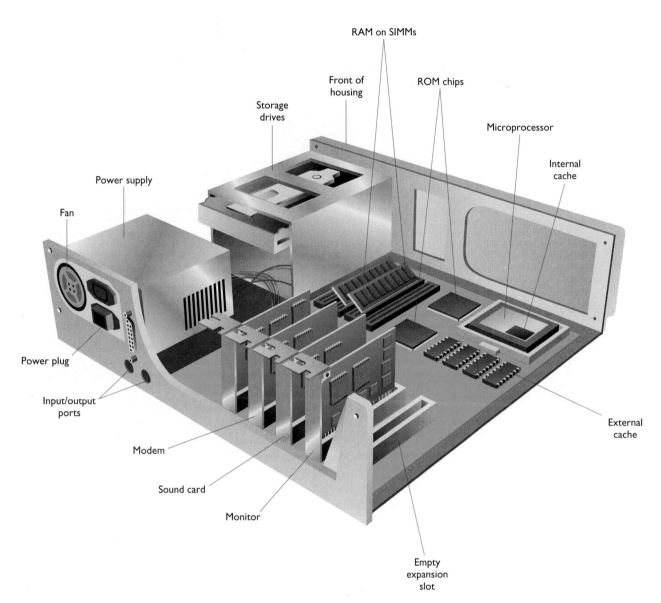

Figure 3-8 Motherboard. When the cover of a personal computer is removed, the motherboard, to which various chips are attached, can be seen inside the housing. All components of a computer are connected through the circuitry on the motherboard.

Memory Components

The first part of this chapter described the central processing unit and how it works with memory. Next is an examination of the memory components. Historically, memory components have evolved from primitive vacuum tubes to today's modern semiconductors. (You may read more about this in Appendix A, *History and Industry.*)

Semiconductor Memory   Most modern computers use semiconductor memory because it has several advantages: reliability, compactness, low cost, and lower power usage. Since semiconductor memory can be mass-produced economically, the cost of memory has been considerably reduced. Chip prices have fallen and risen and fallen again, based on a

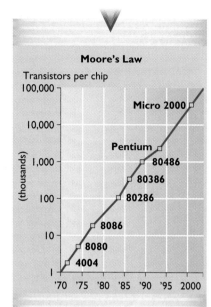

Moore's Law

Moore's Law

Anyone who has been around the computer industry for a while has probably heard of Moore's Law. Way back in 1965 a young fellow named Gordon Moore, an Intel co-founder, suggested that the performance of chip technology, as measured against its price, would double approximately every 18 months. As you can see from the chart, which shows the number of transistors on various Intel microprocessors, he was right.

Figure 3-9 A microprocessor chip. This Pentium chip is shown on a flower to give perspective to its small size.

variety of economic and political factors, but they remain a bargain. Semiconductor memory is **volatile**, that is, it requires continuous electric current to represent data. If the current is interrupted, the data is lost.

Semiconductor memory is made up of thousands of very small circuits—pathways for electric currents—on a silicon chip. A chip is described as **monolithic** because all the circuits on a single chip constitute an inseparable unit of storage. Each circuit etched on a chip can be in one of two states: either conducting an electric current or not—on or off. The two states can be used to represent the binary digits 1 and 0. As noted earlier, these digits can be combined to represent characters, thus making the memory chip a storage bin for data and instructions.

One important type of semiconductor design is called **complementary metal oxide semiconductor (CMOS)**. This design is noted for using relatively little electricity. This makes it especially useful for computers requiring low power consumption, such as portable computers. However, now big computers are getting into the act. IBM is basing its latest mainframe computers on CMOS technology, which can be air-cooled, a vast improvement over older chips that were hotter and thus needed messy water cooling systems.

RAM and ROM   Memory keeps the instructions and data for whatever programs you happen to be using at the moment. Memory is referred to as RAM—random-access memory—in this discussion, both to emphasize its random function and to distinguish it from ROM. Data in mem-

Getting Practical

SHOULD YOU BUILD YOUR OWN COMPUTER?

Building your own computer may seem like a fanciful idea indeed, especially if you have not even decided whether to buy a computer that comes prepackaged. However, the option of building a computer, once the territory of hard-core techies, is now a possibility for mainstream consumers. Some people like the idea of the adventure, and they also like the cost savings.

What skills do you need? And what equipment? Surprisingly, very little of either. You will not need to do anything as dramatic as welding. In truth, your task is really to acquire and then assemble the various components, screwing and snapping them into place, rather like an electronic Lego set.

Let us begin with the shopping list. You will need a motherboard, microprocessor, RAM, case with power supply, diskette drive, hard drive, video card, monitor, keyboard, and mouse. You will likely also want a modem, CD-ROM drive, sound card, and speakers. Now the questions become which ones. A visit to your local electronics store can be a high-tech reconnaissance mission, in which you can gather information from both sales people and fellow customers. Be sure to check the store's return policy; you should be able to return any component unconditionally within a certain time frame. If reduced personal service is an acceptable trade-off for lower costs, you may prefer to buy from a mail-order house; check the advertising section of any major computer magazine. But do buy the major components from the same company to cut down on compatibility problems.

We do not have the space here to describe the components in detail, much less the assembly process. Detailed instructions, which you should read carefully, accompany each hardware item. You can get further advice from magazines, perhaps a local computer club, and the Internet.

We mentioned cost savings, but most of the savings are not up front. The total component cost will not be significantly less than what you would pay for a fully assembled computer. The real savings come in the future when you are able to upgrade your computer on your own, adding more memory, a new microprocessor, a new hard drive, or whatever, rather than buying a new computer.

Building a computer can be a satisfying experience, but it is not for everyone. Generally speaking, if you have any doubts, don't do it.

ory can be accessed randomly, no matter where it is, in an easy and speedy manner. RAM is usually volatile; as noted above, this means that its contents are lost once the power is shut off. RAM can be erased or written over at will by the computer software.

Figure 3-10 DRAM chip. This DRAM chip is smaller than a button.

In recent years the amount of RAM storage in a personal computer has increased dramatically. An early personal computer, for example, was advertised with "a full 4K RAM." Now 16MB RAM or even more is common. More memory has become a necessity because sophisticated personal computer software requires significant amounts of memory. You can augment your personal computer's RAM by buying extra memory chips to install in your memory board or by purchasing a **single in-line memory module (SIMM)**, a board that contains memory chips. The SIMM board plugs into sockets on the computer's motherboard, which is more convenient than attaching individual chips. In general, the more memory your computer has, the more (and bigger) tasks the computer can do.

RAM is often divided into two types: static RAM **(SRAM)** and dynamic RAM **(DRAM)**. DRAM must be constantly refreshed (recharged) by the central processing unit or it will lose its contents; hence the name dynamic. Although SRAM is faster, DRAM is used in most personal computer memory because of its size and cost advantages (Figure 3-10).

Read-only memory (ROM) contains programs and data that are permanently recorded into this type of memory at the factory; they can be read and used, but they cannot be changed by the user. For example, a personal computer probably has a program for calculating square roots in ROM. ROM is nonvolatile—its contents do not disappear when the power is turned off.

Using specialized tools called **ROM burners**, the instructions within some ROM chips can be changed. These chips are known as **PROM** chips, or **programmable read-only memory** chips. There are other variations on ROM chips, depending on the methods used to alter them. Programming and altering ROM chips is the province of the computer engineer.

▶ Speed and Power

The characteristic of speed is universally associated with computers. Power is a derivative of speed as well as of other factors such as memory size. What makes a computer fast? Or, more to the point, what makes one computer faster than another? Several factors are involved, including microprocessor speed, bus line size, and the availability of cache. A user who is concerned about speed will want to address all of these. More sophisticated approaches to speed include flash memory, RISC computers, and parallel processing. A discussion of each follows.

Computer Processing Speeds

Although all computers are fast, there is a wide diversity of computer speeds. The execution of an instruction on a very slow computer may be measured in less than a **millisecond**, which is one-thousandth of a second. Most computers can execute an instruction measured in **microseconds**, each of which is one-millionth of a second. Some modern computers have reached the **nanosecond** range—one-billionth of a second. Still to be broken is the **picosecond** barrier—one-trillionth of a second.

Microprocessor speeds are usually expressed in **megahertz (MHz)**, millions of machine cycles per second. Thus, a personal computer listed at

100MHz has a processor capable of handling 100 million machine cycles per second. A top-speed personal computer can be more than twice as fast.

Another measure of computer speed is **MIPS**, which stands for one *million instructions per second.* For example, a computer with speed of .5 MIPS can execute 500,000 instructions per second. High-speed personal computers can perform at 100 MIPS and higher. MIPS is often a more accurate measure than clock speed, because some computers can use each tick of the clock more efficiently than others. A third measure of speed is the **megaflop**, which stands for one *million floating-point operations per second.* It measures the ability of the computer to perform complex mathematical operations.

Bus Lines

As is so often the case, the computer term *bus* is borrowed from its common meaning—a mode of transportation. A **bus line** is a set of parallel electrical paths, usually copper tracing on the surface of the motherboard, that internally transports data from one place to another within the computer system. The amount of data that can be carried at one time is called the bus width, which indicates the number of electrical paths. The greater the width, the more data can be carried at a time. A larger bus size means

- The computer can transfer more data at a time, making the computer faster
- The computer can reference larger memory address numbers, allowing more memory
- The computer can support a greater number and variety of instructions

In general, the larger the word size or bus width, the more powerful the computer.

Cache

A **cache** (pronounced "cash") is a relatively small block of very fast memory designed for the specific purpose of speeding up the internal transfer of data and software instructions. Think of cache as a selective memory: The data and instructions stored in cache are those that are most recently or most frequently used. When the processor first requests data or instructions, these must be retrieved from main memory, which is delivered at a pace that is relatively slow compared to the microprocessor. As they are retrieved, those same data or instructions are stored in cache. The next time the microprocessor needs data or instructions, it looks first in cache; if the needed items can be found there, they can be transferred at a rate that far exceeds a trip from main memory. Of course, cache is not big enough to hold everything, so the wanted data or instructions may not be there. But there is a good chance that frequently used items will be in cache. Thus, since the most frequently used data and instructions are kept in a handy place, the net result is an improvement in processing speed.

Caching has become such a vital technique that some newer microprocessors offer **internal cache** built right into the processor's design. This is the fastest sort, since it is right there for the microprocessor to access. However, cache memory takes up precious space on the micro-

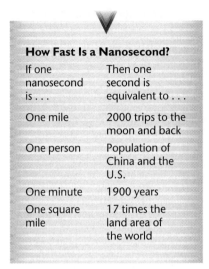

How Fast Is a Nanosecond?	
If one nanosecond is . . .	Then one second is equivalent to . . .
One mile	2000 trips to the moon and back
One person	Population of China and the U.S.
One minute	1900 years
One square mile	17 times the land area of the world

A Family of Chips

The Intel Corporation has provided personal computer makers with several generations of microprocessor chips. The first was a standard-setter: the 8088 chip used by the first IBM PC (introduced in 1981) and its many imitators. The next member of the family, the 80186 chip, was merely a transitional chip, soon replaced by the 80286 chip, which powered the IBM PC AT and, again, a slew of clones.

Intel moved to increase power and flexibility with the introduction of the 80386 chip, first brought to the market in the Compaq 386. Close on the heels of the 80386 chip was the 80486 (the "486"), a chip whose speed and power made it popular through the early 1990s.

The next chip, trotted out in 1993, was expected to be christened the 80586. However, citing proprietary problems, Intel called it Pentium, based on the Latin root word meaning *five*. The amazing Pentium, nicknamed P5 by techies, is twice as fast as the fastest 486 chip.

The next in line, initially christened the P6, was designed to be used as a group to power server computers and is now used in personal computers as the Pentium Pro.

Each new Intel chip has been increasingly powerful. In terms of MIPS, the 486 processes almost 50 million instructions per second, compared to the Pentium at about 100 million and the P6 at well over 250 million instructions per second.

Figure 3-11 The Intel Pentium Pro microprocessor. Intel has embedded 256KB of cache in the same ceramic housing as the microprocessor. The cache is on the left, the microprocessor on the right.

processor, so a processor would probably have only about 8KB of onboard cache. Most computers include **external cache** on separate chips. Although some computers offer 512KB of external cache, most offer at least 256KB. Obviously, the more cache a computer has, the more likely it is to have the instructions or data the processor needs in the cache. Intel's P6 chip packages external cache in the same housing as the microprocessor (Figure 3-11).

Flash Memory

We have stated that memory is volatile—that it disappears when the power is turned off—hence the need for secondary storage to keep data on a more permanent basis. A long-standing speed problem has been the slow rate at which data is accessed from a secondary storage device such as a disk, a rate significantly slower than internal computer speeds. It seemed unimaginable that data might someday be stored on nonvolatile memory chips—nonvolatile RAM—close at hand. A breakthrough has emerged in the form of nonvolatile **flash memory.** Flash chips are currently being used in cellular phones and cockpit flight recorders, and they are replacing disks in some handheld computers.

Flash memory chips are being produced in credit card–like packages, which are smaller than a disk drive and require only half the power; that is why they are being used in notebook computers and the handheld personal digital assistants.

Although flash memory is not yet commonplace, it seems likely that it will become a mainstream component. Since data and instructions will be ever closer to the microprocessor, conversion to flash memory chips would have a pivotal impact on a computer's processing speed.

NEW DIRECTIONS

CHIPS IN YOUR FUTURE

We already know about unseen microchips in everyday appliances—refrigerators, clocks, and microwave ovens. But these are trifling compared to what is in store.

Here are some scenarios in sight in the near future. At the airport your suitcase will be tagged with a tiny chip that identifies it and allows it to be—properly—tracked through the airline system to its destination. In the supermarket chip-

operated machines will dispense dog food or potato chips or soda with the exact amounts the cus-

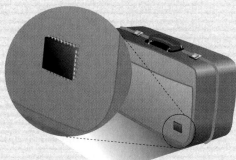

tomer specifies. Out in the elements, your chip-embedded coat will sense the temperature and puff up as the mercury drops. Chips implanted in your car's tire treads will monitor tire pressure, balance, and tread wear. At home, your pill bottle will speak up to remind you that it is time to take your medication, and even better, your TV remote control will answer when you call out to find it.

RISC Technology: Less Is More

It flies in the face of computer tradition: Instead of reaching for more variety, more power, more everything-for-everyone, proponents of **RISCs—reduced instruction set computers**—suggest that we could get by with a little less. In fact, reduced instruction set computers offer only a small subset of instructions; the absence of bells and whistles increases speed. So there is a back-to-basics movement in computer design.

RISC supporters say that on conventional computers (called **CISCs**, or **complex instruction set computers**), a hefty chunk of the instruction set is rarely used. Those underused instructions, they note, are an impediment to speedy performance. RISC computers, with their stripped-down instruction sets, zip through programs like racing cars—at speeds four to ten times those of CISC computers. This is heady stuff for the merchants of speed who want to attract customers by offering more speed for the money.

Parallel Processing

The ultimate speed solution is **parallel processing**, a method of using several processors at the same time. Consider the description of computer processing you have seen so far in this chapter: The processor gets an instruction from memory, acts on it, returns processed data to memory, and then repeats the process. This is conventional **serial processing**, the execution of one instruction at a time. A variation on this approach is **pipelining**, in which an instruction's actions—fetch, decode, execute, store—need not be complete before the next instruction is begun. For example, once fetch is complete for an instruction and it moves to decode, fetch is begun for the next instruction.

The problem with the conventional computer is that the single electronic pathway, the bus line, acts like a bottleneck. The computer has a one-track mind because it is restricted to handling one piece of data at a time. For many applications, such as simulating the air flow around an entire airplane in flight, this is an exceedingly inefficient procedure. A better solution? Many processors, each with its own memory unit, working at the same time: parallel processing. Some parallel processors are capable of operating in terms of **teraflops**—that is, *trillions* of floating-point instructions per second. Recall, for comparison, that a megaflop is a mere one million floating-point operations per second.

A number of parallel processors are being built and sold commercially. However, do not look for parallel processing in personal computers just yet. Thus far, this technology is limited to larger computers.

The future holds some exciting possibilities for computer chips. New speed breakthroughs certainly will continue. One day we may see computers that operate using light (photonics) rather than electricity (electronics) to control their operation. Light travels faster and is less likely to be disrupted by electrical interference. Also, light beams can pass through one another, alleviating some of the problems that occur in the design of electronic components, in which wires should not cross. And would you believe that someday computers might actually be grown as biological cultures? So-called biochips may replace today's silicon chip. As research continues, so will the surprises.

Whatever the design and processing strategy of a computer, its goal is the same: to turn raw input into useful output. Input and output are the topics of the next chapter.

CHAPTER REVIEW

Summary and Key Terms

- The **central processing unit (CPU)** is a complex set of electronic circuitry that executes program instructions, consisting of a control unit and an arithmetic/logic unit.

- The central processing unit interacts closely with primary storage, or memory. Memory provides temporary storage of data while the computer is executing the program. Secondary storage holds the data that is permanent or semipermanent.

- The **control unit** of the central processing unit coordinates execution of the program instructions by communicating with the arithmetic/logic unit and memory—the parts of the system that actually execute the program.

- The **arithmetic/logic unit (ALU)** contains circuitry that executes the arithmetic and logical operations. The unit can perform four **arithmetic operations**: addition, subtraction, multiplication, and division. Its **logical operations** usually involve making comparisons that test for three conditions: the **equal-to condition**, the **less-than condition**, and the **greater-than condition**. The computer can test for more than one condition at once, so it can discern three other conditions as well: less than or equal to, greater than or equal to, and less than or greater than.

- Symbols called **relational operators** (=, <, >) can define the comparison to perform.

- **Registers** are areas for temporary data storage. A register might be an **accumulator**, which collects the results of computations. An **address register** keeps track of where data is stored in memory. A **storage register** temporarily holds data taken from or about to be sent to memory. A **general-purpose register** is used for several functions.

- **Memory** is the part of the computer that temporarily holds data and instructions before and after they are processed by the arithmetic/logic unit. Memory is also known as **primary storage**, **primary memory**, **main storage**, **internal storage**, and **main memory**. Manufacturers often use the term **RAM**, which stands for *random-access memory*.

- The central processing unit follows four main steps when executing an instruction: It (1) fetches—gets—the instruction from memory, (2) decodes the instruction and gives instructions for the transfer of appropriate data from memory to the ALU, (3) directs the ALU to perform the actual operation on the data, and (4) directs the ALU to store the result of the operation in memory or a register. The first two steps are called **I-time** (instruction time), and the last two steps are called **E-time** (execution time).

- A **machine cycle** is the combination of I-time and E-time. The internal **clock** of the central processing unit produces pulses at a fixed rate to synchronize computer operations. A machine-cycle instruction may include many subinstructions, each of which must take at least one clock cycle. Each central processing unit has a set of commands it can understand. Together, these commands are called an **instruction set**.

- The location in memory for each instruction and each piece of data is identified by an **address**. Address numbers remain the same, but the contents of the locations change. A meaningful name given to a memory address is called a **symbolic address**.

- Since a computer can recognize only whether electricity is on or off, data is represented by an on/off **binary system**, represented by the digits 1 and 0.

- Each 0 or 1 in the binary system is called a **bit** (binary digit). A group of bits (usually 8 bits) is called a **byte**, which usually represents one **character** of data, such as a letter, digit, or special character. Memory capacity is expressed in **kilobytes (KB or K)**. One kilobyte equals 1024 bytes. A **megabyte (MB)** equals about one million bytes, and a **gigabyte (GB)** equals about one billion bytes.

- A computer **word** is the number of bits that make up a unit of data, as defined by the computer system.

- A common coding scheme for representing characters is **ASCII** (American Standard Code for Information Interchange), which uses 7-bit characters. A variation of the code, called ASCII-8, uses 8 bits per character.

- The **motherboard**, the flat board within the personal computer housing, holds the chips and circuitry that organize the computer's activities. The motherboard also holds **expansion slots** into which other circuit boards can be inserted to link peripheral devices to the processor.

- A central processing unit, or processor, on a chip is a **microprocessor,** or **microchip** for short. A microprocessor may be called a **logic chip** when it is used to control specialized devices. Microprocessors contain tiny **transistors,** electronic switches that may or may not allow current to pass through, representing a 1 or 0 bit, respectively.

- The **MMX** (for **multimedia extensions**) chip boosts a computer's ability to produce graphics, video, and sound. The more functions that are combined on a microprocessor, the faster the computer runs, the cheaper it is to make, and the more reliable it is.

- **Semiconductor memory**, thousands of very small circuits on a silicon chip, is **volatile.** A chip is described as **monolithic** because the circuits on a single chip constitute an inseparable unit of storage.

- Most modern computers use semiconductor memory because it has the advantages of reliability, compactness, low cost, and lower power usage.

- An important type of semiconductor design is called **complementary metal oxide semiconductor (CMOS);** it is noted for using little electricity, making it especially useful for computers requiring low power consumption, such as portable computers.

- **Random-access memory (RAM)** keeps the instructions and data for whatever programs you happen to be using at the moment. RAM is usually volatile.

- A **single in-line memory module (SIMM)** is a plug-in board that contains memory chips.

- RAM is often divided into two types: static RAM **(SRAM),** which is faster, and dynamic RAM **(DRAM),** which is smaller and less expensive.

- **Read-only memory (ROM)** contains programs and data that are permanently recorded into this type of memory at the factory; they can be read and used, but they cannot be changed by the user. ROM is nonvolatile. The instructions within some ROM chips can be changed using **ROM burners;** these chips are known as **PROM** chips, or **programmable read-only memory** chips.

- Computer instruction speeds fall into various ranges, from a **millisecond**, which is one-thousandth of a second; to a **microsecond,** one-millionth of a second; to a **nanosecond,** one-billionth of a second. Still to be achieved is the **picosecond** range—one-trillionth of a second.

- Microprocessor speeds are usually expressed in **megahertz (MHz),** millions of machine cycles per second. Another measure of computer speed is **MIPS,** which stands for one million instructions per second. A third measure is the **megaflop,** which stands for one million floating-point operations per second.

- A **bus line** is a set of parallel data paths that transports data from one place to another internally within the computer system. The amount of data that can be carried at one time is called the bus width.

- A **cache** is a relatively small amount of very fast memory that stores data and instructions that are used frequently, resulting in an improved processing speed. **Internal cache,** the fastest kind, refers to cache built right into the processor's design. Most computers include **external cache** on separate chips.

- The emerging technology of **flash memory** will provide memory chips that are nonvolatile.

- **RISCs—reduced instruction set computers—**are fast because they use only a small subset of instructions. Conventional computers, called **CISCs,** or **complex instruction set computers,** include many instructions that are rarely used.

■ Conventional **serial processing** uses a single processor and can handle just one instruction at a time. **Pipelining** means that an instruction's actions—fetch, decode, execute, store—need not be complete before the next instruction is begun. **Parallel processing** uses several processors in the same computer at the same time. Some parallel processors are capable of operating in terms of **teraflops**—that is, trillions of floating-point instructions per second.

Quick Poll

Compare your answers to those of your colleagues or classmates.

1. The large number of technical terms in this chapter
   ❏ a. Are useful for a general background in computers
   ❏ b. Are needed only by people pursuing technical careers
   ❏ c. May at least be useful when checking out new computers
2. Keeping up with changing microchip technology is
   ❏ a. A key to following the computer industry
   ❏ b. Of interest only from a historical standpoint
   ❏ c. Useful information when considering a computer purchase
3. I find the idea of building my own computer
   ❏ a. Intriguing
   ❏ b. Practical
   ❏ c. A waste of time

Discussion Questions

1. Why is writing instructions for a computer more difficult than writing instructions for a person?
2. Do you think there is a continuing need to increase computer speed? Can you think of examples in which more speed would be desirable?
3. It will soon be possible to have microchips implanted in our bodies to monitor or improve our physical conditions. Do you think this is a good or bad idea? Would you personally consider such a thing?

Student Study Guide

Multiple Choice

1. The electrical circuitry that executes program instructions:
   a. register
   b. accumulator
   c. central processing unit
   d. bus line
2. The entire computer system is coordinated by
   a. the ALU
   b. the control unit
   c. the accumulator
   d. arithmetic operators
3. A bus line consists of
   a. registers
   b. parallel data paths
   c. accumulators
   d. machine cycles
4. Equal to, less than, and greater than are examples of
   a. logical operations
   b. subtraction
   c. locations
   d. arithmetic operations
5. The primary storage unit is also known as
   a. storage registers
   b. mass storage
   c. accumulators
   d. memory
6. Data and instructions are put into primary storage by
   a. memory
   b. secondary storage
   c. the control unit
   d. the ALU
7. Registers that collect the results of computations are
   a. general-purpose
   b. storage registers
   c. main storage
   d. accumulators
8. During E-time the ALU
   a. examines the instruction
   b. executes the instruction
   c. enters the instruction
   d. elicits the instruction
9. When the control unit gets an instruction it is called
   a. E-time
   b. I-time
   c. machine time
   d. ALU time
10. When the control unit directs the ALU to perform an operation on the data, the machine cycle is involved in its
    a. first step
    b. second step
    c. third step
    d. fourth step
11. Computer operations are synchronized by
    a. the CPU clock
    b. the binary system
    c. megabytes
    d. E-time
12. Another name for primary storage is
    a. secondary storage
    b. binary system
    c. ROM
    d. main storage
13. Which is *not* another name for memory?
    a. primary storage
    b. internal storage
    c. main storage
    d. secondary storage
14. Another name for a logic chip is
    a. PROM
    b. microprocessor
    c. memory
    d. ROM
15. Data is represented on a computer by a two-state on/off system called
    a. a word
    b. a byte
    c. the binary system
    d. RAM

16. A letter, number, or special character is represented by a
    a. bit   c. kilobyte
    b. byte   d. megabyte
17. Memory capacity may be expressed in
    a. microseconds   c. kilobytes
    b. bits   d. cycles
18. Which is *not* a kind of register?
    a. storage   c. address
    b. accumulator   d. variable
19. A type of computer that is faster because it has fewer instructions:
    a. symbolic   c. RISC
    b. ASCII-8   d. ROM burner
20. An emerging technology that provides nonvolatile memory chips:
    a. flash memory   c. PROM
    b. CMOS   d. CISC
21. The data coding scheme that is the American standard:
    a. ASCII   c. KB
    b. SIMM   d. gigabyte
22. Tools to change PROM chips are called
    a. chip kits   c. RAM burners
    b. PROM burners   d. none of these
23. An approach to increase speed:
    a. CISC   c. parallel processing
    b. serial processing d. CMOS
24. The shortest period of time:
    a. millisecond   c. nanosecond
    b. picosecond   d. microsecond
25. A trillion floating-point instructions per second:
    a. MIPS   c. teraflop
    b. CISC   d. MHz

True/False

T F   1. The control unit consists of the CPU and the ALU.
T F   2. Secondary storage holds data only temporarily.
T F   3. The control unit directs the entire computer system.
T F   4. MIPS is an abbreviation for megaflop.
T F   5. The electronic circuitry that controls all arithmetic and logical operations is contained in the ALU.
T F   6. The three basic logical operations may be combined to form a total of nine commonly used operations.
T F   7. Memory allows fast access to instructions in secondary storage.
T F   8. Registers are temporary storage areas located in memory.
T F   9. Address registers hold the addresses of locations containing data needed for an instruction.

T F 10. RISC computers use fewer instructions than traditional computers.
T F 11. All computers except personal computers can execute more than one instruction at a time.
T F 12. The machine cycle consists of four steps, from the first step of fetching the instruction to the last step of storing the result in memory.
T F 13. The internal clock of the CPU produces pulses at a fixed rate to synchronize all computer operations.
T F 14. A cache is a small amount of secondary storage.
T F 15. Computers represent data using the two-state binary system.
T F 16. A bit is commonly made up of 8 bytes.
T F 17. A kilobyte (KB) is 1024 bytes.
T F 18. The MMX chip includes the ability to produce video and sound.
T F 19. Another name for memory is secondary storage.
T F 20. Serial processing is replacing parallel processing.
T F 21. Addition and subtraction are logical operations.
T F 22. Primary storage is part of the central processing unit.
T F 23. Memory is usually volatile.
T F 24. A microsecond is briefer than a millisecond.
T F 25. The ASCII coding scheme is accepted as the American standard.

Fill-In

1. A millionth of a second is called

   _____

2. The unit that consists of both the control unit and the arithmetic/logic unit: _____

3. Processing instructions one at a time is called

   _____

4. List five other names for memory.
   a. _____
   b. _____
   c. _____
   d. _____
   e. _____

5. MHz is an abbreviation for

   _____

6. The abbreviation for memory chips that can be

   altered: _____

7. The combination of I-time and E-time is called

   _____

8. The name for the symbols =, <, and > is

   _____

9. Each memory location is identified by

   _____

10. A 0 or 1 in the binary system is called

    _____

11. MIPS stands for _____

12. A disadvantage of semiconductor memory:

    _____

13. An electronic path to transfer data:

    _____

14. RAM stands for _____

15. The main circuit board: _____

16. Type of chip that holds programs that will not be

    altered: _____

17. Register type that holds data taken from or sent to

    memory: _____

18. The name for comparing operations:

    _____

19. The concept of many processors working at the

    same time: _____

20. When the control unit decodes an instruction, is

    the machine cycle in I-time or E-time?

    _____

Answers

Multiple Choice

1. c	6. c	11. a	16. b	21. a
2. b	7. d	12. d	17. c	22. d
3. b	8. b	13. d	18. d	23. c
4. a	9. b	14. b	19. c	24. b
5. d	10. c	15. c	20. a	25. c

True/False

1. F	6. F	11. F	16. F	21. F
2. F	7. F	12. T	17. T	22. F
3. T	8. F	13. T	18. T	23. T
4. F	9. T	14. F	19. F	24. T
5. T	10. T	15. T	20. F	25. T

Fill-In

1. microsecond
2. central processing unit
3. serial processing
4. a. main storage
   b. internal storage
   c. primary storage
   d. primary memory
   e. main memory
5. megahertz
6. PROM
7. a machine cycle
8. relational operators
9. an address
10. a bit
11. one million instructions per second
12. it is volatile
13. bus line
14. random-access memory
15. motherboard
16. ROM
17. storage register
18. logical operations
19. parallel processing
20. I-time

PLANET INTERNET

Добро пожаловать
в Санкт-Петербург!
—————— switch to english ——————

GLOBAL VILLAGE

The Internet is big, really big. Some say that working on the Internet gives new meaning to the word *infinity*. One way to grasp the vastness of the 'Net is to link to sites in other countries.

So far away. As intriguing as these faraway sites may be, it can take some time to access them. An option that may be available is a *mirror site*, a nearby site that has the identical offering. The WebMuseum site in Paris, for example, which offers paintings from the Louvre on your screen, urges you right away to switch (link) to one of the mirror sites on its list. Using a mirror site dramatically improves the speed of data access.

The CERN site. It is entirely appropriate that we mention the CERN site, a laboratory for particle physics in Geneva, Switzerland. CERN, as described in Chapter 7, is the birthplace of the World Wide Web. This site includes a link to the history of CERN's relationship with the Web.

English or not English. Many foreign sites offer an English version of their site to visitors whose language is English; you could just as easily

be in Kansas. They usually offer a choice: Would you prefer English or Swedish? Others simply launch into their native tongue. You either speak it or just go along for the pictures. More-sophisticated sites note your location and immediately present their site in English, with an option to switch to the native tongue. That is the case with the site to tour St. Petersburg in Russia, whose opening page logo is shown here. We chose the native version because it is fascinating to see the Russian alphabet on the screen as you tour, but notice that a return to English is always an option.

Worth the trip? You decide. A good place to begin is the World Communities site, where you can hop from country to country. Be prepared for the fact that some developing countries have relatively primitive offerings at this point; in fact, despite being on the list, some cannot be reached at all. But many sites are fascinating. The sites may offer detailed information about the native country. Others officially represent the commercial and tourist interests of the country or community; the logo on the Singapore home page shown here is typical.

Global information at home. Businesses with a global presence need to maintain a global awareness. There are many sites devoted to information about international customs and trade, represented by the Internationalist logo shown here. The tourist industry has a significant presence on the Internet; you can learn about all kinds of package tours and countries to visit, as indicated by the All about Rio logo shown here.

The Internationalist®
The Center for International Business Information

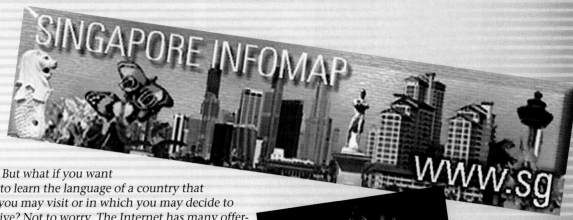

But what if you want to learn the language of a country that you may visit or in which you may decide to live? Not to worry. The Internet has many offerings in that department, as indicated by the Watch Your Language image shown here.

Internet Exercises

1. **Structured exercise.** Begin with the AWL URL, http://hepg.awl.com/capron/planet/, and use the link supplied to go to the CERN site. Reminder: You can link to any site mentioned in this *Planet Internet* via the AWL URL.

2. **Freeform exercise.** Beginning with the World Communities site, compare the home pages you find for countries in Europe, Asia, the Pacific, and South America.

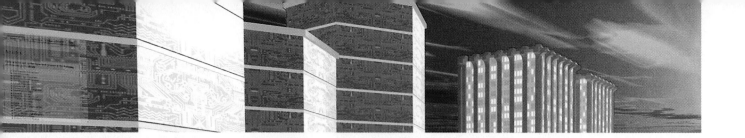

By the time he went to medical school, Miguel Hernandez was no stranger to computers. As an undergraduate, he had used word processing to prepare assignments and term papers, desktop publishing to produce a biology report that included photos of lab specimens, and even (once) the Internet to shop for casual clothing.

Miguel did not pause to consider how his actions demonstrated some of the forms of input and output of computer usage, but there were several. He used a keyboard to input the text of his papers, and a mouse to assist with commands. He used a scanner to input the photos of his lab specimens. He produced output both on the computer screen and on the printer. When he placed his order over the Internet, his input triggered more output than he could have imagined—a shipping label and a backorder notice for him and, for the company's internal records, entries reflecting his purchases on inventory, reorder, and demographic reports. These are routine input/output activities. None come close to the drama of the computer input and output that awaited him in his medical school classes.

Medical students study, among other things, the anatomy of the human body. These days, that study is enhanced by computer software that lets students perform exploratory actions on the screen. For example, Miguel can input changes to the program that shows a close-up of a leg to remove layers of tissue and thus reveal the muscles and bone underneath. The screen displays (as output) the changes, allowing Miguel to simulate exploration and even surgery on the computer.

Most of us will not be executing input with such dramatic results. But it is certain that we will be giving the computer input and accepting computer output in more ways than we can now imagine.

Input and Output

The User Connection

▶ How Users See Input and Output

The central processing unit is the unseen part of a computer system, and users are only dimly aware of it. But users are very much aware of the input and output associated with the computer. They submit input data to the computer to get processed information, the output.

Sometimes the output is an instant reaction to the input. Consider these examples:

- Zebra-striped bar codes on supermarket items provide input that permits instant retrieval of outputs—price and item name—right at the checkout counter.
- A forklift operator speaks directly to a computer through a microphone. Words like *left*, *right*, and *lift* are the actual input data. The output is the computer's instant response, which causes the forklift to operate as requested.
- A sales representative uses an instrument that looks like a pen to enter an order on a special pad. The handwritten characters are displayed as "typed" text and are stored in the pad, which is actually a small computer.
- Factory workers input data by punching in on a time clock as they go from task to task. The time clock is connected to a computer. The outputs are their weekly paychecks and reports for management that summarize hours per project on a quarterly basis.

Input and output may be separated by time or distance or both. Here are some examples:

- Data on checks is used as input to the bank computer, which eventually processes the data to prepare a bank statement once a month.

MAKING THE RIGHT CONNECTIONS

COMPUTER, PHONE HOME

Lost, strayed, stolen? A missing computer can just make the right connections and be on its way home again. A missing computer is most likely a stolen computer. But not to worry; some crafty software can help the computer rescue itself.

The software instructs the computer to phone a toll-free hot line and, using the phone company's Caller ID option, report its location. It makes the call once a week. If the computer remains with its proper owner, the phone calls are simply logged and stored. But if the computer is reported stolen, the phone calls are carefully monitored and the new location identified. If the

thief is using the phone line or if the modem is not yet hooked up, the software simply bides its time and makes the phone call later.

The software, called Compu-Trace, is stealthy. It will not show up in a list of files, and it can survive having the entire hard drive reformatted—made clean as new. It even turns off the modem speaker temporarily so that no one can hear it dialing.

Making Microchips

Computer power in the hands of the people—we take it for granted now, but not so long ago computers existed only in enormous rooms behind locked doors. The revolution that changed all that was ignited by chips of silicon smaller than your fingernail: microchips.

Silicon is one of the most common elements on Earth, but there is nothing commonplace about designing, manufacturing, testing, and packaging the microprocessors that are made from silicon. In this gallery we will explore the key elements in the process by which those marvels of miniaturization—microchips—are made.

The Idea Behind the Microchip

Microchips form the lightning-quick "brain" of a computer. These devices, though complex, work on a very simple principle: They "know" when electric current is on and when it is off. They can process information because it is coded as a series of on-off electric signals. Before the invention of microchips, these signals were controlled by thousands of separate devices laboriously wired together to form a single circuit. However, thousands of circuits can be embedded on a single microchip; a microchip is often called an integrated circuit.

Silicon is a semiconductor—it conducts electricity only "semi" well. This does not sound like such an admirable trait, but the beauty of silicon is that it can be doped, or treated, with different materials to make it conduct electricity well or not at all. By doping various areas of a silicon chip differently, pathways can be set up for electricity to follow. The pathways consist of grooves that are etched into layers placed over a silicon substrate. The silicon is doped so that the pathways conduct electricity. The surrounding areas do not conduct electricity at all.

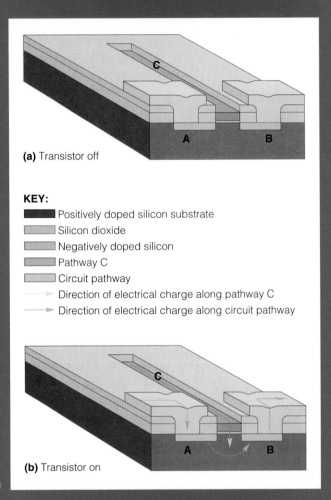

(a) Transistor off

KEY:
- Positively doped silicon substrate
- Silicon dioxide
- Negatively doped silicon
- Pathway C
- Circuit pathway
- → Direction of electrical charge along pathway C
- → Direction of electrical charge along circuit pathway

(b) Transistor on

1. This simplified illustration shows the layers and grooves within a transistor, one of thousands of circuit components on a single chip. Pathway C controls the flow of electricity through the circuit. (a) When no electric charge is added to pathway C, electricity cannot flow along the circuit pathway from area A to area B. Thus, the transistor is "off." (b) A charge added to pathway C temporarily allows electricity to travel from area A to area B. Now the transistor is "on," and electricity can continue to other components in the circuit. The control of electricity here and elsewhere in the chip makes it possible for the computer to process information coded as "on-off" electric signals.

Preparing the Design

2

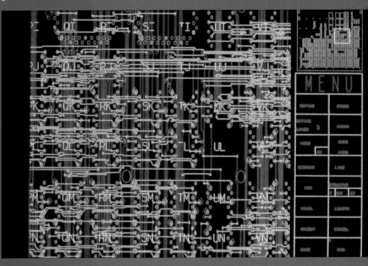

3

4

Each microprocessor is constructed like a multistory building, with multiple layers of material combining to create a single, complex unit. Try to imagine figuring out a way to place thousands of circuit components next to one another so that electricity flows through the whole integrated circuit the way it is supposed to. That is the job of chip designers. Essentially, they are trying to put together a gigantic multilayered jigsaw puzzle.

The circuit design of a typical chip requires over a year's work by a team of designers. Computers assist in the complex task of mapping out the most efficient pathways for each circuit layer.

2. A designer can arrange and modify circuit patterns and display them on a screen. Superimposing the color-coded circuit layers allows the designer to evaluate the relationships between them. The computer allows the designer to electronically store and retrieve previously designed circuit patterns.

3. Here the designer has used computer graphics software to display a screen image of the circuit design.

4. The computer system can also provide a printed version of any or all parts of the design. This large-scale printout allows the design team to discuss and modify the entire chip design.

Manufacturing the Chip

The silicon used to make computer chips is extracted from common rocks and sand. It is melted down into a form that is 99.9 percent pure silicon and then doped with chemicals to make it either electrically positive or electrically negative.

5. The molten silicon is then "grown" into cylindrical ingots in a process similar to candle dipping.

5

6

6. A diamond saw slices each ingot into circular wafers 4 or 6 or 8 inches in diameter and four-thousandths of an inch thick. The wafers are sterilized and polished to a perfectly smooth, mirror-like finish. Each wafer will eventually contain hundreds of identical chips. One silicon wafer can produce more than 100 microprocessors.

Since a single speck of dust can ruin a chip, chips are manufactured in special laboratories called clean rooms. The air in clean rooms is filtered, and workers dress in "bunny suits" to lessen the chance of chip contamination. A manufacturing lab is 100 times cleaner than a hospital operating room.

7. Chip-manufacturing processes vary, but one step is common: Electrically positive silicon wafers are placed in an open glass tube and inserted in a 1200° Celsius oxidation furnace. Oxygen reacts with the silicon, covering each wafer with a thin layer of silicon dioxide, which does not conduct electricity well. Each wafer is then coated with a gelatin-like substance called photoresist, which hardens. The final design of each circuit layer must be reduced to the size of the chip. A stencil called a mask, representing the schematic design of the circuit, is placed over the wafer. Ultraviolet light is shined through the mask, softening the exposed—nonmasked—photoresist on the wafer.

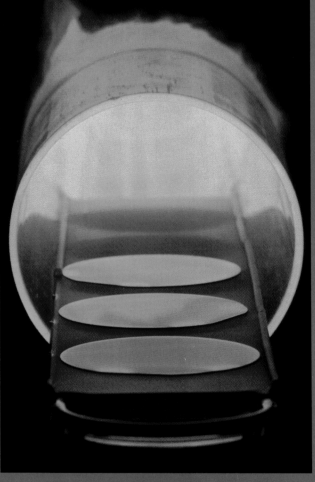

7

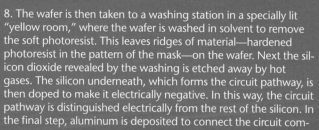

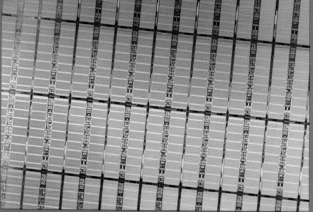

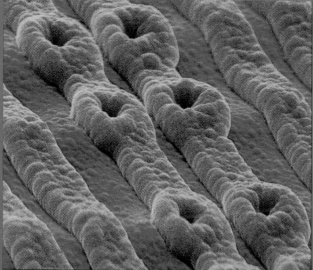

8. The wafer is then taken to a washing station in a specially lit "yellow room," where the wafer is washed in solvent to remove the soft photoresist. This leaves ridges of material—hardened photoresist in the pattern of the mask—on the wafer. Next the silicon dioxide revealed by the washing is etched away by hot gases. The silicon underneath, which forms the circuit pathway, is then doped to make it electrically negative. In this way, the circuit pathway is distinguished electrically from the rest of the silicon. In the final step, aluminum is deposited to connect the circuit com-

ponents and form the bonding pads to which wires will later be connected.
9. The result: one wafer with many chips.
10. Computerized coloration enhances this close-up view of a wafer with chips.
11. This image shows circuit paths on a microprocessor chip magnified 3000 times.

Testing the Chip

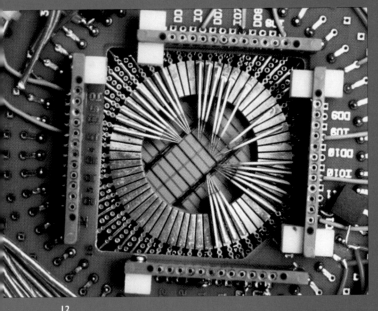

12

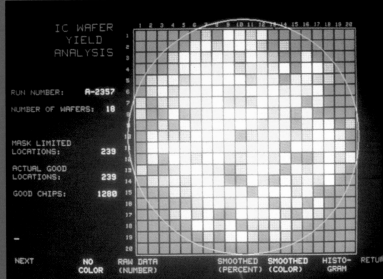

IC WAFER
YIELD
ANALYSIS

RUN NUMBER: A-2357

NUMBER OF WAFERS: 18

MASK LIMITED
LOCATIONS: 239

ACTUAL GOOD
LOCATIONS: 239

GOOD CHIPS: 1280

NEXT   NO   RAW DATA   SMOOTHED   SMOOTHED   HISTO-   RETU
            COLOR   (NUMBER)   (PERCENT) (COLOR)   GRAM

13

Although chips on a particular wafer may look identical, they do not perform identically.

12. A probe machine must perform millions of tests on each chip, to determine whether it conducts electricity in the precise way it was designed to. The needle-like probes contact the bonding pads, apply electricity, measure the results, and mark ink spots on defective chips.

13. A defect review performed by a computer finds and classifies defects in order to eliminate them from the wafer.

14. After the initial testing, a diamond saw cuts each chip from the wafer, and defective chips are discarded.

14

Packaging the Chip

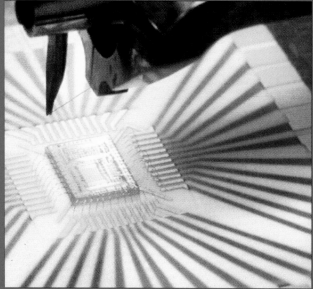

15

16

Each acceptable chip is mounted on a protective package.

15. An automated wire-bonding device wires the bonding pads of the chip to the electrical leads on the package, using aluminum or gold wire thinner than a human hair. A variety of packages are in use today.

16. Dual in-line packages have two rows of legs that are inserted into holes in a circuit board.

17. Square pin-grid array packages, which are used for chips requiring many electrical leads, look like a bed of nails. The pins are inserted into holes in a circuit board. In this photo the protective cap has been cut away, revealing the ultrafine wires connecting the chip to the package.

17

From Chip to Computer

19

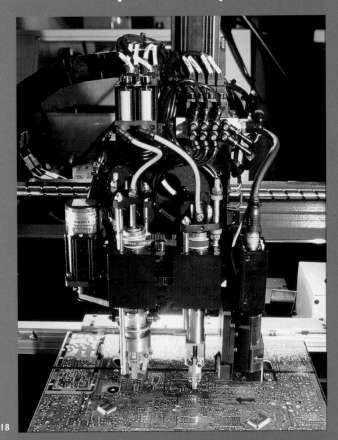

18

21

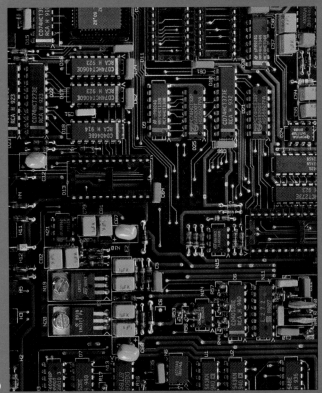

20

At a factory that manufactures circuit boards, 18. a robot makes a circuit board and 19. another robot inserts a pin-grid package into holes in a circuit board. Several surface mount packages have already been placed on the board.
20. Dual in-line packages of various sizes have been attached to this circuit board.
21. This circuit board is being installed in a Compaq computer.

■ Charge-card transactions in a retail store provide input data that is processed monthly to produce customer bills.

■ Water-sample data is collected at lake and river sites, keyed in at the environmental agency office, and used to produce reports that show patterns of water quality.

The examples in this section show the diversity of computer applications, but in all cases the process is the same: input–processing–output. The topic of processing was covered in the previous chapter. This chapter examines input and output methods in detail.

▶ Input: Getting Data from the User to the Computer

Some input data can go directly to the computer for processing. Input in this category includes bar codes, speech that enters the computer through a microphone, and data entered by means of a device that converts motions to on-screen action. Some input data, however, goes through a good deal of intermediate handling, such as when it is copied from a **source document** (jargon for the original written data) and translated to a medium that a machine can read, such as a magnetic disk. In either case the task is to gather data to be processed by the computer—sometimes called *raw data*—and convert it into some form the computer can understand.

Keyboard

A **keyboard**, which usually is similar to a typewriter keyboard, may be part of a personal computer or part of a terminal that is connected to a computer somewhere else (Figure 4-1a). Not all keyboards are traditional, however. A fast-food franchise like McDonald's, for example, uses keyboards whose keys represent items such as large fries or a Big Mac (Figure 4-1b). Even less traditional is the keyboard shown in Figure 4-1c, which is used to enter Chinese characters. Figure 4-2 shows the complete layout of a traditional keyboard.

Mouse

A **mouse**, which has a ball on its underside, is rolled on a flat surface, usually the desk on which the computer sits (Figure 4-3a and b). The rolling movement causes a corresponding movement on the screen. Moving the mouse and then clicking it at the desired location on the screen allows you to reposition the **pointer**, or **cursor**, an indicator on the screen that shows the insertion point. (The cursor can also be moved by pressing various keyboard keys.) You can also use the mouse to communicate commands to the computer by clicking a button on top of the mouse. In particular, a mouse button is often used to click on an **icon** (Figure 4-3c), a pictorial symbol on a screen; the icon represents a computer activity—a command to the computer—so clicking the icon invokes the command. This process of communicating with the computer by clicking on icons is referred to as a **graphical user interface (GUI)**.

Mice have evolved, adding new features and new buttons. Some are even cordless. Microsoft's IntelliMouse offers an extra wheel, positioned

(a)

(b)

(c)

Figure 4-1 Keyboards. (a) A traditional computer keyboard. (b) Workers at McDonald's press a key for each item ordered. The amount of the order is totaled by the computer system and then displayed on a small screen so that the customer can see the amount owed. (c) Chinese characters are significantly more complicated than the letters and digits found on a standard keyboard. To enter Chinese characters into the computer system, a person uses a special keyboard. Each letter key shows the characters that a user can type by holding down other keys while pressing that letter (as you would hold down a Shift key to make capital letters).

FINDING YOUR WAY AROUND A KEYBOARD

Most personal computer keyboards have three main parts: function keys, the main keyboard in the center, and numeric keys to the right. Extended keyboards, such as the keyboard shown here, have additional keys between the main keyboard and the numeric keys and status lights in the upper-right corner.

Function Keys

The function keys (highlighted in tan on the diagram) are an easy way to give certain commands to the computer. What each function key does is defined by the particular software you are using.

Main Keyboard

The main keyboard includes the familiar keys found on a typewriter keyboard (dark blue), as well as some special command keys (light blue). The command keys have different uses that depend on the software being used. Some of the most common uses are listed here.

 The Escape key, Esc, is used in different ways by different programs; often it allows you to "escape" to the previous screen of the program.

 The Tab key allows you to tab across the screen and set tab stops as you would on a typewriter.

 When the Caps Lock key is pressed, uppercase letters are pro-

duced. Numbers and symbols are not affected—the number or symbol shown on the bottom of a key is still produced. When the Caps Lock key is pressed, the status light under "Caps Lock" lights up.

 The Shift key allows you to produce uppercase letters and the upper symbols shown on the keys.

 The Control key, Ctrl, is pressed in combination with other keys to initiate commands as specified by the software.

The Alternate key, Alt, is also used in combination with other keys to initiate commands.

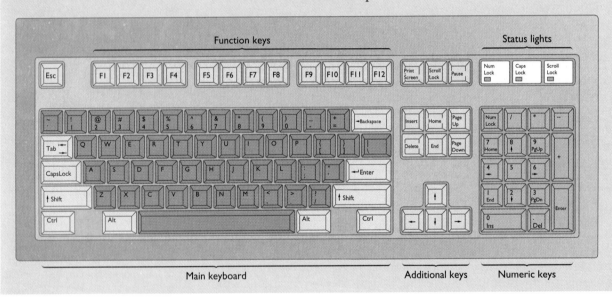

Figure 4-2 Finding your way around a keyboard.

between the two mouse buttons, that can be clicked like a button or rolled to affect the cursor (Figure 4-3d). With software designed to be used with this mouse, it can move though a document line by line or page by page or zoom in on a special spreadsheet cell or flip backwards through web pages already seen.

Trackball

A variation on the mouse is the **trackball.** You may have used a trackball to play a video game. The trackball is like an upside-down mouse—you

The Backspace key is most often used to delete a character to the left of the cursor, moving the cursor back one position. (The cursor is the flashing indicator on the screen that shows where the next character will be inserted.)

 The Enter key moves the cursor to the beginning of the next line. It is used at the end of a paragraph, for instance.

Numeric Keys

The numeric keys (purple) serve one of two purposes, depending on the status of the Num Lock key. When the computer is in the Num Lock mode, these keys can be used to enter numeric data and mathematical symbols (/ for "divided by," * for "multiplied by," -, and +). In the Num Lock mode, the status light under "Num Lock" lights up. When the computer is not in the Num Lock mode, the numeric keys can be used to move the cursor and perform other functions. For example:

 In some programs the End key moves the cursor to the bottom-left corner of the screen.

 This key moves the cursor down.

 The Page Down key, PgDn, advances one full screen while the cursor stays in the same place.

 This key moves the cursor to the left.

 This key moves the cursor to the right.

 In some programs the Home key moves the cursor to the top-left corner of the screen.

 This key moves the cursor up.

 The Page Up key, PgUp, backs up to the previous screen while the cursor stays in the same place.

 The Insert key, Ins, when toggled off, causes keyed characters to override existing characters.

 The Delete key, Del, deletes a character, space, or selected text.

Additional Keys

Extended keyboards include additional keys (green) that duplicate the cursor movement functions of the numeric keys. Users who enter a lot of numeric data can leave their computers in the Num Lock mode and use these additional keys to control the cursor.

The Arrow keys, to the left of the numeric keys, move the cursor position, just as the numeric keys 2, 4, 6, and 8 do when they are not in the Num Lock mode.

Just above the arrow keys are six keys—Insert, Delete, Home, End, Page Up, and Page Down—which duplicate functions of the numeric keys 0, decimal point (Del), 7, 1, 9, and 3.

At the top of the keyboard, to the right of the function keys, are keys that perform additional tasks. For example:

 The Print Screen key causes the current screen display to be printed. However, some programs will print a screen only when a printed page is full, so you may have to press the Print Screen key more than once.

 The Scroll Lock key causes lines of text—not the cursor—to move when cursor keys are used. When the computer is in the Scroll Lock mode, the status light under "Scroll Lock" lights up.

 The Pause key causes the screen to pause when information is appearing on the screen too fast to read.

roll the ball directly with your hand. The popularity of the trackball surged with the advent of laptop computers, when traveling users found themselves without a flat surface on which to roll the traditional mouse. Trackballs are often built in on portable computers, but they can also be used as separate input devices with standard desktop computers (Figure 4-4).

A variation on this theme is the **track pad**, with your finger as the pointer (Figure 4-5). Just wiggle your finger across the pad of the tiny surface and corresponding movements will be made on the screen. Tabs at the bottom of the unit serve the same functions as mouse buttons.

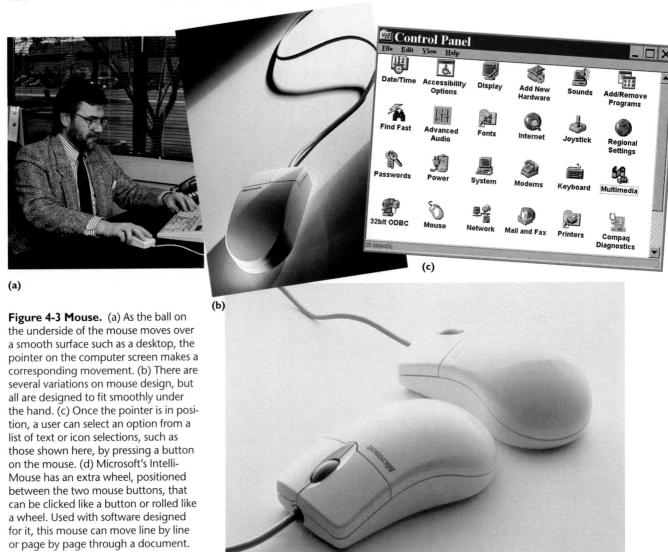

(a)

(b)

(c)

(d)

Figure 4-3 Mouse. (a) As the ball on the underside of the mouse moves over a smooth surface such as a desktop, the pointer on the computer screen makes a corresponding movement. (b) There are several variations on mouse design, but all are designed to fit smoothly under the hand. (c) Once the pointer is in position, a user can select an option from a list of text or icon selections, such as those shown here, by pressing a button on the mouse. (d) Microsoft's Intelli-Mouse has an extra wheel, positioned between the two mouse buttons, that can be clicked like a button or rolled like a wheel. Used with software designed for it, this mouse can move line by line or page by page through a document.

Source Data Automation: Collecting Data Where It Starts

Efficient data input means reducing the number of intermediate steps required between the origination of data and its processing. This is best accomplished by **source data automation**—the use of special equipment to collect data at the source, as a by-product of the activity that generates the data, and send it directly to the computer. Recall, for example, the supermarket bar code, which can be used to send data about the product directly to the computer. Source data automation eliminates keying, thereby reducing costs and opportunities for human-introduced mistakes. Since data about a transaction is collected when and where the transaction takes place, source data automation also improves the speed of the input operation.

For convenience, this discussion is divided into the primary areas related to source data automation: magnetic-ink character recognition, scanners and other optical recognition devices, and even your own voice, finger, or eye.

(a)

(b)

Figure 4-4 Trackball. The rotation of the ball causes a corresponding movement of the cursor on the screen. (a) Trackballs are often used with laptop computers because, especially on an airplane, there may be no handy surface on which to roll a mouse. Notice that the ball is placed in the center, both for compactness and to accommodate both right- and left-handed users. (b) This trackball, looking rather like an oversized egg, is called EasyBall because it can be grasped and manipulated by a child's small hand.

Magnetic-Ink Character Recognition

Abbreviated **MICR**, **magnetic-ink character recognition** involves using a machine to read characters made of magnetized particles. The most common example of magnetic characters is the array of numbers across the bottom of your personal check. Figure 4-6 shows what some of these numbers and symbols represent.

Most magnetic-ink characters are preprinted on your check. If you compare a check that you wrote that has been cashed and cleared by the bank with those that are still unused in your checkbook, you will note that the amount of the cashed check has been reproduced in magnetic characters in the lower right corner. These characters were added by a person at the bank by using an **MICR inscriber**.

Figure 4-5 Track pad. Use your finger on this pad to move the cursor on the screen. The tabs at the bottom serve the same functions as mouse buttons.

Scanner

There was a time when the only way to transfer an existing document into the computer was to retype it. Now, however, a **scanner** can convert text or even a drawing or picture into computer-recognizable data by using a form of optical recognition. **Optical recognition** systems use a light beam to scan input data and convert it into electrical signals, which are sent to the computer for processing. Optical recognition is by far the most common type of source input. Although there are many ways to use optical recognition, scanning is the method most likely to be used by personal computer users.

Just think of all those drawers filled with receipts, warranties, and old checks. If you would let the computer take care of them, you could save space and, even better, be able to find an item when you want it. In a process called **imaging**, a scanner converts those papers to an electronic version, which can then be stored on disk and retrieved when needed.

Business people also find imaging useful, since they can view an exact computer-produced replica of the original document at any time. Processed by related software, the words and numbers of the document

Do You Have Your Card Yet?

Your photo ID card identifies you as a student and lets you unlock doors, make phone calls, and buy anything from a vending machine. But that is just the small stuff. The same card can be used to register for classes, pay tuition, borrow library books, and purchase cafeteria meals. Called the Campus Connection card and first used at Florida State University, this ID card has magnetized stripes on the back to store student data that is used as input to the various systems. The card makes life a little easier for students, who do not have to juggle multiple cards or carry much cash.

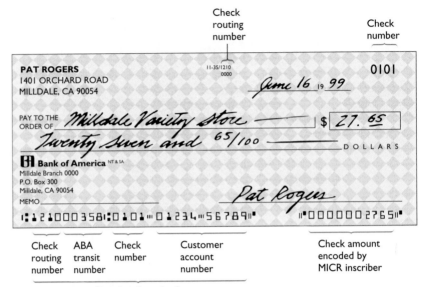

Figure 4-6 The symbols on your check. Magnetic-ink numbers and symbols run along the bottom of a check. The symbols on the left are preprinted. The MICR characters in the lower right corner of a cashed check are entered by the bank that receives it; these numbers should correspond to the amount of the check.

can be manipulated by word processing and other software. The Internal Revenue Service uses imaging to process 17,000 tax returns per hour, a significant improvement over hand processing.

Scanners fall into three categories. A **flatbed scanner** typically scans one sheet at a time, although some offer an attachment for scanning multiple sheets. Flatbed scanners are space hogs, taking up about as much room as a tabletop copy machine (Figure 4-7a). The advantage of a flatbed scanner is that it can be used to scan bound documents, such as pages from books and other bulky items. In a **sheetfeed scanner,** motorized rollers feed the sheet across the scanning head. A key attraction of sheetfeed scanners is that they are usually designed to fit neatly between the keyboard and the monitor (Figure 4-7b). Some computer manufacturers offer such scanners as part of the computer package. A **handheld scanner,** the least expensive and least reliable of the three, is a handy portable option (Figure 4-7c). It is often difficult to get a good scan with a handheld scanner, because the user must move the scanner in a straight line at a fixed rate.

Many users like scanners because they can use them to feed photographs directly into the computer. If, however, you want to scan text and then be able to edit it using word processing, you need special software—usually called OCR software, for *optical character recognition*—that can identify the individual letters as opposed to treating the entire text document as one big picture. Most scanners come packaged with OCR software.

More Optical Recognition Methods

In addition to text and images, optical recognition can process data appearing in a variety of forms: optical marks, optical characters, bar codes, and even handwritten characters.

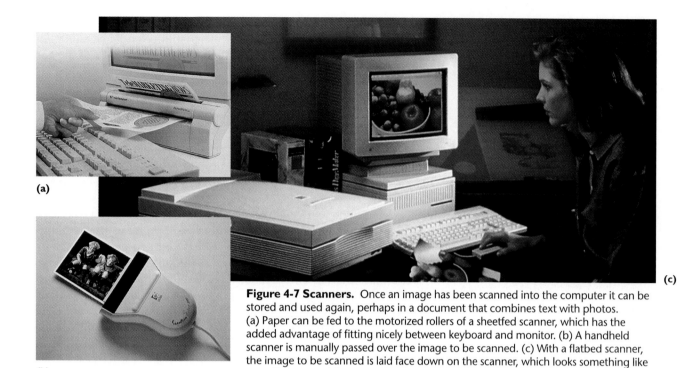

(a)

(b)

(c)

Figure 4-7 Scanners. Once an image has been scanned into the computer it can be stored and used again, perhaps in a document that combines text with photos. (a) Paper can be fed to the motorized rollers of a sheetfed scanner, which has the added advantage of fitting nicely between keyboard and monitor. (b) A handheld scanner is manually passed over the image to be scanned. (c) With a flatbed scanner, the image to be scanned is laid face down on the scanner, which looks something like a small copy machine.

Optical Mark Recognition   Abbreviated **OMR, optical mark recognition** is sometimes called mark sensing, because a machine senses marks on a piece of paper. As a student, you may immediately recognize this approach as the technique used to score certain tests. Using a pencil, you make a mark in a specified box or space that corresponds to what you think is the answer. The answer sheet is then graded by an optical device that recognizes the patterns and converts them to computer-recognizable electrical signals.

Optical Character Recognition   Abbreviated **OCR, optical character recognition** devices also use a light source to read special characters and convert them into electrical signals to be sent to the central processing unit. The characters—letters, numbers, and special symbols—can be read by both humans and machines. They are often found on sales tags on store merchandise. A standard typeface for optical characters, called **OCR-A**, has been established by the American National Standards Institute (Figure 4-8).

The handheld **wand reader** is a popular input device for reading OCR-A. There is an increasing use of wands in libraries, hospitals, and factories, as well as in retail stores. In retail stores the wand reader is connected to a **point-of-sale (POS) terminal**. This terminal is somewhat like a cash register, but it performs many more functions. When a clerk passes the wand reader over the price tag, the computer uses the input merchandise number to retrieve a description (and possibly the price, if it is not on the tag) of the item. A small printer produces a customer receipt that shows the item description and price. The computer calculates the subtotal, the sales tax (if any), and the total. This information is displayed on the screen and printed on the receipt.

The raw purchase data becomes valuable information when it is summarized by the computer system. This information can be used by the

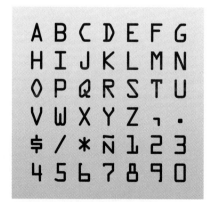

Figure 4-8 Reading the OCR-A typeface. This is a common typeface for optical character recognition.

accounting department to keep track of how much money is taken in each day, by buyers to determine what merchandise should be reordered, and by the marketing department to analyze the effectiveness of their ad campaigns.

Bar Codes   Each product on the store shelf has its own unique number, which is part of the **Universal Product Code (UPC).** This code number is represented on the product label by a pattern of vertical marks, or bars, called **bar codes.** (UPC, by the way, is an agreed-upon standard within the supermarket industry; other kinds of bar codes exist. You need only look as far as the back cover of this book to see an example of another kind of bar code.) These zebra stripes can be sensed and read by a **bar code reader,** a photoelectric device that reads the code by means of reflected light. Like the wand reader in a retail store, the bar code reader in a bookstore or grocery store is part of a point-of-sale terminal. When you buy, say, a can of corn at the supermarket, the checker moves it past the bar code reader (Figure 4-9a). The bar code merely identifies the product to the store's computer; the code does not contain the price, which may vary. The price is stored in a file that can be accessed by the computer. (Obviously, it is easier to change the price in the computer than it is to restamp the price on each can of corn.) The computer automatically tells the point-of-sale terminal what the price is; a printer prints the item description and price on a paper tape for the customer. Some supermarkets are moving to do-it-yourself-scanning, putting the bar code reader—as well as the bagging—in the customer's hands.

Although bar codes were once found primarily in supermarkets, there are a variety of other interesting applications. Bar coding has been described as an inexpensive and remarkably reliable way to get data into a computer. It is no wonder that virtually every industry has found a niche for bar codes. Federal Express, for example, attributes a large part of the corporation's success to the bar coding system it uses to track packages (Figure 4-9b). Each package is uniquely identified by a ten-digit bar code, which is input to the computer at each point as the package travels through the system. An employee can use a computer terminal to query the location of a given shipment at any time; the sender can request a status report on a package and receive a response within 30 minutes.

Figure 4-9 Bar codes. (a) This photoelectric bar code scanner, often seen at supermarket checkout counters, reads the product's zebra-stripe bar code. The bar code identifies the product for the store's computer, which retrieves price and description information. The price is then automatically rung up on the point-of-sale terminal. (b) Bar codes are often used to sort, route, and inventory packages.

(a)

(b)

Handwritten Characters   Machines that can read handwritten characters are yet another means of reducing the number of intermediate steps between capturing data and processing it. In many instances it is preferable to write the data and immediately have it usable for processing rather than having data entry operators key it in later. However, not just any scrawl will do; the rules as to the size, completeness, and legibility of the handwriting are fairly rigid (Figure 4-10).

Figure 4-10 Handwritten characters. Legibility is important in making handwritten characters readable by optical recognition.

	Good	Bad
1. Make your letters big	EWING	EWING
2. Use simple shapes	57320	57320
3. Use block printing	KENT	Kent
4. Connect lines	5BE4	5BE4
5. Close loops	9068	9068
6. Do not link characters	LOOP	LOOP

Voice Input

Speaking to a computer, known as **voice input** or **speech recognition**, is another form of source input. **Speech recognition devices** accept the spoken word through a microphone and convert it into binary code (0s and 1s) that can be understood by the computer (Figure 4-11). Typical users are the disabled, those with "busy hands" or hands too dirty for the keyboard, and those with no access to a keyboard. Uses for speech recognition include changing radio frequencies in airplane cockpits, controlling inventory in an auto junkyard, asking for stock-market quotations over the phone, inspecting

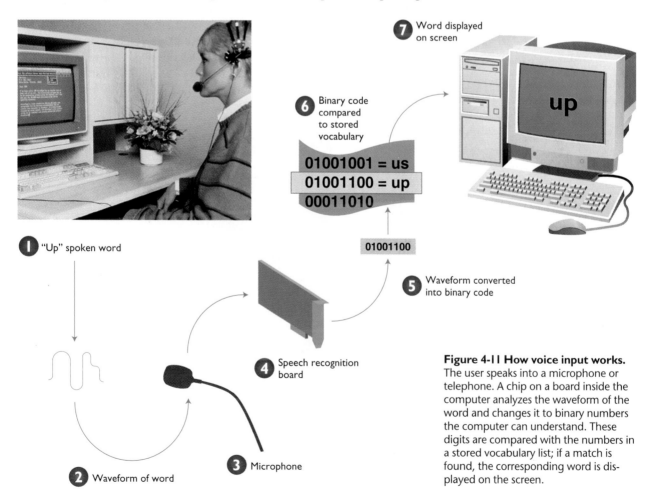

7 Word displayed on screen

6 Binary code compared to stored vocabulary

01001001 = us
01001100 = up
00011010

01001100

5 Waveform converted into binary code

1 "Up" spoken word

4 Speech recognition board

3 Microphone

2 Waveform of word

Figure 4-11 How voice input works. The user speaks into a microphone or telephone. A chip on a board inside the computer analyzes the waveform of the word and changes it to binary numbers the computer can understand. These digits are compared with the numbers in a stored vocabulary list; if a match is found, the corresponding word is displayed on the screen.

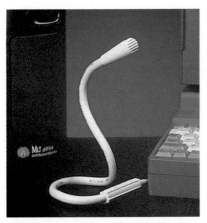

Figure 4-12 Microphone. This twistable—and inexpensive—microphone is as much a conversation piece as it is a personal computer input device.

items moving along an assembly line, and allowing physically disabled users to issue commands (Figure 4-12).

Most speech recognition systems are speaker dependent—that is, they must be separately trained for each individual user. The speech recognition system "learns" the voice of the user, who speaks isolated words repeatedly. The voiced words the system "knows" are then recognizable in the future.

Speech recognition systems that are limited to isolated words are called **discrete word systems**, and users must pause between words. Experts have tagged speech recognition as one of the most difficult things for a computer to do. Eventually, **continuous word systems** will be able to interpret sustained speech, so that users can speak normally; so far, such systems are limited by vocabulary to a single subject, such as insurance or the weather. A key advantage of delivering input to a computer in a normal speaking pattern is ease of use.

Touch Screens

One way of getting input directly from the source is to have a human simply point to a selection. The edges of a **touch screen** emit horizontal and vertical beams of light that crisscross the screen. When a finger touches the screen, the interrupted light beams can pinpoint the location selected on the screen. Kiosks are self-contained self-help boxes often found in public places such as malls and government offices (Figure 4-13). Kiosks offer a variety of services via touch screens. They are ideal for the casual passerby who may not have a pencil handy. Also, a touch screen is so easy to use that it attracts users. An insurance company kiosk will let you select a policy, or a government kiosk will let you order a copy of your birth certificate. Kiosks are also found in private stores. Wal-Mart, for example, uses kiosks to let customers find needed

Figure 4-13 Touch screen kiosk. This kiosk is in a grocery store in Avon, Connecticut. Customers can touch the screen to make a series of choices, and a suitable recipe is then printed out.

auto parts. Many delicatessens use kiosks to let you point to salami on rye, among the other selections.

Looking

Delivering input simply by looking at the computer would seem to be the ultimate in capturing data at the source. The principles involved are similar to those used in making a screen selection by touching the screen with a finger. Electrodes attached to the skin around the eyes respond to movement of the eye muscles, which produce tiny electric signals when they contract. The signals are read by the computer system, which determines the location on the screen where the user is looking.

Such a system is not yet in the mainstream. The first people to benefit will likely be those who, due to disabilities or busyness, cannot use their hands or voices for input.

▶ Output: Information for the User

As noted earlier, computer output usually takes the form of screen or printer output. Other forms of output include voice, sound, and various forms of graphics output.

A computer system often is designed to produce several kinds of output. An example is a travel agency that uses a computer system. If a customer asks about airline connections to, say, Toronto, Calgary, and Vancouver, the travel agent will probably make a few queries to the system and receive on-screen output indicating availability on the various flights. After the reservations have been confirmed, the agent can ask for printed output that includes the tickets, the traveler's itinerary, and the invoice. In addition, agency management may periodically receive printed reports and charts, such as monthly summaries of sales figures or pie charts of regional costs. First in line is the most common form of output, computer screens.

Another Line to Skip

It's not that they don't like people. Business travelers are just busy and weary. After an arduous trip, a business person wants to collapse in the hotel room. Quickly. That is why, at Hyatt Hotels, they gladly bypass the registration desk and instead use the handy kiosk. A traveler simply swipes a credit card through a card reader, keys in name and address, scoops up a room key, and heads for the elevator.

Computer Screen Technology

A user's first interaction with a computer screen may be to view the screen response to the user's input. When data is entered, it appears on the screen. Furthermore, the computer response to that data—the output—also appears on the screen. The screen is part of the computer's **monitor,** which also includes the housing for its electrical components. Monitors usually include a stand that can be tilted or swiveled to allow the monitor to be easily adjusted to suit the user.

Screen output is known in the computer industry as **soft copy** because it is intangible and temporary, unlike **hard copy,** produced by a printer on paper, which is tangible and can be permanent.

Computer screens come in many varieties, but the most common kind is the **cathode ray tube (CRT).** Most CRT screens use a technology called **raster scanning,** a process of sweeping electron beams across the back of the screen. The backing of the screen display has a phosphorous coating that glows whenever it is hit by a beam of electrons. But the phosphorous does not glow for very long, so the image must be **re-**

NEW DIRECTIONS

IS THE PAPERLESS OFFICE FINALLY IN SIGHT?

As far back as the 1970s, computer gurus were predicting that it was just a matter of time until computers replaced paper. It hasn't worked out that way. In fact, now that people can use desktop publishing to produce reports that are more attractive than ever, paper use is actually increasing.

Administrators know that their organizations are drowning in paper. For example, a manager in an insurance company walked around the offices and made special marks on the stacks of paper reports he found everywhere. When he returned in a week he was not surprised to see that they had not been touched. Another manager discovered that a customer statement was automatically produced in quintuplicate,

four of which disappeared into filing cabinets, never to be seen again.

Faced with these grim realities, managers have turned to the computer technologies that can provide relief. Imaging is one approach—placing all documents on the computer so that they exist in just one paperless place. Employees at desktop computers

are encouraged to communicate via e-mail—and not print the results. Mobile employees are induced to keep all records on their laptop computers and send reports directly from there to the main computer. These and other technologies were designated to stem the flow.

The results? Only feeble. People cling to the tactile touch of paper. Also, paper is in many ways a rational choice: A person can read a long report in a more comfortable place than a computer chair and possibly avoid computer-induced eye strain. Finally, as one employee put it, "Human beings just trust the printed word."

No, the paperless office is not yet in sight.

freshed often. If the screen is not refreshed often enough, the fading screen image appears to flicker. A **scan rate**—the number of times the screen is refreshed—of 60 times per second is usually adequate to retain a clear screen image. As the user, you tell the computer what image you want on the screen, by typing, say, the letter *M*, and the computer sends the appropriate image to be beamed on the screen. This is essentially the same process used to produce television images.

A computer display screen that can be used for graphics is divided into dots that are called addressable because they can be *addressed* individually by the graphics software. Each dot can be illuminated individually on the screen. Each dot is potentially a *pic*ture *el*ement, or **pixel.** The **resolution** of the screen—its clarity—is directly related to the number of pixels on the screen: The more pixels, the higher the resolution. Another factor of importance is **dot pitch**, the amount of space between the dots. The smaller the dot pitch the better the quality of the screen image.

Some computers come with built-in graphics capability. Others need a device, called a **graphics card** or **graphics adapter board**, that has to be added.

There have been several color screen standards, relating particularly to resolution. The first color display was **CGA** (color graphics adapter), which had low resolution by today's standards (320x200 pixels). This

Chapter Four   Input and Output   **109**

Getting Practical

GETTING YOUR PHOTOS INTO YOUR COMPUTER

There are lots of reasons that you may want to put snapshots in the computer—to brighten up newsletters, to add them to holiday greetings, or to add to your own Internet web page. Some simply see the computer in its conventional keeping-track-of-things role, in this case photographs. Indeed, once the photos are in the computer, they can be sorted and filed, but they can also be changed. The traditional photo shown here was gleefully distorted by Power Goo software.

But how does one get the photos in the computer in the first place? There are several possibilities. One choice is simply to scan photos into the computer. If you do not have a scanner, your local print shop can do this for you. A direct approach is to use a digital camera, which records the pictures you take on a camera-embedded chip. For most cameras, pictures are downloaded by means of a cable hooked up to your computer's serial port, a plug-like input in the back. A caveat: The cameras are still rather expensive and the picture quality still marginal. For good quality, the best option is to have film that was shot with a conventional camera returned as digitized pictures on a diskette instead of the usual prints or

slides. Finally, if your photo interest goes beyond family snapshots, you can, if you have permission, download images from professional services on the Internet.

Once the photos are accessible in your computer, you may wish to edit or resize them with some kind of image-editing software. This software may also let you change or enhance the colors and contrast in the photograph. This kind of software usually comes with a hardware purchase such as a scanner. Several photo-editing packages can be found on the usual software racks. Now you can take that photo of Grandpa holding a minnow on his fishing line and blow the fish up to shark size.

was followed by the sharper **EGA** (enhanced graphics adapter), featuring 640x350 pixels. Next came **VGA** (video graphics array) with 640x480 pixels. **SVGA** (super VGA), the common standard today, offers 800x600 pixels or 1024x768 pixels, the latter having by far the best clarity.

Is bigger really better? Screen sizes are measured diagonally. However, unlike television screens, computer screen size is not regulated. Manufacturers sometimes fudge a bit, perhaps including the part covered by the monitor housing. When making comparisons, a user would do well to bring a ruler. A typical office worker who handles light word processing and spreadsheet duties will probably find a 15-inch screen adequate. A user involved with high-powered graphics will probably want at least a 17-inch screen. At the high end, screens can be purchased that are as large as television sets, 21 inches and up.

To answer the question, yes, bigger is usually better, but it is also more expensive. For your own personal computer, once you try a larger screen you will not want to go back. In addition to the reduced strain on the eyes, it is particularly useful for web pages, page layout, graphics, and large photos and illustrations.

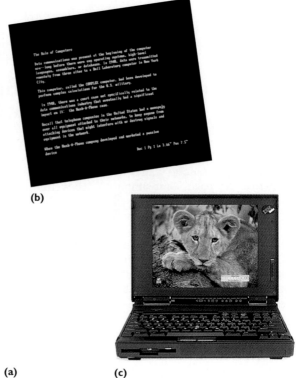

(b)

(a)   (c)

Figure 4-14 A variety of screens.
(a) This high-resolution brilliance is available only on a color graphics display.
(b) Monochrome screens are used in applications such as order entry, where no color is needed. (c) Laptop computers, once limited to monochrome screens, now usually have color screens.

Types of Screens

Cathode ray tube monitors that display text and graphics are in common use today. Although most CRTs are color (Figure 4-14a), some are **monochrome**, meaning that only one color, usually green, appears on a dark background (Figure 4-14b). Monochrome screens, which are less expensive than those with color, are used in business applications such as customer inquiry or order entry, which have no need for color. Another type of screen technology is the **liquid crystal display (LCD)**, a flat display often seen on watches and calculators. LCD screens are used on laptop computers (Figure 4-14c). Some LCDs are monochrome, but color screens are popular.

Terminals

A screen may be part of the monitor of a self-contained personal computer, or it may be part of a terminal attached to a large computer. A **terminal** consists of an input device, an output device, and a communications link to the main computer. Most commonly, a terminal has a keyboard for an input device and a screen for an output device, although there are many variations on this theme. Most terminals these days have some processing ability of their own—a CPU—and are thus called **smart terminals.**

Printers

A **printer** is a device that produces information on paper output. Some printers produce only letters and numbers, but most printers used with personal computers can also produce information in graphic form.

There are two ways of printing an image on paper: the impact method and the nonimpact method. An **impact printer** uses some sort of physical contact with the paper to produce an image, physically striking paper, ribbon, and print hammer together. Mainframe users who are

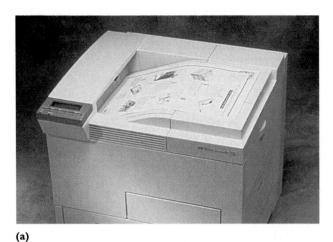

(a)

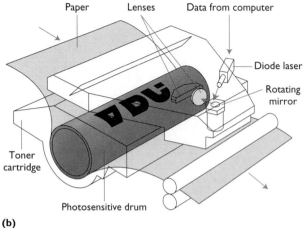

Paper   Lenses   Data from computer

Diode laser

Rotating mirror

Toner cartridge

Photosensitive drum

(b)

Figure 4-15 Laser printers. (a) The high-quality print and durability of the Hewlett-Packard laser printers make them best-sellers. (b) A laser printer works like a photocopy machine. Using patterns of small dots, a laser beam conveys information from the computer to a positively charged drum inside the laser printer. Wherever an image is to be printed, the laser beam is turned on, causing the drum to become neutralized. As the drum passes by a toner cartridge, toner sticks to the neutral spots on the drum. The toner is then transferred from the drum to a piece of paper. In the final printing step, heat and pressure fuse the toner to the paper. The drum is then cleaned for the next pass.

more concerned about high volume than high quality usually use line printers—impact printers that print an entire line at a time. Such organizations are likely to print hearty reports, perhaps relating to payroll or costs, for internal use. Impact printers are needed when multiple copies of a report are printed; the impact carries the output through to the lower copies.

A **nonimpact printer** places an image on a page without physically touching the page. The major technologies competing in the nonimpact market are laser and ink-jet, the two kinds of printers you will find in your local computer store. **Laser printers** use a light beam to help transfer images to paper (Figure 4-15). Today's laser printers print 600 **dpi (dots per inch)**, producing extremely high-quality results. Laser printers print a page at a time at impressive speeds. Organizations use laser printers to produce high-volume, customer-oriented reports. Low-end black-and-white laser printers for use with personal computers can now be purchased for a few hundred dollars. Color laser printers are more expensive.

Ink-jet printers, which spray ink from multiple jet nozzles, can print in both black and white and several different colors of ink to produce excellent graphics (Figure 4-16). However, the print quality of an ink-jet printer, although more than adequate, usually will not match that of a laser printer. Nor will the printing be as speedy. Furthermore, ink-jet printers need a fairly high quality of paper so that the ink does not smear. Nevertheless, low-end ink-jet printers, which cost just a few hundred dollars, are a bargain for users who want color output capability.

If you choose a color printer, whether ink-jet or laser, you will find that their colors are not perfect. The color you see on your computer screen is not necessarily the exact color you will see on the printed output. Nor is it likely to be the color you would see on a professional four-color offset printing press.

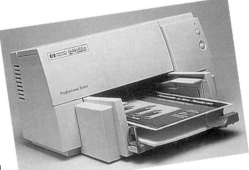

Figure 4-16 Ink-jet printers. A color ink-jet printer is an affordable and popular addition to many computer systems.

Choosing between a laser printer and an ink-jet printer comes down to a few factors. If printing speed is important to you, or if the quality of the printed text is a top priority, you probably want a black-and-white laser printer. If you cannot resist the prospect of color and are not overly concerned about text quality or speed, an ink-jet may be your best choice. If you want it all, color laser printers are available, but in a higher price range.

My First Laptop

Priced at about $50, this bright little gadget costs significantly less than a real laptop computer. But it should not be dismissed as a worthless toy. Designed for three-year-olds, the machine will teach tots counting, the alphabet, and even geometry. More significantly, it can be connected to a desktop computer, where it can interface with a CD-ROM that teaches exercises that develop motor skills.

Voice Output

We have already examined voice input in some detail. As you will see in this section, however, computers are frequently like people in the sense that they find it easier to talk than to listen. **Speech synthesis**—the process of enabling machines to talk to people—is much easier than speech recognition. "The key is in the ignition," your car says to you as you open the car door to get out. Machine voices are not real human voices. They are the product of **voice synthesizers** (also called **voice-output devices** or **audio-response units**), which convert data in main storage to vocalized sounds understandable to humans.

There are two basic approaches to getting a computer to talk. The first is **synthesis by analysis**, in which the device analyzes the input of an actual human voice speaking words, stores and processes the spoken sounds, and reproduces them as needed. The second approach to synthesizing speech is **synthesis by rule**, in which the device applies a complex set of linguistic rules to create artificial speech. Synthesis based on the human voice has the advantage of sounding more natural, but it is limited to the number of words stored in the computer.

Voice output has become common in such places as airline and bus terminals, banks, brokerage houses, and even some automobiles. It is typically used when an inquiry is followed by a short reply, such as a bank balance or flight time. Many businesses have found other creative uses for voice output over the telephone. Automatic telephone voices take surveys, inform customers that catalog orders are ready to be picked up, and, perhaps, remind consumers that they have not paid their bills.

Music Output and Other Sounds

In the past, personal computer users occasionally sent primitive musical messages, feeble tones that wheezed from the tiny internal speaker. Today's personal computers can be equipped with speakers placed on either side of the computer or, in some cases, mounted on the sides of the monitor or buried in the computer housing. Users want good-quality sound from certain kinds of software, especially the sophisticated CD-ROM offerings called *multimedia*, which will be examined in more detail in Chapter 5. Even the zap-and-crash sounds of action games deserve to be heard. To enhance the listening experience further, manufacturers are now producing audio chips that, by varying the frequencies and timing of the sound waves as they reach the human ear, can fool the brain into thinking that it is hearing three-dimensional sound from two speakers.

Professional musicians use special sound chips that simulate different instruments. A sound card installed internally in the computer and, of course, speakers, complete the output environment. Now, using appropriate software, the computer can produce the sound of an orchestra or a rock band.

▶ Computer Graphics

Now for everyone's favorite, computer graphics. Just about everyone has seen TV commercials or movies that use computer-produced animated graphics. Computer graphics can also be useful in education, computer art, science, sports, and more (Figure 4-17). But perhaps their most prevalent use today is in business.

Figure 4-17 Computer graphics. This work is by computer graphic artist Matthew Lechner.

Business Graphics

Graphics can be a powerful way to impart information. Colorful graphics, maps, and charts can help managers compare data more easily, spot trends, and make decisions more quickly. Also, the use of color helps people get the picture—literally. Although color graphs and charts have been used in business for years—usually to make presentations to upper management or outside clients—the computer allows them to be rendered quickly, before information becomes outdated. One user refers to business graphics as "computer-assisted insight" (Figure 4-18).

Video Graphics

Video graphics can be as creative as an animated cartoon (Figure 4-19). Although they operate on the same principle as a moving picture or cartoon—one frame at a time in quick succession—**video graphics** are produced by computers. Video graphics have made their biggest splash on television, but many people do not realize they are watching a computer at work. The next time you watch television, skip the trip to the kitchen and pay special attention to the commercials. Unless there is a live human in the advertisement, the moving objects you see, such as floating cars and bobbing electric razors, are doubtless computer output. Another fertile ground for video graphics is a television network's logo

The Universal Serial Bus

Adding new peripherals to a personal computer—say a scanner or a faster modem—has not always been easy. Users who wanted to expand their computer's capabilities have had to open the computer case to install some physical components, fiddle with switches, and make sure all the components worked together.

Now many personal computers support a technology called the Universal Serial Bus (USB), which can connect the central processing unit to the new peripheral. The new item is automatically configured to the computer. Furthermore, the USB can support many devices in a daisy-chain arrangement: The first device is connected to the computer, the second to the first, the third to the second, and so forth.

Personal computer industry giants—Compaq, Intel, Microsoft, IBM, and more—worked together to create the new bus standard because they realized that ease of use was the most important facet of personal computer technology.

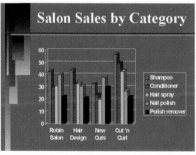

(a)

(b)

Figure 4-18 Business graphics. These charts were made with powerful but easy-to-use graphics software.

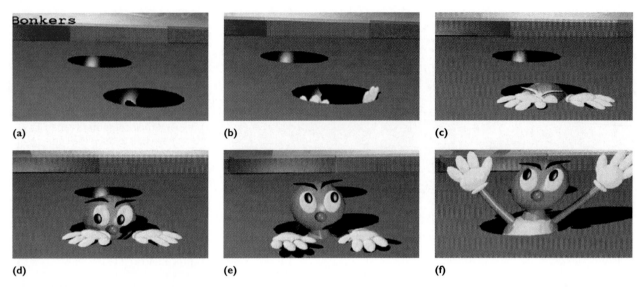

(a)   (b)   (c)

(d)   (e)   (f)

Figure 4-19 Video graphics. These images are part of a 500-frame set developed by a college student. The movie, called Bonkers, includes a sound track and runs for several seconds.

and theme. Accompanied by music and swooshing sounds, the network symbol spins and cavorts and turns itself inside out, all with the finesse that only a computer could supply.

Computer-Aided Design/ Computer-Aided Manufacturing

For more than a decade, computer graphics have also been part and parcel of a field known by the abbreviation **CAD/CAM**, short for **computer-aided design/computer-aided manufacturing**. In this area computers are used to create two- and three-dimensional pictures of everything from hand tools to tractors to highway designs. CAD/CAM provides a bridge between design (planning what a product will be) and manufacturing (actually making the planned product). As a manager at Chrysler said, "Many companies have design data and manufacturing data, and the two are never the same. At Chrysler, we have only one set of data that everyone dips into." Keeping data in one place, of course, makes changes easier and encourages consistency. For an example of Chrysler's efforts, see Figure 4-20.

Graphics Input Devices

There are many ways besides the mouse to produce and interact with screen graphics. The following are some other common devices that allow the user to interact with screen graphics. A **digitizing tablet** lets you create your own images (Figure 4-21). This device has a special stylus that you can use to draw or trace images, which are then converted to digital data that can be processed by the computer.

For direct interaction with your computer screen, the **light pen** is ideal. It is versatile enough to modify screen graphics or make a menu selection—that is, to choose from a list of activity choices on the screen. A light pen has a light-sensitive cell at one end. When you place the light pen against the screen, it closes a photoelectric circuit that pinpoints the spot the pen is touching. This tells the computer where to enter or modify pictures or data on the screen.

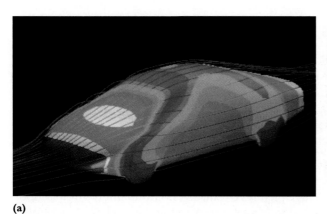

(a)

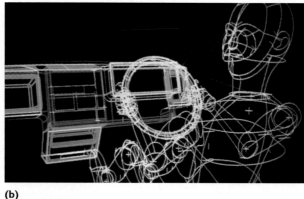

(b)

Figure 4-20 CAD/CAM. With computer-aided design and computer-aided manufacturing (CAD/CAM), the computer can keep track of all details, maintain designs of parts in storage, and combine parts electronically as required. (a) A computer-aided design wireframe of a car used to study design possibilities. (b) Engineers also use graphics to test designs relative to the consumer.

Finally, a well-known graphics input device is the **joystick**, dear to the hearts of video game fans. This device allows fingertip control of figures on a CRT screen.

Graphics Output Devices

Just as there are many different ways to input graphics to the computer, there are many different ways to output graphics. Graphics are most commonly output on a screen or printed on paper, as previously discussed. Another popular graphics output device is the **plotter**, which can draw hard-copy graphics output in the form of maps, bar charts, engineering drawings, and even two- or three-dimensional illustrations. Plotters often come with a set of four pens in four different colors. Most plotters also offer shading features.

Figure 4-21 Digitizing tablet. This engineer is using a digitizing tablet to input his drawing to the computer.

▶ Ethics and Data

Few people pause to ponder the relationship between ethics and data, but it is an important one. Once the data is in the computer, there are many ways it can be used, sold, or even altered. Data can also be input and be stored in a great variety of ways.

Consider these data ethics issues, all of which are at least debatable and most of which could be defensible in some situations:

- Is it ethically acceptable to use a computer to alter photographs? Is it ethical to substitute one person for another in a photograph? Should we be able to change pictures of ourselves? Group photos from school or work? Is it ethical to use a computer to add a celebrity to a photo? Does it matter if the celebrity is alive or dead?
- Suppose you perceive that the contents of certain e-mail messages may be of interest to a plaintiff suing your company. Is it ethical to just erase them?
- A friend who has worked on a political campaign has a disk file of donors. Is it ethical to use that same list to solicit for your candidate?

Note that none of these scenarios inherently require a computer. But the computer makes it that much easier.

New forms of computer input and output are announced regularly, often with promises of multiple benefits and new ease of use. Part of the excitement of the computer world is that these promises are usually kept, and users reap the benefits directly. Input and output just keep getting better.

CHAPTER REVIEW

Summary and Key Terms

- A **keyboard** is a common input device that may be part of a personal computer or a terminal connected to a remote computer. A **source document** is the original written input data to be keyed into the computer.

- A **mouse** is an input device with a ball on its underside, whose movement on a flat surface causes a corresponding movement on the screen. Moving the mouse (or pressing keyboard keys) allows you to reposition the **pointer**, or **cursor**, an indicator on the screen that shows where the next interaction with the computer can take place. An **icon**, a pictorial symbol on a screen, can be clicked to invoke a command to the computer, a process called a **graphical user interface (GUI).**

- A **trackball** is like an upside-down mouse—the ball is rolled with the hand. A **track pad** invokes a command with finger movement.

- **Source data automation** involves the use of special equipment to collect data at its origin and send it directly to the computer.

- **Magnetic-ink character recognition (MICR)** allows a machine to read characters made of magnetized particles, such as the preprinted characters on a personal check. Some characters are preprinted, but others, such as the amount of a check, are added by a person using an **MICR inscriber.**

- A **scanner** can convert text or even a drawing or picture into computer-recognizable form by using **optical recognition**, a system that uses a light beam to scan input data and convert it into electrical signals that are sent to the computer for processing. In a process called **imaging**, a scanner converts those papers to an electronic version, which can then be stored on disk and retrieved when needed.

- A **flatbed scanner,** a tabletop machine, typically scans a sheet at a time, although some offer an attachment for scanning multiple sheets. A **sheetfeed scanner,** usually designed to fit neatly between the keyboard and the monitor, uses motorized rollers to feed the sheet across the scanning head. A **handheld scanner,** the least expensive and least reliable of the three, is handy for portability.

- **Optical mark recognition (OMR)** devices recognize marks on paper. **Optical character recognition (OCR)** devices read special characters, such as those on price tags. These characters are often in a standard typeface called **OCR-A.** A commonly used OCR device is the handheld **wand reader,** which is often connected to a **point-of-sale (POS) terminal** in a retail store. A **bar code reader** is a photoelectric scanner used to input a **bar code,** a pattern of vertical marks that represents the **Universal Product Code (UPC)** that identifies a product. Some optical scanners can read precise handwritten characters.

- **Voice input,** or **speech recognition,** is the process of presenting input data to the computer through the spoken word. **Speech recognition devices** convert spoken words into a digital code that a computer can understand. The two main types of devices are **discrete word systems,** which require speakers to pause between words, and **continuous word systems,** which allow a normal rate of speaking.

- Input can be given directly to a computer via a **touch screen;** a finger touching the screen interrupts the light beams on the monitor edge, pinpointing the selected screen location.

- A user can deliver input to a computer by looking at a screen, assuming electrodes are attached to the skin near the user's eyes so that their signals can be read by the computer system.

- The **monitor** features the computer's screen, includes the housing for its electrical components, and probably sits on a stand that tilts and swivels. Screen output is known in the computer industry as **soft copy** because it is intangible and temporary, unlike **hard copy,** produced by a printer on paper, which is tangible and can be permanent.
- The most common kind of computer screen is the **cathode ray tube (CRT).** Most CRT screens use a technology called **raster scanning,** in which the backing of the screen display has a phosphorous coating, which will glow whenever it is hit by a beam of electrons. The screen image must be **refreshed** often to avoid flicker. A **scan rate**—the number of times the screen is refreshed—of 60 times per second is usually adequate to retain a clear screen image.
- A computer display screen that can be used for graphics is divided into dots that are called addressable because they can be *addressed* individually by the graphics software. Each screen dot is called a **pixel.** The more pixels, the higher the screen **resolution,** or clarity. **Dot pitch** is the amount of space between the dots on a screen. A computer must either come with built-in graphics capability or have a **graphics card** or **graphics adapter board** added.
- Color screen standards are the relatively low-resolution **CGA** (color graphics adapter); **EGA** (enhanced graphics adapter); **VGA** (video graphics array), with 640x480 pixels; and today's higher-resolution **SVGA** (super VGA), with 800x600 pixels or 1024x768 pixels.
- Some computer screens are **monochrome**—the characters appear in one color, usually green, on a dark background.
- A **liquid crystal display (LCD)** is a type of flat screen found on laptop computers.
- A screen may be the monitor of a self-contained personal computer, or it may be part of a **terminal,** an input-output device linked to a main computer. Most terminals these days have some processing ability of their own—a CPU—and are thus called **smart terminals.**
- **Printers** produce printed paper output. Printers can be classified as either **impact printers,** which form characters by physically striking the paper, or **nonimpact printers, laser** and **ink-jet printers,** which use a noncontact printing method. Today's laser printers print 600 **dpi (dots per inch),** producing extremely high-quality results.
- Computer **speech synthesis** has been accomplished through **voice synthesizers** (also called **voice-output devices** or **audio-response units**). One approach to speech synthesis is **synthesis by analysis,** in which the computer analyzes stored tapes of spoken words. In the other approach, called **synthesis by rule,** the computer applies linguistic rules to create artificial speech.
- **Video graphics** are a series of computer-produced pictures.
- In **computer-aided design/computer-aided manufacturing (CAD/CAM),** computers are used to create two- and three-dimensional pictures of manufactured products such as hand tools and vehicles.
- Common graphics input devices include the **digitizing tablet, light pen,** and **joystick.**
- Graphics output devices include screens, printers, and **plotters.**

Quick Poll

Compare your answers to those of your colleagues or classmates.

1. Excluding the keyboard and mouse, the input method that seems most useful is
   - ❑ a. Trackball
   - ❑ b. Scanner
   - ❑ c. Bar code
   - ❑ d. Speech recognition
   - ❑ e. Touch screen

2. For personal use, the printer I would choose is
   - ❏ a. Laser (black and white)
   - ❏ b. Ink-jet
   - ❏ c. Color laser
3. A scanner attached to my computer
   - ❏ a. Would soon be put to work
   - ❏ b. Would be fun for pictures
   - ❏ c. Is just another frill

Discussion Questions

1. For this question, use your knowledge from either reading or experience, or imagine the possibilities. What kind of input device might be convenient for these types of jobs or situations? (a) A supermarket stock clerk who takes inventory by surveying items currently on the shelf; (b) a medical assistant who must input existing printed documents to the computer; (c) an airport automated luggage-tracking system; (d) a telephone worker who takes orders over the phone; (e) a restaurant in which customers place their own orders from the table; (f) an inspector at the United States Bureau of Engraving who monitors and gives a go/no go response on printed money passing by on an assembly line; (g) a retailer who wants to move customers quickly through checkout lines; (h) a psychologist who wants to give a new client a standard test; (i) an environmental engineer who hikes through woods and streams to inspect and report on the effects of pollutants; (j) a small business owner who wants to keep track of employee work hours.
2. Do you think that continued research into voice input is worthwhile? In your answer, consider the practicality of current and potential uses.
3. What should a buyer consider when comparing different models of printers? If price were not a consideration, what kind of printers would you buy for your home or business personal computers?

Student Study Guide

Multiple Choice

1. The amount of space between the dots on a screen:
   - a. OCR
   - b. LCD
   - c. dot pitch
   - d. OMR
2. A pictorial screen symbol that represents a computer activity is called a(n)
   - a. pointer
   - b. icon
   - c. touch screen
   - d. MICR
3. Using computers to design and manufacture products is called
   - a. inscribing
   - b. CAD/CAM
   - c. detailing
   - d. imaging
4. Soft copy refers to
   - a. OCR-A
   - b. music sounds
   - c. screen output
   - d. digitizing
5. The CRT technology with the best resolution:
   - a. MICR
   - b. SVGA
   - c. VGA
   - d. LCD
6. An ink-jet printer is an example of a(n)
   - a. laser printer
   - b. impact printer
   - c. LCD printer
   - d. nonimpact printer
7. Entering data as a by-product of the activity that generates the data is
   - a. source data automation
   - b. a discrete word system
   - c. CAD/CAM
   - d. MICR entry
8. The rate of screen refreshment is called
   - a. pixel speed
   - b. bit-map speed
   - c. raster rate
   - d. scan rate
9. Magnetic characters are produced on your bank checks by
   - a. bar code readers
   - b. mice
   - c. MICR inscribers
   - d. OCR
10. "Mark sensing" is another term for
    - a. MICR
    - b. POS
    - c. OMR
    - d. VGA
11. A device used for optical character recognition is a(n)
    - a. wand reader
    - b. cursor
    - c. pen
    - d. MICR reader
12. OCR-A is a
    - a. plotter
    - b. standard typeface
    - c. wand reader
    - d. bar code
13. POS terminals are similar to
    - a. calculators
    - b. touch-tone telephones
    - c. UPCs
    - d. cash registers
14. A one-color screen on a black background is called
    - a. monochrome
    - b. blank
    - c. addressable
    - d. liquid crystal display
15. Voice input devices convert voice input to
    - a. digital codes
    - b. bar codes
    - c. OCR-A
    - d. optical marks
16. Imaging uses what device to input data?
    - a. scanner
    - b. bar code reader
    - c. icon
    - d. tablet
17. The cursor can be moved by rolling this device on a flat surface:
    - a. mouse
    - b. trackball
    - c. wand reader
    - d. interactive tablet
18. Which input device is often attached to laptop computers?
    - a. trackball
    - b. graphic display
    - c. inscriber
    - d. wand reader

19. A screen that is lighter and slimmer than a CRT is a(n)
    a. OCR
    b. graphics card
    c. flat panel
    d. terminal
20. Computer animation is a form of
    a. LCD
    b. CAD/CAM
    c. video graphics
    d. color printer output
21. A color screen with the best resolution has the most
    a. CRT
    b. OCR
    c. VGA
    d. pixels
22. The name for the screen's clarity:
    a. resolution
    b. discrete
    c. pixel
    d. LCD
23. A bar code represents the product's
    a. CGA
    b. OMR
    c. LCD
    d. UPC
24. The type of scanner that fits between the keyboard and the monitor:
    a. sheetfeed
    b. handheld
    c. flatbed
    d. plotter
25. Another word for pointer:
    a. monochrome
    b. pixel
    c. monitor
    d. cursor

True/False

T F 1. The greater the number of pixels, the poorer the screen clarity.
T F 2. Printers produce hard copy.
T F 3. Video graphics are computer-produced pictures.
T F 4. Discrete word systems allow a normal rate of speaking.
T F 5. Data is scanned into the computer using a mouse.
T F 6. In a discrete word system, the user must pause between words.
T F 7. CRT stands for computer remote terminal.
T F 8. Optical recognition technology is based on magnetized data.
T F 9. OMR senses marks on paper.
T F 10. A wand reader can read OCR characters.
T F 11. A color screen is called monochrome.
T F 12. LCD is a type of flat screen found on laptop computers.
T F 13. LCD stands for liquid crystal display.
T F 14. The screen standard with the highest resolution is CGA.
T F 15. A mouse can be clicked to invoke a command.
T F 16. The MICR process is used mainly by retail stores.
T F 17. A cursor indicates the location of the next interaction on the screen.
T F 18. Dot pitch refers to the number of pixels on a screen.
T F 19. The best way to scan a page from a book is with a flatbed scanner.
T F 20. The color screen standard today is CGA.
T F 21. Pixel is short for picture element.
T F 22. A screen must be refreshed to avoid flicker.
T F 23. Optical marks may be used to record test answers.
T F 24. Nonimpact printers are quieter than impact printers.
T F 25. Laser printers use a light beam to transfer images to paper.

Fill-In

1. Original written input data to be keyed into the computer: _____
2. LCD stands for _____
3. The standard optical typeface: _____
4. POS stands for _____
5. Another name for a pictorial screen symbol that represents a command: _____
6. MICR stands for _____
7. Using a scanner to input documents to the computer: _____
8. The phrase used to describe collecting computer data at the source: _____
9. UPC stands for _____
10. The input method used mainly by banks for processing checks: _____
11. The general term for systems that use a light source to read data: _____
12. The method that uses a light beam to sense marks on machine-readable test forms: _____
13. The tabletop scanner that can handle a book page: _____
14. Which technology is more challenging, voice input or voice output? _____
15. The kind of terminal that may read bar codes but is like a cash register: _____
16. Screen output is called _____

17. Printed computer output is called

    _____

18. A type of nonimpact printer that uses a light source:

    _____

19. An input device that reads OCR tags:

    _____

20. A screen that accepts input from a pointing finger:

    _____

21. The number of times a screen is refreshed is called

    its _____

22. CAD/CAM stands for _____

23. The Universal Product Code is represented on a

    package by a _____

24. A speech recognition system limited to isolated

    words is called _____

25. Screen clarity is called _____

26. The amount of space between dots on a screen:

    _____

27. A type of screen in which characters appear in only

    one color, usually on a dark background:

    _____

28. The input device, controlled by hand movements,

    that is often found on a laptop computer:

    _____

29. The CRT technology in which the phosphorous-

    coated screen glows when it is hit by a beam of elec-

    trons: _____

30. The type of scanner that accepts of sheet of paper

    with motorized rollers: _____

Answers

Multiple Choice

1. c	6. d	11. a	16. a	21. d
2. b	7. a	12. b	17. a	22. a
3. b	8. d	13. d	18. a	23. d
4. c	9. c	14. a	19. c	24. a
5. b	10. c	15. a	20. c	25. d

True/False

1. F	6. T	11. F	16. F	21. T
2. T	7. F	12. T	17. T	22. T
3. F	8. F	13. T	18. F	23. T
4. F	9. T	14. F	19. T	24. T
5. F	10. T	15. T	20. F	25. T

Fill-In

1. source document
2. liquid crystal display
3. OCR-A
4. point of sale
5. icon
6. magnetic-ink character recognition
7. imaging
8. source data automation
9. Universal Product Code
10. MICR
11. optical recognition
12. OMR
13. flatbed
14. voice input
15. POS terminal
16. soft copy
17. hard copy
18. laser
19. wand reader
20. touch screen
21. scan rate
22. computer-aided design/computer-aided manufac-
    turing
23. bar code
24. discrete word system
25. resolution
26. dot pitch
27. monochrome
28. trackball
29. raster scanning
30. sheetfeed

PLANET INTERNET

FAQS AND HELP

When people begin to learn something new, they usually have many questions. In fact, beginners on the same subject often have the same questions. Rather than answer each question individually, it makes sense to keep the most frequently asked questions—FAQs—in a handy place that anyone can access. FAQs are a long-standing tradition on the Internet.

Where are FAQs on the Internet? The use of FAQs is so widespread that you are likely to come across them on many sites. However, some sites specialize in comprehensive FAQs—and

answers—for beginners, notably the World Wide Web FAQs. Another excellent source is the long-standing Boutell's Internet FAQs. Another good place to start is Beginner's Central. Several sites offer lists of Internet-related definitions; these include the World Wide Web Starter Kit and Net Lingo sites.

For information about resources needed for Internet access, see the World Wide Web Starter Kit. If you would like a better idea of Internet resources worldwide, the Virtual Tourist World Map site, which lists Internet service providers worldwide, can provide information by geographic location.

Can I get some general information about the Internet? Some sites include a history of the Internet as one of many offerings. Others, like the History of the Internet, Net History, Hobbes Internet Timeline, and Web Origins and Beyond sites, offer a long and detailed history, with names, organizations, and timelines. You can get demographic information about the Internet—official and unofficial statistics—from sites such as Internet FAQs and Stats or Internet Statistics.

What is Doonesbury doing over there? Look closely and you will see that one of the circles contains the cartoon's artist, Garry Trudeau, with "FAQs" printed nearby. This icon links to a portion of the site where the artist answers questions about the strip. Similarly, the Car Talk image represents a page that offers, among other things, a list of FAQs on car repair. These two

home   www FAQ   c.i.w. announce   wusage   mapedit   cgic   gd   perl MUD   aunt squishy   verbiage   world birthday web   activism

sites typify the use of FAQs related to the material on individual sites, as opposed to topics related to the Internet as a whole.

What about going beyond the basic facts to get help on making a home page? Advice abounds. Most users with an interest in making a web page start with information about HTML. Perhaps the best-known site is the Beginner's Guide to HTML. Another is the HTML Guide, whose clickable reference-book logo is shown here. There are dozens of HTML sites. If you find one HTML site, it probably will have a list of links to others.

Anything else for making a page? There are many sites that offer design advice and free clip art images. Bobaworld is a popular home page advice site. Other images, as indicated by the cartoon here, are available for a fee.

Are there other places to get help? There are several possibilities besides teaching yourself. Many colleges include home page creation as part of an Internet course. Private firms advertise courses to teach you the basics in a few hours. Serious users, usually businesses that want a "Web presence," may engage the services of consultants who can create a sophisticated home page.

Internet Exercises

1. **Structured exercise.** Begin with the AWL URL, http://hepg.awl.com/capron/planet/, and link to the World Wide Web FAQs.
2. **Freeform exercise.** Go to the Beginner's Guide to HTML and click on some of the links listed there.

© 1996 Interactive Features Syndicate

Author	About	The Missing	Character sets	Comprehensive	Documented	Forms	Image maps	Input	Bulltin Pk.	Obsolete	Undocumented
I	II	III	IV	V	VI	VII	VIII	IX	X	XI	XII

Keisha Brown was employed as a graphics artist when she realized that, for personal reasons, she needed to work at home two or three days a week. She prepared a plan, which included buying her own personal computer for home use, and convinced her boss to go along.

As an experienced computer user, Keisha had little trouble deciding on the basic computer hardware she wanted to purchase. But in view of her profession, she looked very carefully at storage options. She knew that the software she needed, the same software she used at work, would take up many millions of bytes of hard disk space. She also knew that sophisticated graphics image files take up a lot of storage space, often 300,000 bytes or more each. She did not hesitate about making sure that the computer package included a hard disk that would hold several gigabytes.

A bigger problem was deciding on a method for moving image files between home and office. She decided it would be inconvenient and possibly insecure to send the files via data communications. A diskette would be an easy transfer device, but it would hold only a few image files. As she looked over the computer she was going to purchase, she realized that there was an empty drive bay—appearing as a blank rectangle on the computer housing near the diskette and CD-ROM drives. After noting that there was a similar unused drive bay in her work computer, Keisha bought drives to hold removable hard disk cartridges for both home and office. The removable cartridge holds almost 100 times more data than a high-density diskette. Although just a bit more unwieldy, it fits nicely in her briefcase. Furthermore, a full cartridge can be replaced with a fresh one when needed.

A rule of thumb among computer professionals is to estimate disk needs generously and then double that amount. But estimating future needs is rarely easy.

Storage and Multimedia

The Facts and More

The Benefits of Secondary Storage

Picture, if you can, how many filing-cabinet drawers would be required to hold the millions of files of, say, tax records kept by the Internal Revenue Service or historical employee records kept by General Motors. The record storage rooms would have to be enormous. Computers, in contrast, permit storage on tape or disk in extremely compressed form. Storage capacity is unquestionably one of the most valuable assets of the computer.

Secondary storage, sometimes called **auxiliary storage**, is storage separate from the computer itself, where you can store software and data on a semipermanent basis. Secondary storage is necessary because memory, or primary storage, can be used only temporarily. However, you probably want to reuse the data you have used or the information you have derived from processing; that is why secondary storage is needed.

The benefits of secondary storage can be summarized as follows:

- **Space.** Organizations may store the equivalent of a roomful of data on sets of disks that take up less space than a breadbox. A simple diskette for a personal computer can hold the equivalent of 500 printed pages, or one book. An optical disk can hold the equivalent of approximately 500 books.
- **Reliability.** Data in secondary storage is basically safe, since secondary storage is physically reliable. (We should note, however, that diskettes sometimes fail.) Also, it is more difficult for unscrupulous people to tamper with data on disk than with data stored on paper in a file cabinet.
- **Convenience.** With the help of a computer, authorized users can locate and access data quickly.
- **Economy.** Together the three previous benefits indicate significant savings in storage costs. It is less expensive to store data on tape or disk (the principal means of secondary storage) than to buy and house filing cabinets. Data that is reliable and safe is less expensive to maintain than data subject to errors. But the greatest savings can be found in the speed and convenience of filing and retrieving data.

These benefits apply to all the various secondary storage devices but, as you will see, some devices are better than others. The discussion begins with a look at the various storage media, including those used for personal computers, and then moves to what it takes to get data organized and processed.

Magnetic Disk Storage

Diskettes and hard disks are magnetic media; that is, they are based on a technology of representing data as magnetized spots on the disk—with a magnetized spot representing a 1 bit and the absence of such a spot representing a 0 bit. Reading data from the disk means converting the magnetized data to electrical impulses that can be sent to the processor. Writing data to disk is the opposite; it involves sending electrical impulses from the processor to be converted to magnetized spots on the disk. As Figure 5-1 shows, the surface of each disk has concentric tracks on it. The number of tracks per surface varies with the particular type of disk.

Figure 5-1 Surface of a disk. Note that each track is a closed circle. This drawing illustrates the location of the tracks; you cannot actually see the tracks on the disk surface.

NEW DIRECTIONS

BUT WHERE ARE THE BOOKS?

It certainly is wonderful that computer storage can hold vast amounts of library materials and that those materials can be readily called up on a handy computer screen. But, as some would lament, we have gotten used to actual books. Not to worry. The online library still has books, but it will make everything in the library, including elusive research materials, much more available than when they were buried in the stacks.

The San Francisco Public Library is boldly designed and technologically outfitted for the 21st century. The seven-story building, flooded with natural light, has 300 computer terminals that can access card catalogs, databases, and the Internet. A huge children's area has its own array of computers on child-size tables. And, yes, there are still lots of open stacks for browsing.

From Sarasota to San Diego, cities across the country are racing to rethink and retool their libraries. But the books are still around. As one librarian put it, "Technology merely complements the books."

Diskettes

Made of flexible mylar, a **diskette** can record data as magnetized spots on tracks on its surface. Diskettes became popular along with the personal computer. Most computers use the 3½-inch diskette (Figure 5-2). The diskette has the protection of a hard plastic jacket and fits conveniently in a shirt pocket or purse. Diskettes offer particular advantages that, as you will see, are not readily available with a hard disk:

- **Portability.** Diskettes easily transport data from one computer to another. Workers, for example, carry their files from office computer to home computer and back on a diskette instead of carrying a stack of papers in a briefcase. Students use the campus computers but keep their files on their own diskettes.

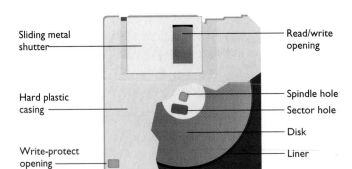

Labels (clockwise):
Sliding metal shutter · Read/write opening · Hard plastic casing · Spindle hole · Sector hole · Disk · Liner · Write-protect opening

Figure 5-2 Diskette. A cutaway view of a 3½-inch diskette.

- **Backup.** It is convenient to place an extra copy of a hard disk file on a diskette.
- **New software.** Although for convenience software is kept on a hard disk, new software out of the box may come on diskettes (it also may come on CD-ROMs, a topic coming up shortly).

The venerable diskette, so light and so handy, does have its limitations. Although some newer diskettes hold much more data, most hold a relatively limited amount. This can be problematic if, for example, you want to take a large file back and forth between your office and home computers. One possibility is **data compression**, the process of squeezing a big file into a small place. The compression temporarily removes nonessential but space-hogging items such as tab marks and double-spacing. To be used again the file must, of course, be uncompressed. Incidentally, to speed up the transfer, many users choose to compress files that will be sent from one computer to another via data communications.

Hard Disks

A **hard disk** is a metal platter coated with magnetic oxide that can be magnetized to represent data. Hard disks come in a variety of sizes (Figure 5-3). Several disks can be assembled into a **disk pack.** There are different types of disk packs, with the number of platters varying by model. Each disk in the pack has top and bottom surfaces on which to record data. Many disk devices, however, do not record data on the top of the top platter or on the bottom of the bottom platter.

A **disk drive** is a device that allows data to be read from a disk or written on a disk. A disk pack is mounted on a disk drive that is a separate unit connected to the computer. Large computers have dozens or even hundreds of disk drives. In a disk pack all disks rotate at the same time, although only one disk is being read from or written on at any one time. The mechanism for reading or writing data on a disk is an **access arm**; it moves a read/write head into position over a particular track (Figure 5-4a). The **read/write head** on the end of the access arm hovers just above the track but does not actually touch the surface. When a read/write head does accidentally touch the disk surface, it is called a **head crash** and all data is destroyed. Data can also be destroyed if a read/write head encounters even minuscule foreign matter on the disk surface (Figure 5-4b). A disk pack has a series of access arms that slip in between the disks in the pack (Figure 5-4c). Two read/write heads are on each arm, one facing up to access the surface above it and one facing down to

(a)

(b)

Figure 5-3 Magnetic disks. (a) Hard magnetic disks come in a variety of sizes. Shown here is a 3½-inch hard drive for a personal computer. (b) These 3½-inch diskettes are protected by a firm plastic exterior cover.

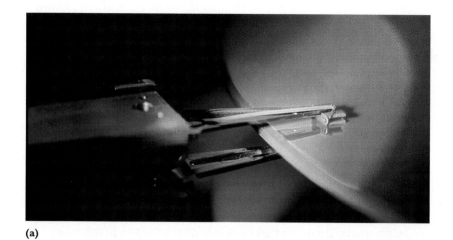

(a)

(b)

(c)

Figure 5-4 Read/write heads and access arms. (a) This photo shows a read/write head on the end of an access arm poised over a hard disk. (b) When in operation the read/write head comes very close to the surface of the disk. On a disk, particles as small as smoke, dust, a fingerprint, and a hair loom large. If the read/write head encounters one of these, data is destroyed and the disk damaged. (c) Note that there are two read/write heads on each access arm. Each arm slips between two disks in the disk pack. The access arms move simultaneously, but only one read/write head operates at any one time.

Getting Practical

DISKETTE CARE

Although the 3½-inch diskette is rugged, you should take precautions to protect diskettes—disks—from damage.

- Never put anything heavy on a disk or pile disks on top of one another; they should be stored vertically.
- Do not put disks near a magnet or anything that could generate a magnetic field, such as telephones and stereo speakers.
- Keep disks away from sunlight and excessive heat, including the vent from your car heater.
- Do not move the sliding metal shutter on a disk or touch the disk inside; fingerprints leave an oily residue that could prevent the read/write head from accessing data.
- Never attempt to clean the surface of the inner disk. Even the softest cleaning cloth could damage it.

- Keep your disks away from food, drink, and smoke.
- Keep your disks in an environment as free from dust as possible.
- Do not use disk labels in layers, lest the disks get too thick and become stuck in the drive.
- Never attempt to force a disk into the drive nor to remove a stuck disk; get help.
- Never remove a disk from the drive when the drive light is on; the light tells you the disk is in use, and removing it could damage the data.
- Do not remove a disk from the drive too quickly; if you pop the button and remove the disk almost at the same time the metal shutter can get bent.

- If a disk holds important data, you can make sure it is not accidentally overwritten by using the write-protect tab in the lower left corner of the disk. Simply slide the tab to expose—open—the hole. (On the other hand, if you find you cannot write to a certain disk when you want to, make sure the hole is covered so that writing is permitted.)

Following these simple rules should keep your data safe. But disks sometimes fail for no apparent reason, so be sure to make copies of your disks.

16 tons

---

access the surface below it. However, only one read/write head can operate at any one time.

Most disk packs combine the disks, access arms, and read/write heads in an airtight sealed module. These disk assemblies are put together in clean rooms so that even microscopic dust particles do not get on the disk surface.

Hard disks for personal computers are 3½-inch disks in sealed modules (Figure 5-5). Hard disk capacity for personal computers has soared in recent years; older hard disks have capacities of hundreds of megabytes, but new ones offer multiple gigabytes of storage. Terabyte capacity is on the horizon. Although an individual probably cannot imagine generating enough output—letters, budgets, reports, and so forth—to fill a hard disk, software packages take up a lot of space and can make a dent rather quickly. Furthermore, graphics images and audio and video files require large amounts of disk space. Perhaps more important than capacity, however, is the convenience of speed. Personal computer users find that accessing files on a hard disk is significantly faster and more convenient than accessing files on a diskette.

Personal computer users, who never seem to have enough hard disk storage space, may turn to a **removable hard disk cartridge.** Once full, a removable hard disk cartridge can be replaced with a fresh one. In effect, a removable cartridge is as portable as a diskette, but the disk car-

Figure 5-5 Hard disk for a personal computer. The innards of a 3½-inch hard disk with the access arm visible.

How High Can You Count?

It is only in recent years that disk space has been measured in gigabytes instead of megabytes. It is easy to predict that in the future storage space will be described in terabytes.

Kilo =
1,000
Thousand
Mega =
1,000,000
Million
Giga =
1,000,000,000
Billion
Tera =
1,000,000,000,000
Trillion
Peta =
1,000,000,000,000,000
Quadrillion
Exa =
1,000,000,000,000,000,000
Quintillion
Bronto =
1,000,000,000,000,000,000,000
Sextillion

tridge holds much more data. Iomega's Zip drive, and 100 MB Zip disks, provide 70 times the capacity of traditional floppy disks (Figure 5-6). There are even removable cartridges that hold gigabytes of data. Removable units also are important to businesses concerned with security, because the units can be used during business hours but locked away during off-hours. A disadvantage of a removable hard disk is that it takes longer to access data than on a built-in hard drive.

Hard Disks in Groups

No storage system is completely safe, but a **redundant array of inexpensive disks,** or simply **RAID,** comes close. RAID storage uses several small hard disks that work together as a unit. The most basic RAID system—RAID level 1—simply duplicates data on separate disk drives, a concept called **data mirroring** (Figure 5-7b). Thus, no data is lost if one drive fails. This process is reliable but expensive. Expense, however, may not be an issue when the value of the data is considered.

Higher levels of RAID take a different approach called **data striping** (Figure 5-7c), which involve spreading the data across several disks in the array, with one disk used solely as a check disk, to keep track of what data is where. If a disk fails, the check disk can reconstitute the data. Higher levels of RAID process data more quickly than simple data mirroring does. RAID is now the dominant form of storage for mainframe computer systems.

How Data Is Organized on a Disk

There is more than one way of physically organizing data on a disk. The methods considered here are the sector method and the cylinder method.

The Sector Method   In the **sector method** each track on a disk is divided into sectors that hold a specific number of characters (Figure

Figure 5-6 A removable hard disk drive.

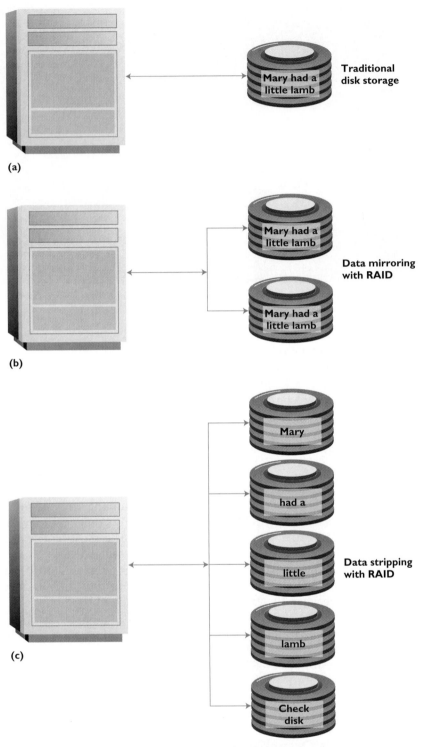

Figure 5-7 RAID storage. (a) Data is stored on disk in traditional fashion. (b) Disk mirroring with RAID stores a duplicate copy of the data on a second disk. (c) In a system called data striping with RAID, data is scattered among several disks, with a check disk that keeps track of what data is where so that data lost on a bad disk can be re-created.

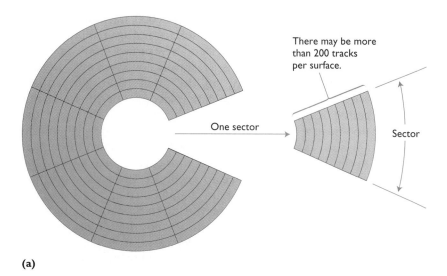

(a)

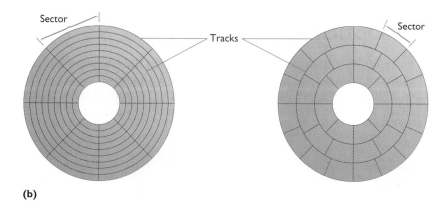

(b)

Figure 5-8 Sectors and zone recording. (a) When data is organized by sector, the address is the surface, track, and sector where the data is stored. (b) If a disk is divided into traditional sectors, as shown here on the left, each track has the same number of sectors. Sectors near the outside of the disk are wider, but they hold the same amount of data as sectors near the inside. If the disk is divided into recording zones, as shown on the right, the tracks near the outside have more sectors than the tracks near the inside. Each sector holds the same amount of data, but since the outer zones have more sectors, the disk as a whole holds more data than the disk on the left.

5-8a). Data on the track is accessed by referring to the surface number, track number, and sector number where the data is stored. The sector method is used for diskettes.

The fact that a disk is circular presents a problem: The distance around the tracks on the outside of the disk is greater than that around the tracks on the inside. A given amount of data that takes up 1 inch of a track on the inside of a disk might be spread over several inches on a track near the outside of a disk. This means that the tracks on the outside are not storing data as efficiently.

Zone recording takes maximum advantage of the storage available by dividing a disk into zones and assigning more sectors to tracks in outer zones than to those in inner zones (Figure 5-8b). Since each sector on the disk holds the same amount of data, more sectors mean more data storage than if all tracks had the same number of sectors.

The Cylinder Method   A way to organize data on a disk pack is the **cylinder method,** shown in Figure 5-9. The organization in this case is vertical. The purpose is to reduce the time it takes to move the access arms of a disk pack into position. Once the access arms are in position, they are in the same vertical position on all disk surfaces.

To appreciate this, suppose you had an empty disk pack on which you wished to record data. You might be tempted to record the data horizon-

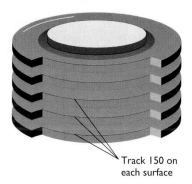

Track 150 on each surface

Figure 5-9 Cylinder data organization. To visualize the cylinder form of organization, imagine dropping a cylinder such as a tin can straight down through all the disks in the disk pack. Within cylinder 150, the track surfaces are vertically aligned and are numbered vertically from top to bottom.

tally—to start with the first surface and fill track 000, track 001, track 002, and so on and then move to the second surface and again fill tracks 000, 001, 002, and so forth. Each new track and new surface, however, would require movement of the access arms, a relatively slow mechanical process.

Recording the data vertically, on the other hand, substantially reduces access arm movement. The data is recorded on the tracks that can be accessed by one positioning of the access arms—that is, on one **cylinder.** To visualize cylinder organization, pretend that a cylindrically shaped item, such as a tin can, was dropped straight down through all the disks in the disk pack. All the tracks thus encountered, in the same position on each disk surface, make up a cylinder. The cylinder method, then, means that all tracks of a certain cylinder on a disk pack are lined up one beneath the other, and all the vertical tracks of one cylinder are accessible by the read/write heads with one positioning of the access arms mechanism. Tracks within a cylinder are numbered according to this vertical perspective, from 0 on the top down to the last surface on the bottom.

▶ Optical Disk Storage

The explosive growth in storage needs has driven the computer industry to provide inexpensive and compact storage with greater capacity. This demanding shopping list is a description of the **optical disk** (Figure 5-10a). The technology works like this: A laser hits a layer of metallic

(a)

(b)

Figure 5-10 Optical disks. (a) Optical disks store data using laser beam technology. (b) Many laptop computers include a CD-ROM drive. Laptop users can use CD-ROM applications to make on-the-road presentations or can pop in a CD-ROM encyclopedia to find some needed information.

material spread over the surface of a disk. When data is being entered, heat from the laser produces tiny spots on the disk surface. To read the data, the laser scans the disk, and a lens picks up different light reflections from the various spots.

Mostly Reading

Optical storage technology is categorized according to its read/write capability. **Read-only media** are disks recorded by the manufacturer and can be read from but not written to by the user. Such a disk cannot, obviously, be used for your files, but manufacturers can use it to supply software. An applications software package could include a dozen diskettes or more; all these can fit on one optical disk with room to spare. Furthermore, software can be more easily installed from a single optical disk than from a pile of diskettes.

Write-once, read-many media, also called **WORM media**, may be written to once. Once filled, a WORM disk becomes a read-only medium. A WORM disk is nonerasable. For applications demanding secure storage of original versions of valuable documents or data, such as legal records, the primary advantage of nonerasability is clear: Once they are recorded, no one can erase or modify them.

Magneto-Optical

A hybrid type of disk, called **magneto-optical (MO)**, combines the best features of magnetic and optical disk technologies. A magneto-optical disk has the high-volume capacity of an optical disk but can be written over like a magnetic disk. The disk surface is coated with plastic and embedded with magnetically sensitive metallic crystals. To write data, a laser beam melts a tiny spot on the plastic surface and a magnet aligns the crystals before the plastic cools. The crystals are aligned so that some reflect light and others do not. When the data is later read by a laser beam, only the crystals that reflect light are picked up.

CD-ROM

A variation on optical storage technology is the **CD-ROM**, for **compact disk read-only memory.** CD-ROM has a major advantage over other optical disk designs: The disk format is identical to that of *audio* compact disks, so the same dust-free manufacturing plants that are now stamping out digital versions of Kenny G or Jewel can easily convert to producing anything from software to a digitized encyclopedia. Furthermore, CD-ROM storage is gargantuan—up to 660 megabytes per disk, the equivalent of more than four hundred standard 3½-inch diskettes, or 10,000 printed pages.

Keep in mind that a CD-ROM cannot be used in your personal computer's diskette drive; you must have a CD-ROM drive on your computer. Today, even some laptop computers have CD-ROM drives (Figure 5-10b). Although CD-ROMs are read-only, a different technology called **CD-R** permits writing on optical disks. CD-R technology requires a CD-R drive, CD-R disks, and the accompanying software. Once a CD-R disk is written on, it can be read not only by the CD-R drive but by any CD-ROM drive.

Just Who Do You Think You Are?

Not all CD-ROM offerings focus on sight and sound. Some use the large CD capacity to offer many layers of text and attractive screen presentations. This describes a CD-ROM personality test called Who Do You Think You Are? Anyone with a bent for introspection will enjoy working through the profile.

Written by two psychologists, the software presents hundreds of questions, each presented on-screen in large text. The analyzed results are displayed with colorful graphs. This is followed by a candid description of your personality type and short biographies of famous people whose personalities are similar to yours.

DVD-ROM

The storage technology that outpaces all others is called **DVD-ROM,** for **digital video disk.** Think of a DVD, as it is called for short, as an over-achieving CD-ROM. Although the two look the same, a DVD has an astonishing 4.7-gigabyte capacity, seven times more than that of the CD-ROM. And that is just the plain variety. DVDs have two layers of information, one clear and one opaque, on a single side; this so-called double-layered DVD surface can hold about 8.5GB. Furthermore, DVDs can be written on both sides, bumping capacity to 17GB. And a DVD-ROM drive can also read CD-ROMs.

Operating very much like CD-ROM technology, DVD uses a laser beam to read microscopic spots that represent data. But DVD uses a laser with a shorter wavelength, permitting it to read more densely packed spots, thus increasing the disk capacity. The benefits of this storage capacity are many—full-length movies, exquisite sound, and, eventually, high-volume business data. It is just a matter of time until all new personal computers will come with a DVD drive as standard equipment. However, not all software makers are jumping on the DVD bandwagon. The reason is the Internet. Software can be continually updated on the Internet without redistributing disks, and even the expansive DVD capacity is dwarfed by the virtually unlimited capacity of the Internet.

If you have a CD-ROM drive—or perhaps even a DVD-ROM drive—you can be on your way to one of the computer industry's great adventures: multimedia.

➤ Multimedia

Multimedia stirs the imagination. For example, have you ever thought that you could see a film clip from *Gone with the Wind* on your computer screen? One could argue that such treats are already available on video-cassette, but the computer version provides an added dimension for this and other movies: reviews by critics, photographs of movie stars, lists of Academy Awards, the possibility of user input, and much more. Software described as **multimedia** typically presents information with text, illustrations, photos, narration, music, animation, and film clips (Figure 5-11). Until the optical disk, placing this much data on a disk was impossible. However, the large capacity of optical disks means that the kinds of data that take up huge amounts of storage space—photographs, music, and film clips—can now be accommodated.

Multimedia Requirements

To use multimedia software, you must have the proper hardware. In addition to the aforementioned CD-ROM drive, you also need a sound card (installed internally) and speakers, which may rest externally on either side of the computer or be built into the computer housing. Special software accompanies the drive and sound card. In particular, if full-motion video is important to you, be sure your computer includes **MPEG (Motion Picture Experts Group),** a set of widely accepted video standards. Another video-related issue is the speed of the CD-ROM drive. As anyone who tries to keep a computer system up-to-date knows, the single-speed drive was quickly doubled, then doubled again to the "quad" speed 4X, and then to 8X and beyond. The higher the drive

(a)

(b)

(c)

(d)

Figure 5-11 Multimedia applications. Multimedia applications on CD-ROM offer everything from games to business advice. These four samples include (a) the study of ancient lands, including maps; (b) a tour of the interior of the Titanic, including the grand staircase shown here; (c) archived issues of *Life* magazine, including a photo of young John Kennedy Jr. in the White House; and (d) detailed wedding advice on flowers, the guest list, the ceremony, and who pays for what.

speed, the faster the transfer of data and the smoother the video showing on the screen.

Should your next computer be a multimedia personal computer? Absolutely. There is no doubt that multimedia is the medium of choice for all kinds of software.

Multimedia Applications

If you take a moment to peruse the racks of multimedia software in your local store, you can see that most of the current offerings come under the categories of entertainment or education—or possibly both. You can study *and hear* works by Stravinsky or Schubert. You can explore the planets or the ocean bottom through film clips and narrations by experts. You can be "elected" to Congress, after which you tour the Capitol, decorate your office, hire staff, and vote on issues. You can study the

Figure 5-12 Magnetic tape units.
Tapes are always protected by glass from outside dust and dirt. These modern tape drives, called "stackers," accept several cassette tapes, each with its own supply and take-up reel.

battle of Gettysburg—and even change the outcome. You can study the Japanese language, seeing the symbols and hearing the intonation. You can buy multimedia versions of reference books, magazines, children's books, and entire novels.

But this is just the beginning. Businesses are already moving to this high-capacity environment for street atlases, national phone directories, and sales catalogs. Coming offerings will include every kind of standard business application, all tricked out with fancy animation, photos, and sound. Educators will be able to draw upon the new sight and sound for everything from human anatomy to time travel. And just imagine the library of the future, consisting of not only the printed word but also photos, film, animation, and sound recordings—all flowing from the computer.

▶ Magnetic Tape Storage

We saved magnetic tape storage for last because it has taken a subordinate role in storage technology. **Magnetic tape** looks like the tape used in music cassettes—plastic tape with a magnetic coating. As in other magnetic media, data is stored as extremely small magnetic spots. Tapes come in a number of forms, including ½-inch-wide tape wound on a reel, ¼-inch-wide tape in data cartridges and cassettes, and tapes that look like ordinary music cassettes but are designed to store data instead of music. The amount of data on a tape is expressed in terms of **density**, which is the number of **characters per inch (cpi)** or **bytes per inch (bpi)** that can be stored on the tape.

The highest-capacity tape is the **digital audio tape**, or DAT, which uses a different method of recording data. Using a method called **helical scan recording**, DAT wraps around a rotating read/write head that spins vertically as it moves. This places the data in diagonal bands that run across the tape rather than down its length. This method produces high density and faster access to data.

Figure 5-12 shows a **magnetic tape unit** that might be used with a mainframe. The tape unit reads and writes data using a **read/write head.** When the computer is writing on the tape, the **erase head** first erases any data previously recorded.

Two reels are used, a **supply reel** and a **take-up reel.** The supply reel, which has the tape with data on it or on which data will be recorded, is the reel that is changed. The take-up reel always stays with the magnetic tape unit. Many cartridges and cassettes have the supply and take-up reels built into the same case.

Tape now has a limited role because disks have proved the superior storage medium. Disk data is quite reliable, especially within a sealed module. Furthermore, as will be shown, disk data can be accessed directly, as opposed to data on tape, which can be accessed only by passing by all the data ahead of it on the tape. Consequently, the primary role of tape today is as an inexpensive backup medium.

▶ Backup Systems

Although a hard disk is an extremely reliable device, it is subject to electromechanical failures that cause loss of data. Furthermore, data files, particularly those accessed by several users, are subject to errors introduced by users. There is also the possibility of errors introduced by software. With any method of data storage, a **backup system**—a way of storing data in more than one place to protect it from damage and errors—is vital. As already noted, magnetic tape is used primarily for backup purposes. For personal computer users, an easy and inexpensive way to back up a hard disk file is simply to copy it to a diskette whenever it is updated. But this is not practical for a system with many files or many users.

Personal computer users have the option of purchasing their own tape backup system, to be used on a regular basis for copying all data from hard disk to a high-capacity tape. Data thus saved can be restored to the hard disk later if needed. A key advantage of a tape backup system is that it can copy the entire hard disk in minutes; also, with the availability of gigabytes of hard disk space, it is not really feasible to swap diskettes in and out of the machine. Further, tape backup can be scheduled to take place when you are not going to be using the computer.

▶ Organizing and Accessing Stored Data

As users of computer systems, we just offer data as we are instructed to do, such as punching in our identification code at an automated teller machine or perhaps filling out a form with our name and address. But data cannot be dumped helter-skelter into a computer. Some computer professional—probably a programmer or systems analyst—has to have planned how data from users will be received, organized, and stored, and also in what manner data will be processed by the computer.

This kind of storage goes beyond what you may have done to store a memo created in word processing. Organizations that store data usually need a lot of data on many subjects. For example, a charitable organization would probably need detailed information about donors, names and schedules of volunteers, perhaps a schedule of fundraising events, and more. A factory would need to keep track of inventory (name, identification number, location, quantity, and so forth), the scheduled path of the product through the assembly line, records of quality-control checkpoints, and much more. All this data must be organized and stored according to a plan. First consider how data is organized.

Data: Getting Organized

To be processed by the computer, raw data is organized into characters, fields, records, files, and databases. First is the smallest element, the character.

- A **character** is a letter, digit, or special character (such as $, ?, or *).
- A **field** contains a set of related characters. For example, suppose that a health club is making address labels for a mailing. For each person it might have a member-number field, a name field, a street address field, a city field, a state field, a zip code field, and a phone number field.
- A **record** is a collection of related fields. Thus, on the health club mailing list, one person's member number, name, address, city, state, zip code, and phone number constitute a record.

Multimedia Forever?

As promising as multimedia technology is, its peak is already in view. That is, multimedia that comes on CD-ROMs may diminish. The spoiler is—surprise—the Internet. Many web sites now offer what they describe as "the full multimedia experience." Although sometimes certain software is needed to appreciate all the sights and sounds, that software is often offered for downloading right at the site. It is just a matter of time until interested users are fully outfitted to satisfy their multimedia needs from the Internet.

Software called Shockwave can be downloaded from the Macromedia site, shown here. Once it has been added to your browser, you can view sites animated by Shockwave.

Figure 5-13 How data is organized.
Whether stored on tape or on disk, data is organized into characters, fields, records, and files. A file is a collection of related records. These drawings represent (a) magnetic tape and (b) magnetic disk.

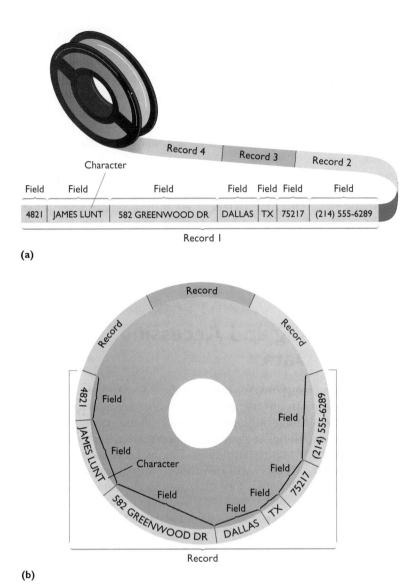

(a)

(b)

- A **file** is a collection of related records. All the member records for the health club compose a file. Figure 5-13 shows how data for a health club member might look.
- A **database** is a collection of interrelated files stored together with minimum redundancy. Specific data items can be retrieved for various applications. For instance, if the health club is opening a new outlet, it can pull out the names of people with zip codes near the new club and send them an announcement.

A field of particular interest is the **key**, a unique identifier for a record. It might seem at first that a name—of a person, say, or a product—would be a good key; however, since some names may be the same, a name field is not a good choice for a key. When a file is first computerized, existing description fields are seldom used as keys. Although a file describing people might use a Social Security number as the key, it is more likely that a new field will be developed that can be assigned unique values, such as customer number or product number.

In addition to organizing the expected data, a plan must be made to access the data on files.

The File Plan: An Overview

Now that you have a general idea of how data is organized, you are ready to look at the process used to decide how to place data on a storage medium. Consider this chain: (1) It is the application—payroll, airline reservations, inventory control, whatever—that determines how the data must be accessed by users. (2) Once an access method has been determined, it follows that there are certain ways the data must be organized so that the needed access is workable. (3) The organization method, in turn, limits the choice of storage medium. The discussion begins with an appreciation of application demands, then moves to a detailed look at organization and access.

The following application examples illustrate how an access decision might be made.

1. A department store offers its customers charge accounts. When a customer makes a purchase, a sales clerk needs to be able to check the validity of the customer's account while the customer is waiting. The clerk needs immediate access to the individual customer record in the account file.
2. A major oil company supplies its charge customers with credit cards, which it considers sufficient proof for purchase. The charge slips collected by gas stations are forwarded to the oil company, which processes them in order of account number. Unlike the retail example just given, the company does not need access to any one record at a specific time but merely needs access to all customer charge records when it is time to prepare bills.
3. A city power and light company employee accepts reports of burned-out streetlights from residents over the phone. Using a key made up of unique address components, the clerk immediately finds the record for the offending streetlight and prints out a one-page report that is routed to repair units within 24 hours. To produce such quick service based on an individual streetlight, the employee needs to be able to access the individual streetlight record.
4. Next-month schedules for airline flight attendants are computer-produced monthly and delivered to the attendants' home-base mailboxes. The schedules are put together from information based on flight records, whose entire file can be accessed monthly at the convenience of the airline and the computer-use plan.

As you can see, the question of access seems to come down to whether a particular record is needed right away, as it was in examples 1 and 3. This immediate need for a particular record means access must be *direct*. It follows that the organization must also be direct, or at least *indexed*, and that the storage medium must be disk. Furthermore, the type of processing, a related topic, must be *transaction processing*. The critical distinction is whether or not immediate access to an individual record is needed. The following discussion examines all these topics in detail. Although organization type is determined by the type of access required, the file must be organized before it can be accessed, so organization is the first topic.

File Organization: Three Methods

There are three major methods of storing files of data in secondary storage:

- Sequential file organization, in which records are organized in a particular order
- Direct file organization, in which records are not organized in any special order
- Indexed file organization, in which records are organized sequentially but indexes are built into the file to allow a record to be accessed either sequentially or directly

Sequential File Organization   **Sequential file processing** means that records are in order according to a key field. As noted earlier, a file containing information on people will be in order by a key that uniquely identifies each person, such as Social Security number or customer number. If a particular record in a sequential file is wanted, all the prior records in the file must be read before the desired record is reached. Tape storage is limited to sequential file organization. Disk storage may be sequential, but records on disk can also be accessed directly.

Direct File Organization   **Direct file processing**, or **direct access**, allows the computer to go directly to the desired record by using a record key; the computer does not have to read all preceding records in the file as it does if the records are arranged sequentially. Direct processing requires disk storage; in fact, a disk device is called a **direct-access storage device (DASD)** because the computer can go directly to the desired record on the disk. It is this ability to access any given record instantly that has made computer systems so convenient for people in service industries—for catalog order-takers determining whether a particular sweater is in stock, for example, or bank tellers checking individual bank balances. An added benefit of direct access organization is the ability to read, change, and return a record to its same place on the disk; this is called **updating in place.**

Obviously, if we have a completely blank area on the disk and can put records anywhere, there must be some predictable system for placing a record at a disk address and then retrieving the record at a subsequent time. In other words, once the record has been placed on a disk, it must be possible to find it again. This is done by choosing a certain formula to apply to the record key, thereby deriving a number to use as the disk address. **Hashing**, or **randomizing**, is the name given to the process of applying a mathematical operation to a key to yield a number that represents the address. Even though the record keys are unique, it is possible for a hashing scheme to produce the same disk address, called a **synonym**, for two different records; such an occurrence is called a **collision.** There are various ways to recover from a collision; one way is simply to use the next available record slot on the disk.

There are many different hashing schemes; although the example in Figure 5-14 is too simple to be realistic, you can get a general idea of how the process works. An example of how direct processing works is provided in Figure 5-15.

Indexed File Organization   Indexed file processing, or **indexed processing**, is a third method of file organization, and it represents a com-

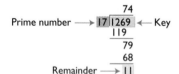

Figure 5-14 A hashing scheme. Dividing the key number 1269 by the prime number 17 yields a remainder of 11, which can be used to indicate the address on a disk.

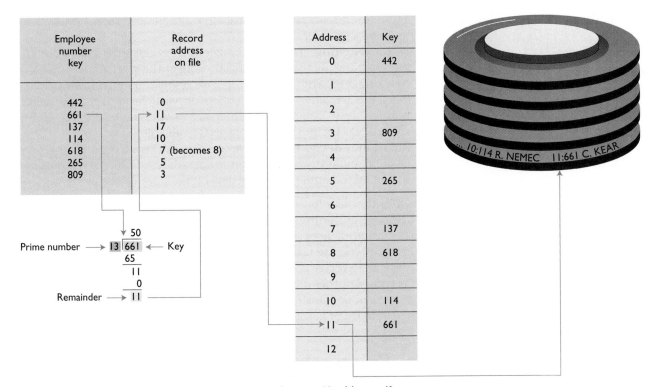

Figure 5-15 An example of direct access. Assume there are 13 addresses (0 through 12) available in the file. Dividing the key number 661, which is C. Kear's employee number, by the prime number 13 yields a remainder of 11. Thus, 11 is the address for key 661. However, for the key 618, dividing by 13 yields a remainder of 7, a synonym, since this address has already been used by the key 137, which also has a remainder of 7. Hence, the address becomes the next location—that is, 8. Note, incidentally, that keys (and therefore records) need not appear in any particular order. (The 13 record locations available are, of course, too few to hold a normal file; a small number was used to keep the example simple.)

promise between the sequential and direct methods. It is useful in applications where a file needs to be in sequential order but, in addition, access to individual records is needed.

An indexed file works as follows: Records are stored in the file in sequential order, but the file also contains an index. The index contains entries consisting of the key to each record stored on the file and the corresponding disk address for that record. The index is like a directory, with the keys to all records listed in order. For a record to be accessed directly, the record key must be located in the index; the address associated with the key is then used to locate the record on the disk. Accessing the entire file of records sequentially is simply a matter of beginning with the first record and proceeding one a a time through the rest of the records.

Before proceeding with the actual processing of data, consider the physical activity of the disk as it accesses records directly.

Disk Access to Data

Three primary factors determine **access time**, the time needed to access data directly on disk:

■ **Seek time.** This is the time it takes the access arm to get into position over a particular track. Keep in mind that all the access arms move as a unit, so they are simultaneously in position over a set of tracks that make up a cylinder.

- **Head switching.** The access arms on the access mechanism do not move separately; they move together, all at the same time. However, only one read/write head can operate at any one time. Head switching is the activation of a particular read/write head over a particular track on a particular surface. Since head switching takes place at the speed of electricity, the time it takes is negligible.
- **Rotational delay.** Once the access arm and read/write head are in position and ready to read or write data, the read/write head waits for a short period until the desired data on the track moves under it.

Once the data has been found, the next step is **data transfer**, the process of transferring data between memory and the place on the disk track—from memory to the track if you are writing, from the track to memory if you are reading. One measure for the performance of disk drives is the average access time, which is usually measured in milliseconds (ms). Another measure is the **data transfer rate**, which tells how fast data can be transferred once it has been found. This usually will be stated in terms of megabytes of data per second.

▶ Processing Stored Data

Once there is a plan for accessing the files, they can be processed. There are several methods of processing data files in a computer system. The two main methods are batch processing (processing data in groups at a more convenient later time) and transaction processing (processing data immediately, as it is received).

Batch Processing

Batch processing is a technique in which transactions are collected into groups, or batches, to be processed at a time when the computer may have few online users and thus be more accessible, usually during the night. Unlike transaction processing, a topic coming up momentarily, batch processing involves no direct user interaction. Let us consider updating the health club address-label file. The **master file**, a semipermanent set of records, is, in this case, the list of all members of the health club and their addresses. The **transaction file** contains all changes to be made to the master file: additions (transactions to create new master records for new members), deletions (transactions with instructions to delete master records of members who have resigned from the health club), and revisions (transactions to change items such as street addresses or phone numbers in fields in the master records). Periodically, perhaps monthly or weekly, the master file is **updated** with the changes called for in the transaction file. The result is a new, up-to-date master file (Figure 5-16).

In batch processing, before a transaction file is matched against a master file, the transaction file must be sorted (usually by computer) so that all the transactions are in sequential order according to a key field. In updating the health club address-label file, the key is the member number assigned by the health club. The records on the master file are already in order by key. Once the changes in the transaction file are sorted by key, the two files can be matched and the master file updated.

MAKING THE RIGHT CONNECTIONS

SPEED ISN'T EVERYTHING

What good will raw speed be on the racetrack if the car breaks down for mechanical reasons? For that matter, what use are the best pit mechanics if no one is aware of the car's needs?

Not to worry. The computer is standing by. Alongside the mechanics, a notebook computer is "making the right connections" with the car. The driver may be alone in the cockpit, but technology connects the driver to the pit crew. The team engineer, using a notebook computer and a wireless connection system, monitors key engine readings produced by on-board computers—from generic measurements such as rpm, temperature, pressure, and fuel consumption to detailed readings as specific as the right-rear wheel-bearing temperature, which is crucial when racing on oval tracks.

The connections are one-way. The engineer is not permitted to tweak any of the car's calibrations remotely. However, the computer has done its part: The engineer radios instructions to the driver, who then makes adjustments by hand.

During processing, the computer matches the keys from the master and transaction files, carrying out the appropriate action to add, revise, or delete. At the end of processing, a newly updated master file is created; in addition, an error report is usually printed. The error report shows actions such as an attempt to delete a nonexistent record or an attempt to add a record that already exists.

Transaction Processing

Transaction processing is a technique of processing transactions—a bank withdrawal, an address change, a credit charge—in random order, that is, in any order they occur. Note that although batch processing also uses transactions, in that case they are grouped together for processing; the phrase "transaction processing" means that each transaction is handled immediately. Transaction processing is real-time processing. **Real-time processing** means that a transaction is processed fast enough for the result to come back and be acted upon right away. For example, a teller at a bank can find out immediately what your bank balance is. For processing to be real-time, it must also be **online**—that is, the terminals must be connected directly to the computer. Transaction processing systems use disk storage because the disk drive can move directly to the desired record.

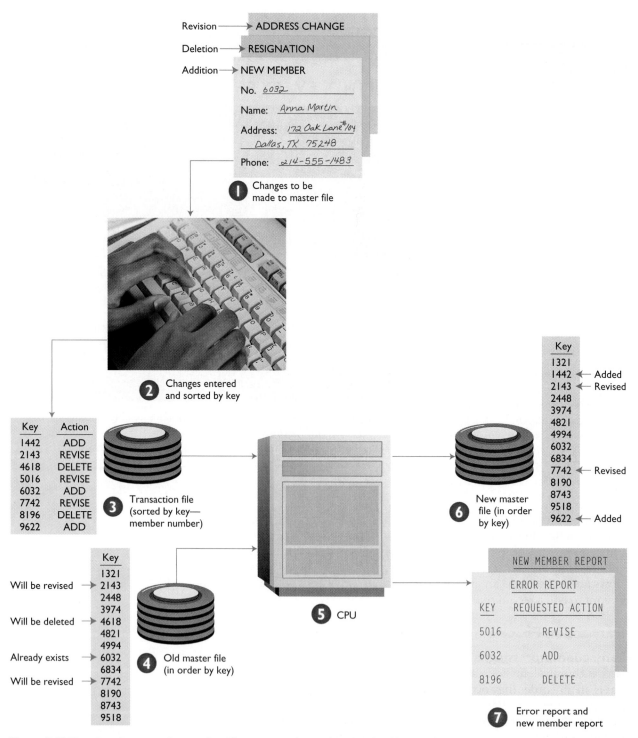

Figure 5-16 How batch processing works. The purpose of this system is to update the health club's master address-label file. The updating will be done sequentially. ① Changes to be made (additions, deletions, and revisions) are input with ② a keyboard, sorted, and sent to a disk, where they are stored in ③ the transaction file. The transaction file contains records in sequential order, according to member number, from lowest to highest. The field used to identify the record is called the key; in this instance the key is the member number. ④ The master file is also organized by member number. ⑤ The computer matches transaction file data and master file data by member number to produce ⑥ a new master file and ⑦ an error report and a new member report. Note that since this was a sequential update, the new master file is a completely new file, not just the old file updated in place. The error report lists member numbers in the transaction file that were not in the master file and member numbers that were included in the transaction file as additions that were already in the master file.

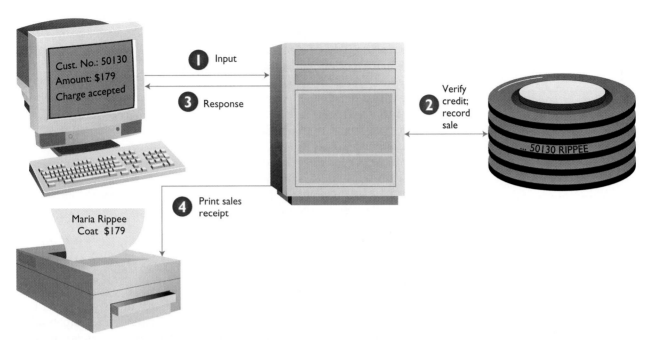

Figure 5-17 How transaction processing works. The purposes of this retail sales system are to verify that a customer's credit is good, record the credit sale on the customer's record, and produce a sales receipt. Since customers may have the same name, the file is organized by customer account number rather than by name. Here Maria Rippee, account number 50130, wishes to purchase a coat for $179. ① The sales clerk uses the terminal to input Maria's account number and the sale. ② When the computer receives the data from the clerk, it uses the account number to find Maria's record on the disk file, verify her credit, and record the sale so that she will later be billed for it. ③ The computer returns an acceptance back to the clerk's terminal. ④ The computer sends sales receipt information to the clerk's printer. All this is done within seconds while the customer is waiting. This example is necessarily simplified, but it shows a system that is real-time (immediate response) and online (directly connected to the computer).

Advantages of transaction processing are immediate access to stored data (and thus immediate customer service) and immediate updating of the stored data. A sales clerk, for example, could access the computer via a terminal to verify the customer's credit and also record the sale via the computer (Figure 5-17). Later, by the way, those updated records can be batch processed to bill all customers.

Batch and Transaction Processing: The Best of Both Worlds

Numerous computer systems combine the best features of both methods of processing. A bank, for instance, may use transaction processing to check your balance and individually record your cash withdrawal transaction during the day at the teller window. However, the deposit that you leave in an envelope in an "instant" deposit drop may be recorded during the night by means of batch processing. Printing your bank statement is also a batch process. Most store systems also combine both methods: A point-of-sale terminal finds the individual item price as a sale is made, but that same process captures inventory data, which may be batched and totaled to produce inventory reports.

Police license-plate checks for stolen cars work the same way. As cars are sold throughout the state, the license numbers, owners' names, and so on, are updated in the motor vehicle department's master file, usually via batch processing on a nightly basis. But when police officers see a car they suspect may be stolen, they can radio headquarters, where an operator with a terminal uses transaction processing to check the master file immediately to see if the car has been reported missing. Some officers have a laptop computer right in the car and can check the information themselves.

Auto junkyards, which often are computerized big businesses, can make an individual inquiry for a record of a specific part needed by a customer waiting on the phone or in person. As parts are sold, sales records are kept to update the files nightly using batch processing.

★ ★ ★ ★

What is the future of storage? Perhaps holographic storage, which would be able to store thousands of pages on a device the size of a quarter and would be much faster than even the fastest hard drives. Whatever the technology, it seems likely that there will be greater storage capabilities in the future to hold the huge data files for law, medicine, science, education, business, and, of course, the government.

To have access to all that data from any location, we need data communications, the subject of the next chapter.

CHAPTER REVIEW

Summary and Key Terms

- **Secondary storage**, sometimes called **auxiliary storage**, is storage separate from the computer itself, where software and data can be stored on a semipermanent basis. Secondary storage is necessary because memory, or primary storage, can be used only temporarily.

- The benefits of secondary storage are space, reliability, convenience, and economy.

- Diskettes and hard disks are magnetic media, based on a technology of representing data as magnetized spots on the disk—with a magnetized spot representing a 1 bit and the absence of such a spot representing a 0 bit. The surface of each disk has concentric tracks on it.

- **Diskettes** are made of flexible mylar. Advantages of diskettes, compared to hard disks, are portability, backup, and delivery of new software to consumers.

- **Data compression** makes a large file smaller by temporarily removing nonessential but space-hogging items such as tab marks and double-spacing.

- A **hard disk** is a metal platter coated with magnetic oxide that can be magnetized to represent data. Several disks can be assembled into a **disk pack.**

- A **disk drive** is a machine that allows data to be read from a disk or written on a disk. A disk pack is mounted on a disk drive that is a separate unit connected to the computer. The disk **access arm** moves a **read/write head** into position over a particular track, where the read/write head hovers above the track. A **head crash** occurs when a read/write head touches the disk surface and causes all data to be destroyed. Most disk packs combine the disks, access arms, and read/write heads in a sealed module.

- Hard disks for personal computers are 3½-inch disks in sealed modules. Hard disk capacity for personal computers can be hundreds of millions of bytes, or gigabytes; much of this will be for storing software. Personal computer users may supplement hard disk storage with a **removable hard disk cartridge**, which, once filled, can be replaced with a fresh one.

- A **redundant array of inexpensive disks**, or simply **RAID**, uses several small hard disks that work together as a unit. RAID level 1 duplicates data on separate disk drives, **data mirroring.** Higher levels of RAID use **data striping**, spreading the data across several disks in the array, with one disk used solely as a check disk to keep track of what data is where.

- The **sector method** of recording data on a disk divides each track into sectors that hold a specific number of characters. Data on the track is accessed by referring to the surface number, track number, and sector number where the data is stored. **Zone recording** involves dividing a disk into zones to take maximum advantage of the storage available by assigning more sectors to tracks in outer zones than to those in inner zones.

- The **cylinder method** is a vertical organization of data on a disk pack. When the access arms are in position, they are in the same vertical position for all disk surfaces. The set of tracks that can be accessed by one positioning of the access arms is called a **cylinder.**

- **Optical disk** technology uses a laser beam to enter data as spots on the disk surface. To read the data, the laser scans the disk, and a lens picks up different light reflections from the various spots. **Read-only media** are recorded on by the manufacturer and can be read from but not written to by the user. **Write-once, read-many media**, also called **WORM media**, may be written to once. A hybrid type of disk, called **magneto-optical (MO)**, has the large capacity of an optical disk but can be written over like a magnetic disk. **CD-ROM**, for **compact disk read-only memory**, which has a disk format identical to that of audio compact disks, can hold up to 660 megabytes per disk. CD-R technology permits writing on optical disks. **DVD-ROM**, for **digital video disk**, has astonishing storage capacity, up to 17GB if both layers and both sides are used.

- **Multimedia** software typically presents information with text, illustrations, photos, narration, music, animation, and film clips—possible because of the large capacity of optical disks. **MPEG (Motion Picture Experts Group)** is a set of widely accepted video standards.

- **Magnetic tape** stores data as extremely small magnetic spots. The amount of data on a tape is expressed in terms of **density**, which is the number of **characters per inch (cpi)** or **bytes per inch (bpi)** that can be stored on the tape. The highest-capacity tape is **digital audio tape**, or **DAT**, which uses a different method of recording data. Using a method called **helical scan recording**, the data is placed in diagonal bands that run across the tape rather than down its length.

- A **magnetic tape unit** reads and writes data using a **read/write head;** when the computer is writing on the tape, the **erase head** first erases any data previously recorded. Two reels are used, a **supply reel** that has the data tape and a **take-up reel** that stays with the magnetic tape unit.

- A **backup system** is a way of storing data in more than one place to protect it from damage and loss. Most backup systems use tape.

- A **character** is a letter, digit, or special character (such as $, ?, or *). A **field** contains a set of related characters. A **record** is a collection of related fields. A **file** is a collection of related records. A **database** is a collection of interrelated files stored together with minimum redundancy; specific data items can be retrieved for various applications.

- The application determines the way the data must be accessed by users, and it follows that there are certain ways the data must be organized to provide the needed access. The organization method, in turn, limits the choice of storage medium.

- **Sequential file processing** means that records are in a certain order by a unique identifier field called a **key.** If a particular record in a sequential file is wanted, then all the prior records in the file must be read before the desired record is reached.

- **Direct file processing**, or **direct access**, allows the computer to go directly to the desired record by using a record key. Direct processing requires disk storage; a disk device is called a **direct-access storage device (DASD)**. In addition to instant access to any record, an added benefit of direct access organization is the ability to read, change, and return a record to its same place on the disk; this is called **updating in place. Hashing**, or **randomizing**, is the name given to the process of applying a formula to a key to yield a number that represents the address for the record that has that key. A hashing scheme may produce the same disk address, called a **synonym**, for two different records; such an occurrence is called a **collision.**

- **Indexed file processing**, or **indexed processing**, stores records in the file in sequential order, but the file also contains an index of keys; the address associated with the key is then used to locate the record on the disk.

- Three factors determine **access time**, the time needed to access data directly on disk: **seek time**, the time it takes to get the access arm into position over a particular track; **head switching**, the activation of a particular read/write head over a particular track on a particular surface; and **rotational delay**, the brief wait until the desired data on the track moves under the read/write head. Once data has been found, **data transfer**, the transfer of data between memory and the place on the disk track, occurs.

- Access time is usually measured in milliseconds (ms). The **data transfer rate**, which tells how fast data can be transferred once it has been found, is usually stated in terms of megabytes of data per second.

- **Batch processing** is a technique in which transactions are collected into groups, or batches, to be processed at a time when the computer has few online users and thus is more accessible. A **master file** is a semipermanent set of records. A **transaction file**, sorted by key, contains all changes to be made to the master file: additions, deletions, and revisions. The master file is **updated** periodically with the changes called for in the transaction file.

- **Transaction processing** is a technique of processing transactions in any order they occur. **Real-time processing** means that a transaction is processed fast enough for the result to come back and be acted upon right away. **Online** processing means that the terminals must be connected directly to the computer.

Quick Poll

Compare your answers to those of your colleagues or classmates.

1. The most important files to consider when planning storage needs:
   - ❏ a. Software
   - ❏ b. Data
2. For convenience, I prefer to work with files stored on
   - ❏ a. Diskette
   - ❏ b. CD-ROM
   - ❏ c. Hard disk
   - ❏ d. Removable hard disk cartridge
3. The most likely reason I would neglect to back up my files:
   - ❏ a. No time
   - ❏ b. Unlikely to be a problem
   - ❏ c. Forget

Discussion Questions

1. If you were buying a personal computer today, what would you choose for secondary storage?
2. Can you imagine new multimedia applications that take advantage of sound, photos, art, and perhaps video?
3. Provide your own example to illustrate how characters of data are organized into fields, records, files, and (perhaps) databases. If you wish, you may choose one of the following examples: department store data, airline reservations, or Internal Revenue Service data. Would you organize these files directly or sequentially? Would your examples use batch processing, transaction processing, or a combination of the two?

Student Study Guide

Multiple Choice

1. The density of data stored on magnetic tape is expressed as
   - a. units per inch
   - b. tracks per inch
   - c. packs per inch
   - d. bytes per inch
2. Another name for secondary storage:
   - a. cylinder
   - b. density
   - c. auxiliary
   - d. memory
3. A magnetized spot represents:
   - a. cpi
   - b. 0 bit
   - c. MB
   - d. 1 bit
4. A field contains one or more
   - a. characters
   - b. databases
   - c. records
   - d. files
5. The reel that is changed on a magnetic tape unit:
   - a. take-up reel
   - b. RAID
   - c. supply reel
   - d. record
6. A hard disk can be backed up efficiently using
   - a. zoning
   - b. a tape backup system
   - c. a transaction file
   - d. WORM
7. Relatively permanent data is contained in
   - a. a field
   - b. memory
   - c. a transaction
   - d. a master file
8. A limitation of magnetic tape as a method of storing data:
   - a. not reusable
   - b. organized sequentially
   - c. expensive
   - d. not portable
9. DASD refers to
   - a. disk storage
   - b. tape storage
   - c. fields
   - d. sorting
10. Optical disk technology uses
    - a. helical scanning
    - b. DAT
    - c. a laser beam
    - d. RAID
11. The mechanism for reading or writing data on a disk:
    - a. track
    - b. WORM
    - c. key
    - d. access arm
12. Higher levels of RAID spread data across several disks, a method called
    - a. helical scanning
    - b. hashing
    - c. data striping
    - d. duplication
13. The time required to position the access arm over a particular track:
    - a. rotational delay
    - b. seek time
    - c. data transfer
    - d. head switching
14. A way of organizing data on a disk pack to minimize seek time:
    - a. sequential file
    - b. the cylinder method
    - c. in sequential order
    - d. hashing
15. The speed with which a disk can find data being sought:
    - a. access time
    - b. direct time
    - c. data transfer time
    - d. cylinder time

16. The disk storage that uses both a magnet and a laser beam:
    a. hashing
    b. CD-ROM
    c. magneto-optical
    d. WORM
17. The RAID method of duplicating data:
    a. zoning
    b. the sector method
    c. data mirroring
    d. data striping
18. Before a sequential file can be updated, the transactions must first be
    a. numbered
    b. sorted
    c. labeled
    d. updated
19. Hashing, to get an address, is the process of applying a formula to a
    a. key
    b. file
    c. record
    d. character
20. Personal computer users can increase hard disk storage capacity with
    a. higher density
    b. read-only media
    c. CD-R
    d. removable hard disk cartridge
21. A CD-ROM has the same format as a(n)
    a. backup tape
    b. diskette
    c. RAID
    d. audio compact disk
22. Several small disk packs that work together as a unit:
    a. CD-ROM
    b. WORM
    c. RAID
    d. MO
23. Assigning more sectors to outer disk tracks:
    a. zone recording
    b. data transfer
    c. randomizing
    d. sectoring
24. The ability to return a changed disk record to its original location is called
    a. magneto-optical
    b. multimedia
    c. rotational delay
    d. updating in place
25. Processing transactions in groups is called
    a. data transfer
    b. transaction processing
    c. head switching
    d. batch processing

True/False

T F 1. Real-time processing means that a transaction is processed fast enough for the result to come back and be acted upon right away.
T F 2. CD-R technology permits writing on CD-ROMs.
T F 3. A 0 bit is represented on magnetic disk by a magnetized spot.
T F 4. A magnetic tape unit records data on tape but cannot retrieve it.
T F 5. A transaction file contains records to update the master file.
T F 6. WORM can be written once; then it becomes read-only.
T F 7. Rotational delay comes before seek time.
T F 8. Density is the number of characters per inch.
T F 9. The most common backup medium is CD-ROM.

T F 10. Another name for randomizing is zoning.
T F 11. Transaction processing systems are real-time systems.
T F 12. Multimedia software can include film clips.
T F 13. Nonremovable hard disks have disks, access arms, and read/write heads in a sealed module.
T F 14. Magneto-optical refers to a special type of tape that records data diagonally.
T F 15. A magnetic disk has concentric tracks.
T F 16. Access time is measured in terms of megabytes.
T F 17. Data compression makes files smaller by eliminating text.
T F 18. A synonym is another name for a database.
T F 19. Zone recording takes full advantage of the space on a disk track.
T F 20. Hashing is a process used to locate records sequentially.
T F 21. RAID uses several large disks in place of several small disks.
T F 22. A field is a set of related records.
T F 23. Auxiliary storage can be used only temporarily.
T F 24. A database is a collection of interrelated records.
T F 25. Indexed records are stored in sequential order.

Fill-In

1. Adding more sectors to the outer tracks of a disk is called _____

2. Processing transactions in a group:

   _____

3. Four benefits of secondary storage:

   a. _____

   b. _____

   c. _____

   d. _____

4. The type of software that can offer photos, narration, music, and more: _____

5. DASD stands for _____

6. The type of access required by a file is determined by _____

7. Two types of RAID:

    a. _____

    b. _____

8. If a read/write head touches a hard disk surface, this

    is called _____

9. What does CD-ROM stand for?

    _____

10. The disk that has magnetically sensitive metallic

    crystals embedded in the plastic coating:

    _____

11. The concept of using several disks together as a

    unit: _____

12. The primary advantage of optical disk technology:

    _____

13. The three kinds of components in a sealed data

    module:

    a. _____

    b. _____

    c. _____

14. The three primary factors that determine access

    time for disk data:

    a. _____

    b. _____

    c. _____

15. Three major methods of file organization:

    a. _____

    b. _____

    c. _____

16. Required before transactions can be used to update

    a sequential file: _____

17. A unique identifier for a record:

    _____

18. The smallest unit of raw data:

    _____

19. The method of organizing data vertically on a disk

    pack: _____

20. Another name for hashing:

    _____

Answers

Multiple Choice

1. d	6. b	11. d	16. c	21. d
2. c	7. d	12. c	17. c	22. c
3. d	8. b	13. b	18. b	23. a
4. a	9. a	14. b	19. a	24. d
5. c	10. c	15. a	20. d	25. d

True/False

1. T	6. T	11. T	16. F	21. F
2. T	7. F	12. T	17. F	22. F
3. F	8. T	13. T	18. F	23. F
4. F	9. F	14. F	19. T	24. T
5. T	10. F	15. T	20. F	25. T

Fill-In

1. zone recording
2. batch processing
3. a. space
   b. reliability
   c. convenience
   d. economy
4. multimedia
5. direct-access storage device
6. the application
7. a. disk mirroring
   b. data striping
8. head crash
9. compact disk read-only memory
10. magneto-optical
11. redundant array of inexpensive disks (RAID)
12. high capacity
13. a. disks
    b. access arms
    c. read/write heads
14. a. seek time
    b. head switching
    c. rotational delay
15. a. sequential file
    b. direct file
    c. indexed file
16. sorting transactions by key
17. key
18. character
19. cylinder method
20. randomizing

PLANET INTERNET

FREE OR NOT FREE

Many people, especially those associated with schools and government organizations, have free access to the Internet. But is the information available on Internet sites also free? Often, the answer is yes.

What information is free and what isn't? There are no uniform rules to guide you. Although some information providers make a blanket "help yourself" statement, much information is unaccompanied by a proprietary statement. However, business people and others who do not want their works

copied post clear notices on their pages, using phrases such as *copyrighted* and *all rights reserved*.

Freebies. Several types of information tend to be free. Categories of free information include health care, the environment, government agencies, humor, lists of events, family issues, the weather, hobby information, clip art, web design and home page advice, academic offerings, and most topics found on individual home pages. The solar system shown here, for example, is from a government agency site. Note the cartoon, shown here, of a woman leaning against a door. The room behind the door is bursting with files of clip art, which are always free. Clip art is handy for building home pages.

As a category, software is not generally free. However, many sites do offer free software, usually to be downloaded directly to a user's computer. The PC Computing site, whose Free Stuff on the Web image is shown here, often includes a comprehensive list of free software offerings.

Some companies on the Web offer free samples of their products. For example, the Jelly Belly and Snapple sites offer free samples that they send through the mail. Of course, this means providing your

Free Beans   History   Factory Tour   Q & A   Menu   Recipes   Gifts   Art Gallery   Bean me home.

mailing address. The form you fill out probably will ask for other information too, especially your e-mail address, all of which the company can use for promotional purposes.

Not free. Business products and services are likely to have a fee. What's more, businesses are running, not walking, to the Internet, so the proportion of for-a-fee offerings can only increase. Even information on sites related to sports and entertainment may not be freely available.

Art and photography. Many artists and photographers put their works on the Internet to be shared freely by all. Most browsers allow you to capture such items by clicking the right mouse button and then Save (back to the left button) to save the image to a file. Another possibility is screen capture software.

However, many artist and photographers, usually professionals, state that their works are copyrighted and may be used only with permission. An example is the Stock Solution, whose logo is shown here. The Stock Solution is an

agency that represents professional photographers whose works can be seen right on your screen. But you must agree to a lease fee before you can make any further use of the photos.

Internet Exercises

1. **Structured exercise.** Begin with the AWL site with URL http://hepg.awl.com/capron/planet/, and examine the free (save frog lives!)Virtual Frog Dissection Kit.
2. **Freeform exercise.** Beginning with Yahoo or your own favorite online directory, find the maps to track the weather in your home state.

Spreading good taste all over the place.

Within the image, the following text appears on screen:

S E A R C H
What's New
Distributors
Product Catalog
Tech. Support
Distributors
Contact Us

Internet
BUSINESS PARK

Internet

Tools

Kim Warren has heard a lot about the information superhighway. She read that the pieces are being assembled by a hodgepodge of computer and software vendors, by phone and cable companies, and by any other visionary who wants to jump aboard. Yet, she read, this project lacks a central architect and a basic blueprint. The articles go on and on, in every newspaper and magazine. In fact, a recent article noted that more has been written about the information superhighway than was written about personal computers when they first came out. But a personal computer, unlike the information superhighway, is something real that Kim can see and even buy.

Kim has a personal computer, her third. And she understands the basics of the information superhighway—that eventually information will be readily available to almost anyone from almost any place. She also knows that the information sending/receiving devices will be computers in some form and that the "highway" carrying the information will be some assemblage of communications equipment such as telephone and cable lines. Even if it is not yet a reality, Kim believes most of the predictions about the information superhighway, particularly that it will be pervasive.

Kim wants to get a head start. She has taken three approaches. First, she has equipped her own computer with the hardware and software needed to communicate with other computers. Second, she has signed up for the Internet, which some consider to be the early stages of the information superhighway, and has begun investigating its many options. Third, she has taken a two-week after-hours course offered by her employer to learn about the basics of communications. Kim is well-positioned at an on-ramp for the information superhighway.

Networking

Computer Connections

▶ Data Communications: How It All Began

Mail, telephone, TV and radio, books, newspapers, and periodicals—these are the principal ways users send and receive information, and they have not changed appreciably in a generation. However, **data communications systems**—computer systems that transmit data over communications lines such as telephone lines or cables—have been gradually evolving since the mid-1960s. Let us take a look at how they came about.

In the early days of computing, **centralized data processing** placed everything—all processing, hardware, and software—in one central location. Computer manufacturers responded to this trend by building even larger general-purpose mainframe computers so that all departments within an organization could be serviced. Eventually, however, total centralization proved inconvenient and inefficient. All input data had to be physically transported to the computer, and all processed material had to be picked up and delivered to the users. Insisting on centralized data processing was like insisting that all conversations between people occur face to face in one designated room.

The next logical step was **teleprocessing** systems—terminals connected to the central computer via communications lines. Teleprocessing systems permitted users to have remote access to the central computer from their terminals in other buildings and even other cities. However, even though access to the computer system was decentralized, all processing was still centralized—that is, performed by a company's one central computer.

In the 1970s businesses began to use minicomputers, which were often at a distance from the central computer. These systems were clearly decentralized because the smaller computers could do some processing on their own, yet some also had access to the central computer. This new setup was labeled **distributed data processing**. It is similar to telepro-

Figure 6-1 Local area network. Although allocated to individual workers, the computers shown here are wired together so that their users can communicate with one another.

cessing, except that it accommodates not only remote *access* but also remote *processing*. A typical application of a distributed data processing system is a business or organization with many locations—perhaps branch offices or retail outlets.

The whole picture of distributed data processing has changed dramatically with the advent of networks of personal computers. A **network** is a computer system that uses communications equipment to connect two or more computers and their resources. Distributed data processing systems are networks. But of particular interest in today's business world are *local area networks (LANs)*, which are designed to share data and resources among several individual computer users in an office or building (Figure 6-1). Networking will be examined in more detail in later sections of this chapter.

The next section previews the components of a communications system, to give you an overview of how these components work together.

➤ Putting Together a Network: A First Look

Even though the components needed to transmit data from one computer to another seem quite basic, the business of putting together a network can be extremely complex. This discussion begins with the initial components and then moves to the list of factors that a network designer needs to consider.

Getting Started

The basic configuration—how the components are put together—is pretty straightforward, but there is a great variety of components to choose from, and the technology is ever changing. Assume that you have some data—a message—to transmit from one place to another. The basic components of a data communications system used to transmit that message are (1) a sending device, (2) a communications link, and (3) a receiving device. Suppose, for example, that you work at a sports store. You might want to send a message to the warehouse to inquire about a Wilson tennis racket, an item you need for a customer. In this case the sending device is your computer terminal at the store, the communications channel is the phone line, and the receiving device is the computer at the warehouse. As you will see later, however, there are many other possibilities.

There is another often-needed component that must be mentioned in this basic configuration, as you can see in Figure 6-2. This component is a modem, which is usually needed to convert computer data to signals that can be carried by the communications channel and vice versa. Modems will be discussed in detail shortly.

Large computer systems may have additional components. At the computer end, data may travel through a communications control unit called a **front-end processor,** which is actually a computer in itself. Its purpose is to relieve the central computer of some of the communications tasks and thus free it for processing applications programs. In addition, a front-end processor usually performs error detection and recovery functions.

1 Sending device

2 Modem

3 Communications link

5 Central processing unit or terminal

4 Modem

Figure 6-2 Communications system components. Data originating from ① a sending device is ② converted by a modem to data that can be carried over ③ a communications link and ④ reconverted by a modem at the receiving end before ⑤ being received by the destination computer.

Network Design Considerations

The task of network design is a complex one, usually requiring the services of a professional specifically trained in that capacity. Although you cannot learn how to design a network in this brief chapter, you can ask some questions that can help you appreciate what the designer must contemplate. Here, in the vernacular, is a list of questions that might occur to a customer who was considering installing a network; these questions also provide hints of what is to come in the chapter.

Question: I've heard that modems send data at different speeds. Does that matter?

Answer: Yes. The faster the better. Generally, faster means lower transmission costs, too. That also goes for synchronous transmission, which permits data to be sent quickly in big clumps.

Question: Am I limited to communicating via the telephone system?

Answer: Not at all. There are all kinds of communications media, with varying degrees of speed, reliability, and cost. There are trade-offs. A lot depends on distance, too—you wouldn't choose a satellite, for example, to send a message to the office next door.

Question: So the geographical area of the network is a factor?

Answer: Definitely. In fact, network types are described by how far-flung they are: *a wide area network* might span the nation or even the globe, but a *local area network* would probably be in an office or possibly just a department. The computers vary, too; generally, smaller networks can be served by small computers.

Question: Can I just cable the computers together and start sending data?

Answer: Not quite. You must decide on some sort of plan. There are various standard ways, called *topologies*, to physically lay out the computers and other elements of a network. Also available are standard software packages, which provide a set of rules, called a *protocol*, that defines how computers communicate.

Question: I know one of the advantages of networking is sharing disk files. Where are the files kept? And can any user get any file?

Answer: The files are usually kept with a particular computer, one that is more powerful than the other computers on the network. Access depends on the network setup. In some arrangements, for example, a

MAKING THE RIGHT CONNECTIONS

THE INFORMATION SUPERHIGHWAY

Just what is the information superhighway? The name is based on an analogy. Everyone understands what a highway is. Before the interstate highway system existed, just about everything you purchased was grown or built locally. It would have been pretty unusual for someone in Florida to be eating apples that were grown in Washington. But once the highway system was in place, in the 1950s, it opened up new markets. It really did not matter where goods were produced; they could be sold anywhere in the country.

Now the same thing is happening for information services. It does not matter where the information is located. A person in Oregon does not have to get on an airplane and fly to Washington, D.C., to gain access to the Library of Congress. The information is available by tapping into the information superhighway. Any information that is available any place can be accessed anywhere in the country if you are on the information superhighway. And, of course, information travels much faster than a truckload of apples from Washington to Florida.

Is the information superhighway really just another name for kinds of

computer services I have heard about, such as America Online? Not quite. Those services are early versions of the information superhighway. The problem is that they must be accessed through a computer, and computers are not in every home. But almost every home in the United States does have a telephone and a television set, and almost everyone knows how to use them. These are the sort of components to consider for the information superhighway.

What will the people connection to the information superhighway actually look like? The truth is that no one really knows. In one approach, industry is making major investments to incorporate the television system as part of the information superhighway. Thus we have the network computer, sometimes offered as a "Web TV." Your television will be like a computer screen, but it won't have a keyboard or anything like that. You will use some sort of

remote control device, sort of like the one you use with your television now, to make selections from menus of services and information. The fact that there might be a computer embedded in that television set is pretty much immaterial to the person who is using the television set.

Others believe that it will be easier to broaden the use of computers and make them easier to use, thus making them more palatable for the general population. This might be more realistic than making computer users out of couch potatoes. But keep in mind that computers are in only about a third of all homes and that not all of them have connectivity.

When will an information superhighway be in place? Despite all the current hype, it will probably take ten years, if not longer, to develop an information superhighway that is as universal as the phone system. However, in the next few years there should be a significant change in government regulation for communications. There will be much greater competition, which will encourage a greater variety of services and also lower prices to consumers.

user might be sent a whole file, but in others the user would be sent only the particular records needed to fulfill a request. The latter is called *client/server,* a popular alternative.

Question: This is getting complicated.

Answer: Yes.

These and other related topics will be presented first, followed by an example of a complex network or, rather, a set of networks. You need not understand all the details, but you will have an appreciation for the effort required to put together a network. Let us see how the components of a communications system work together, beginning with how data is transmitted.

▶ Data Transmission

A terminal or computer produces digital signals, which are simply the presence or absence of an electric pulse. The state of being on or off represents the binary number 1 or 0, respectively. Some communications lines accept digital transmission directly, and the trend in the communications industry is toward digital signals. However, most telephone lines through which these digital signals are sent were originally built for voice transmission, and voice transmission requires analog signals. The next section describes these two types of transmission and then discusses modems, which translate between them.

Digital and Analog Transmission

Digital transmission sends data as distinct pulses, either on or off, in much the same way that data travels through the computer. However, most communications media are not digital. Communications devices such as telephone lines, coaxial cables, and microwave circuits are already in place for voice (analog) transmission. The easiest choice for most users is to piggyback on one of these. Thus, the most common communications devices all use **analog transmission**, a continuous electrical signal in the form of a wave.

Figure 6-3 Analog signals. (a) An analog carrier wave moves up and down in a continuous cycle. (b) The analog waveform can be converted to digital form through amplitude modulation. As shown, the wave height is increased to represent a 1 or left the same to represent a 0. (c) In frequency modulation the amplitude of the wave stays the same but the frequency increases to indicate a 1 or stays the same to indicate a 0.

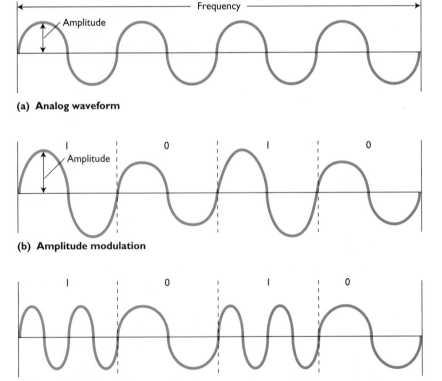

Frequency

Amplitude

(a) Analog waveform

Amplitude

(b) Amplitude modulation

(c) Frequency modulation

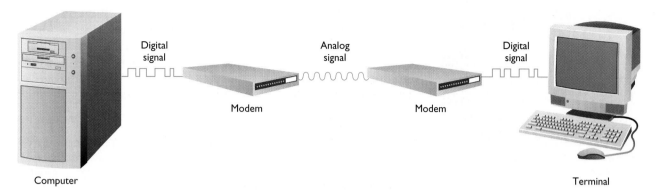

Digital signal   Analog signal   Digital signal

Computer   Modem   Modem   Terminal

Figure 6-4 Modems. Modems convert—modulate—digital data signals to analog signals for sending over communications links, then reverse the process—demodulate—at the other end.

To be sent over analog lines, a digital signal must first be converted to an analog form. It is converted by altering an analog signal, called a **carrier wave**, which has alterable characteristics (Figure 6-3a). One such characteristic is the **amplitude**, or height of the wave, which can be increased to represent the binary number 1 (Figure 6-3b). Another characteristic that can be altered is the **frequency**, or number of times a wave repeats during a specific time interval; frequency can be increased to represent a 1 (Figure 6-3c).

Conversion from digital to analog signals is called **modulation**, and the reverse process—reconstructing the original digital message at the other end of the transmission—is called **demodulation.** (You probably know amplitude and frequency modulation by their abbreviations, AM and FM, the methods used for radio transmission.) An extra device is needed to make the conversions: a modem.

Modems

A **modem** is a device that converts a digital signal to an analog signal and vice versa (Figure 6-4). Modem is short for *mo*dulate/*dem*odulate.

Types of Modems   Modems vary in the way they connect to the telephone line. There are two main types: acoustic coupler modems and direct-connect modems. **Acoustic coupler modems** include a cradle to hold the telephone handset. Most modems today, however, are directly connected to the phone system by a cable that runs from the modem to the wall jack.

A **direct-connect modem** is directly connected to the telephone line by means of a telephone jack. An **external modem** is separate from the computer (Figure 6-5). Its main advantage is that it can be used with a variety of computers. If you buy a new personal computer, for example, you can probably keep the same external modem. For those personal computer users who regard an external modem as one more item taking up desk space, new modem-on-a-chip designs have produced a modem that is so small you will hardly notice it. For a modem that is out of sight—literally—an **internal modem** board can be inserted into the computer by the user; in fact, most personal computers today come with an internal modem as standard equipment. As we will discuss shortly, most modems today also have fax capability.

Figure 6-5 An external modem.

Figure 6-6 A PC card modem. This PC card modem, although only the size of a credit card, packs a lot of power: transmission at 56,000 bytes-per-second. The card, shown here is resting against a laptop keyboard, is slipped into a slot on the side of the keyboard. Look closely at the right end of the modem and you can see the pop-out jack. So, in this order: slide in the card, pop out the jack, and snap in the phone cord.

Table 6-1 Data transfer rates compared	
Rate (bps)	Time to transmit a 20-page single-spaced report
1,200	10 minutes
2,400	5 minutes
9,600	1.25 minutes
14,400	50 seconds
28,800	25 seconds
33,600	30 seconds
56,000	12.5 seconds

Notebook and laptop computers often use modems that come in the form of **PC cards**, originally known as PCMCIA cards, named for the Personal Computer Memory Card International Association. The credit card–sized PC card slides into a slot in the computer (Figure 6-6). A cable runs from the PC card to the phone jack in the wall. PC cards have given portable computers full connectivity capability outside the constraints of an office.

Modem Data Speeds   The World Wide Web has given users an insatiable appetite for fast communications. This, and costs based on time use of services, provide strong incentives to transmit as quickly as possible. The old—some *very* old—standard modem speeds of 1200, 2400, 9600, 14,400, and 28,800 **bits per second (bps)** have now been superseded by modems that transmit 33,600 bps. Most people today measure modem speed by bits per second, but another measure is **baud rate**, the number of times that the signal being used to transmit data changes. At lower modem speeds, each signal change represents one bit being sent, so bits per second and baud are the same. At higher speeds, more than one bit may be sent per signal change, so bits per second will be greater than the baud rate.

Since modems work over the phone lines, which are designed to carry tones of different pitches, the limited number of pitches holds the top modem speed to about 30,000 bps—or so it was thought. Now, using compression techniques, modems can send data at an astonishing 56,000 bps. This speed is limited to one direction, from the Internet to the user, but that fits perfectly with what users usually do—download files from the Internet. Note the transmission time comparisons in Table 6-1.

ISDN

As noted earlier, communication via phone lines requires a modem to convert between the computer's digital signals and the analog signals used by phone lines. But what if another type of line could be used directly for digital transmission? That technology is called **Integrated Services Digital Network**, but it is usually known by its acronym, **ISDN**. The attraction is that an **ISDN adapter** can move data at 128,000 bps, a vast speed improvement over any modem. Another advantage is that an ISDN circuit includes two phone lines, so a user can use one line to connect to the Internet and the other to talk on the phone at the same time. Still, ISDN is not a panacea. Although prices are coming down, initial costs are not inexpensive. You need both the adapter and phone service and possibly even a new line, depending on your current service. Also, ongoing monthly fees may be significant. Furthermore, ISDN is unavailable in some geographic areas.

Asynchronous and Synchronous Transmission

Sending data off to a far destination works only if the receiving device is ready to accept it. But *ready* means more than just available; the receiving device must be able to keep in step with the sending device. Two techniques commonly used to keep the sending and receiving units dancing to the same tune are asynchronous and synchronous transmission.

When **asynchronous transmission** (also called **start/stop transmission**) is used, a special start signal is transmitted at the beginning of each

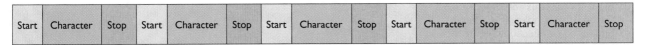

(a) Asynchronous transmission

(b) Synchronous transmission

Figure 6-7 Asynchronous and synchronous transmission. (a) Asynchronous transmission uses start/stop signals surrounding each character. (b) Page width constraints preclude showing the true amount of continuous data that can be transmitted synchronously between start and stop characters. Unlike asynchronous transmission, which has one start/stop set per character, synchronous transmission can send many characters, even many messages, between one start/stop set. Note that synchronous transmission requires a set of error check bits to make sure all characters were received properly.

group of message bits—a group is usually just a single character. Likewise, a stop signal is sent at the end of the group of message bits (Figure 6-7a). When the receiving device gets the start signal, it sets up a timing mechanism to accept the group of message bits.

Synchronous transmission is a little trickier because characters are transmitted together in a continuous stream (Figure 6-7b). There are no call-to-action signals for each character. Instead, the sending and receiving devices are synchronized by having their internal clocks put in time with each other via a bit pattern transmitted at the beginning of the message. Furthermore, error check bits are transmitted at the end of each message to make sure all characters were received properly. Synchronous transmission equipment is more complex and more expensive but, without all the start/stop bits, transmission is much faster.

Simplex, Half-Duplex, and Full-Duplex Transmission

Data transmission can be characterized as simplex, half duplex, or full duplex, depending on permissible directions of traffic flow (Figure 6-8). **Simplex transmission** sends data in one direction only; everyday examples are television broadcasting and arrival/departure screens at airports. **Half-duplex transmission** allows transmission in either direction, but only one way at a time. An analogy is talk on a CB radio. In a bank a teller using half-duplex transmission can send the data about a deposit and, after it is received, the computer can send a confirmation reply. **Full-duplex transmission** allows transmission in both directions at once. An analogy is a telephone conversation in which, good manners aside, both parties can talk at the same time.

Data transmission has been discussed at some length. Now it is time to turn to the actual media that transmit the data.

▶ Communications Links

The cost for linking widely scattered computers is substantial, so it is worthwhile to examine the communications options. Telephone lines are the most convenient communications channel because an extensive

Figure 6-8 Transmission directions.
(a) Seldom-used simplex transmission sends data in one direction only. (b) Half-duplex transmission can send data in either direction, but only one way at a time. (c) Full-duplex transmission can send data in both directions at once.

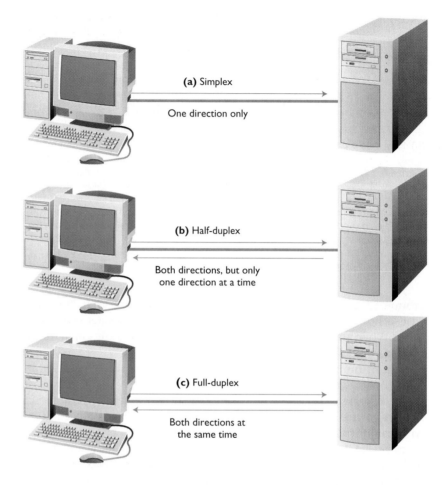

(a) Simplex
One direction only

(b) Half-duplex
Both directions, but only one direction at a time

(c) Full-duplex
Both directions at the same time

system is already in place, but there are many other options. A communications **link** is the physical medium used for transmission.

Types of Communications Links

There are several kinds of communications links. Some may be familiar to you already.

Wire Pairs   One of the most common communications media is the **wire pair,** also known as the **twisted pair.** Wire pairs are wires twisted together to form a cable, which is then insulated (Figure 6-9a). Wire pairs are inexpensive. Further, they are often used because they have already been installed in a building for other purposes or because they are already in use in telephone systems. However, they are susceptible to electrical interference, or noise. **Noise** is anything that causes distortion in the signal when it is received. High-voltage equipment and even the sun can be sources of noise.

Coaxial Cables   Known for sending a strong signal, a **coaxial cable** is a single conductor wire within a shielded enclosure (Figure 6-9b). Bundles of cables can be laid underground or undersea. These cables can transmit data much faster than wire pairs and are less prone to noise.

Fiber Optics   Traditionally, most phone lines transmitted data electrically over wires made of metal, usually copper. These metal wires had to be protected from water and other corrosive substances. **Fiber optics** technology eliminates this requirement (Figure 6-9c and d). Instead of using electricity to send data, fiber optics uses light. The cables are made of glass fibers, each thinner than a human hair, that can guide light beams for miles. Fiber optics transmits data faster than some technologies, yet the materials are substantially lighter and less expensive than wire cables. It can also send and receive a wider assortment of data frequencies at one time. The range of frequencies that a device can handle is known as its **bandwidth;** bandwidth is a measure of the capacity of the link. The broad bandwidth of fiber optics translates into promising multimedia possibilities, since fiber optics is well suited for handling all types of data—voice, pictures, music, and video—at the same time.

Microwave Transmission   Another popular medium is **microwave transmission,** which uses what is called line-of-sight transmission of data signals through the atmosphere (Figure 6-10a). Since these signals cannot bend to follow the curvature of the earth, relay stations—often antennas in high places such as the tops of mountains and buildings—are positioned at points approximately 30 miles apart to continue the transmission. Microwave transmission offers speed, cost-effectiveness, and ease of implementation. Unfortunately, in major metropolitan areas tall buildings may interfere with microwave transmission.

Satellite Transmission   The basic components of **satellite transmission** are **earth stations,** which send and receive signals, and a satellite component called a transponder. The **transponder** receives the transmission from an earth station, amplifies the signal, changes the frequency, and retransmits the data to a receiving earth station (Figure 6-10b). (The frequency is changed so that the weaker incoming signals will not be impaired by the stronger outgoing signals.) This entire process takes only a few seconds.

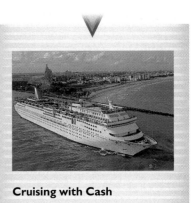

Cruising with Cash

Customers on cruises have often found themselves isolated from land in more ways than one. A distinct handicap for tourists cruising the Caribbean was lack of access to cash. Although vacationers can run up a tab for most services and purchases, certain items, such as day trips and tips for the crew, require cash.

Carnival Cruise Lines was the first to address the problem. Each ship provides on-board automated teller machines, which bounce data off a satellite to a bank in Fort Lauderdale, Florida. Now cash is just as available aboard ship as it is on land.

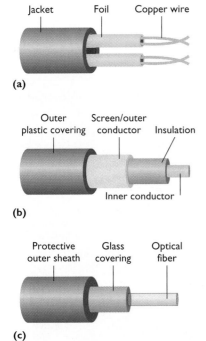

(a)

(b)

(c)

(d)

Figure 6-9 Communications links. (a) Wire pairs are pairs of wires twisted together to form a cable, which is then insulated. (b) A coaxial cable is a single conductor wire surrounded by insulation. (c) Fiber optics consists of hair-like glass fibers that carry voice, television, and data signals. (d) This photo shows light emitted from a handful of fiber optic cables.

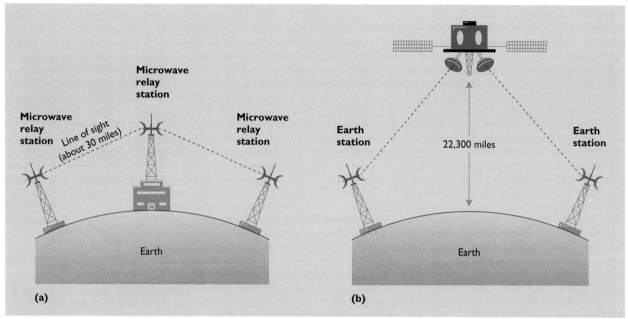

Figure 6-10 Microwave and satellite transmission. (a) To relay microwave signals, dish-shaped antennas such as these are often located atop buildings, towers, and mountains. Microwave signals can follow a line-of-sight path only, so stations must relay this signal at regular intervals to avoid interference from the curvature of the earth. (b) In satellite transmission, a satellite acts as a relay station and can transmit data signals from one earth station to another. A signal is sent from an earth station to the relay satellite, which changes the signal frequency before transmitting it to the next earth station.

If a signal must travel thousands of miles, satellites are usually part of the link. A message being sent around the world probably travels by cable or some other physical link only as far as the nearest satellite earth transmission station (Figure 6-11). From there it is beamed to a satellite, which sends it back to earth to another transmission station near the data destination. Communications satellites are launched into space, where they are suspended about 22,300 miles above the earth. Why 22,300 miles? That is where satellites reach geosynchronous orbit—the orbit that allows them to remain positioned over the same spot on the earth.

Mixing and Matching   A network system is not limited to one kind of link and, in fact, often works in various combinations, especially over long distances. An office worker who needs data from a company com-

Figure 6-11 A Satellite dish. A satellite dish is not usually the prettiest site on the horizon, but a photographer has taken this shot of a dish with an exaggerating "fish eye" lens, emphasizing the relationship of the dish with the signals that come from the satellite in space.

puter on the opposite coast will most likely use wire pairs in the phone lines, followed by microwave and satellite transmission (Figure 6-12). Astonishingly, the trip across the country and back, with a brief stop to pick up the data, may take only seconds.

Protocols

A **protocol** is a set of rules for the exchange of data between a terminal and a computer or between two computers. A protocol is embedded in the network software. Think of protocol as a sort of pre-communication to make sure everything is in order before a message or data is sent. Protocols are handled by software related to the network, so that users need only worry about their own data.

Protocol Communications   Two devices must be able to ask each other questions (Are you ready to receive a message? Did you get my last message? Is there trouble at your end?) and to keep each other informed (I am sending data now). In addition, the two devices must agree on how data is to be transferred, including data transmission speed and duplex setting. But this must be done in a formal way. When communi-

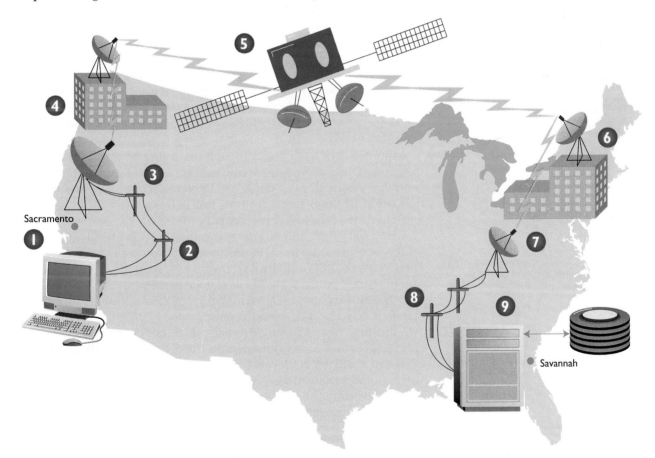

Figure 6-12 A variety of communications links. Say an accountant working in the Sacramento office needs certain tax records from the headquarters computer files in Savannah. One possibility for the route of the user request and the response is as follows. ① The accountant makes the request for the records, which ② goes out over the local phone system to ③ a nearby microwave station, which transmits the request to ④ the nearest earth satellite transmission station, where ⑤ it is relayed to a satellite in space, which relays it back to earth ⑥ to an earth satellite station near Savannah, where it is sent to ⑦ a microwave station and then ⑧ via the phone lines to ⑨ the headquarters computer. Once the tax records are retrieved from the Savannah computer files, the whole process is reversed as the requested records are sent back to Sacramento.

Directly from the Satellite

Can't wait for the evening news? Snatch the news from the sky as it happens—and show it right on your computer screen. You do not even need a modem.

The pyramid-shaped News-Catcher is a wireless device that receives signals from a satellite and passes them on to your computer via a cable from the News-Catcher to one of the serial port plugs on the back of your computer. Once you have set up the accompanying software, you may select the types of news you wish to receive, such as headline news, business news, weather reports, sports scores, and more.

NewsCatcher starts itself whenever you turn on your computer and remains at the ready all day, showing a narrow band across the top of your screen. You may choose which subject windows to show on the screen and dispense with them at your pleasure. The display shown here displays Headline News in the upper right corner of the screen. News items, constantly updated, scroll by, independently of other action on the screen.

cation is desired among computers from different vendors (or even different models from the same vendor), the software development can be a nightmare because different vendors use different protocols. Standards would help.

Setting Standards   Standards are important in the computer industry; it saves money if users can all coordinate effectively. Nowhere is this more obvious than in data communications systems, where many components must "come together." But it is hard to get people to agree to a standard.

Communications standards exist, however, and are constantly evolving and being updated for new communications forms. Standards provide a framework for how data is transmitted. Perhaps the most important protocol is the one that makes Internet universality possible. Called **Transmission Control Protocol/Internet Protocol (TCP/IP)**, this protocol permits any computer at all to communicate with the Internet. This is rather like everyone in the world speaking one language.

▶ Network Topologies

As noted earlier, a network is a computer system that uses communications equipment to connect computers. They can be connected in different ways. The physical layout of a network is called a **topology**. There are three common topologies: star, ring, and bus networks. In a network topology, a component is called a **node**, which is usually a computer on a network. (The term *node* is also used to refer to any device connected to a network, including the server, computers, and peripheral devices such as printers.)

A **star network** has a hub computer that is responsible for managing the network (Figure 6-13a). All messages are routed through the central computer, which acts as a traffic cop to prevent collisions. Any connection failure between a node and the hub will not affect the overall system. However, if the hub computer fails, the network fails.

A **ring network** links all nodes together in a circular chain (Figure 6-13b). Data messages travel in only one direction around the ring. Any data that passes by is examined by the node to see if it is the addressee; if not, the data is passed on to the next node in the ring. Since data travels in only one direction, there is no danger of data collision. However, if one node fails, the entire network fails.

A **bus network** has a single line to which all the network nodes are attached (Figure 6-13c). Computers on the network transmit data in the hope that it will not collide with data transmitted by other nodes; if this happens, the sending node simply tries again. Nodes can be attached to or detached from the network without affecting the network. Furthermore, if one node fails, it does not affect the rest of the network.

▶ Wide Area Networks

There are different kinds of networks. It is appropriate to begin with the geographically largest, a wide area network.

A **wide area network (WAN)** is a network of geographically distant computers and terminals. A network that spans a large city is sometimes

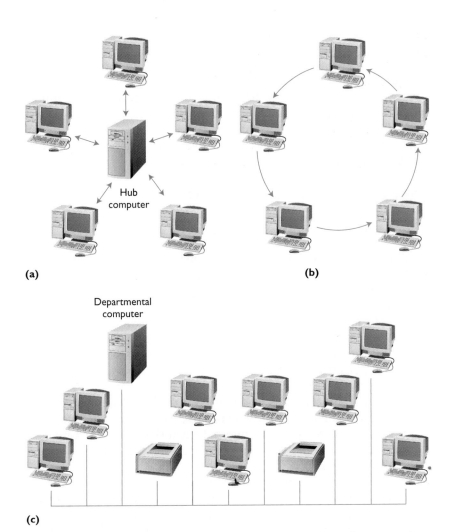

(a)   (b)

(c)

Figure 6-13 Topologies. (a) The star network topology has a central computer that runs the network. (b) The ring network topology connects computers in a circular fashion. (c) The bus network topology connects all nodes in a line and can preserve the network if one computer fails.

called a **metropolitan area network**, or **MAN.** In business, a personal computer sending data any significant distance is probably sending it to a minicomputer or mainframe computer. Since these larger computers are designed to be accessed by terminals, a personal computer can communicate with a minicomputer or mainframe only if the personal computer emulates, or imitates, a terminal. This is accomplished by using **terminal emulation software** on the personal computer. The larger computer then considers the personal computer or workstation as just another user input/output communications device—a terminal.

When smaller computers are connected to larger computers, the result is sometimes referred to as a **micro-to-mainframe** link. The larger computer to which the terminal or personal computer is attached is called the **host computer.** If a personal computer is being used as a terminal, **file transfer software** permits users to download data files from the host or upload data files to the host. To **download** a file means to retrieve it from another computer and to send it to the computer of the user who requested the file. To **upload** a file, a user sends a file to another computer.

▶ Local Area Networks

A **local area network (LAN)** is a collection of computers, usually personal computers, that share hardware, software, and data. In simple terms, LANs hook personal computers together through communications media so that each personal computer can share the resources of the others. As the name implies, LANs cover short distances, usually one office or building or a group of buildings that are close together.

Local Area Network Components

LANs do not use the telephone network. Networks that are LANs are made up of a standard set of components.

- All networks need some system for interconnection. In some LANs the nodes are connected by a shared **network cable**. Low-cost LANs are connected with twisted wire pairs, but many LANs use coaxial cable or fiber optic cable, which may be more expensive but faster. Some local area networks, however, are **wireless**, using infrared or radio wave transmissions instead of cables. Wireless networks are easy to set up and reconfigure, since there are no cables to connect or disconnect, but they have slower transmission rates and limit the distance between nodes.
- A **network interface card**, sometimes called a **NIC**, connects each computer to the wiring in the network. A NIC is a circuit board that fits in one of the computer's internal expansion slots. The card contains circuitry that handles sending, receiving, and error checking of transmitted data.
- Similar networks can be connected by a **bridge**, a hardware/software combination that recognizes the messages on a network and passes on those addressed to nodes in other networks. For example, a fabric designer whose computer is part of a department LAN for a textile manufacturer could send cost data, via a bridge, to someone in the accounting department whose computer is part of another company LAN, one used for financial matters. It makes sense for each department, design and finance, to maintain separate networks because their interdepartmental communication is only occasional. A **router** is a special computer that directs communications traffic when several networks are connected together. If traffic is clogged on one path, the router can determine an alternate path. More recently, now that many networks have adopted the Internet protocol (IP), routers are being replaced with **IP switches**, which are less expensive and, since no translation is needed, faster than routers.
- A **gateway** is a collection of hardware and software resources that lets a node communicate with a computer on another dissimilar network. One of the main tasks of a gateway is protocol conversion. A gateway, for example, could connect an attorney on a local area network to a legal service offered through a wide area network.

Now let us move on to the types of local area networks. Two ways to organize the resources of a LAN are client/server and peer-to-peer.

Client/Server Networks

A **client/server** arrangement involves a **server,** the computer that controls the network. In particular, a server has hard disks holding shared files and often has the highest-quality printer, another resource to be shared (Figure 6-14). The clients are all the other computers on the network. Under the client/server arrangement, processing is usually done by the server, and only the results are sent to the client. Sometimes the server and the client computer share processing. For example, a server, upon request from the client, could search a database of cars in the state of Maryland and come up with a list of all Jeep Cherokees. This data could be passed on to the client computer, which could process the data further, perhaps looking for certain equipment or license plate letters. This method can be contrasted with a **file server** relationship, in which the server transmits the entire file to the client, which does all its own processing. Using the Jeep example, the entire car file would be sent to the client, instead of just the extracted Jeep Cherokee records (Figure 6-15).

Client/server has attracted a lot of attention because a well-designed system reduces the volume of data traffic on the network and allows faster response for each client computer. Also, since the server does most of the heavy work, less-expensive computers can be used as nodes.

Peer-to-Peer Networks

All computers in a **peer-to-peer** arrangement have equal status; no one computer is in control. With all files and peripheral devices distributed across several computers, users share one another's data and devices as needed. An example might involve a corporate building in which marketing wants its files kept on its own computer, public relations wants its files kept on its own computer, personnel wants its files kept on its own computer, and so on; all can still gain access to the other's files when needed. The main disadvantage is lack of speed—peer-to-peer networks slow down under heavy use. Many networks are hybrids, containing elements of both client/server and peer-to-peer arrangements.

Local Area Network Protocols

As already noted, networks must have a set of rules—protocols—that are used to access the network and send data. Recall that a protocol is embedded in the network software. The two most common network protocols for LANs are Ethernet and the Token Ring network.

Ethernet, the network protocol that dominates the industry, uses a high-speed network cable. Ethernet uses a bus topology and is inexpensive and relatively simple to set up. Since all the computers in a LAN use the same cable to transmit and receive data, they must follow a set of rules about when to communicate; otherwise, two or more computers could transmit at the same time, causing garbled or lost messages. Operating much like a party line, before transmitting data a computer "listens" to find out if the cable is in use. If the cable is in use, the computer

Figure 6-14 Server and peripheral hardware. In this network for a clinic with seven doctors, the daily appointment records for patients are kept on the hard disk associated with the server. Workers who, using their own computers, deal with accounting, insurance, and patient records can access the daily appointment file to update their own files.

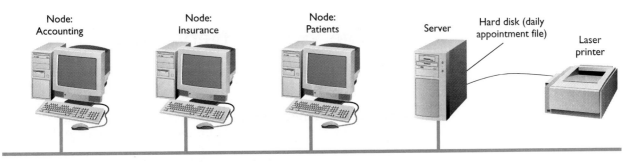

Node: Accounting   Node: Insurance   Node: Patients   Server   Hard disk (daily appointment file)   Laser printer

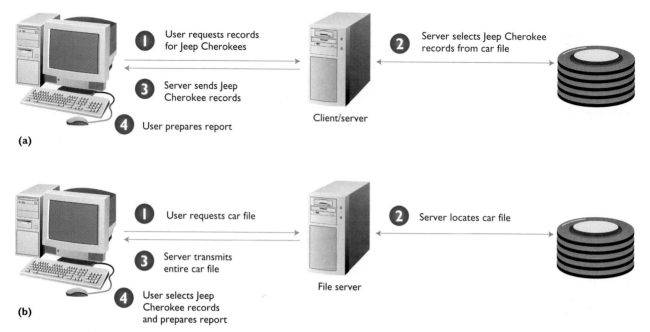

Figure 6-15 Client/server contrasted with file server. (a) In a client/server relationship, ① a user makes a request to the server to select only Jeep Cherokee records from a state car file; ② the server does so and ③ sends the records back to the user, who ④ uses those specific records to prepare a report. (b) In a file server relationship, ① a user asks for the entire state car file, which ② the server locates and then ③ transmits to the user, who then ④ selects the Jeep Cherokee records and prepares a report. The client/server setup places most of the processing burden on the more powerful server and also significantly reduces the amount of data being transferred between server and user.

must wait. When the cable is free from other transmissions, the computer can begin transmitting immediately. This transmission method is called by the fancy name of **carrier sense multiple access with collision detection**, or **CSMA/CD**.

If by chance two computers transmit data at the same time, the messages collide. When a **collision** occurs, a special message, lasting a fraction of a second, is sent out over the network to indicate that it is jammed. Each computer stops transmitting, waits a random period of time, and then transmits again. Since the wait period for each computer is random, it is unlikely that they will begin transmitting at the same time again. This all happens without the user being aware of it.

A **Token Ring network**, which is closely associated with IBM, works on the concept of a ring network topology, using a token—a kind of electronic signal. The method of controlling access to the shared network cable is called **token passing**. The idea is similar to the New York City subway: If you want to ride—transmit data—you must have a token. However, unlike the subway, there is only one token available. The token circulates from computer to computer along the ring-shaped LAN.

Only one token is available on the network. When a computer on the network wishes to transmit, it first captures the token; only then can it transmit data. When the computer has sent its message, it releases the token back to the network. Since only one token is circulating around the network, only one device is able to access the network at a time.

▶ The Work of Networking

Think of the millions of telephones installed throughout the world; theoretically, you can call any one of them. Further, every one of these phones has the potential to be part of a networking system. Although other communications media have been discussed, it is still the telephone that is the basis for action for the user at home or in the office.

Revolutionary changes are in full swing in both places, but particularly in the office.

The use of automation in the office is as varied as the offices themselves. As a general definition, however, **office automation** is the use of technology to help people do their jobs better and faster. Much automated office innovation is based on communications technology. This section begins with several important office technology topics—electronic mail, voice mail, facsimile technology, groupware, teleconferencing, and electronic data interchange.

Electronic Mail

Electronic mail, or **e-mail**, is the process of sending messages directly from one computer to another. A user can send data to a colleague downstairs, a message across town to that person who is never available for phone calls, a query to the headquarters office in Switzerland, and even memos simultaneously to regional sales managers in Chicago, Raleigh, and San Antonio.

Electronic mail works, of course, only if the intended receiver has a computer to receive the message. There are several electronic mail options. One option is for a user to enlist a third-party service bureau that provides electronic mail service for its customers. Another option is to use a public data network such as the Internet.

Electronic mail users shower it with praise. It crosses time zones, can reach many people with the same message, reduces the paper flood, and does not interrupt meetings the way a ringing phone does.

Voice Mail

Another method that releases workers from the tyranny of the telephone is **voice mail.** Here is how voice mail typically works from the point of view of the user. If the person being called does not answer, the caller is given instructions to dictate a message to the system. The voice mail computer system stores the message in the recipient's "voice mailbox." Later, when the recipient dials the mailbox, the system delivers the message.

Is voice mail just a fancy answering machine? They serve similar purposes, but they do not use the same storage techniques. A voice mail system translates the words of a message into digital impulses, which it then stores on disk, just as it does any other data. Later, the stored message is reconverted to audio form (Figure 6-16). Voice mail may seem like a spoken version of electronic mail. There is one big difference between electronic mail and voice mail, however. To use electronic mail, you and the mail recipient must have computers and be able to use them. In contrast, telephones are everywhere, and everyone already knows how to use them.

Facsimile Technology

Operating something like a copy machine connected to a telephone, **facsimile technology** uses computer technology and communications links to send quality graphics, charts, text, and even signatures almost anywhere in the world. The drawing—or whatever—is placed in the facsimile machine at one end, where it is digitized (Figure 6-17). Those digits are transmitted across the miles and then reassembled at the other

E-mail Emotions

People communicate emotions to one another by facial expressions in person or by tone of voice over the phone. Over e-mail, some people compensate by using combinations of punctuation marks called smileys. Notice that you must tilt your head to the left to see what they are. Some samples:

: –)	Happy, smiling
; –)	Winking
>:-(	Frowning
:'–(	Crying
O:-)	Angelic
{gms}	Hug, with person's initials in center
—<—@	A rose

Keep in mind that not everyone appreciates smileys, especially if they are overused.

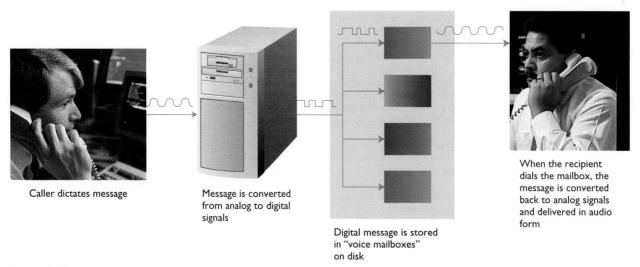

Caller dictates message

Message is converted from analog to digital signals

Digital message is stored in "voice mailboxes" on disk

When the recipient dials the mailbox, the message is converted back to analog signals and delivered in audio form

Figure 6-16 A voice mail system. The caller's message is stored in the recipient's voice mailbox on disk. Later, the recipient can check his mailbox to get the message.

Figure 6-17 Faxing it. This facsimile machine can send and receive text, drawings, and graphs long-distance.

end to form a nearly identical version of the original picture. All this takes only minutes—or less. Facsimile is not only faster than overnight delivery services, it is less expensive. Facsimile is abbreviated **fax**, as in "I sent a fax to the Chicago office."

Personal computer users can send and receive faxes directly by means of a **fax modem**, which also performs the usual modem functions. A user can send computer-generated text and graphics as a fax. When a fax comes in, it can be reviewed on the computer screen and printed out. The only missing ingredient in this scheme is paper; if the document to be sent is available only on paper, it must be scanned into the computer first or else be sent using a separate fax machine.

Groupware

As we noted in Chapter 2, **groupware** is any kind of software that lets a group of people share things or track things together. The data the workers share is in a database on disk. But the key to their being able to share that data is their access to it via communications lines. We mention groupware in this chapter only to emphasize the role of communications systems in letting people, who may be in far-flung locations, work together.

Teleconferencing

An office automation development with cost-saving potential is **teleconferencing**, a method of using technology to bring people and ideas together despite geographic barriers (Figure 6-18). There are several varieties of teleconferencing, but most common today is **videoconferencing**, whose components usually include a large screen, video cameras that can send live pictures, and an online computer system to record communication among participants. Although this setup is expensive to rent and even more expensive to own, the costs seem trivial when compared to travel expenses—airfare, lodging, meals—for in-person meetings.

Videoconferencing has some drawbacks. Some people are uncomfortable about their appearance on camera. A more serious fear is that the loss of personal contact will detract from some business functions, especially those related to sales or negotiations.

Figure 6-18 A videoconferencing system. Geographically distant groups can hold a meeting with the help of videoconferencing. A camera transmits images of local participants for the benefit of distant viewers.

Electronic Data Interchange

Businesses use a great deal of paper in transmitting orders. One method devised to cut down on paperwork is **electronic data interchange (EDI)**. EDI is a series of standard formats that allow businesses to transmit invoices, purchase orders, and the like electronically. In addition to eliminating paper-based ordering forms, EDI can help to eliminate errors in transmitting orders that result from transcription mistakes made by people. Since EDI orders go directly from one computer to another, the tedious process of filling out a form at one end and then keying it into the computer at the other end is eliminated.

Many firms use EDI to reduce paperwork and personnel costs. A study done by a cookie company found that processing a typical paper-based purchase order cost about $70, but processing the same order via EDI cost less than a dollar. Some large firms, especially discounters such as Wal-Mart, require their suppliers to adopt EDI and, in fact, have direct computer hookups with their suppliers.

Electronic Fund Transfers: Instant Banking

Using **electronic fund transfers (EFTs)**, people can pay for goods and services by having funds transferred from various accounts electronically, using computer technology. One of the most visible manifestations of EFT is the ATM—the **automated teller machine** that people use to obtain cash quickly (Figure 6-19). A high-volume EFT application is the disbursement of millions of Social Security payments by the government directly into the recipients' checking accounts. Unlike those sent via U.S. mail, no such payment has ever been lost.

Electronic funds transfers are not limited to transfers between institutions and individuals. Banks and other financial institutions transfer funds among themselves electronically, on both the national and international level.

The Check Is Not in the Mail

As of January 1, 1999, all payments from the federal government, including Social Security checks, are made directly to bank accounts, using electronic funds transfers.

Since it costs approximately 42¢ to issue and mail a paper check but only 2¢ to process an electronic payment, the government saves many millions of dollars every year. There are advantages to recipients too: the payments arrive exactly on time and, unlike paper checks, cannot be lost in the mail.

Figure 6-19 An automated teller machine. Users can obtain bank services 24 hours a day through ATMs.

Computer Commuting

A logical outcome of computer networks is **telecommuting**, the substitution of communications and computers for the commute to work (Figure 6-20). That is, a telecommuter works at home on a personal computer and probably uses the computer to communicate with office colleagues or customers. In fact, some telecommuters are able to link directly to the company's network. Although the original idea was that people would work at home all the time, telecommuting has evolved into a mixed activity. That is, many telecommuters stay home two or three days a week and come into the office the other days. Time in the office permits the needed face-to-face communication with fellow workers and also provides a sense of participation and continuity.

The ideal telecommuting candidate is one who needs little personal contact with colleagues, has access to a quiet work space at home, is able to work with little supervision, and reports to a supervisor who manages by results rather than by surveillance or a time clock. Telecommuting was once considered a privilege granted to certain employees, but now employers often embrace telecommuting because they see advantages such as enhanced worker productivity, the ability to retain valuable employees, and increased employee loyalty. Although only a half mil-

Figure 6-20 Telecommuters. (a) This financial advisor has all the equipment he needs to work at home. (b) Using CAD/CAM software, an architect can work at home. (c) This telecommuter, a designer, works out of her home four days a week. (d) This insurance adjuster is in the office one day a week, in the field two days a week, and at home on the computer two days a week.

(a)

(b)

(c)

(d)

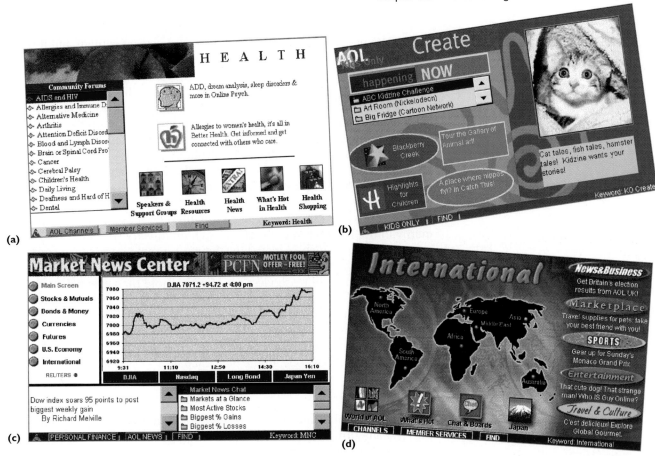

Figure 6-21 Online services. Computer users can use their personal computers to get information on a variety of topics through online services such as America Online. Shown here are (a) the opening menu for health topics, (b) a colorful screen to encourage kid creativity, (c) a snapshot of the financial market news, and (d) a clickable international screen.

lion workers telecommuted in 1992, almost eight million are forecasted to do so by the year 2002. The numbers surely will continue to rise.

Potential benefits of telecommuting include savings in fuel costs and commuting time, more flexible hours, and greater availability to family. Some people also appreciate not having to dress in formal work attire. There are, of course, some problems. A common complaint is that at-home employees miss the interaction with co-workers at the office, and worry about losing the game of office politics. At the head of the list, however, is this, from the telecommuters themselves: They work too much!

Online Services

Some companies offer a wide range of services. Users can connect their personal computers to commercial, consumer-oriented communications systems via telephone lines. These services, formally called **information utilities**, or, more popularly, **online services**, are widely used by both home and business customers. Popular online services include America Online and the Microsoft Network. You need only set up the software, provided free by the service, and answer questions about how you will arrange to pay (probably a credit card).

These online services each offer myriad choices, including news, weather, shopping, games, educational materials, electronic mail, forums, financial information, and software product support (Figure 6-21). America Online offers a superior, easy-to-use graphical environment, with mouse-controlled icons and overlaid screen windows. The Microsoft Network is the newest of the two and thus the slimmest on content, but it is well organized and has an excellent Internet browser.

Charges for online services vary. Most offer the software free. Often package deals are available. One possibility is a monthly fee that includes all basic services and a certain amount of connection time, with extra charges for extra time. For a higher monthly fee, a user can purchase unlimited access. People who live in densely populated areas can connect to the service through a local phone number, avoiding extra phone charges. However, people in remote areas may have to access the service through a long-distance phone number, a disadvantage that can generate a shocking phone bill for the uninitiated.

Online services also offer access to the Internet. A user interested primarily in the Internet might prefer to sign up directly with an Internet service provider, which, as noted in Chapter 1, provides the server computer and the software needed to connect to the Internet. Faced with this competition, online services are offering more than ever before. In addition to an easy-to-use structure, online services have expanded their services, enhanced their splashy graphics, and added entertainment activities such as celebrity appearances. We will address the prospect of a direct link to an Internet service provider, and provide some information on how to choose one, in the next chapter.

The Internet

The Internet, as indicated earlier in this book, is not just another online activity. The other topics discussed in this section pale in comparison (Figure 6-22). The Internet is considered by many to be the defining technology of the end of this century, and it may well hold that status into the next century. Since we are devoting a separate chapter and features exclusively to the Internet, we mention it here only to make the list complete.

(b)

(a)

Figure 6-22 Internet screens. (a) This serious-looking site is for Price Waterhouse, a serious financial company. All the words on the left are links to be clicked. In addition, the page allows selections—by industry, service, and so on—using a clickable arrow that will cause choices to be displayed. (b) Royal Caribbean operates cruise ships. Almost any word or picture you see on its opening page is a link that can be clicked to be transported to another part of the company's site.

NEW DIRECTIONS

HOTELING

Many companies do not talk about telecommuting or "work at home" programs anymore. Instead, they talk about working "anywhere, any time." Laptop computers, fax machines, cellular phones, networks, e-mail, and voice mail are making a portable workforce a way of doing business. But what happens when those same mobile workers come into the office for a day? Or two. Perhaps only a few days a month. Do their own offices, complete with family pictures, await them? Not if the company has adopted a concept called *hoteling*. And no, it will not look like the hotel shown here.

The company supplies a number of empty "hotel offices" that any telecommuter or mobile worker can use. Each such office has a custom-made desk, whose

drawers are replaceable, and a computer hooked up to the network. Furthermore, each worker has his or her own "pedestal," a cart on wheels that contains file drawers that slide into the desk and a separate filing cabinet, all containing the worker's own files. A worker need only call ahead for a "reservation" for a day or week. That worker's pedestal will be rolled from a storage room into a spare hotel office and its contents quickly set up before the worker arrives. The worker can even dig in the desk drawer and pull out family photos for the day.

▶ The Complexity of Networks

Networks can be designed in an amazing variety of ways, from a simple in-office group of three personal computers connected to a shared printer to a global spread including thousands of personal computers, minicomputers, and mainframes. The latter, of course, would not be a single network but, instead, a collection of connected networks.

You have already glimpsed the complexity of networks. Review Figure 6-12, for example, showing the variety of communications links that can be used in a nation-spanning network. Now let us consider a set of networks for a toy manufacturer (Figure 6-23).

The toy company has a bus local area network for the marketing department, consisting of six personal computers, a modem used by outside field representatives to call in for price data, and a server with a shared laser printer and shared marketing program and data files. The LAN for the design department, also a bus network, consists of three personal computers and a server with shared printer and shared files. Both LANs use the Ethernet protocol and have client/server relationships. The design department sometimes sends its in-progress work to the marketing representatives for their evaluation; similarly, the marketing department sends new ideas from the field to the design department. The two departments communicate, one LAN to another, via a bridge. It makes sense to have two separate LANs, rather than one big LAN, because the two departments need to communicate with each other only occasionally.

In addition to communicating with each other, users on each LAN, both marketing and design, occasionally need to communicate with the mainframe computer, which can be accessed through a gateway. All com-

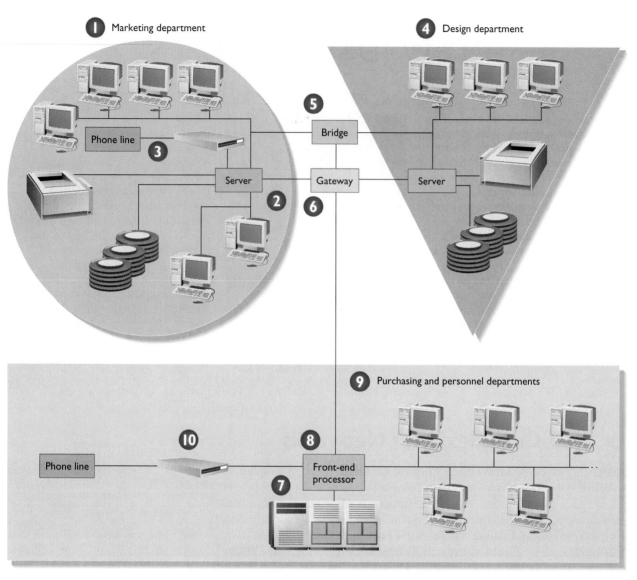

Figure 6-23 Example of a network. In this set of networks for a toy manufacturer, ① the marketing department has a bus local area network whose six personal computers use a shared printer. Both program and data files are stored with the ② server. Note ③ the modem that accepts outside inquiries from field representatives. ④ The design department, with just three personal computers, has a similar LAN. The two LANs can communicate via ⑤ a bridge. Either LAN, via ⑥ a gateway, can access ⑦ the mainframe computer, which uses ⑧ a front-end processor to handle communications. Users in ⑨ the purchasing and personnel departments have terminals attached directly to the mainframe computer. The mainframe computer also has ⑩ a modem that connects to the telephone lines and then, via satellite, to the mainframe at the headquarters office in another state.

munications for the mainframe are handled by the front-end processor. Users in the purchasing, administrative, and personnel departments have terminals connected directly to the mainframe computer. The mainframe also has a modem that connects to telephone lines and then, via satellite, to the mainframe computer at corporate headquarters in another state.

Network factors that add to complexity but are not specifically addressed in Figure 6-23 include the electronic data interchange setups

Getting Practical

SHOULD YOU CHOOSE AN ONLINE SERVICE OR AN INTERNET SERVICE PROVIDER?

Online services such as America Online offer a variety of services. First and foremost is e-mail, which is, of course, available from both online services and ISPs. But online services go significantly beyond e-mail, providing content on every conceivable topic, all in a colorful, clickable environment that a child could use.

In fact, children's needs are a major staple of online services, from games to cartoons to encyclopedias. There is even more content for adults: stock market news, shopping malls, and every sort of information about travel reservations, computers, health, hobbies, sports, and music.

Some people are attracted to the social interaction of online services, which feature buddy lists, real-time trivia games, chat rooms, and much more. In addition to all this, online services also provide their own browsers and offer access to the Internet. So why go anywhere else?

Scenario	Best choice
You are new to data communications	Online service
Most of your friends and colleagues use the same online service	Online service
People of different ages and skill levels will use your computer to go online	Online service
You want to control what your children see online	Online service
You want the most Internet hours for the least money	Internet service provider
You want a choice of browsers	Internet service provider
You plan to use an ISDN line	Internet service provider
You want to publish a Web home page	Internet service provider

For some people, an Internet service provider is a better choice. These people are usually less interested in the managed resources of an online service and more interested in a free-wheeling Internet experience that they can control themselves. They also may prefer a different browser. These are usually experienced folks who may also be interested in writing their own web pages.

Consider the factors in the attached table in your decision. However, keep in mind that no decision is irrevocable. You could, as many people do, start out with an online service and later change to an Internet service provider.

---

between the toy manufacturer's purchasing department and seven of its major customers, the availability of electronic mail throughout the networks, and the fact that—via a modem to an outside line—individual employees can access the Internet.

★ ★ ★ ★

The near future in data communications is not difficult to see. The demand for services is just beginning to swell. Electronic mail already pervades the office and the campus and is beginning to reach the home. Expect instant access to all manner of information from a variety of convenient locations. Prepare to become blasé about communications services available in your own home and everywhere you go.

CHAPTER REVIEW

Summary and Key Terms

- **Data communications systems** are computer systems that transmit data over communications lines, such as telephone lines or cables.
- **Centralized data processing** places all processing, hardware, and software in one central location.
- In **teleprocessing** systems, terminals at various locations are connected by communications lines to the central computer that does the processing.
- Businesses with many locations or offices often use **distributed data processing**, which allows both remote access and remote processing. Processing can be done by the central computer and the other computers that are hooked up to it.
- A **network** is a computer system that uses communications equipment to connect two or more computers and their resources.
- The basic components of a data communications system are a sending device, a communications link, and a receiving device.
- Data may travel to a large computer through a communications control unit called a **front-end processor,** which is actually a computer in itself. Its purpose is to relieve the central computer of some communications tasks.
- **Digital transmission** sends data as distinct on or off pulses. **Analog transmission** uses a continuous electric signal in a **carrier wave** having a particular **amplitude** and **frequency.**
- Computers produce digital signals, but most types of communications equipment use analog signals. Therefore, transmission of computer data involves altering the analog signal, or carrier wave. Digital signals are converted to analog signals by **modulation** (change) of a characteristic, such as the amplitude of the carrier wave. **Demodulation** is the reverse process; both processes are performed by a device called a **modem.**
- **Acoustic coupler modems** include a cradle to hold the telephone handset. A **direct-connect modem** is connected directly to the telephone line by means of a telephone jack. An **external modem** is not built into the computer and can therefore be used with a variety of computers. An **internal modem** is on a board that fits inside a personal computer. Notebook and laptop computers often use a **PC card** modem that slides into a slot in the computer.
- Modem speeds are usually measured in **bits per second (bps)**, but another measure is **baud rate**, the number of times that the signal being used to transmit data changes.
- An **ISDN adapter**, based on **Integrated Services Digital Network (ISDN)**, can move data at 128,000 bps, a vast improvement over any modem.
- Two common methods of coordinating the sending and receiving units are **asynchronous transmission** and **synchronous transmission**. The asynchronous, or **start/stop,** method keeps the units in step by including special signals at the beginning and end of each group of message bits—a group is usually a character. In synchronous transmission the internal clocks of the units are put in time with each other at the beginning of the transmission, and the characters are transmitted in a continuous stream.
- **Simplex transmission** allows data to move in only one direction (either sending or receiving). **Half-duplex transmission** allows data to move in either direction but only one way at a time. With **full-duplex transmission**, data can be sent and received at the same time.
- A communications **link** is the physical medium used for data transmission. Common communications links include **wire pairs** (or **twisted pairs**), **coaxial cables, fiber**

optics, **microwave transmission**, and **satellite transmission.** In satellite transmission, which uses **earth stations** to send and receive signals, a **transponder** ensures that the stronger outgoing signals do not interfere with the weaker incoming ones. **Noise** is anything that causes distortion in the received signal. **Bandwidth** refers to the number of frequencies that can fit on one link at the same time, or the capacity of the link.

- A **protocol** is a set of rules for exchanging data between a terminal and a computer or between two computers. The protocol that makes Internet universality possible is **Transmission Control Protocol/Internet Protocol (TCP/IP),** which permits any computer at all to communicate with the Internet.

- The physical layout of a local area network is called a **topology.** A **node** usually refers to a computer on a network. (The term *node* is also used to refer to any device connected to a network, including the server, computers, and peripheral devices such as printers.) A **star network** has a central computer, the hub, that is responsible for managing the network. A **ring network** links all nodes together in a circular manner. A **bus network** has a single line, to which all the network nodes and peripheral devices are attached.

- Computers that are connected so that they can communicate among themselves are said to form a network. A **wide area network (WAN)** is a network of geographically distant computers and terminals. A network that spans a large city is sometimes called a **metropolitan area network,** or **MAN.** To communicate with a mainframe, a personal computer must employ **terminal emulation software.** When smaller computers are connected to larger computers, the result is sometimes referred to as a **micro-to-mainframe** link. The large computer to which a terminal or personal computer is attached is called the **host computer.** In a situation in which a personal computer or workstation is being used as a network terminal, **file transfer software** enables a user to **download** files (retrieve them from another computer and store them) and **upload** files (send files to another computer).

- A **local area network (LAN)** is usually a network of personal computers that share hardware, software, and data. The nodes on some LANs are connected by a shared **network cable** or by **wireless** transmission. A **network interface card (NIC)** may be inserted into a slot inside the computer to handle sending, receiving, and error checking of transmitted data.

- If two LANs are similar, they may send messages among their nodes by using a **bridge.** A **router** is a special computer that directs communications traffic when several networks are connected together. Since many networks have adopted the Internet protocol (IP), some use **IP switches,** which are less expensive and faster than routers. A **gateway** is a collection of hardware and software resources that connect two dissimilar networks, including protocol conversion.

- A **client/server** arrangement involves a **server,** a computer that controls the network. The server has hard disks holding shared files and often has the highest-quality printer. Processing is usually done by the server, and only the results are sent to the node. A **file server** transmits the entire file to the node, which does all its own processing.

- All computers in a **peer-to-peer** arrangement have equal status; no one computer is in control. With all files and peripheral devices distributed across several computers, users share each other's data and devices as needed.

- **Ethernet** is a type of network protocol that accesses the network by first "listening" to see if the cable is free; this method is called **carrier sense multiple access with collision detection,** or **CSMA/CD.** If two nodes transmit data at the same time, this is called a **collision.** A **Token Ring network** controls access to the shared network cable by using **token passing.**

- **Office automation** is the use of technology to help people do their jobs better and faster. **Electronic mail (e-mail)** allows workers to transmit messages to other people's computers. **Voice mail** lets a caller dictate a message, which is translated into digital impulses, stored, and later delivered in audio form. **Facsimile technology (fax)** can transmit text, graphics, charts, and signatures. **Fax modems** for personal computers can send or receive faxes, as well as handle the usual modem functions.

- **Groupware** is any kind of software that lets a group of people share things or track things together, often using data communications to access the data.
- **Teleconferencing** is usually **videoconferencing**, in which computers are combined with cameras and large screens. **Electronic data interchange (EDI)** allows businesses to send common business forms electronically.
- In **electronic fund transfers (EFTs)**, people pay for goods and services by having funds transferred from various checking and savings accounts electronically, using computer technology. The **ATM**—the **automated teller machine**—is a type of EFT.
- **Telecommuting** means a worker works at home on a personal computer and probably uses the computer to communicate with office colleagues or customers.
- America Online and the Microsoft Network are examples of major commercial communications services, called **information utilities** or **online services.**

Quick Poll

Compare your answers to those of your colleagues or classmates.

1. How determined are you to have speedy downloads from the Internet?
   - ❑ a. A 33,600 bps modem is good enough for my purposes.
   - ❑ b. More speed, please. A 56,000 bps modem would be my choice.
   - ❑ c. I must have ISDN and I am willing to pay more to get it.
2. Assuming you are suitably equipped, what would be your choice for online access?
   - ❑ a. I prefer the structure of an online service, which gives me the Internet too.
   - ❑ b. Skip the in-between layers and give me the straight Internet.
   - ❑ c. I would probably make a decision based strictly on value for the money.
3. Regarding networking:
   - ❑ a. I'd like the advantages but want to concentrate on my own work rather than how the network operates.
   - ❑ b. Networking is a critical technology and I at least want to keep up in a general way.
   - ❑ c. I am seriously interested in networking and hope to make some phase of networking a part of my career.

Discussion Questions

1. Suppose you ran a business out of your home. Pick your own business or choose one of the following: catering, motorcycle repair, financial services, a law office, roofing, photography, or photo research. Now, assuming that your personal computer is suitably equipped, determine for what purposes you might use one or more—or all—of the following: e-mail, fax modem, online services such as America Online, the Internet, electronic fund transfers, and electronic data interchange.
2. Discuss the advantages and disadvantages of telecommuting versus working in the office.
3. Do you expect to have a computer on your desk on your first full-time job? Do you expect it to be connected to a network? In the kind of work you expect to do, would a network provide advantages to you as a worker?

Student Study Guide

Multiple Choice

1. Internet protocol:
   a. EFT
   b. TCP/IP
   c. MAN
   d. EDI

2. Centralized processing but with access from terminals is known as
   a. a teleprocessing system
   b. MAN
   c. EDI
   d. telecommuting

3. Using data communications equipment to connect computers and their resources:
   a. host computer systems
   b. teleprocessing
   c. networks
   d. centralized systems

4. Housing all hardware, software, storage, and processing in one location:
   a. a time-sharing system
   b. a distributed system
   c. centralized processing
   d. a host computer system

5. Transmission permitting data to move only one way at a time:
   a. half-duplex
   b. full-duplex
   c. simplex
   d. start/stop

6. The process of converting from analog to digital:
   a. modulation
   b. telecommuting
   c. line switching
   d. demodulation

7. The device used with satellite transmission that ensures that strong outgoing signals do not interfere with weak incoming signals:
   a. microwave
   b. cable
   c. transponder
   d. modem

8. A network that spans a large city:
   a. ISDN
   b. MAN
   c. LAN
   d. NIC

9. The Token Ring network controls access to the network using
   a. facsimile
   b. ISDN
   c. a bus
   d. token passing

10. The arrangement in which most of the processing is done by the server:
    a. simplex transmission
    b. file server
    c. electronic data interchange
    d. client/server

11. A computer-based system in which a telephone message is recorded in digital form and then forwarded to others:
    a. teleconferencing
    b. topology
    c. voice mail
    d. telecommuting

12. One or more computers connected to a hub computer is a(n)
    a. ring network
    b. CSMA
    c. node
    d. star network

13. A connection for similar networks:
    a. router
    b. bridge
    c. gateway
    d. fax

14. The physical layout of a LAN:
    a. topology
    b. link
    c. contention
    d. switch

15. A network type in which all computers have equal status:
    a. communications link
    b. WAN
    c. peer-to-peer
    d. gateway

16. The type of modulation that changes the height of the signal:
    a. frequency
    b. amplitude
    c. phase
    d. prephase

17. A network that places all nodes on a single cable:
    a. star
    b. switched
    c. ring
    d. bus

18. Signals produced by a computer to be sent over phone lines must be converted to
    a. modems
    b. digital signals
    c. analog signals
    d. microwaves

19. The device used between LANs that use the Internet protocol:
    a. bus
    b. gateway
    c. IP switch
    d. token

20. Microwave transmission, coaxial cables, and fiber optics are examples of
    a. modems
    b. communication links
    c. routers
    d. ring networks

21. A network of geographically distant computers and terminals is called a(n)
    a. bus
    b. ATM
    c. WAN
    d. LAN

22. Two dissimilar networks can be connected by a
    a. gateway
    b. bus
    c. node
    d. server

23. Graphics and other paperwork can be transmitted directly using
    a. CSMA/CD
    b. facsimile
    c. token passing
    d. transponder

24. The number of frequencies that can fit on a link:
    a. WAN
    b. bandwidth
    c. EFT
    d. EDI

25. Software used to make a personal computer act like a terminal:
    a. fax
    b. bridge
    c. videoconferencing
    d. emulation

True/False

T F   1. Frequency modulation varies the position in time of a complete wave cycle.

T F   2. Local area networks are designed to share data and resources among several computers in the same geographical location.

T F   3. A WAN is usually limited to one office building.

T F   4. A front-end processor is a computer.

T F   5. Teleprocessing allows a user to make queries of a computer 1000 miles away.

T F 6. An internal modem is normally used with a variety of computers.

T F 7. A modem can be used for either modulation or demodulation.

T F 8. Start/stop transmission transmits characters in a stream.

T F 9. A transponder ensures that the stronger incoming signals do not interfere with the weaker outgoing ones.

T F 10. Full-duplex transmission allows transmission in both directions at once.

T F 11. Fiber optics are a cheaper form of communication than wire cables.

T F 12. A standard modem can transmit data faster than ISDN.

T F 13. Another name for file server is peer-to-peer.

T F 14. A digital signal can be altered by frequency modulation.

T F 15. Synchronous transmission is also called start/stop transmission.

T F 16. Interactions among networked computers must use a protocol.

T F 17. The term *node* may refer to any device connected to a network.

T F 18. Ethernet and Token Ring are identical protocols.

T F 19. A ring network has no central host computer.

T F 20. A file server usually transmits the entire requested file to the user.

T F 21. A gateway connects two similar computers.

T F 22. A bus network uses a central computer as the server.

T F 23. Fax boards can be inserted inside computers.

T F 24. Ethernet systems "listen" to see if the network is free before transmitting data.

T F 25. Telecommuting is a type of information utility.

Fill-In

1. The term for computer systems that transmit data over telephone lines: _____

2. TCP/IP stands for _____

3. The kind of signal most telephone lines require: _____

4. What device converts a digital signal to an analog signal and vice versa? _____

5. What are America Online and CompuServe examples of? _____

6. Distortion in the received signal: _____

7. The number of frequencies that can fit on a link at one time: _____

8. What is the general term for the use of technology in the office? _____

9. The name of the extra computer often used by large computers to perform communications functions: _____

10. What kind of network links distant computers and terminals? _____

11. The physical layout of a network: _____

12. A type of server that delivers the entire file to a user node: _____

13. How does a Token Ring network control access to the cable? _____

14. Another name for information utility: _____

15. NIC stands for _____

16. What is the term for computer networks that share resources in a limited geographical location? _____

17. To move files from the user's computer to another computer: _____

18. Personal computers and other hardware attached to a LAN are called _____

19. A network in which all computers have equal status and share resources: _____

20. ISDN stands for _____

21. What hardware device connects two dissimilar networks? _____

22. The protocol that uses CSMA/CD: _____

23. To communicate with a larger computer, a personal computer must use what kind of software?

_____

24. Changing a signal from digital to analog is called

_____

25. Another name for the start/stop method of data transmission: _____

26. MAN stands for: _____

27. The data transmission method that permits data to travel in only one direction:

_____

28. Analog transmission uses what kind of wave signal:

_____

29. EDI stands for: _____

30. Adding cameras to teleconferencing makes it

_____

31. A set of rules for exchanging electronic data:

_____

32. Signals are transmitted to satellites from:

_____

33. Another name for wire pairs:

_____

34. Laptop computer often use this kind of modem, which slides into a slot in the computer:

_____

35. The height of a carrier wave is called its

_____

Answers

Multiple Choice

1. b	6. d	11. c	16. b	21. c
2. a	7. c	12. d	17. d	22. a
3. c	8. b	13. b	18. c	23. b
4. c	9. d	14. a	19. c	24. b
5. a	10. d	15. c	20. b	25. d

True/False

1. T	6. F	11. T	16. T	21. F
2. T	7. T	12. F	17. T	22. F
3. F	8. F	13. F	18. F	23. T
4. T	9. F	14. F	19. T	24. T
5. T	10. T	15. F	20. T	25. F

Fill-In

1. data communications systems
2. Transmission Control Protocol/Internet Protocol
3. analog
4. a modem
5. information utilities, or online services
6. noise
7. bandwidth
8. office automation
9. front-end processor
10. wide area network
11. topology
12. file server
13. token passing
14. online service
15. network interface card
16. local area network
17. upload
18. nodes
19. peer-to-peer
20. Integrated Services Digital Network
21. gateway
22. Ethernet
23. terminal emulation software
24. modulation
25. asynchronous
26. Metropolitan Area Network
27. simplex
28. carrier
29. electronic data interchange
30. videoconferencing
31. protocol
32. earth stations
33. twisted pairs
34. PC card
35. amplitude

PLANET INTERNET

So many stores. The term *electronic mall* refers to a group of Internet stores that rivals physical malls in size and variety. A good place to start is the Hall of Malls, which lists dozens of malls, each of which has many stores. There are many similar malls, as well as thousands of individual retail sites. Many shoppers find that, in a rather short time, they have stumbled on favorite stores. We offer these from our list: Patagonia, Cybershop, Bagel Oasis, Mexican Pottery, Southpaw Enterprises, and the Chocolate Lovers' Page. You can use the Addison Wesley Longman URL to check these out, but you will soon make your own list.

Finding what you want. It is all well and good to know the names and the URLs of several shopping sites. But, although shopping on the Internet is more convenient than traipsing around by car and foot, you are still faced with the prospect of searching for what you want, store by Internet store. What if there was a better way? What if you could just say what you wanted and have

the computer search through the "stores" for you? One possibility is a *search engine*, described in Chapter 7, a site that allows you to type in a request of one or more words. The search engine then returns lists of sites matching your search words. You merely click on the name of a desired site to be transported there. Search engines, by the way, are not just for shopping; they can come in handy any time you need to find something specific on the 'Net.

SHOPPING TOUR

Shopping conveniences have existed since catalogs were invented. Convenience is at a high point today because computer shopping offers goods and services handily bundled together. The variety of available goods is stunning. What would you like to buy? A watch? A book? A kite? Fashionable clothing? Perhaps you need something more expensive, like a computer. Gateway 2000 is a computer manufacturer that sells a significant portion of its computers from its web site. The cows are part of Gateway's overall marketing theme. If you really want to go to the top end financially, look up the Porsche site to see many images of cars. All of these products are available from companies that sell their wares on the Internet. As for the service, with a few clicks of a mouse and taps on the keyboard, an order can be on its way to you. However, no one will be sending a Porsche through the mail.

The Visual Internet

Internet Site Designers

Compared to plain text, graphic images have far more bytes. A single image may take a half-million bytes. The more bytes of data in a web site, the longer it takes the site to load. Since site owners do not want visitors to be discouraged by a long wait, most limit their graphics to a few small images. Thus, it is not common to find graphics-rich sites.

However, people who specialize in designing web sites want to show their wares, so they usually display more graphics than the average site. But even their graphics are moderate; they are just more skilled at presenting them. The Dahlin Smith White site, shown on the opening page, uses modest graphics to convey a whimsical effect. Each icon represents information available on the site, only a click away.

There are hundreds, perhaps thousands, of web site designers. Here are some of the best. On this page: Brad Johnson (top) and Dan Design (bottom). On the facing page: Primo Angeli, Oden, Avalanche, Verso, and John Hersey.

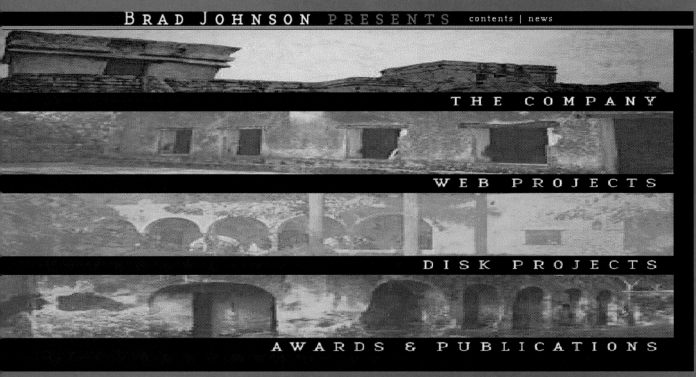

HOME BRANDING CLIENTS CAPABILITIES PROFILE RESPOND

PRIMO ANGELI INC.

MAKING PEOPLE RESPOND
DESIGN FOR MARKETING & COMMUNICATION

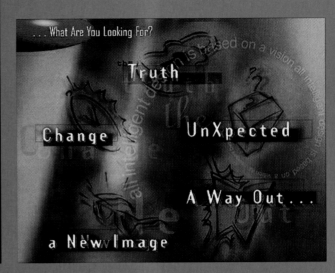

. . . What Are You Looking For?

Truth

Change   UnXpected

A Way Out...

a NewImage

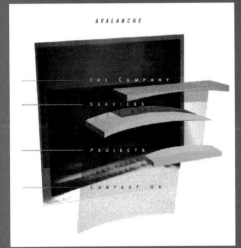

AVALANCHE

THE COMPANY

SERVICES

PROJECTS

CONTACT US

verso

HOME WORK METHOD PEOPLE

Cool Companies

Even in cyberspace, some of our old favorites look familiar—with the use of graphics. Notice that the appearance of lavish graphics is really caused by a series of well-placed small images, whether of bagels, animals, or shirts drying on the clothesline. Although the L. L. Bean graphic is a solid image, it takes up a relatively small part of the home page.

BAGEL OASIS®

BAGEL INGREDIENTS:

OURS: THEIRS:

Don't forget to bookmark this page!

BAGEL OASIS   WE SHIP ANYWHERE IN THE U.S.

Food For Thought Fact Book

Products

About Iams

Customer Service

Employment

Ask the Veterinarian

Our Mission:
To enhance the well-being of dogs and cats by providing world-class quality foods.

THE **Tide** ClothesLine

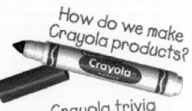

Crayola®

BINNEY & SMITH

Do Your Own Jazzy Thing!

JazzY™ ★

No boys allowed!!

PLAY TO WIN! A ROOM FULL OF FUN! VALUED AT $25,000! PLUS 50,000 INSTANT WIN PRIZES!

How do we make Crayola products?

Crayola trivia

Fresh Out of the Box

Stain Removal Tips

Crayola History

Multimedia

The sites shown here are all have animation and sound powered by the popular software plug-in called *Shockwave.* The Shockwave player software is included with many popular browsers and is also available free from the Macromedia site. You can download *Shockwave,* and it will be "plugged in" to your browser. It is in Macromedia's interest to have many users able to appreciate "shocked" sites, because it helps sell the software that generates the animation and sound.

A key application for animation and sound is on-screen games. People who want to play a game may be more patient

than, say, a potential business customer when it comes to waiting for the site to download. This is just as well because a multimedia-rich site can take an inordinate amount of time to download, depending, of course, on the speed of the data transmission vehicle. The Candystand and Chips Ahoy sites shown here, although commercial sites, offer extensive games to attract users.

However, many sites take clever advantage of just a small animation subset. The Nike screen shown here, for example, merely changes the shoe image repeatedly. The boat in the Water Cycle screen veers into the site but then just sits there while the action focuses on a small circle. The Windows CE site lets a user click on an image on the small screen to see its function. Andy's Garage limits itself to some flashing lights and muffled giggles. At the Warner site, the baby's vocabulary varies from *Mommy* to *Tolstoy* to *existential.* Even more amusing is the Columbia coffee pot, in which a voice-over intones the benefits of full-flavored biscuit or ham-and-eggs coffee. The One Stop Jazz screen offers some floating images, but its main attraction is the jazz you can hear when you visit the site.

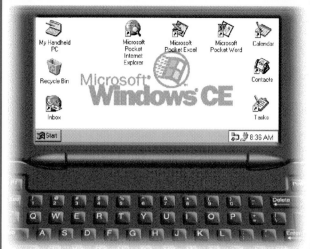

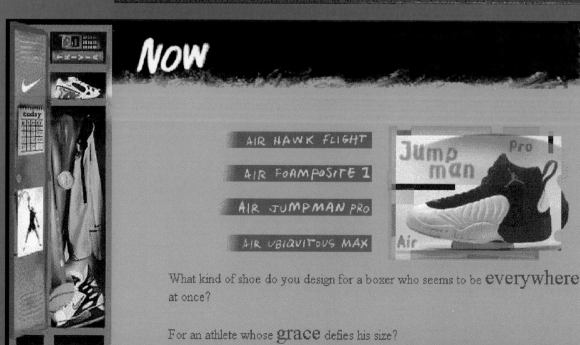

What kind of shoe do you design for a boxer who seems to be everywhere at once?

For an athlete whose grace defies his size?

Just Two More

Note the effective use of graphics in these two sites. Although the Rollerblade site projects action, there is really just one relatively small detailed graphic.

WHAT'S NEW
Site updates and in-line skating news.

AGGRESSIVE
What's up in street and vert.

SKATE SCENES
The scenes, the moves and the skaters.

SKATES & GEAR
The new '97 product line.

TECHNOLOGY/INNOVATIONS
Only from Rollerblade

GETTING STARTED
How to catch up to your friends.

IN-LINE DIRECTORIES
Places to skate and associations.

NATIONAL EVENTS
When and where it's at.

ROLLERBLADE

The Nature Conservancy site uses small images with halo effects to set them off against the dark background.

The Nature Conservancy

WELCOME
WHAT'S NEWS
NATURE CHAT
WHERE WE WORK
DOMESTIC
INTERNATIONAL
CONSERVATION
SCIENCE
GET INVOLVED
JOIN
BACK BUTTON HELP
HOME
SEARCH
COMMENT
INDEX
Copyright 1996 The Nature Conservancy

wired for conservation
WEB SITE OF THE NATURE CONSERVANCY
SPECIAL EVENT
A Place for 500,000 stars to shine

Photo Contest

Sierra de las Minas
HABITAT AT RISK

MINNESOTA
Spectacle of the Season

This exciting area of cyberspace is made possible in par by the HEINZ FOUNDATION

MALL BOOKSHOP

What if I don't want to buy anything? No problem. It's just like old-fashioned window shopping, where you are welcome to look to your heart's content. Of course, as do retailers in real stores, they hope you will see something you want to buy.

Charge it? Standards for secure transmission of transactions through the Internet are still evolving. For this reason, some people prefer to do their shopping on the 'Net but to place the actual order by telephone or some other secure means.

Such a bargain! If you are a comparison shopper, you will be delighted to discover that merchandise offered via the 'Net is often a bargain. This is because overhead is low when compared to physical retail stores and even when compared to shopping by mail. No attractive displays, no sales people, no security devices clipped to merchandise, no printed catalogs, and possibly even no advertising. And, of course, a successful business has a potentially worldwide audience and can thus purchase in high volume and pass the savings on to consumers.

Internet Exercises

1. **Structured exercise.** Begin with the AWL site with URL http://hepg.awl.com/capron/planet/ and go to the Bookshop site. Check the price of a certain title and then call your local bookstore for a comparison price.
2. **Freeform exercise.** This is obvious: Head right down the Hall of Malls.

Whitney Bonilla had heard about the Internet, although she did not know quite what it was. She thought it had something to do with connecting to other people in other places. She also thought that it somehow contained a lot of information, information that might be handy for research for her college papers. She was right on both counts.

During her first week on campus, Whitney set out to hunt down the Internet. She discovered that there were several computer labs on campus and that one specialized in helping students get started on the Internet. But Whitney needed a lab pass to gain entry. A lab pass, for a fee, entitles a student to a certain number of hours on the Internet. The lab passes went first to students enrolled in computer classes and then to other students on a first-come, first-served basis. Unfortunately, Whitney was not among the first and was not able to get a pass at all.

All was not lost, however. Whitney found Internet access at the main library on campus. A librarian (who liked to call herself a "cybrarian") offered an hour-long beginners' class, repeated every day at noon and available to any student. Although subsequent computer access was limited to 30 minutes per session and no more than twice a week, Whitney found this sufficient to get her feet wet. She learned to get on the Internet, to move from site to site, and to find what she wanted.

She registered at the earliest possible date for the following quarter and included a beginning Internet course in her class schedule. She also got a lab pass.

The Internet

A Resource for All of Us

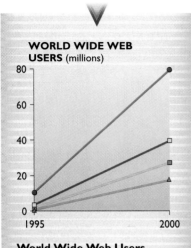

WORLD WIDE WEB USERS (millions)

World Wide Web Users

This chart shows the exponential growth of the World Wide Web as the year 2000 approaches. The red bar on the top represents growth in the United States. The other bars, top to bottom, represent Asia, Western Europe, and the rest of the world.

The Internet as a Phenomenon

The Internet is a loosely configured, rapidly growing labyrinth of networks of computers from around the world, from corporations, organizations, and individuals. Since the numbers change daily, the growth rate of Internet sites and Internet users can only be described as unprecedented. Ironically, the original idea behind the personal computer was to provide individual—and separate—computing. But, instead of remaining solo acts, users find the greatest utility by connecting to every resource they can find. Although the growth of personal computers over the last few decades has been noteworthy, the increase has been steady rather than spectacular. The rise of connectivity, especially the use of the Internet, has been much faster. Millions and millions of users hook up to the Internet every day. Some people have tried to figure out who all those users are.

Some have guessed that it is mostly teenage boys who hang out on the Internet, and that they are there for hours and hours at a time. This is partly right. There are certainly lots of teenage boys on the Internet, and they probably have more time than most of us to surf the 'Net. But they are by no means the majority. Although statistics are fleeting, Internet demographic trends have been evident for some time.

To begin with, almost half of the users of the Internet are female, and the vast majority are adults. About 40 percent have a college degree. Three-fourths of them own their own home computers. Just over 10 percent consider themselves computer professionals. Furthermore, according to a Neilsen survey—the same folks who do the famous Neilsen TV ratings—more than two-thirds of users reach the Internet from their place of work and stay there an average of only five hours per week. Finally, more than half the sites on the Web are business sites, presumably visited by people with business interests. Clearly, the Internet has gone beyond teenagers and has become a fixture in serious places.

To many people who are recent users, it seems as if the Internet sprang up overnight. That, of course, is not true, but its popularity caught a lot of people by surprise. A look at its history explains why.

Don't Know Much About History

The history of the Internet bears telling. It is mercifully short. The reason that there is little to say is that it slumbered and stuttered for approximately 25 years before the general public even knew it existed. The 'Net was started by obscure military and university people as a vehicle for their own purposes. They never in their wildest dreams thought it would become the international giant it is today. Let us look back briefly, to understand their point of view.

First Stirrings at the Department of Defense

Ever heard of a fallout shelter? In the Cold War of the 1950s, people worried about "the bomb," a nuclear attack whose radiation aftereffects—fallout—would be devastating. Some people built underground shelters, usually under their own houses, to protect themselves. It was in this climate of fear that the United States Department of Defense became concerned that a single bomb could wipe out its computing capabilities.

Working with the RAND Corporation, they decided to rely on not one but several computers, geographically dispersed. No one computer would be in charge.

A message to be sent to another computer would be divided up into **packets**, each labeled with its destination address. Each packet would wind its way individually through the network, probably taking different routes, but each heading in the direction of its destination and eventually being reconstituted into the original message at the end of the journey. The idea was that even if one computer was knocked out, the others could still carry on by using alternative routes. A packet can travel a variety of paths; the chosen path does not matter as long as the packet reaches its destination. The software that took care of the packets was Transmission Control Protocol/Internet Protocol (TCP/IP), the universal standard that was described in Chapter 6. TCP does the packeting and reassembling of the message. The IP part of the protocol handles the addressing, seeing to it that packets are routed across multiple computers.

They called the new set of connections **ARPANet**, an acronym that stands for Advanced Research Projects Agency Network. The year was 1969. Before long, computers from research universities and defense contractors joined the network. But the network was limited to people who had some technical expertise—a major reason why it was not yet of particular interest to the general public.

Tim and Marc

Tim Berners-Lee is arguably the pivotal figure in the surging popularity of the Internet: He made it easy. In 1990, Dr. Berners-Lee, a physicist at a laboratory for particle physics in Geneva, Switzerland, perceived that his work would be easier if he and his far-flung colleagues could easily link to one another's computers (Figure 7-1). He saw the set of links from computer to computer to computer as a spider's web; hence the name **Web**. The **CERN site**, the name of the particle physics laboratory where Dr. Berners-Lee worked, is considered the birthplace of the **World Wide Web.**

A **link** on a web site is easy to see: it is either colored text called **hypertext** or an icon or image called a **hyperregion** (Figure 7-2). A mouse click on the link appears to transport the user to the site represented by the link, and in common parlance one speaks of moving or transferring to the new site; actually, data from the new site is transferred to the user's computer.

Marc Andreessen was only a student when, in 1993, he led a team that invented the *browser,* software used to explore the Internet (Figure 7-3). The browser featured a graphical interface, so that users could see and click on pictures as well as text. That first browser was named **Mosaic**, and it made web page multimedia possible. For the viewing public, the 'Net now offered both easy movement with Dr. Berners-Lee's links and attractive images and a graphical interface provided by the browser. Today there are many competitive browsers, one of which is Netscape Navigator, produced by a company founded by Marc Andreessen and others.

The Internet Surges Ahead

TCP/IP is software in the public domain. Since no one was really in charge of the network, there was no one to stop others from just barging

Figure 7-1 Dr. Tim Berners-Lee. Working at a physics lab in Geneva, Switzerland, Dr. Berners-Lee invented a method of linking from site to site so that he could easily communicate with his colleagues worldwide. Thus was born the World Wide Web or, simply, the Web.

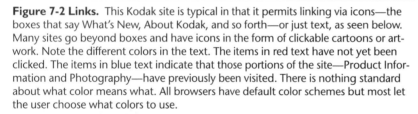

Figure 7-2 Links. This Kodak site is typical in that it permits linking via icons—the boxes that say What's New, About Kodak, and so forth—or just text, as seen below. Many sites go beyond boxes and have icons in the form of clickable cartoons or artwork. Note the different colors in the text. The items in red text have not yet been clicked. The items in blue text indicate that those portions of the site—Product Information and Photography—have previously been visited. There is nothing standard about what color means what. All browsers have default color schemes but most let the user choose what colors to use.

Figure 7-3 Marc Andreessen. As a college student, Mr. Andreessen led a team that developed the first browser, called Mosaic. He later developed the Netscape Navigator browser, which was an instant success and is widely used on the 'Net.

in and linking up wherever they could. The network became steadily more valuable as it embraced more and more networks. Meanwhile, corporate networks, especially LANs of personal computers, were growing apace. Companies and organizations, noting an opportunity for greater communication and access to information, hooked their entire networks to the burgeoning network. A new name, taken from the name of the TCP/IP protocol, evolved: the Internet. The original ARPANet eventually disappeared altogether. Its users hardly noticed. Its functions continued and improved under the broader Internet.

In summary, the emergence of the Internet is due to four factors: (1) the universal TCP/IP standard, (2) the web-like ability to link from site to site, (3) the ease of use provided by the browser's graphical interface, and (4) the growth of personal computers and their local area networks that could be connected to the Internet.

Although statistics and projections vary, the growth of the Internet has been swift and unprecedented. No one thinks it is a fad. Almost everyone agrees that it is a true technological revolution.

► Getting Started

History is interesting, but most people want to know how to *use* the Internet, or at least how to get started. We cannot be specific here because many factors—computers, servers, browsers, and more—vary from place to place. But we can talk about overall strategy and what the various services and software applications have to offer.

The Internet Service Provider and the Browser

An Internet user needs a computer with a modem and its related software, an Internet service provider, and a browser. As noted in Chapter 1, an **Internet service provider (ISP)** provides the server computer and the software to connect to the Internet. A **browser** is the software on the user's computer that allows the user to access the Internet via the service provider, using a graphical interface. If accessing the Internet from a school, an organization, or a workplace, it is likely that these elements are already in place. The only task would be to activate the browser and know how to use it.

If you wish to access the Internet from your own personal computer, one possibility, as noted in Chapter 6, is to sign up for an online service that includes Internet access. The Internet service provider and browser are included in the package, and thus Internet access is available to you as soon as you have signed up for the online service.

If you elect to go directly to an Internet service provider, you will first need to select one. Some people seek advice from friends; others begin with advertisements in their phone books or the business section of the newspaper. Note the Getting Practical feature called *Choosing an Internet Service Provider*. Once you have arranged to pay the fees (probably an installation fee and certainly a monthly fee), you will set up your ISP interaction according to your provider's directions. The ISP may provide a disk that, once installed on your computer, will automatically set up the software, dial up the ISP, and set up your account, all with minimal input from you.

The next step is to install browser software on your computer. You can purchase a browser in your local software retail outlet or, if you have some other online access vehicle, possibly download it free from the browser vendor's web site. As you are installing the browser, you will be asked for information about your ISP, for which your ISP will have prepared you. (An ISP typically furnishes several pages of detailed instructions.) Once you are set up, you invoke the browser as you would any software on your computer, and it will begin by dialing the Internet service provider for you. You are on your way to the Internet experience.

The Browser in Action

As mentioned earlier, a browser is software used to explore the Internet. When they first came on the scene, browsers were a great leap forward in Internet friendliness. In just a few years, vigorous competition among browsers has made them ever more attractive and useful.

A number of browsers are available, some better organized and more useful than others. Two well-designed browsers are Netscape Navigator and Microsoft's Internet Explorer (Figure 7-4).

When you invoke your browser software, it will dial up the Internet service provider and, once successfully connected, display either the **home page**—initial page—of the web site that created your particular browser or some other site designated by your ISP (Figure 7-5). The browser shows three parts on the screen: two very obvious chunks and a third that is just a line at the bottom. The top part is the *browser control panel,* consisting of lines of menus and buttons, to be described momentarily. The lower part, by far the largest part of the screen, is the *browser display window*. At the very bottom of the screen is a *status line,* which indicates the progress of data being transferred as you move from site to site. The

The Latest and Greatest

Computer users are sometimes so anxious to make sure that they have the best and latest that they stand frozen in time, afraid to buy something that might be out of date in moments. The software called Oil Change addresses that issue by making sure your computer is running the most current version of any software you use.

Oil Change first makes a list of all the software on your hard disk. Then it scouts out the latest versions of the software on the Internet. The new versions of the software arrive from the Internet via your modem and self-install. It doesn't get any easier than that.

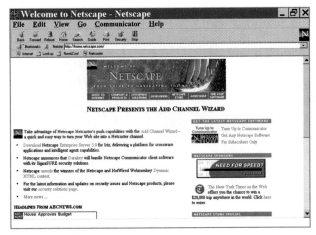

(a)

(b)

Figure 7-4 Browser home pages.
(a) The Netscape home page features its ship image logo and links to various products and services. The Netscape browser used to access this home page is the Communicator version, which although functionally equivalent, has a control panel somewhat different in appearance from other Netscape versions. (b) The Microsoft Internet Explorer home page promotes its own products and services for business and home users.

status line may also show other messages, depending on the browser. The browser control panel stays the same as you travel through the Web; the browser display window changes, showing, in turn, each new Internet site you visit.

When you first invoke the browser, the web site window usually shows material according to the browser vendor's wishes, usually useful information and possibly advertisements for their products. Note that the site display is not limited to the size of your screen. The page can be **scrolled**—moved up and down—by using the **scroll bar** on the right; simply press your mouse button over a scroll bar arrow to see the page move. As you move the page, note that the browser control panel stays in place; it is always available no matter what the browser display window shows.

Browser Functions and Features

Next, let us examine the functions of the browser control panel. You can follow along on Figure 7-5 as you read these descriptions. Again, this discussion is necessarily generic and may vary from browser to browser. First, note the browser's welcome banner, touting its own name, across the top of the screen. Next, usually off to the right, is the browser logo, such as the N shown in Figure 7-5. The logo is active—shimmering, changing colors, *something*—when it wants to let you know that it is in the process of moving you to a new site. Since this sometimes takes a while, it would be disconcerting to stare at a static screen and think nothing is happening. Note also that the status line at the bottom of the page will provide information about the progress in contacting and receiving data from the desired site. If the transfer to the new site takes too long, you can cancel the move by clicking the browser's Stop button.

Menus and Buttons   Using a mouse lets you issue commands through a set of **menus**, a series of choices normally laid out across the top of the screen. The menus are called **pull-down menus** because each initial choice, when clicked with a mouse, reveals lower-level choices that pull down like a window shade from the initial selection at the top of the screen. You can also invoke commands using **buttons** for functions such as Print to print the current page, Home to return to the browser home page, and—perhaps the ones you will use the most—Back and Forward,

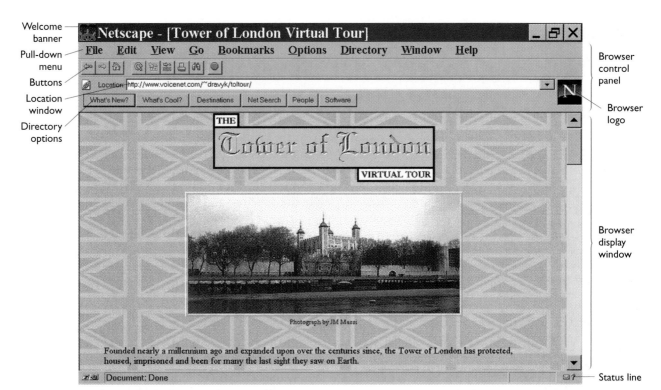

Welcome banner
Pull-down menu
Buttons
Location window
Directory options

Browser control panel
Browser logo
Browser display window
Status line

Figure 7-5 Browser control panel. Most browsers offer pretty much the same functions; the example here is a popular browser called Netscape. Just below the browser's welcome banner, displaying the name of the browser and the name of the web site on display, is a set of pull-down menus: each such menu has several submenus. The button line just below includes buttons for (left to right) Back, Forward, Home (return to browser's home page), Reload (redo the current site), Load images, Open (a new file or location), Print (the contents of the browser display window), Find (some text within the current site on display), and Stop (to stop an incoming site that, perhaps is taking too long to load or that, after just a brief look, you wish to see no further). Below the button line is the Location window (sometimes called Netsite or Address window), which contains the URL of the site in the browser display window. Below that is a line of various directory-like options containing sets of links chosen by the browser.

to help you retrace sites you have recently traversed. If you rest the cursor over a button for just a few seconds, a small text message will reveal its function. Other buttons on the lower line offer directory options, most especially the Net Search option, which you can click to go to a site that will perform searches for you. (Searches are discussed in more detail later in this chapter.) Note that all functions are listed in the pull-down menus; the buttons are just convenient repetitions of the most commonly used functions.

URL The location slot, sometimes called the address window, will usually contain a **Uniform Resource Locator (URL)**, a rather messy-looking string of letters and symbols, which is the unique address of a web page or file on the Internet. An URL has a particular format (Figure 7-6). A web page URL (pronounced "earl") begins with the protocol *http,* which stands for **HyperText Transfer Protocol.** This protocol is the means of communicating by using links, the clickable text or image that transports a user to the desired site. Next comes the **domain name**, which is the address of the Internet service provider (ISPs, by the way, must register each domain name and pay an ongoing fee). The last part of the domain name, *com* in Figure 7-6, is called a **top-level domain** and represents the purpose of the organization or entity—in this case *com* for "commercial." In some cases, the end of the domain name stands for the country of ori-

```
URL:
http://www.intel.com/homecomputing/index.htm
```

| Protocol | ISP address (domain) | Path, directory, file name |

Figure 7-6 A dissected URL. The Uniform Resource Locator represents a unique address of an Internet site or file. Whenever you are looking at a web site, you can see its URL near the top of the screen in the browser's control panel, in the location (address) slot. The example here shows a web address for the Intel host, using a file called index.htm in the homecomputing directory.

gin. Note the usage of top-level domain names in Figure 7-7. The last part of the URL, usually the most complex, contains directories and file names to help zero in on a very specific part of a site. Parts of the URL to the right of the domain, that is, the directory and file names, are case sensitive; that is, you must type uppercase or lowercase exactly as indicated.

Many URLs end right after the domain. Although there may be many pages that are part of the site and thus have longer URLs, it is simplest to start at the top with the short URL. In fact, many advertised URLs neglect to even mention the *http://* part of their address, partly because newer browser versions do not require the *http://* if the first part of the domain name is *www*. For those who use other browsers, advertisers figure that a user who knows enough to get on the 'Net to find the site also knows enough to add the needed *http://* prefix.

No one likes to type URLs. There are several ways to avoid it. The easy way, of course, is simply to click links to move from one site to another. Another way is to click a pre-stored link on your browser's **hot list**—called Bookmarks or Favorites or something similar—where you can store your favorite sites and their URLs.

Frames Several browsers support a concept called **frames**, which allow a given page to be divided into rectangular sections, each of which can operate independently of the others (Figure 7-8). It is like having several small pages on the same screen, each of which can be scrolled up and down. The advantage is that a site can offer several different functions or areas of focus. A disadvantage of frames is that a small screen, notably a laptop screen, may look cluttered. Further, a site probably cannot be viewed at its best by a user whose browser does not support frames.

Competition Glitz Not just functional buttons, but buttons that illuminate when the cursor passes over them. Not just English, but French, German, and Italian. Not just frames, but borderless frames. You begin to get the idea. Browsers can only get fancier. And we, the users, presumably get more browser functionality. In addition to the browsers themselves, various vendors offer **plug-ins**, software that enhances the value of a browser by increasing its functionality or features. Typical plug-ins can enhance a site's audio-video experience or improve image viewing.

Java

In the early days of the Web, everything presented on a web page was static, just material that had already been prepared. A user was basically

Figure 7-7 Domain breakdown. This pie chart shows the approximate relative sizes of top-level Internet domain names. "Country" domains use two letters; typical examples are jp (Japan), fi (Finland), us (United States), uk (United Kingdom), de (Germany), ca (Canada), au (Australia), nl (Netherlands), and se (Sweden) Seven new top-level domain names have been added: *firm* firm for business sites, *store* for sites offering goods to purchase, *web* for sites emphasizing activities related to the WWW, *arts* for sites emphasizing cultural and entertainment activities, *rec* for sites emphasizing recreation/entertainment activities, *info* for sites providing information services, and *nom* for those wishing individual or personal nomenclature.

(Pie chart labels: com 25%, edu 19%, net 8%, org 3%, gov 3%, mil 3%, countries 28%, other 11%)

Getting Practical

CHOOSING AN INTERNET SERVICE PROVIDER

If you have decided that you want to connect your computer to the Internet directly via an Internet service provider, you have to choose among many offerings. Many ISPs are national in scope; others are regional or local services. The best rates are usually from local ISPs. In fact, it is hard to keep track of them all; new ones pop up weekly. Prepare to do some digging.

You can begin by checking the Yellow Pages of your local phone directory, which probably has listings under "Internet." Check out ISP advertisements in monthly computer magazines and, in urban areas, in your local newspaper. Many advertisements include a toll-free number that you can call for free software and a free "trial subscription" of a month or a certain number of online hours.

An online resource called The List is by far the most comprehensive and useful list of ISPs (http://www.thelist.iworld.com). It is, of course, available only to people who are already able to get online. However, you may be able to persuade a friend or colleague to access the site for you. It features more than 1500 ISPs and is searchable by state, province (in Canada), and telephone area code.

Further tips:

- Look for an ISP whose access is only a local phone call away. Otherwise, phone charges will figure prominently in your monthly Internet bill. Even if a seemingly toll-free number is offered, the provider will recoup the cost in charges to you.
- Seek a provider with speedy access. That number is relative and changeable, so we will not fixate on it now. But do not assume that all ISPs have the same access speed. Ask and compare.
- Ideally, find a provider with software that will automate the registration process. Configuring the right connections on your own is not a trivial task.
- Figure out how likely you are to get help. At the very least, ask for the phone numbers and hours of the help line. If help is available only via e-mail, take your business elsewhere.

Finally, don't fall for an unrealistic bargain. Like anything else, if it sounds too good to be true, it probably is. You will probably find that a "bargain" service is oversubscribed, underpowered, and full of busy signals. Even worse, your call for technical help may garner only a "this number has been disconnected" message. Stability is worth something.

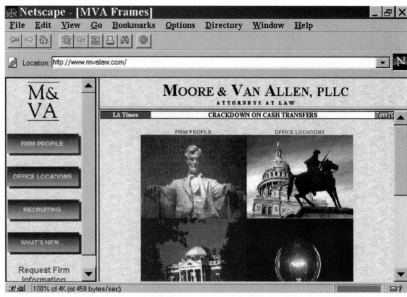

Figure 7-8 Frames. Notice that the browser display window for this law firm is divided into three parts, called frames. The content of the top frame, holding the firm name, stays the same. The other two frames, on the right and left, have their own scroll bars so the information they contain can be manipulated separately. As a point of interest, notice also that the right frame includes a separate display window that rotates news items from various sources; currently you can see an item from the *LA Times* about a crackdown on cash transfers.

accessing the electronic version of a printed page. Even though that access was certainly a convenience, the content of the web page offered nothing innovative. Until Java. It is Java that permits the dancing icons, sound clips, flashing messages, banners that scroll across the page—and much more. **Java** is a programming language, developed by Sun Microsystems, that is used to write software that can run on any machine, hence its appeal to the multifaceted Internet.

The programs that provide the moving images and sound clips on a web page are called **applets**, a sort of abbreviation for "little applications" (Figure 7-9). Applets can make web pages perform virtually any task—display animations, receive input, perform calculations, and so forth. Java also provides the possibility of dynamic interaction, where the user can receive immediate feedback and the programs actually do things on their own.

To benefit from applets, a user must have a browser that is capable of running Java, as, indeed, the most popular browsers are. If you are thus equipped, you will doubtless see many applets in action as you cruise the Web. If you have a particular interest in Java applets, check out Sun's web page, which has links to test applets of various kinds.

Moving from Site to Site

There are several ways to leave your browser's home page and start moving to other sites. Most browsers provide a list of clickable categories, such as sports, weather, news, technology, and even comic strips. Also a button click away are lists of new sites, cool sites, and various comprehensive directories. All of these come under the category of—yes—browsing.

Figure 7-9 Applets. Applets are extremely common on web sites; you probably will see a great variety. In these applets, the flag waves, the WOW bounces, and the cow's propeller spins.

NEW DIRECTIONS

INTERNET UNIVERSITY

Learning from a distance is already available on the Internet in a variety of forms. But there is also something different, something more grand: a virtual university. This university goes beyond a course or two; it offers a four-year degree. The school is sponsored by ten western states (excluding California), created in response to the high costs of educating college students on-site. Called the Western Governors University, the school is an accredited regional university that exists solely in cyberspace.

The building shown here is merely symbolic; the university has no physical facilities at all.

The key here is *accredited,* meaning that the degree will be recognized by other institutions, including graduate schools, throughout the country.

Students get learning materials from electronic databases, turn in papers by e-mail, and meet in online sessions using video and voice links. Studies show that among adults, distance learning is as effective as traditional classroom instruction.

But suppose you have something more specific in mind. If you know the URL for a desired site, delete the current URL in the location box, then type in the new one—carefully—and press *Enter* on the keyboard. You will be moved to the site just as if you had clicked a link. Sometimes—too often—an URL does not work. That is, a message is returned saying Unable to Locate Server or, simply, Not Found. The former may mean that you typed the URL incorrectly. The latter probably means that the specific site you want is no longer on that ISP. People do move around, and they do not always provide a forwarding address.

Keep in mind that moving from site to site, whether by link or URL, is not magic. Although the movement from site to site is relatively effortless for the user, all the concepts described here and in Chapter 6 are in play. That is, link requests move from your computer to your server and across networks of computers, all using TCP/IP, until the destination site is reached. Then, carrying the desired information, the process is reversed.

▶ Searching the Internet

Although a browser, true to its name, lets a user browse by listing clickable categories of information—sports, business, kids, whatever—most users soon want to find something specific. A **search engine** is software, usually located at its own web site, that lets a user specify search terms; the search engine then finds sites that fit those terms. The search engine will present the list of sites in some format, which varies by search engine. In fact, the nature of the search varies according to the search engine. Each search engine is associated with a constantly updated database of sites and related keywords. A browser usually offers links to one or more search engines, or a user can simply link to the site of a favorite search engine. Initially, users are astonished at the number of sites found by the search engine, often hundreds and perhaps thousands.

Narrowing the Search

A simple one-word search will yield many sites, most of which will be irrelevant to your purposes. Suppose, for example, you are considering a driving trip through Utah. If you submit the word *Utah* as your search criterion, you will retrieve everything from Utah Lake to the Utah Jazz basketball team. The trick is to customize your search criteria. In this case, adding the word *vacation* to the search criteria will produce a list that begins with various hotels and parks in Utah. You can refine and narrow your search repeatedly.

There are more sophisticated methods for narrowing your search and for getting it right the first time. Different search engines offer different methods. Take a look at the search site's page, and you will probably see a clickable phrase such as Custom Search or Advanced Search or Options. Click the phrase to see how your request can be made to order. For example, the AltaVista search engine permits quotation marks. If you type *"World Trade Center"* as your search criterion, you will get results that focus on that institution. If, instead, you type *World, Trade,* and *Center* as just three words in a row, the search engine will find every instance of each of the three words, alone and in combination—possibly several thousand sites. Alas, even the quote method is imperfect. For example, a site on a completely different topic will show up if the words *World Trade Center* appear anywhere in the site.

OPERATOR	USE	EXAMPLE
AND	Include both requested terms in selected sites	life AND insurance
OR	Include either or both requested terms in selected sites	university OR college
NOT	Exclude any site with terms preceded by NOT	browsers AND NOT Microsoft

Figure 7-10 Boolean search terms.

Most search engines offer operators with special functions, based on a mathematical system called **Boolean logic.** The operators most commonly used are AND, OR, and NOT. The words can be further qualified with parentheses. AND means both; OR means either or both. Used correctly, these simple words can reduce search output to a dozen relevant sites instead of thousands of unrelated ones (Figure 7-10). Some examples: You want information on the companies called Cirrus and Intel. Key *Cirrus OR Intel* for output that gives any site that mentions either or both companies. Suppose you need the population of the country of Jordan. If you key Jordan, you will see many sites for Michael Jordan, among others. Instead, key *Jordan AND NOT Michael.* Most requests combine several terms and operators. For example, suppose you want to go to school in Illinois but want to live in a town smaller than Chicago, and you want to inquire about tuition. Try *Illinois AND NOT Chicago AND (college OR university) AND tuition AND admission.* This query is quite specific and it will produce mostly desired sites.

Hot Search Engines

The title of this section is somewhat facetious, since a new "hot" search engine can show up overnight. Further, some early search engines, less than half a dozen years old, are considered hackneyed and dull. Nevertheless, of the dozens of search engines in existence, a list of a few useful search engines is appropriate. Note that the use of these search engines is free, although you will, of course, encounter some advertising. See the comparison chart in Table 7-1.

Although it may seem that the same search query ought to produce the same list of sites no matter what the search engine, this is hardly the

Table 7-1 Top search engines

	Search Engine	Features
	AltaVista	Very fast. Indexes every word on every page of every site. Searches Usenet too.
	Infoseek	Searches not only the Web but also newsgroups, FAQs, and e-mail addresses. Limited Boolean operations, but ranks the results well.
	Open Text Index	Full set of Boolean operators. Web only but indexes every word on every site.
	HotBot	Fast. Unique search options let you restrict searches. Very comprehensive.
	Excite	Conceptual searching finds ideas related to your original terms. Not easy to narrow searches.
	Lycos	An established site full of good information.
	WebCrawler	Another venerable site. Searches the Web only.
	Yahoo	Web only. Well-organized categories let the user switch from browsing to searching in a certain area. But finds only keywords, not any word on a site.

case. Search engines vary widely in size, content, and search methodology. Keeping this in mind, serious researchers sometimes put the same query to each of several search engines.

The ultimate search device is software that searches the search engines. That is, it runs your query on several different search engines, probably the top seven or eight, simultaneously. Another approach, instead of doing the searches yourself, is to use your own software agent.

➤ Your Own Home Page

If you want to have your own site on the Web, commonly called a "home page" because it is often a single page, you must have a service

MAKING THE RIGHT CONNECTIONS

RATING SYSTEMS

Suppose you have indeed made "the right connections" and are surfing the Internet. How likely are you to find anything of quality? If you stick with sites listed in the directories of established web sites, the sites you see will be somewhere between passable and good. If you stray into uncharted waters, perhaps looking at every home page on a local Internet service provider, you are likely to find the blandest of the bland. After you view a few dozen of them, they seem almost interchangeable ("My hobbies are . . .").

Suppose, instead, that you are determined to see the very best the Web has to offer. This goal is not too lofty, mostly because others have been there before you. In fact, the "raters" have drawn conclusions and given awards to sites they find worthy. If you follow the accolades you should have a rewarding experience.

Some of the web rating sites are CNET Best of the Web, Yahoo Internet Life Reviews, Netguide Live's Best of the Web, and Point Communications' Top 5% Sites, whose logo, affixed to a winning site, is shown here. It was probably inevitable that someone would make a Bottom 95% Sites logo, which, of course, can be awarded to everyone else.

provider that will store it for you and let it be accessible to other people. You also must have some software with which to write it, and you must know how to use that software. In an academic environment, you may be permitted to keep your work on the school's computer, at least temporarily, and you can probably find a class that teaches you how to create a home page. You could even teach yourself. Ready to get started? Not by a long shot. What most page makers fail to understand is that they need to have *something to say*. A page that describes yourself ("I'm cool"), your pet ("So cute!"), and your hobbies ("I like jazz and collecting barbecue recipes") will not make a contribution to the Internet.

Start with the assumption, since you are going to go to the trouble of making it, that you would like others to visit your page. Your friends will come no matter what—once. If you want the general public to drop by, your page needs to offer something of value: information. The topic matters less than what you have to say about it. Once you have determined how your page will have some value, you can turn to its design. An attractive, uncluttered design adds to a page's value.

Once you have some instruction, even self-instruction, creating a home page is not at all difficult. It is also very satisfying to see your own page, finished and available to the world. Even if you soon abandon the page, you will have acquired skills and resources. If, however, your interest is sustained, you must update your page on a regular basis, or people will lose interest. That is, your page is never finished.

Web pages are often written directly in a language called **HyperText Markup Language**, more commonly known as **HTML**. The HTML code uses a set of **tags** that tell your web browser how to format, load, and align text and graphics on your page. A tag, for example, might note that a particular line should be a title or a heading or be bulleted. Nothing stands still for long in the computer world, so others have come along with easier software to provide a simple user interface for writing HTML code. They essentially just offer easier ways to specify what you want, then they convert it to HTML for you.

Business on the Internet

Businesses large and small have embraced the Internet. But businesses can find the Internet frustrating because they must sit idly by, so to speak, and hope that users will visit their sites. That is, in the jargon of the trade, they await users to *pull* data from their sites. The answer to this problem is the opposite approach: push technology.

Push Technology

Think of it this way: *pull* is like going to the newsstand to pick up a paper, but *push* is like having it delivered to your door. More precisely, **push technology** refers to software that automatically sends—pushes—information from the Internet to a user's personal computer. From the sender's point of view, this process is akin to TV broadcasting, so push technology is sometimes called **webcasting.** Proponents laud push technology as a timesaver for users: Instead of browsing and searching the Internet for what you want, customized information is gathered up for you from various sites and sent to you automatically. Detractors view it in less flattering terms, seeing it as marketing hype that will clog the Internet with frivolous graphics and unwanted advertising.

The pushing, however, begins only with the consent of the recipient. The concept was pioneered by PointCast Inc., which delivers information in the form of a screen saver (Figure 7-11). It works like this. You download the push software from the company's web site and install it. Then, using the software, you select "channels" you want to receive. The list of channels includes generic channels such as sports and business, and also brand name channels such as CNN and the New York Times. You can narrow selections further within the channels. Then the push

Figure 7-11 Push technology. PointCast downloads information in varioius categories from the Internet to the user's personal computer. Categories range from headline news to sports to lifestyles to business, as shown here. The information is displayed as a screen saver when the computer is temporarily idle. Stock quotes and sports scores stream across the bottom of the screen. Screens also show commercials; notice the VISA ad in the box on the left.

software goes out to the Internet and retrieves, from various sites, information related to your declared interests—and ads. These are presented on your screen, complete with stock quotes and sports scores flowing across the bottom of the screen.

This concept works best for users who have a persistent connection via the office computer network. The information is downloaded to a corporate server and then relayed to employees. News and information is updated throughout the day. For people using the software on a personal computer at home, the service can only push information to you if you make a connection. You click the push software's update button whenever you want the latest information; the push software will dial a connection, gather information from the Internet, disconnect itself, then display the new information on your screen. Further, the software can be set to connect and update automatically at regular intervals.

Both the software and the information-gathering service are free. You must, of course, have the ability to connect to the Internet.

Although many businesses use the Internet to promote their products and services to the public, they are finding that an even more useful application is for their own internal purposes; hence, the intranet.

Intranets

Vendors promoting their intranet software products in magazine advertisements often make a play on the word, perhaps InTRAnet or even Intranet. They do not want you to think that they are simply misspelling Internet. In fact, an **intranet** is a private Internet-like network internal to a certain company. The number of intranets has been growing rapidly. Every Fortune 500 company either has an intranet or is planning one; Levi Strauss, Ford, Silicon Graphics, and U.S. West are examples of early users. Part of the reason for the phenomenal growth is the ease in setting up an intranet.

Setting Up an Intranet   It's fast, it's easy, it's inexpensive. Relatively speaking, of course. The components of an intranet are familiar ones: the same ones used for the Internet. Hardware requirements include a server and computers used for access. These probably exist because most companies already have local area networks; hence, the setup designation of fast-easy-inexpensive. The Internet TCP/IP protocols must be in place. The server, which will act as a clearinghouse for all data regardless of source, needs its own software. The server will process requests and also perhaps pull data from traditional sources such as a mainframe computer. As on the Internet, each access computer needs a browser.

The intranet developers will doubtless devote the most time and attention to writing the web pages that employees will see and use. The pages must be well designed and easy to follow. A typical opening page, for example, would probably have an attractive company logo and several clickable generic icons to represent functions. One click leads to a more detailed page, and so on. By presenting information the same way to every computer, the developers can pull all the computers, software, and data files that dot the corporate landscape into a single system that helps employees find information wherever it resides.

Intranets at Work   A well-designed intranet can be used by most employees from day one. They can point and click and link to sites that contain information previously locked away behind functionaries and forms. Suppose, for example, that an employee needs to check up on the status of her benefits. Traditionally, she would probably have to find the right form, fill it out correctly, submit it, and wait a few days for a response. Now, it is point and click, give some identifying information such as Social Security number, and the information shows up on the screen and can be printed.

Employee information is just the beginning. Typical applications are internal job openings, marketing, vacation requests, and corporate policy information. Some even include the local weather report and the daily cafeteria menu. Intranets even cut down on the flow of e-mail. A manager can, instead of sending out mass e-mail to employees, post notices on his own web site and leave it to employees to check it regularly.

The Internet Too   An intranet can remain private and isolated, but most companies choose to link their intranets to the Internet. This gives employees access to Internet resources and to other employees in geographically dispersed places, with their own intranets.

Taking the intranet one step further, intranet-to-intranet, that is, hooking up the intranets of two companies, is called an **extranet.** Some companies are finding that their long-standing relationships with customers and suppliers can often be handled more easily and more inexpensively than with more traditional electronic data interchange—EDI—systems.

> Traffic Jams

The Internet was not planned for its current users. The original Internet was a low-speed, text-based network designed to send messages between a few government sites and the research and defense contracting community. No one envisioned today's millions of users, some surfing for hours at a time and sending high-volume multimedia data. The Internet is a victim of its own success, its arteries so clogged that a user often crawls and stutters through cyberspace.

Numerous solutions to the speed problem have been proposed. Still more are on the drawing table. Most solutions are aimed at increasing bandwidth, just expanding "the pipes" so that more data can flow through. Some current options were mentioned in Chapter 6, from a souped-up 56Kbps modem to ISDN at 128Kbps.

Another approach, now available in limited markets, is a **cable modem,** a speedster that uses the coaxial television cables already in place without interrupting normal cable TV reception. Cable modems can be stunningly fast: 10 *million* bps. See Figure 7-12 for a comparison. Furthermore, a cable modem is always "on," like a TV channel, and does not require dialing or placing a call to get started. But problems remain, notably the necessary upgrades to the cable infrastructure for data communications.

The problem is complicated by the fact that the Internet comprises many communication links, and no one "fix" can affect them all. The major links that tie servers across wide geographical areas are called the **backbone** of the Internet. Links that form the backbone bear well-known commercial names such as Sprint and MCI and UUNet, and are noted for significant bandwidth. Suppose, however, that many users increase their home access bandwidth. Widespread use of high-speed

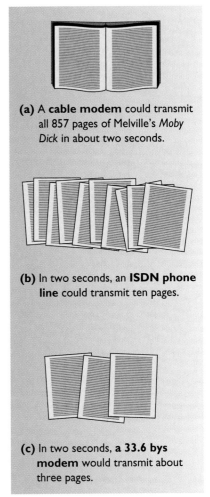

(a) A **cable modem** could transmit all 857 pages of Melville's *Moby Dick* in about two seconds.

(b) In two seconds, an **ISDN phone line** could transmit ten pages.

(c) In two seconds, a **33.6 bys modem** would transmit about three pages.

Figure 7-12 Just how fast? A comparison of data capacity for different modes of transmission.

BTW, I'm ROFL

People who regularly post messages on newsgroups have developed their own shorthand, which you might find puzzling at first glance. Here are some clues. BTW stands for *by the way*. ROFL means *rolling on the floor laughing*. Or try IMHO for *in my humble opinion*; FWIW, *for what it's worth*; CUL, *see you later*; or (if you are up to it) TTFN, *ta ta for now*.

home access systems will place even more demands on the backbone, and that will, in turn, slow everyone's access to the system.

Part of the reason for Internet congestion, and thus slower speeds, is that people have not been charged based on their usage of the Internet. In forum after forum, experts predict that users are going to have to pay for Internet use. A heavy user, it is thought, should pay more than an occasional browser. Economists venture that, as in other segments of society, if people do not pay for what they consume, there will be no economic incentive to keep building the Internet.

▶ Branching Out

Although the World Wide Web is usually the focus of any Internet discussion, there are other parts of the 'Net that deserve attention. All of them, in fact, predate the Web. One way to identify such sites is to observe the protocol. Instead of *http*, to which you may be accustomed for web sites, you may see *news*, *Gopher*, or *ftp*.

Newsgroups

Usenet is an informal network of computers that allows the posting and reading of messages in newsgroups that focus on specific topics. A more informal name is simply **newsgroups.** Topics of newsgroup discussions cover almost any subject you could imagine. If you have a passion for herbal remedies or for Macintosh computers or for Chinese politics, you can find not just one person but an entire group of people who share your interest and have something to say about it. Today there are more than 10,000 newsgroups. All of them offer conversation, and many offer files to download.

Think of a newsgroup as one large bulletin board, marked off by category. If you happen along, you can read other people's postings. If you wish to respond to a message or just contribute your own original thought, you leave a message. The process is just about that simple. Using your browser, you click the newsgroup icon, then pick the topic that interests you. Some refinements are available, such as reading messages posted only after a certain date, so that you do not see messages you have already read.

A suggested rule is that you observe the newsgroup for a while, an activity called **lurking,** before you jump in. That is, just read messages without writing any. That way you will get the flavor of the group before you participate. Another suggested rule is to skip participation in a group if you do not accept their underlying premise. For example, an atheist should not join a newsgroup of priests discussing canonical matters. You do not have to agree; just go away.

There are a few problems associated with newsgroups. The one that can affect anyone is that newsgroups are a great source for picking up e-mail addresses, which can then be used for directed advertising. If you were selling, say, a recipe for homemade acne relief, for example, what better target for your sales pitch than the participants in the herbal remedies newsgroup? Of course, mass advertising on the 'Net is not only frowned upon, it is discouraged with unpleasant e-mail responses and other sanctions, such as blocking incoming mail from a certain address. Sanctions help, but they cannot really stop a determined marketer (who, among other things, can just move to a different address). The result is that you, as the addressee, will have more unwanted e-mail.

A more insidious problem possibly awaits those who participate in unsavory groups, often with the prefix *alt*, for alternative. Many alt groups—algebra or aliens, for example—are of little concern to any but the participants. But parents are concerned about "adult" forums that may be accessed by minors. It is partly these groups that have inspired legislation aimed at restricting certain Internet content.

Newsgroups are among the oldest and most cherished institutions on the Internet. They were around long before the mass participation of users in the Web and will continue, no doubt, to revel in their own special subject matters.

Gopher Searches

In any part of the Internet, a user needs to be able to find information. One of the attractions of the Web is the ease of using search engines to do so. Another tactic, a non-Web approach, is to use a Gopher search. **Gopher**, named for the mascot at the University of Minnesota where it was developed, lets you "go fer" a certain file through a series of menus that zero in on your choice. The Gopher software, also accessed by a click on your browser menu, uses a hierarchical menu structure to organize, search, and deliver information on the Internet. For example, if you wanted to find information about banking in China, you might first go to business, then select banking, then international banking.

There are other tools that can help search Gopher files. Their names—acronyms—are easy to remember, even if the words the acronyms represent seem a bit contrived. We will mention the words anyway, just so you will have seen them once and will not have to wonder what they are. **Veronica** (Very Easy Rodent Oriented Netwide Index to Computerized Archives) is software that searches for keywords in Gopher menus. An alternative, which also searches for Gopher keywords, is **Jughead** (Jonzy's Universal Gopher Hierarchy Excavation and Display).

FTP: Downloading Files

You already know that you can access files that reside on remote computers through the Internet and view them on your own computer screen. That is, you are allowed to look at them. But what if you wanted to keep a file; that is, what if you wanted your own copy of a file on your own computer? It may be possible to download—get—the file from the distant computer and place it on the hard disk of the computer you are using.

Whether or not a file is available for downloading depends on two things: (1) whether you are allowed to download files to the hard disk of the computer you are using, and (2) whether the file you want is available for copying. You should be able to find out whether or not you are permitted to download files to the computer you are using. Disk space is at a premium in some locations. Of course, if you are using your own personal computer, you may do whatever you like.

Many computer files are proprietary, and a user who wants them must have an account on that computer and a password. The files available for you to copy are not proprietary. All kinds of files—programs, text, graphics images, even sounds—are available to be copied. The free files are public archives, often associated with an educational institution or the government.

There are many reasons you might want someone else's file. Perhaps, for example, a colleague in another city has just written a 150-page grant proposal and wants to send it to you; it is not convenient to send large files via e-mail. Perhaps you want some NASA space photos or some game software. Perhaps you have nothing particular in mind but, knowing the free stuff is out there, simply go to a popular FTP site and look around. You can also upload—send your own files to another computer—but most people do a lot more downloading than uploading.

Computers on the Internet have a standard way to transfer copies of files, a program called **FTP**, for **file transfer protocol**. The term has become so common that FTP is often used as a verb, as in "Jack FTP-ed that file this morning." Most downloading is done by a method called **anonymous FTP.** This means that instead of having to identify yourself with a proper account on the remote computer, you can simply call yourself Anonymous. Also, instead of a password, you just use your e-mail address. This is merely background information; your browser will do all this work for you when you indicate that you want to transfer to an FTP site to select a file and download it.

An FTP site arranges files hierarchically by subject matter, but the various layers are linked so that you need only click repeatedly in your area of interest to narrow down to a specific file name. Once you have identified the file, you can click its name to download it. Many files available for downloading are compressed or "zipped" to save space. Some of these files automatically decompress—unzip—themselves when they are executed. Others must be uncompressed by software for this purpose; such software is usually available to download from FTP sites.

▶ Not Quite Perfect Yet

The Internet has been heaped with well-deserved praise. But still there are concerns. To begin with, no one really knows exactly who is out there on the 'Net and what they are doing online. It's a little worrisome. On the other hand, many users find the freewheeling, no-controls aspect of the Internet appealing. Many fear government attempts, such as the Telecommunications Bill of 1996, which proposed fines and jail time for offenders, to tame the Internet. Although this bill was struck down by the courts, the issues remain.

Behavior Problems

There really are some behavior problems on the Internet. But there are behavior problems in any aspect of society, from the playground to the boardroom. Those who abuse the 'Net are, relatively speaking, small in number. One solution is a proposed ratings system, with software for parental control of the types of sites or newsgroups accessed.

Meanwhile, the community of Internet users has made serious efforts to monitor behavior on the 'Net. One consistent effort is **netiquette**, which refers to appropriate behavior in network communications. For example, users are admonished not to type in caps (IT'S LIKE SHOUTING). Netiquette rules are published on several sites and in every book about the Internet. Users who stray may be subjected to **flaming**, in which angry e-mail is directed to someone on the 'Net who has done something egregious, such as the mass advertising mentioned earlier.

Useless, Overburdened, and Misinformed

Some people consider some home pages useless. In fact, there is a site called Useless Pages that maintains a listing of pages the site manager deems useless. However, many people are willing to pay for the connection to a web server in order to promote a home page they fancy, whatever anyone else may think. Others put out birth or wedding announcements, complete with photos. One useless page does nothing except count the number of times the page is accessed. At the other end of the spectrum are sites that, apparently, have so much value that their popularity renders them mostly inaccessible. Any list of "cool" sites, a favorite Web word, is likely to be crowded.

There are no guarantees. The Internet is full of misinformation. Just because something is on the Internet does not mean it is true. If someone steps up to announce that the government uses black helicopters to spy on us or that tapes sound better if you soak them in water first, you need not accept such information as fact. It's not that people intend to be wrong, it's just that they sometimes are. If you are doing serious research on the Internet, be sure to back it up with other sources, especially non-Internet sources.

The Internet is interesting and even fun. Perhaps the best aspect of the Internet is that even a novice computer user can learn how to move from site to site on the Internet with relative ease.

CHAPTER REVIEW

Summary and Key Terms

- In the 1950s the United States Department of Defense became concerned that a single bomb could wipe out its computing capabilities. Working with the RAND Corporation, they decided to rely on not one but several computers, geographically dispersed.

- A message to be sent to another computer is divided up into **packets**, each labeled with its destination address; the packets are reassembled at the destination address.

- The software that takes care of the packets is Transmission Control Protocol/Internet Protocol (TCP/IP). TCP does the packeting and reassembling of the message. The IP part of the protocol handles the addressing, seeing to it that packets are routed across multiple computers.

- The new set of connections, officially established in 1969, was called **ARPANet**, for Advanced Research Projects Agency Network.

- In 1990, **Dr. Tim Berners-Lee** made getting around the Internet easier by designing a set of links for one computer to connect to another. He saw the set of links as a spider's web; hence the name **Web**. The **CERN site** at this laboratory is considered the birthplace of the **World Wide Web**. A **link** on a web site is easy to see: it is colored text called **hypertext** or an icon or image called a **hyperregion**. A mouse click on the link transports the user to the site represented by the link.

- As a student, **Marc Andreessen**, in 1993, led a team that invented the *browser*, graphical interface software used to explore the Internet. That first browser was named **Mosaic.**

- The emergence of the Internet is due to four factors: (1) the universal TCP/IP standard, (2) the web-like ability to link from site to site, (3) the ease of use provided by the browser's graphical interface, and (4) the growth of personal computers and their local area networks that could be connected to the Internet.

- An Internet user needs a computer with a modem and its related software, an Internet service provider, and a browser. An **Internet service provider (ISP)** provides the server computer and the software to connect to the Internet. A **browser** is the software on the user's computer that allows the user to access the Internet via the service provider, using a graphical interface.

- If you elect to go directly to an Internet service provider you will need to select one, arrange to pay the fees, and set up your ISP interaction according to their directions.

- As you are installing the browser, you will be asked for information about your ISP, for which your ISP vendor has prepared you. Once you are set up, you invoke the browser as you would any software on your computer, and it will begin by dialing the Internet service provider for you.

- When you invoke your browser software, it will dial up the Internet service provider and, once successfully connected, display the **home page** of the browser's web site. The browser shows three parts on the screen, the *browser control panel*, consisting of lines of menus and buttons; the *browser display window* to show the current site; and a *status line* at the bottom. The page can be **scrolled**—moved up and down—by using the **scroll bar** on the right.

- Using a mouse permits commands to be issued through a series of **menus**, a series of choices normally laid out across the top of the screen. The menus are called **pull-down menus** because each initial choice, when clicked with a mouse, reveals lower-level choices. **Buttons** can also invoke commands.

- The **Uniform Resource Locator (URL)** is a string of letters and symbols that is the unique address of a web page or file on the Internet. A web page URL begins with the protocol *http*, which stands for **HyperText Transfer Protocol**, the means of communicating using links. Next comes the **domain name**, which is the address of the Internet service provider. The last part of the domain name is called a **top-level domain** and represents the purpose of the organization or entity.

- A **hot list**—called Bookmarks or Favorites or something similar—stores favorite sites and their URLs.

- In browsers, **frames** allow a given page to be divided into rectangular sections, each of which can operate independently of the other. A **plug-in** is software that enhances the functionality of a browser.

- **Java**, a programming language developed by Sun Microsystems, can be used to write software that can be used on any machine. Java **applets** are the small programs that provide dancing icons, scrolling banners, and the like on web pages.

- Methods of moving to other sites from the initial browser page include clicking categories, typing in a new URL for a desired site, or using a search engine.

- A **search engine** is software that lets a user specify search terms; the search engine then finds sites that fit those terms. The search can be narrowed by refining the search criteria.

- Another way to narrow a search is to use a mathematical system called **Boolean logic**, which uses the operators AND, OR, and NOT.

- Search engines vary widely in size, content, and search methodology.

- To make a home page on the Web, you need a service provider, software with which to write it and the ability to use that software, and something to say. A home page that has value must offer information and at least a passable design.

- Web pages were originally written in a language called **HyperText Markup Language**, more commonly known as **HTML**. The HTML code uses a set of **tags** that tell your web browser how to format, load, and align text and graphics on your page. Now easier software simplifies the process of creating HTML code.

- **Push technology**, also called **webcasting**, refers to software that automatically sends—pushes—information from the Internet to a user's personal computer.

- An **intranet** is a private Internet-like network internal to a certain company.

- An **extranet** is a network of two or more intranets.

- Numerous solutions to the Internet's sluggish speed have been proposed, including a **cable modem,** a speedster that uses the coaxial television cables already in place without interrupting normal cable TV reception. The major communication links that tie servers across wide geographical areas are called the **backbone** of the Internet. Widespread use of high-speed home access systems will place even more demands on the backbone, and that will, in turn, slow everyone's access to the system.

- **Usenet** is an informal network of computers that allow the posting and reading of messages in newsgroups that focus on specific topics. A more informal name is simply **newsgroups.** The more than 10,000 newsgroups cover every imaginable topic. Users can read and contribute messages to the newsgroup. A suggested rule is that you observe the newsgroup for a while, just reading messages without writing any—an activity called **lurking.**

- **Gopher**, named for the mascot at the University of Minnesota where it was developed, lets you "go fer" a certain file through a series of menus that zero in on your choice. The Gopher software, also accessed by a click on your browser menu, uses a hierarchical menu structure to organize, search, and deliver information on the Internet. **Veronica** and **Jughead** are software that searches for keywords in Gopher menus.

- Computers on the Internet have a standard way to transfer copies of files, a set of rules called **FTP,** for **file transfer protocol.** Most downloading is done by a method called **anonymous FTP,** meaning that a user can be named Anonymous and the password just the user's e-mail address.

- **Netiquette** refers to appropriate behavior in network communications. Netiquette rules are published on several sites and in every book about the Internet. Users who stray may be subjected to **flaming,** in which angry e-mail is directed to someone on the 'Net who has done something egregious, such as mass advertising.

Quick Poll

Compare your answers to those of your colleagues or classmates.

1. My reaction to newsgroups:
   - ❏ a. Too time-consuming, and not much use.
   - ❏ b. Can be very helpful on a given topic.
   - ❏ c. I can spend hours just watching these people.
2. Regarding writing my own home page:
   - ❏ a. Not where I want to put my time.
   - ❏ b. The knowledge would be valuable.
   - ❏ c. I'd like to learn all the ins and outs.
3. My vote for a search engine (even if I have not used them all) is
   - ❏ a. Infoseek
   - ❏ b. Excite
   - ❏ c. AltaVista
   - ❏ d. Open Text Index
   - ❏ e. HotBot
   - ❏ f. Other

Discussion Questions

1. How reliable are search engines? Why might one give a different set of results than another?
2. On what topic(s) might you write a home page?
3. After he left school, Marc Andreessen, in his own words, wanted to make a "Mosaic killer." He felt he had not been given sufficient credit for his college efforts and set out to make his fortune commercially with Netscape Navigator. He did. Dr. Tim Berners-Lee, however, rejected numerous commercial offerings. He felt that if he cashed in on his invention it would compromise the Web, which he wanted available to everyone. Are both these positions defensible? Comment.

Student Study Guide

Multiple Choice

1. The author of the Web:
   - a. RAND Corporation
   - b. ARPANet
   - c. Tim Berners-Lee
   - d. Marc Andreessen
2. Which is *not* a Boolean operator:
   - a. OR
   - b. IN
   - c. AND
   - d. NOT
3. The software that uses a hierarchical menu structure to organize and search the Internet:
   - a. TCP/IP
   - b. Gopher
   - c. HTML
   - d. FTP

4. The action of moving a page up or down on the screen:
   - a. scrolling
   - b. linking
   - c. lurking
   - d. framing
5. The software on a user's computer that uses a graphical interface to access the Internet:
   - a. Veronica
   - b. FTP
   - c. ISP
   - d. browser
6. Which factor was *not* a major contributor to the emergence of the Internet:
   - a. linking
   - b. browser
   - c. frames
   - d. TCP/IP
7. The first browser:
   - a. Internet Explorer
   - b. Jughead
   - c. Netscape Navigator
   - d. Mosaic
8. The birthplace of the World Wide Web:
   - a. RAND Corporation
   - b. CERN
   - c. ARPA
   - d. Gopher
9. The name for the major links that tie servers across wide geographical areas:
   - a. Gopher
   - b. backbone
   - c. HTML
   - d. ARPANet
10. A browser's ability to divide a page into independent rectangles:
    - a. Boolean logic
    - b. URLs
    - c. frames
    - d. plug-in

True/False

T F   1. The emergence of the Internet is due primarily to its ability to perform hierarchical searches.

T F   2. In an URL, the domain name is the address of the ISP.

T F   3. The inventor of the browser is Marc Andreessen.

T F   4. TCP/IP is the standard Internet protocol.

T F   5. Dr. Tim Berners-Lee started ARPANet.

T F   6. A cable modem is slower than a traditional modem.

T F   7. The first ISP was Mosaic.

T F   8. Veronica and Jughead are Gopher searches.

T F   9. *Com* is an example of a top-level domain.

T F 10. A link on a web site is usually colored text or an image or icon.

T F 11. Newsgroup users prefer that new people offer comments immediately so they can assess the new person's viewpoint.

T F 12. A message to be sent from one computer to another on the Internet is divided up into packets.

T F 13. Boolean logic operators are used primarily in HTML code.

T F 14. HTML uses a set of tags.

T F 15. An ISP is needed only if a user does not have a browser.

T F 16. The birthplace of the World Wide web is considered the CERN site.

T F 17. The Department of Defense worked with CERN to develop ARPANet.

T F 18. To go to a new site, an Internet user must type the site's URL.

T F 19. Files can be transferred using the Gopher protocol.

T F 20. The TCP/IP protocol is used in the United States and Canada, but the rest of the world uses other protocols.

Fill-In

1. The inventor of the first browser:

   _____

2. The process of watching a newsgroup before participating: _____

3. TCP/IP stands for _____

4. Software that organizes and searches hierarchically on the Internet: _____

5. HTML stands for _____

6. Moving a page up and down on the screen:

   _____

7. *Gov, edu,* and *com* are examples of

   _____

8. Usenet is a formal name for

   _____

9. FTP stands for _____

10. ARPA stands for _____

11. ISP stands for _____

12. The first page of a web site:

    _____

13. A message to be sent over the Internet is divided into _____

14. The major links that tie servers across wide geographical areas are called _____

15. The division of a web page into independent rectangles: _____

16. The inventor of the technique of using links to access other Internet sites:

    _____

17. The "think tank" that worked with the U.S. Department of Defense to configure ARPANet:

    _____

18. The mathematical system used as a basis for narrowing searches: _____

19. The first browser: _____

20. The birthplace of the World Wide Web:

    _____

Answers

Multiple Choice

1. c	6. c
2. b	7. d
3. b	8. b
4. a	9. b
5. d	10. c

True/False

1. F	6. F	11. F	16. T
2. T	7. F	12. T	17. F
3. T	8. T	13. F	18. F
4. T	9. T	14. T	19. F
5. F	10. T	15. F	20. F

Fill-In

1. Marc Andreessen
2. lurking
3. Transmission Control Protocol/Internet Protocol
4. Gopher
5. HyperText Markup Language
6. scrolling
7. top-level domains
8. newsgroups
9. file transfer protocol
10. Advanced Research Projects Agency
11. Internet service provider
12. home page
13. packets
14. backbone
15. frames
16. Dr. Tim Berners-Lee
17. RAND Corporation
18. Boolean logic
19. Mosaic
20. CERN site

PLANET INTERNET

CAREER SO NEAR

Many people, whether college students or experienced employees, dread the prospect of facing the world and begging for a job. Resources for this onerous task are often limited to the classified ads and perhaps a placement center. You need have no such limitation if you have access to the Internet. A number of services specialize in matching employers with job seekers. However, although assistance is available for first-time job seekers, and some sites even specialize in helping college students, it would be fair to say that many jobs posted on the Internet lean toward experienced people in the computer field.

Online help for students. The Online Career Center offers career support services such as a list of keywords to use to search for jobs from thousands of companies. The e-span site features a searchable list of jobs and, in addition, lets job seekers type in a location and get the advertisements for that geographic area. JobWeb offers employment information, job listings, and tips; it also permits a job seeker to fill out a form online to create a listing on its pages. JobTrak is the largest online job listing service in the United States and, as you can see from its home page image, shown here, offers a large variety of services. Career Mosaic, whose on-screen logo is shown here, lists high-powered employers and offers a variety of support for job seekers.

These sites, and others like them, have one thing in common: They all promote their list of job seekers to employers. This is their profit center. For a fee, an employer can search the site's database of job candidates. The database search can be narrowed by using keywords that represent job titles or particular skills required. This connection between employer and job seeker is much more efficient and speedy than the traditional shuffling of piles of résumés.

Your home page résumé. Some job seekers have taken advantage of Web exposure by developing their own home page résumés. This goes so far beyond the traditional résumé that a new name should be invented for it. Typically, the candidate

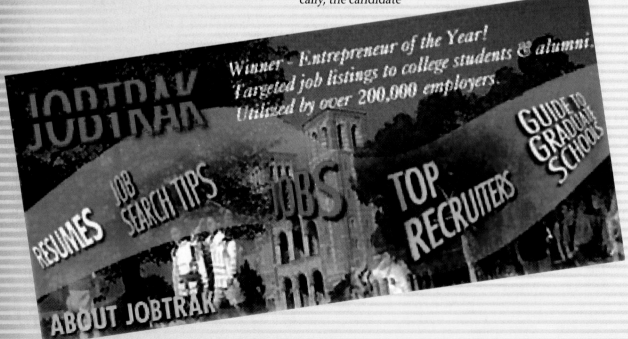

includes a nice photo and then offers perhaps a 10- to 15-line résumé. Why so short? Each résumé line has links! For example, one line may refer to classes taken, with classes being a link. A potential employer merely clicks on the word *classes* to pop up a list of classes the job seeker has taken. Similarly, links can be made to intern work, laboratory assignments, extracurricular activities, work experience, special skills, and so forth. A person developing such a home page from scratch can make the résumé as varied as desired. Some schools permit students to post résumés on their site for a certain time period.

There are a few dozen sites devoted exclusively to résumés. They usually offer, among other things, tips on résumé writing. Other sites feature a résumé service as one of many options; the Virtual Job Fair site, whose opening image is shown here, offers résumé services. As so many sites do, this one will let you post your résumé on its site. Résumé service is sometimes free, but more often a fee is required.

On being a webmaster. One special career worth mentioning is webmaster, particularly because it may be available to new graduates. A webmaster's duties vary, but the overall mission is the design and monitoring of the company's site. Some companies are willing to hire a webmaster right out of college if he or she has had

spend a lot of time meeting with people who have a vested interest in the site, such as company employees from the marketing department. Other assets for a potential webmaster are experience in design, even if it was just a newsletter, and marketing experience.

Although they are still sparse and undefined, a handful of formal certificate programs are available for would-be webmasters. Check out some of the many sites devoted to webmasters.

Internet Exercises

1. **Structured exercise.** Hooking up to the AWL site with URL http://hepg.awl.com/capron/planet/, take a look at the Virtual Job Fair site. Find out what you have to do to submit a résumé for posting on this site.
2. **Freeform exercise.** To expand your set of resources, begin with the Yahoo site. Find and click on Business and then, under Business, click Employment.

experience designing a web site. That site, of course, would have to be fairly sophisticated. Employers usually require knowledge of Unix, the operating system most often associated with the Internet. The next requirement is not technical but is a necessity in any team environment: communication skills. The reason for this is that most webmasters must

Harley Bjornson owns his own manufacturing company, a company begun by his father. His father had come to America from Norway and knew something about fishing boats. As a young man, the father invented and received a patent for a winch of particular interest to gill-netters. That invention has been a large part of the success of the company, now run by Harley and his son Erik.

It was Erik who pushed Harley into the computer age, making a case for seven networked personal computers. The two of them, working with a consultant, gave a lot of thought to what business functions could be computerized and who should use the computers for what purpose. They even planned to access the Internet. They gave no thought, however, to security or privacy. They came to regret that oversight in January 1997, the month of the mudslide. That month, as it turned out, was significant in more ways than one.

The mudslide followed two weeks of first snow and then torrential rains. Harley's office building, at the bottom of a hill, was overcome by a mudslide that ruined all the furniture—and the four computers—on the first floor. The server, fortunately, was on the second floor. Harley had no disaster plan in place. Replacing the computers was the least of it; several files that had been scattered among them were lost, and there were no backup copies. The business limped along for several weeks while the files were painstakingly reconstructed.

Harley contracted with computer professionals to help sort out the mess. In the process, a consultant discovered that their network had been invaded by intruders. In particular, a patent application that his son was preparing on a new invention, possibly another breakthrough in winch technology, had been tampered with. Looking further, they also discovered that the records for one employee showed a trail of Internet access to distinctly unbusinesslike sites. Finally, old e-mail records showed that one employee sent hundreds of non-business communications, some of them complaining about the boss. Rather overwhelmed, Harley and Erik sat down for a serious discussion with the computer professionals. They mapped out a disaster plan and employee computer-use policies.

They also built a large retaining wall between the hill and their office building.

Security and Privacy

Computers and the Internet

➤ A First Look at Security and Privacy

There was a time when security and privacy issues related to computers were easily managed: simply lock the computer room door. Those centralized days are, of course, long gone. Now, in theory, anyone can hook up to any computer from any location. In light of data communications access, the first issue is security. The vast files of computer-stored information must be kept secure—safe from destruction, accidental damage, theft, even espionage.

A second issue is privacy. Private data—salaries, medical information, Social Security numbers, bank balances, and much more—must be kept from prying eyes. The problems are many and the solutions complex. The advent of the Internet and its escalating expansion has only heightened the existing problems and added new problems of its own.

These issues and more will be addressed in this chapter as we march through security, privacy, and the specific problems associated with the Internet. However, we begin with a fascinating aspect of the security problem: computer crime.

➤ Computer Crime

It was 5 o'clock in the morning, and 14-year-old Randy Miller was startled to see a man climbing in his bedroom window. "FBI," the man announced, "and that computer is mine." So ended the computer caper in San Diego where 23 teenagers, ages 13 to 17, had used their home computers to invade computer systems as far away as Massachusetts. The teenagers are **hackers**, people who attempt to gain access to computer systems illegally, usually from a personal computer, via a data communications network.

The term *hacker* used to mean a person with significant computer expertise, but the term has taken on the more sinister meaning with the advent of computer miscreants. In this case the hackers did not use the system to steal money or property. But they did create fictitious accounts and destroyed or changed some data files. The FBI's entry through the bedroom window was calculated: The agents figured that, given even a moment's warning, the teenagers were clever enough to alert each other via computer.

This story—except for the name—is true. Hackers ply their craft for a variety of reasons but most often to show off for their peers or to harass people they do not like. A favorite trick, for example, is to turn a rival's telephone into a pay phone, so that when his or her parents try to dial a number an operator would interrupt to say, "Please deposit 25 cents." A hacker may have more sinister motives, such as getting computer services without paying for them or getting information to sell.

You will probably not be surprised to learn that hackers have invaded web sites. These vandals show up with what amounts to a digital spray can, defacing sites with taunting boasts, graffiti, and their own private jokes. Although the victims feel violated, the perpetrators view their activities as mere pranks.

Hackers and Other Miscreants

Hacking has long been thought the domain of teenagers with time on their hands. The pattern is changing, however. A recent government survey showed that the computer systems of over half of the largest U.S. corporations had been invaded, but not by teenagers. Most intruders were competitors stealing proprietary information. For example, suppose a biomedical company discovers just one little research secret in a competitor's computer files; the snooping company may then be the first to market with a drug that the invaded company has been working on for years. Even more astounding, federal investigators told a U.S. Senate hearing that the U.S. Department of Defense computers are attacked more than 200,000 times per year. Most worrisome is the emerging computer attack abilities of other nations, which, in a worst-case scenario, could seriously degrade the military's ability to deploy and sustain military forces.

Hackers ply their craft by surprisingly low-tech means. Using what is called **social engineering**, a tongue-in-cheek term for con artist actions, hackers simply persuade unsuspecting people to give away their passwords over the phone. Recognizing the problem, employers are educating their employees to be alert to such scams.

Getting Practical

KEEPING A SECRET

Employers wish that computer passwords were better-kept secrets. Here are some hints on password use.

- Do not name your password after your child or car or pet, an important date, or your phone number. Passwords that are easy to remember are also easy to crack.
- Make passwords as random as possible. Include both letters and numbers. The more characters the better. Embed at least one nonalphabetic character, and consider mixing upper- and lowercase letters. Example: Go*TOP6.
- Keep your password in your head or in a safe. Astonishingly, an occasional thoughtless user will scribble the password on paper and stick it on the computer screen where anyone can see it.
- Change your password often, at least once a month. In some installations, passwords are changed so seldom that they become known to many people, thus defeating the purpose.
- Do not fall for hacker phone scams—"social engineering"—to obtain your password. Typical ruses are callers posing as a neophyte employee ("Gosh, I'm so confused, could you talk me through it?"); a system expert ("We're checking a problem in the network that seems to be coming from your workstation. Could you please verify your password?"); a telephone company employee ("There seems to be a problem on your phone line"); or even an angry top manager ("This is outrageous! How do I get into these files anyway?").

Most people are naturally inclined to be helpful. Do not be inappropriately so. Keep in mind that you will be—at the very least—embarrassed if you are the source of information to a hacker who damages your company.

Hackers are only a small fraction of the security problem. The most serious losses are caused by electronic pickpockets who are usually a good deal older and not so harmless. Consider these examples:

- A brokerage clerk sat at his terminal in Denver and, with a few taps of the keys, transformed 1700 shares of his own stock, worth $1.50 per share, to the same number of shares in another company worth ten times that much.
- A Seattle bank employee used her electronic fund transfer code to move certain bank funds to an account held by her boyfriend as a "joke"; both the money and the boyfriend disappeared.
- A keyboard operator in Oakland, California, changed some delivery addresses to divert several thousand dollars' worth of department store goods into the hands of accomplices.
- A ticket clerk at the Arizona Veteran's Memorial Coliseum issued full-price basketball tickets for admission and then used her computer to record the sales as half-price tickets and pocketed the difference.

These stories point out that computer crime is not always the flashy, front-page news about geniuses getting away with millions of dollars. These people are ordinary employees in ordinary businesses—committing computer crimes.

The problems of computer crime have been aggravated in recent years by increased access to computers (Figure 8-1). More employees now have access to computers on their jobs. In fact, computer crime is often just white-collar crime with a new medium: Every time an employee is trained on the computer at work, he or she also gains knowledge that—potentially—could be used to harm the company.

The Changing Face of Computer Crime

Computer crime once fell into a few simple categories, such as theft of software or destruction of data. The dramatically increased access to networks has changed the focus to damage that can be done by unscrupulous people with online access. The most frequently reported computer crimes fall into these categories:

- **Credit card fraud.** Customer numbers are floating all over public and private networks, in varying states of protection. Some are captured and used fraudulently.
- **Data communications fraud.** This category covers a broad spectrum, including piggybacking on someone else's network, the use of an office network for personal purposes, and computer-directed diversion of funds.
- **Unauthorized access to computer files.** This general snooping category covers everything from accessing confidential employee records to the theft of trade secrets and product pricing structure.
- **Unlawful copying of copyrighted software.** Whether the casual sharing of copyrighted software among friends or assembly line copying by organized crime, unlawful copying incurs major losses for software vendors.

Although it is not our purpose to write a how-to book on computer crime, the margin note called *Some "Bad Guy" Tricks* mentions the methods some criminals use.

Disgruntled or militant employee could

- Sabotage equipment or programs
- Hold data or programs hostage

Competitor could

- Sabotage operations
- Engage in espionage
- Steal data or programs
- Photograph records, documentation, or CRT screen displays

Data control worker could

- Insert data
- Delete data
- Bypass controls
- Sell information

Clerk/supervisor could

- Forge or falsify data
- Embezzle funds
- Engage in collusion with people inside or outside the company

System user could

- Sell data to competitors
- Obtain unauthorized information

Operator could

- Copy files
- Destroy files

User requesting reports could

- Sell information to competitors
- Receive unauthorized information

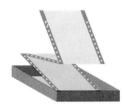

Engineer could

- Install "bugs"
- Sabotage system
- Access security information

Data conversion worker could

- Change codes
- Insert data
- Delete data

Programmer could

- Steal programs or data
- Embezzle via programming
- Bypass controls

Report distribution worker could

- Examine confidential reports
- Keep duplicates of reports

Trash collector could

- Sell reports or duplicates to competitors

Figure 8-1 The perils of increased access. By letting your imagination loose, you can visualize many ways in which people can compromise computer security. Computer-related crime would be far more rampant if all the people in these positions took advantage of their access to computers.

Discovery and Prosecution

Prosecuting the computer criminal is difficult for several reasons. To begin with, discovery is often difficult. Many times the crime simply goes undetected. In addition, crimes that are detected are—an estimated 85 percent of the time—never reported to the authorities. By law, banks have to make a report when their computer systems have been compromised, but other businesses do not. Often they choose not to report such crimes because they are worried about their reputations and credibility in the community.

Most computer crimes are discovered by accident. For example, a bank employee changed a program to add 10¢ to every customer service charge under $10 and $1 to every charge over $10. He then placed this overage into the last account, a bank account he opened himself in the name of Zzwicke. The system worked fairly well, generating several hundred dollars each month, until the bank initiated a new marketing campaign in which it singled out for special honors the very first depositor—and the very last. In another instance some employees of a city welfare department created a fictitious work force, complete with Social Security numbers, and programmed the computer to issue paychecks, which the employees would then intercept and cash. They were discovered when a police officer investigated an illegally parked overdue rental car and found the fraudulent checks inside.

Even if a computer crime is detected, prosecution is by no means assured. There are a number of reasons for this. First, some law enforcement agencies do not fully understand the complexities of computer-related fraud. Second, few attorneys are qualified to handle computer crime cases. Third, judges and juries are not always educated about computers and may not understand the nature of the violation or the seriousness of the crime.

In short, the chances of having a computer crime go undetected are, unfortunately, good. And the chances that, if detected, there will be no ramifications are also good: A computer criminal may not go to jail, may not be found guilty if prosecuted, and may not even be prosecuted.

But this situation is changing. Since Congress passed the **Computer Fraud and Abuse Act** in 1986, there has been a growing awareness of computer crime on the national level. This law is supplemented by state statutes; most states have passed some form of computer crime law. Computer criminals who are successfully prosecuted are subject to fines, jail time, and confiscation of their computer equipment.

▶ Security: Playing It Safe

As you can see from the previous section, the computer industry has been vulnerable in the matter of security. **Security** is a system of safeguards designed to protect a computer system and data from deliberate or accidental damage or access by unauthorized persons. That means safeguarding the system against such threats as natural disasters, fire, accidents, vandalism, theft or destruction of data, industrial espionage, and hackers (Figure 8-2).

Identification and Access: Who Goes There?

How does a computer system detect whether you are the person who should be allowed access to it? Various means have been devised to give

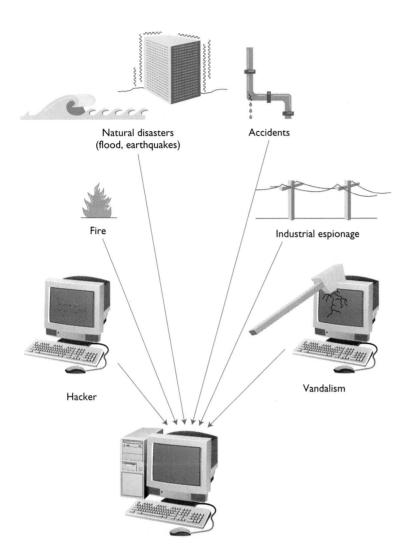

access to authorized people without compromising the system. These means fall into four broad categories: what you have, what you know, what you do, and what you are.

- **What you have.** You may have a key, badge, token, or plastic card to give you physical access to the computer room or to a locked-up terminal or personal computer. A card with a magnetized strip, for example, can give you access to your bank account via a remote cash machine. Taking this a step further, some employees begin each business day by donning an **active badge**, a clip-on identification card with an embedded computer chip. The badge signals its wearer's location—legal or otherwise—by sending out infrared signals, which are read by sensors sprinkled around the building.
- **What you know.** Standard what-you-know items are a password or an identification number for your bank cash machine. Cipher locks on doors require that you know the correct combination of numbers.
- **What you do.** In their daily lives people often sign documents as a way of proving who they are. Though a signature is difficult to copy, forgery is not impossible. Today, software can verify both scanned and online signatures.
- **What you are.** Now it gets interesting. Some security systems use **biometrics**, the science of measuring individual body characteristics.

(a)

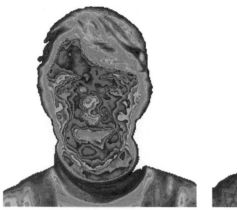
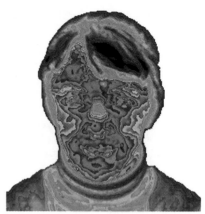

(b)

Figure 8-3 Identification. (a) The eye can be a means of personal identification. A user first keys a unique identification code number. The security system then matches the person's unique retina pattern to the individual's computer-stored retina pattern for conclusive identification of authorized users. (b) A person's entire face is used for identification in some security systems. Identification is based on a unique pattern of heat radiating from an individual's facial blood vessels.

Fingerprinting may seem to be old news, but not when you simply insert your finger into an identification machine. Some systems use the characteristics of the entire hand. Another approach is identification by voice recognition. Even newer is the concept of identification by the retina of the eye, which has a pattern that is harder to duplicate than a voiceprint (Figure 8-3a), or by the entire face, which draws its uniqueness from heat radiating from blood vessels (Figure 8-3b).

Some systems use a combination of the preceding four categories. For example, access to an automated teller machine requires both something you have—a plastic card—and something you know—a personal identification number (PIN).

When Disaster Strikes: What Do You Have to Lose?

In New York a power outage shut down computer operations and effectively halted business, air traffic, and transportation throughout the United States. In Italy armed terrorists singled out corporate and state computer centers as targets for attack and, during a ten-month period, bombed ten such centers throughout the country. In California a poem, a pansy, a bag of cookies, and a message, "Please have a cookie and a nice day," were left at the Vandenberg Air Force Base computer installation—along with five demolished mainframe computers. Computer installations of any kind can be struck by natural or man-made disasters that can lead to security violations. What kinds of problems might this cause an organization?

Your first thoughts might be of the hardware, the computer and its related equipment. But loss of hardware is not a major problem in itself; the loss will be covered by insurance, and hardware can be replaced. The true problem with hardware loss is the diminished processing ability that exists while managers find a substitute facility and return the installation to its former state. The ability to continue processing data is critical. Some information industries, such as banking, could literally go out of business in a matter of days if their computer operations were suspended. Loss of software should not be a problem if the organization has heeded industry warnings—and used common sense—to make backup copies of program files.

A more important problem is the loss of data. Imagine trying to reassemble lost or destroyed files of customer records, accounts receivable, or design data for a new airplane. The costs would be staggering. Software and data security will be presented in more detail later in this chapter. First, however, consider an overview of disaster recovery, the steps to restoring processing ability.

Disaster Recovery Plan

A **disaster recovery plan** is a method of restoring computer processing operations and data files if operations are halted or files are damaged by major destruction. There are various approaches. Some organizations revert temporarily to manual services, but life without the computer can be difficult indeed. Others arrange to buy time at a service bureau, but this is inconvenient for companies in remote or rural areas. If a single act, such as a fire, destroys your computing facility, it is possible that a mutual aid pact will help you get back on your feet. In such a plan two or more companies agree to lend each other computing power if one of them has a problem. This would be of little help, however, if there were a regional disaster and many companies needed assistance.

Banks and other organizations with survival dependence on computers sometimes form a **consortium**, a joint venture to support a complete computer facility. Such a facility is completely available and routinely tested but used only in the event of a disaster. Among these facilities, a **hot site** is a fully equipped computer center, with hardware, environmental controls, security, and communications facilities. A **cold site** is an environmentally suitable empty shell in which a company can install its own computer system.

The use of such a facility or any type of recovery at all depends on advance planning—specifically, the disaster recovery plan. The idea of such a plan is that everything except the hardware has been stored in a safe place somewhere else. The storage location should be several miles away, so it will not be affected by local physical forces, such as a hurricane. Typical items stored at the backup site are program and data files, program listings, program and operating systems documentation, hardware inventory lists, output forms, and a copy of the disaster plan manual.

The disaster recovery plan should include a list of priorities identifying the programs that must be up and running first, plans for notifying employees of changes in locations and procedures, a list of needed equipment and where it can be obtained, a list of alternative computing facilities, and procedures for handling input and output data in a different environment.

Computer installations actually perform emergency drills. At some unexpected moment a notice is given that "disaster has struck," and the computer professionals must run the critical systems at some other site.

Software Security

Software security has been an industry concern for years. Initially, there were many questions: Who owns custom-made software? Is the owner the person who wrote the program or the company for which the author wrote the program? What is to prevent a programmer from taking copies of programs from one job to another? The answer to these questions are well established. If the author of the software—the programmer—is in the employ of the organization, the software belongs to the organization, not the programmer. The programmer may not take the software along to

LEAVING CANADA

STOP AND REPORT TO U.S. CUSTOMS

They Know My Voice at the Border

If you have ever crossed the border between the United States and Canada, you may have waited in a long line of cars. But if you happened to pass through at night, you were probably processed quickly. Both of these statements apply, however, only at major border crossings, which are open 24 hours a day.

If you want to pass through an obscure open-only-sometimes crossing, you may have to make a run for it at closing time. This is especially hard on the locals who must cross often. If you miss the border opening times at Scobey, Montana, for example, you face a 120-mile detour to the nearest crossing. But help is now in place. It is computer help, of course: an electronic border crossing.

After applying to the local Immigration and Naturalization office, an approved user receives an ID card, is assigned a four-digit number, and records a brief voice phrase. To get across an unattended border, a user need only punch in the number and then speak the prerecorded words, and—presto—the gate opens.

the next job. If the programmer is a consultant, however, the ownership of the software produced should be spelled out specifically in the contract—otherwise, the parties enter extremely murky legal waters. According to a U.S. Supreme Court decision, software can be copyrighted.

Data Security

We have discussed the security of hardware and software. Now consider the security of data, which is one of an organization's most important assets. Here too there must be planning for security. Usually, this is done by security officers who are part of top management.

What steps can be taken to prevent theft or alteration of data? There are several data-protection techniques; these will not individually (or even collectively) guarantee security, but they make a good start.

Secured Waste   Discarded printouts, printer ribbons, and the like can be sources of information to unauthorized persons. This kind of waste can be made secure by the use of shredders or locked trash barrels.

Internal Controls   Internal controls are controls that are planned as part of the computer system. One example is a transaction log. This is a file of all accesses or attempted accesses to certain data.

Auditor Checks   Most companies have auditors go over the financial books. In the course of their duties, auditors frequently review computer programs and data. From a data security standpoint, auditors might also check to see who has accessed data during periods when that data is not usually used. Today auditors can use off-the-shelf audit software, programs that assess the validity and accuracy of the system's operations and output.

Applicant Screening   The weakest link in any computer security system is the people in it. At the very least, employers should verify the facts that job applicants list on their résumés to help weed out dishonest applicants before they are hired.

Passwords   A password is a secret word or number, or a combination of the two, that must be typed on the keyboard to gain access to a computer system. Cracking passwords is the most prevalent method of illicit entry to computer systems.

Built-in Software Protection   Software can be built into operating systems in ways that restrict access to the computer system. One form of software protection system matches a user number against a number assigned to the data being accessed. If a person does not get access, it is recorded that he or she tried to tap into some area to which that person was not authorized. Another form of software protection is a user profile: Information is stored about each user, including the files to which the user has legitimate access. The profile also includes each person's job function, budget number, skills, areas of knowledge, access privileges, supervisor, and loss-causing potential. These profiles are available for checking by managers if there is any problem.

Worms and Viruses: Uninvited Guests

Worms and *viruses* are rather unpleasant terms that have entered the jargon of the computer industry to describe some of the insidious ways that computer systems can be invaded.

A **worm** is a program that transfers itself from computer to computer over a network and plants itself as a separate file on the target computer's disks. One newsworthy worm, originated by Robert Morris when he was a student at Cornell University, traveled the length and breadth of the land through an electronic mail network, shutting down thousands of computers. The worm was injected into the network and multiplied uncontrollably, clogging the memories of infected computers until they could no longer function.

A virus, as its name suggests, is contagious. That is, a **virus,** a set of illicit instructions, passes itself on to other programs or documents with which it comes in contact. In its most basic form, a virus is the digital equivalent of vandalism. It can change or delete files, display words or obscene messages, or produce bizarre screen effects. In its most vindictive form, a virus can slowly sabotage a computer system and remain undetected for months, contaminating data or, in the case of the famous Michelangelo virus, wiping out your entire hard drive. A virus may be dealt with by means of a **vaccine,** or **antivirus,** a computer program that stops the spread of and often eradicates the virus. However, a **retrovirus** has the ability to fight back and may even delete antivirus software.

Viruses seem to show up when least expected. In one instance a call came to a company's information center at about 5:00 p.m. The caller's computer was making a strange noise. With the exception of an occasional beep, computers performing routine business chores do not usually make noises. Soon employees were calling from all over the company, all with "noisy" computers. One caller said that it might be a tune coming from the computer's small internal speaker. Finally, one caller recognized a tinny rendition of "Yankee Doodle," confirmation that an old virus had struck once again. The Yankee Doodle virus, once attached to a system, is scheduled to go off at 5:00 p.m. every eight days. Viruses, once considered merely a nuisance, are costing American business over $2 billion a year. Unfortunately, viruses are easily transmitted.

You may wonder who produces viruses. At one point, the mischief makers were merely teenagers with too much time on their hands. Now, virus makers are older and actually trade notes and tips on the Internet. They do what they do, psychologists say, mostly to impress their friends. Experts have estimated that there are hundreds of virus writers worldwide. However, although there are thousands of known viruses, most of the damage is caused by only a dozen or so.

Transmitting a Virus   Consider this typical example. A programmer secretly inserts a few viral instructions into a game called Kriss-Kross, which she then offers free to others via the Internet. Any takers download the game to their own computers. Now, each time a user runs Kriss-Kross—that is, loads it into memory—the virus is loaded too. The virus stays in memory, infecting any other program loaded until the computer is turned off again. The virus now has spread to other programs, and the process can be repeated again and again. In fact, each newly infected program becomes a virus carrier. Although many viruses are

Figure 8-4 An example of a virus invasion.

ORIGINATION
A programmer writes a tiny program —the virus—that has destructive power and can reproduce itself. The virus is introduced to the computer via disk or downloading.

TRANSMISSION
Most often, the virus is attached to a normal program; unknown to the user, the virus spreads to other software.

REPRODUCTION
The virus is passed to other users who use other computers. The virus remains dormant as it is passed on.

INFECTION
At a predetermined time, prompted by the computer's internal clock, the attack begins: A benign virus may just print an unexpected message, but a vicious virus may destroy data files and gobble up memory.

```
Hold down  he space bar
and the ha  d too
app  ars. P  sh th
but  on dow   on t  e
mou  e and   old i   while
mov  ng and  the s  reen
wil   scrol   in t  e
opo  ite di  ectio   of
you   hand  oveme  t. Use
thi   repea  edly   o g
to   arious  parts  of
you   docum  nt.
          e    t       o
              l   o
```

Figure 8-5 The Cascade virus. This virus attaches itself to the operating system and causes random letters in text to "drop" to a pile at the bottom of the screen display.

transmitted just this way via networks, the most common method is by passing diskettes from computer to computer (Figure 8-4).

Here is another typical scenario. An office worker puts a copy of a report on a diskette and slips it into her briefcase to take home. After shooing her children away from the new game they are playing on the computer, she sits down to work on the report. She does not know that a virus, borne by the kids' new software, has infected the diskette. When she takes the disk back to work, the virus is transmitted from her computer to the entire office network.

The most insidious viruses attach to the operating system. One virus, called Cascade, causes random text letters to "drop" to a pile at the bottom of the screen (Figure 8-5). Viruses attached to the operating system itself have greater potential for mischief.

A relative newcomer to the virus scene is the macro virus, which uses a program's own macro programming language to distribute itself. Unlike previous viruses, a macro virus does not infect a program; it infects a document. When you open the document that has the virus, any other documents opened in same session may get the virus too.

Damage from Viruses   Most viruses remain dormant until triggered by some activity. For example, a virus called Jerusalem B activates itself every Friday the 13th and proceeds to erase any file you may try to load from your disk. Another virus includes instructions to add 1 to a counter each time the virus is copied to another disk. When the counter reaches 4, the virus erases all data files. But this is not the end of the destruction, of course; the three copied disks have also been infected.

The Concept virus, a relatively benign macro virus, refuses to let you save your document after you have made changes, saying the file is "read only." However, the Nuclear macro virus, among other things, destroys vital operating system files on any April 5th.

Prevention   A word about prevention is in order. Although viruses are most commonly passed via diskettes, viruses can propagate by other means, such as local area networks, electronic mail, and the Internet. If your personal computer has a disk drive, a modem, or a network connector, it is vulnerable. Furthermore, viruses are rampant on some college campuses, a source of considerable annoyance to students. Use these commonsense approaches to new files:

- Never install a program unless the diskette comes in a sealed package.
- Be especially wary of software that arrives unexpectedly from companies with whom you have not done business.
- Use virus-scanning software to check any file or document, no matter what the source, before loading it onto your hard disk.
- If your own diskette was used in another computer, scan it to see if it caught a virus.

Although there have been isolated instances of viruses in commercial software, viruses tend to show up on free software or software acquired from friends or the Internet. Antivirus software can be installed to scan your hard disk every time you boot the computer or, if you prefer, at regularly scheduled intervals.

Personal Computer Security

One summer evening two men in coveralls with company logos backed a truck up to the building that housed a university computer lab. They showed the lab assistant, a part-time student, an authorization slip to move 23 personal computers to another lab on campus. The assistant was surprised but not shocked, since lab use was light in the summer quarter. The computers were moved, all right, but not to another lab. In another case a ring of thieves mingled with students in computer labs at various West Coast universities and stole hundreds of microprocessor chips from the campus computers.

There is an active market for stolen personal computers and their internal components. As these unfortunate tales indicate, personal computer security breaches can be pretty basic. One simple, though not foolproof, remedy is to secure personal computer hardware in place with locks and cables. Also, most personal computers have an individual cover lock that prevents access to internal components.

In addition to theft, personal computer users need to be concerned about the computer's environment. Personal computers in business are not coddled the way bigger computers are. They are designed, in fact, to withstand the wear and tear of the office environment, including temperatures set for the comfort of people. Most manufacturers discourage eating and smoking near computers and recommend some specific cleaning techniques, such as vacuuming the keyboard. The response to these recommendations is directly related to the awareness level of the users.

Several precautions can be taken to protect disk data. One is to use a **surge protector**, a device that prevents electrical problems from affecting computer data files. The computer is plugged into the surge protector, which is plugged into the outlet. Diskettes should be under lock and key. The most critical precaution, however, is to back up your files.

Prepare for the Worst: Back Up Your Files

A computer expert, giving an impassioned speech, said, "If you are not backing up your files regularly, you *deserve* to lose them." Strong words. Although organizations recognize the value of data and have procedures in place for backing up data files on a regular basis, personal computer users are not as devoted to this activity. In fact, one wonders why, with continuous admonishments and readily available procedures, some people still leave their precious files unprotected.

What Could Go Wrong?   If you use software incorrectly or simply input data incorrectly, it may be some time before the resulting erroneous data is detected. You then need to go back to the time when the data files were still acceptable. Sometimes the software itself can harm data, or a hard disk could physically malfunction, making your files inaccessible. Although none of these are too likely, they certainly do happen. It is even less likely that you would lose your hard disk files to fire or flood, but this is also possible. The most likely scenario is that you will accidentally delete some files yourself. One fellow gave a command to delete all files with the file name extension BAK—there were four of them—but accidentally typed *BAT* instead, inadvertently wiping out 57 files. (Deleted files, we should mention, can probably be recovered using utility software if the action is taken right away, before other data is written over the deleted files.) Finally, there is always the possibility of your files being infected with a virus. Experts estimate that average users experience a significant disk loss once every year.

Ways to Back Up Files   Some people simply make another copy of their hard disk files on diskette. This is not too laborious if you do so as you go along. If you are at all vulnerable to viruses, you should back up all your files on a regular basis.

A better way is to back up all your files on a tape. Backing up to a tape drive is safer and faster. You can also use software that will automatically back up all your files at a certain time of day, or on command. Sophisticated users place their files on a mirror hard disk, which simply makes a second copy of everything you put on the original disk; this approach, as you might expect, is expensive.

Keep backed-up files in a cool, dry place off-site. For those of you with a home computer, this may mean keeping copies of your important files at a friend's house; some people even use a bank safety deposit box for this purpose.

▶ Privacy: Keeping Personal Information Personal

Think about the forms you have willingly filled out: paperwork for loans or charge accounts, orders for merchandise through the mail, magazine subscription orders, applications for schools and jobs and clubs, and on and on. There may be some forms you filled out with less delight—for taxes, military draft registration, court petitions, insurance claims, or a stay in the hospital. And remember all the people who got your name and address from your check—fund-raisers, advertisers, and petitioners. These lists may not have covered all the ways you have supplied data, but you can know with certainty where it went: straight to computer files.

Passing Your Data Around

Where is that data now? Is it shared, rented, sold? Who sees it? Will it ever be deleted? Or, to put it more bluntly, is *anything* private anymore?

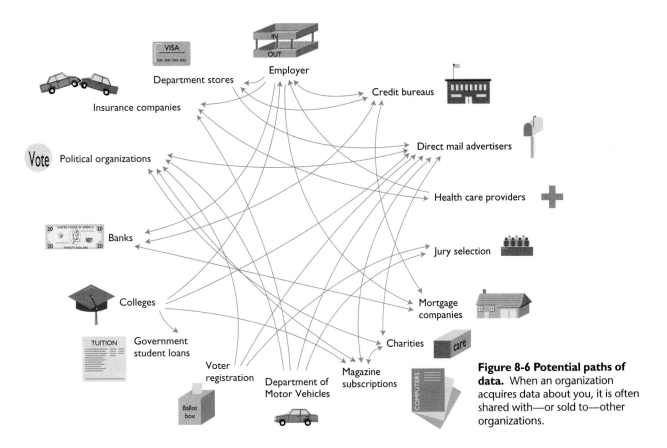

Figure 8-6 Potential paths of data. When an organization acquires data about you, it is often shared with—or sold to—other organizations.

In some cases one can only guess at the answers. It is difficult to say where your data is now, and bureaucracies are not eager to enlighten you. The data may have been moved to other files without your knowledge. In fact, much of the data is most definitely passed around, as anyone with a mailbox can attest. Even online services sell their subscriber lists, neatly ordered by zip code and computer type.

As for who sees your personal data, the answers are not comforting. Government agencies, for example, regularly share data that was originally filed for some other purpose. IRS records, for example, are compared with draft registration records to catch draft dodgers, and also with student loan records to intercept refunds to former students who have defaulted on their loans. The IRS created a storm of controversy by announcing a plan to use commercial direct-mail lists to locate tax evaders. Many people are worried about the consequences of this kind of sharing (Figure 8-6). For one thing, few of us can be certain that data about us, good or bad, is deleted when it has served its legitimate purpose.

The unfortunate fact is that, for very little money, anybody can learn anything about anybody—through massive databases. There are matters you want to keep private. You have the right to do so. Although you can do little to stop data about you from circulating through computers, there are some laws that give you access to some of it. Let us see what kind of protection is available to help preserve privacy.

Privacy Legislation

Significant legislation relating to privacy began with the **Fair Credit Reporting Act** in 1970. This law allows you to have access to and gives

NEW DIRECTIONS

TIGER TEAMS

Faced with threats on every side, some network-laced companies have chosen a proactive stance. Rather than waiting for the hacks and snoops and thieves to show up, they hire professionals to beat them to it. Called tiger teams or sometimes "intrusion testers" or "hackers for hire," these highly trained technical people are paid to try to break into a computer system before anyone else does.

Using the same kind of finesse and tricks a hacker might, tiger team members exploit the system weaknesses. Once such chinks are revealed, they can be protected. The team's first approach, typically, is to access the company's system from the Internet. The quality of security varies from company to company. Sometimes security is fairly tight; other times,

as one tiger team member put it, "It's a cakewalk."

Sometimes companies will hire one company to establish security and then hire a tiger team to try to defeat it. The company may not even alert its own employees to the tiger team activities, preferring to see whether the intrusions are detected and, if so, how employees react.

you the right to challenge your credit records. In fact, this access must be given to you free of charge if you have been denied credit. Businesses usually contribute financial information about their customers to a community credit bureau, which gives them the right to review a person's prior credit record with other companies. Before the Fair Credit Reporting Act, many people were—without explanation—turned down for credit because of inaccurate financial records about them. Because of the act, people may now check their records to make sure they are accurate.

The **Freedom of Information Act** was also passed in 1970. This landmark legislation allows ordinary citizens to have access to data about them that was gathered by federal agencies (although sometimes a lawsuit has been necessary to pry data loose).

The most significant legislation protecting the privacy of individuals is the **Federal Privacy Act** of 1974. This act stipulates that there can be no secret personnel files; individuals must be allowed to know what is stored in files about them and how the data is used, and must be able to correct it. The law applies not only to government agencies but also to private contractors dealing with government agencies. These organizations cannot obtain data willy-nilly, for no specific purpose; they must justify obtaining it.

A more recent law is the **Video Privacy Protection Act** of 1988, which prevents retailers from disclosing a person's video rental records without a court order; privacy supporters want the same rule for medical and insurance files. Another step in that direction is the **Computer Matching and Privacy Protection Act** of 1988, which prevents the government from comparing certain records in an attempt to find a match. However, most comparisons are still unregulated.

▶ The Internet: Security and Privacy Problems

Networks, whether connected to the Internet or not, pose unique security and privacy problems. Many people have access to the system, often

MAKING THE RIGHT CONNECTIONS

YOU HAVE NO PRIVACY WHATEVER

No privacy on the company e-mail, that is. Your employer can snoop into messages you send or receive even if you think you erased them. You have only erased them from their current hard drive location; copies are still in the company computer files. In fact, most companies archive all such files on tape and store them for the foreseeable future. Companies may fail to convey the message that e-mail, as a company conduit, is not private. Employees are often startled, after the fact, to discover that their messages have been invaded.

Furthermore, some people specialize in extracting deleted messages for use as evidence in court. E-mail can be a dangerous time bomb because litigators argue that, more than any other kind of written communication, e-mail reflects the real, unedited thoughts of the writer. This candid form of corporate communication increasingly is providing the most incriminating evidence used against companies in litigation.

What to do? It is certainly degrading to have something you thought was private waved in front of you as evidence of malingering. As one computer expert put it, if nothing is private, just say so. Companies have begun doing exactly that. The company policy on e-mail is—or should be—expressed in a clear, written document and routinely disseminated to all employees. However, even that step is probably insufficient. People tend to forget or get

complacent. Reminders should be given through the usual company conduits—bulletin boards, posters, and so forth.

What about the e-mail you send and receive at home—do you at least have privacy in your own home? Maybe not. You certainly cannot count on it if the

computer of the party at the other end is in an office. Further, keep in mind that messages sent across the Internet hop from computer to computer, with (depending on the service used) the sender having little say about its route. There are many vulnerable spots along the way.

from remote locations. Clearly, questions arise: If it is so easy for authorized people to get data, what is to stop unauthorized people from tapping it? Organizations must be concerned about unauthorized people intercepting data in transit, whether hackers or thieves or industrial spies.

One fundamental approach to network security is to dedicate one computer, called a **firewall**, whose sole purpose is to talk to the outside world. A firewall will provide an organization with greatly increased security because only one network computer is accessible to people outside the network, and that one computer accepts only appropriate access.

Encryption

Data being sent over communications lines may be protected by scrambling the messages—that is, putting them in code that can be broken only by the person receiving the message. The process of scrambling messages is called **encryption.** The American National Standards Institute has endorsed a process called the **Data Encryption Standard (DES),** a standardized public key by which senders and receivers can scramble and unscramble their messages. Although the DES code is well known, companies still use it because the method makes it quite expensive to intercept coded messages. Thus, interlopers are forced to use other methods of gathering data—methods that carry greater risk of detection. Encryption software is available for personal computers. A typical package, for example, offers a variety of security features: file encryption, keyboard lock, and password protection.

Privacy Problems for Networked Employees

Although employees do not have expectations of total privacy at the office, they are often shocked when they discover that the boss has been spying on them via the network, even their comings and goings on the Internet. The boss, of course, is not spying at all, merely "monitoring." This debate has been heightened by the advent of software that lets managers check up on networked employees without their ever knowing that they are under surveillance. With a flick of a mouse button, the boss can silently pull up an employee's current computer screen.

Surveillance software is not limited to checking screens. It can also check on e-mail, count the number of keystrokes per minute, note the length of a worker's breaks, and monitor what computer files are used and for how long.

Worker associations complain that workers who are monitored suffer much higher degrees of stress and anxiety than nonmonitored workers. However, vendors defend their products by saying that they are not "spy software" but rather products designed for training, monitoring resources, and helping employees. Privacy groups are lobbying legislators at both the state and federal levels to enact legislation that requires employers to alert employees that they are being monitored.

People who feel invaded at work may be shocked to find out that they are also being watched when online—from the privacy of their homes. This time it is not the boss but the web site owners who are watching you.

You Are Being Watched

It may seem to be the ultimate in privacy invasion. When you visit a web site, it can easily collect the city you are calling from, the site from which you just came, and, of course, everything you do while you are at the site. Software can also discover and record the hardware and software you use. That's the good part. Software can even monitor a user's **click**

stream, the series of mouse clicks that link from site to site. Thus, a history of what a user chooses to view on the web can be recorded and used for a variety of purposes by managers and marketers.

If your computer is identifiable, presumably by an e-mail address, then the web site adds a record to a special file called a **cookie.** To add insult to injury, the file—actually called *cookie*—is kept right on your own computer, without your permission and probably without your knowledge. (Go ahead, check your computer's files.) The next time you show up at that web site, it checks what it knows about you on your cookie file.

In true computer industry style, however, anonymity software can now defeat the snooping software. The anonymous software, where you must begin each web session, acts as a middleman, retrieving sites and documents without revealing your identity.

Junk E-mail

Privacy invasion in the form of junk e-mail has become, unfortunately, a common event. Furthermore, it promises to get worse. The volume of junk e-mail will only soar as marketers discover how cheap it is. A postal mailing to a million people costs about $800,000, including postage and printing. Internet marketers can reach the same number of people by making a phone call and paying a few hundred dollars for time spent online. The software that makes mass advertising—called **spamming**—possible both gathers e-mail addresses and sends e-mail messages for marketers—thousands and thousands every day. One of the most annoying aspects of e-mail is that, unlike postal junk mail, which at least arrives at no cost to you, a user who pays for online usage may be paying for part of the cost of junk e-mail delivery.

Enraged spam recipients sometimes respond to the perpetrator by **flaming**, sending insulting messages in return. Experienced spammers, however, may have already abandoned the originating site and, most likely, moved to another one.

If you want to maximize your privacy and reduce your chances of getting junk e-mail, be careful where you leave your e-mail address. As noted in Chapter 7, a prime source of e-mail addresses is newsgroup messages, whose e-mail addresses will likely be gathered up and sold. Further, Internet business sites entice visitors to supply personal data that can be used for marketing and promotion. An e-mail address is their most treasured commodity.

Government Intervention?

The invasion of privacy online, especially through the Internet, may be that rare problem that, in the opinion of some communications experts, requires government intervention. Such laws would have to carefully carve out a middle ground between preserving new opportunities for the legitimate needs of business people, researchers, and investigators on the one hand, and preserving the right to privacy on the other.

➤ Ethics and Privacy

Snooping did not begin with computers. Neither did improper dissemination of personal information. But computers have elevated those problems to a much more serious level. As we have already noted, just about everything there is to know about you is already on a computer file, more likely several computer files. The thorny issues center around appropriate ethical treatment of that data by those who control it or merely have access to it. It is not unlikely that, in the course of your career, you will see personal data about other people. Consider these scenarios:

■ Suppose that, as a programmer, you work on software that uses the company personnel files. Is it legitimate to look up salary data for people you know? If you see such data in the normal course of your work, is it appropriate to let those individuals know that you saw it?

■ Suppose that you had access to data about bank loan applications, some of which appeared in test reports on which you are working. If someone takes these from your desktop while you are on your lunch break, is this an ethical breach on your part?

■ Suppose that you are a programmer for a medical organization and, in the normal course of your work, see records about a celebrity. Is it ethical to describe the medical treatment to your friends, saying that it is a celebrity but not giving the name? Is it ethical to mention that the named celebrity uses your clinic without giving any medical details?

The above descriptions involve programmers, who are likely to see considerable private data over the course of a career. But people in many walks of life—accountants, tellers, nurses, contractors, and more—see data that resides on a computer. All of us need to respect the privacy of personal data.

The issues raised in this chapter are often the ones we think of after the fact—that is, when it is too late. Security and privacy factors are somewhat like insurance that we wish we did not have to buy. But we do buy insurance for our homes and cars and lives because we know we cannot risk being without it. The computer industry also knows that it cannot risk being without safeguards for security and privacy. As a computer user, you will share responsibility for addressing these issues.

CHAPTER REVIEW

Summary and Key Terms

- The word **hacker** originally referred to an enthusiastic, self-taught computer user, but now the term usually describes a person who gains access to computer systems illegally. Using **social engineering**, a tongue-in-cheek term for con artist actions, hackers persuade unsuspecting people to give away their passwords over the phone.

- The changing face of computer crime includes credit card fraud, data communications fraud, unauthorized access to computer files, and unlawful copying of copyrighted software.

- Prosecution of computer crime is often difficult because law enforcement officers, attorneys, and judges are unfamiliar with the issues involved. However, in 1986 Congress passed the latest version of the **Computer Fraud and Abuse Act**, and most states have passed some form of computer crime law.

- **Security** is a system of safeguards designed to protect a computer system and data from deliberate or accidental damage or access by unauthorized persons.

- The means of giving access to authorized people are divided into four general categories: (1) **what you have** (a key, badge, or plastic card); (2) **what you know** (a system password or identification number); (3) **what you do** (such as signing your name); and (4) **what you are** (by making use of **biometrics**, the science of measuring individual body characteristics such as fingerprints, voice, and retina). An **active badge**, a clip-on employee identification card with an embedded computer chip, signals its wearer's location—legal or otherwise—by sending out infrared signals, which are read by sensors sprinkled around the building.

- Loss of hardware and software is generally less of a problem than loss of data. Loss of hardware should not be a major problem, provided that the equipment is insured and a substitute processing facility is found quickly. Loss of software should not be critical, provided that the owner has taken the practical step of making backup copies. However, replacing lost data can be quite expensive.

- A **disaster recovery plan** is a method of restoring data processing operations if they are halted by major damage or destruction. Common approaches to disaster recovery include relying temporarily on manual services; buying time at a computer service bureau; making mutual assistance agreements with other companies; or forming a **consortium**, a joint venture with other organizations to support a complete computer facility used only in the event of a disaster.

- A **hot site** is a fully equipped computer facility with hardware, environmental controls, security, and communications equipment. A **cold site** is an environmentally suitable empty shell in which a company can install its own computer system.

- A disaster recovery plan should include a list of priorities identifying the programs that must be up and running first, plans for notifying employees of changes in locations and procedures, a list of needed equipment and where it can be obtained, a list of alternative computing facilities, and procedures for handling input and output data in a different environment.

- If a programmer is employed by an organization, any program written for the organization belongs to the employer. If the programmer is a consultant, however, the contract must clearly state whether it is the organization or the programmer that owns the software. Software can be copyrighted.

- Common means of protecting data are secured waste, internal controls, auditor checks, applicant screening, passwords, and built-in software protection.

- A **worm** is a program that transfers itself from computer to computer over a network, planting itself as a separate file on the target computer's disks. A **virus** is a set of illicit instructions that passes itself on to other programs with which it comes in contact. A **vaccine**, or **antivirus**, is a computer program that stops the spread of the virus and eradicates it. A **retrovirus** can fight back and may delete antivirus software.
- Personal computer security includes such measures as locking hardware in place; providing an appropriate physical environment; and using a **surge protector**, a device that prevents electrical problems from affecting computer data files.
- Files are subject to various types of losses and should be backed up on disk or tape.
- The security issue extends to the use of information about individuals that is stored in the computer files of credit bureaus and government agencies. The **Fair Credit Reporting Act** allows individuals to check the accuracy of credit information about them. The **Freedom of Information Act** allows people access to data that federal agencies have gathered about them. The **Federal Privacy Act** allows individuals access to information about them that is held not only by government agencies but also by private contractors working for the government. Individuals are also entitled to know how that information is being used. The **Video Privacy Protection Act** and the **Computer Matching and Privacy Protection Act** have extended federal protections.
- A **firewall** is a dedicated computer whose sole purpose is to talk to the outside world and decide who gains entry.
- The process of scrambling messages is called **encryption.** The American National Standards Institute has endorsed a process called the **Data Encryption Standard (DES)**, a standardized public key by which senders and receivers can scramble and unscramble their messages.
- Software can monitor a user's **click stream,** the series of mouse clicks that link from site to site, providing a history of what a user chooses to view on the Web.
- If your computer is identifiable, the web site can add a record of your activity to a **cookie** file that is stored on your computer.
- Privacy invasion in the form of junk e-mail has become a common event and will get worse because it is inexpensive. Mass advertising on the Internet is called **spamming.** Enraged spam recipients sometimes respond to the perpetrator by **flaming,** sending insulting messages in return.
- To reduce your chances of getting junk e-mail, be careful where you leave your e-mail address.

Quick Poll

Compare your answers to those of your colleagues or classmates.

1. Regarding security and privacy overall:
   - ❏ a. I can see that I need to pay more attention.
   - ❏ b. I will seek out my employer's policies to make sure I stay out of trouble.
   - ❏ c. These topics will be a key concern as I use computers.
2. Regarding viruses:
   - ❏ a. No encounters thus far; they seem to be only a moderately serious problem.
   - ❏ b. They are an occasional problem for me and for friends.
   - ❏ c. They are a major problem.
3. Regarding privacy on the Internet:
   - ❏ a. I provide no personal information. Period.
   - ❏ b. I may give my e-mail address to a reputable site, other information rarely.
   - ❏ c. They can find out anything; if I were that worried I'd just stay off the 'Net.

Discussion Questions

1. Before accepting a particular patient, a doctor might like access to a computer file listing patients who have been involved in malpractice suits. Before accepting a tenant, the owner of an apartment building might want to check a file that lists people who have previously sued landlords. Should computer files be available for such purposes?
2. Discuss the following statement: An active badge may help an organization maintain security, but it also erodes the employee's privacy.
3. Why do some people consider computer viruses important? Discuss your answer from the point of view of the professional programmer, the MIS manager, and the hacker.

Student Study Guide

Multiple Choice

1. Persuading people to tell their passwords:
   a. social engineering   c. biometrics
   b. flaming   d. encryption
2. History of a user's movements from site to site:
   a. worm   c. consortium
   b. vaccine   d. click stream
3. One safeguard against theft or alteration of data is the use of
   a. DES   c. identical passwords
   b. the Trojan Horse   d. data diddling
4. Legislation that prohibits government agencies and contractors from keeping secret personal files on individuals:
   a. Federal Privacy Act   c. Fair Credit Reporting Act
   b. Computer Abuse Act   d. Freedom of Information Act
5. Mass advertising via the Internet:
   a. hacking   c. social engineering
   b. spamming   d. flaming
6. Computer crimes are usually
   a. easy to detect   c. prosecuted
   b. blue-collar crimes   d. discovered accidentally
7. The "what you are" criterion for computer system access involves
   a. a badge   c. biometrics
   b. a password   d. a magnetized card
8. The key factor in a computer installation that has met with disaster is the
   a. equipment replacement   c. loss of hardware
   b. insurance coverage   d. loss of processing ability

9. In anticipation of physical destruction, every computer organization should have a
   a. biometric scheme   c. disaster recovery plan
   b. DES   d. set of active badges
10. A file with a record of web site activity:
    a. hot file   c. click file
    b. cookie file   d. active file
11. Networked employees may be monitored with
    a. disaster recovery plan   c. surveillance software
    b. DES   d. biometrics
12. Secured waste, auditor checks, and applicant screening all aid
    a. data security   c. built-in software protection
    b. license protection   d. piracy detection
13. The weakest link in any computer system:
    a. the people in it   c. hardware
    b. passwords   d. software
14. A device that prevents electrical problems from affecting data files:
    a. site license   c. Trojan Horse
    b. hot site   d. surge protector
15. One form of built-in software protection for data is
    a. secured waste   c. applicant screening
    b. user profiles   d. auditor checks
16. An identification card with an embedded chip to signal its wearer's location:
    a. antivirus   c. active badge
    b. site license   d. consortium
17. An empty shell in which a company may install its own computer is called a
    a. restoration site   c. cold site
    b. hot site   d. hardware site
18. A program written when the programmer is employed by an organization is owned by
    a. the programmer   c. no one
    b. the state   d. the organization
19. Security protection for personal computers includes
    a. internal components   c. locks and cables
    b. software   d. all of these
20. The secret words or numbers to be typed in on a keyboard before any activity can take place are called
    a. biometric data   c. data encryptions
    b. passwords   d. private words
21. Another name for an antivirus:
    a. vaccine   c. worm
    b. Trojan Horse   d. DES
22. Sending insulting messages to mass advertisers:
    a. surging   c. clicking
    b. flaming   d. spamming
23. A virus that replicates itself is called a
    a. bug   c. worm
    b. vaccine   d. bomb
24. A program whose sabotage depends on certain conditions is called a
    a. bug   c. worm
    b. vaccine   d. bomb

25. A person who gains illegal access to a computer system:
   a. hacker
   c. worm
   b. software pirate
   d. zapper

True/False

T F   1. Most computer organizations cannot afford consortiums.
T F   2. Vaccine is another name for antivirus software.
T F   3. The Trojan Horse is an embezzling technique.
T F   4. If a computer crime is detected, prosecution is assured.
T F   5. Computer security is achieved by restricting physical access to the computer.
T F   6. Fingerprints are an example of biometrics.
T F   7. The actual loss of hardware is a major security problem due to its expense.
T F   8. If a user is identifiable, a web site may add a record to the user's spam file.
T F   9. A victim of mass advertising may respond by flaming.
T F 10. Most computer crimes are not detected.
T F 11. The science of studying individual body characteristics is called biometrics.
T F 12. Passwords are best changed annually.
T F 13. The spread of a vaccine is usually stopped by an antivirus.
T F 14. Data diddling is a criminal method whereby data is modified before it goes into a computer file.
T F 15. Although hackers have invaded corporate and government mainframes, they have thus far respected web sites.
T F 16. A mutual aid pact with another computer facility is one possibility for a disaster recovery plan.
T F 17. A cookie file holds records on Web activities right on the user's disk.
T F 18. The Data Encryption Standard is a standardized list of passwords for software security.
T F 19. By allowing a programmer also to be a computer operator, a computer organization can improve security.
T F 20. Increasing access to networks has changed the nature of computer crime.
T F 21. Mass advertising is called flaming.
T F 22. Most states have passed some form of computer crime law.
T F 23. A cold site is an environmentally suitable empty shell in which a company can install its own computer system.
T F 24. Social engineering is a movement to improve password protection.
T F 25. Users concerned about privacy should withhold personal information but need not worry about giving out their e-mail address.

Fill-In

1. An environmentally suitable empty shell into which a computer organization can put its computer system: _____

2. A system of safeguards to protect a computer system and data from damage or unauthorized access: _____

3. Bypassing security systems with an illicitly acquired software package is called _____

4. The field concerned with the measurement of individual body characteristics: _____

5. The name for a fully equipped computer center to be used in the event of a disaster: _____

6. What is the assurance to individuals that personal property is used properly called? _____

7. A person who gains access to a computer system illegally is called _____

8. A standardized public key by which senders and receivers can scramble and unscramble their messages: _____

9. The four categories of authorized access to a computer system:
   a. _____
   b. _____
   c. _____
   d. _____

10. The file on your own computer that has records of Web activity: _____

11. The law, passed in 1970, that allows ordinary citizens to have access to data gathered by federal agencies: _____

12. The law that prohibits government agencies and their private contractors from keeping secret personal files: _____

13. The Fair Credit Reporting Act of 1970 gives people access to this information: _____

14. Another name for mass advertising on the Internet: _____

15. Does a program belong to the employed programmer or the employing organization? _____

16. Which is potentially the least damaging type of security violation: hardware, software, or data? _____

17. The salami technique is which type of method? _____

18. Placing an illicit program within a completed program, allowing unauthorized entry: _____

19. Sending insulting messages to those who send mass advertising: _____

20. Persuading people to give away their passwords: _____

21. Another name for a vaccine: _____

22. An illegal program that transfers itself from computer to computer over a network: _____

23. A user's movements from site to site: _____

24. A device that prevents electrical problems from affecting computer files: _____

25. The name for the identification card that can track the wearer's location: _____

Answers

Multiple Choice

1. a	6. d	11. c	16. c	21. a
2. d	7. c	12. a	17. c	22. b
3. a	8. d	13. a	18. d	23. c
4. a	9. c	14. d	19. d	24. d
5. b	10. b	15. b	20. b	25. a

True/False

1. T	6. T	11. T	16. T	21. F
2. T	7. F	12. F	17. T	22. T
3. F	8. F	13. F	18. F	23. T
4. F	9. T	14. T	19. F	24. F
5. F	10. T	15. F	20. T	25. F

Fill-In

1. cold site
2. security
3. zapping
4. biometrics
5. hot site
6. privacy
7. hacker
8. Data Encryption Standard (DES)
9. a. what you have
   b. what you know
   c. what you do
   d. what you are
10. cookie
11. Freedom of Information Act
12. Federal Privacy Act
13. credit reports
14. spamming
15. the organization
16. hardware
17. embezzlement
18. trapdoor
19. flaming
20. social engineering
21. antivirus
22. worm
23. click stream
24. surge protector
25. active badge

PLANET INTERNET

Unexpected. Even so, you can easily come across sites that feature subjects you never expected to find on the Web. For example, few would expect to come across a panhandler site; he wants a handout. He prefers credit card donations but will accept cash through the mail. Been thinking about prisons lately? Probably not. But there it is, the Alcatraz prison site. An even more somber site is the World Wide Cemetery, in which you can post dedications to departed loved ones.

Not your everyday pursuit. You might whip up some interest in gold prospecting when you see all the links on the site. And speaking of riches, the Found Money site suggests that "you may be rich and not even know it!" You can check their database to see if you have any money lying around.

YOU JUST NEVER KNOW WHAT YOU'LL FIND

You never know what you might find on the Internet. If you deliberately put provocative words through a search engine, even something as tame as *strange,* you may find some of the sites returned to be disconcerting or even alarming. But it is pretty easy to stay away from such sites if you tread the beaten paths.

You didn't know you needed this. Have Cyrano write love letters for you. See the clever ArtsWire site for the Mona Lisa links. Hear what the flake man has to say about his collection of classic cereal boxes. Read the southern cooking recipes at the Grits site. Take the survey; they want to include you in their Internet demographics compilation. Finally, take a hint and write a letter to Dear Mom.

Dear Timmy,
I'll always be here when you need me. A nice card from you would make any day special.

ps: Write more often. You know how your mother worries.

A **YEAR ROUND** Tribute to Mom.

Gold Prospecting

Internet Exercises

1. **Structured exercise.** Begin with the AWL URL, http://hepg.awl.com/ capron/planet/ and take a tour of Alca- traz. Visit the bookstore.
2. **Freeform exercise.** Use the WebCrawler's Search Ticker to check out a few of its randomly selected sites.

GRITS

"NO ONE CAN EAT JUST ONE!"

Art Room

Art News

Pet Peeves

Art Jobs

Art Stuff

Guest Book

Lessons

Art Site of the Week

Awards

AEAI

Cartoons

SUR☑EY.NET

TM

Applications

Tools

Jane Duffin, a physical therapist in the Mount Tahoma School District, appreciates the interaction between her students and computers. In particular, she has observed them using software specially designed to help physically challenged students communicate.

Until recently, however, Jane has done most of her own paperwork by hand. Other paperwork, primarily the dreaded end-of-year reports, were typed and retyped by a secretary. For Jane, everything changed the day the district administrators announced that professional employees would get their own computers to take home with them. The administrators also required a series of classes on how to use the computer software.

Jane learned word processing, a type of software that let her prepare and print text documents such as memos and reports. She made her first tentative foray into word processing by typing a memo. She was not concerned about typing mistakes she made but simply corrected them on-screen before she printed the memo.

That was the beginning. With a speed that surprised her, Jane found herself moving all her paperwork to the computer: individualized child service plans, bus schedules, academic and physical progress reports, and her own time records for each child. At first Jane composed what she wanted to communicate on paper and then keyed it into the word processing program. Before long she became comfortable enough to compose directly on the computer. Furthermore, she saw her overall communication improve as she wrote memos to parents, teachers, doctors, and staff members.

A few months later Jane decided to use her word processing skills to tackle the annual grant proposal document. In past years the entire proposal, running some 40 pages, had to be typed from scratch. This was true even though much of the proposal was the same from year to year. A word-processed document can be handled differently: Only the new or changed material has to be keyed, and then the entire document can be printed as if new. Relishing the thought of how easy it was going to be *next* year, Jane set out to produce the grant proposal in word-processed form.

Jane could also improve the document's attractiveness by using features such as boldface, underlining, and even line drawings. Best of all, she could make the document look professionally printed by choosing an attractive typeface—font—from her word processing package.

Jane is still a busy physical therapist. But thanks to her computer and its word processing software, she has more time for her first love: children.

Word Processing and Desktop Publishing

Printing It

Supertypist Mavis Beacon

Many people who want to use the computer to take typing lessons select a package called Mavis Beacon Teaches Typing. Mavis's picture graces the box, and her image appears in both computer graphics and in advertisements promoting the product. Mavis Beacon has been a computer icon for more than ten years, guiding thousands of people as they learn to type.

There is just one catch. Mavis Beacon does not exist. The photo is of a fashion model named Renee Lesperance. The name of the fictional typing teacher has two origins: Mavis was a favorite of the software author, and the second name is from beacon, as in a guiding light.

Word Processing as a Tool

Word processing software lets you create, edit, format, store, retrieve, and print a text document. Let us examine each part of the definition. A *text document* is any text that can be keyed in, such as a memo. *Creation* is the original composing and keying in of the document. *Editing* is making changes to the document to fix errors or improve its content—for example, deleting a sentence, correcting a misspelled name, or moving a paragraph. *Formatting* refers to adjusting the appearance of the document to make it look appropriate and attractive. For example, you might want to center a heading, make wider margins, or use double spacing. *Storing* the document means saving it on disk so that it can be accessed on demand. (Although beginners usually think in terms of saving the completed document, all users, whether experienced or inexperienced, should save a document at regular intervals as it is being keyed to avoid losing work if something should go wrong.) *Retrieving* the document means bringing the stored document from disk back into computer memory so that it can be used again or changed in some way. *Printing* is producing the document on paper, using a printer connected to the computer.

Some people think of word processing as just glorified typing, but consider the advantages of word processing over typing: Word processing lets you see on the screen what you type before you print it, remembers what you type and lets you change it, and prints the typed document at your request. A word processing package is a sophisticated tool with many options. This chapter discusses several of them. First, here is an overview of how word processing works.

An Overview: How Word Processing Works

Think of the computer's screen as a page of typing paper. When you type, you can see the line of text you are typing on the screen—it looks just like a line of typing on paper. You are not really typing on the screen, of course; the screen merely displays what you are entering into memory. As you type, the program displays a **cursor** to show where the next character you type will appear on the screen. The cursor is usually a blinking dash or line or rectangle that you can easily see. Although this chapter examines word processing in a general way that applies to any word processing software, occasionally, as here, a point will be demonstrated with Microsoft Word (Figure 9-1).

Scrolling

A word processing program lets you type page after page of material. Most programs show a horizontal line on the screen to mark where one printed page will end and another will begin; this line does not appear on the printed document. Most word processing programs also display, at the bottom of the screen, the number of the page on which you are currently typing and also an indicator of the line, either by line number or by inches from the top of the printed page. Although the screen display size is limited, your document size is not. As you add new lines at

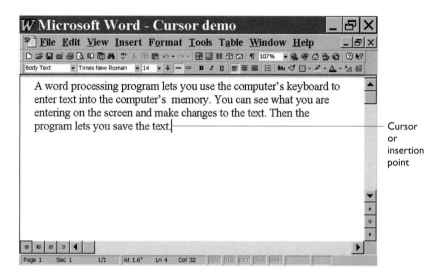

Cursor
or
insertion
point

Figure 9-1 Entering text with word processing software. As you type in your text, the position of the cursor (the vertical line just to the right of the last word on the screen) shows where the next character will be placed.

the bottom of the screen, the lines you typed earlier move up the screen. Eventually, the first line you typed disappears off the top of the screen. The line has not disappeared from the document or from the computer's memory.

To see lines that have disappeared from the top, you can move the cursor up to the top of the screen and press the up arrow key; lines that had disappeared drop back down onto the screen. You can also use a mouse to accomplish the same thing by clicking over the up arrow of the scroll bar to the right of the screen. You can use opposite movements to send screen lines in the upward direction. This process, called **scrolling**, lets you see any part of the document—but only one screen at a time.

No Need to Worry About the Right Side

After you start to type the first line of a document, you will eventually get to the right edge of the screen. If there is not enough room at the end of a line to complete the word you are typing, the program automatically starts that word at the left margin of the next line down. This feature is called **word wrap.** With word wrap you do not have to push a carriage return key (on the computer, the *Enter* key) at the end of each line as you would with a typewriter; in fact, you should *not* press *Enter* at the end of a line, or the word wrap feature will not work properly. You should only press *Enter* when you want a blank line or to signal the end of a paragraph.

Easy Corrections

What if you make a mistake while you are keying? No problem: Move the cursor to the position of the error and make the correction. Use the **Backspace key** to delete characters to the left of the cursor, or use the **Delete key** to delete the character under the cursor or just to the right of the cursor. Word processing programs let you delete characters or whole words or lines that you have already typed; the resulting spaces are closed up automatically.

You can also insert new characters in the middle of a line or a word without typing over (and erasing) the characters that are already there. The program automatically moves the existing characters to the right of

Getting Practical

TO YOUR HEALTH

Can all this computing be good for you? Are there any unhealthy side effects? The computer seems harmless enough. How bad can it be, sitting in a padded chair in a climate-controlled office?

How bad is it? Health questions have been raised by the people who sit all day in front of computer screens. What about eyestrain? And what about the age-old back problem? Then there is repetitive strain injury (RSI), dubbed "the occupational disease of the '90s," related to workers who hold their hands over a keyboard. RSI is caused by speed, repetition, awkward positioning, and holding a static position for a long period of time.

Ergonomics. Workers can do a number of things to take care of themselves. A good place to begin is with an ergonomically designed workstation. *Ergonomics* is the study of human factors related to computers. A

properly designed workstation takes a variety of factors into account, such as the distance from the eyes to the screen and the angle of the arms and wrists.

How we cope. Experts recommend these steps to prevent injury:

- Turn the screen away from the window to reduce glare, and cover your screen with a glare deflector. Turn off overhead lights; illuminate your work area with a lamp.
- Put your monitor on a tilt-and-swivel base.
- Get a pneumatically adjustable chair. Position the seat back so that your lower back is supported.
- Place the keyboard low enough to avoid arm and wrist fatigue. Do not bend your wrists when you type. Use an inexpensive raised wrist rest. Do not rest your wrists on a sharp edge.
- Sit with your feet firmly on the floor.
- Exercise at your desk, occasionally rotating your wrists, rolling your shoulders, and stretching. Better yet, get up and walk around at regular intervals.
- Finally, keep your fingernails short, or at least not long.

the insertion as you type the new characters and rewraps the text. However, if you wish, the word processing program also lets you *overtype* (replace) characters you typed before.

Menus and Buttons: At Your Command

Most word processing packages permit commands to be given via **menus**, a set of choices normally laid out across the top of the screen. The menus are called **pull-down menus** because each initial choice, when clicked with a mouse, reveals lower-level choices that pull down like a window shade from the initial selection at the top of the screen. For example, an initial selection of Format may reveal several submenus; the submenu Font has its own set of selections (Figure 9-2). A mouse user can also invoke commands using **buttons**, such as those shown at the top of the screen in Figure 9-2. For example, the top leftmost buttons on

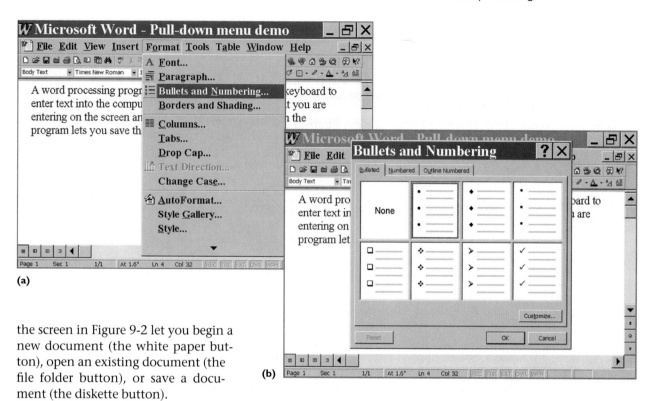

(a)

(b)

the screen in Figure 9-2 let you begin a
new document (the white paper button), open an existing document (the
file folder button), or save a document (the diskette button).

Figure 9-2 Pull-down menus.
(a) When the Format menu is clicked
with a mouse, a submenu of choices
appears. The submenu Bullets and
Numbering is highlighted. If it is clicked,
the submenu shown in (b) appears.
(b) Some submenus have their own submenus; here, the submenu Bullets and
Numbering has further selections.
    Note also the vertical scroll bar on the
right side of the screen. When a mouse is
used to click one of the large up or down
arrows on the scroll bar, the document
moves down or up, respectively. A mouse
can also move the square within the scroll
bar, the document moves down or up,
respectively. A mouse can also move the
square within the scroll bar up or down,
causing rapid movement through the document.

▶ Word Processing Features

All word processing users begin by learning the basics: Invoke the word
processing software, key in the document, change the document, and
save and print the document. However, most users also come to appreciate the various features offered by word processing software (Figure 9-3).

Formatting

The most commonly used features are those that control the **format**—
the physical appearance of the document. Format refers to centering,
margins, tabs and indents, justification, line spacing, emphasis, and all
the other factors that affect appearance. Note the examples in Figure 9-3
as some formatting options are described.

Vertical Centering   A short document such as a memo starts out
bunched at the top of the page. Vertical centering adjusts the top and
bottom margins so that the text is centered vertically on the printed
page. This eliminates the need to calculate the exact number of lines to
leave at the top and bottom, a necessary process if you are using a typewriter.

Line Centering   Any line can be individually **centered** between the
left and right margins of the page. Headings and titles are usually centered; other lines, such as addresses, may also be appropriately centered.

Margins   Some settings, called **default settings**, are used automatically
by the word processing program; they can be overridden by the user. The

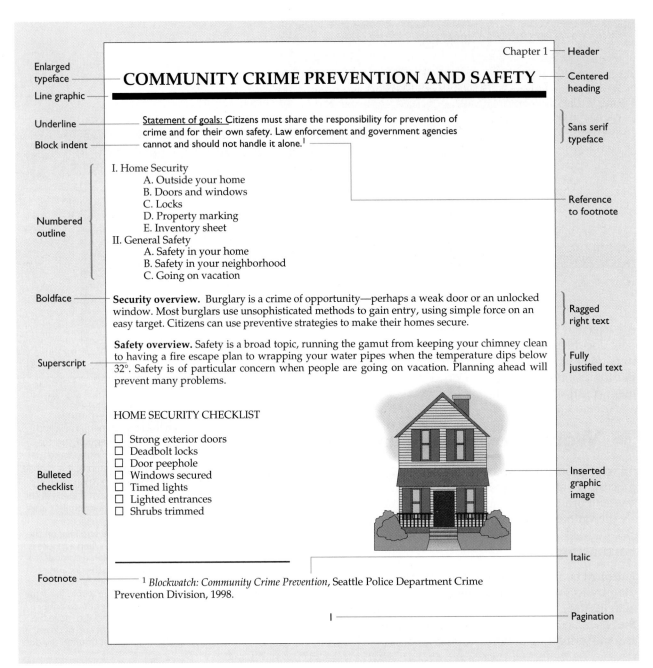

Enlarged typeface

Line graphic

Underline

Block indent

Numbered outline

Boldface

Superscript

Bulleted checklist

Footnote

Header

Centered heading

Sans serif typeface

Reference to footnote

Ragged right text

Fully justified text

Inserted graphic image

Italic

Pagination

Figure 9-3 Word processing features. Although it is not possible to show all word processing features on a single page, this page illustrates many of the capabilities available.

default left and right margins are usually 1¼ inches wide. Documents are often typed using the default margin settings. However, if the document would look better with narrower or wider margins, the margin settings can be changed accordingly.

When the margin settings are changed, word processing software automatically adjusts the text to fit the new margins. This process is called **automatic reformatting.**

Tabs and Indentation   It is common to **tab** just once to begin a paragraph. Some users need a set of tab positions across the page to make items align. It is also possible to **indent** an entire paragraph, and even to indent it from two sides, so that it stands out.

Justification   The evenness of text at the side margins is called justification. A document of several paragraphs is often most attractive if it is **fully justified**, that is, has an even margin down each side. The program adjusts each line so that it ends exactly at the right margin, spacing the words evenly. There are occasions, perhaps to spot any unintentional spaces, when only left justification is desired; this is referred to as **ragged right** text because of the uneven appearance of the unjustified right side.

Line Spacing   Most of the time you will want your documents—letters, memos, reports—to be single spaced. But on occasion you will find it is convenient or necessary to double space or even triple space a document. Word processing lets you do this with ease.

Boldface, Italic, and Underlining   Certain words or phrases, or even entire paragraphs, can be given emphasis by using a darker text known as **boldface** text, or by using the slanted type called *italic,* or by underlining important words.

Fonts   Most word processing packages offer several fonts. A **font** is a set of characters – letters, punctuation, and numbers—of the same design. Everyday fonts can generally be grouped into serif and sans serif fonts (*sans* means without). On a **serif** font, each character includes small marks called serifs, thought to help the eye travel more easily from character to character, making reading easier. A **sans serif** font is clean and stark, with no serif marks (Figure 9-4). In this book, the main text uses a serif font, but the margin notes use a sans serif font. The fonts in word processing packages can be augmented by separate software that offers an amazing variety of fonts (Figure 9-5).

Other Important Features

Popular word processing packages offer more features than most people use. Although it is not possible to discuss every feature here, this list contains a few that you may find handy.

Search   Imagine working with a 97-page study called *Western Shorebirds,* all nicely prepared as a word-processed document. There has been an additional sighting of the white-rumped sandpiper, and it has fallen to you to make a change in the report. You could, of course, leaf through the printed report to find out where to put the change. Alternatively, you could scroll the report on the screen, hoping to see the words *white-rumped sandpiper* pass by. The fast and easy way, however, is to use the **search command**, also called the **find command**. Just invoke the search command, key in the word or words you are looking for, and the exact page and place where it is located will appear on the screen.

Find and Replace   Suppose you type a long report in which you repeatedly and incorrectly spell the name of a client as *Mr. McDonald.* To make

---

Squeezing or Stretching a Document

There are times when you want certain text to fit into a certain space. For example, an instructor could suggest that a term paper be at least ten double-spaced pages, or a potential employer could suggest a résumé of no more than two pages. Or perhaps the problem is something as simple as reducing a memo that runs three pages plus two lines to just three pages. There are several ways to use word processing features to adjust the length of a document:

■ Adjust the margins, both sides and top and bottom, larger to stretch the number of pages, smaller to reduce the number.

■ Try different line spacing. One-and-a-half line spacing, available with most word processing programs, looks quite similar to double spacing.

■ Experiment with fonts. Some take up much less room than others at the same point size. And, of course, point size is a variable you can adjust.

(a) The quick brown fox jumped over the lazy dog.

(b) The quick brown fox jumped over the lazy dog.

Figure 9-4 Comparing serif and sans serif fonts. (a) This popular serif font is called Times Roman. (b) This sans serif font is called Helvetica Light.

this font is called Hogarth

this font is called Surf Style

this font is called City

this font is called Commerce Lean

this font is called Rage

this font is called Arriba Arriba

THIS FONT IS CALLED BANG

this font is called Laser Chrome

this font is called Gotisch

this font is called Journal Ultra

a change, you could search for each individual occurrence of *McDonald*, replacing each incorrect *Mc* with the correct *Mac*. There is, however, a more efficient way—using the **find and replace function.** You make a single request to replace one word or phrase with another. Then, find and replace quickly searches through the entire document, finding each instance of the word or phrase and replacing it with the word or phrase you designated. Most word processing programs also offer **conditional replace**, which asks you to verify each replacement before it takes place.

Pagination   Displaying page numbers in a document is a normal need for most users. Word processing programs offer every imaginable paging option, permitting the page number to be located at the top or bottom of the page and to the left, right, or center, or even alternating left and right.

Print Preview   Many users call this their favorite feature. With a single command a user can view on the screen in reduced size an entire page or two facing pages or even several consecutive pages. This gives a better overall view than the limited number of lines available on a screen.

Footnotes   A user need only give the footnote command and type the footnote. The word processing program keeps track of space needed and automatically renumbers if a new footnote is added.

Headers and Footers   Unlike footnotes, which appear just once, headers (top of the page) and footers (bottom of the page) appear on every page of a document (see Figure 9-3). A number of variations are available, including placement, size, and font.

Text Blocks: Moving, Copying, and Deleting

Text block techniques comprise a powerful set of tools. A **text block** is a unit of text in a document. A text block can consist of one or more words, phrases, sentences, paragraphs, or even pages. Text blocks can be moved, copied, or deleted.

Consider this example. Robert Merino is the manager of the Warren Nautilus Club, a fitness center just seven blocks from the state university he attends. Last December, just before the student holidays, Robert used word processing to dash off a notice to the members, informing them of changes in the holiday schedule (Figure 9-6a).

Now, four months later, Robert wants to produce a similar notice regarding schedule changes during spring break. Rather than beginning anew, Robert will retrieve his old document from the disk and key in the changes. After Robert has given the command to retrieve the document, the current version of the notice, just as he saved it on disk, is loaded into memory and displayed on the screen. Robert plans to make changes so that the new notice will be as shown in Figure 9-6b. In particular, Robert uses text block commands to move a paragraph.

Marking a Text Block   Whenever action is to be taken on a block of text, that block must first be **marked**, which is a form of identification. Marking a block is sometimes called **selection**, since you are selecting text with which to work. A block usually is marked by placing the mouse at the beginning of the block, holding the mouse button down, and dragging the mouse to the end of the block. In Robert's memo the block to be marked is the paragraph with the special offer. On the screen the marked block is now highlighted, probably by **reverse video**—the print in the marked text is the color of the normal background and the background is the color of the normal text. Once the block is marked, it can be moved, copied, or deleted.

Figure 9-6 Moving a text block.
(a) Robert's original memo. (b) Robert begins by deleting *assistant* so that his title reflects his recent promotion to manager. He next uses the find and replace command to change each mention of December to March. He takes a few moments to delete the old dates and times, add the new ones, and add *April 1st* as the deadline for the new member promotion. Finally, since the notice is supposed to be about the changed schedule, he uses text block commands to move the "special offer" paragraph to the end of the notice. The result is the revised memo shown here.

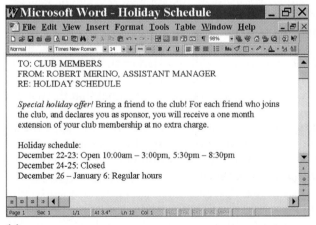

(a)

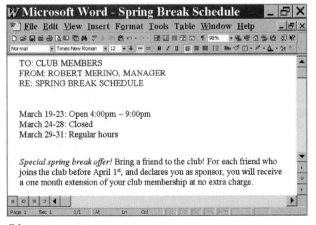

(b)

Moving a Text Block   Moving a block of text removes it from its original location and places it in another location. The block still appears only once in the document. Moving a block from one location to another is also called **cutting and pasting,** a reference to what you literally would have to do if you were working with a document on paper. Some word processing programs use the actual words *cut* and *paste* as command names: The cut command removes the block from its old location, and the paste command places the block in its new location, as indicated by the cursor location. To summarize the move operation: (1) mark the block, (2) cut, (3) move the cursor to the new destination, and (4) paste.

Copying a Text Block   The copy command leaves the block intact in its original location but also inserts it in a designated new location; now there are two copies of the block. Typical commands for copying a block are copy and paste. To summarize the copy operation: (1) mark the block, (2) copy, (3) move the cursor to the new destination, and (4) paste.

Deleting a Text Block   Deleting a block of text is easy. In fact, it has already been described. Once a block is marked and cut, it is effectively deleted. An easy alternative is to mark a block and then press the *Delete* key.

▷ Spelling Checker and Thesaurus Programs

A **spelling checker** program finds spelling errors you may have made when typing a document. The program compares each word in your document to the words it has in its dictionary. If the spelling checker program finds a word that is not in its list, it assumes that you have misspelled or mistyped that word. The spelling checker draws attention to the offending word in some way, perhaps by reversing the screen colors. Then it displays words from its dictionary that are close in spelling or sound to the word you typed (Figure 9-7). If you recognize the correct spelling of the highlighted word in the list you are given, you can replace the incorrect word with the correct word from the list.

Spelling checkers often do not recognize proper names (such as *Ms. Verwys)* or acronyms *(NASA)* or technical words specific to some disciplines *(orthotroid).* So you must decide if whether the word is actually misspelled. If it is, you can correct it easily with the word processing software. If the word is correct, the software lets you signal that the word is acceptable and, if you wish, even add it to the dictionary.

A **thesaurus** program offers synonyms (words with the same meaning) and antonyms (words with the opposite meaning) for common words. Suppose you find a word in your document that you have used too frequently or that does not seem suitable. Place the cursor on the word. Then click the menu or button that activates the thesaurus program. The program provides a list of synonyms for the word you want to replace (Figure 9-8). A click on the chosen new word replaces the word in your document with the synonym you prefer. It is easy, and even painlessly educational.

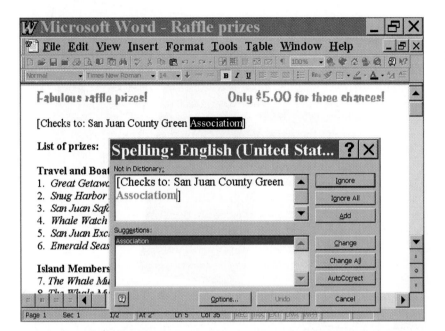

Figure 9-7 Spelling checker. The highlighted word, *associatiom*, is misspelled, so the spelling checker offers an alternative—*association*—in the suggestion window. In this case selecting Change replaces the misspelled word with the correct spelling.

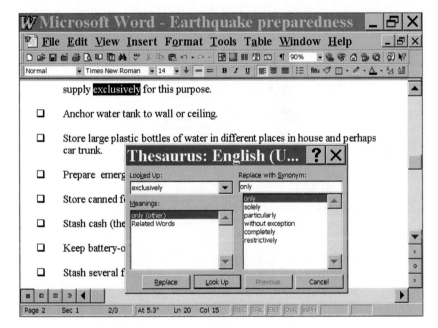

Figure 9-8 A thesaurus program. The words on the list are synonyms for the highlighted word *exclusively*.

▶ Desktop Publishing: An Overview

Would you like to be able to produce well-designed pages that combine elaborate charts and graphics with text and headlines in a variety of fonts? You can, with a technology called **desktop publishing.** You can use desktop publishing software to design sophisticated pages and, with a high-quality printer, print a professional-looking final document (Figure 9-9).

Unlike word processing, desktop publishing gives you the ability to do **page composition,** deciding where you want text and pictures on a page, what fonts to use, and what other design elements to include.

Figure 9-9 Desktop publishing. With desktop publishing software and a high-quality laser printer, you can create professional-looking newsletters and documents.

Desktop publishing fills the gap between word processing and professional typesetting (Figure 9-10).

▷ The Publishing Process

Desktop publishing gives the user full control over the editing and design of the document. Desktop publishing also eliminates the time-consuming measuring and cutting and pasting involved in traditional production techniques.

The Art of Design

One part of the design of a document is **page layout**—how the text and pictures are arranged on the page. For example, magazine publishers have found that text organized in columns and separated by a solid vertical line is an effective page layout. If pictures are used, they must be inserted into the text. Picture size needs to be adjusted for proper fit on the page. In addition to page layout, designers must take into account such factors as headings, type sizes, and fonts. Are general headings used? Do separate sections or articles need their own subheadings? Does the size of the type need to be increased or decreased to fit a story into a predetermined space? What is the best font to use? Should more than one kind of font be used on a page?

To help you understand how some of these decisions are made, it is necessary to discuss some of the publishing terminology involved.

Fonts: Sizes and Styles

The type that a printer uses is described by its size, font, weight, and style. **Type size** is measured by a standard system that uses points. A **point** equals about ½ inch. Point size is measured from the top of the letter that rises the highest above the baseline (a letter such as *h* or *l*) to the bottom of the letter that descends the lowest (a letter such as *g* or *y*). Figure 9-11 shows type in different sizes.

The shapes of the letters and numbers in a published document are determined by the font selected. Recall that a **font** is a set of characters of the same design. A font can be printed in a specific **weight**, such as boldface, which is darker than usual, or in a specific **style**, such as italic. Changes in font provide emphasis and variety.

As shown in Figure 9-12a, varying the size and style of the type used in a publication can improve the appearance of a page and draw attention to the most important sections. However, using too many different

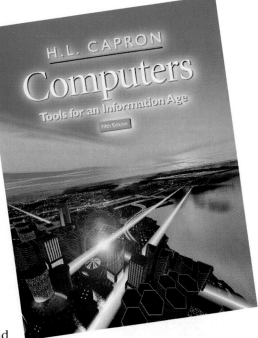

Figure 9-10 High-end desktop publishing. The cover of this book was produced with the latest computer technology. Using cross-country conference calls, e-mail, and modem file transfers, the Santa Rosa, California, artist developed his ideas in collaboration with the designer in San Francisco and the art director in Massachusetts. The image was rendered using 3-D modeling software. Drawn elements were seamlessly blended with textures, light effects, and shadows. A final high-resolution file was imported into a page layout program, then sent to Massachusetts to be converted to film.

Times New Roman (12)

Times New Roman (18)

Times New Roman (24)

Times New Roman (36)

Times New Roman (48)

Figure 9-11 Different point sizes. This figure shows a variety of different point sizes in a popular font called Times New Roman. The smallest shown here, point size 12, is often used for long text passages, such as correspondence. The larger sizes probably would be used only for headings or titles.

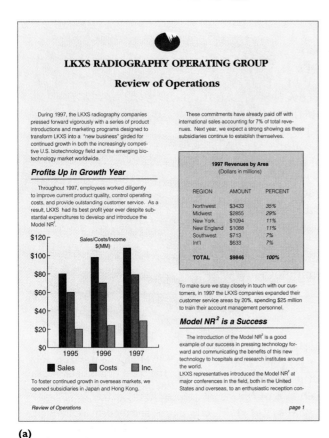

(a)

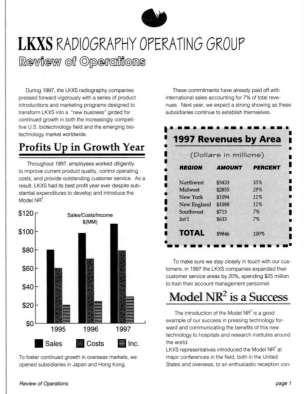

(b)

Figure 9-12 Sample designs. (a) This example uses complementary fonts to produce a professional-looking document. (b) The same page created with clashing fonts and other distractions.

fonts or using clashing fonts can create a page that is unattractive and hard to read (Figure 9-12b). Combine fonts with discretion.

Most printers used in desktop publishing store a selection of fonts in a ROM chip in the printer. These are called the printer's **internal fonts.** Also, most desktop publishing programs provide a **font library** on a disk. A font library contains a wide selection of type fonts called **soft fonts.** A soft font can be sent, or downloaded, from the library disk in the computer's disk drive to the computer, from which it then can be sent to the printer.

Leading and Kerning

Two terms you will encounter when you begin desktop publishing are *leading* and *kerning.* **Leading** (pronounced "ledding") refers to the spacing between the lines of type on a page. Leading is measured vertically from the base of one line of type to the base of the line above it. The greater the leading, the more white space between lines. Leading, just like type size, is measured in points.

Kerning refers to adjusting the space between the characters in a word. In desktop publishing software, each font has a default kerning. An example of kerning is shown in Figure 9-13.

Halftones

Halftones, which resemble photographs, appear in newspapers, magazines, books, and documents produced by desktop publishing. Halftones are representations made up of black dots printed on white paper. Vary-

(a) Unkerned:

WAVE

(b) Kerned:

WAVE

Figure 9-13 Kerning. (a) In this example the space between the characters is not altered. (b) Kerning, or adjusting the space between the characters, can improve the overall appearance of the word.

MAKING THE RIGHT CONNECTIONS

THE VIRTUAL OFFICE

The word *virtual* is applied in various computer settings, but it always means the same thing: the appearance of something that really does not exist. The computer somehow masks the reality and permits benefits similar to those offered by the real thing. In this discussion of the virtual office, the office as we know it—a physical place with a desk and a chair and office supplies—does not actually exist. But its functions do exist.

Consider the way Nora Mathison runs her sprinkler installation business in Phoenix. She relies on a toll-free phone number, voice mail, a cellular phone, and a notebook computer with a fax modem. No building, no office, no desk.

Nora advertises her toll-free number in the Yellow Pages; potential customers in the urban/suburban area can call the number without charge. When they

do, they are advised to leave a voice mail message. Nora, working on site in some customer's yard, can retrieve her voice mail messages and return the calls on her cell phone. She can use software on her notebook computer to work up a bid right at a customer site, or she can do the work later and fax the results to the customer. She also uses the notebook computer for scheduling, work flow, and billing.

In addition to convenience, the virtual office can minimize start-up costs for fledgling entrepreneurs. For business people who spend most of their time out of the office anyway, the virtual office is an ongoing asset.

ing the number and size of dots in a given space produces shades of gray. As you can see in Figure 9-14, the smaller the dot pattern used, the clearer the halftone.

➤ Using Desktop Publishing Software

The page composition program is the key ingredient of a desktop publishing system. **Page composition programs**, also called **page makeup programs,** let you design each page on the computer screen. You can determine the number and the width of the columns of text to be printed on the page. You can also indicate where pictures, charts, graphs, and headlines are to be placed. Once you have created the page design, you can use the page composition program to insert text and graphics into it. Text may be keyed as you prepare the page or imported as a file created by a word processing program. Page composition programs also let you move blocks of text and pictures around on your page. If you are not satisfied with the way the page looks, you can change the size of the type or the pictures.

Figure 9-14 Halftones. Halftones consist of a series of dots. Reducing the size of the dots makes the resulting halftone clearer.

Principles of Good Typography

Word processing and desktop publishing programs put many different fonts at your disposal, but you can overwhelm a document if you use overly fancy fonts or too many fonts. A general rule is "less is better." The guidelines that follow promote a clean and attractive look for your document.

- Use only two or three fonts in a document.
- Be conservative: Limit the use of decorative or unusual fonts. In particular, use stylized fonts such as QUAKE or **MACHINE** or CUTOUT only for signs and titles, never for passages of text.
- Use different sizes and styles of one font to distinguish between different heading levels, rather than using several different fonts.
- Never type body text in all capital letters.
- Do not use type that is too small to read easily just to fit everything on one page.
- Use a sans serif font only for short text passages; for long passages use a serif font, which is easier to read.
- Use italic or boldface, rather than underlining, for emphasis.

Some desktop publishing programs offer **templates**, predetermined page designs that you can use quickly by filling in your own text. Templates typically offered include those for newsletters, flyers, greeting cards, banners, calendars, and even business forms. Page composition programs can also integrate **clip art**—images already produced by professional artists for public use—into your publication to enliven your

Figure 9-15 Clip art. A variety of clip art software can be purchased and used to improve the appearance of a document. Most clip art is mundane—primitive sketches of everyday items such as kittens, household implements, and grinning pumpkins. The items pictured here offer a little more visual enhancement than the usual clip art.

NEW DIRECTIONS

DIGITAL ART

Imagine the day when, instead of a minimalist collection of clip art, you had the works of the masters at your disposal—Matisse, Renoir, van Gogh, and Klee (shown here). Now add the works of famous photographers such as Ansel Adams. If we had such collections available at the click of a mouse, we could indeed produce impressive output.

A company called Corbis Publishing is taking the first steps in this direction. Corbis is not the usual high-tech company; art history majors and librarians outnumber techies. The company has acquired the digital rights—usually nonexclusive—to several collections. In fact, over a million works of fine art and photographs have been archived. But the value of these works is that they are in digital form and thus can become a primary visual resource for the consumer, education, and publishing markets.

Some word processing and desktop publishing packages already offer a limited set of photographs and artwork, along with the usual clip art.

text. Most desktop publishing programs include a library of clip art. You can purchase disks of additional clip art. Figure 9-15 shows examples of illustrations in a clip art library.

★ ★ ★ ★

By now you should be convinced that word processing is probably essential for your career and, further, that desktop publishing is a valuable tool for individuals as well as businesses.

CHAPTER REVIEW

Summary and Key Terms

- **Word processing** is the creating, editing, formatting, storing, retrieving, and printing of a text document.
- A text document is any text that can be keyed in, such as a memo. *Creation* is the original composing and keying in of the document, *editing* is making changes to the document, *formatting* is adjusting the appearance of the document, *storing* is saving the document to disk, *retrieving* is bringing the stored document from disk back into computer memory, and *printing* is producing the document on paper.
- **Scrolling**, done by moving the cursor, lets you display any part of the document on the screen.
- **Word wrap** automatically starts a word on the next line if it does not fit on the previous line.
- Use the **Backspace key** to delete characters to the left or the **Delete key** to delete the character under the cursor or to the right of the cursor.
- Mouse users issue commands through a series of **menus**, called **pull-down menus**, which offer initial choices and submenus, or by using **buttons** at the top of the screen.
- The **format** is the physical appearance of the document.
- **Vertical centering** adjusts the top and bottom margins so that the text is centered vertically on the printed page.
- Any line can be individually **centered** between the left and right margins of the page.
- Settings automatically used by the word processing program are called **default settings**.
- When the margin settings are changed, word processing software adjusts the text to fit the new margins; this process is called **automatic reformatting.**
- Users can **tab** just once to begin a paragraph or can **indent** an entire paragraph.
- **Justification** refers to the evenness of the text at the side margins. A document is **fully justified** when it has an even margin down each side. Left justification causes an unjustified right side, which is referred to as **ragged right** text.
- **Line spacing** variations include single spaced, double spaced, and even triple spaced.
- Certain words or phrases or even entire paragraphs can be given special emphasis by using a darker text known as **boldface** text, or by using the slanted type called *italic*, or by underlining.
- A **font** is a set of characters—letters, punctuation, and numbers—of the same design. On a **serif** font, each character includes small marks, known as serifs. A **sans serif** font is clean and stark, with no serif marks.
- The **search command**, also called the **find command**, displays on the screen the exact page and place where a word or phrase is located. The **find and replace function** finds each instance of a certain word or phrase and replaces it with another word or phrase. A **conditional replace** asks you to verify each replacement.
- Word processing programs offer **pagination** options, permitting the page number to be located at the top or bottom of the page and to the left, right, or center, or even alternating left and right.
- With a single command, a user can see in reduced size a **print preview** of an entire page or two facing pages or even several consecutive pages.
- A word processing program keeps track of space needed for a **footnote** and automatically renumbers if a new footnote is added.
- **Headers** (top) and **footers** (bottom) appear on every page of a document. A number of variations are available, including placement, size, and font.

■ A **text block** can be moved, copied, or deleted. To manipulate a block of text, you must first **mark** (or **select**) the block, which then usually appears in **reverse video** (in which the background color becomes the text color and vice versa). The block move command, also known as **cut and paste**, moves the text to a different location. The block copy command copies the block of text into a new location, leaving the text in its original location as well. Block delete removes the block entirely.

■ A **spelling checker** program includes a built-in dictionary. A **thesaurus** program supplies synonyms and antonyms.

■ A **desktop publishing** program lets you produce professional-looking documents containing both text and graphics.

■ One part of the overall design of a document is **page layout**—how text and pictures are arranged on the page. Adding text to a layout is called **page composition.**

■ Type is described by **type size, font, weight,** and **style.** Type size is measured by a standard system based on the **point.**

■ Most printers used in desktop publishing contain **internal fonts** stored in a ROM chip. Most desktop publishing programs provide a **font library** on disk, containing additional fonts called **soft fonts.**

■ **Leading** refers to the spacing between the lines of type on a page. **Kerning** refers to adjusting the space between the characters in a word.

■ A **halftone** is a photographic representation made up of dots.

■ **Page composition programs,** also called **page makeup programs,** let the user design the page layout. Some desktop program packages offer **templates,** predetermined page designs. Page composition programs also allow the incorporation of electronically stored **clip art**—professionally produced images for public use.

Quick Poll

Compare your answers to those of your colleagues or classmates.

1. My personal use of word processing:
   ❑ a. I use college computers for college papers.
   ❑ b. It is sufficiently important that I want my own computer.
   ❑ c. It will be critical in almost everything I do.
2. My personal use of desktop publishing:
   ❑ a. I can get what I need from word processing only.
   ❑ b. I'd like to have it but it seems a luxury.
   ❑ c. I see it as an important tool for business and/or personal use.
3. The most important tool in my opinion:
   ❑ a. Spelling checker
   ❑ b. Thesaurus

Discussion Questions

1. Suppose you are an editorial assistant at a publishing house. As part of your job, you prepare the schedule for book development and production. You circulate your first cut of the schedule to various editors and designers (usually about six people), who return their copies with changes for you to incorporate. Contrast the differences in this process if you were using a typewriter and if you were using word processing.
2. You are producing a monthly newsletter for your volunteer organization, which helps illiterate adults learn to read. You prepare the first two issues using word processing, and these seem adequate. But you have seen newsletters that are more sophisticated and discover that they are made with desktop publishing software, with which you are not

familiar. Assuming that the cost of the software is not a problem, what would it take for you to make the switch?

3. Consider all the uses you might make of desktop publishing at home. Consider, for example, items such as birthday cards and banners.

Student Study Guide

Multiple Choice

1. A set of choices on the screen is called a(n)
   a. menu
   b. reverse video
   c. editor
   d. template
2. A program that provides synonyms is called a(n)
   a. indexing program
   b. form letter program
   c. editing program
   d. thesaurus program
3. An image made up of dots:
   a. pull-down menu
   b. block
   c. headers
   d. halftone
4. A type of menu that shows further subchoices:
   a. reverse
   b. scrolled
   c. pull-down
   d. wrapped
5. The feature that keeps track of the right margin is
   a. find and replace
   b. word wrap
   c. ragged right
   d. right justified
6. If using verification with the find and replace feature, this is called
   a. verified replace
   b. conditional replace
   c. questionable replace
   d. "what-if" replace
7. The feature that allows viewing of any part of a document on the screen is
   a. searching
   b. scrolling
   c. pasting
   d. editing
8. Transferring text to another location without deleting it from its original location is called
   a. scrolling
   b. searching
   c. copying
   d. moving
9. Ragged right means the right margin is set to be
   a. uneven
   b. variable
   c. even
   d. wide
10. Spelling checker programs use
    a. tab settings
    b. pasting
    c. pagination
    d. a dictionary

True/False

T F 1. Formatting refers to the physical appearance of a document.

T F 2. A thesaurus program supplies both synonyms and antonyms.

T F 3. A spelling checker program can detect spelling errors and improper use of language.

T F 4. Right justified means that the right margin will be ragged right.

T F 5. The move command moves text to another place and deletes it from its original place.

T F 6. A footer appears on the bottom of each page of the document.

T F 7. The feature that word processing and typing have in common is permanent marks made on paper as the document is keyed.

T F 8. When margin settings are changed, automatic reformatting adjusts the text to fit the new margins.

T F 9. The copy command moves text to another place and deletes it from its original place.

T F 10. A template is a set of clip art.

T F 11. A pull-down menu can be clicked with a mouse to show submenus.

T F 12. Text is centered vertically by adjusting the right margin.

T F 13. Clip art is art that is designed by the user of a desktop publishing program.

T F 14. A conditional replace asks a user to verify each replacement.

T F 15. Another phrase for marking a text block is selecting a text block.

T F 16. Print preview permits a user to view one or more pages on-screen before printing.

T F 17. A sans serif font is clean, with no serif marks.

T F 18. Another name for the search command is the find command.

T F 19. Internal fonts are stored on hard disk.

T F 20. The cursor is usually a blinking dash or line or rectangle.

T F 21. The quality of the printer is important for desktop publishing.

T F 22. Graphics capability is not required for desktop publishing.

T F 23. Most desktop publishing systems include an inexpensive printer.

T F 24. A halftone usually appears in reverse video on the screen.

T F 25. For most companies, printing costs are a relatively small part of the budget.

T F 26. Pagination options limit the page number to the left, center, or right on the bottom of the page.

T F 27. Desktop publishing is suitable for most in-house publications.

T F 28. Few businesses today can afford desktop publishing.

T F 29. The cursor can be moved by movement of the mouse.

T F 30. The top and bottom margins of a page can be adjusted to make the page text vertically centered.

Fill-In

1. Settings automatically used by the word processing program unless overridden by the user are called

   _____

2. A line that appears on the top of each page of the document: _____

3. Copy and move commands are generally known as:

   _____

4. Which feature permits a user to view any part of a document, about 20 lines at a time?

   _____

5. Resetting what will make a document shorter and wider? _____

6. Which feature finds and changes text?

   _____

7. What are words printed in darker type said to be?

   _____

8. Before a block of text can be copied or moved, what must be done first? _____

9. An even right margin is said to be

   _____

10. What is the verification feature with find and replace called? _____

11. Synonyms and antonyms can be supplied by

    _____

12. A set of drawings stored on disk:

    _____

13. Printers used for desktop publishing must have what software on a ROM chip?

    _____

14. The fonts stored in the printer are called

    _____

15. Adding type to a layout is called

    _____

16. Adjusting the space between characters in a word is called _____

17. Italic is an example of what font characteristic?

    _____

18. Boldface is an example of what font characteristic?

    _____

19. A set of characters of the same design:

    _____

20. The feature that automatically moves a word to the next line if it does not fit on the previous line:

    _____

Answers

Multiple Choice

1. a	6. b
2. d	7. b
3. d	8. c
4. c	9. a
5. b	10. d

True/False

1. T	7. F	13. F	19. F	25. F
2. T	8. T	14. T	20. T	26. F
3. F	9. F	15. T	21. T	27. T
4. F	10. F	16. T	22. F	28. F
5. T	11. T	17. T	23. F	29. T
6. T	12. F	18. T	24. F	30. T

Fill-In

1. default settings
2. header
3. cut and paste
4. scrolling
5. margins
6. find and replace
7. boldface
8. mark the text
9. justified
10. conditional replace
11. a thesaurus program
12. clip art
13. internal fonts
14. internal fonts
15. page composition
16. kerning
17. style
18. weight
19. font
20. word wrap

PLANET INTERNET

MULTIMEDIA

For users who are Internet-savvy, a key buzzword is *multimedia*. The concept covers a lot of ground and, more specifically, much exciting software.

I think I understand the term *multimedia* in a general sense—text, images, photographs, sound effects, and even motion—but what does it mean on the Internet? Pretty much the same thing. Text, of course, has always been a component of the Internet. Images and photographs became easily available with the advent of browser software. Now users can hear narrations and music and other sounds. The advent of Java and other software has also made motion a possibility.

So I can hear music and see movement just by showing up at a site that has them? Not quite. You must have a browser that is up to the task. The newer versions of modern browsers can do some of these things. Some special effects require special software additions to your browser, called plug-ins. If your browser cannot take advantage of the full "experience," you will probably see a message on the site that tells you so—and urges you to get a better browser (often one they suggest). They may also suggest that you get some specific software that will enhance site enjoyment. If so, they probably include a link to the site that offers the software, often for free downloading to your computer.

How do I get this plug-in software and then get it to work with my browser? Go to the site of the software developer that makes the plug-in. You won't have to look far for a clickable download icon. Read the instructions carefully to make sure that you select the software that works with your browser and your operating system. You may also be asked to choose the directory—folder—in which you want the software placed; the default location is usually in the same place as your browser. You may be offered instructions, and it is usually suggested that you print them for later reference. These include installation instructions, that is, how to plug the new software into your browser once it is downloaded. This usually involves running one of the programs downloaded.

Are there some standard software plug-ins that I should be sure to check out? Tough question. Standards are evolving. Once the standards battles

274

are settled, it is likely that plug-in functions will be subsumed eventually into evermore sophisticated browsers. Meanwhile, there are definitely some software products that are widely used.

Can I see some sites that use these popular plug-ins? Yes, but first you need to have the plug-in software in order to appreciate their value to the site. (By the way, you can usually still see the multimedia site even if you don't have a suitable browser or required plug-in software to appreciate its multimedia aspects; you just see more of a "plain vanilla" site.) Before you do any downloading, the best approach is probably to go to the site of the software developer and see all the action with the plug-in software supplied on the site.

Let us consider two popular plug-ins. *Shockwave*, which can be seen and downloaded from the Macromedia site, can provide amazing animation. Text and images swoop and swirl and stream across the screen as the site loads, usually with audio accompaniment. Shockwave makes the site come alive. Shockwave is the main attraction on tens of thousands of sites, including the well-known Disney and Nike sites as well as less well-known sites such as the Blue Platypus.

As an example, the World Wildlife Fund's Living Planet Campaign site opens with growling animals to lend ambience. Also, looking at the screen shown here, imagine the letters on the left side swooping into the site as you watch. For another example, check out Revenge of the Cowboy, a game site that should appeal to both kids and adults. Since *Shockwave* supplies action, it makes sense that it would be used to enable action-packed games.

Another popular add-on is *RealAudio*, from Progressive Networks. RealAudio sounds are suf-

ficiently sophisticated to provide entire broadcasts, such as baseball games. RealAudio is part of a larger audio/video package called RealPlayer. Your browser, by the way, can probably support some sound; try the BigEye or Historical Speeches sites.

Serious stuff. If you want to be a serious multimedia player, a site of note is Gamelan, which has been designated by Sun Microsystems' Java-Soft as the official directory for Java resources. Featuring the world's largest directory of reviewed Java resources, Gamelan is an indispensable site for Java developers and users. Gamelan offers comprehensive information, including a detailed FAQ list that should be useful to both beginners and seasoned users.

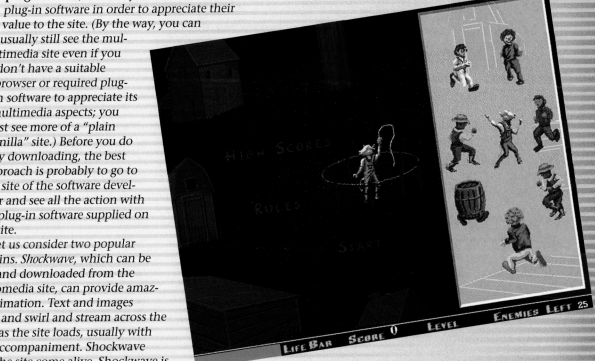

Internet Exercises

1. **Structured exercise.** Begin with the AWL URL, http://hepg.awl.com/capron/planet/, and link to the Macromedia (Shockwave) site.
2. **Freeform exercise.** Put the word *multimedia* through a search engine and see what you find.

Tom Shaffer earned his degree in accounting just before the revolution—the computer revolution, that is. He learned to balance corporate budgets by using a desktop calculator, a paper ledger, and a pencil with an eraser.

After he had been on the job for several years, Tom saw an electronic spreadsheet for the first time at a business convention. The convention crowd focused on the Apple exhibit, where the black-and-white screen of an Apple II computer displayed VisiCalc, the first widely available electronic spreadsheet software.

Tom was not impressed at first. The little Apple screen showed only a few rows and columns of numbers. The only way to see the whole ledger at once was to print it. Yes, the machine-printed ledger was attractive. But a secretary could type a table of numbers on a typewriter and make it look even better. Nevertheless, Tom began to listen to the sales representative.

The first advantage of electronic spreadsheets that Tom noticed was that no erasers were required. When the sales rep made a mistake or wanted to make a change, she just backspaced over it and entered the correct number. However, the greater advantage was one that had not been at all apparent at first. The sales representative pointed out that not all the numbers in the spreadsheet had been keyed in manually; several of the columns of numbers had been calculated automatically by the computer. As the sales rep made changes to some of the manually entered numbers, Tom watched the automatically calculated figures change accordingly. A change in one number—an interest rate, for instance—could result in the automatic updating of half the numbers in the spreadsheet.

Back at the office, Tom lobbied hard for a desktop computer and electronic spreadsheet software. Now Tom works on a personal computer much more powerful than his first Apple II, and with spreadsheet software many times more sophisticated than VisiCalc—the software that brought personal computers into the business mainstream. He moves rows and columns of data with the click of the mouse. A color screen shows him high-quality graphs automatically constructed from the spreadsheet data.

Tom went from skeptic to computer enthusiast in one afternoon. Not everyone is that quick to see how to apply a computer-based tool to a particular line of work. However, once experienced, it is hard to live without the computer advantage.

Spreadsheets and Business Graphics

Facts and Figures

The Nature of Spreadsheets

A worksheet that presents business data in a grid of rows and columns is called a **spreadsheet** (Figure 10-1a). The manually constructed spreadsheet, on paper, has been used as a business tool for centuries. Spreadsheets can be used to organize and present business data, thus aiding managerial decisions. However, spreadsheets are not limited to businesses. Personal and family budgets, for example, are often organized on spreadsheets. Furthermore, nonfinancial or even nonnumeric data can be analyzed in a spreadsheet format.

Unfortunately, creating a large spreadsheet manually is time-consuming and tedious, even when you use a calculator or copy results from a computer printout. Another problem with manual spreadsheets is that making a mistake is too easy. If you do not discover the mistake, the consequences can be serious. If you discover the mistake after the spreadsheet is finished, you must manually redo all the calculations that used the wrong number.

	JAN.	FEB.	MAR.	APR.	TOTAL
SALES	1750	1501	1519	1430	6200
COST OF GOODS SOLD	964	980	932	943	3819
GROSS MARGIN	786	521	587	487	2381
NET EXPENSE	98	93	82	110	383
ADM EXPENSE	77	79	69	88	313
MISC EXPENSE	28	45	31	31	135
TOTAL EXPENSES	203	217	182	229	831
AVERAGE EXPENSE	68	72	61	76	277
NET BEFORE TAXES	583	304	405	258	1550
FEDERAL TAXES	303	158	211	134	806
NET AFTER TAX	280	146	194	124	744

(a)

Figure 10-1 Manual versus electronic spreadsheets. (a) This manual spreadsheet is a typical spreadsheet consisting of rows and columns. (b) The same spreadsheet created with a spreadsheet program.

Microsoft Excel - Net after taxes

File Edit View Insert Format Tools Data Window Help

Arial   10   B I U $ % A

H19   =

	A	B	C	D	E	F	G
1		JAN.	FEB.	MAR.	APR.	TOTAL	
2							
3	Sales	$ 1,750	$ 1,501	$ 1,519	$ 1,430	$ 6,200	
4	Cost of goods sold	964	980	932	943	3819	
5	Gross margin	786	521	587	487	2381	
6							
7	Net expense	98	93	82	110	383	
8	Adm. expense	77	79	69	88	313	
9	Misc. expenses	28	45	31	31	135	
10	Total expenses	203	217	182	229	831	
11	Average expense	68	72	61	76	277	
12							
13	Net before tax	583	304	405	258	1550	
14	Federal tax	303	158	211	134	806	
15	Net after tax	$280	$146	$194	$124	$744	
16							

Sheet1 / Sheet2 / Sheet3 /

Ready

(b)

Electronic Spreadsheets

An **electronic spreadsheet**, or **worksheet**, is a computerized version of a paper spreadsheet (Figure 10-1b). Working with a spreadsheet on a computer eliminates much of the toil of setting up a manual spreadsheet. In general, an electronic spreadsheet works like this: You enter the data you want on your spreadsheet and then key in the types of calculations you need. The electronic spreadsheet program automatically does all the calculations for you, completely error-free, and produces the results in your spreadsheet. You can print a copy of the spreadsheet and store the data on your disk so that the spreadsheet can be used again. By the way, although this chapter examines spreadsheets in a general way, we will illustrate spreadsheets using software called Microsoft Excel, as shown here in Figure 10-1b. Thus, although the screen is realistic, our area of concern is merely the spreadsheet, not the various menus and buttons that come with this specific software.

By far the greatest labor-saving aspect of the electronic spreadsheet is **automatic recalculation:** When you change one value or calculation on your spreadsheet, all dependent values on the spreadsheet are automatically recalculated to reflect the change. Suppose, to use a common example, that one entry on a spreadsheet is RATE, another is HOURS, and another is SALARY, which is the product of RATE and HOURS. Values for RATE and HOURS will be entered, but SALARY will be calculated by the spreadsheet software. But what if RATE changes? RATE can be entered anew, but the person entering the data need not worry about SALARY because the spreadsheet will recalculate SALARY using the new value for RATE. Although this example may seem trivial, the automatic recalculation principle has significant consequences for large, complex spreadsheets. A change in a single value could affect dozens or even hundreds of calculations, which, happily, the spreadsheet will perform.

"What-If" Analysis

Automatic recalculation is valuable for more than just fixing mistakes. If a number is changed—not because it is incorrect but because a user wants to see different results—related calculations will also be changed at the same time. This ability to change a number and have the change automatically reflected throughout the spreadsheet is the foundation of **"what-if" analysis**—the process of changing one or more spreadsheet values and observing the resulting calculated effect. Consider these examples:

- What if a soap manufacturer were to reduce the price of a certain brand by 5 percent; how would the net profit be affected? How about 10 percent? 15 percent?
- What if a general contractor were to subcontract with several workers, but one of them reneged and the contractor had to hire someone more expensive; how would that affect the total cost?
- What if the prime lending rate were raised or lowered; how would this affect interest moneys for the bank or the cost of a loan for bank customers?

Once the initial spreadsheet is set up, any of these "what-if" scenarios can be answered by changing one value and examining the new, recalculated results.

▶ Spreadsheet Fundamentals

Before you can learn how to use a spreadsheet, you must understand some basic spreadsheet features. The characteristics and definitions that follow are common to all spreadsheet programs.

Cells and Cell Addresses

Figure 10-2 shows one type of spreadsheet—a teacher's grade sheet. Notice that the spreadsheet is divided into rows (horizontal) and columns (vertical). The rows have *numeric labels* and the columns have *alphabetic labels*. There are actually more rows and columns than you can see on the screen. Some spreadsheets have thousands of rows and hundreds of columns—probably more than you will ever need to use.

The intersection of a row and column forms a cell. A **cell** is a storage area on a spreadsheet. When referring to a cell, you use the letter and number of the intersecting column and row. For example, in Figure 10-2, cell B7 is the intersection of column B and row 7—in this example, the grade of 25 for Vedder on Quiz 1. This reference name is known as the **cell address**, or **cell reference**. Notice that the alphabetic column designation always precedes the row number: B7, not 7B.

On a spreadsheet one cell is always known as the **active cell**, or **current cell**. When a cell is active you can enter data or edit that cell's contents. Typically, the active cell is marked by highlighting in reverse video or with a heavy border drawn around it. The active cell in Figure 10-2 is cell A1.

You can use a mouse or the cursor-movement (arrow) keys to scroll through a spreadsheet both vertically and horizontally.

Contents of Cells: Labels, Values, and Formulas

Each cell can contain one of three types of information: a label, a value, or a formula. A **label** provides descriptive text information about entries in the spreadsheet, such as a person's name. A cell that contains a label is not generally used to perform mathematical calculations. For example, in Figure 10-2, cells A1, A9, and F1, among others, contain labels. A **value**

Getting Practical

QUESTIONS AND ANSWERS

Sooner or later most computer users need answers to questions. Help is usually available over the phone from staff employed by the software maker. Typically, assistance is free for a certain time period, perhaps 90 days from the first phone call, but then there is a charge to the user. To make the best use of your time on the phone, do some advance preparation.

Before you call:
- Have your software documentation handy.
- Place your phone near your computer.
- Know your computer type and model and the version of your software package.
- Write down the exact wording of any error messages.

When you call:
- Give identifying information when asked.
- State the problem clearly.
- Tell the technician what you have already tried.
- Be ready to explore solutions on the computer as you talk.

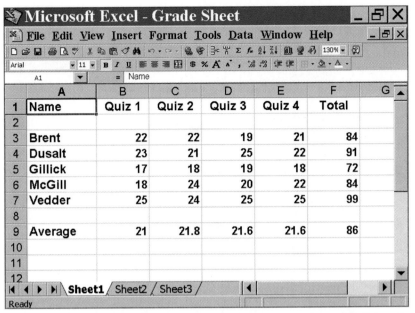

Figure 10-2 Anatomy of a spreadsheet screen. This screen shows a typical spreadsheet—a teacher's grade sheet. It shows space for 13 rows numbered down the side and 7 columns labeled A through G. The intersection of a row and column forms a cell. Here, cell A1 is the active cell—the cell into which a user may key data. Only one cell may be active at a given time.

Planning Your Spreadsheet

Unless you are an experienced spreadsheet user, you will want to take time to plan your spreadsheet before you invoke the spreadsheet software.

1. Determine the results you want to display on your spreadsheet by mapping it out on paper.
2. Determine the data you have to input to your spreadsheet to calculate the results you want.
3. Write down the names of the input and output values that you will use in your spreadsheet and the equations you will use. Record the exact form in which you will enter them in your spreadsheet.
4. Write down the formulas for converting the spreadsheet's inputs to its outputs.

---

is an actual number entered into a cell to be used in calculations. In Figure 10-2, for example, cell B3 contains a value.

A **formula** is an instruction to the program to calculate a number. A formula generally contains cell addresses and one or more arithmetic operators: a plus sign (+) to add, a minus sign (–) to subtract, an asterisk (*) to multiply, and a slash (/) to divide. When you use a formula rather than entering the calculated result, the software can automatically recalculate the result if you need to change any of the values on which the formula is based.

In addition to the types of calculations just mentioned, a formula can include one or more functions. A **function** is like a preprogrammed formula. Two common functions are the SUM function, which adds numbers together, and the AVG function, which calculates the average of a group of numbers. Most spreadsheet programs contain many functions for a variety of uses, from mathematics to statistics to financial applications. A formula or function does not appear in the cell; instead, the cell shows the result of the formula or function. The result is called the **displayed value** of the cell. The formula or function is the **content** of the cell.

Ranges

Sometimes it is necessary to specify a range of cells in order to build a formula or perform a function. A **range** is a group of one or more adjacent cells occurring in a rectangular shape; the program treats the range as a unit during an operation. Figure 10-3 shows some ranges. To define a range, you must indicate the upper left and lower right cells of the block. Depending on the particular spreadsheet software you are using, the cell addresses are separated by a colon or by two periods. For example, in Fig-

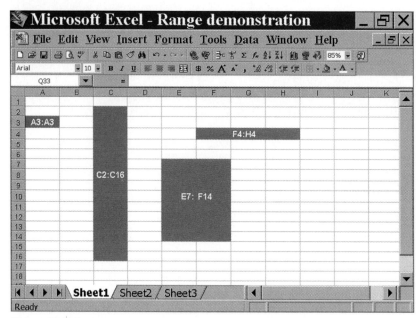

Figure 10-3 Ranges. A range is a group of one or more cells arranged in a rectangle. You can name a range or refer to it by using the addresses of the upper left and lower right cells in the group.

ure 10-2, the Quiz 1 range is B3:B7 (or B3..B7), and the Brent quiz range is B3:E3 (or B3..E3).

▶ Spreadsheet Features

Once spreadsheet users master the basics, they are usually eager to learn the extra features, especially formatting and graphics, that make their work more useful or attractive. Formatting features take a worksheet beyond the historically plain page full of numbers. Here is a partial list of features you will probably find included with spreadsheet software:

■ **Column width.** Columns containing labels—words—usually need to be wider than columns for numbers. Note, for example, that the leftmost column in Figure 10-1 is wider than the other columns to accommodate the data. Columns can also be made narrower. (Incidentally, although less common, it is also possible to alter the height of a row.)

■ **Headings.** If a heading is desired, it can be invoked as a wide column and can even be centered.

■ **Number symbols**. If appropriate, a number value can be shown with a dollar sign ($), a percent sign (%), and commas and decimal places, as desired.

■ **Appearance of data.** Spreadsheet data can be presented in one of many proffered fonts and in boldface or italic. Furthermore, data can be centered within the cell or can be justified right or left within the cell. Often an entire column of cells will be justified right or left. In Figure 10-2, for example, all data in column A is left justified, whereas data in columns B through F are right justified.

■ **Printing.** When a user is developing and experimenting with a spreadsheet, he or she is looking at the spreadsheet on the screen. But the finished product, or even a series of variations of the product, will probably be printed for distribution and examination. Spreadsheet software offers several printing options. For example, a spreadsheet may be centered on the printed page. Margins may be altered. The entire page may be printed sideways, that is, horizontally instead of vertically. Vertical and horizontal grid lines may be hidden on the printed spreadsheet.

■ **Decoration.** Many spreadsheet packages include decorative features, such as borders and color options.

The change from numbers to pictures—graphics—is a refreshing variation. Most spreadsheet software makes it fairly easy to switch from numbers to pictures. That is, once you prepare a spreadsheet, you can show your results in graphic form. The value of business graphics will be discussed in detail later in the chapter.

▶ A Problem for a Spreadsheet

Jean Lake, at age eight, was an entrepreneur. One hot summer day she borrowed some sugar and lemons from the kitchen and stirred up a pitcher of lemonade, which she proceeded to sell from a stand in front of her house. By the end of the day, she had gone through three pitchers and had taken in $6.25. Her joy, however, subsided when her mother explained that a business person has to pay for supplies—in this case, the sugar and lemons. But Jean was not deterred for long. In her growing-up years, she sold bird houses, a neighborhood newsletter, and sequined hair barrettes. In the process, she learned that it was important to keep good business records.

A New Business

When Jean attended Ballard Community College, she noticed that the only beverages available were milk, coffee, and canned soft drinks. Thinking back to her early days, Jean got permission to set up a lemonade stand on campus. In addition to fresh lemonade, she sold bagels and homemade cookies. The stand was soon successful, and eventually Jean hired other students to manage stands on nearby campuses: Aurora, Eastlake, and Phinney.

Using Spreadsheets for the Business

When Jean took a computer applications course at the college, she decided that spreadsheets were appropriate for keeping track of her business. She began by comparing sales for the four campuses for the fourth quarter of the year. She sketched her spreadsheet on paper (Figure 10-4). As she invoked the spreadsheet software, Jean decided that she also would add some headings. In her first cut at the spreadsheet, Jean keyed in the campus names in column A and the campus sales for each of the three months in columns B, C, and D.

Jean does not, of course, have to compute totals—the spreadsheet software will do that. In fact, the obvious solution is to key formulas using the SUM function to compute both column and row totals. In cell E6, for example, Jean keys =SUM(B6:D6). This instructs the software to sum the values in cells B6, C6, and D6 and place the resulting sum in cell E6. Even

Spreadsheets in the Home
Family budgeting is the most common home use for spreadsheets. However, some people are more interested in "what-if" scenarios, for which spreadsheets are the perfect tool. Here are some examples users have dreamed up:

■ **What if I go back to work . . .** is it really worth it? You can factor in all the expenses of employment—travel, wardrobe, child care, taxes, and other disbursements—and compare the total against the income received.
■ **What if I start my own business . . .** can I make a go of it? Although estimates may be sketchy at best, a budding entrepreneur can approximate expenses (for materials, tools, equipment, office rental, and so forth) and compare them to anticipated revenues from clients over different periods of time.
■ **What if I save $50 per month for my child's education . . .** how much money would be saved (with accumulated interest) by the time the child is 18? What if I were to save $75 or $100 per month?
■ **What if I jump into the stock market . . .** or stick to a more conservative investment approach? A popular sport among investors is running dollar amounts and anticipated growth rates of various investment opportunities through spreadsheets. The results may give them a glimpse of their future financial picture.

Figure 10-4 Spreadsheet planning. A sketch of a spreadsheet is useful before invoking the software. This plan includes one row per campus and the monthly totals, and one column for the campus names, each month's sales, and the campus totals.

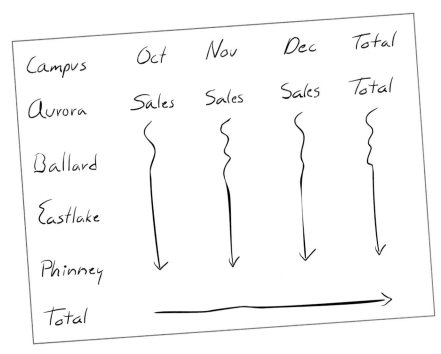

Figure 10-5 First draft of sales spreadsheet. This initial look at Jean's spreadsheet shows the headings and data keyed into the spreadsheet. Jean keyed formulas that include the SUM function in cells E5, E6, E7, E8, B10, C10, D10, and E10. Later, Jean will make a change to a data item. She will also format the spreadsheet to improve its appearance; for example, the month headings (OCT, NOV, and so forth) need to be centered over their appropriate columns.

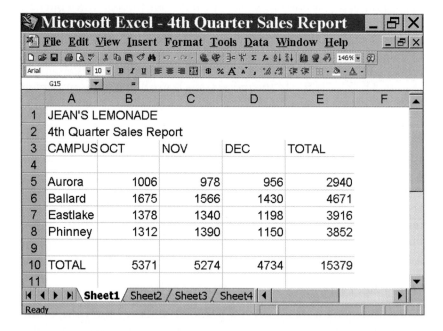

though she typed a formula in the cell, the result is a value, in this case 4671 (Figure 10-5). Keep in mind that the resulting value in any cell containing a formula will change if any of the values in the cells in the formula change. For cell E6 the resulting value would change if there were a change to the values in cell B6, C6, or D6. The other cells containing totals (E5, E7, E8, B10, C10, D10, and E10) also contain formulas that will calculate values. Cell E10, by the way, could sum up either column E (=SUM(E5:E8)) or row 10 (=SUM(B10:D10)). The result is the same either way.

Jean has been saving her spreadsheet on disk as she goes along. Now that the basic spreadsheet is complete, Jean saves it one more time and then prints it.

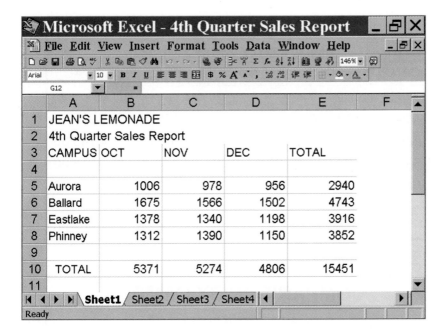

**Figure 10-6 The altered spreadsheet,
reflecting automatic recalculations.**
Jean changed the value in cell D6, causing an automatic change to calculated
values in cells E6, D10, and E10.

Changing the Spreadsheet: Automatic Recalculation

Jean has discovered an error in her spreadsheet: cell D6, rather than containing 1430, should be 1502. Again using her spreadsheet software, she
needs merely to retrieve the spreadsheet from disk and make the single
change to cell D6 (Figure 10-6). Note, however, that cell D6 is used for
the totals calculations in cells E6 and D10. Furthermore, because either
column E or row 10 is used to compute the final total in E10, either
changed cell E6 or changed cell D10 will cause a change in the value calculated in cell E10. All these changes are made by the spreadsheet software automatically. Indeed, note the changed values in cells E6, D10,
and E10—all the result of a single change to cell D6.

Formatting and Printing

Now that Jean is satisfied with her spreadsheet calculations, she decides
to make some formatting changes and then print the spreadsheet. She
uses the spreadsheet software to make the changes (to see the changes,
you can look ahead to Figure 10-7a). Here is a list of the changes she
wants to make:

- Center the two major headings.
- Use a different font on the two major headings, and change them to
  boldface.
- Center CAMPUS, OCT, NOV, DEC, and both TOTAL labels, each
  within its own cell, and boldface each label.
- Put each campus name in italic.
- Present the sales figures as currency by adding dollar signs ($) and
  decimal points.
- Use a vertical double border to separate the campus names from the
  sales figures, a horizontal double border to separate the headings from
  the sales figures, and a single horizontal border to separate the top
  two heading rows from the rest of the spreadsheet.
- Remove the spreadsheet grid lines.

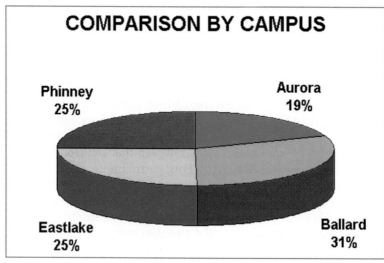

JEAN'S LEMONADE 4th Quarter Sales Report				
CAMPUS	OCT	NOV	DEC	TOTAL
Aurora	$1,006.00	$ 978.00	$ 956.00	$ 2,940.00
Ballard	$1,675.00	$1,566.00	$1,502.00	$ 4,743.00
Eastlake	$1,378.00	$1,340.00	$1,198.00	$ 3,916.00
Phinney	$1,312.00	$1,390.00	$1,150.00	$ 3,852.00
TOTAL	$5,371.00	$5,274.00	$4,806.00	$15,451.00

(a)

(b)

Figure 10-7 The finished spreadsheet and a matching graph. (a) On the final version of her spreadsheet, printed here, Jean has boldfaced and centered the headings and changed their fonts, added vertical and horizontal borders, used italics and boldface on certain cells, and expressed the sales figures as currency. (b) This simple pie chart shows the figures from the rightmost column of the spreadsheet, the campus totals, as percentages of total sales.

Note that the printed result need not include the alphabetic column labels or the numeric row labels (Figure 10-7a).

A Graph from Spreadsheet Data

Jean decides to make a chart to contrast the sales totals among the four campuses. These figures already exist in the last column of the spreadsheet, cells E5 through E8. Using the software's charting capability, Jean can select those cells and then request a three-dimensional pie chart to display them. She decides to specify that the sales figures be shown as percentages of total sales, and that each pie wedge be further labeled with the campus name, supplied from column A on the spreadsheet. After adding a title, Comparison by Campus, Jean saves and prints the finished chart (Figure 10-7b).

Units Sold Each Month

Material	Jan.	Feb.	Mar.	Apr
Copper	6	10	13	22
Bronze	18	28	36	60
Iron	9	15	19	32
Gold	32	52	64	110
Silver	20	32	40	68
Totals:	85	137	172	292

(a)

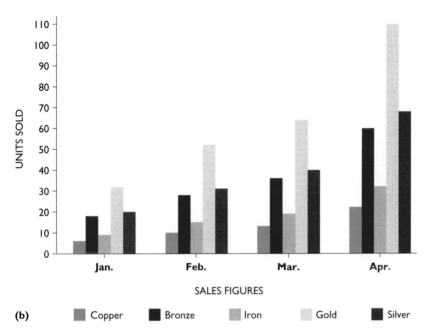

(b)   ■ Copper   ■ Bronze   ■ Iron   ■ Gold   ■ Silver

Figure 10-8 Business graphics. (a) A large amount of data can be translated into (b) one simple, clear bar graph.

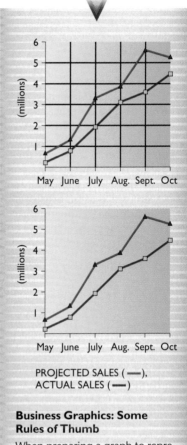

PROJECTED SALES (—),
ACTUAL SALES (—)

Business Graphics: Some Rules of Thumb

When preparing a graph to represent numbers in a spreadsheet, it is easy to mindlessly click the "draw graph" button and expect the resulting graph to be meaningful and attractive. This will probably not be the case unless you have done some planning.

■ Think in detail about what you want to the graph to represent. What variables will you use? What labels and titles would help explain your graph?

■ Keep the graph simple. Include only the minimum amount of information needed to convey the point you are trying to make.

■ Make an uncluttered graph. For example, gridlines are usually distracting and unnecessary. Choose the option to eliminate them when you print. (Note the examples with and without gridlines above.)

▶ Business Graphics

Graphics can show words and numbers and data in ways that are meaningful and quickly understood. This is the key reason they are valuable. Personal computers give people the capability to store and use data about their businesses. These same users, however, sometimes find it difficult to convey this information to others—managers or clients—in a meaningful way. **Business graphics**—graphics that represent data in a visual, easily understood format—provide an answer to this problem.

Why Use Graphics?

Graphics generate and sustain the interest of an audience by brightening up any lesson, report, or business document. In addition, graphics can help get a point across by presenting numeric data (Figure 10-8a) in one simple, clear graph (Figure 10-8b). What is more, that simple graph can reveal a trend that could be lost if buried in long columns of numbers. In addition, a presenter who uses graphics often appears more prepared and organized than one who does not. To sum up, most people use busi-

NEW DIRECTIONS

A SPREADSHEET FOR THE WORLD

It seems inevitable that with worldwide communication readily available on the Internet, people would want to combine local information in some way that was useful. This is already happening with the help of schoolchildren.

Sponsored by an organization called Landmark, the project encourages teachers to send children out to their local grocery stores to find prices of standard items in standard amounts—rice, chocolate, and the like. Landmark provides a form that can be filled in and sent via e-mail to the Landmark Internet site. That data is combined with like data from many other locations into a large spreadsheet, which the teacher can download. In addition to allowing comparison of all the original data, the spreadsheet calculates minimums, maximums, and averages.

The spreadsheet portion shown here lists only U.S. locations. It gets more complex when many countries are considered. Measuring methods—grams versus ounces, and so forth—and local currencies can be factored in by the computer.

City	Alton	Cocoa	Antioch	Archbold
State or Province	Iowa	Florida	California	Ohio
Country	USA	USA	USA	USA
Currency	Dollars	Dollars	Dollars	Dollars
HAMBURGER	$1.59	$1.61	$1.52	$1.69
RICE	$0.69	$0.94	$0.62	$0.97
ORANGES	$0.59	$0.70	$0.40	$1.29
SUGAR	$2.19	$0.49	$1.56	$1.98
ALL PURPOSE FLOUR	$1.85	$1.08	$1.16	$1.29
WHOLE MILK	$2.19	$2.50	$2.71	$2.21
CHOCOLATE	$4.19	$2.45	$2.14	$3.05
POTATOES	$1.29	$1.65	$1.54	$1.48
BUTTER	$1.19	$1.16	$1.50	$1.59
CORN	$0.45	$0.53	$0.55	$0.61
PEANUT BUTTER	$2.79	$1.67	$2.00	$1.20
COFFEE	$3.64	$3.23	$4.94	$4.09

ness graphics software for two reasons: (1) to view and analyze data and (2) to make a positive impression during a presentation. To satisfy these different needs, two types of business graphics programs have been developed: analytical graphics and presentation graphics.

Analytical Graphics

Analytical graphics programs are designed to help users analyze and understand specific data. Sometimes called analysis-oriented graphics programs, these programs use already-entered spreadsheet or database data to construct and display line, bar, and pie chart graphs (Figure 10-9a through c). Spreadsheet software usually provides this option.

Although analytical graphics programs do a good job of producing simple graphs, these programs are too limited and inflexible for a user who needs to prepare elaborate presentations. Analytical graphics programs, for example, let you choose from only a small number of graph types, and the formatting features—graph size, color, and lettering—are limited. These restrictions may be of little concern to some users, but

Computer Graphics

The Artist's Subject

The computer artwork that opens this gallery, by artist Bill Frymire, expresses the impact of computers on the world.

The computer artworks on these pages, created by various artists, show the diversity of subject matter open to any artist, from the exotic to the serious to the whimsical.

1. This white mask, by artist Huan Le Tran, reflects beauty from the artifacts of his culture.
2. Artist Radim Mojzis chose donating blood to the Red Cross as his subject matter. His Drops of Life won Best of Show in the annual CorelDraw competition.
3. In an entirely different direction, artist John Stephens produced this charming drawing based on the story of The Lady of Shallot.
4. Artist Eric Yang's image reflects an interest in football.
5. This image, called Sentries and based on an allegorical tale, was produced by artist Judy York.
6. Artist Marcia Broderick produced this image partly as an environmental statement.
7. This simple still life of dishes was produced by artist Tomasz Wawrzyczek.

The Drops of Life

Gift of Blood-Gift of Life ✚ Different ways to Help

ic yang

4

5

6

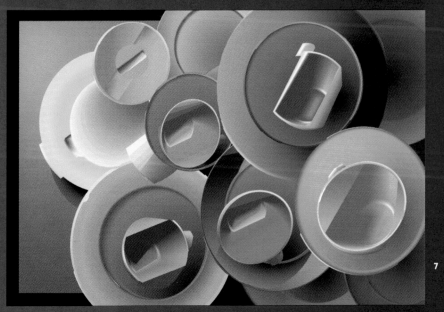

7

3

The Artist's Style

Anyone who might think that using a computer inhibits an artist's style need only see the amazing variety of approaches used by computer artists. As in hand-produced art, there are as many styles as there are artists.

8. Artist Diane Fenster often uses a collage of images, overlapping and intertwining them.

9. Artist Michael Bruggemen clearly prefers a realistic approach to showing off a 1957 Chevy.

10. Wendy Grossman's artwork is often extremely detailed and composed of a number of smaller images.

11. Artist Gerry Wilson adds his own whimsy to this realistic night skyline.

12. Artist Glen Mitsui presents his clear images with clean lines and uncomplicated colors.

13. Bill Frymire produced this work, which is something of a classic in graphics circles. The artist scanned his own thumb print to be used as the background. But all eyes are on Rex, his pet iguana. Altogether, the style is half-real/half not.

14. Two artists, Georgina Curry and Gerry Moss, worked together to produce this image in an altogether different style, which resembles a mosaic.

8

The 1957 Chevy

9

10

11

12

13

14

Ray Tracing

An important aspect of realistic perspective is the use of light and shadow. Rather than adding these elements individually, graphic artists can use software to enhance their works. The "ray" in ray tracing refers to light rays, whose direction can be "traced" by the software. For example, a user can specify the location—point of view—of a light element, such as light from the sun or a nearby window, and the software will add appropriate shadows. The light source need not actually be included in the image; it could be "off screen" but still cause shadows.

The works shown here were all entries in the International Ray Tracing Competition, which has a new contest every few months on a different theme. Examine them carefully to see how the artists made use of light and shadow.

15. This green vase by artist Nikita Beliaev took third place in the Glass competition. In the competition called School, 16. Ian Armstrong won first place with this entry in the Time competition. 17. In the competition called School, this library scene, which the artist calls Philosophy 101, was submitted by Derek Owens. 18. In the competition with a Time theme, Adrian Baumann won second place with this Admiral watch. 19. Steve Gowers won first prize in the Summer theme contest with his rendition of a bucket of shells. 20. Called Physics at Play, this work was entered in the Physics and Math contest by artist Rob Bolin. In the Flight category, 21. Nathan O'Brien took second place with The Flight of the Atlantis and 22. Ian Armstrong won honorable mention. 23. John McIvor calls this work of different mathematical shapes, entered in the Physics and Math competition, Transcendentia.

15

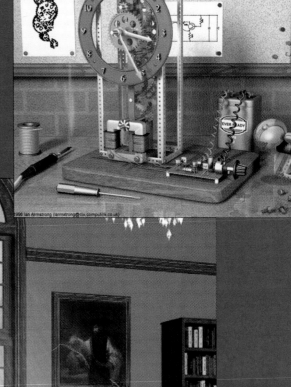

16

17

18

19

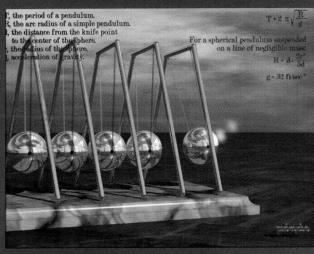

T, the period of a pendulum.
R, the arc radius of a simple pendulum.
the distance from the knife point
to the center of the sphere.
the radius of the sphere.
acceleration of gravity.

$$T = 2\pi\sqrt{\frac{R}{g}}$$

For a spherical pendulum suspended
on a line of negligible mass:

$$R = d + \frac{2r^2}{5d}$$

g = 32 ft/sec²

20

21

23

22

24

25

26

Pictures Do Lie

The works on this page show how photographs can be manipulated by the computer. Begin with 24., a photo of a building interior. Then consider 25., photos of strolling tourists, a statue, and a painting. These four photos have been scanned into the computer and manipulated to become 26., a museum with artworks and tourists to view them. Note in particular the adjusted shape of the painting and the computer artist's addition of clouds in the skylight.

27. Here is the intriguing result of computer imaging of four photos. The original photos were of trees, a sunset, a swan, and a red world logo.

28. Here the artist has produced various computer-manipulated versions of an original photo of a child.

27

28

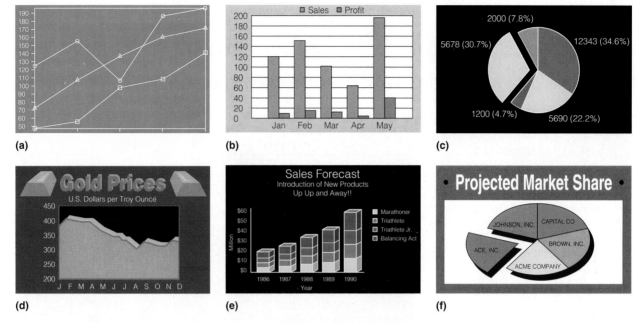

Figure 10-9 Analytical graphics compared to presentation graphics. Analytical graphics (a, b, and c) are certainly serviceable, but they lack the clarity and appeal of presentation graphics (d, e, and f). Compare the line graphs (a and d), bar graphs (b and e), and pie charts (c and f).

those who require sophisticated graphics will want to consider presentation graphics.

Presentation Graphics

Presentation graphics programs are also called **business-quality graphics.** These programs let you produce charts, graphs, and other visual aids that look as if they were prepared by a professional graphic artist (Figure 10-9d through f). However, you can control the appearance of the product when you create it yourself, and you can produce graphics faster and make last-minute changes if necessary.

Most presentation graphics programs help you do several kinds of tasks:

- Edit and enhance charts, such as analytical graphs, created by other programs.
- Create charts, diagrams, drawings, and text slides from scratch.
- Use a library of symbols, drawings, and pictures called **clip art** that comes with the graphics program.
- Permit an animated presentation so that, for example, letters of a title can swoop in one by one to create a dynamic effect.
- Use small files that come with the program to add sounds—chimes, applause, swoosh, and even thunk—to your presentation.

Although graphics hardware requirements vary, be aware that to use presentation graphics you will need a high-resolution color monitor, possibly a color printer, and perhaps some method of transferring your computer-produced results to slides or transparencies or to a projector that can show computer screen output on a wall screen.

MAKING THE RIGHT CONNECTIONS

PLUGGING IN THE PUBLIC

It is Saturday and you forgot to report that burned-out streetlight during regular working hours. No problem. Just turn to your modem-equipped home computer, and tap into a color screen of icons for city and county government. Dash off a note to the city light department: "The streetlight at 2137 Argyle Dr. N. is out. Can you get it fixed soon?" Click on the Send Mail icon and then on the City Light icon. Done.

Next, you have read that a bill has been introduced in the legislature to expand the use of home incarceration for nonviolent first-time offenders. Again using your computer, you dial up the legislative hotline and have a copy of the bill downloaded to your computer's hard drive for analysis later.

You also need to pay that parking ticket. Click over to that department and enter your Visa card number.

Finally, you tap into one of the many county databases, this time

regarding a business rating system for local insurance agencies. You read a dozen articles and download three that interest you to your own computer.

Far-fetched? Not at all. The technology is available to have a public access system in place

today. Local governments are already experimenting with computer systems that give the public two-way communication with just about any government service, department, or agency.

▶ Some Graphics Terminology

To use a graphics program successfully, you should know some basic concepts and design principles. Let us begin by exploring the types of graphs you can create.

Line Graphs

One of the most useful ways of showing trends or cycles over a period of time is to use a **line graph.** For example, the graph in Figure 10-10 shows company costs for utilities, supplies, and travel during a five-month period. Line graphs are appropriate when there are many values or complex data. In the business section of a newspaper, line graphs are used to show complex trends in gross national product, stock prices, or employment changes over a period of time. Also, corporate profits and losses are often illustrated by line graphs.

Notice, in Figure 10-10, the line that runs vertically on the left and the one that runs horizontally across the bottom; each line is called an **axis.** (The plural of *axis* is *axes.*) The horizontal line, called the **x-axis,** often

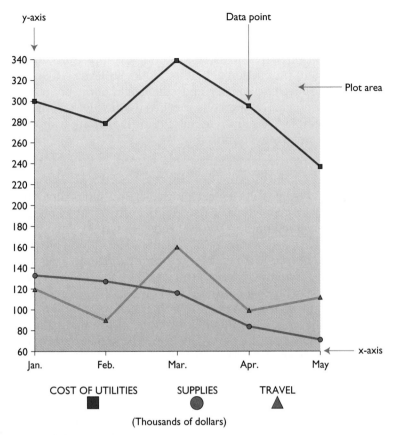

Figure 10-10 A line graph. Line graphs are useful for showing trends over a period of time. In many analytical programs, different symbols are used to show the different types of data being plotted.

represents units of time, such as days, months, or years; it can also represent characteristics, such as model number, brand name, or country. The vertical line, called the **y-axis**, usually shows measured values or amounts, such as dollars, staffing levels, units sold, and so on. The area above and to the right of the axes is called the **plot area**—the space in which the graph is plotted, or drawn.

Graphics programs automatically scale (arrange the units or numbers on) the x-axis and y-axis so that the graph of your data is nicely proportioned and easy to read. When you become proficient with a graphics program, you can select your own scaling for the axes. Each dot or symbol on a line graph represents a single numeric quantity called a **data point.** You must specify the data to be plotted on the graph; many graphs are produced from the data stored in the rows and columns of spreadsheet files. This data is usually referred to as the set of *values.* The items that the data points describe are called **variables.** For example, in Figure 10-10 the variable Utilities includes the values 300, 280, 340, 300, and 240; the top line in the plot area shows how these values are graphed.

To make the graph easier to read and understand, **labels** are used to identify the categories along the x-axis and the units along the y-axis. **Titles** summarize the information in the graph and are used to increase comprehension.

Bar Graphs

Bar graphs are used for graphing the same kinds of data that line graphs represent. They are often used to illustrate multiple comparisons, such as sales, expenses, and production activities. Notice in Figure 10-9b that **bar graphs** shade a rectangular area up to the height of the point being plotted, creating a bar. These graphs can be striking and informative when they are simple. Bar graphs are useful for presentations because the comparisons are easy to absorb.

Pie Charts

Representing just a single value for each variable, a **pie chart** shows how various values make up a whole. These charts really look like pies; the whole amount is represented by a circle, and each wedge of the pie—a portion of the whole—represents a value. Figure 10-9c shows a pie chart.

Pie charts can show only the data for one time period, such as a single month. However, of all the graphics, the pie chart does the best job of showing the proportions for different variables. If a pie chart for expenses, for example, showed that more than half went for rent, that half-pie is easy to spot. Figure 10-9f shows one of the wedges pulled slightly away from the pie, for emphasis. This type of pie chart is called an **exploded pie chart.**

★ ★ ★ ★

Of the three chapters on applications software, the first, on word processing and desktop publishing, dealt with communicating with words. This chapter has addressed analyzing and communicating with numbers. The upcoming chapter on databases takes a different approach, offering a way for users to keep and retrieve data conveniently.

CHAPTER REVIEW

Summary and Key Terms

- Forms that are used to organize business data into rows and columns are called **spreadsheets**. An **electronic spreadsheet**, or **worksheet**, is a computerized version of a manual spreadsheet.
- The greatest labor-saving aspect of the electronic spreadsheet is **automatic recalculation:** When one value or calculation in a spreadsheet is changed, all dependent values on the spreadsheet are automatically recalculated to reflect the change.
- **"What-if" analysis** is the process of changing one or more spreadsheet values and observing the resulting calculated effect.
- The intersection of a row and column forms a **cell.** The letter and number of the intersecting column and row is the **cell address**, or **cell reference.**
- The **active cell**, or **current cell**, is the cell in which you can type data.
- Each cell can contain one of three types of information: A **label** provides descriptive information about entries in the spreadsheet; a **value** is an actual number entered into a cell; and a **formula** is an instruction to the program to perform a calculation. A **function** is like a preprogrammed formula. Sometimes you must specify a **range** of cells, a group of adjacent cells in a rectangular area, to build a formula or perform a function.
- To create a spreadsheet you enter labels, values, formulas, and functions into the cells. Formulas and functions do not appear in the cells; instead, the cell shows the result of the formula or function. The result is called the **displayed value** of the cell. The formula or function is the **content** of the cell, or the **cell content.**
- **Business graphics** represent business data in a visual, easily understood format.
- **Analytical graphics** programs help users analyze and understand specific data by presenting data in visual form. **Presentation graphics** programs, or **business-quality graphics** programs, produce sophisticated graphics. Presentation graphics programs contain a library of symbols and drawings called **clip art** and also offer animation and sounds.
- A **line graph**, which uses a line to represent data, is useful for showing trends over time. A reference line on a line graph is an **axis.** The horizontal line is called the **x-axis**, and the vertical line is called the **y-axis.** The area above the x-axis and to the right of the y-axis is the **plot area.** Each dot or symbol on a line graph is a **data point.** Each data point represents a value. The items that the data points describe are called **variables.** Labels identify the categories along the x-axis and the units along the y-axis. **Titles** summarize the information in the graph.
- **Bar graphs** show data comparisons by the lengths or heights of bars.
- A **pie chart** represents a single value for each variable. A wedge of an **exploded pie chart** is pulled slightly away from the pie, to emphasize that share of the whole.

Quick Poll

Compare your answers to those of your colleagues or classmates.

1. As for using spreadsheets for personal use,
   - ❏ a. It seems like too much work for the return.
   - ❏ b. I wouldn't mind starting out small and building on it.
   - ❏ c. I see spreadsheets as a convenient way to manage some aspects of my life.

2. As for spreadsheets in business,
   ❏ a. In my line of work, I doubt that I will use them or even encounter them.
   ❏ b. I am not sure whether I will need spreadsheets, but I want at least minimum knowledge just in case.
   ❏ c. No question about it; I'll need spreadsheets and want to maximize my advantage.
3. Regarding clip art in presentations,
   ❏ a. Using text only is more suitable for business presentations.
   ❏ b. Clip art adds interest no matter who the audience is.
   ❏ c. Clip art is too primitive; formal art or photos would be better.

Discussion Questions

1. Consider more "what-if" scenarios. *What if I save $100 a month . . .* how soon can I buy a car? What if I save $125 or $150 per month? If you have a price in mind for a car, what information could such a spreadsheet give you? What information could you get by varying interest rates and the price of the car? *What if I buy the house by the lake . . .* instead of the house near work? The houses have different price tags and different expenses. These factors and others can be built into a spreadsheet and used to calculate monthly payments and other factors that might affect your budget. What factors might you include in your spreadsheet? Hint: one factor may be reduced transportation costs for the house near work.
2. How might you use a spreadsheet in your career? What use might these workers have for a spreadsheet: video store manager, dietitian, civil engineer who designs bridges, day care supervisor.
3. Business people who only occasionally give presentations say that one reason they prefer using graphics is that graphics focus the audience on the screen and thus reduce the nervousness of the speaker. What other advantages do graphics offer to the speaker?

Student Study Guide

Multiple Choice

1. The active cell:
   a. current cell   c. formula
   b. range   d. cell address

2. A preprogrammed formula:
   a. function   c. range
   b. graph   d. cell
3. A chart that represents only one value for each variable:
   a. function   c. pie
   b. line   d. bar
4. Business-quality graphics:
   a. recalculation   c. analytical
   b. range   d. presentation
5. Intersection of a row and column:
   a. active address   c. cursor
   b. formula   d. cell
6. The result of a formula in a cell:
   a. label   c. range
   b. value   d. displayed value
7. Text information in a cell:
   a. label   c. formula
   b. value   d. cell address
8. A dot or symbol on a line graph:
   a. label   c. variable
   b. data point   d. axis
9. Summarizes information related to a graph:
   a. plot area   c. label
   b. title   d. axis
10. Computer-prepared art:
    a. cell   c. clip art
    b. analytical   d. range

True/False

T F   1. Another name for the content of a cell is its displayed value.
T F   2. A group of cells in a rectangular form is called a range.
T F   3. Another name for the active cell is the cell reference.
T F   4. A manual spreadsheet is capable of automatically recalculating totals when changes are made to figures in the spreadsheet.
T F   5. A disadvantage of business graphics is that they depict data in a manner that is hard to grasp.
T F   6. The displayed value of a cell is its formula or function.
T F   7. The shape of the set-apart portion of an exploded pie chart is a wedge.
T F   8. A function is like a preprogrammed formula.
T F   9. Another name for the current cell is a labeled cell.
T F 10. In a spreadsheet, both column width and row height can be altered.
T F 11. Analytical graphics let you construct line, bar, and pie chart graphs.
T F 12. Many presentation graphics programs can edit and enhance charts created by other programs.

T F 13. Presentation graphics appear professionally produced.
T F 14. Column widths in spreadsheets are fixed.
T F 15. Analytical graphics use a library of symbols to enhance output.
T F 16. The active spreadsheet cell is marked by the pointer.
T F 17. Labels identify categories along graph axes.
T F 18. On an exploded pie chart, one wedge is slightly removed from the pie for emphasis.
T F 19. The greatest labor-saving aspect of an electronic spreadsheet is its ability to recalculate dependent values when the value it depends on is changed.
T F 20. In a spreadsheet a label cannot be used for calculations.

Fill-In

1. List the three types of information a user can enter in a spreadsheet cell.

   a. _____

   b. _____

   c. _____

2. What is the name of the kind of analysis that lets a user change spreadsheet values and then observe the resulting effect? _____

3. What are enhanced graphics called?

   _____

4. In a spreadsheet a formula or function is called the cell content; what is the calculated result called?

   _____

5. What is the intersection of a row and column on a spreadsheet called? _____

6. Plain line graphs are an example of what kind of graphics? _____

7. Another name for a cell address:

   _____

8. Another name for the active cell:

   _____

9. In a line graph the horizontal axis is called

   _____

10. A preprogrammed formula is called

    _____

11. A group of cells in a rectangular form:

    _____

12. The type of chart that has a single wedge separate from the rest of the chart: _____

13. When one value or calculation on a spreadsheet is changed, all dependent calculations are also changed by the software. This is called

    _____

14. The letter and number of the intersecting column and row of a cell is called _____

15. An actual number entered into a cell:

    _____

Answers

Multiple Choice

1. a	6. d
2. a	7. a
3. c	8. b
4. d	9. b
5. d	10. c

True/False

1. F	6. F	11. T	16. F
2. T	7. T	12. T	17. T
3. F	8. T	13. T	18. T
4. F	9. F	14. F	19. T
5. F	10. T	15. F	20. T

Fill-In

1. a. labels
   b. numbers
   c. formulas
2. "what-if" analysis
3. presentation
4. displayed value
5. cell
6. analytical
7. cell reference
8. current cell
9. x-axis
11. range
12. exploded pie chart
13. automatic recalculation
14. cell address
15. value

PLANET INTERNET

SERIOUS BUSINESS

The Internet was started by the military and long remained the province of the government and educational institutions. Businesses wondered if commercial enterprises were even permitted on the 'Net. The answer, a resounding yes, has led to an explosion of activity.

Big companies too? You may have heard about individuals starting their own small business on the Internet. There are many thousands of them.

But what about the big companies that have been established for decades? Are serious businesses interested in the Internet? You bet. Much of the Internet is embraced by—and supported by—business. More than half of Internet networks are business related.

A Web presence. Just being "on the Web" is probably not enough. The issue is whether a business site has established a Web presence—an oft-visited site respected for its value and content. Notice that the web sites shown here for Computer World, Kellogg, and Land Rover are both attractive and useful; each has many clickable icons as links to informational parts of their sites. The image of buildings, for example, is part of the ComputerWorld site. Click on any company name, and you will be given the latest information about that company.

Success factors. The secret to a successful page is that users accept the invitation to visit the site and, more importantly, keep coming back to it. If they form a habit of visiting a page, they will be more disposed to buying products and services. The primary reason users come back is that they know they can expect some useful content. Selling food? Include recipes at your site. Offering golf equipment? Report the latest information on tournaments and courses. In fact, many sites begin by offering useful information and, once

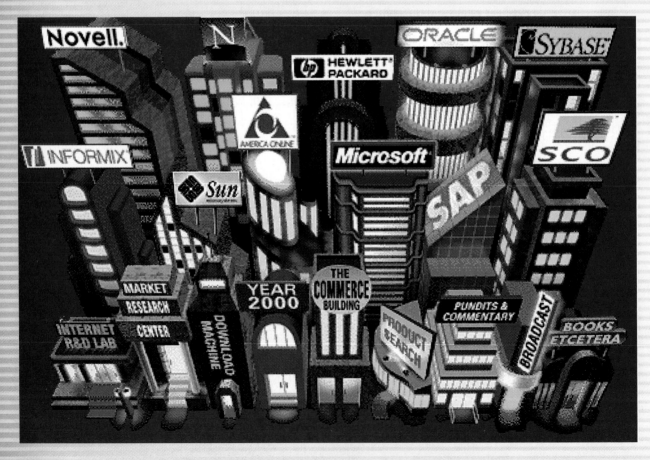

themselves and their preferences, a process called *registration*. A more likely method is to offer something of value in return for the user's name, e-mail address, and other information. For this reason, the Internet abounds with contests, sweepstakes, drawings, and prizes.

Sending mail. An obvious interactive technique for a business site is to offer an e-mail option. Users who take the trouble to write, to ask questions, or even to complain supply valuable marketing data to the company. The business, of course, must respond to all e-mail messages promptly.

The future. The Internet has both short-term and long-term benefits for businesses and for their users. For business people, in the short term there is e-mail, information gathering, and even direct marketing. For users, business sites provide information and convenience. Long term, the most compelling benefit for both groups is that the Internet represents the way business is going to be transacted in the future.

an audience is established, start offering products.

Advertising. There are different approaches to advertising on the Internet. A business can, of course, pitch its products or services on its own site. Many businesses now trumpet their web sites by including their Internet address in their television or print advertisements. Another approach is to buy advertising on a popular site—perhaps Yahoo or ESPNET SportsZone. The point is to pick a site that has a lot of traffic; a click on your advertising banner or icon takes the user to your own site.

Targeting users. What business people on the Internet desperately want is measurements. How many people visit the site? Who are they? What hardware and software do they have? Is this their first time, or are they repeat visitors? If they have been here before, what parts of the site did they visit? If they had the answers to these questions, they could tailor their sites to the user and improve their prospects. Some information is relatively easy to gather. For example, even a novice can include a counter on a web page, so the number of visits—if not visitors—is easily known. Also, a multipaged site can use software to track a user's journey through the site.

One on one. Successful business sites take advantage of the Internet's unique characteristic, its interactivity. A business that prepares a television commercial is pitching to a passive audience. But an ad on the Internet can be a two-way activity between the business, as represented by the site, and the user. The most straightforward way to take advantage of interactivity is to ask users to voluntarily give some information about

Internet Exercises

1. **Structured exercise.** Begin with the AWL URL, http://hepg.awl.com/capron/planet/. Choose a business directory to see what kinds of sites are on the 'Net.
2. **Freeform exercise.** Think of a business product or service that interests you—computers, chocolate, motorcycles, whatever. Feed that word to a search engine and see what business sites you find.

Suppose you had a really terrific recipe for chocolate chip cookies. In fact, your friends and family rave about your oatmeal raisin cookies too, not to mention your snicker-doodles and macadamia nut specials. Thus encouraged, you open a small cookie shop. Just one. It is not too difficult to keep track of supplies—just multiply the ingredients of a few recipes.

But that simplicity has changed for Debbi Fields, whose Mrs. Fields Cookies have blossomed from a single store in Palo Alto, California, to a chain of more than 600 stores in almost every state and several foreign countries. Fortunately, her husband, Randy Fields, a computer programmer, put together a team of technicians to provide databases with every kind of information a store might need.

Recipes and ingredients are just the beginning. The databases specialize in planning and marketing strategies. For example, from data gathered and stored over a period of time, the database knows how meteorological conditions affect sales at each store. In Seattle, rain means more cookies sales; in Los Angeles, rain means fewer cookie sales. Stores in either city can plan the amount of cookies to bake accordingly. But the weather is only one factor. Cookies sold and dollars generated are updated at each store hourly. These records can be accessed in the future to predict sales. If, for example, a store sees that its sales are below predictions, workers are authorized to offer specials—say, a free soft drink or "buy 5 get 2 free."

Employees at Mrs. Fields Cookies find it easy to learn to use the database software. The databases have many advantages, in particular, keeping consistent standards at each store. But the bottom line is that the computer databases squeeze out higher productivity.

Database Management Systems

Getting Data Together

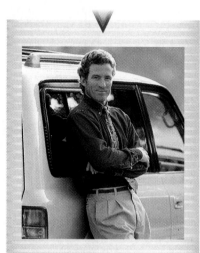

Own a Car? Your Name and Address Are Probably for Sale

In approximately two-thirds of the states, it is perfectly legal to obtain the identification of car owners. Anyone can jot down a license plate number and go to the motor vehicles department to get the owner's name and address. Some states go even further, selling information—name, address, height, weight, age, vision, and type of car—on computer tapes to all comers, from insurance companies to marketers to detectives. California, spurred by privacy invasions by crazed movie fans, has passed a law to keep such information private.

▶ Getting It Together: Database Systems

A **database** is an organized collection of related data. In a loose sense you are using a database when you use a phone book or when you take papers from a file cabinet. Unfortunately, as the amount of data increases, creating, storing, changing, sorting, and retrieving data become overwhelming tasks.

Suppose you had a collection of names and addresses, each on a separate index card, stored in an index-card file (Figure 11-1). If you had only 25 cards, sorting the cards into alphabetical order or even finding all the people who have the same zip code would be fairly easy. But what if you had 100, or 1000, or 10,000 cards? What if you had several different boxes, one organized by names, one by cities, and one by zip codes? What if different file clerks added more cards each day, not knowing whether they were duplicating cards already in the file? And what if another set of clerks was trying to update the data on the same cards? As you can see, things might get out of hand. Enter computers and database management software.

A **database management system (DBMS)** is software that helps you organize data in a way that allows fast and easy access to the data. In essence, the program acts as an efficient and elaborate file system. With a database program you can enter, modify, store, and retrieve data in a variety of ways.

Databases Are Different

Before proceeding further, it should be noted that database systems are different from word processing or spreadsheet software. Generally, most users have a good understanding of both word processing and spreadsheets. They enter and use the data in the same form as that in which it resides on disk. Data in databases, however, could reside on the disk in ways unknown to a user. In particular, sophisticated database systems, particularly those designed for a mainframe computer environment, are complex and must be planned and managed by computer professionals.

However, even though the underlying technology may be complex, such databases are available to the average user. Users are trained to input data to and retrieve data from the database system by using appropriate software; they can do this successfully without ever having to understand the underlying technology.

On the other hand, database software is available for personal computers that a novice user can apply to simple or moderately complex problems. That is, in contrast to complex databases that must be set up by professionals, a user could both set up and use a database on a personal computer. That is the kind of database we will be examining in this chapter.

Figure 11-1 An index-card database. Each card in this index-card file contains one person's name and address. The cards are arranged alphabetically by last name.

MAKING THE RIGHT CONNECTIONS

THE CASE OF THE DANGEROUS INTERSECTION

Ethan Leonard, an insurance man, looked at the report and scratched his head. A carload of people had been injured when the insured car had rear-ended it. The injured passengers suffered sprains, strains, and whiplash, the so-called soft tissue injuries that cannot be confirmed by an X ray. And the accident had taken place at the corner of Chicago's North Avenue and North Shore Drive—again.

In fact, the whole scenario sounded so familiar that Ethan looked up some recent reports. He found not only similar scenarios at the same site, but also the same attorneys representing the injured parties and the same doctors attesting to their injuries.

The insurance company initiated a full investigation. It tapped remotely into two insurance industry databases that contain

information about claimants, including their names and addresses, and the names of their lawyers and doctors. The matchups went well beyond coincidence. The investigation was able

to uncover a ring of 21 lawyers, doctors, chiropractors, and street organizers—the people who lined up the "victims" to stage the sudden-stop accidents. Lawsuits for fraud are in process.

Advantages of Databases

Several advantages are generally associated with databases.

- **Reduced redundancy.** Data stored in separate files, as opposed to in a database, tends to repeat some of the same data over and over. A college, for example, needs to have various kinds of information for a student—perhaps financial, academic, and career data. If each of these sets of data is in a separate file, some repetition is inevitable—such as each student's name, address, and Social Security number or other identification. In a database most of this information would appear just once.
- **Integrated data.** Rather than being in separate and independent files, data in a database is considered integrated because any item of data can be used to satisfy an inquiry or a report. This advantage is related to the reduced redundancy advantage: Since data can be retrieved from any place in the database, many specific data items need not be repeated.
- **Integrity.** People who maintain any kind of file hope that it has integrity, that is, that the file is accurate and up-to-date. Integrity concerns increase as the sophistication of the data increases. Reduced redundancy increases the likelihood of data integrity.

Databases and the Arts

Some people are surprised to learn that performing arts groups use computers as standard business tools. The groups find databases particularly useful. Database software, for example, can search for the names of musical pieces—all 20-minute violin pieces by German composers, for example.

The managers of the American Ballet Theatre take their computers on tour: One database plots rehearsal schedules; another keeps track of sets, lighting, and costumes. Other databases are used to coordinate ticket sales with fund-raising; if you are a patron, this probably means that you will receive your tickets with great efficiency and then be solicited for a donation.

▶ Database Concepts

There are many DBMS programs on the market today. Covering all the operations, features, and functions of each package would be impossible. Instead, this chapter examines database management in a generic way. The features discussed are common to most database software packages.

Database Models

The way a database organizes data depends on the type, or **model**, of the database. There are three main database models: hierarchical, network, and relational. Each type structures, organizes, and uses data differently. Hierarchical and network databases are usually used with mainframes and minicomputers and will not be discussed here. However, relational databases are used with personal computers as well as mainframes. A **relational database** organizes data in a table format consisting of related rows and columns. Figure 11-2a shows an address list; in Figure 11-2b this data is laid out as a table.

Fields, Records, and Files

Notice in Figure 11-2b that each box in the table contains a single piece of data, known as a **data item**, such as the name of one city. Each column of the table represents a **field**, which is a type of data item. The specific data items in a field may vary, but each field contains the same type of data item—for example, first names or zip codes. The full set of data in any given row is called a **record**. Each record has a fixed number of fields. The fields in a particular record contain related data—for example, the name and address of a person. A collection of related records make up a **file**. In a relational database a file is also called a **relation**. There can be a variable number of records in a given relation; Figure 11-2b shows five records—one for each person. There can also be more than one file in a database.

Database Power

Now that you know what *field, record, file,* and *relation* mean, you are ready to glimpse the real power of databases. The power is in the connection: A relational system can relate data in one file to data in another file, allowing a user to tie together data from several files. To understand how this works, consider the database called MOORE that uses a set of four related files—four relations—to constitute one database. These four files have some fields in common (Figure 11-3). The files are part of a database for Moore Contax, Inc., a company that warehouses computer equipment and supplies. Moore needs to keep track of its sales representatives, customers, orders, and inventory.

Now look at a detailed version of these relations (Figure 11-4). The Sales Representative file has six fields: REP-ID (representative identification), LNAME (last name), FNAME (first name), REGION (geographic area), HDATE (hire date), and PHONE. Similarly, Customer file has four fields, Order file has four fields, and Inventory file has three fields (QOH stands for quantity on hand). The interesting point about these relations is that they are connected. Both the Sales Representative file and the Customer file have a REP-ID field. The Customer file and the Order file

Akers, Ted
4302 Lemon Ave.
Oakland, CA 94709

Brown, Ann
345 Willow Rd.
Palo Alto, CA 94025

Chandler, Joy
4572 College Ave.
Berkeley, CA 94705

James, Susan
822 York St.
San Francisco, CA 94103

Mead, Ken
8 Rocklyn Ave.
Tiburon, CA 94903

(a)

Field

LAST NAME	FIRST NAME	STREET	CITY	STATE	ZIPCODE
AKERS	TED	4302 LEMON AVE.	OAKLAND	CA	94709
BROWN	ANN	345 WILLOW RD.	PALO ALTO	CA	94025
CHANDLER	JOY	4572 COLLEGE AVE.	BERKELEY	CA	94705
JAMES	SUSAN	822 YORK ST.	SAN FRANCISCO	CA	94103
MEAD	KEN	8 ROCKLYN AVE.	TIBURON	CA	94903

(b)

Data item

Figure 11-2 A relational database. In this example the address list in (a) is organized as a relational database in (b). Note that the data is laid out in rows and columns; each field is equivalent to a column, and each record is equivalent to a row.

are connected by the field CUST-NO. The Order file and the Inventory file are connected by the field ITEM-NO. These sample files are, of course, rather primitive, but they illustrate the point of connectivity.

These connections allow users to extract information across several relations, something that would not be possible if each relation was an independent file instead of a file within a database. Suppose, for example, that Anthony Harl, an employee for Moore Contax, receives a phone call inquiring about an order for Computer City. The folks at Computer City are concerned because a promised order is overdue and they have not heard from their sales representative. Anthony has, of course, a computer on his desk. Keep in mind that Anthony need not be concerned with how the relations are set up and may not even know what a relation is. From his training, however, he has a pretty good idea of what information he can get from the database system.

Anthony can, by using commands appropriate to his database software, ask a question that is the equivalent of this: What is the status of Computer City's order? The database software would look to the Customer file (follow along in Figure 11-4), find CUST-NO 3007 for Computer City, and then go to the Order file and look up the order lines for CUST-NO 3007. From the 3007 line in the Order file, the software could pick up ITEM-NO data 7639; using that data and now moving to the Inventory file, it can be seen that item 7639, a sound card, is out of stock. All this scrambling around is **transparent** to the user; that is, the user is not aware of the specific searches through the files but is merely given a response to the request. Anthony gets a message

Figure 11-3 Conceptual diagram of the files in the MOORE database. The files are Sales Representative, Customer, Order, and Inventory. Note the common fields.

Database on disk

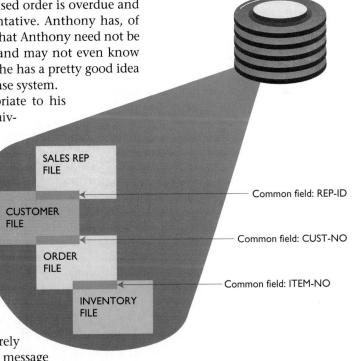

SALES REP FILE

CUSTOMER FILE

ORDER FILE

INVENTORY FILE

Common field: REP-ID

Common field: CUST-NO

Common field: ITEM-NO

Figure 11-4 Records in the four files in the MOORE database. Observe that there are common fields among the files, enabling the files to reference one another.

SALES REPRESENTATIVE FILE

REP-ID	LNAME	FNAME	REGION	HDATE	PHONE
114	Abele	Lori	SW	10-15-86	(602) 624-9384
159	Higgins	Heatheryn	SE	12-16-91	(404) 524-8472
230	Sullivan	Pat	SE	2-21-88	(305) 734-2987
386	Speed	Kristen	MW	6-14-90	(708) 823-8222
349	Demaree	Donn	NW	7-10-93	(206) 634-1955

CUSTOMER FILE

CUST-NO	CNAME	CITY	REP-ID
2934	Ballard Computer	Seattle	349
3007	Computer City	Miami	230
4987	Laser Systems	Atlanta	159
8987	Varner User Systems	Naperville	386
9185	CGI Computers	Spokane	349
9876	Computing Solutions	Tucson	114

ORDER FILE

CUST-NO	DATE	ITEM-NO	QTY
3007	8-12-99	7639	11
4987	8-12-99	6720	15
8987	8-13-99	2378	14
9185	8-10-99	1628	10
9876	8-14-99	6720	20

INVENTORY FILE

ITEM-NO	DESCR	QOH
1628	Hand scanner	191
2378	Modem	453
3457	Hard drive	294
5647	Printer pack	676
6720	3 1/2" disk holder	982
6599	CD-ROM drive	817
7639	Sound card	0
8870	Mouse	296
9037	Monitor	152

back on his screen with the net result: On Computer City's order, item 7639, sound card, is out of stock. Anthony can convey this information to the customer waiting on the line.

Furthermore, Anthony can, again by using commands appropriate to his database software, ask about Computer City's sales representative. The database software, looking in the Customer file, can see that Computer City's REP-ID is 230. Moving now to the Sales Representative file, REP-ID 230 is Pat Sullivan, whose phone number is (305) 734-2987. When a message to this effect comes back on the screen, Anthony can pass this information along to the customer on the phone line.

▶ A Problem Fit for a Database

The next sections focus on just one database file and show, generally, how data can be planned and entered. Bess Deck is a convention plan-

NEW DIRECTIONS

BUSTING LOOSE: DATA IN THE 21ST CENTURY

Before long, it is going to seem old-fashioned to call it data. Traditional data in columns and rows, good for accounting and customer lists and inventory, is making room for audio, video, text, and images. The idea, in theory, is simple: anything that can be conceived can be defined and captured. Once captured, it then can be converted to the basic zeros and ones required for computer processing.

It is unlikely that you will see voice or video or Internet transactions in a corporate database any time soon. But many database management software vendors are laying the groundwork now for a new generation of databases that will manage a broad spectrum of data.

Working with a database will change too. The vehicle of choice will likely be an Internet site connected to a database in a way that is transparent—not obvious—to the user. For example, the screen could show a shiny car, say a red Corvette. By clicking on the car, a General Motors marketer could bring up a profile of Corvette buyers. Clicking on a nearby map could show sales patterns by geographic region. From there, the marketer could view a sales training video to see if the video fit the pattern for the particular region.

Future thinkers wonder if the name *database* is too mundane to convey the source of all this information. Perhaps. But the concepts of data storage and retrieval are still the same. Only the kinds of data and the elaborate retrieval methods will really change.

ner. She lives in Seattle and contracts with various organizations who plan to hold conventions in that city. Bess and her staff of five coordinate every physical aspect of the convention, including transportation, housing, catering, meeting rooms, services, tours, and entertainment.

Bess began moving her files to a computer three years ago. She has found database software useful because of its ability to cross-reference several files and, in particular, to answer inquiries about the data. Bess thinks the time is ripe to set up a database file for the tours she offers. She has noticed that clients ask many questions about the tours available, including times, costs, and whether or not food is included. Also, clients want to know if much walking is included on the tour and whether or not there are stairs.

In answer to these kinds of questions, Bess or one of her staff now has to shuffle through a thick folder of brochures and price lists. Bess knows that she will be able to respond more quickly to client inquiries if this information is in her database file.

➤ Creating and Using a Database

After you have considered your needs, such as what reports and inquiries you will want to make, there are two steps to creating a database file: (1) designing the structure of the file and (2) entering the data into the file. Look ahead to Figure 11-8 if you want to see what Bess's final database will look like.

Determining the File Structure

Bess begins creating what will be called the TOUR database by sketching on paper the **file structure**—what kind of data she wants in each column (Figure 11-5). To create the file structure, she must choose meaningful fields. The fields she chooses should be based on the data she will want to retrieve from the database. Let us take a look at each type.

Getting Practical

UNINSTALL

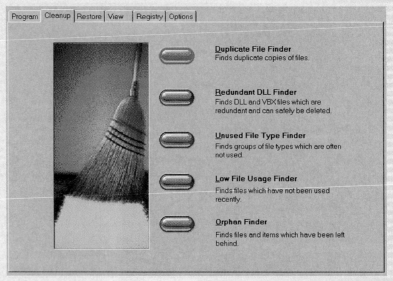

A person with a new computer, bent on adding software to it, usually does not see the software future clearly. The problem is not with software purchases, which most likely will be copied onto the hard drive. The problem, in the not-so-distant future, is going to be how to get rid of software on the hard drive.

There are a number of reasons for removing software from the hard drive, "uninstalling" it. If the software turns out to have little value, a user may simply want to clear it out. If the hard drive is getting crowded, the software could be considered expendable. In a simpler time, a user could simply delete a program file, and that would be the end of it. Software installed under Microsoft Windows, however, involves the addition of several related files and changes to others. The average person does not know how to hunt them all down in order to do a complete uninstall.

Software labeled "Designed for Windows 95 or later" must include a program that can uninstall the software completely, removing all traces from the hard drive. However, many software packages do not have that designation. An alternative is to purchase special uninstall software, priced very reasonably, that will take care of the task. You will be able to find three or four offerings, such as Clean Sweep, shown here, at your software retailer.

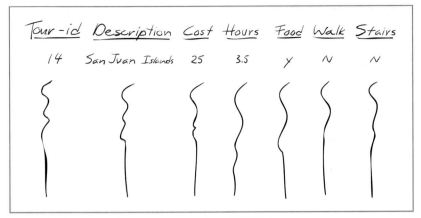

Figure 11-5 Sketch of the structure of the TOUR database.

Field Name Names of the types of data you want to use are called **field names.** Each field must have a unique name. Bess plans to use these field names for her TOUR database: Tour-ID (identifying number for the tour), Description (description of the tour), Cost (cost of the tour), Hours (number of hours the tour takes), Food (yes or no on whether food is included in the tour), Walk (yes or no regarding much walking on the tour), and Stairs (yes or no on whether there are stairs on the tour).

Field Type Although different software packages offer different field types, there are four commonly used types of fields: character fields, numeric fields, date fields, and logical fields. **Character fields** contain descriptive data, such as names, addresses, and telephone numbers. **Numeric fields** contain numbers used for calculations, such as rate of pay. When you enter a numeric field, you must specify the number of decimal places you wish to use. Bess will use two decimal places for Cost and one decimal place for Hours. **Date fields** are usually limited to eight characters, including the slashes used to separate the month, day, and year. **Logical fields** are used to keep track of true/false, yes/no conditions. For example, Bess can keep track of which tours include food by making Food a logical field; when entering data for that field, she indicates Yes or No. Note that in Microsoft Access, the software used here, this is indicated by checking (Yes) or not checking (No) a box.

Field Widths The **field width** determines the maximum number of characters or digits to be contained in the field, including decimal points.

Key Fields One or more **key fields** can be designated as a field on which an inquiry to the database can be based. A key field is sometimes called an *index field.* For example, if Bess will want to ask the database to list all tours that take less than two hours, she will declare the Hours field to be a key field.

Setting Up the File Structure

We have used Microsoft Access to demonstrate how database software can accept a database file structure (Figure 11-6). Access presents the *design view* to accept the file structure (note the words *design view* in the

Legal Databases

You have seen the formal photo-graph of the judge, the attorney, the politician—each with a solid wall of law books in the back-ground. Those books are not just decoration, however. Workers in any law office need to be able to research legal precedents and related matters.

But why not take the informa-tion in those books and just "drop it" into a computer? That is, in essence, what has been done. The books have been converted into computer-accessible data-bases, and the result is that legal research time has decreased sig-nificantly. Two common comput-erized legal research systems are LEXIS and WESTLAW, available in most law libraries and law firms.

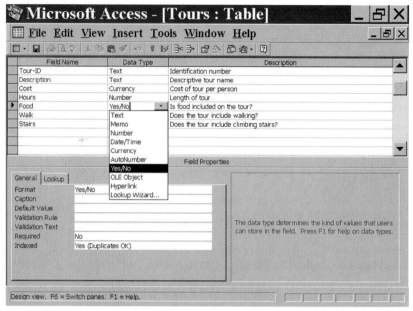

Figure 11-6 File structure. On the Microsoft Access design view, one line is entered for each field. These field entries establish the structure of the TOUR data-base. Options, as shown in the lower left, are available for each field. Note, in particu-lar, the option to have the field defined as an index (a key field). Also, a submenu is shown for the Data Type for the Food entry. Keep in mind that the structure only describes what kind of data will be entered into the database; no actual data has been entered yet.

lower left corner of Figure 11-6). Bess will type one line for each field in her database. At a glance, the line consists of the field name (Tour-ID for the first field), Data Type (Text), and an optional Description. But the procedure is slightly more complex. For each part of each line, there are options in the lower left part of the screen, with hints about how to use them to the right. For example, a text field would require a width. In par-ticular, Access lets Bess indicate that a field is designated a key field by choosing Yes for Indexed (see Figure 11-6, lower left).

Furthermore, when typing in the Date Field, an arrow in the right of the field can be clicked to provide many choices for the Date Field. In the example shown in Figure 11-6, working on the line for the field Food (as indicated by the arrow on the left), the Yes/No choice has been selected for the Data Type, indicating that Food is a logical field requir-ing Yes/No data. Bess proceeds to enter one line for each field in her database on the design view screen.

Entering the Data

When it is time to key in the records in the file, Access presents a table called *datasheet view*. The fields that Bess defined in the file structure—the design view—are presented as headings across the datasheet (Figure 11-7). Bess keys the appropriate data under each name—14 for Tour-ID, San Juan Islands for Description, and so on. The ID heading to the far left is generated automatically by Access; in fact, (AutoNumber), trun-cated in this figure, appears on the next line, now awaiting data.

After Bess has filled in all the data for the first record, the database program automatically displays another blank input line so that she can enter the data items for the fields in the second record. She will continue

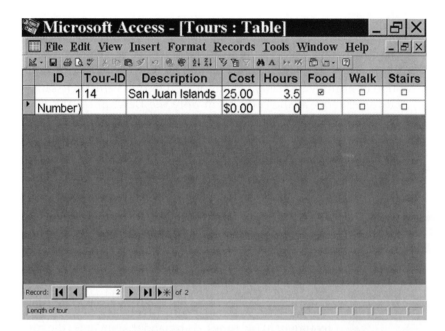

Figure 11-7 **The first record for the TOUR database.** The field names are across the top of the datasheet. The data items are keyed in under the appropriate field name. This process is repeated for each record.

Figure 11-8 **The complete set of records for the TOUR database.**

ID	Tour-ID	Description	Cost	Hours	Food	Walk	Stairs
1	14	San Juan Islands	$25.00	3.5	☑	☐	☐
3	16	Local ferry ride	$2.50	1	☐	☐	☐
4	23	Boeing plant	$0.00	2.4	☐	☑	☑
5	26	Museum tour	$15.50	0	☐	☑	☐
6	34	Cityscape bus tour	$24.00	2.5	☑	☐	☐
7	35	Chinatown at night	$30.00	3	☑	☑	☐
8	36	Name droppers tour	$25.00	3	☐	☐	☐
9	47	Northwest Trek	$12.50	4	☑	☐	☐
10	58	Mount Rainier	$22.00	5	☑	☑	☐
11	79	Seattle Locks	$0.00	2	☐	☑	☐
12	81	Underground tour	$5.50	1.5	☐	☑	☑

this pattern for each record. Eventually, she will signal the database software that she has entered all the records (Figure 11-8).

Other Options

Since this chapter is not describing a specific software package, it is not practical to demonstrate options that are available to modify the database. The following are descriptions of operations available with any database software package.

■ **List the records.** Bess could ask for a list of all existing records, either displayed on the screen or printed out on paper. If she is displaying the records on-screen, the software displays only as many records as will fit on the screen. Scrolling up or down displays additional records. If there were a large number of fields in a record, Bess could **pan**—scroll horizontally across the screen—to the left or right. Panning is a horizontal version of scrolling.

■ **List specific fields.** In addition to printing all records, Bess has the option of printing just certain fields of each record. Perhaps, to satisfy a customer request, she could print only the Description and Cost fields for each record. The software also offers the option of printing the fields in any order requested, not just the order in which they appear in the record. For example, Bess could request a list of these fields in this order: Description, Tour-ID, Walk, and Hours.

■ **Query.** Bess can make a query—ask a question—about the records in the file. She will need to use a **relational operator** when entering instructions that involve making comparisons. Table 11-1 shows the relational operators that are commonly used. These operators are particularly useful when you want to locate specific data items. Suppose, for example, that, based on a client request, Bess wants to find all the tours that cost less than $15. She could issue a query to the database software to find records that meet this requirement by using a command that includes the stipulation Cost < 15. Note that Cost is a key field. The software would respond with a list of all records that meet the requirement, in this case a local ferry ride, the Boeing plant, Northwest Trek, the Seattle Locks, and the underground tour.

Table 11-1	Relational Operators
Command	**Explanation**
<	Less than
>	Greater than
=	Equal to
<=	Less than or equal to
>=	Greater than or equal to
<>	Not equal to

■ **Add new records.** Bess can add records for new tours at any time.

■ **Modify existing records.** Bess may need to change an existing record. In the TOUR file, it would not be uncommon, for example, for the price of a tour to change.

■ **Delete records.** Sometimes a record must be removed, or deleted, from a database file. In the TOUR file, perhaps a tour no longer exists or Bess, for whatever reason, no longer wants to promote the tour. Database software provides this option.

There are many database options beyond the basic features this chapter has discussed. Those options are beyond the scope of this book, but you may have an opportunity in the future to learn all the bells and whistles of a database management package.

CHAPTER REVIEW

Summary and Key Terms

- A **database** is an organized collection of related data. A **database management system (DBMS)** is software that creates, manages, protects, and provides access to a database.
- Advantages of databases are **reduced redundancy, integrated data,** and **integrity.**
- A database can store data relationships so that files can be integrated. The way the database organizes data depends on the type, or **model,** of database. There are three main database models—hierarchical, network, and relational.
- A **relational database** organizes data in a table format consisting of related rows and columns. Each location in the table contains a single piece of data, known as a **data item.** Each column of the table represents a **field,** which consists of data items. The full set of data in any given row is called a **record.** Related records make up a **file.** In a relational database a file is also called a **relation.**
- Computer activities are considered **transparent** if a user is unaware of them as they are taking place.
- The power of databases is in the connection: A relational system can relate data in one file to data in another file, allowing a user to tie together data from several files.
- There are two steps to creating a database file: (1) designing the **file structure** and (2) entering the data.
- When a file structure is defined, many database programs require the user to identify the **field types, field names,** and **field widths.** There are four commonly used types of fields: **character fields, numeric fields, date fields,** and **logical fields.** The field width determines the maximum number of letters, digits, or symbols to be contained in the field. One or more **key fields** can be designated as a field on which a query to the database can be based.
- Once a file structure is defined, it is presented to the user as an input form so that data for each record may be entered.
- At times you may have to **pan**—scroll horizontally across the screen—to view all the fields in a database record.
- A **relational operator** is needed when making comparisons or when entering instructions.

Quick Poll

Compare your answers to those of your colleagues or classmates.

1. Regarding database management software:
   - ❏ a. It seems much less practical than word processing.
   - ❏ b. I expect to use databases in business no matter what I do.
   - ❏ c. It is just a matter of time until we are all accessing massive databases routinely.
2. Regarding databases about people:
   - ❏ a. Extensive people databases are a valuable tool for marketers and for societal reasons such as finding everyone from missing persons to deadbeats.
   - ❏ b. There needs to be a balance between the needs of marketers and privacy rights, perhaps with government monitoring.
   - ❏ c. People databases are a menace. I am extremely careful about giving out personal data, especially my Social Security number.

3. Regarding personal use of database management software:
   - ❑ a. It is mostly a tool for businesses with lots of data to manage and access. I don't see any practical application on a personal basis.
   - ❑ b. I have a vague notion of parts of my life I might want to manage using database software—perhaps hobby collections or information related to a volunteer activity.
   - ❑ c. I want to use database software myself both to manage my own activities and to become as knowledgeable as possible about what I perceive as the main software for future business use.

Discussion Questions

1. Consider these workers as possible users of a database: a crime lab technician handling evidence, a tulip bulb grower who produces 47 varieties for more than 200 customers, a runners club that tracks meets and member data. What data might they want to look up? What data would they need to store? What fields might be key fields?

2. An environmental organization concerned about preserving undeveloped land keeps a database of its donors with these fields: last name, first name, street address, city, state, zip code, phone number, amount of last donation, date of last donation, amount of highest donation, date of highest donation, amount of average donation, code for special interests (M for mountains, R for rivers, and so forth). The organization regularly sends out form letters soliciting donations. The form letters are keyed to a particular donor population, for example, those who have not sent a donation in six months or those who might want to give to a special shorebirds preserve. Among the fields listed, which might be key fields?

3. For the data mentioned in question 2, list some relational operators and appropriate fields that might be used for making a query to the database. Examples: Use the "equal to" operator to find donors in a certain zip code: ZIP = 22314; use "greater than" to find donors whose average donation is over $100: AVGDON > 100.

Student Study Guide

True/False

T   F   1. A logical operator, such as =, <, or >, is needed when making database comparisons.

T   F   2. There are two commonly used types of fields: character and index.

T   F   3. In a database, only one field can be designated as the key field.

T   F   4. A database is a collection of data prepared for a particular user in separate files.

T   F   5. Panning means to move across the screen to view all fields in a database.

T   F   6. Two key benefits of database processing are shared data and segregated files.

T   F   7. One disadvantage of databases is that they can be used by only a single user.

T   F   8. The two steps to creating a file are designing its structure and entering the data.

T   F   9. The power of a relational database is related to connections among files.

T   F   10. Database records may be entered and modified but not deleted.

T   F   11. The database model most commonly used on personal computers is the hierarchical model.

T   F   12. A record is made up of fields.

T   F   13. An advantage of databases is that redundancy is reduced.

T   F   14. A database is an organized collection of related data.

T   F   15. Computer activities are considered transparent if a user is unaware of them when they are taking place.

T   F   16. A user may request to print only certain fields of a database.

T   F   17. A DBMS is software.

T   F   18. Field widths may vary for character fields but are always the same for numeric fields.

T   F   19. Users can use a database successfully only if they understand the underlying technology.

T   F   20. A database is an unorganized collection of related data.

T   F   21. In a relational database a file is also called a relation.

T   F   22. When planning the file structure of a database, a user types in the data that will be used in the database.

T   F   23. In a database, field names must be unique.

T   F   24. The three main database models are hierarchical, network, and relational.

T   F   25. The data item in a field is the same for each row of a relation.

T   F   26. A user enters data in a database one column at a time.

T   F   27. Dates, including month and year, are usually stored in logical fields.

T   F   28. The fields in a particular database record contain unrelated data.

T   F   29. A relational database organizes data in a table of rows and columns.

T   F   30. There is exactly one file per database.

Fill-In

1. The abbreviation for a database management system is _____

2. Advantages of databases: _____

3. A designated field on which a query to a database can be based: _____

4. Symbols such as =, >, and < are called

   _____

5. As related to databases, network, hierarchical, and relational are each a type of _____

6. In a relational database another name for a file is

   _____

7. To move sideways across the screen:

   _____

8. The four most common field types:

   a. _____

   b. _____

   c. _____

   d. _____

9. When planning a database, the first step is to determine the rows and columns that together form the

   _____

10. The database model usually used on personal computers: _____

11. Each location in a relational database table contains: _____

12. Computer activities of which users are unaware are said to be _____

13. Each field is represented in a relational table by a

    _____

14. Each record of data in a relational table is represented by a _____

15. The kind of field that would hold only Yes or No:

    _____

Answers

True/False

1. F	6. F	11. F	16. T	21. T	26. F
2. F	7. F	12. T	17. T	22. F	27. F
3. F	8. T	13. T	18. F	23. T	28. F
4. F	9. T	14. T	19. F	24. T	29. T
5. T	10. F	15. T	20. F	25. F	30. F

Fill-In

1. DBMS
2. reduced redundancy, integrated data, integrity
3. key field
4. relational operators
5. model
6. relation
7. pan
8. a. character, b. numeric, c. date, d. logical
9. file structure
10. relational
11. data item
12. transparent
13. column
14. row
15. logical

PLANET INTERNET

ENTREPRENEURS

Starting your own business on the Internet is a game anyone can play. And we do mean anyone, from those involved in agriculture to real estate to finance. Even the smallest entrepreneur can get in on the act. Individuals can gain access to people and markets—including global markets— not readily affordable or even available elsewhere. For a minimum investment, far less than that needed for a physical store or office, you can have a server link and a smashing home page that exactly expresses the nature of your business. You can even alter the page as your business grows and changes.

Not a level playing field. The statements just made are true, if a bit rosy in color. Even though "anyone can play," the Internet is not a level playing field. Firms with multimillion-dollar marketing budgets and customer bases in the hundreds of thousands are more likely to be able to draw large numbers of people to their web sites than the most creative garage-based entrepreneur. Does this mean that the little guys do not have a chance? They have a chance, but not a level playing field.

Content. Nothing guarantees success, defined as making a profit from your Internet business. It can be done, and most certainly *is being done*, but business on the Internet is not a panacea. Just as in a regular store, the key success factor for any commercial web site is repeat business. How do you keep customers coming back? The answer is content. The site must offer something—preferably several somethings—to keep interest up. What will it be? News about the product, scores, contests, searches, and much more. Observe the variety of content as you examine business sites. The site cannot be static. If it is exactly the same as on a previous visit, most users will not bother returning.

Be unique. One recommendation for success is to have a specialty, something not offered elsewhere. Twins Jason and Matthew Olim, jazz fans who had trouble finding a good selection of recordings in their local stores, decided to set up a web site that they called CDnow, offering every jazz album made in the United States and thousands of imports. The beauty of the scheme was that there was no initial outlay for a store or even for inventory. A shopper places an order with CDnow, which in turn contacts distributors. The disk is usually delivered within 24 hours. CDnow eventually added other kinds of music and also movies. Another successful specialty site is Hot Hot Hot, whose logo is shown here, offering an enormous variety of hot sauces from around the world. Note that in each of these two examples, the site not only offers something unique but also appeals to an audience that will be repeat customers.

Community. A key to the success of a commercial site is a sense of community. An outstanding

example of this is the Amazon Books site, whose logo is shown here. Amazon features notes from authors about their own books and lets any customer write a review about a book. Customers perusing book offerings can just click an icon to read the reviews for a certain book. People who love books return again and again to this site. Customers who agree to register by filling out an on-screen form are eligible for book prizes. The prizes are attractive, and the registration data—name, e-mail address, and possibly book interests—provides Amazon with future marketing information.

More success stories. The name is inspired by Shakespeare's *As You Like It*: "I met a fool i' the forest, a motley fool." Despite their trademark jester costumes, no one would take brothers David and Tom Gardner, shown here, for fools. The Motley Fool is the name of their online forum, which lets investors ask questions and share knowledge. Hundreds of thousands of visitors, frustrated by lack of investing knowledge from traditional sources, visit the site each month.

Golf Web began cleverly by concentrating on content, such as descriptions of courses, tournament calendars, instruction, the latest golf news, and photos of golf professionals in action. Only when an audience was well established did Golf Web add products.

Real World Interface offers mobile robots, such as the all-terrain outdoor robot shown here.

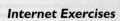

An interesting side note is that the owner, Grinnell More, decided to spark interest with a name-the-robot contest, offering prizes to robotics researchers who submitted their names and e-mail addresses. He got more than he bargained for. People who use search engines to find contests discovered this one and bombarded the site with many thousands of entries.

Waiting for success. One reason that some businesses are successful on the Internet is simply the passage of time. Several small businesses have been on the Web for a few years. Although they may have lost money initially, they have had time to tinker with their formulas, creating new business models and web pages that work for them.

Internet Exercises

1. **Structured exercise.** Begin with the AWL URL, http://hepg.awl.com/capron/planet/. Look up two or three of the entrepreneurial sites mentioned here. Assuming that you had some interest in the topic, do they provide content that might keep you coming back?
2. **Freeform exercise.** Assume that you want to start your own business, using the Internet as your forum. Using a search engine, choose words related to that business to find sites that you can use as a source of information and inspiration.

Software

Tools

Roberta Matnick and Sean O'Connor met as freshmen at Ohio State University in an introductory business class. They became fast friends when they discovered that they were both majoring in accounting. The next semester they signed up for an introductory computer course to get a good foundation in computer technology and, in particular, to become proficient in the use of spreadsheets.

After studying what programmers do, however, Roberta recalled her rusty BASIC programming from high school and decided to take a closer look. She signed up for a learn-at-your-own-pace lab course in BASIC programming. From there she gravitated to the computer science department, where she studied more languages and took a variety of theoretical courses. Roberta eventually decided on a computer science major but minored in accounting. Sean was not as taken with computers, particularly with the details of programming, and he remained an accounting major. After graduation, each found a job in his or her own field.

Their paths crossed again by chance seven years later when they began attending an evening M.B.A. program at a private university. Both accounting skills and computer skills were needed for various projects in the program. Roberta and Sean were able to help each other out, each contributing specific expertise. In particular, Sean came to appreciate the care and precision needed to write a computer program.

Programming and Languages

Telling the Computer What to Do

Doomsday: January 1, 2000

Tick, tick, tick. Some computer professionals are predicting a doomsday scenario when the clock passes midnight and we plunge into a new century—the year 2000. The problem is the date, specifically the year, which has been recorded in millions of computer files in a two-digit format: MM/DD/YY. The year 1990 was recorded as 90, 1995 as 95, and so forth. The year 2000 would be recorded as 00.

This seeming bit of trivia will cause serious problems after the year 2000 in such time-related computer program activities as determining age and computing interest. Suppose, for example, that your birth year is 1978. In 1999 the computer can subtract 78 from 99 to reveal your age correctly as 21. In the year 2000, however, a similar subtraction, 78 from 00, would present your age as –78.

Various solutions have been proposed but the most common one is to go into existing programs and change any date-sensitive code. As straightforward as this sounds, experts estimate the programming to adjust all systems for the year 2000 at approximately $50 *billion*.

Why Programming?

You may already have used software, perhaps for word processing or spreadsheets, to solve problems. Perhaps now you are curious to learn how programmers develop software. As noted earlier, a **program** is a set of step-by-step instructions that directs the computer to do the tasks you want it to do and produce the results you want. A set of rules that provides a way of telling a computer what operations to perform is called a **programming language**. There is not, however, just one programming language; there are many.

In this chapter you will learn about controlling a computer through the process of programming. An important point before proceeding: You will not be a programmer when you finish reading this chapter or even when you finish reading the final chapter. Programming proficiency takes practice and training beyond the scope of this book. However, you will become acquainted with how programmers develop solutions to a variety of problems.

What Programmers Do

In general, the programmer's job is to convert problem solutions into instructions for the computer. That is, the programmer prepares the instructions of a computer program and runs those instructions on the computer, tests the program to see if it is working properly, and makes corrections to the program. The programmer also writes a report on the program. These activities are all done for the purpose of helping a user fill a need, such as paying employees, billing customers, or admitting students to college.

The programming activities just described could be done, perhaps, as solo activities, but a programmer typically interacts with a variety of people. For example, if a program is part of a system of several programs, the programmer coordinates with other programmers to make sure that the programs fit together well. If you were a programmer, you might also have coordination meetings with users, managers, and systems analysts, as well as with peers who evaluate your work—just as you evaluate theirs.

The Programming Process

Developing a program involves steps similar to any problem-solving task. There are five main ingredients in the programming process: (1) defining the problem, (2) planning the solution, (3) coding the program, (4) testing the program, and (5) documenting the program.

Let us discuss each of these in turn.

1. Defining the Problem

Suppose that, as a programmer, you are contacted because your services are needed. You meet with users from the client organization to analyze the problem, or you meet with a systems analyst who outlines the project. Specifically, the task of defining the problem consists of identifying what it is you know (input—the data given) and what it is you want to

Getting Practical

SO YOU WANT TO BE A PROGRAMMER

There is a shortage of qualified personnel in the computer field, but, paradoxically, there are many people at the front end trying to get entry-level programming jobs. Before you join their ranks, consider the advantages of the computer field and what it takes to succeed in it.

The joys of the field. Although many people make career changes into the computer field, few choose to leave it. In fact, surveys of computer professionals, especially programmers, consistently report a high level of job satisfaction. There are several reasons for this contentment. One is the challenge; most jobs in the computer industry are not routine. Another is security, since established computer professionals can usually find work. And that work pays well—you should certainly be comfortable and, if you should happen to be part of an organization that offers stock options to all employees, possibly very comfortable. The computer industry has historically been a rewarding place for women and minorities. And finally, the industry holds endless fascination, since it is always changing.

What it takes. Although some people buy a book and teach themselves a programming language, this is unlikely to lead to a

job. You need some credentials, most often a two- or four-year degree in computer information systems or computer science (note that this degree will require math and science courses). The requirements and salaries vary by the organization and the region, so we will not dwell on these here. Beyond that, the person most likely to land a job and move up the career ladder is one with excellent communication skills, both oral and written. These are also the qualities that can be observed by potential employers in an interview. Promotions are sometimes tied to advanced degrees (an M.B.A. or an M.S. in computer science).

Open doors. The overall outlook for the computer field is promising. The Bureau of Labor Statistics projects, through the 1990s, a 72 percent increase in the number of programmers and a 69 percent increase in the number of systems analysts. Further, these two professions are predicted to be the number two and number three high-growth jobs into the next century. (In case you are curious, the number one high-growth job area is predicted to be the paralegal profession.) The reasons for the continued job increase in the computer field are more computers, more applications of computers, and more computer users.

Traditionally, career progression in the computer field was a path from programmer to systems analyst to project manager. This is still a popular direction, but it is complicated by the large number of options open to computer professionals. Computer professionals sometimes specialize in some aspect of the industry, such as communications, database management, personal computers, graphics, and, most especially, the Internet. Others may specialize in the computer-related aspects of a particular industry, such as banking or insurance. Still others strike out on their own, becoming consultants or entrepreneurs.

obtain (output—the result). Eventually, you produce a written agreement that, among other things, specifies the kind of input, processing, and output required. This is not a simple process. It is closely related to the process of systems analysis, which will be discussed in Chapter 14.

2. Planning the Solution

Two common ways of planning the solution to a problem are to draw a flowchart and to write pseudocode, or possibly both. Essentially, a **flowchart** is a pictorial representation of a step-by-step solution to a prob-

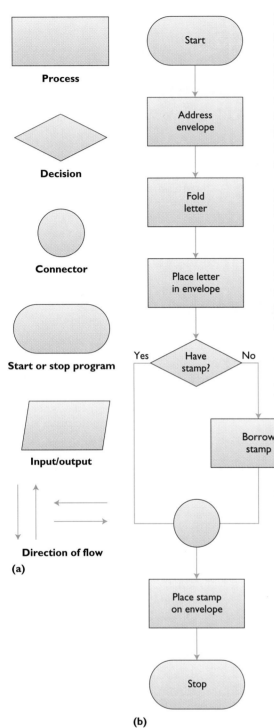

Figure 12-1 Flowchart symbols and a simple flowchart. (a) The ANSI standard flowchart symbols. (b) A flowchart shows how the standard symbols might be used to prepare a letter for mailing. There can be as many flowcharts to represent the task as there are ways of mailing a letter.

lem. It consists of arrows representing the direction the program takes and boxes and other symbols representing actions. It is a map of what your program is going to do and how it is going to do it. The American National Standards Institute (ANSI) has developed a standard set of flowchart symbols. Figure 12-1 shows the symbols and how they might be used in a simple flowchart of a common everyday act—like preparing a letter for mailing. As a practical matter, few programmers use flowcharting in their work, but flowcharting retains its value as a visual representation of the problem-solving process.

Pseudocode is an English-like nonstandard language that lets you state your solution with more precision than you can in plain English but with less precision than is required when using a formal programming language. Pseudocode permits you to focus on the program logic without having to be concerned just yet about the precise rules of a particular programming language. However, pseudocode is not executable on the computer. These two approaches, flowcharting and pseudocode, will be illustrated later in this chapter, when focusing on language examples.

3. Coding the Program

As the programmer, your next step is to code the program—that is, to express your solution in a programming language. You will translate the logic from the flowchart or pseudocode or some other tool to a programming language. There are many programming languages: BASIC, COBOL, Pascal, FORTRAN, and C are some examples. The different types of languages will be discussed in detail later in this chapter.

Although programming languages operate grammatically, somewhat like the English language, they are much more precise. To get your program to work, you have to follow exactly the rules—the **syntax**—of the language you are using. Of course, using the language correctly is no guarantee that your program will work, any more than speaking grammatically correct English means you know what you are talking about. The point is that correct use of the language is the required first step. You will key your program as you compose it, using a terminal or personal computer.

One more note here: Programmers usually use a **text editor**, which is somewhat like a word processing program, to create a file that contains the program. However, as a beginner, you will probably want to write your program code on paper first.

4. Testing the Program

In theory, a well-designed program can be written correctly the first time. However, the imperfections of the world are still with us, so most programmers get used to the idea that their newly written programs probably have a few errors. Therefore, after coding the program, you must prepare to test it on the computer. This step involves these phases:

- **Desk-checking.** In desk-checking you simply sit down and mentally trace, or check, the logic of the program to attempt to ensure that it is error-free and workable. Many organizations take this phase a step further with a **walkthrough**, a process in which a group of programmers—your peers—review your program and offer suggestions in a collegial way.

- **Translating.** A **translator** is a program that (1) checks the syntax of your program to make sure the programming language was used correctly, giving you all the syntax-error messages, called **diagnostics**, and then (2) translates your program into a form the computer can understand. The mistakes are called **syntax errors.** The translator produces descriptive error messages. For instance, if in FORTRAN you mistakenly write N = 2*(I + J))—with two closing parentheses instead of one—you will get an error message that might say, "UNMATCHED PARENTHESES." Programs are most commonly translated by a **compiler**, which translates your entire program at one time. As shown in Figure 12-2, the translation involves your original program, called a **source module**, which is transformed by a compiler into an **object module.** Prewritten programs from a system library may be added during the **link/load phase**, resulting in a **load module**, which can be executed by the computer.

- **Debugging.** A term used extensively in programming, debugging means detecting, locating, and correcting bugs (mistakes), usually by running the program. These bugs are **logic errors**, such as telling a computer to repeat an operation but not telling it how to stop repeating. In the debugging phase you run the program using test data that you devise. You must plan the test data carefully to make sure you test every part of the program.

5. Documenting the Program

An ongoing process, **documentation** is a detailed written description of the programming cycle and specific facts about the program. Typical program documentation materials include the origin and nature of the problem, a brief narrative description of the program, logic tools such as flowcharts and pseudocode, data-record descriptions, program listings, and testing results. Comments in the program itself are also considered an essential part of documentation. Many programmers document as they code. In a broader sense, program documentation can be part of the documentation for an

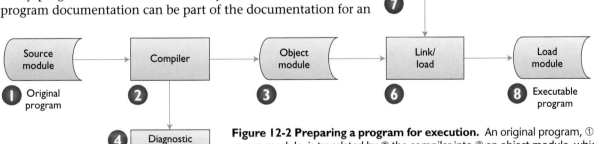

Figure 12-2 Preparing a program for execution. An original program, ① the source module, is translated by ② the compiler into ③ an object module, which represents the program in a form the machine can understand. The compiler may produce ④ diagnostic messages, indicating syntax errors. ⑤ A listing of the source program may also be output from the compiler. After the program successfully compiles, the object module is linked in the ⑥ link/load phase with ⑦ system library programs as needed, and the result is ⑧ a load module, or executable program.

entire system, as you will learn in Chapter 14, which discusses systems analysis and design.

Levels of Language

There are several programming languages in common use today. Before turning to specific languages, however, we need to discuss levels of language. Programming languages are said to be "lower" or "higher," depending on how close they are to the language the computer itself uses (0s and 1s—low) or to the language people use (more English-like—high). There are five levels of language, numbered 1 through 5 to correspond to levels, or generations. In terms of ease of use and capabilities, each generation is an improvement over its predecessors. The five generations of languages are (1) machine language, (2) assembly languages, (3) high-level languages, (4) very high-level languages, and (5) natural languages.

Machine Language

Humans do not like to deal in numbers alone; they prefer letters and words. But, strictly speaking, numbers are what machine language is. This lowest level of programming language, **machine language**, represents data and program instructions as 0s and 1s, binary digits corresponding to the on and off electrical states in the computer. This is really the only language the computer truly understands; all other languages must be translated to the machine language before execution (Figure 12-3). Each type of computer has its own machine language. Primitive by today's standards, machine language programs are not convenient for people to read and use. The computer industry quickly moved to develop assembly languages.

Assembly Languages

Today, **assembly languages** are considered very low level—that is, they are not as convenient for people to use as more recent languages. At the time they were developed, however, they were considered a great leap forward. To replace the 0s and 1s used in machine language, assembly languages use mnemonic codes, abbreviations that are easy to remember: A for add, C for compare, MP for multiply, STO for storing information in memory, and so on. Furthermore, assembly languages permit the use of names—perhaps RATE or TOTAL—for memory locations instead of actual address numbers. As with machine language, each type of computer has its own assembly language.

Since machine language is the only language the computer can actually execute, a translator, called an **assembly program**, is required to convert the assembly language program into machine language. Assembly language may be easier to read than machine language, but it is still tedious (Figure 12-4).

High-Level Languages

The first widespread use of **high-level languages** in the early 1960s transformed programming into something quite different from what it had been. Programs were written in an English-like manner, thus making them more convenient to use. As a result, a programmer could

```
FD    71    431F    4153
F3    63    4267    4321
96    F0    426D
F9    10    41F3    438A
47    40    40DA
47    F0    4050
```

Figure 12-3 Machine language. True machine language is all binary—only 0s and 1s—but since an example would take too much space here, we are showing an example of machine language in the hexadecimal (base 16) numbering system. (The letters A through F in hexadecimal represent the numbers 10 through 15 in the decimal system.) The computer commands shown, taken from machine language for an IBM mainframe computer, are operation codes instructing the computer to divide two numbers, compare the quotient, move the result into the output area of the system, and set up the result so it can be printed.

```
                PRINT   NOGEN
PROG8           START   0
CARDFIL         DTFCD   DEVADDR=SYSRDR,RECFORM=FIXUNB,IOAREA1=CARDREC,C
                        TYPEFLE=INPUT,BLKSIZE=80,EOFADDR=FINISH
REPTFIL         DTFPR   DEVADDR=SYSLST,IOAREA1=PRNTREC,BLKSIZE=132
BEGIN           BALR    3,0                     REGISTER 3 IS BASE REGISTER
                USING   *,3
                OPEN    CARDFIL,REPTFIL    OPEN FILES
                MVC     PRNTREC,SPACES     MOVE SPACES TO OUTPUT RECORD
READLOOP        GET     CARDFIL            READ A RECORD
                MVC     OFIRST,IFIRST      MOVE ALL INPUT FIELDS
                MVC     OLAST,ILAST        TO OUTPUT RECORD FIELDS
                MVC     OADDR,IADDR
                MVC     OCITY,ICITY
                MVC     OSTATE,ISTATE
                MVC     OZIP,IZIP
                PUT     REPTFIL            WRITE THE RECORD
                B       READLOOP           BRANCH TO READ AGAIN
FINISH          CLOSE   CARDFIL,REPTFIL    CLOSE FILES
                EOJ                        END OF JOB
CARDREC         DS      0CL80              DESCRIPTION OF INPUT RECORD
IFIRST          DS      CL10
ILAST           DS      CL10
IADDR           DS      CL30
ICITY           DS      CL20
ISTATE          DS      CL2
IZIP            DS      CL5
                DS      CL3
PRNTREC         DS      0CL132             DESCRIPTION OF OUTPUT RECORD
                DS      CL10
OLAST           DS      CL10
                DS      CL5
OFIRST          DS      CL10
                DS      CL15
OADDR           DS      CL30
                DS      CL15
OCITY           DS      CL20
                DS      CL5
OSTATE          DS      CL2
                DS      CL5
OZIP            DS      CL5
SPACES          DC      CL132' '
                END     BEGIN
```

accomplish more with less effort, and programs could now direct much more complex tasks.

Of course, a translator is needed to translate the symbolic statements of a high-level language into computer-executable machine language; this translator is usually a compiler. There are many compilers for each language and at least one for each type of computer.

Very High-Level Languages

Languages called **very high-level languages** are often known by their generation number; that is, they are called **fourth-generation languages** or, more simply, **4GLs.** The 4GLs are essentially shorthand programming languages. An operation that requires hundreds of lines in a third-generation language typically requires only five to ten lines in a 4GL. However, beyond the basic criterion of conciseness, 4GLs are difficult to describe because there are so many different types.

Figure 12-4 Assembly language. This example shows the IBM assembly language BAL used in a program for reading a record and writing it out again. The left column contains symbolic addresses of various instructions or data. The second column contains the actual operation codes to describe the kind of activity needed; for instance, MVC stands for move characters. The third column describes the data on which the instructions are to act. The far right column contains English-like comments related to the line or lines opposite. This entire page of instructions could be compressed to a few lines in a high-level language.

Most experts say the average productivity improvement factor is about 10; that is, you can be ten times more productive in a fourth-generation language than in a third-generation language. Consider this request: Produce a report showing the total units sold for each product, by customer, in each month and year, and with a subtotal for each customer. In addition, each new customer must start on a new page. A 4GL request looks something like this:

```
TABLE FILE SALES
SUM UNITS BY MONTH BY CUSTOMER BY PRODUCT
ON CUSTOMER SUBTOTAL PAGE BREAK
END
```

Even though some training is required to do even this much, you can see that it is pretty simple. The third-generation language COBOL, however, typically requires more than 500 statements to fulfill the same request. It would be naïve, however, to assume that all programs should be written using 4GLs; a third-generation language makes more sense for commercial applications that require a high degree of precision.

A variation on fourth-generation languages is **query languages**, which can be used to retrieve information from databases. Data is usually added to databases according to a plan, and planned reports may also be produced. But what about a user who needs an unscheduled report or a report that differs somehow from the standard reports? A user can learn a query language fairly easily and then request and receive the resulting report on his or her own terminal or personal computer.

Natural Languages

The word *natural* has become almost as popular in computing circles as it has in the supermarket. The newest level of language, called fifth-generation languages is even more ill-defined than fourth-generation languages. They are most often called **natural languages** because of their resemblance to the "natural" spoken English language; that is, they resemble the way that you speak. A user of one of these languages can say the same thing in any number of ways. For example, "Get me tennis racket sales for January" works just as well as "I want January tennis

Figure 12-5 A natural language. This package, called Cash Management System, uses a language that is so "natural" that some might think it a little too cute, as in "Just a sec." You can follow the dialogue more easily by noting that, in this demonstration, the command from the user is in reverse video and the response from the computer is not.

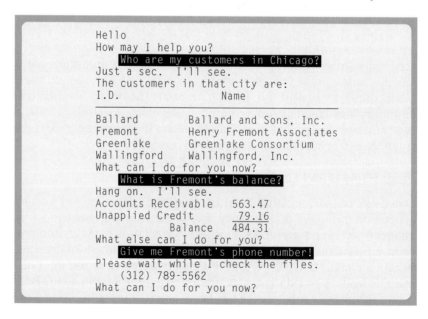

```
Hello
How may I help you?
Who are my customers in Chicago?
Just a sec.  I'll see.
The customers in that city are:
I.D.                Name

Ballard           Ballard and Sons, Inc.
Fremont           Henry Fremont Associates
Greenlake         Greenlake Consortium
Wallingford       Wallingford, Inc.
What can I do for you now?
What is Fremont's balance?
Hang on.  I'll see.
Accounts Receivable    563.47
Unapplied Credit        79.16
          Balance      484.31
What else can I do for you?
Give me Fremont's phone number!
Please wait while I check the files.
   (312) 789-5562
What can I do for you now?
```

racket revenues." The natural language translates human instructions—bad grammar, slang, and all—into code the computer understands. If it is not sure what the user has in mind, it politely asks for further explanation. An example of a natural language is shown in Figure 12-5.

Choosing a Language

How do you choose the language with which to write your program? There are several possibilities. In a work environment, your company may decree that everyone on your project will use a certain language, possibly because there is a need to interface with other programs written in that language. If a program is to be run on different computers, it must be written in a language that is portable—suitable on each type of computer—so that the program need be written only once but will run on all of the various computers.

Perhaps the simplest reason for choosing a language, one that applies to many amateur programmers, is that they know the language called BASIC because it came with, or was inexpensively purchased with, their personal computers.

Major Programming Languages

The following sections on individual languages will give you an overview of some third-generation languages in use today: FORTRAN, COBOL, BASIC, Pascal, and C. You will see a program written in each of these languages, as well as the output produced by each program. Each program is designed to find the average of three numbers; the resulting average is shown in the sample output matching each program. Since all of the programs perform the same task, you will see some of the differences and similarities among the languages. You are not expected to understand these programs; they are here merely to let you glimpse each language. Figure 12-6 presents the flowchart and pseudocode for the task of averaging numbers. This logic will be used for each of the programs.

FORTRAN: The First High-Level Language

Developed by IBM and introduced in 1954, **FORTRAN**—for FORmula TRANslator—was the first high-level language. FORTRAN is a scientifically oriented language; in the early days use of the computer was primarily associated with engineering, mathematical, and scientific research tasks.

FORTRAN is noted for its brevity, and this characteristic is part of the reason it remains popular. This language is very good at serving its primary purpose, which is the execution of complex formulas such as those used in economic analysis and engineering. Figure 12-7 shows a FORTRAN program and sample output from the program.

COBOL: The Language of Business

In the 1950s FORTRAN had been developed, but there was still no accepted high-level programming language appropriate for business. The U.S. Department of Defense in particular was interested in creating such a standardized language and called together a committee that, in 1959, introduced **COBOL**, for COmmon Business-Oriented Language.

The First Bug Was Real

Computer literacy books are bursting with bits and bytes and disks and chips and lessons on writing programs in BASIC. All this is to provide quick enlightenment for the computer illiterate. But the average newly computer-literate person has not been told about the bugs.

It is a bit of a surprise, then, to find that the software you are using does not always work quite right. Or perhaps the programmer who is doing some work for you cannot seem to get the program to work correctly. Both problems are "bugs," errors that were introduced unintentionally into a program when it was written.

The term *bug* comes from an experience in the early days of computing. One summer day in 1945, according to computer pioneer Grace M. Hopper, the Mark I computer came to a halt. Working to find the problem, computer personnel actually found a moth inside the machine (see photo above). They removed the offending bug, and the computer was fine. From that day forward, any mysterious problem or glitch was said to be a bug.

Figure 12-6 Flowchart and pseudocode for averaging numbers. (a) This flowchart, along with (b) matching pseudocode, shows the logic for a program to let a user enter numbers through the keyboard; the program then averages the numbers. The user can make any number of entries, one at a time. To show when he or she is finished making entries, the user enters 999. The logic to enter the numbers forms a loop: entering the number, adding it to the sum, and adding 1 to the counter. When 999 is keyed, the loop is exited. Then the machine computes the average and displays it on the screen. This logic is used for the programs, in various languages, shown in Figures 12-7 through 12-11.

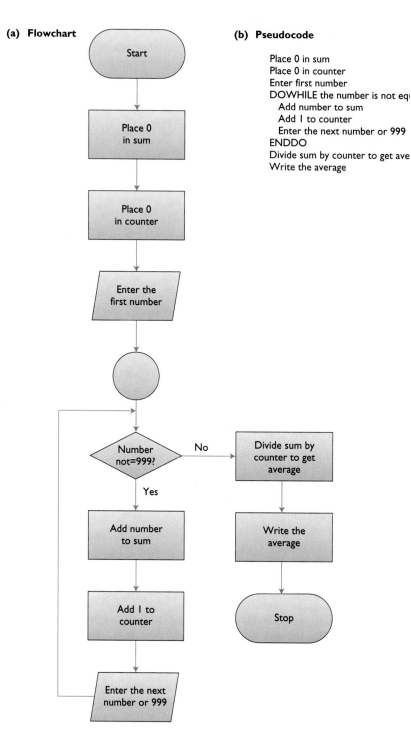

(a) Flowchart

(b) Pseudocode

Place 0 in sum
Place 0 in counter
Enter first number
DOWHILE the number is not equ
    Add number to sum
    Add 1 to counter
    Enter the next number or 999
ENDDO
Divide sum by counter to get ave
Write the average

COBOL is very good for processing large files and performing relatively simple business calculations, such as payroll or interest. COBOL is English-like; even if you know nothing about programming, you may still understand what the program does. However, the feature that makes COBOL so useful—its English-like appearance and easy readability—is also a weakness, because a COBOL program can be incredibly verbose (Figure 12-8).

```
C       FORTRAN PROGRAM
C       AVERAGING INTEGERS ENTERED THROUGH THE KEYBOARD
        WRITE (6,10)
        SUM = 0
        COUNTER = 0
        WRITE (6,60)
        READ (5,40) NUMBER
   1    IF (NUMBER .EQ. 999) GOTO 2
        SUM = SUM + NUMBER
        COUNTER = COUNTER + 1
        WRITE (6,70)
        READ (5,40) NUMBER
        GO TO 1
   2    AVERAGE = SUM / COUNTER
        WRITE (6,80) AVERAGE
  10    FORMAT (1X, 'THIS PROGRAM WILL FIND THE AVERAGE OF',
      * 'INTEGERS YOU ENTER ',/1X, 'THROUGH THE ',
      * 'KEYBOARD. TYPE 999 TO INDICATE END OF DATA.',/)
  40    FORMAT (13)
  60    FORMAT (1X, 'PLEASE ENTER A NUMBER ')
  70    FORMAT (1X, 'PLEASE ENTER THE NEXT NUMBER ')
  80    FORMAT (1X, 'THE AVERAGE OF THE NUMBERS IS ',F6.2)
        STOP
        END
```

(a)

```
THIS PROGRAM WILL FIND THE AVERAGE OF INTEGERS YOU ENTER
THROUGH THE KEYBOARD.  TYPE 999 TO INDICATE END OF DATA.
PLEASE ENTER A NUMBER     6
PLEASE ENTER THE NEXT NUMBER     4
PLEASE ENTER THE NEXT NUMBER     11
PLEASE ENTER THE NEXT NUMBER     999
THE AVERAGE OF THE NUMBERS IS     7.00
```

(b)

Figure 12-7 FORTRAN program and sample output. This program is interactive, prompting the user to supply data. (a) The first two lines are comments, as they are in the rest of the programs in this chapter. The WRITE statements send output to the screen in the format called for by the second numeral in the parentheses, which represents the line number containing the format. The READ statements accept data from the user and place it in location NUMBER, where it can be added to the accumulated total, SUM. The IF statement checks for 999 and, when 999 is received, diverts the program logic to statement 2, where the average is computed. The average is then displayed. (b) This screen display shows the interaction between program and user.

A Programming Pioneer: Grace Hopper

When Grace M. Hopper died in 1992 at the age of 85, she left behind the legacy of a true programming pioneer—involvement with the first computers and the first business programming language.

As a Phi Beta Kappa graduate of Vassar College with an M.A. and Ph.D. from Yale University, Hopper joined the U.S. Naval Reserve in 1943. She was assigned to the Bureau of Ordnance Computation Project at Harvard, where she learned to program the first large-scale digital computer, the Mark I.

In 1948 Hopper became senior mathematician at the Eckert-Mauchly Computer Corporation. Later she became senior programmer on the team that created the first commercial large-scale electronic computer, UNIVAC I. In the 1950s she coauthored the COBOL compiler and programming language.

Among all her achievements, the one she liked best was her promotion to the rank of Rear Admiral in the U.S. Naval Reserve.

Figure 12-8 COBOL program and sample output. The purpose of the program and its results are the same as those of the FORTRAN program, but (a) the look of the COBOL program is very different. Note the four divisions: identification, environment, data, and procedure. In particular, note that the logic in the procedure division uses a series of PERFORM statements, which divert action to other places in the program. After a prescribed action has been performed, the computer returns to the procedure division, to the statement after the one that was just completed. DISPLAY writes to the screen, and ACCEPT takes user input. (b) This screen display shows the interaction between program and user.

```
****************************************************************
IDENTIFICATION DIVISION.
****************************************************************
PROGRAM-ID.  AVERAGE.
* COBOL PROGRAM
* AVERAGING INTEGERS ENTERED THROUGH THE KEYBOARD.
****************************************************************
ENVIRONMENT DIVISION.
****************************************************************
CONFIGURATION SECTION.
SOURCE-COMPUTER.          H-P 9000.
OBJECT-COMPUTER.          H-P 9000.
****************************************************************
DATA DIVISION.
****************************************************************
FILE SECTION.
WORKING-STORAGE SECTION.
01 AVERAGE        PIC ---9.99.
01 COUNTER        PIC 9(02)         VALUE ZERO.
01 NUMBER-ITEM    PIC S9(03).
01 SUM-ITEM       PIC S9(06)        VALUE ZERO.
01 BLANK-LINE     PIC X(80)         VALUE SPACES.
****************************************************************
PROCEDURE DIVISION.
****************************************************************
100-CONTROL-ROUTINE.
    PERFORM 200-DISPLAY-INSTRUCTIONS.
    PERFORM 300-INITIALIZATION-ROUTINE.
    PERFORM 400-ENTER-AND-ADD
            UNTIL NUMBER-ITEM = 999.
    PERFORM 500-CALCULATE-AVERAGE.
    PERFORM 600-DISPLAY-RESULTS.
    STOP RUN.
200-DISPLAY-INSTRUCTIONS.
    DISPLAY
      "THIS PROGRAM WILL FIND THE AVERAGE OF INTEGERS YOU ENTER".
    DISPLAY
      "THROUGH THE KEYBOARD. TYPE 999 TO INDICATE END OF DATA.".
    DISPLAY BLANK-LINE.
300-INITIALIZATION-ROUTINE.
    DISPLAY "PLEASE ENTER A NUMBER".
    ACCEPT NUMBER-ITEM.
400-ENTER-AND-ADD.
    ADD NUMBER-ITEM TO SUM-ITEM.
    ADD 1 TO COUNTER.
    DISPLAY "PLEASE ENTER THE NEXT NUMBER".
    ACCEPT NUMBER-ITEM.
500-CALCULATE-AVERAGE.
    DIVIDE SUM-ITEM BY COUNTER GIVING AVERAGE.
600-DISPLAY-RESULTS.
    DISPLAY "THE AVERAGE OF THE NUMBERS IS ",AVERAGE.
```

(a)

```
        THIS PROGRAM WILL FIND THE AVERAGE OF
        INTEGERS YOU ENTER THROUGH THE KEYBOARD.
        TYPE 999 TO INDICATE END OF DATA.

        PLEASE ENTER A NUMBER
        6
        PLEASE ENTER THE NEXT NUMBER
        4
        PLEASE ENTER THE NEXT NUMBER
        11
        PLEASE ENTER THE NEXT NUMBER
        999
        THE AVERAGE OF THE NUMBERS IS   7.00
```

(b)

Today, many consider COBOL old-fashioned and inelegant. In fact, many companies devoted to fast, nimble program development have converted to the language called C.

BASIC: For Beginners and Others

BASIC—Beginners' All-purpose Symbolic Instruction Code—is a common language that is easy to learn. Developed at Dartmouth College, BASIC was introduced by John Kemeny and Thomas Kurtz in 1965 and was originally intended for use by students in an academic environment. The use of BASIC has extended to business and personal computer systems.

The primary feature of BASIC is one that may be of interest to many readers of this book: BASIC is easy to learn, even for a person who has never programmed before. Thus, the language is often used to train students in the classroom. An example of a BASIC program and its output are shown in Figure 12-9.

```
'BASIC PROGRAM
'AVERAGING INTEGERS ENTERED THROUGH THE KEYBOARD
CLS
PRINT "THIS PROGRAM WILL FIND THE AVERAGE OF INTEGERS YOU ENTER"
PRINT "THROUGH THE KEYBOARD. TYPE 999 TO INDICATE END OF DATA."
PRINT
SUM=0
COUNTER=0
PRINT "PLEASE ENTER A NUMBER"
INPUT NUMBER
DO WHILE NUMBER <> 999
      SUM=SUM+NUMBER
      COUNTER=COUNTER+1
      PRINT "PLEASE ENTER THE NEXT NUMBER"
      INPUT NUMBER
LOOP
AVERAGE=SUM/COUNTER
PRINT "THE AVERAGE OF THE NUMBERS IS"; AVERAGE
END
```
(a)

Figure 12-9 BASIC program and sample output. (a) PRINT displays data right in the statement on the screen. INPUT accepts data from the user. (b) This screen display shows the interaction between program and user.

```
THIS PROGRAM WILL FIND THE AVERAGE OF INTEGERS YOU ENTER
THROUGH THE KEYBOARD. TYPE 999 TO INDICATE END OF DATA.

PLEASE ENTER A NUMBER
?6
PLEASE ENTER THE NEXT NUMBER
?4
PLEASE ENTER THE NEXT NUMBER
?11
PLEASE ENTER THE NEXT NUMBER
?999
THE AVERAGE OF THE NUMBERS IS    7
```
(b)

Pascal: The Language of Simplicity

Named for Blaise Pascal, the seventeenth-century French mathematician, **Pascal** was developed as a teaching language by a Swiss computer scientist, Niklaus Wirth, and first became available in 1971. Since that time its use spread first in Europe and then in the United States, particularly in schools offering computer science programs, although its popularity has declined.

An attractive feature of Pascal is that it is simpler than other languages—it has fewer features and is less wordy than most. In addition to being popular in college computer science departments, the language has also made large inroads in the personal computer market as a simple yet sophisticated alternative to BASIC. Today, Borland's Turbo Pascal is used by the business community and is often the choice of nonprofessional programmers who need to write their own programs. An example of a Turbo Pascal program and its output are shown in Figure 12-10.

C: A Portable Language

A language invented by Dennis Ritchie at Bell Labs in 1972, **C** produces code that approaches assembly language in efficiency while still offering the features of a high-level language. C was originally designed to write systems software but is now considered a general-purpose language. C contains some of the best features from other languages, including Pascal. C compilers are simple and compact. A key attraction is that there are C compilers available for different operating systems, a fact that contributes to the portability of C programs.

An interesting side note is that the availability of C on personal computers has greatly enhanced the value of personal computers for budding software entrepreneurs. Today C is fast being replaced by its enhanced cousin, C++, a language that will be discussed shortly. An example of a C++ program and its output are shown in Figure 12-11.

Java

Programming languages rarely attain media darling status. But it seems that the language called **Java**, from developers at Sun Microsystems, has had more coverage in the computer press than the president gets in the mainstream press. Java is a network-friendly programming language, derived from the C++ language, that permits a piece of software to run on many different platforms. A **platform** is the hardware and software combination that comprises the basic functionality of a computer. For example, a popular platform today is based on some version of Microsoft's Windows operating system and Intel's processors, a combination nicknamed *Wintel*.

Traditionally, programmers have been limited to writing a program for a single platform. Coding has had to be redone for other platforms. But a programmer can write a program in Java, which operates across platforms, and have it run anywhere. So how does Java accomplish this cross-platform feat? The programs that programmers write in Java can be understood by a universal platform, called the Java platform, that sits atop a computer's regular platform. Essentially, then, this universal platform is an extra layer of software that has been accepted as a standard by

```
PROGRAM AverageofNumbers;
(*Pascal Program
   averaging integers entered through the keyboard*)

USES
   crt;

VAR
   counter, number, sum : integer;
   average : real ;

BEGIN (*main*)
   WRITELN ('THIS PROGRAM WILL FIND THE AVERAGE OF INTEGE
   WRITELN ('THROUGH THE KEYBOARD. TYPE 999 TO INDICATE E
   WRITELN;
   sum :=0;
   counter :=0;
   WRITELN ('PLEASE ENTER A NUMBER');
   READLN (number);
   WHILE number <> 999 DO
       Begin  (*while loop*)
           sum := sum + number;
           counter := counter + 1;
           WRITELN ('PLEASE ENTER THE NEXT NUMBER');
           READ (number);
       END; (*while loop*)
   average := sum / counter;
   WRITELN ('THE AVERAGE OF THE NUMBERS IS ', average:6:2
END.  (*main*)
```

(a)

```
THIS PROGRAM WILL FIND THE AVERAGE OF INTEGERS YOU ENTER
THROUGH THE KEYBOARD. TYPE 999 TO INDICATE END OF DATA.

PLEASE ENTER A NUMBER
6
PLEASE ENTER THE NEXT NUMBER
4
PLEASE ENTER THE NEXT NUMBER
11
PLEASE ENTER THE NEXT NUMBER
999
THE AVERAGE OF THE NUMBERS IS   7.00
```

(b)

Figure 12-10 Pascal program and sample output. (a) Comments are from
(* to *). Each variable name must be declared. The symbol := assigns a value to the
variable to its left; the symbol < > means not equal to. WRITELN by itself puts a blank
line on the screen. (b) This screen display shows the interaction between program
and user. The program was written in Turbo Pascal.

Pay or You Don't Play

Some programmers earn their living as consultants, writing programs on a contract basis. Working for yourself has many
advantages. A disadvantage,
however, is the possibility of not
getting paid in full or on time.

Some consultants tackle this
problem by planting logic bombs
in their programs. That is, if the
buyer does not pay up, he or she
will discover a glitch in the program, possibly even one that will
mutate into a full system crash
without the proper "antidote"
provided by its creator.

This approach, considered
unethical in the computer industry, is not recommended to programmers. Instead, prepare a
well-defined contract that
includes exactly when, and under
what conditions, payments are
made. There is, of course, legal
recourse for breach of contract.

This information is more of a
caveat to those who contract for
programming services. Check the
reputation of the programmer(s)
in advance, obtain a clear and
signed contract—and pay your
bills.

```
// C++ PROGRAM
// AVERAGING INTEGERS ENTERED THROUGH THE KEYBOARD

#include <iostream.h>
main ()
{
  float average;
  int number, counter = 0; int sum = 0;
  cout << "THIS PROGRAM WILL FIND THE AVERAGE OF INTEGERS YOU ENTER \ n";
  cout << "THROUGH THE KEYBOARD.  TYPE 999 TO INDICATE END OF DATA. \ n";
  cout << "PLEASE ENTER A NUMBER";
  cin >> number;
  while (number !=999)
    {
      sum := sum + number;
      counter ++;
      cout << "\nPLEASE ENTER THE NEXT NUMBER";
      cin >> number;
    }
  average = sum / counter;
  cout << "\nTHE AVERAGE OF THE NUMBERS IS " << average
}
```
(a)

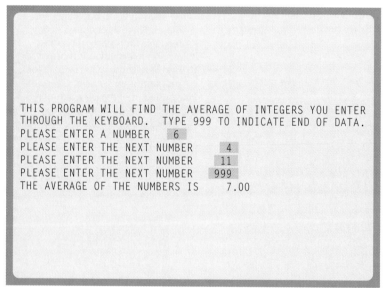

(b)

Figure 12-11 C++ program and sample output. (a) The symbol // marks comment lines. All variable names, such as number, must be declared. The command *cout* sends output to the screen, and *cin* takes data from the user. (b) This screen display shows the interaction between program and user. The program was written in Turbo C++.

most of the computer industry—no small feat. The Java platform translates Java instructions into instructions that the platform underneath can understand.

When you consider that Java can run across many platforms, it is easy to see why it is relevant to Internet development; in fact, Java's earliest incarnations were on web applications. Java has a good start on becoming the universal language of Internet computing.

▶ Object-Oriented Programming

The approach called **object-oriented programming (OOP)** is relatively new and distinctly different. Since this topic is an important emerging trend, it deserves its own section. It is possible here only to introduce the concepts and terminology of object technology. There is no expectation that you will understand exactly how object-oriented programming works; even professional programmers can take months to gain that knowledge.

What Is an Object?

Consider items that, in everyday parlance, might be called objects—for instance, a tire or a cat. Now affix known facts to those everyday objects. Without trying to be exhaustive, it can be said that a tire may be round and black and that a cat has four feet and fur. Taking this further, each object also has functions: a tire can roll or stop or go flat, and a cat can eat or purr or howl. In the world of object orientation, an object includes the item itself and also related facts and functions. More formally, in a programming environment, an **object** is a self-contained unit that contains both data and related facts and functions—the instructions to act on that data. This is in direct contrast to traditional programming, in which procedures are defined in the program separate from the data.

The word that is used to describe an object's self-containment is *encapsulation*: An object **encapsulates** both data and its related instructions. In an object, related facts are called **attributes**, and the instructions that tell the data what to do are called **methods** or **operations**. A specific occurrence of an object is called an **instance**; your pet kitty Tschugar is an instance of the object Cat.

Beginnings: Boats as Objects

Object orientation was first conceived in 1969 by Dr. Kristin Nygaard, who was trying to develop a computer model of boats passing through Norwegian fjords. As Dr. Nygaard wrestled with the complex components of waves, tides, an irregular coastline, and moving boats, he hit upon the idea of isolating each component into autonomous elements—objects—and then modeling the relationships among the elements. Consider the object Boat, shown in Figure 12-12. The object called Boat consists of the boat itself, its attributes, and its methods—descriptions of the things it does, such as float or sink. It should be noted, however, that in practice few objects have an inner life and can invoke their own methods spontaneously. Thus, methods in most cases are actions from the outside that change the state of the object.

Using object-oriented programming, programmers define classes of objects. Each **class** contains the characteristics that are unique to objects of that class. In Figure 12-12, for example, a Boat object is an instance of the Boats class. In addition to classes, objects may be formed from subclasses. Objects are arranged hierarchically in classes and subclasses by their dominant characteristics. In Figure 12-12, some kinds of boats—sailboats, powerboats, and canoes—are subclasses of the object Boat.

Figure 12-12 Object classes and subclasses. The subclasses Sailboat, Powerboat, and Canoe inherit the characteristics float and sink from the higher-class object Boat. Furthermore, each subclass, under the property of polymorphism, can respond to the message "move" by using its own methods.

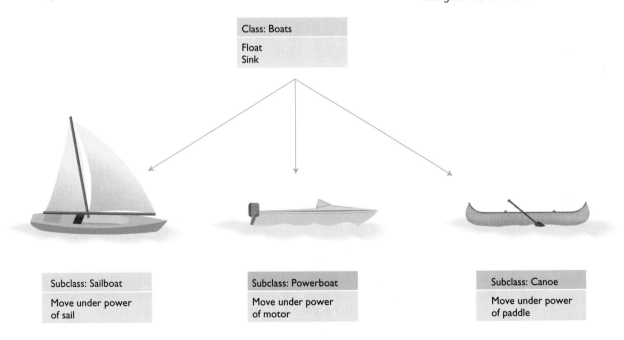

Class: Boats

Float
Sink

Subclass: Sailboat

Move under power
of sail

Subclass: Powerboat

Move under power
of motor

Subclass: Canoe

Move under power
of paddle

NEW DIRECTIONS

COMPUTERS AND CURVES

Frank Gehry, an iconoclastic architect, professes to hate computers. He describes seeing his architectural designs on the screen as "agony." He prefers to work with blocks. Gehry begins the design process by placing colored blocks together, blue for public areas, red for offices, yellow for parking, and so forth—a process that can take weeks. He then makes sketches of the block designs. Gehry never met a straight line he liked, so the straight lines of the blocks become curves in his sketches. Gehry's curves define buildings all over the world, such as the in-process Walt Disney Concert Hall shown here.

But his sketches must be converted to drawings that can be used by contractors to actually build the buildings, and therein lies the problem. Translating the calculus of these shapes is a daunting task. So, because crunching numbers is exactly what computers do best, it is to computers that Gehry has turned. Computers both speed up and sharpen the design process. The computer also improves Gehry's communication with contractors and artisans and thus allows problems to be solved earlier in the building process, preventing costly delays or refabrications.

An object in a subclass automatically possesses all the characteristics of the class from which it is derived; this property is called **inheritance**. The subclass object Canoe, for example, contains not only its own characteristics, such as a need to be paddled, but also characteristics such as the ability to float or sink inherited from the higher object class called Boats. The characteristics from the class that a subclass is derived from need not be repeated in each subclass. This means that, in a programming environment, a programmer would not have to repeat the instructions for characteristics that are inherited, saving both time and money.

Even more savings accrue from the ability to reuse objects. As object technology is used by an organization, the organization gradually builds a library of classes. Once a class has been created, tested, and found useful, it can be reused—used again. In fact, classes may be used and reused in future program applications. Because each class is self-contained, it need not be altered for use in future applications. This reduces errors significantly, since new programs can be constructed largely of pretested error-free classes. Of course, organizations will not reap the benefits of reuse until they are a few projects down the line.

MAKING THE RIGHT CONNECTIONS

NETWORKED CHILDREN

Fifth graders in Wauwatosa, Wisconsin, are corresponding via e-mail with pen-pals in all 50 states. They ask probing questions, from "What is your state's most important problem?" to "How much does a pizza cost?" This activity has paid several dividends, from increased student interest in geography to a greater understanding of how people live in large cities.

Early educational software was numbingly dull, used mostly for rote arithmetic or grammar lessons. Today's software is sophisticated and enticing, but the real breakthrough is the possibility of connecting to the world outside the classroom walls. Schools all over the land are gearing up to take advantage of Internet access, where they can plug into the Library of Congress, write to an astronaut, and even send questions to Thomas Jefferson. Students find the Internet more fun than picking up an encyclopedia.

Activating the Object

Since an object is self-contained, how do you get it to do something? A command, called a **message**, is sent to the object from outside it. The message tells the object what needs to be done, and just how it is done may be contained in the object's methods. For example, the message "move" could be sent to objects belonging to any subclass of the Boats class—Sailboat, Powerboat, or Canoe. This brings up a fancy word that goes a long way toward revealing the value of object technology: *polymorphism*. When a message is sent, the property of **polymorphism** allows an individual object receiving the message to know how, using its own methods, to process the message in the appropriate way for that particular object. For example, when the message "move" is received, the object Sailboat knows it is supposed to move under power of sail, the object Powerboat knows that it moves by means of a motor, and the object Canoe knows that it moves by being paddled. In each case the object merely had to be told to move and it did move, using its own built-in methods.

Object-Oriented Languages: C++ and Smalltalk

The object-oriented language that currently dominates the market is C++, which is the object-oriented version of the programming language

Figure 12-13 Visual Basic. On this screen you can see part of the program, as well as the visual result being achieved.

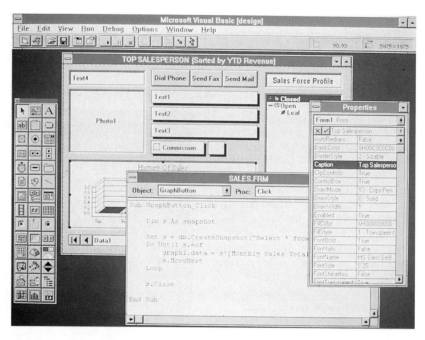

Figure 12-13 Visual Basic. On this screen you can see part of the program, as well as the visual result being achieved.

C (recall Figure 12-11). Versions of C++ are available for large systems and personal computers.

Smalltalk, which was one of the first object-oriented languages on the market, is making inroads. Smalltalk signaled a dramatic departure from traditional computer languages because it supports an especially visual system. Smalltalk works by using a keyboard to enter text, but all other interaction takes place through a mouse and icons. There are other languages that have object-oriented versions, notably Pascal and Microsoft's Visual Basic (Figure 12-13).

Object Technology in Business

When businesses approach object technology, they are more likely to be interested in invoices and payroll checks than cats or boats. Business items have their own attributes and methods, which can be coded into objects. Once the objects exist, they can inherit characteristics from objects in higher classes. For example, subclass objects relating to a customer account could inherit the address of the customer, which need not then be repeated in each subclass object. In the fashion of object technology, business objects can also respond to messages and, of course, can be reused.

★ ★ ★ ★

The essential power of any computer is managed by its operating system. The next chapter describes operating systems, the background software that allows computers to manage their own resources.

CHAPTER REVIEW

Summary and Key Terms

- A **programming language** is a set of rules for instructing the computer what operations to perform.
- A programmer converts solutions to the user's problems into instructions for the computer. These instructions are called a **program.** Writing a program involves defining the problem, planning the solution, coding the program, testing the program, and documenting the program.
- Defining the problem means discussing it with the users or a systems analyst to determine the necessary input, processing, and output.
- Planning can be done by using a **flowchart,** which is a pictorial representation of the step-by-step solution, and by using **pseudocode,** which is an English-like outline of the solution. Pseudocode is not executable on the computer.
- Coding the program means expressing the solution in a programming language. Programmers usually use a **text editor,** which is somewhat like a word processing program, to create a file that contains the program.
- Testing the program consists of desk-checking, translating, and debugging. The rules of a programming language are referred to as its **syntax. Desk-checking** is a mental checking or proofreading of the program before it is run. A **walkthrough** is a process in which a group of programmers—your peers—review your program and offer suggestions in a collegial way. In translating, a **translator** program converts the program into a form the computer can understand and in the process detects programming language errors, which are called **syntax errors.** A common translator is a **compiler,** which translates the entire program at one time and gives error messages called **diagnostics.** The original program, called a **source module,** is translated to an **object module,** to which prewritten programs may be added during the **link/load phase** to create an executable **load module. Debugging** involves running the program to detect, locate, and correct mistakes known as **logic errors.**
- Typical **documentation** contains a detailed written description of the programming cycle and the program along with the test results and a printout of the program.
- Programming languages are described as being lower level or higher level, depending on how close they are to the language the computer itself uses (0s and 1s—low) or to the language people use (more English-like—high). There are five main levels, or generations, of languages: (1) machine language, (2) assembly languages, (3) high-level languages, (4) very high-level languages, and (5) natural languages.
- **Machine language,** the lowest level, represents data as 0s and 1s, binary digits corresponding to the on and off electrical states in the computer.
- **Assembly languages** use letters as mnemonic codes to replace the 0s and 1s of machine language. An **assembler program** is used to translate the assembly language into machine language.
- **High-level languages** are written in an English-like manner. Each high-level language requires a different compiler, or translator program, for each type of computer on which it is run.
- **Very high-level languages,** also called **fourth-generation languages (4GLs),** are basically shorthand languages. A variation on 4GLs are **query languages,** which can be used to retrieve data from databases.
- Fifth-generation languages are often called **natural languages** because they resemble "natural" spoken language.

- The first high-level language, **FORTRAN** (FORmula TRANslator), is a scientifically oriented language that was introduced by IBM in 1954. Its brevity makes it suitable for executing complex formulas.
- **COBOL** (COmmon Business-Oriented Language) was introduced in 1959 as a standard programming language for business.
- When **BASIC** (Beginners' All-purpose Symbolic Instruction Code) was developed at Dartmouth and introduced in 1965, it was intended for instruction. Now its uses include business and personal computer applications.
- **Pascal**, named for the French mathematician Blaise Pascal, first became available in 1971. It is popular in college computer courses.
- Invented at Bell Labs, **C** offers high-level language features such as structured programming. C code is almost as efficient as assembly language, and it is suitable for writing portable programs that can run on more than one type of computer.
- **Java** is a network-friendly programming language, derived from the C++ language, that permits a piece of software to run on many different **platforms**, the hardware and software combination that comprises the basic functionality of a computer.
- The approach called **object-oriented programming (OOP)** uses **objects**, self-contained units that contain both data and related facts and functions—the instructions to act on that data. An object **encapsulates** both data and its related instructions. In an object, related facts are called **attributes**, and the instructions that tell the data what to do are called **methods** or **operations**. A specific occurrence of an object is called an **instance**.
- An object **class** contains the characteristics that are unique to that class. Objects are arranged hierarchically in classes and subclasses by their dominant characteristics. An object in a subclass automatically possesses all the characteristics of the class to which it belongs; this property is called **inheritance**.
- Once an object has been created, tested, and found useful, it can be used and reused in future program applications.
- A command called a **message**, telling what—not how—something is to be done, activates the object. **Polymorphism** means that an individual object receiving a message knows how, using its own methods, to process the message in the appropriate way for that particular object.
- The object-oriented language that currently dominates the market is **C++**, which is the object-oriented version of the programming language C. Versions of C++ are available for large systems and personal computers. The language called **Smalltalk**, which supports an especially visual system, is making inroads.

Quick Poll

Compare your answers to those of your colleagues or classmates.

1. If you were a programmer, what aspect might interest you the most?
   - ❏ a. Code, code, code. The more the better.
   - ❏ b. Working with users to make sure they are in on the planning and are satisfied with the results.
   - ❏ c. Documentation. I know this isn't usually a favored chore, but I like to wrap up the whole package so that the program can be easily understood by me or someone else in the future.
2. Regarding program testing:
   - ❏ a. I would want to test on my own first and catch as many of my mistakes as possible before anyone else sees the results. Then I'd like to test enough so that the user is satisfied that everything works.
   - ❏ b. As quick and dirty as possible. No need to hold up the schedule with endless testing if the program has been planned and coded with skill.

❏ c. I am not sure any amount of testing would be enough. Who can say that every error has been found?

3. Become a programmer?
   ❏ a. That's why I'm here.
   ❏ b. Not a chance. I'm not into the nuts and bolts. I'm more interested in using software that someone else had to write.
   ❏ c. I can see myself dabbling, maybe just as a hobby, maybe as a hobby that turns into something more.

Discussion Questions

1. It has been noted that, among other qualities, good programmers are detail-oriented. Why might attention to detail be important in the programming process?
2. In addition to insisting on proper documentation, managers encourage programmers to write straightforward programs that another programmer could easily follow. Discuss occasions in which a programmer may have to work with a program written by another programmer. Under what circumstances might a programmer completely take over the care of a program written by another? If you inherited someone else's program, about which you knew nothing, would you be dismayed to discover minimal documentation?
3. Should students taking a computer literacy course be required to learn some programming?

Student Study Guide

Multiple Choice

1. The presence of both data and its related instructions in an object:
   a. C++   c. encapsulation
   b. orientation   d. inheritance
2. In preparing a program, one should first
   a. plan the solution   c. code the program
   b. document the program d. define the problem
3. During the development of a program, drawing a flowchart is a means to
   a. plan the solution   c. code the program
   b. define the problem   d. analyze the problem
4. An English-like language that one can use as a program design tool:
   a. BASIC   c. pseudocode
   b. COBOL   d. Pascal

5. In preparing a program, desk-checking and translating are examples of
   a. coding   c. planning
   b. testing   d. documenting
6. The process of detecting, locating, and correcting logic errors:
   a. desk-checking   c. translating
   b. debugging   d. documenting
7. Comments in the program itself are part of
   a. compiling   c. translating
   b. linking   d. documenting
8. The hardware/software combination that comprises a computer's functionality:
   a. platform   c. class
   b. pseudocode   d. syntax
9. The first high-level language to be introduced:
   a. COBOL   c. FORTRAN
   b. Pascal   d. BASIC
10. The ability of an object to interpret a message using its own methods:
    a. polymorphism   c. encapsulation
    b. inheritance   d. messaging
11. The language named for a French mathematician:
    a. C   c. FORTRAN
    b. Pascal   d. COBOL
12. Specifying the kind of input, processing, and output required for a program occurs when
    a. planning the solution c. flowcharting the problem
    b. coding the program   d. defining the problem
13. Error messages provided by a compiler:
    a. bugs   c. diagnostics
    b. translations   d. mistakes
14. After stating a solution in pseudocode, the next step would be
    a. testing the program   c. coding the program
    b. implementing the   d. translating the
       program   program
15. The highest-level languages are called
    a. 4GLs   c. high-level
    b. assembly   d. natural
16. To activate an object, send
    a. a message   c. an instance
    b. a method   d. an attribute
17. Popular object-oriented languages:
    a. Pascal, COBOL   c. C++, Smalltalk
    b. C++, FORTRAN   d. COBOL, BASIC
18. Software that translates assembly language into machine language:
    a. a binary translator c. a compiler
    b. an assembler   d. a link-loader
19. A standardized business language:
    a. Pascal   c. BASIC
    b. COBOL   d. FORTRAN

20. In developing a program, documentation should be done
    a. as the last step
    b. only to explain errors
    c. throughout the process
    d. only during the design phase

21. A fourth-generation language used for database retrieval:
    a. high-level language
    b. query language
    c. assembly language
    d. machine language

22. The network-friendly language derived from C++:
    a. Java
    b. Pascal
    c. Smalltalk
    d. BASIC

23. The lowest level of programming language:
    a. natural language
    b. BASIC
    c. assembly language
    d. machine language

24. An assembly language uses
    a. English words
    b. 0s and 1s
    c. mnemonic codes
    d. binary digits

25. The language Smalltalk is
    a. machine oriented
    b. problem oriented
    c. document oriented
    d. object oriented

True/False

T   F   1. The usual reason for choosing a programming language is simply that it is the one the programmer likes best.

T   F   2. Developing a program requires just two steps, coding and testing.

T   F   3. A flowchart is an example of pseudocode.

T   F   4. Desk-checking is the first phase of testing a program.

T   F   5. A translator is a form of hardware that translates a program into language the computer can understand.

T   F   6. *Wintel* is an example of a platform.

T   F   7. Debugging is the process of locating program logic errors.

T   F   8. The highest level of language is natural language.

T   F   9. Pseudocode can be used to plan and execute a program.

T   F   10. 4GLs increase clarity but reduce user productivity.

T   F   11. An object encapsulates both data and its related instructions.

T   F   12. Pascal is particularly easy to use because it has fewer features than most languages.

T   F   13. COBOL is divided into four parts called areas.

T   F   14. BASIC is especially suited for large and complex programs.

T   F   15. FORTRAN stands for FORms TRANsfer.

T   F   16. Expressing a problem solution in Pascal is an example of coding a program.

T   F   17. Diagnostic messages are concerned with improper use of the programming language.

T   F   18. An assembler program translates high-level language into assembly language.

T   F   19. An object subclass inherits characteristics from higher object classes.

T   F   20. A specific occurrence of an object is called an instance.

T   F   21. Polymorphism means that an object knows how, using its own methods, to act on an incoming message.

T   F   22. Another name for a high-level language is 4GL.

T   F   23. A query language is a type of assembly language.

T   F   24. FORTRAN is used primarily in scientific environments.

T   F   25. Low-level languages are tied more closely to the computer than are high-level languages.

Fill-In

1. The type of language used to access databases:

   _____

2. The type of language that replaced machine language by using mnemonic codes.

   _____

3. The object orientation property that permits a subclass to retain the characteristics of a higher class:

   _____

4. A query language is what level of language?

   _____

5. The name for a translator that translates high-level languages into machine language.

   _____

6. The rules of a programming language are called its

   _____

7. How many levels of language were described in the chapter? _____

8. A source module is translated into a(n)

   _____

9. The object orientation property that permits an object to use its own methods to act on a message is _____

10. Two commonly used OOP languages:

    a. _____

    b. _____

11. The hardware and software combination that comprises the basic functionality of a computer: _____

12. An object module is link-loaded into a _____

13. Languages that resemble spoken languages: _____

14. The high-level language that is scientifically oriented: _____

15. The command that activates an object: _____

16. The programming process step that is best done throughout the process: _____

17. Two common methods of planning the solution to a problem:

    a. _____

    b. _____

18. List the three phases of testing a program.

    a. _____

    b. _____

    c. _____

19. The next step after a programmer has planned the solution: _____

20. The term for the error messages that a translator provides: _____

Answers

Multiple Choice

1. c	6. b	11. b	16. a	21. b
2. d	7. d	12. d	17. c	22. a
3. a	8. a	13. c	18. b	23. d
4. c	9. c	14. c	19. b	24. c
5. b	10. a	15. d	20. c	25. d

True/False

1. F	6. T	11. T	16. T	21. T
2. F	7. T	12. T	17. T	22. F
3. F	8. T	13. F	18. F	23. F
4. T	9. F	14. F	19. T	24. T
5. F	10. F	15. F	20. T	25. T

Fill-In

1. query language
2. assembly language
3. inheritance
4. very high-level language
5. compiler
6. syntax
7. five
8. object module
9. polymorphism
10. C++, Smalltalk
11. platform
12. load module
13. natural languages
14. FORTRAN
15. message
16. documentation
17. a. flowcharting
    b. writing pseudocode
18. a. desk-checking
    b. translating
    c. debugging
19. code the program
20. diagnostics

PLANET INTERNET

ETHICS AND THE INTERNET

Ethics refers to a judgment of what is wrong and what is right. At first, it may seem strange that ethics issues would be attached to something as new and different and ethereal as the Internet. How can the Internet be right or wrong? As it turns out, the issues are many, and they are not so very different from ethical issues in other parts of society. Consider also that any ethics issue may or may not have legal ramifications.

Many people and many organizations have raised concerns about ethics and the Internet. They often make their positions known on their web sites. We will take a brief glance at some of the issues. As with many ethics issues, it is easier to raise questions than to provide answers.

User behavior. As mentioned in Chapter 7, there are many netiquette sites proposing a certain conduct of behavior for Internet users. Some people consider these to be ethical issues, especially if a user is being annoying and thus ruining the 'Net experiences of other users. Others, instead of raising this to the level of an ethical issue, prefer to think of it in terms of courtesy.

Hacking. Is it ethical to give tips to hackers so that they can then proceed to invade computers? Many sites do just that. However, some carefully state that their purpose is only to "increase awareness" and alert security employees to the potential problems they face. There are hundreds of hacker sites, most of them "how-to" sites, loaded with hacking tips and gleeful bragging. Astonishingly, there are developer sites with "challenges" (their word) to hackers: They are invited to try to break an encryption code or penetrate a firewall, with thousands of dollars in prizes for those who are successful. Try sorting out those ethics!

Intellectual property. Some people have the notion that "if I can connect to it, I can treat it as if it's mine to do with as I please." That attitude overlooks federal copyright laws, which protect an individual's original expressions, whether they are a book or a song or a work of art. The originator has exclusive right to his or her works. Their presence on an Internet site does not alter the law.

Privacy. A little tug of war is going on between business interests, who want your e-mail address, and site visitors who prefer to maintain their privacy. People sometimes readily give up their addresses for some enticement such as a contest, only to be surprised when they get junk e-mail. One approach is to use a site like Switchboard as a go-between, to camouflage your identity.

As we noted in Chapter 8, some businesses record cookie files related to site usage on a visitor's hard disk. Some groups are objecting to this practice, both on privacy and property bases. The Internet Engineering Task Force, for example, wrote to several industry and government leaders, promoting "the ability of users to see and exercise control over the disclosure of personally identifiable information."

Get off of my site! Can your site be considered your property and, thus, an unwanted visitor considered to be trespassing? If this makes your head spin, be assured that some legal scholars are pondering this very issue. It can be argued, of course, that it is already possible, using current technology, to admit only selected people to a site or to reject certain others. Businesses do this all the time with their internal sites. But a case could be made that if one puts a notice on a site that certain users are not permitted, perhaps for a nonoffensive reason such as trying to save them money if they pay for access by the minute, then that edict should be honored.

Ethics and the Internet

Fraud. The warnings are the same on the Internet as they are in other parts of society: Look out for scams. A rather famous fraud was the successful promotion of SoftRAM, a software product that allegedly doubles memory without the purchase of new memory chips. Many people liked that idea a lot and continued to buy the product long after it was exposed as a fraud. Interestingly, the bad news came from users across the Internet long before the traditional press caught up with the story. Fraud, of course is not ethical and is well covered by law.

New laws? Many people argue that no new laws are needed for the Internet, because the problems related to the Internet—fraud, theft, copyright infringement, and so forth—are covered by pre-Internet laws. This argument is also made regarding pornography on the 'Net. Why is material that is legally permissible in a bookstore not permissible on a different forum, the Internet? People who take the opposite view argue that the immediacy and availability of Internet materials, especially to children, paints a different and scarier scenario. Each side sees this as an ethical issue. The Communications Decency Act of 1996 proposes penalties for indecent materials on the Internet. The act is, at this writing, before the United States Supreme Court. The full text of the act is on several web sites; you can also link to it from the Addison Wesley Longman site.

The blue ribbons you may see attached to web sites are statements in favor of "free speech" on the Internet; that is, they indicate opposition to the act. (If, by the way, you wonder about ribbons in general and what they mean, see the Ribbons on the Internet site.)

Service. Lest we see nothing but problems, it is appropriate to note that some Internet sites perform a service by proposing ethical codes and behaviors. Others publish the pre-Internet codes of ethics for particular professions or organizations, including medical, business, computer, and sports organizations.

Universal access. An organization called Computer Professionals for Social Responsibility has a comprehensive and serious site representing its members' concerns. A key ethical issue for them is the right of everyone to Internet access. They express this in terms that look not unlike a set of existing non-'Net rights: the right to assemble in online communities, the right to speak freely, the right to privacy, and the right to access regardless of income, location, or disability. They look to the government to make this happen.

Internet Exercises

1. **Structured exercise.** Begin with the AWL URL, http://hepg.awl.com/capron/planet/, and link to the Computer Professionals for Social Responsibility site.
2. **Freeform exercise.** Put the words *computer* and *ethics* through a search engine and check out a few sites that look promising.

When Linda Ronquillo was taking a night class in applications software at a community college four years ago, she did not have to worry much about the operating system, the necessary software in the background. The college personal computers were on a network that managed all the computers. As Linda sat down to begin work, the computer screen showed a menu of numbered choices reflecting the software packages available: (1) WordPerfect, (2) Microsoft Word, (3) Microsoft Excel, and so forth. At the bottom of the screen, Linda was instructed to type the number of her chosen selection; if she typed 1, for example, the system put her into WordPerfect. Linda did have to learn operating system commands to prepare her own diskettes and save data on them so that she could take her work with her, but she had little other contact with the operating system.

On the job as a supervisor for a small airport freight company, Linda needed to use word processing, spreadsheets, and database software packages on her personal computer. But no one had set up a menu shortcut here; with a little advice from colleagues, she learned what she needed to know about the operating system called MS-DOS. She learned, among other things, to execute the software she needed to use and to take care of her data files, copying files from one disk to another and sometimes renaming or deleting them. She eventually felt fairly comfortable with her operating system knowledge.

Two months later, Linda was informed by the company personal computer manager that the company's three personal computers were going to be switched to Microsoft Windows 98, an operating system that included a user-friendly interface. Despite assurances that the new system would be colorful and easy to use, Linda was less than thrilled to be making another change. But she did not say so. She knew that being a computer user meant being willing to adjust to change. So Linda learned to use a mouse and mastered icons, overlapping windows, pull-down menus, and other mysteries.

Approximately six months later, Linda took a job at another, larger airline freight company. Part of the reason she was hired was her response to the revelation that the new company used Windows NT, which, she knew, was yet another operating system. Linda said, "Oh, I have learned several systems. It shouldn't be any problem learning another." She was right, of course. In fact, she had little trouble switching to the new operating system.

Operating Systems

Software in the Background

▷ Operating Systems: Hidden Software

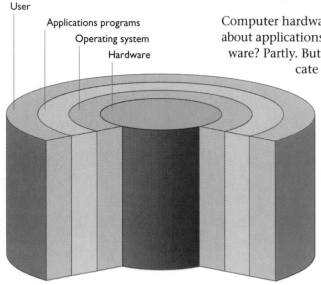

Computer hardware needs software to tell it what to do. Are we talking about applications software, such as word processing or spreadsheet software? Partly. But an applications software package does not communicate directly with the hardware. Between the applications software and the hardware is a software interface—an operating system. An **operating system** is a set of programs that lies between applications software and the computer hardware. Figure 13-1 gives a conceptual picture of operating system software as an intermediary between the hardware and the applications software. Incidentally, the term **system software** is sometimes used interchangeably with *operating system*, but system software means all programs related to coordinating computer operations. System software does include the operating system, but it also includes programming language translators, which we mentioned in Chapter 12, and service programs, which we will discuss briefly in this chapter.

Figure 13-1 A conceptual diagram of an operating system. Closest to the user are applications programs—software that helps a user compute a payroll or play a game or calculate the trajectory of a rocket. The operating system is the set of programs between the applications programs and the hardware.

Note that we said that an operating system is a *set* of programs. The most important program in the operating system, the program that manages the operating system, is the **supervisor program**, most of which remains in memory and is thus referred to as *resident*. The supervisor controls the entire operating system and loads into memory other operating system programs (called *nonresident*) from disk storage only as needed (Figure 13-2).

An operating system has three main functions: (1) manage the computer's resources, such as the central processing unit, memory, disk drives, and printers; (2) establish a user interface; and (3) execute and provide services for applications software. Keep in mind, however, that much of the work of an operating system is hidden from the user; many necessary tasks are performed behind the scenes. In particular, the first listed function, managing the computer's resources, is taken care of without the user being aware of the details. Furthermore, all input and output operations, although invoked by an applications program, are actually carried out by the operating system.

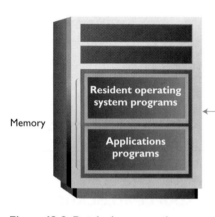

Nonresident operating system programs

Figure 13-2 Retrieving operating system programs from disk. The supervisor program of the operating system is resident in memory and calls in nonresident operating system programs from the disk as needed.

Although much of the operating system functions are hidden from view, you will know when you are using an applications software package, and this requires that you invoke—call into action—the operating system. Thus you establish a user interface and also execute software.

Operating systems for large computers must keep track of several programs from several users, all running in the same time frame. We will examine the inherent complexities of such systems later in the chapter. For now, focus on the interaction between a single user and a personal computer operating system.

➤ Operating Systems for Personal Computers

If you peruse software offerings at a retail store, you will generally find the software grouped according to the operating system on which the software can run. Generally, applications software—word processing, spreadsheets, games, whatever—can run on just one operating system. Just as you cannot place a Nissan engine in a Ford truck, you cannot take a version of WordPerfect designed to run on a computer using the Microsoft Windows operating system, and run it on an Apple Macintosh, which uses the OS8 operating system. The operating systems must certainly be different if the computer's processors are different. Software makers must decide for which operating system to write an applications software package, although some make versions of their software for more than one operating system.

Users do not set out to buy an operating system; they want computers and the applications software to make them useful. However, since the operating system determines what software is available for a given computer, they must at the least be aware of their own computer's operating system.

Although operating systems differ, many of their basic functions are similar. Let us examine some of the basic functions of operating systems by examining MS-DOS.

➤ A Brief Look at MS-DOS

Most users today have a computer with a hard disk drive. No matter what operating system is being used, when the computer is turned on, the operating system will be loaded from the hard drive into the computer's memory, thus making it available for use. The process of loading the operating system into memory is called bootstrapping, or **booting** the system. The word *booting* is used because, figuratively speaking, the operating system pulls itself up by its own bootstraps. When the computer is switched on, a small program (in ROM—read-only memory) automatically pulls up the basic components of the operating system from the hard disk.

If you are using a computer whose operating system is MS-DOS, the net observable result of booting MS-DOS is that the characters C:\> appear on the screen. The C refers to the disk drive; the > is a **prompt**, a signal that the system is *prompting* you to do something. At this point you must give some instruction to the computer. Perhaps all you need to do is key certain letters to make the applications software take the lead. But it could be more complicated than that because C:\> is actually a signal for direct communication between the user and the operating system.

Although the prompt is the only visible result of booting the system, MS-DOS (often called just DOS, to rhyme with *boss*) also provides the basic software that coordinates the computer's hardware components and a set of programs that lets you perform the many computer system tasks you need to do. To execute a given DOS program, a user must type a **command**, a name that invokes a specific DOS program. Entire books have been written about DOS commands, but we will consider just a few that people use for ordinary activities. Some typical tasks that you can

THE MS-DOS COMMANDS YOU WILL USE MOST

These instructions assume you are using a computer with diskette drive A and hard drive C. Instructions for you to type are in this `typeface`.

FORMAT (Prepare an unformatted disk for use)

A new diskette may need to be formatted before it can be used. Caution: *Never* format hard disk drive C; formatting destroys all data on a disk.

1. Insert the blank diskette in drive A.
2. `C:\>CD\DOS`
   Change to the DOS directory.
3. `C:\DOS>FORMAT A:`
   Type the command to format.
4. When asked, press Enter to confirm that a diskette is present and again to skip the volume label.

DIR (Directory)

In no time at all, most computer users have lots of files on lots of disks; you can easily forget where files are. DIR produces an on-screen list of file names. /P and /W add further options.

`C:\>DIR`   Lists one line per file, with name, size in bytes, and date/time created.

`C:\>DIR/W`   Lists file names only, in five columns across the screen.

`C:\>DIR/P`   Lists one line per file, a page at a time; press any key to continue.

`C:\>DIR/W/P`   Lists file names only in five columns, a page at a time.

COPY (Make a copy of a file)

One important reason to copy a file is to produce a backup copy. Another is to copy a data file generated on a community (school or office) hard disk to your own diskette. If we assume the file to be copied is on the current drive, in this case drive C, C need not be mentioned in the command. And, if you want the new file to have the same name in its new location, which is usually the case, you need not key it again on the new drive, in this case A.

`C:\>COPY MRKTDATA.SUM A:`   Copies file MRKTDATA.SUM on drive C to drive A.

`C:\>COPY *.* A:`   Copies all files in the directory to drive A.

DEL or ERASE (Delete a file)

When your disk gets cluttered with files you no longer want, it is time to clean house. Use DEL followed by the name of the file you want to delete.

RENAME (Give a file a new name)

If you decide to change a file name, use the RENAME command, followed by the old name and then the new name. Assume that a file named MRKTDATA.SUM is on a diskette in drive A.

`A:\>RENAME MRKTDATA.SUM SSDATA.CHT`   New name is SSDATA.CHT.

Other simple commands

The following three commands can be invoked by simply keying the commands themselves, without the need for any additional information: *CHKDSK*, meaning check disk, causes a screen display of information about the status of the disk, including number of files, number of bytes used in files, and number of bytes available for use. *CLS* clears the screen. When you key *TIME*, the proper time appears on the screen. If you wish, you can key in a new time; this is convenient for switching back and forth between daylight savings time and standard time. *VER* will provide the current version number of the operating system.

---

perform with DOS commands are list the files on a disk, copy files from one disk to another, and erase files from a disk. For specifics, see the box *The MS-DOS Commands You Will Use Most.*

▶ Microsoft Windows

Today there is another—most say better—way to interact with the computer's operating system. **Microsoft Windows**—Windows for short—uses a colorful graphics interface that, among other things, eases access to the operating system. Microsoft Windows defines the operating environment standard for computers with Intel processors. Most new personal computers come with Windows already installed.

A Windows Overview

The feature that makes Windows so easy to use is a **graphical user interface** (**GUI**, pronounced "*goo*-ee"), in which users work with on-screen pictures called **icons** and with **menus** rather than with keyed-in commands (Figure 13-3). Clicking icons or menu items activates a command or function. The menus in Figure 13-3 are called **pull-down menus** because they appear to pull down like a window shade from the original selection. Some menus, in contrast, called **pop-up menus**, originate from a selection on the bottom of the screen. Furthermore, icons and menus encourage pointing and clicking with a mouse, an approach that can make computer use both fast and easy.

Windows started out as an **operating environment**, another layer added to separate the operating system from the user. This layer is often called a **shell** because it forms a "coating," with icons and menus, over the operating system.

As millions of users can attest, Windows is an unqualified success. But even a popular software product can be improved, hence the subsequent versions called Windows 95 and the latest, Windows 98.

Introducing Mr. Gates

Anyone who has not figured out what the trend is for operating systems has missed the heavy press coverage of billionaire Bill Gates, the founder of the Microsoft Corporation, the largest software company in the world. Mr. Gates has graced the covers of *Time, Fortune,* and any other news magazine you could name. Each time he is interviewed, Mr. Gates makes a pitch for his vision of the future, which features, among other things, Microsoft Windows. (Incidentally, Microsoft was denied a trademark on the word *windows;* it was simply considered too common.)

Figure 13-3 Windows 98. We positioned the Windows Explorer screen on the bottom half of the screen; note the pull-down menu for Tools. Explorer shows file folders on the left and the contents of the open folder—in this case Games—on the right. The top half of the screen shows the desktop, with its clickable program icons. When clicked, the Start button on the lower left issues a pop-up menu with various options, including shutting down. The Start button is part of the task bar, which shows tiny clickable icons for (left to right) TV channels, return to desktop, the Internet, and Microsoft Outlook Express, a program to keep track of e-mail and other functions. To the right of these icons, there is a button for each program currently open, from left to right, Explorer (see above), Microsoft Word (word processing), and PKZip (file compression). Rightmost is the time; if you rest your mouse on it the day and date appear.

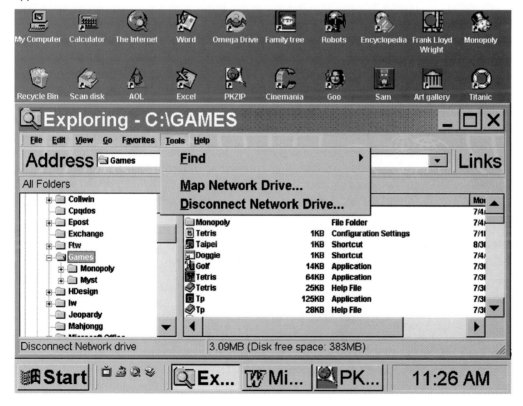

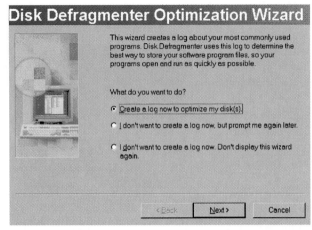

(a)

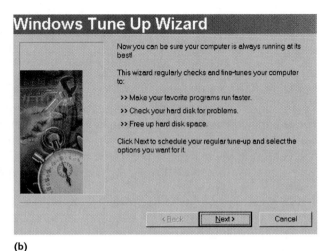

(b)

Figure 13-4 Wizards. These screens show Windows 98 wizards—easy-to-use software—for (a) defragmenting the disk and (b) tuning up the computer. Note a small cosmetic item: Windows 98 permits a two-colored title bar. The user chose blue for the left end and red for the right, and the computer made a color transition between them.

Windows 95

Note, first of all, that Windows 95 is *not* a shell; it is a self-contained operating system, and thus requires no pre-installed DOS. However, DOS commands are still available. But Windows 95 was offered as a new and distinct operating system. Windows 98, as we will see shortly, is a variation on Windows 95 and has much the same screen look.

Perhaps the most obvious change in Windows 95 was the Start button in the lower-left corner just waiting to be clicked (Figure 13-3). From this beginning you can conveniently find a program or a file. Programs can also be invoked by a double-click on an icon on the desktop, the Windows opening screen. In Figure 13-3, the desktop area, with the blue background, is shown toward the top of the screen; you can see several program icons. Perhaps the greatest convenience, as you can see in Figure 13-3, is the task bar along the bottom of the screen, an array of buttons for each program in current use. You can click from program to program as easily as changing channels on your TV. As another example of convenience, long file names, up to 255 characters, are permitted.

Anyone who has added a new component, perhaps a modem or a sound card, to an existing computer knows that it must be configured to the system, a process that may involve some software and even hardware manipulations. Windows 95 supported **plug and play**, a concept that lets the computer configure itself when a new component is added. However, for plug and play to become a reality, hardware components must also feature the plug and play standard. Once a peripheral is built to the plug and play standard, a user can install it simply by plugging it in and turning on the computer. Windows recognizes that a new device has been added and proceeds to configure it.

A Windows 95 technology called **object linking and embedding** (**OLE**—wonderfully pronounced *Oh-LAY*) lets you embed or link one document with another. For instance, you could embed a graphic within a document created in a desktop publishing program that supports OLE. When you click the graphic to edit it, you would be taken to the graphics program in which you created the graphic.

Windows 98

Windows 98 is built on the same code base as Windows 95, so Windows 98 provides the same level of compatibility as Windows 95. Windows 98 offers a variety of improvements, some sophisticated, some cosmetic. As we noted earlier, the screen look is much the same. Further, user interaction has not changed significantly, so a user familiar with Windows 95 can adjust quickly to Windows 98.

The average user will probably be most impacted by these Windows 98 features:

Figure 13-5 Windows CE. This handheld computer, showing a Windows CE screen, rests in a desktop cradle when not on the road.

Internet/intranet browsing capabilities. Microsoft's browser, Internet Explorer, is included with Windows 98. In fact, Windows 98 itself has been made to look more like a browser. Note, for example, in Figure 13-3, the Address slot at the top of the screen; this is reminiscent of a browser screen. Note also, on the left end of the task bar, a series of tiny icons; the earth-shaped icon can be clicked to invoke the Internet Explorer.

Support for state-of-the-art hardware. This includes support for the Universal Serial Bus (USB)(see the margin note in Chapter 4), Digital Video Disk (DVD), and the latest multimedia components.

Support for huge disk drives. Everyone wants more disk space and gigabyte drives provide the answer. Support for high-capacity drives is provided in Windows 98 by FAT 32, a 32-bit file allocation table that records the location of each file on the disk. This replaces FAT 16, an underpowered 16-bit table.

TV viewer and broadcast ability. A broadcast-enabled computer blends television with new forms of information and entertainment. It blurs the line between television, web pages, and computer content. It also enables the reception of broadcast web pages and other live data feeds, such as across-the-screen news headlines and stock quotes. You can see the tiny TV channels icon on the lower left in Figure 13-3.

Wizards. Windows 98 lets users accomplish various tasks using "wizards," software that make tasks user-friendly (Figure 13-4).

Further, Windows 98 includes technologies to help reduce the cost of owning and maintaining a personal computer. Other features include improved backup, improved interfaces with other software, new and improved networking features, and increased security. Finally, Windows 98 includes an improved Dr. Watson, which provides technical information about the state of the computer when it suffers a general protection fault, commonly called a crash.

The stripped-down version called Windows CE (for *consumer electronics*) is meant for handheld organizers and other new digital appliances (Figure 13-5). It is a subset of Windows, scaled back to work with less memory on smaller screens and without much, if any, file storage. It looks roughly like Windows and has rudimentary word processing, spreadsheet, e-mail, and web browsing software. It also allows contact and calendar information, and documents, to be swapped between a desktop personal computer and a handheld computer.

Windows NT

The operating system called Windows NT (for *new technology*) is meant mostly for corporate, networked environments. Beginning with version 4.0, NT looks exactly like Windows 98 and runs most of the software that runs under Windows 98. But beneath the surface, Windows NT is far more robust and heavy-duty. It has been engineered for stability and, as befits a networked environment, has much stronger security features.

Getting Practical

ACCESSIBILITY OPTIONS

Long hours staring at a computer screen can be hard on the eyes. Windows offers, as shown here on the right, the option of enlarged letters and high-contrast colors.

Improved visibility is only part of the story. The Accessibility Options icon, found in the Control Panel, offers aids for seeing, hearing, touching. For example, a hearing-impaired individual can elect to have any computer sound show up as a visual indicator on the screen. Furthermore, spoken words can be shown on the screen as captions.

An option called StickyKeys permits keys that normally must be pressed at the same time in order to invoke a command, such as Ctrl-Alt-Del, to be pressed separately but still achieve the same effect. Another option, handy for anyone who has a habit of inadvertently pressing the Caps Lock key, is to sound a beep whenever the Caps Lock, Num Lock, or Scroll Lock keys are pressed. Mouse movements can also be replaced with the numeric keypad keys.

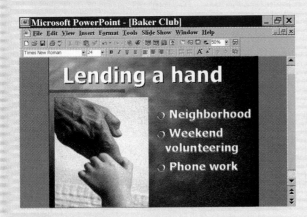 

For home users, the features that make Windows NT attractive to businesses are definitely overkill. Furthermore, Windows NT requires much more memory and hard disk space—probably triple for each—than Windows 98. Technical support costs more too, closer to what a business would expect to pay. It also lacks compatibility in many respects; in particular, it is unable to work with older add-on hardware devices or to run older programs, especially games.

▶ Operating Systems for Networks

An extension of operating systems for personal computers is a **network operating system (NOS)**, which is designed to let computers on a network share resources such as hard disks and printers. A network operating system is similar to a standard operating system but includes special features for handling network functions. Our earlier discussion of Windows NT described the workstation version; the server version of Windows NT is one example of a network operating system. In addition to resource sharing, a NOS supports data security (does this user have the right to that data?), troubleshooting (oops—computer XYZ on the network failed to receive a message intended for it), and administrative control (track the online hours and number of messages to and from each computer).

In a client/server relationship, parts of the NOS (mostly file access and management programs) run on the server computer, while other NOS

NEW DIRECTIONS

TECHNOLOGY FOR TECHNOLOGY'S SAKE

The change in operating systems, say, from MS-DOS to Windows to Windows 98, is one example of the steady march of technology. Hardware changes occur even faster. Some people grumble that all this is just "technology for technology's sake," and that we could make do with existing hardware and software for longer periods of time. Some view the rapid changes as an example of planned obsolescence—the computer companies and their software partners produce a constant stream of new products so that we consumers will continue to buy.

Although it is certainly true that all manufacturers, no matter what the product, need a continuing stream of buyers, something more subtle is going on in the computer industry. Two phenomena are occurring at the same time, and they feed on each other. The first is that hardware manufacturers are, quite naturally, always looking to improve their products. Over the years they have been able to offer greater

capacity in every respect without significant price increases. But why would a consumer give up on a perfectly good computer just

because there is something newer and better on the market? That brings us to the second phenomenon, the increased functionality of software. Software makers also want to improve their products. In particular, they want to make the software easy to use. But the easier the product is to use, the more space is needed both on the hard drive and in memory. Frequently, new software just will not function well on an older computer that has, relatively speaking, limited capacity.

Consumers can resist new software for just so long. In particular, if they cling too long to an older operating system, they will find that no applications software is being written for it. There are several stopgap measures—adding memory, adding a hard drive, upgrading the microprocessor. But most people eventually buy the new computer, one with the capacity to handle all the new software. And then the cycle begins again.

---

components, such as software that permits requests to the server and messages to other computers, run on the client computers.

One of the network operating system's main tasks is to make the resources appear as if they are running from the client computer. Whether issuing commands, running applications software, or sending jobs to a printer, the role of the NOS is to make the desired services appear to be local to that client computer. The whole point of a client/server system is to provide expanded services to individual users at their own networked computers; the network operating system is the software that makes it possible.

▶ Operating Systems for Large Computers

Large computers—mainframes—had been around for more than two decades before anyone thought to make a personal computer. Those big computers usually were owned by businesses and universities, which made them available to many users. So, rather than the scenario with which you may be familiar—one person per personal computer at a time—a large computer is used by many people. This presents special problems, which must be addressed by the operating system.

Since a large computer can handle many programs from many users, questions arise from computer users when they first realize that their program is "in there" with all those other programs.

> *Question*: If my program and another program both want to use the *central processing unit* at the same time, what decides which program gets it first?
>
> *Answer*: The operating system.
>
> *Question*: If several other programs are in *memory* at the same time as my program, what keeps the programs from getting mixed up with one another?
>
> *Answer*: The operating system.
>
> *Question*: I know that for *storage* big computers use big disk packs that can hold files for several users—what keeps the files in some kind of accessible order?
>
> *Answer*: The operating system.
>
> *Question*: Well, the *printer* must be a problem. If we all need it at the same time, what prevents everyone's hard copy output from coming out in one big jumble?
>
> *Answer*: The operating system!

This litany may sound repetitive, but it does make a point: The operating system anticipates these problems and many others so that you, as a user, can share the computer's resources with others with minimum concern about the details of how it is done. Notice that the questions above address sharing problems regarding the central processing unit, memory, storage, and the printer.

▶ Resource Allocation

On a large computer with many users, shared resources are said to be allocated. **Resource allocation** is the process of assigning computer resources to certain programs for their use. Those same resources are deallocated—released—when the program using them is finished, and then they are reallocated elsewhere.

Sharing the Central Processing Unit

Since most computers have a single central processing unit, all programs running on the computer must share it. The sharing process is controlled by the operating system. Two approaches to sharing are multiprogramming and time-sharing. But first, let us distinguish multiprogramming from multiprocessing. **Multiprocessing** refers to the use of a powerful computer with more than one central processing unit, so that multiple programs can run simultaneously, each using its own processor.

Multiprogramming   If there is only one central processing unit (the usual case), it is not physically possible for more than one program to use it at the same time. **Multiprogramming** means that two or more programs are being executed in the same time frame, that is, **concur-**

rently, on a computer. What this really means is that the programs are taking turns; one program runs for a while and then another one runs. The key word here is *concurrently* as opposed to *simultaneously.* One program could be using the CPU while another does something else, such as sending output to the printer. Concurrent processing means that two or more programs are using the central processing unit in the same time frame—during the same hour, for instance—but not at the exact same time. In other words, concurrent processing allows one program to use one resource while another program uses another resource; this gives the illusion of simultaneous processing. As a result, there is less idle time for the computer system's resources. Concurrent processing is effective because CPU speeds are so much faster than input/output speeds. During the time it takes to execute a read instruction for one program, for example, the central processing unit can execute hundreds or even thousands of calculation instructions for another program.

Multiprogramming is **event-driven.** This means that programs share resources based on events that take place in the programs. Normally, a program is allowed to complete a certain activity (event), such as a calculation, before relinquishing the resource (the central processing unit, in this example) to another program that is waiting for it.

The operating system implements multiprogramming through a system of interrupts. An **interrupt** is a signal that causes normal program processing to be suspended temporarily. Suppose, for example, that several programs are running on a large computer, two of them a payroll program and an inventory management program. When the payroll program needs to read the next employee record, that program is interrupted—or, in a sense, interrupts itself—while the operating system takes over to do the actual reading by communicating with the disk drive. Meanwhile, since the payroll program is not using the CPU, the operating system may allocate the CPU to the inventory program to do some calculations. Once the record has been read for the payroll program, the interrupt is over and the payroll program may resume executing, perhaps calculating the employee's overtime pay, subject to the availability of the CPU. The CPU may be available right away or since programs in a multiprogramming environment may be assigned priorities, the CPU may be allocated instead to a different program of higher priority.

The point of this discussion is not to clarify what program does what when. Rather, it is to show that shared resources are being managed by the operating system in the background. Although it may appear to the user that a program is being run continuously from start to finish, in fact it is continuously being interrupted.

In large computer systems, programs that run in an event-driven multiprogramming environment are usually batch programs. Typical examples are programs for payroll, accounts receivable, sales and marketing analysis, financial planning, quality control, and stock reporting.

Time-sharing   A special case of multiprogramming, **time-sharing** is usually **time-driven** rather than event-driven. A common approach is to give each user a **time slice**—a fraction of a second—during which the computer works on a single user's tasks. However, the operating system does not wait for completion of the event; at the end of the time slice—that is, when time is up—the resources are taken away from that user and given to someone else. This is hardly noticeable to the user: When

DEFRAG

Imagine trying to find a rather long report, parts of which have been scattered among various filing cabinets and drawers in your office. You might be able to do it, but it would not be a very efficient use of your time. It would be better, of course, if the report had been stored in one place, where it could be easily found. DEFRAG, an abbreviation of *defragment,* is a utility that can be used in either DOS or Windows to organize disk files whose parts may have been scattered.

To understand how the problem could come about, consider how files are stored on disk. A file is divided into pieces, each of which is stored in its own disk sector. If you begin with a new, unused disk, then a file is simply stored in adjoining sectors, and the next file is stored in the next set of sectors, and so forth. Each of these files can be easily retrieved.

At some point, some files are going to be deleted, leaving available sectors mid-disk. When the next new file is to be stored on disk, the operating system will try to store it in the available sectors. If the new file is too large to fit in one set of sectors, it will overlap to another set of sectors, and perhaps more. A file that is stored in two or more disk areas that are not contiguous—next to each other—is said to be fragmented. As files are added and deleted and the disk fills up, many files may be fragmented. The search for fragmented files is slow, partly because of the physical movement of the disk drive arm as it moves across the disk picking up file parts.

The DEFRAG command undoes the damage. It simply rewrites the disk, arranging each file in contiguous sectors.

you are sitting before a terminal in a time-sharing system, the computer's response time will be quite short—fractions of a second—and it may seem as if you have the computer to yourself.

Response time is the time between your typed computer request and the computer's reply. Even if you are working on a calculation and the operating system interrupts it, sending you to the end of the line until other users have had their turns, you may not notice that you have been deprived of service. Not all computer systems give ideal service all the time, however; if a computer system is trying to serve too many users at the same time, response time may slow down noticeably.

Typical time-sharing applications are those with many users, each of whom has a series of brief, randomly occurring actions; examples include credit checking, point-of-sale systems, and airline reservation systems. Each of these systems has many users, perhaps hundreds, who need to share the system resources.

Sharing Memory

What if you have a very large program for which it might be difficult to find space in memory? Or what if several programs are competing for space in memory? These questions are related to memory management. **Memory management** is the process of allocating memory to programs and of keeping the programs in memory separate from one another.

There are many methods of memory management. Some systems simply divide memory into separate areas, each of which can hold a program. The problem is how to know how big the areas, sometimes called **partitions** or **regions**, should be; at least one of them should be large enough to hold the largest anticipated program. Some systems use memory areas that are not of a fixed size; that is, the sizes can change to meet the needs of the current assortment of programs. In either case, whether the areas are of a fixed or variable size, there is a problem with unused memory between programs. When these memory spaces are too small to be used, space is wasted.

Foreground and Background Large all-purpose computers often divide their memory into foreground and background areas. The **foreground** is generally for programs that have higher priority and therefore receive more CPU time. A typical foreground program is in a time-sharing environment, with the user at a terminal awaiting response. That is, a foreground program is interactive, with the CPU often unused while the user is entering the next request. Thus, there is CPU time available for the waiting background programs. The **background**, as the name implies, is for programs with less pressing schedules and, thus, lower priorities and less CPU time. Typical background programs are batch programs in a multiprogramming environment. Foreground programs are given privileged status—more turns for the central processing unit and other resources—and background programs take whatever they need that is not currently in use by another program. Lists of programs waiting to run are kept in **queues** suitable to their job class.

Virtual Storage Many computer systems manage memory by using a technique called **virtual storage** (also called **virtual memory**). The virtual storage concept means that part of the program is stored on disk and is brought into memory for execution only as needed. (Since only one part of a program can be executing at any given time, the parts not

MAKING THE RIGHT CONNECTIONS

THE NATURE CONSERVANCY ONLINE

The Nature Conservancy is a non-profit organization that buys land, particularly shore and woodlands, to preserve it forever for the public. As all nonprofit organizations must, the conservancy solicits donations to support its cause. The conservancy has found a method to receive donations that is reliable and thrifty: contributions online.

A conservancy donor who agrees to be a sustaining member completes a form agreeing to a stipulated monthly dollar amount to be transferred electronically

from the donor's bank account to the conservancy's bank account. For this service, the conservancy pays 40¢ to a service bureau and

10¢ to the bank, for a total of 50¢ per transaction, as compared to paying 92¢ per transaction for processing checks that come through the mail.

The conservancy has enjoyed other benefits from its online approach, including increased contributions, improved membership retention, and lowered administrative costs. A benefit that is particularly satisfying to the conservancy is that online contributions do not require any paper, thus saving trees.

currently needed are left on the disk). Virtual storage causes the program to appear to be using more memory space than is actually the case. Since only part of the program is in memory at any given time, the amount of memory needed for a program is minimized. Memory, in this case, is considered **real storage**, while the secondary storage (hard disk, most likely) holding the rest of the program is considered virtual storage.

Virtual storage can be implemented in a variety of ways. Consider the paging method, for example. Suppose you have a very large program, which means there will be difficulty finding space for it in the computer's shared memory. If your program is divided into small pieces, it will be easier to find places to put those pieces. This is essentially what paging does. **Paging** is the process of dividing a program into equal-size pieces called **pages** and storing them in equal-size memory spaces called **page frames**. All pages and page frames are the same fixed size, typically 2KB or 4KB. The pages are stored in memory in *noncontiguous* locations, that is, locations not necessarily next to each other.

Even though the pages are not right next to each other in memory, the operating system is able to keep track of them. It does this by using a **page table**, which, like an index, lists each page that is part of the program and the corresponding beginning memory address where it has been placed.

Memory Protection   In a multiprogramming environment it is theoretically possible for the computer, while executing one program, to destroy or modify another program by transferring to the wrong memory locations. That is, without protection, one program might accidentally hop into the middle of another, causing destruction of data and general chaos. This, of course, is not permitted. To avoid this problem, the operating system confines each program to certain defined limits in memory. If a program inadvertently attempts to enter some memory area outside its limits, the operating system terminates the execution of that program. This process of keeping one program from straying into another is called **memory protection**.

Sharing Storage Resources

The operating system keeps track of which file is where and responds to commands to manipulate files. But the situation is complicated by the possibility that more than one user may want to read or write a record from the same disk pack at the same time. Again, it is the operating system that keeps track of the input and output requests and processes them, usually in the order received. Any program instruction to read or write a record is routed to the operating system, which processes the request and then returns control to the program.

Sharing Printing Resources

Suppose a half-dozen programs are active, but the computer has only one printer. If all programs took turns printing out their output a line or two at a time, interspersed with the output of other programs, the resulting printed report would be worthless. To get around this problem, a process called **spooling** is used: Each program writes onto a disk each file that is to be printed. Or, to be more accurate, the program thinks it is writing to the printer, but the operating system intercepts that output and sends it instead to the disk. When the entire file is on the disk, spooling is complete, and the disk files are printed intact.

Spooling also addresses the problem of relatively slow printer speeds. Writing a record on disk is much faster than writing that same record on a printer. A program, therefore, completes execution more quickly if records to be printed are written temporarily on disk. The actual printing can be done at some later time, when printing will not slow program execution. Some installations use a separate (usually smaller) computer dedicated exclusively to the printing of spooled files; some print during off-hours or overnight so that smaller, more immediate jobs can use the printer during the day.

Service Programs

Most of the resource allocation tasks just described are done by the operating system without involvement by a user. For example, activities such as paging and spooling go on without explicit commands from users. But the operating system can also perform explicit services at the request of the user.

Why reinvent the wheel? Duplication of effort is what **service programs**, also known as **utilities**, are supposed to avoid. Such prewritten programs perform many secondary chores, such as backing up and restoring files, compressing files and entire hard disks, locating files, and ferreting out computer viruses. As we have noted, strictly speaking, these utilities are considered part of the system software but not part of the operating system.

★ ★ ★ ★

Now that we have examined two major topics related to programming—the programming process and operating systems—we can put these tasks in perspective. Our next topic is systems analysis and design, which shows you the big picture.

CHAPTER REVIEW

Summary and Key Terms

- An **operating system** is a set of programs that lies between applications software and the computer hardware. **System software** means all programs related to coordinating computer operations, including the operating system, programming language translators, and service programs.

- The **supervisor program**, most of which remains in memory, is called *resident*. The supervisor controls the entire operating system and loads into memory *nonresident* operating system programs from disk storage as needed.

- An operating system has three main functions: (1) manage the computer's resources, such as the central processing unit, memory, disk drives, and printers; (2) establish a user interface; and (3) execute and provide services for applications software.

- Loading the operating system into memory is called **booting** the system.

- The > in C:\> is a **prompt**, a signal that the system is waiting for you to give an instruction to the computer. To execute a given DOS program, a user must type a **command**, a name that invokes a specific DOS program.

- A key product is **Microsoft Windows**, software with a colorful **graphical user interface (GUI)**. Windows offers on-screen pictures called **icons** and both **pull-down** and **pop-up menus**, both of which encourage pointing and clicking with a mouse, an approach that can make computer use faster and easier.

- Early versions of Windows were merely a layer of software over the operating system, called an **operating environment** or **shell**.

- Microsoft Windows 95 is a true operating system and not a shell. A key feature is **plug and play**, a concept that lets the computer configure itself when a new component is added. A Windows technology called **object linking and embedding (OLE)** lets you embed or link one document with another. Windows 98 is built on the same code base as Windows 95, and has a similar look and user interaction. In particular, Windows 98 incorporates Internet Explorer, a browser, into the operating system.

- Windows NT (for *new technology*) is meant mostly for corporate, networked environments. It looks exactly like Windows 95 but has been engineered for stability and has much stronger security features. Windows CE (for *consumer electronics*) is a scaled back version of Windows 98, meant for handheld organizers and other new digital appliances.

- A **network operating system (NOS)** is designed to let computers on a network share resources such as hard disks and printers. A NOS supports resource sharing, data security, troubleshooting, and administrative control. Parts of the NOS run on the server computer, while other NOS components run on the client computers.

- **Resource allocation** is the process of assigning computer resources to certain programs for their use.

- **Multiprocessing** means that a computer with more than one central processing unit can run multiple programs simultaneously, each using its own processor.

- **Multiprogramming** is running two or more programs in the same time frame, **concurrently**, on the same computer. Multiprogramming is **event-driven**, meaning that one program is allowed to use a particular resource (such as the central processing unit) to complete a certain activity (event) before relinquishing the resource to another program. In multiprogramming, the operating system uses **interrupts**, which are signals that temporarily suspend the execution of individual programs.

- **Time-sharing** is a special case of multiprogramming in which several people use one computer at the same time. Time-sharing is **time-driven**—each user is given a **time slice** in which the computer works on that user's tasks before moving on to another user's tasks. **Response time** is the time between the user's typed computer request and the computer's reply.

- **Memory management** is the process of allocating memory to programs and of keeping the programs in memory separate from each other. Some systems simply divide memory into separate areas, sometimes called **partitions** or **regions**, each of which can hold a program. Large all-purpose computers often divide memory into a **foreground** area for programs with higher priority and a **background** area for programs with lower priority. Programs waiting to be run are kept on the disk in **queues.**
- In the **virtual storage** (or **virtual memory**) technique of memory management, part of the application program is stored on disk and is brought into memory only when needed for execution. Memory is considered **real storage;** the secondary storage holding the rest of the program is considered virtual storage.
- Virtual storage can be implemented in several ways, one of which is paging. **Paging** divides a program into equal-size pieces **(pages)** that fit exactly into corresponding noncontiguous memory spaces **(page frames).** The operating system keeps track of page locations using an index-like **page table.**
- In multiprogramming, **memory protection** is an operating system process that defines the limits of each program in memory, thus preventing programs from accidentally destroying or modifying one another.
- **Spooling** writes each file to be printed temporarily onto a disk instead of printing it immediately. When this spooling process is complete, all the appropriate files from a particular program can be printed intact.
- **Service programs,** also called **utilities,** are prewritten standard programs that perform many tasks such as compressing files and ferreting out viruses.

Quick Poll

Compare your answers to those of your colleagues or classmates.

1. Regarding operating systems:
   - ❏ a. I'll be an operating system minimalist. An operating system is necessary, of course, but there's no need to know the nitty-gritty details.
   - ❏ b. I want to know much more, so that I have a thorough background.
   - ❏ c. I want to know all the tricks and tips that will make my computer interface more convenient, but I don't need to know the details behind the scenes.
2. When it comes to learning different operating systems,
   - ❏ a. I'm pretty flexible. Since operating systems are ever-changing, I'll change with them. It is not a problem.
   - ❏ b. I hope I work some place where they have the latest operating system and will keep it for a while, so that I can concentrate on my work.
   - ❏ c. The more variety the better. I'd like to have varied experiences. If nothing else, it looks good on my résumé.

Discussion Questions

1. How would your access to computers be affected if there were no operating systems?
2. How do you explain the rapid acceptance of Microsoft Windows?
3. Which of these kinds of operating systems might you expect to use in your career: Personal computer operating system? Large computer operating system? Network operating system? All of these? Will it depend on the type of job you have?

Student Study Guide

Multiple Choice

1. An operating system is a
   a. set of users
   b. set of programs
   c. form of time-sharing
   d. supervisor program
2. In multiprogramming, two or more programs can be executed
   a. by optimizing compilers
   b. simultaneously
   c. with two computers
   d. concurrently
3. Time-sharing of resources by users is usually
   a. based on time slices
   b. event-driven
   c. based on input
   d. operated by spooling
4. Management of an operating system is handled by
   a. an interpreter
   b. utility programs
   c. the supervisor program
   d. the CPU
5. The process of allocating main memory to programs and keeping the programs in memory separate from one another is called
   a. memory protection
   b. virtual storage
   c. memory management
   d. real storage
6. The Windows version especially planned for strong stability and security:
   a. XL
   b. OL
   c. NT
   d. NS
7. The technique in shared systems that avoids interspersed printout from several programs is
   a. paging
   b. slicing
   c. queuing
   d. spooling
8. The technique whereby part of the program is stored on disk and is brought into memory for execution as needed is called
   a. memory allocation
   b. virtual storage
   c. interrupts
   d. prioritized memory
9. Part of a NOS runs on client computers and part of it runs on the
   a. page frame
   b. page table
   c. server
   d. shell
10. OLE refers to
    a. embedding
    b. events
    c. paging
    d. operating environments
11. Another name for an operating environment is
    a. page
    b. shell
    c. layer
    d. supervisor
12. Loading the operating system into a personal computer is called
    a. booting
    b. interrupting
    c. prompting
    d. paging
13. Which one of the following uses graphical icons?
    a. spool
    b. utility program
    c. page
    d. GUI
14. In multiprogramming, the process of confining each program to certain defined limits in memory is called
    a. spooling
    b. program scheduling
    c. time-sharing
    d. memory protection
15. The corresponding memory spaces for pages are called
    a. page utilities
    b. page blocks
    c. page frames
    d. page modules
16. The time between the user's request and the computer's reply
    a. concurrent time
    b. allocation time
    c. response time
    d. event time
17. An on-screen picture:
    a. page
    b. icon
    c. NOS
    d. spool
18. Running programs with more than one processor:
    a. interrupting
    b. multiprocessing
    c. embedding
    d. multiprogramming
19. Page frames are typically
    a. 1KB or 2KB
    b. 2KB or 3KB
    c. 3KB or 4KB
    d. 2KB or 4KB
20. The memory area for programs with highest priority:
    a. frame
    b. page table
    c. foreground
    d. boot
21. Lists of programs waiting to be run are in
    a. page frames
    b. shells
    c. the background
    d. queues
22. Prewritten standard file-handling programs are called
    a. pull-down menus
    b. supervisors
    c. pages
    d. utilities
23. The signal that the computer is awaiting a command from the user:
    a. prompt
    b. event
    c. time slice
    d. interrupt
24. Another name for virtual memory is
    a. virtual storage
    b. background
    c. foreground
    d. utility
25. NOS refers to
    a. OLE
    b. pages
    c. booting
    d. operating system for a network

True/False

T F 1. A DOS program is invoked by issuing a command.

T F 2. The most important program in an operating system is the supervisor program.

T F 3. Multiprogramming means that two or more programs can run simultaneously.

T F 4. Time-sharing is effective because input/output speeds are so much faster than CPU speeds.

T F   5. Resource allocation means that a given program has exclusive use of computer resources.

T F   6. Background programs are usually batch programs.

T F   7. Virtual storage is a technique of memory management that appears to provide users with more memory space than is actually the case.

T F   8. With the virtual storage technique, secondary storage is considered real storage.

T F   9. Windows uses a graphical interface.

T F   10. In a network operating system, some functions are performed by the server and others by the client computers.

T F   11. Spooling is a process that results in interspersed printout from several programs.

T F   12. Shell is another name for page.

T F   13. An operating system includes system software, programming language translators, and service programs.

T F   14. Utility programs avoid duplication of effort.

T F   15. In a given memory system, all page frames are the same size.

T F   16. Time-sharing is both event-driven and time-driven.

T F   17. Resource allocation means that a NOS distributes most of its functions to the client computers.

T F   18. Virtual memory is another name for virtual storage.

T F   19. Loading the operating system into memory is called booting.

T F   20. An interrupt causes a program to stop temporarily.

T F   21. Time-sharing programs usually operate in the background of memory.

T F   22. Paging divides a program into pieces of various sizes to fit in the available memory spaces.

T F   23. Response time is the time it takes a program to run.

T F   24. OLE lets a user link from one program to another.

T F   25. Multiprocessing is simultaneous processing.

T F   26. The shared resources that the operating system manages includes the CPU, memory, storage devices, and the printer.

T F   27. Multiprogramming is one approach to sharing the CPU.

T F   28. All operating system programs must be in memory during the time an applications program is running.

T F   29. A knowledgeable user can interact directly with the hardware without invoking the operating system.

T F   30. A typical time-sharing application is processing payroll checks.

Fill-In

1. NOS stands for _____

2. The operating system program that remains resident in memory: _____

3. The term used for the time between a user's request at the terminal and the computer's reply:

_____

4. The type of system that lets two or more programs execute concurrently: _____

5. What are the program pieces called in the virtual storage technique of paging? What are the corresponding memory spaces called?

   a. _____
   b. _____

6. Simultaneous processing of more than one program using more than one processor is called

_____

7. Another name for partition:

_____.

8. High-priority programs usually operate in this part of memory: _____

9. The process of assigning computer resources to certain programs for their use is called

_____

10. The operating system keeps track of page locations using a _____

11. The process used by an operating system to avoid interspersing the printout from several programs:

_____

12. A shell program that overlays the operating system to provide a more friendly environment:

_____

13. In time-sharing, each user is given a unit of time called a _____

14. OLE stands for _____

15. Another name for service programs:

_____

16. Loading the operating system into memory is called

_____

17. Time-sharing is time-driven but multiprogramming is _____-driven.

18. How are programs kept on disk while waiting to be run? _____

19. If memory is divided into foreground and background areas, time-sharing applications are likely to be where? _____

20. What does GUI stand for?

_____

21. In multiprogramming, a condition that temporarily suspends program execution:

_____

22. Keeping programs in memory separate is called

_____

23. An alternative name for virtual storage:

_____

24. MS-DOS uses the > symbol as a

_____

25. An operating system feature that automatically configures new hardware is called

_____

Answers

Multiple Choice

1. b	6. c	11. b	16. c	21. d
2. d	7. d	12. a	17. b	22. d
3. a	8. b	13. d	18. b	23. a
4. c	9. c	14. d	19. d	24. a
5. c	10. a	15. c	20. c	25. d

True/False

1. T	6. T	11. F	16. F	21. F	26. T
2. T	7. T	12. F	17. F	22. F	27. T
3. F	8. F	13. F	18. T	23. F	28. F
4. F	9. T	14. T	19. T	24. T	29. F
5. F	10. T	15. T	20. T	25. T	30. F

Fill-In

1. network operating system
2. the supervisor program
3. response time
4. multiprogramming
5. a. pages
   b. page frames
6. multiprocessing
7. region
8. foreground
9. resource allocation
10. page table
11. spooling
12. operating environment
13. time slice
14. object linking and embedding
15. utilities
16. booting
17. event
18. in queues
19. foreground
20. graphical user interface
21. interrupt
22. memory protection
23. virtual memory
24. prompt
25. plug and play

PLANET INTERNET

THE PEOPLE CONNECTION

Although sociologists fret over the potential isolation of people focused on their personal computers, several sites cater to togetherness among online folks, going so far as to call their sites communities. Beyond this, the Internet caters to people-to-people connections by offering searches for lost friends or colleagues, advocating for missing or adoptable children, providing parent-to-parent support, listing class reunions, and even chronicling celebrities.

Virtual communities. The Well is the oldest and perhaps best-known virtual community, and they describe themselves as literate and iconoclastic. The Well has more than 200 "conferences" on topics as varied as parenting, the future, current events, and the Rockies.

Most communities offer live chat, with members contributing to the discussion, shown scrolling on the screen, from their individual computers. The home page logos of other communities also are shown here: Talk City, World Village, the Social Café, and Cybertown. Each is easy to navigate—just click on an icon—and full of content.

People search. Whatever happened to Bob? Bob can possibly be found by using the Internet, even if he never heard of it. In fact *possibly* will soon become *probably*. Two forces are coming together to make this likely. One is the steadily growing number of computers connected to the Internet. The other is the increasing amount of information about people being stored in computer databases. The 'Net provides fast access to those databases.

Standard search engines can find the name of a person if it is mentioned in a web page or in a newsgroup. More-specialized people searchers, such as WhoWhere or Switchboard, can provide an individual's address, phone number, and e-mail address. Note the WhoWhere form shown here; simply fill in the person's name and, if known, city and state, and await the return of more detailed information. Different search sites use different databases, so if you strike out with one, try others.

The Social Cafe

Specialized people-to-people. Many people want to connect with their own kind. Typical affinity groups involve a nationality, school, hobby, common interest, set of shared values, profession, or family name. There are numerous sites in all of these categories and many more. The Tribal Voice logo shown here highlights the home page for certain Native Americans. The Faces of Adoption image represents a site where adopters and children who can be adopted may come together. Reunion sites, listing gatherings by school and class, abound. Finally, if you are interested in tracking your family, look up some of the many genealogy sites.

Internet Exercises

1. **Structured exercise.** Begin with the AWL site with URL http://hepg.awl.com/capron/planet/, and use both the WhoWhere and Switchboard sites to try to locate an old friend.
2. **Freeform exercise.** Hang out in one or more virtual communities and join in the live chat.

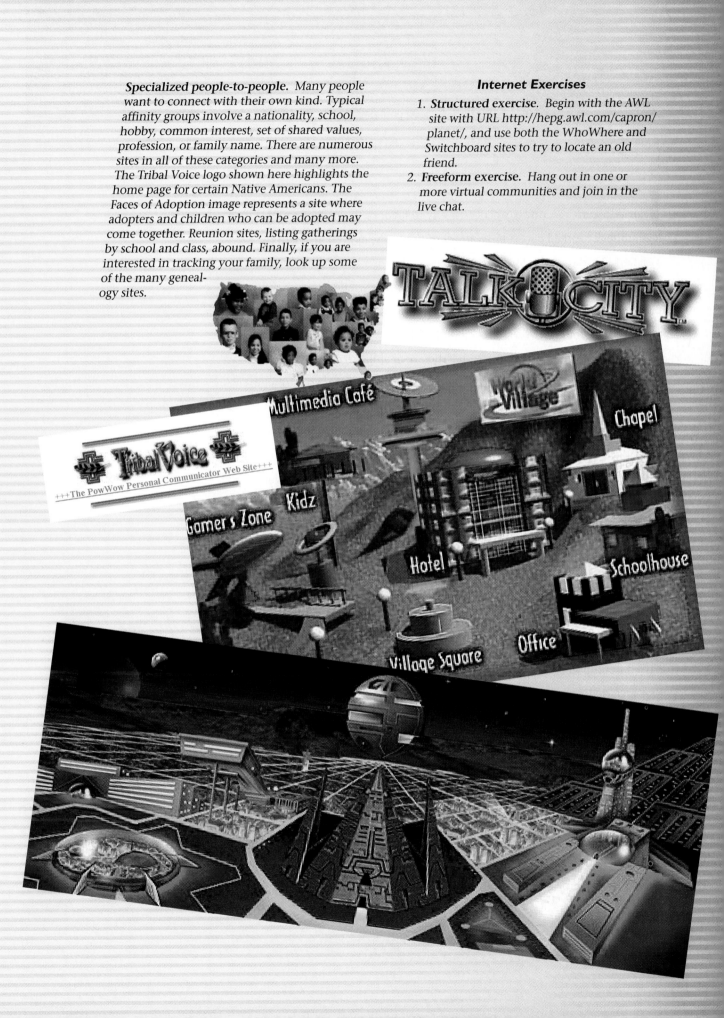

Jean Winston, a second-year college student, worked part-time as an assistant librarian at the Montlake Branch of the Carthage Public Library, which has a central library and four branches. The various libraries cooperated with one another, particularly in the exchange of books needed by library patrons. Unfortunately, the exchange system was cumbersome and unreliable. From her brief study of computers, Jean suspected that a computer system would probably improve service, but she also knew that money was scarce and funds were unlikely to be available for innovations.

The next year, however, the city passed a comprehensive bond issue that included money for the library. The library manager at the central branch immediately engaged an outside company to study how computers could be used in a library system. Jean was delighted but discovered, to her surprise, that the full-time librarians were not. Although the employees were actually in favor of the idea of computers, they were apprehensive in two ways: They worried about whether the computer would prove so efficient that it would eliminate some of their jobs, and they fretted about their own ability to use computers.

This reluctance was soon obvious to the systems analyst who visited the libraries to study the way the current system worked and to interview the library employees. Over time and many discussions, however, the systems analyst was able to reassure the librarians. A new system, whose components included self-service terminals from which customers could order a book from any branch, eventually was put in place.

Systems Analysis and Design

The Big Picture

THE SYSTEMS ANALYST

The Analyst and the System

The Systems Analyst as Change Agent

What It Takes to Be a Systems Analyst

HOW A SYSTEMS ANALYST WORKS: OVERVIEW OF THE SYSTEMS DEVELOPMENT LIFE CYCLE

PHASE 1: PRELIMINARY INVESTIGATION

Problem Definition: Nature, Scope, Objectives

Wrapping Up the Preliminary Investigation

PHASE 2: SYSTEMS ANALYSIS

Data Gathering

Data Analysis

System Requirements

Report to Management

PHASE 3: SYSTEMS DESIGN

Preliminary Design

Prototyping

Detail Design

PHASE 4: SYSTEMS DEVELOPMENT

Scheduling

Programming

Testing

PHASE 5: IMPLEMENTATION

Training

Equipment Conversion

File Conversion

System Conversion

Auditing

Evaluation

Maintenance

> The Systems Analyst

As the opening tale depicts, people are often nervous when they are about to be visited by a systems analyst. A systems analyst with any experience, however, knows that people are uneasy about having a stranger pry into their job situations and that they may be nervous about computers. Before discussing how the systems analyst helps people address change, let us begin with a few basic definitions.

The Analyst and the System

Although a systems project will be described more formally later in the chapter, let us start by defining the words *system, analysis,* and *design.* A **system** is an organized set of related components established to accomplish a certain task. There are natural systems, such as the cardiovascular system, but many systems have been planned and deliberately put into place by people. For example, a fast-food franchise has a system for serving a customer, including taking an order, assembling the food, and collecting the amount due. A **computer system** is a system that has a computer as one of its components.

Systems analysis is the process of studying an existing system to determine how it works and how it meets user needs. Systems analysis lays the groundwork for improvements to the system. The analysis involves an investigation, which in turn usually involves establishing a relationship with the client for whom the analysis is being done and with the users of the system. The **client** is the person or organization contracting to have the work done. The **users** are people who will have contact with the system, usually employees and customers. For instance, in a fast-food system, the client is probably the franchise owner or manager, and the users are both the franchise employees and the customers.

Systems design is the process of developing a plan for an improved system, based on the results of the systems analysis. For instance, an analysis of a fast-food franchise may reveal that customers stand in unacceptably long lines waiting to order. A new system design might involve plans to have employees press buttons that match ordered items, causing a display on an overhead screen that can be seen by other employees who can quickly assemble the order.

The **systems analyst** normally performs both analysis and design. (The term *systems designer* is not common, although it is used in some places.) In some computer installations a person who is mostly a programmer may also do some systems analysis and thus have the title **pro-**

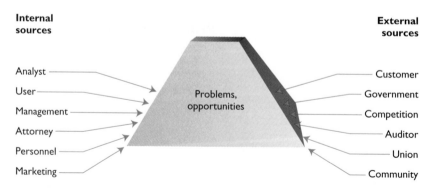

Figure 14-1 Impetus for change.
Internal or external sources can initiate a system change.

grammer/analyst. Traditionally, most people who have become systems analysts started out as programmers.

A systems analysis and design project does not spring out of thin air. There must be an *impetus*—motivation—for change and related *authority* for the change. The impetus for change may be the result of an internal force, such as the organization's management deciding that a computer could be useful in warehousing and inventory, or an external force, such as government reporting requirements or customer complaints about billing (Figure 14-1). Authority for the change, of course, comes from higher management.

The Systems Analyst as Change Agent

The systems analyst fills the role of **change agent**, the catalyst or persuader who overcomes the natural reluctance to change within an organization. The key to success is to involve the people of the client organization in the development of the new system. The common industry phrase is **user involvement**, and nothing could be more important to the success of the system. Some analysts like to think in terms of who "owns" the system. If efforts toward user involvement are successful, the user begins to think of the system as *my* system, rather than *their* system. Once that happens, the analyst's job becomes much easier.

What It Takes to Be a Systems Analyst

Before understanding what kind of person might make a good systems analyst, it is necessary to look at the kinds of things an analyst does. The systems analyst has three principal functions:

- **Coordination.** An analyst must coordinate schedules and system-related tasks with a number of people: the analyst's own manager; the programmers working with the system; the system's users, from clerks to top management; the vendors selling the computer equipment; and a host of others, such as mail-room employees handling mailings and carpenters doing installation.
- **Communication, both oral and written.** The analyst may be called upon to make oral presentations to clients, users, and others involved with the system. The analyst provides written reports—documentation—on the results of the analysis and the goals and means of the design. These documents may range from a few pages long to a few inches thick.
- **Planning and design.** The systems analyst, with the participation of members of the client organization, plans and designs the new system. This function involves all the activities from the beginning of the project until the final implementation of the system.

In light of these principal functions, the kinds of personal qualities that are desirable in a systems analyst become apparent: An *analytical mind* and *good communication skills*. Perhaps not so obvious, however, are qualities such as *self-discipline* and *self-direction*, since a systems analyst often works without close supervision. An analyst must have good *organizational skills* to be able to keep track of all the facts about the system. An analyst also needs *creativity* to envision the new system. Finally, an analyst needs the *ability to work without tangible results*. There can be long dry spells when the analyst moves numbly from meeting to meeting and it can seem that little is being accomplished.

Checking the Classified Ads

Compare these two classified advertisements:

Position Wanted as Systems Analyst. Expertise in systems design. Good technical skills— programming, database design, web site design. Experienced on variety of hardware. References available. Jim. 937-4783.

Wanted: Systems Analyst. Strong user orientation. Ability to assess system impact on user departments. Implementation skills, especially motivation and training of users. Send resume to Athens Chemical, P.O. Box 5, Eugene, OR 97405.

Could Jim be the person who Athens is looking for? Possibly, but you would not know it from their classified ads, which appear to have no common ground. If Jim were asked if he was user-oriented, he would—if he is smart—say yes, and Athens, of course, would be seeking an employee with technical skills as well as user orientation.

Why the contrast in their ads? Systems analysts are often most proud of their technical achievements and think that these skills will be appreciated. But Athens, like other companies, has been around the block a few times and knows that technical skills mean little if the total effort does not serve the user. Managers, in survey after survey, consistently list user needs as their top priority.

Getting Practical

ANSWERING THE KILLER QUESTIONS

You will be job hunting someday, later if not sooner. If you are angling for a highly paid professional position, you can expect to be looked over by several highly paid professional people. Their questions in the interview process will not be trivial. Here are some typical questions—and the hoped-for answers—posed by interviewers to prospective systems analysts.

Question: How would you reinvent our business, from a systems perspective, if you had a blank piece of paper and no constraints? (Well, we said they were killer questions.)

Answer: The interviewer is not really serious about soliciting a plan to reinvent the company. He or she wants to know if you have done your homework on the company and to see if you can come up with some useful-sounding suggestions off the cuff for how business could be better, faster, or cheaper.

Question: Describe a project in which you have been involved that didn't go particularly well. What went wrong and how could it have been more successful?

Answer: They are looking for ownership here—don't point fingers elsewhere. Take some—not all—of the responsibility and say how you learned from the experience.

Question: How can you tell a good program from a bad one?

Answer: User-user-user is your answer. It is good if it meets user specs, fills user needs, makes users happy, and so forth. After you have exhausted that topic, add a few sentences about the program being well planned, easy-to-follow, and well documented. Don't get caught in a techie-talk trap.

Question: When you have had a day at work that makes you really satisfied, what made it a good day? What makes a bad day?

Answer: People alert. Give a people answer, not an I-solved-a-technical-problem answer, at least not right away. Most importantly, don't relate a bad day to a people problem. They want to know that you are more than a technician, that you can work well on a team and with clients.

Although these questions are directed to systems analysts, much of their content shows up in interviews for any type of important job where the focus is on people.

▶ How a Systems Analyst Works: Overview of the Systems Development Life Cycle

Whether you are investigating how to improve a bank's customer relations, or how to track inventory for a jeans warehouse, or how to manage egg production on a chicken ranch, or any other task, you will proceed by using the **systems development life cycle (SDLC)**. The systems development life cycle can be described in five phases:

1. Preliminary investigation—determining the problem
2. Analysis—understanding the existing system

3. Design—planning the new system
4. Development—doing the work to bring the new system into being
5. Implementation—converting to the new system

These simple explanations for each phase will be expanded to full-blown discussions in subsequent sections. It is important to note at this point that moving through these five phases is not necessarily a straightforward, linear process; that is, there will doubtless be adjustments to previous phases as you move along.

As you read about the phases of a systems project, follow the Swift Sport Shoes inventory case study, which is presented in accompanying boxes. Although space limitations prohibit us from presenting a complete analysis and design project, this case study gives the flavor of the real thing.

Phase 1: Preliminary Investigation

The **preliminary investigation**, often called the **feasibility study** or **system survey**, is the initial investigation, a brief study of the problem to determine whether the systems project should be pursued. You, as the systems analyst, need to determine what the problem is and what to do about it. The net result will be a rough plan for how—and whether—to proceed with the project.

Before you can decide whether to proceed, you must be able to describe the problem. To do this, you

CASE STUDY

PRELIMINARY INVESTIGATION

You are employed as a systems analyst by Software Systems, Inc., a company offering packaged software as well as consulting and outsourcing services. Software Systems has received a request for a consultant; the client is Swift Sport Shoes, a chain of stores carrying a huge selection of footwear for every kind of sport. Your boss hands you, a systems analyst, this assignment, telling you to contact company officer Kris Iverson.

In your initial meeting with Mr. Iverson, who is vice president of finance, you learn that the first Swift store opened in San Francisco in 1984. The store has been profitable since the second year. Nine new stores have been added

in the metropolitan area and outlying shopping malls. These stores also show a net profit; Swift has been riding the crest of the fitness boom. But even though sales have been gratifying, Mr. Iverson is convinced that costs are higher than they should be and that customer service has never been adequate.

In particular, Mr. Iverson is disturbed about inventory problems, which are causing frequent stock shortages and increasing customer dissatisfaction. The company has a minicomputer at headquarters, where management offices are. Although there is a small information systems staff, their experience is mainly in batch processing for financial systems. Mr. Iverson envisions more sophisticated technology for an inventory system and figures that outside expertise is needed to design

it. He introduces you to Robin Christie, who is in charge of purchasing and inventory. Mr. Iverson also tells you that he has sent a memo to all company officers and store managers indicating the purpose of your presence and his support of a study of the current system. Before the end of your visit with Mr. Iverson, the two of you construct the organization chart shown in Figure 14-2.

In subsequent interviews with Ms. Christie and other Swift personnel, you find that deteriorating customer service seems to be due to a lack of information about inventory supplies. Together, you and Ms. Christie determine the problem definition, as shown in Figure 14-4. Mr. Iverson accepts your report, in which you outline the problem definition and suggest a full analysis.

will work with the users. One of your tools will be an **organization chart**, which is a hierarchical drawing showing the organization's management by name and title. Figure 14-2 shows an example of an organization chart. Many organizations already have such a chart and can give you a copy. If the chart does not exist, you must ask some questions and then make it yourself. Constructing such a chart is not an idle task. If you are to work effectively within the organization, you need to understand the lines of authority through the formal communication channels.

Problem Definition: Nature, Scope, Objectives

Your initial aim is to define the problem. You and the users must come to an agreement on these points: You must agree on the nature of the problem and then designate a limited scope. In the process you will also determine what the objectives of the project are. Figure 14-3 shows an overview of the problem definition process, and Figure 14-4 gives an example related to the Swift Sport Shoes project.

Nature of the Problem   Begin by determining the true nature of the problem. Sometimes what appears to be the problem turns out to be, on a closer look, only a symptom. For example, suppose that you are examining customer complaints of late deliveries. Your brief study may reveal

Figure 14-2 An organization chart. The chart shows the lines of authority and formal communication channels. This example shows the organizational setup for Swift Sport Shoes, a chain of stores.

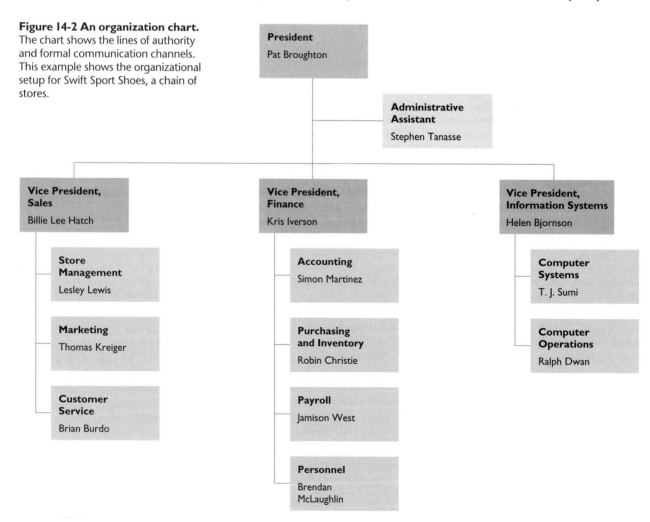

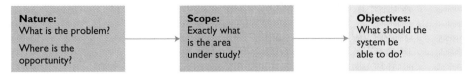

Figure 14-3 Problem definition overview.

that the problem is not in the shipping department, as you first thought, but in the original ordering process.

Scope   Establishing the scope of the problem is critical because problems tend to expand if no firm boundaries are established. Limitations are also necessary to stay within the eventual budget and schedule. So in the beginning the analyst and user must agree on the scope of the project: what the new or revised system is supposed to do—and not do.

Objectives   You will soon come to understand what the user needs— that is, what the user thinks the system should be able to do. You will want to express these needs as objectives. Examine the objectives for the Swift inventory process. The people who run the existing inventory system already know what such a system must do. It remains for you and them to work out how this can be achieved on a computer system. In the next phase, the systems analysis phase, you will produce a more specific list of system requirements based on these objectives.

SWIFT SPORT SHOES: PROBLEM DEFINITION

True Nature of the Problem

The nature of the problem is the existing manual inventory system. In particular:

- Products are frequently out of stock
- There is little interstore communication about stock items
- Store managers have no information about stock levels on a day-to-day basis
- Ordering is done haphazardly

Scope

The scope of the project will be limited to the development of an inventory system using appropriate computer technology.

Objectives

The new automated inventory system should provide the following:

- Adequate stock maintained in stores
- Automatic stock reordering
- Stock distribution among stores
- Management access to current inventory information
- Ease of use
- Reduced operating costs of the inventory function

Figure 14-4 Problem definition. The nature and scope of the problem along with system objectives are shown for the Swift Sport Shoes system.

Some Tips for Successful Interviewing

- Plan questions in advance, even if you vary from them during the interview.
- Dress and behave in a businesslike manner.
- Avoid technical jargon.
- Respect the respondent's schedule. Make an appointment; do not just drop in.
- Listen carefully to the answers and observe the respondent's voice inflection and body movements for clues to evaluate responses.
- Avoid office gossip and discussion of the respondent's personal problems.

Wrapping Up the Preliminary Investigation

The preliminary investigation, which is necessarily brief, should result in some sort of report, perhaps only a few pages long, telling management what you have found and listing your recommendations. Furthermore, money is always a factor in all go/no-go decisions: Is the project financially feasible? At this point management has three choices: They can (1) drop the matter; (2) fix the problem immediately, if it is simple; or (3) authorize you to go on to the next phase for a closer look.

▶ Phase 2: Systems Analysis

Let us suppose that management has decided to continue. Remember that the purpose of systems analysis is to understand the existing system. A related goal is to establish the system requirements. The best way to understand a system is to gather all the data you can about it; this data must then be organized and analyzed. During the systems analysis phase, then, you will be concerned with (1) data gathering and (2) data analysis. Keep in mind that the system being analyzed may or may not already be a computerized system.

Data Gathering

Data gathering is expensive and requires a lot of legwork and time. There is no standard procedure for gathering data because each system is unique. But there are certain sources that are commonly used: written documents, interviews, questionnaires, observation, and sampling. Sometimes you will use all of these sources, but in most cases it will be appropriate to use some and not others.

Written Documents These include procedures manuals, reports, forms, and any other kind of material bearing on the problem that you find in the organization. Take time to get a copy of each form an organization uses.

Interviews A key advantage of interviews is their flexibility; as the interviewer, you can change the direction of your questions if you discover a productive area of investigation. Another bonus is that you can probe with open-ended questions that people would balk at answering on paper. You can also observe the respondent's voice inflection and body motions, which may tell you more than words alone. Finally, of course, there is the bonus of getting to know clients better and establishing a rapport with them, an important factor in promoting user involvement in the system from the beginning. Interviews have certain drawbacks: they are time-consuming and therefore expensive. If you need to find out about procedures from 40 mail clerks, you are better off using a questionnaire.

There are two types of interviews, structured and unstructured. A **structured interview** includes only questions that have been planned and written out in advance. A structured interview is useful when it is desirable—or required by law—to ask identical questions of several people. However, the **unstructured interview** is often more productive, since the interviewer may stray from the line of questioning if appropriate.

Questionnaires   Unlike interviews, questionnaires can be used to get information from large groups. Also, due to the large number of respondents, sometimes a trend or problem pattern emerges that would not be evident from a small number of interviews. They allow people to respond anonymously and, presumably, more truthfully. Questionnaires do have disadvantages, however, including the problem of getting them returned and the possibility of biased answers.

Observation   As an analyst and observer, you go into the organization and watch who interrelates with whom. In particular, you observe how data flows: from desk to desk, fax to fax, or computer to computer. Note how data comes into and leaves the organization. Initially, you make arrangements with a group supervisor and make everyone aware of the purpose of your visit. Be sure to return on more than one occasion so that the people under observation become used to your presence. One form of observation is **participant observation;** in this form the analyst temporarily joins the activities of the group.

Sampling   You may need to collect data about quantities, costs, time periods, and other factors relevant to the system. For example, how many phone orders can be taken by an order entry clerk in an hour? If you are dealing with a major mail-order organization, such as L. L. Bean in Maine, this type of question may be best answered through a procedure called sampling: Instead of observing all 125 clerks filling orders for an hour, you pick a sample of 3 or 4 clerks. Or, in a case involving a high volume of paper output, such as customer bills, you could collect a random sample of a few dozen bills. Although the actual methods are beyond the scope of this book, it should be mentioned that there are statistical techniques that can determine exactly what sample size will yield accurate results.

Data Analysis

Your data-gathering processes will probably produce an alarming amount of paper and a strong need to get organized. It is now time to turn your attention to the second activity of this phase, data analysis. A variety of tools—charts and diagrams—are used to analyze data, not all of them appropriate for every system. You should become familiar with the techniques favored by your organization and then use the tools that suit you at the time. Two typical tools are data flow diagrams and decision tables. Data analysis shows how the current system works and helps determine the system requirements. In addition, data analysis materials will serve as the basis for documentation of the system.

Data Flow Diagrams   A **data flow diagram (DFD)** is a sort of road map that graphically shows the flow of data through a system. It is a valuable tool for depicting present procedures and data flow. Although data flow diagrams can be used in the design process, they are particularly useful for facilitating communication between you and the users during the analysis phase. Suppose, for example, you spend a couple of hours with a McDonald's franchise manager, talking about the paperwork that keeps the burgers and the customers flowing. You would probably make copious notes about what goes on where. But that is only the data-gathering function; now you must somehow analyze your findings.

CASE STUDY

SYSTEMS ANALYSIS

With the assistance of Ms. Christie, you learn more about the current inventory system. She helps set up interviews with store managers and arranges to have you observe procedures in the stores and at the warehouse. As the number of stores has increased, significant expansion has taken place in all inventory-related areas: sales, scope of merchandise, and number of vendors.

Out-of-stock situations are common. The stock shortages are not uniform across all ten stores, however; frequently, one store will be out of an item that the central warehouse or another store has on hand. The present system is not able to recognize this situation and transfer merchandise on a timely basis. There is a tendency for stock to be reordered only when the shelf is empty or nearly so. Inventory-related costs are significant, especially those for special orders of some stock items. Reports to management are minimal and often too late to be useful. Finally, there is no way to correlate order quantities with past sales records, future projections, or inventory situations.

During this period you also analyze the data as it is gathered. You prepare data flow diagrams of the various activities relating to inventory. Figure 14-6 shows the general flow of data to handle purchasing in the existing system. You prepare various decision tables, such as the one shown in Figure 14-7b.

Your written report to Mr. Iverson includes the list of system requirements in Figure 14-8.

You could come back on another day with pages of narrative for the manager to review or, instead, show an easy-to-follow picture. Most users would prefer the picture.

There are a variety of notations for data flow diagrams. The notation used here has been chosen because it is informal and easy to draw and read. The elements of a data flow diagram are processes, files, sources and sinks, and vectors, as shown in Figure 14-5. Note also the DFD for Swift Sport Shoes (Figure 14-6) as you follow this discussion.

Decision Tables   A **decision table**, also called a **decision logic table**, is a standard table of the logical decisions that must be made regarding potential conditions in a given system. Decision tables are useful in cases that involve a series of interrelated decisions; their use helps to ensure that no alternatives are overlooked. Programmers can code portions of a program right from a decision table. Figure 14-7a shows the format of a decision table; Figure 14-7b gives an example of a decision table that applies to the Swift Sport Shoes system.

System Requirements

As noted earlier, the purpose of gathering and analyzing data is twofold: to understand the system and, as a by-product of that understanding, to establish the **system requirements**, a detailed list of the things the system must be able to do. You need to determine and document specific user needs. A system that a bank teller uses, for example, needs to be able to retrieve a customer record and display it on a screen within five seconds.

The importance of accurate requirements cannot be overemphasized, because the design of the new system will be based on the system requirements. Furthermore, the analyst

Figure 14-5 Symbols used in data flow diagrams. Circles represent *processes*, the actions taken on the data—comparing, checking, stamping, authorizing, filing, and so forth. An open-ended box represents a *file*, a repository of data: a disk file, a set of papers in a file cabinet, or even mail in an in-basket or blank envelopes in a supply bin. A *source* is a data origin outside the system under study. An example is a payment sent to a department store by a charge customer; the customer is a source of data. A *sink* is a destination for data going outside the system; an example is the bank that receives money deposits from the accounts receivable department. A source or a sink is represented by a square. *Vectors* are simply arrows, lines with directional notations showing the flow of data.

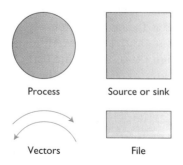

Process   Source or sink

Vectors   File

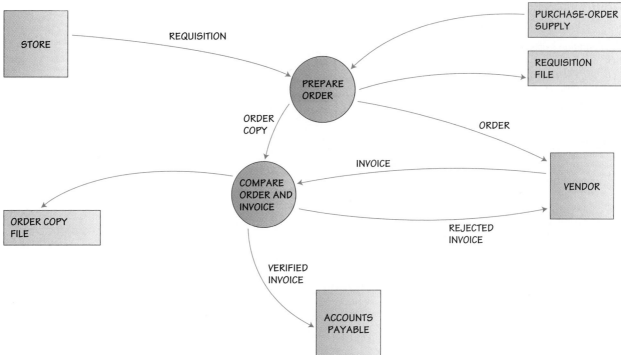

and management must come to clear agreement on the system requirements, since a misunderstanding can result in a poor evaluation of the
new system and even cause a delay in project completion. Note the
requirements for the Swift system shown in Figure 14-8.

Report to Management

When you have finished the systems analysis phase, you present a
report to management. This report summarizes the problems you found
in the current system, describes the requirements for the new system,
includes a cost analysis, and makes recommendations on what course to
take next. If the project is significant, you may also make a formal presentation, including visual displays. If management decides to pursue
the project, you move on to phase 3.

➤ Phase 3: Systems Design

The systems design phase is the phase in which you actually plan the new
system. This phase is divided into two subphases: **preliminary design**, in
which the analyst establishes the new system concept, followed by **detail
design**, in which the analyst determines exact design specifications. The
reason this phase is divided into two parts is that an analyst wants to
make sure management approves the overall plan before spending time
and money on the details of the new system.

Preliminary Design

The first task of preliminary design is to review the system requirements
and then consider some of the major aspects of a system. Should the system be centralized or distributed? Should the system be online? Can the

Figure 14-6 A data flow diagram.
This "map" shows the current flow of
data in the purchasing department at
Swift Sport Shoes. The diagram (greatly
simplified) includes authorization for
purchases of goods, purchase-order
preparation, and verification of the vendor's invoice against the purchase order.
Note that the stores, vendors, and
accounts payable are in square boxes
because they are outside the purchasing
department.

Figure 14-7 Decision tables. (a) The format of a decision table. The table is organized according to the logic that "If this condition exists or is met, then do this." (b) A decision table example. This decision table, which describes the current ordering procedure at Swift Sport Shoes, takes into consideration whether a requisition for goods from a store is valid, the availability of the wanted goods in the warehouse or some other Swift store, whether the quantity ordered warrants an inventory order, and whether the order is a special order for a customer. Examine rule 4. The requisition is valid, so proceed. The desired goods are not available in either the warehouse or in another store, so they must be ordered. However, there is not the required volume of customer demand to place a standard inventory order now, so the requisition is put on hold until there is. (In other words, this order will be joined with others.) And finally, since this is a special customer order and the order is on hold, a back-order notice is sent.

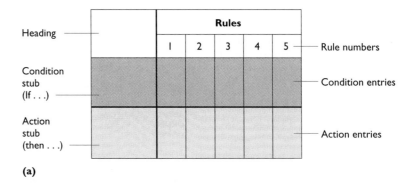

(a)

Order procedure	Rules					
	1	2	3	4	5	6
Valid requisition	Y	Y	Y	Y	Y	N
Available warehouse	Y	N	N	N	N	—
Available another store	—	Y	N	N	N	—
Required order volume	—	—	Y	N	N	—
Special customer order	—	—	—	Y	N	—
Transfer goods from warehouse	X					
Transfer goods from store		X				
Determine vendor			X			
Send purchase order			X			
Hold requisition				X	X	
Send back order notice				X		
Reject requisition						X

(b)

SWIFT SPORT SHOES: REQUIREMENTS

The requirements for the Swift Sport Shoes inventory system are as follows:

- Capture inventory data from sales transactions
- Implement automatic inventory reordering
- Implement a standardized interstore transfer system
- Provide both on-demand and scheduled management reports
- Provide security and accounting controls throughout the system
- Provide a user-oriented system whose online usage can be learned by a new user in one training class
- Reduce operating costs of the inventory function by 20%

Figure 14-8 System requirements. These are the requirements for an inventory system for Swift Sport Shoes.

system be run on the users' personal computers? How will input data be captured? What kind of reports will be needed? The questions can go on and on.

A key question that should be answered early on is whether packaged software should be purchased, as opposed to having programmers write custom software. That is, instead of designing, developing, and implementing a new system from scratch, you may be able to obtain an existing system—**acquisition by purchase**—that meets your client's requirements. This may be tricky because clients often think that their problems are unique. However, if the new system falls into one of several major categories, such as accounting or inventory control, you will find that many software vendors offer packaged solutions. A packaged solution should meet at least 75 percent of client requirements. For the remaining 25 percent, the client can adjust ways of doing business to match the package software or, more expensively, **customize**, or alter, the packaged software to meet the client's special needs.

Another possibility is **outsourcing**, which means turning the system over to an outside agency to develop. Large organizations that employ their own computer professionals may outsource certain projects, especially if the subject matter is one in which a reputable outsourcing firm specializes. The outsourcing company then turns the completed system over to the client. Some organizations outsource most or all of their computer projects, preferring to avoid bearing the costs of keeping their own staff. (In fact, organizations that do not retain their own computer professionals usually outsource the entire project from its inception; this is the case, for example, in the accompanying case study, in which Swift Sport Shoes engages Systems Software, Inc.)

If you proceed with an in-house design, then, together with key personnel from the client organization, you determine an overall plan. In fact, it is common to offer alternative plans, called **candidates**. Each candidate meets the client's requirements but with variations in features and costs. The chosen candidate is usually the one that best meets the client's current needs and is flexible enough to meet future needs.

At this stage it is wise to make a formal presentation of the selected plan, or possibly of all the alternatives. The point is that you do not want to commit time and energy to—nor does the client want to pay for—a detailed design until you and the client agree on the basic design. Such presentations often include a drawing of the system from a user's perspective, such as the one shown in Figure 14-9 for the Swift Sport Shoes system. This is the time to emphasize system benefits; see the list in Figure 14-10.

Prototyping

Building a prototype—a sort of guinea-pig model of the system—has become a standard approach in many organizations. Considered from a systems viewpoint, a **prototype** is a limited working system, or a subset of a system, that is developed quickly, sometimes in just a few days. Some organizations use prototyping very loosely, so that it has no true functionality but can produce output that *looks like* output of the finished system, so that users can see and evaluate it. The idea is that users can get an idea of what the system might be like before it is fully developed. Many organizations develop a prototype as a working model, one that can be tinkered with and fine-tuned. No one expects users to be

Presentations

Presentations often come at the completion of a phase, especially the analysis and design phases. They give you an opportunity to formalize the project in a public way and to look good in front of the brass. The full range of presentation techniques—using visuals, planning logistics, keeping the audience focused, communicating effectively, and minimizing stage fright—must be topics for another book, but we can consider presentation content here.

- **State the problem.** Although you do not want to belabor the problem statement, you do want to show you understand it.
- **State the benefits.** These are a new system's whole reason for being, so your argument here should be carefully planned. Will the system improve accuracy, speed turnaround, save processing time, save money? The more specific you can be, the better. Use terminology appropriate to your audience; do not lapse into technical jargon.
- **Explain the analysis/design.** Here you should give a general presentation and then be prepared to take questions about specifics. Remember that higher management will not be interested in hearing all the details.
- **Present a schedule.** How long will it take to carry out the plan? Give your audience the time frame.
- **Estimate the costs.** The costs include development costs (those required to construct the system) and operating costs (the ongoing costs of running the system). You will also need to tell your audience how long it is going to be before they get a return on their original investment.
- **Answer questions.** A good rule of thumb is to save half the allotted time for questions.

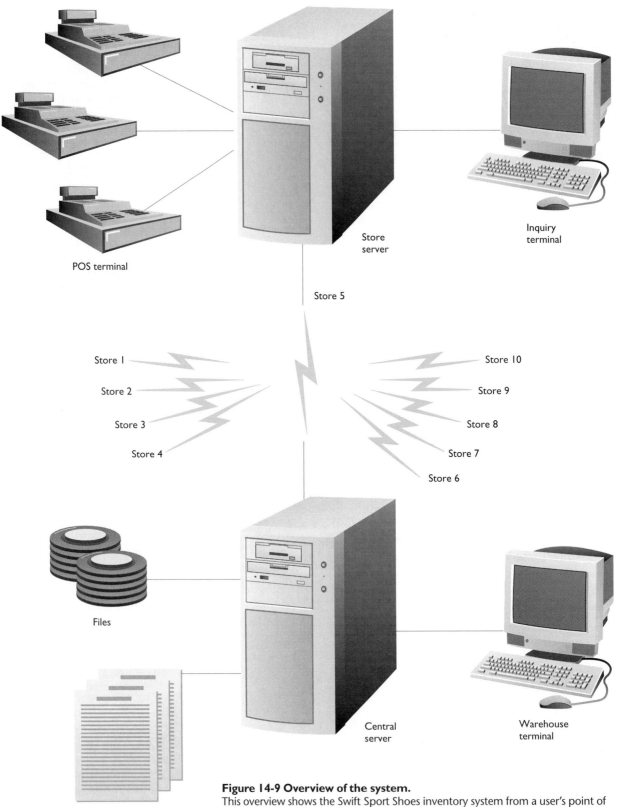

POS terminal

Store
server

Inquiry
terminal

Store 5

Store 1

Store 2

Store 3

Store 4

Store 10

Store 9

Store 8

Store 7

Store 6

Files

Central
server

Warehouse
terminal

Reports

Figure 14-9 Overview of the system.
This overview shows the Swift Sport Shoes inventory system from a user's point of
view. Sales transactions begin at the point-of-sale terminals in the store, which get
pricing data from the local server in the store. Once a day, the sales data is uploaded
over ISDN lines to the central server, which, among other things, updates the inventory files and produces reports. Also, store employees can use a local terminal to pose
stock availability queries, via its own server, to the central server, which can send
appropriate routing information to the warehouse.

CASE STUDY

SYSTEMS DESIGN

The store managers, who were uneasy at the beginning of the study, are by now enthusiastic participants in the design of the new system they are counting on for better control of their inventory. As part of the preliminary design phase, you offer three alternative system candidates for consideration.

The first is a centralized system, with all processing done at the headquarters computer and batch reports generated on a daily basis and delivered by messenger to the stores. This system would provide little control in the stores and thus was not considered seriously; it was mentioned only because of its relatively low cost. The third candidate takes the opposite approach, placing all processing in the stores on their own computers. This approach was attractive to the store managers but did not give the headquarters staff as much control or vision as they needed.

The second candidate, the one eventually selected, is a client/server network system that would use point-of-sale (POS) terminals and a server in each store, and a larger server at the headquarters office. The POS terminals will be connected to the in-store server, which supplies prices and also captures sales transaction data. The captured sales data will be sent to the main server at the end of the day, where it will be used to update the inventory file and to produce inventory transfer reports that will be sent to the warehouse and reorder reports that will be sent to purchasing. A key ingredient of the proposed solution is an automatic reorder procedure: The computer generates orders for any product shown to be below the preset reorder mark. A further enhancement is that each store will have a terminal devoted to inquiries via a server program about product availability, with the capability of ordering product transfers from another store. This fairly simple system is appropriate for the size of the organization, with only 10 stores, but will continue to be workable for growth to 20 stores. Figure 14-9 shows the overall design from a user's viewpoint.

You make a formal presentation to Mr. Iverson and other members of company management. Slides you prepared on a personal computer (with special presentation software) accent your points visually. After a brief statement of the problem, you list anticipated benefits to the company; these are listed in Figure 14-10. You explain the design in general terms and describe the expected costs and schedules. With the money saved from the reduced inventory expenses, you project that the system development costs will be repaid in four years. Swift Sport Shoes management accepts your recommendations, and you proceed with the detail design phase.

You design printed reports and screen displays for managers; samples are shown in Figures 14-11 and 14-12. There are many other exacting and time-consuming activities associated with detail design. Although space prohibits discussing them, here is a list of some of these tasks, to give you the flavor of the complexity: You must plan the use of wand readers to read stock codes from merchandise tags, plan to download the price file daily to be available to the store sever and thus the POS terminals, plan all files on disk with regular backups on tape, design the records in each file and the methods to access the files, design the data communications system, draw diagrams to show the flow of the data in the system, and prepare structure charts of program modules. Figure 14-14 shows a skeleton version of a systems flowchart that represents part of the inventory processing. Some of these activities, such as data communications, require certain expertise, so you may be coordinating with specialists. Several systems controls are planned, among them a unique numbering system for stock items and validation of all data input at the terminal.

You make another presentation to managers and more technical people, including representatives from information systems. You are given the go-ahead.

SWIFT SPORT SHOES: ANTICIPATED BENEFITS

- Better inventory control
- Improved customer service
- Improved management information
- Reduced inventory costs
- Improved employee morale

Figure 14-10 Benefits. Benefits are usually closely tied to the system objectives. These are the anticipated benefits of the new Swift Sport Shoes inventory system.

NEW DIRECTIONS

DATA WAREHOUSING

Computer systems have been produced by companies large and small for decades. Many companies have dozens of systems—payroll, personnel, accounting, product design, inventory, sales, and more. In most cases, each system has its own data, in files or databases. The data is useful for each system's tasks. For example, employee data such as name, pay rate, and hours worked is needed to produce paychecks and related reports.

What if a manager needs to base a decision on data from a variety of files? Can she, for example, combine data from product design and personnel files to find employees who might be suitable

for a certain design team? Can a manager considering an acquisition quickly access and combine data from accounting, inventory, and sales files? Probably not. Generally, data is set up to work with its own system and is not in a format readily available for these kinds of cross-system questions. These systems are sometimes called *legacy systems* because they were probably developed long ago and have been "inherited" by today's employees. The data in a legacy system may not be avail-

able online and thus not subject to even the simplest kind of query from a networked manager.

A recent approach to this problem is *data warehousing*, the process of combining and reformatting data into a single system that can then be used as a basis for management queries. Companies that specialize in data warehousing offer software to set up and update a data warehouse from existing files and also easy-to-use software that managers can invoke to ask their questions.

Data warehousing is neither easy nor inexpensive. But some companies are finding it necessary in order to give managers the information they need.

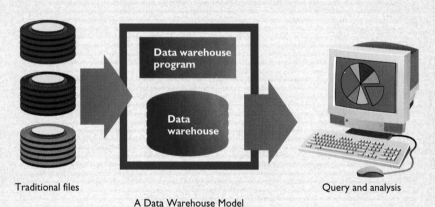

Traditional files

Data warehouse program

Data warehouse

Query and analysis

A Data Warehouse Model

completely satisfied with a prototype, so requirements can be revised before a lot has been invested in developing the new system.

Could you adopt this approach to systems development? It seems at odds with this chapter's systems development life cycle, which promotes doing steps in the proper order. And yet many analysts in the computer industry are making good use of prototypes. The prototype approach exploits advances in computer technology and uses powerful, high-level software tools. These software packages allow analysts to build systems quickly in response to user needs. In particular, recall the fourth-generation languages discussed in Chapter 12. One of their key advantages is that they can be used to produce something quickly. The systems produced can then be refined as they are used until the fit between user and system is acceptable.

Detail Design

Let us say that the users have accepted your design proposal and you are on your way. You must now develop detailed design specifications, or a detail design. This is a time-consuming part of the project, but it is rela-

detail design. This is a time-consuming part of the project, but it is relatively straightforward.

In this phase every facet of the system is considered in detail. Here is a list of some detail design activities: designing output forms and screens, planning input data forms and procedures, drawing system flowcharts, planning file access methods and record formats, planning database interfaces, planning data communications interfaces, designing system security controls, and considering human factors. This list is not comprehensive, nor will all activities listed be used for all systems. Some analysts choose to plan the overall logic at this stage, preparing program structure charts, pseudocode, and the like.

Normally, in the detail design phase, parts of the system are considered in this order: output requirements, input requirements, files and databases, systems processing, and systems controls and backup.

Output Requirements   Before you can do anything, you must know exactly what the client wants the system to produce—the output. As an analyst, you must also consider the *medium* of the output—paper, computer screen, and so on. In addition, you must determine the *type* of reports needed (summary, exception, and so on) and the *contents* of the output—what data is needed for the reports. The *forms* that the output will be printed on are also a consideration; they may need to be custom-printed if they go outside the organization to customers or stockholders. You may wish to determine the report format by using a **printer spacing chart**, which shows the position of headings, the spacing between columns, and the location of date and page numbers (Figure 14-11). You may also use screen reports, mock-ups on paper of how the screen will respond to user queries. A sample screen report is shown in Figure 14-12.

Input Requirements   Once your desired output is determined, you must consider what kind of input is required to produce it. First you must consider the input *medium:* Will you try to capture data at the source via point-of-sale (POS) terminals? Must the input be keyed from a source document? Next you must consider *content* again—what fields

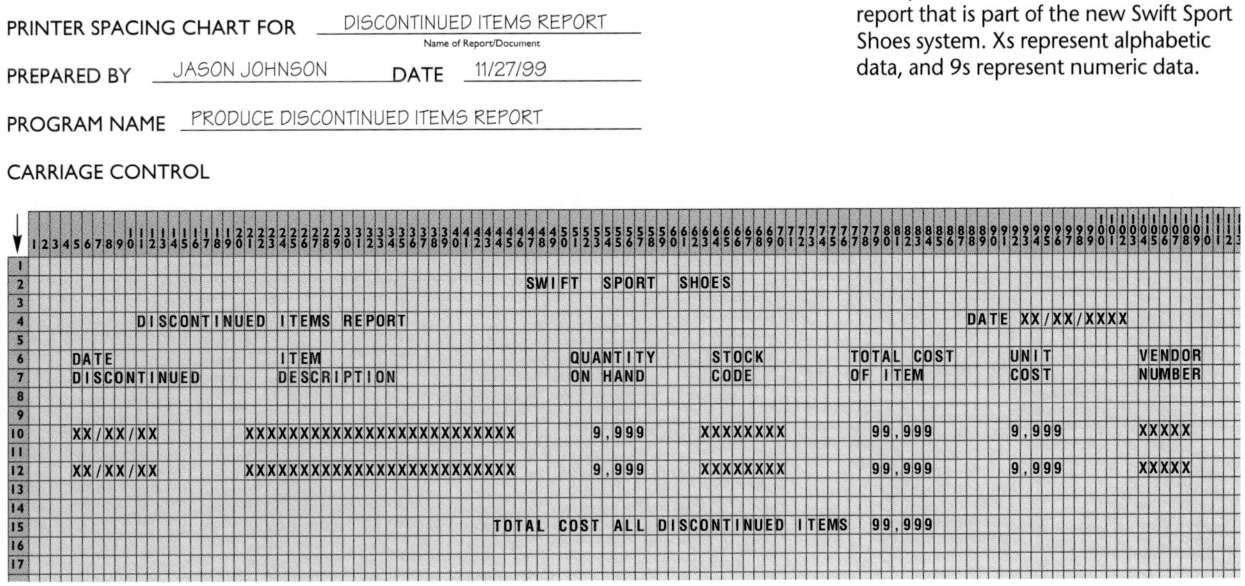

Figure 14-11 Example of a printer spacing chart. This chart shows how a systems analyst wishes the report format to look—headings, columns, and so on—when displayed on a printer. This example shows discontinued items, a report that is part of the new Swift Sport Shoes system. Xs represent alphabetic data, and 9s represent numeric data.

Figure 14-12 Example of a screen report. This screen report layout has been designed as part of the Swift Sport Shoes system. The purpose of the screen is to give information about how much of a given stock item is in each store. The report shows an approximation of what the user will see on the screen after entering a stock code.

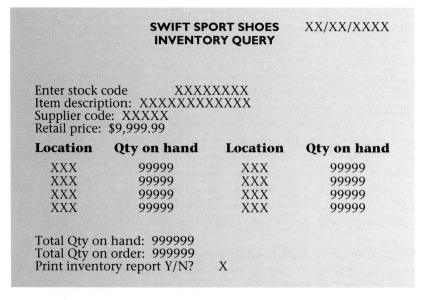

SWIFT SPORT SHOES INVENTORY QUERY   XX/XX/XXXX

```
Enter stock code        XXXXXXXX
Item description:  XXXXXXXXXXXX
Supplier code:  XXXXX
Retail price:  $9,999.99
```

Location	Qty on hand	Location	Qty on hand
XXX	99999	XXX	99999
XXX	99999	XXX	99999
XXX	99999	XXX	99999
XXX	99999	XXX	99999

```
Total Qty on hand:  999999
Total Qty on order:  999999
Print inventory report Y/N?      X
```

are needed, the order in which they appear, and the like. This in turn may involve designing *forms* that will organize data before it is entered. You need to plan some kind of input *validation* process, a check that data is reasonable as well as accurate; you would not expect a six-figure salary, for example, for someone who works in the mail room. Finally, you need to consider input *volume*, particularly the volume at peak periods. Can the system handle it? A mail-order house, for instance, may have to be ready for higher sales of expensive toys during the December holiday season than at other times of the year.

Files and Databases   You need to consider how the files in your computer system will be organized: sequentially, directly, or by some other

Figure 14-13 ANSI systems flowchart symbols. These are some of the symbols recommended by the American National Standards Institute for systems flowcharts, which show the movement of data through a system.

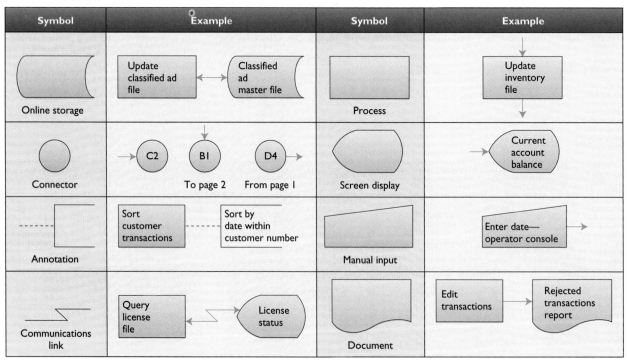

method. You also need to decide how the files should be accessed, as well as the format of records making up the data files. If the system has one or more databases or accesses databases used in other systems, you will have to coordinate your design efforts with the database administrator, the person responsible for controlling and updating databases.

Systems Processing   Just as you drew a data flow diagram to describe the old system, now you need to show the flow of data in the new system. One method is to use standard ANSI flowchart symbols (Figure 14-13) to illustrate what will be done and what files will be used. Figure 14-14 shows a resulting **systems flowchart**. Note that a systems flowchart is

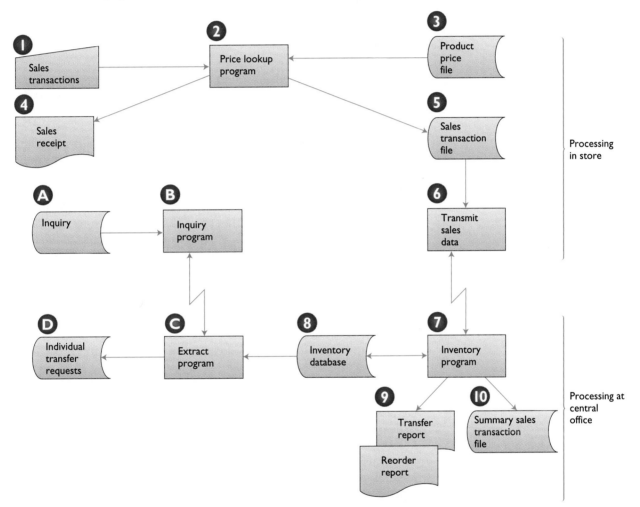

Figure 14-14 Systems flowchart. This very simplified systems flowchart shows part of the processing for the new Swift Sport Shoes inventory system. Note that the top half of the drawing shows processing that occurs in the store. Initial processing is the retrieval of the product price from the store server to the POS terminal as a customer proceeds through checkout. The bottom part of the drawing shows aggregate processing of all sales transactions from all stores, done on the computer at the central headquarters site. Also shown, on the left side of the chart, is an inquiry from a store to the central server. Step by step: The sales clerk ① inputs sales transaction data, prompting ② the POS terminal to look up the item price via an in-store server program that gets the information from ③ the product price file, and then ④ prints a sales receipt for the customer and also stores ⑤ the sales transaction data on a file. At the end of the sales day, ⑥ the store server runs a program to transmit the stored sales transactions over ISDN data communications lines to the central server, which ⑦ processes it for inventory purposes by updating the ⑧ inventory database, producing ⑨ transfer and reorder reports, and placing the sales transaction in ⑩ a file for subsequent auditing. In a separate process, in any store, an employee can use Ⓐ a terminal to invoke Ⓑ the store server program to send a product availability inquiry to Ⓒ a program on the central server, which checks the inventory database and sends a response, and possibly also sends Ⓓ a message for action to the warehouse.

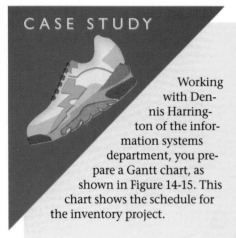

SYSTEMS DEVELOPMENT

Working with Dennis Harrington of the information systems department, you prepare a Gantt chart, as shown in Figure 14-15. This chart shows the schedule for the inventory project.

Program design specifications are prepared using pseudocode, the design tool Mr. Harrington thinks will be most useful to programmers. The programs will be written in C++, since that is the primary language of the installation and it is suitable for this application. Three programmers are assigned to the project.

You work with the programmers to develop a test plan. Some inventory data, both typical and atypical, is prepared to test the new system. You and the programmers continue to build on the documentation base by implementing the pseudocode and by preparing detailed data descriptions, logic narratives, program listings, test data results, and related material.

not the same as the logic flowchart used in programming. The systems flowchart describes only the big picture; a logic flowchart represents the flow of logic within a single program.

Systems Controls and Backup   To make sure that data is input and processed correctly, and to prevent fraud and tampering with the computer system, you will need to institute appropriate controls. In a batch system, in which data for the system is processed in groups, begin with the source documents, such as time cards or sales orders. Each document should be serially numbered so that the system can keep track of it. Documents are time-stamped when received and then grouped in batches. Each batch is labeled with the number of documents per batch; these counts are balanced against totals of the processed data. The input is controlled to make sure that the data is accurately converted from source documents to machine-processable form. Data input to online systems is backed up by **system journals**, files that record every transaction processed at each terminal, such as an account withdrawal through a bank teller. Processing controls include the data validation procedures mentioned in the section on input requirements.

It is also important to plan for the backup of system files; copies of transaction and master files should be made on a regular basis. These file copies are stored temporarily in case the originals are inadvertently lost or damaged. Often the backup copies are stored off- site for added security.

As before, the results of this phase are documented. The resulting report, usually referred to as the detail design specifications, is an outgrowth of the preliminary design document. The report is probably large and detailed. A presentation often accompanies the completion of this stage.

▶ Phase 4: Systems Development

Finally, the system is actually going to be developed. As a systems analyst you prepare a schedule to monitor the principal activities in **systems development**—programming and testing.

Scheduling

Figure 14-15 shows what is known as a **Gantt chart**, a bar chart commonly used to depict schedule deadlines and milestones. In our example

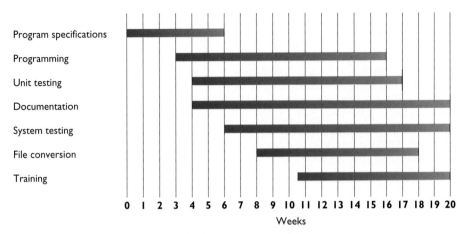

Figure 14-15 Gantt chart. This bar chart shows the scheduled tasks and milestones of the Swift Sport Shoes project. Notice that some phases overlap.

the chart shows the work to be accomplished over a given period. It does not, however, show the number of work hours required. If you were the supervisor, it would be common practice for you to ask others on the development team to produce individual Gantt charts of their own activities. Organizations that want further control may use **project management software**, which offers additional features, such as allocating people and resources to each task, monitoring schedules, and producing status reports.

Programming

Until this point there has been no programming, unless, that is, some prototyping was done. So usually, before programming begins, you need to prepare program design specifications. Program development tools must be considered. Some of this work may already have been done as part of the design phase, but usually programmers participate in refining the design at this point. Program design specifications can be developed through detailed logic flowcharts and pseudocode, among other tools.

Testing

Would you write a program and then simply turn it over to the client without checking it over first? Of course not. Thus, programmers perform **unit testing**, meaning that they individually test their own program pieces (units), using test data. Programmers try even bad data so that they can be confident that their program can handle it appropriately. This is followed by **system testing**, which determines whether all the program units work together satisfactorily. During this process the development team uses test data to test every part of the programs. Finally, **volume testing** uses real data in large amounts. Volume testing sometimes reveals errors that do not show up with test data, especially errors in storage or memory usage. In particular, volume testing of online systems will reveal problems that are likely to occur only under heavy use.

As in every phase of the project, documentation is required. In this phase documentation describes the program logic and detailed data formats.

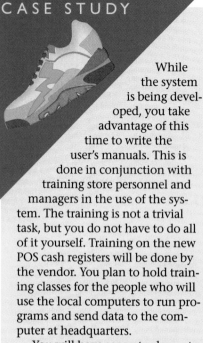

IMPLEMENTATION

While the system is being developed, you take advantage of this time to write the user's manuals. This is done in conjunction with training store personnel and managers in the use of the system. The training is not a trivial task, but you do not have to do all of it yourself. Training on the new POS cash registers will be done by the vendor. You plan to hold training classes for the people who will use the local computers to run programs and send data to the computer at headquarters.

You will have separate classes to teach managers to retrieve data from the system via terminal commands. In both cases training will

be hands-on. Company personnel should find the training enjoyable because the on-screen dialogue is user-friendly—the user is instructed clearly every step of the way.

File conversion is painful. One evening after closing time, the staff works into the evening to take inventory in the stores. Temporary personnel are hired to key an inventory master file from this data. Transactions for the master file are accumulated as more purchases are made, up until the time the system is ready for use; then the master will be updated from these transactions. After discussing the relative merits of the various system conversion methods, you and Ms. Christie agree that a pilot conversion would be ideal. Together you decide to bring up the original store first, then add

other stores to the system one or two at a time.

To evaluate the new system, Mr. Iverson puts together a local team consisting of Ms. Christie, a programmer, and an accountant. Since your documentation is comprehensive, it is relatively easy for the team to check the system completely to see if it is functioning according to specifications. The evaluation report notes several positive results: out-of-stock conditions have almost disappeared (only two instances in one store in one month), inventory transfer among stores is a smooth operation, and store managers feel an increased sense of control. Negative outcomes are relatively minor and can be fixed in a system maintenance operation.

▶ Phase 5: Implementation

You may think that implementation means stopping the old system and starting the new system. You are not alone. Many companies believe that also, but they find out that there is much more to it. Even though **implementation** is the final phase, a good deal of effort is still required, including the following activities: training, equipment conversion, file conversion, system conversion, auditing, evaluation, and maintenance.

Training

Often systems analysts do not give training the attention it deserves, because they are so concerned about the computer system itself. But a system can be no better than the people using it. A good time to start training—for at least a few of the users—is at some point during the testing, so that people can begin to learn how to use the system even as the development team is checking it out. Do not be concerned that these users will see a not-yet-perfect system; users actually gain confidence in a budding system as errors get fixed and the system improves every day.

An important training tool is the user's manual, a document prepared to aid users not familiar with the computer system. Some organizations employ technical writers to create the user's manual while the system is being developed. But documentation for the user is just the beginning. Any teacher knows that students learn best by doing. Besides, users are as likely to read a thick manual as they are to read a dictionary. The message is clear: Users must receive hands-on training to learn to use the system. The trainer must prepare exercises that simulate the tasks users will be required to do. For example, a hotel clerk learning a new online reservation system is given typical requests to fulfill—a family of four for three nights—and uses a terminal to practice. The user's manual is used as a reference guide. Setting all this up is not a trivial task. The trainer must consider class space, equipment, data, and the users' schedules.

Equipment Conversion

Equipment considerations vary from almost none to installing a main-frame computer and all its peripheral equipment. If you are implementing a small- or medium-size system on established equipment in a major information systems department, your equipment considerations may simply involve negotiating scheduled run time and disk space. If you are purchasing a moderate amount of equipment, such as terminals or personal computers, you will be concerned primarily with delivery schedules, networking, and compatibility.

A major equipment purchase demands a large amount of time and attention. The planning for such a purchase, of course, must begin long before the implementation phase. For a major equipment purchase you will need site preparation advice from vendors and other equipment experts.

Personal computer systems are less demanding, but they too require site planning in terms of the availability of space, accessibility, and cleanliness. And, as the analyst, you may be the one who does the actual installation.

File Conversion

File Conversion may be very tricky if the existing files are being handled manually. The data must be prepared in such a way that it is accessible to computer systems. All of the contents of the file drawers in the personnel department, for instance, must be keyed, or possibly scanned, to be stored on disk. Some scheme must be used to input the data files and keep them updated. You may need to employ temporary help. The big headache during this process is keeping all file records up-to-date when some are still manual and some have been keyed in preparation for the new system.

If you are modifying an existing computer system and thus have files already in computer-accessible form, you may need to have a program written to convert the old files to the format needed for the new system. This is a much speedier process than having to key in data from scratch. Nevertheless, it is not unusual for file conversion to take a long time.

System Conversion

During the system conversion stage, you actually "pull the plug" on the old system and begin using the new one. There are four ways of handling the conversion.

Direct conversion means that the user simply stops using the old system and starts using the new one—a somewhat risky method, since there is no other system to fall back on if anything goes wrong. This procedure is best followed only if the old system is very small or in unusable

MAKING THE RIGHT CONNECTIONS

MARTHA DOES MORE THAN TALK

You may have seen Martha Stewart on television, dispensing advice on home and garden. Or perhaps you have seen one of her many books on the same topics. Or maybe her magazine, her newspaper column, her mail-order catalog, or even "Ask Martha" online. She also has several operations in the works—her own lines of furniture, bedding, china, and hybrid tea roses. Overall, she is famously busy, wildly successful, and on the move.

Martha Stewart is a hands-on decision maker, with a need to maintain close control of opera-

tions. Whether at home or on the road, being out of touch is out of

the question. Martha needs connectivity. To this end, she uses both a desktop computer and a notebook computer, both with fax modems. Her suburban van is equipped with a disk recorder for dictation, a small TV, headphones, and mobile navigation software. But the most important tool is her go-everywhere notebook computer. As Martha says, "I have to be able to communicate, and I have an awful lot of communicating to do. My notebook computer faxes from the airplane, from the car, from home, wherever I am."

condition. A **phased conversion** is one in which the organization eases into the new system one step at a time so that all the users are working with some of the system. In contrast, in a **pilot conversion** the entire system is used by a designated set of users and is extended to all users once it has proved successful. This works best when a company has several branch offices or separate divisions. In a **parallel conversion**, the most prolonged and expensive method, the old and new systems are operated simultaneously for some time, until users are satisfied that the new system performs to their standards.

System conversion is often a time of stress and confusion for all concerned. As the analyst, your credibility is on the line. During this time users are often doing double duty, trying to perform their regular jobs and simultaneously cope with a new computer system. Problems seem to appear in all areas, from input to output. Clearly, this is a period when your patience is needed.

Auditing

Security violations, whether deliberate or unintentional, can be difficult to detect. Data begins from some source, perhaps a written source document or a transaction, for which there must be a record log. Eventually, the data is part of the system on some medium, probably disk. Once the data is on disk, it is possible for an unauthorized person to alter it in some illicit way. How would anyone know that the disk files had been changed and, in fact, no longer match the original source documents from which the data came? To guard against this situation, the systems analyst designs an **audit trail** to trace output back to the source data. In real-time systems, security violations can be particularly elusive unless all transactions are recorded on disk for later reference by auditors. Modern auditors no longer shuffle mountains of paper; instead, they have computer programs of their own to monitor applications programs and data.

Evaluation

Is the system working? How well is it meeting the original requirements, benefits, and budgets? Out of such evaluation will come adjustments that will improve the system. Approaches to evaluation vary. Sometimes the systems analyst and someone from the client organization evaluate the system against preset criteria directly related to the requirements that were determined during the systems analysis phase. Some organizations prefer to bring in an independent evaluating team, on the assumption that independent members will be free from bias and expectations.

Maintenance

Many consider maintenance to be a separate phase, one that begins only when the initial system effort is implemented and complete. In any case **maintenance** is an ongoing activity, one that lasts the lifetime of the system. Monitoring and making necessary adjustments continue so that the computer produces the expected results. Maintenance tasks also include making revisions and additions to the computer system.

The preceding discussion may leave the impression that, by simply following a formula, one can develop a system. In fact, novice analysts often believe this to be true. Each system is unique, however, so no one formula can fit every project. It would be more correct to say that there are merely guidelines.

CHAPTER REVIEW

Summary and Key Terms

- A **system** is an organized set of related components established to accomplish a certain task. A **computer system** has a computer as one of its components. A **client** requests a **systems analysis,** a study of an existing system, to determine both how it works and how well it meets the needs of its **users,** who are usually employees and customers. Systems analysis can lead to **systems design,** the development of a plan for an improved system. A **systems analyst** normally does both the analysis and design. Some people do both programming and analysis and have the title **programmer/analyst.** The success of the project requires both impetus and authority within the client organization to change the current system.

- The systems analyst must be a **change agent** who encourages **user involvement** in the development of a new system.

- The systems analyst has three main functions: (1) **coordinating** schedules and task assignments, (2) **communicating** analysis and design information to those involved with the system, and (3) **planning and designing** the system, with the help of the client organization. A systems analyst should have an analytical mind, good communication skills, self-discipline and self-direction, good organizational skills, creativity, and the ability to work without tangible results.

- The **systems development life cycle (SDLC)** can be described in five phases: (1) preliminary investigation, (2) analysis, (3) design, (4) development, and (5) implementation.

- Phase 1, **preliminary investigation,** also known as the **feasibility study** or **system survey,** is the preliminary investigation of the problem to determine how—and whether—an analysis and design project should proceed. Aware of the importance of establishing a smooth working relationship, the analyst refers to an **organization chart** showing the lines of authority within the client organization. After determining the **nature and scope of the problem,** the analyst expresses the users' needs as **objectives.**

- In phase 2, systems analysis, the analyst gathers and analyzes data from common sources such as written documents, interviews, questionnaires, observation, and sampling.

- The analyst must evaluate the relevance of **written documents** such as procedure manuals and reports. **Interview** options include the **structured interview,** in which all questions are planned and written in advance, and the **unstructured interview,** in which the questions can vary from the plan. **Questionnaires** can save time and expense and allow anonymous answers, but response rates are often low. Another method is simply **observing** how the organization functions, sometimes through **participant observation,** which is temporary participation in the organization's activities. Statistical **sampling** is also useful, especially when there is a large volume of data.

- The systems analyst may use a variety of charts and diagrams to analyze the data. A **data flow diagram (DFD)** provides an easy-to-follow picture of the flow of data through the system. Another common tool for data analysis is the **decision table,** or **decision logic table,** a standard table indicating alternative actions under particular conditions.

- The analysis phase also includes preparation of **system requirements,** a detailed list of the things the system must be able to do.

- Upon completion of the systems analysis phase, the analyst submits to the client a report that includes the current system's problems and requirements, a cost analysis, and recommendations about what course to take next.

- In phase 3, systems design, the analyst submits a general preliminary design for the client's approval before proceeding to the specific detail design.

- **Preliminary design** begins with reviewing the system requirements, followed by considering **acquisition by purchase** (perhaps to be **customized** for the client), **outsourcing** to an outside firm, or in-house development with, perhaps, alternative **candidates**. The analyst presents the plan in a form the users can understand.
- The analyst may also develop a **prototype**, a limited working system or part of a system that gives users a preview of how the new system will work.
- **Detail design** normally involves considering the parts of the system in the following order: output requirements, input requirements, files and databases, systems processing, and systems controls and backup. **Output requirements** include the medium of the output, the type of reports needed, the contents of the output, and the forms on which the output will be printed. The analyst might determine the report format by using a **printer spacing chart**, which shows the position of headings, columns, dates, and page numbers. **Input requirements** include the input medium, the content of the input, and the design of data entry forms. The analyst also plans an input validation process for checking whether the data is reasonable, and the analyst makes sure that the system can handle variations in input volume. The organization of **files and databases** must be specified. **Systems processing** must also be described, perhaps by using a **systems flowchart** that uses ANSI flowchart symbols to illustrate the flow of data or by using the hierarchical organization of a structure chart. The analyst must also spell out **systems controls and backup**. Data input to online systems must be backed up by **system journals**, files that record transactions made at the terminal. Processing controls involve data validation procedures. Finally, copies of transaction and master files should be made regularly.
- Phase 4, **systems development**, consists of scheduling, programming, and testing. Schedule deadlines and milestones are often shown on a **Gantt chart**. **Project management software** allocates people and resources, monitors schedules, and produces status reports. The programming effort involves selecting the program language and developing the program design specifications. Programmers then do **unit testing** (individual testing of their own programs), which is followed by **system testing** (assessing how the programs work together). **Volume testing** tests the entire system with real data. Documentation of phase 4 describes the program logic and the detailed data formats.
- Phase 5, **implementation**, includes **training**, to prepare users of the new system; **equipment conversion**, which involves ensuring compatibility and providing enough space and electrical capacity; **file conversion**, making old files accessible to the new system; system conversion; **auditing**, the design of an **audit trail** to trace data from output back to the source documents; **evaluation**, the assessment of system performance; and **maintenance**, the monitoring and adjustment of the system.
- **System conversion** may be done in one of four ways: **direct conversion**, immediately replacing the old system with the new system; **phased conversion**, easing in the new system a step at a time; **pilot conversion**, testing the entire system with a few users and extending it to the rest when proved successful; and **parallel conversion**, operating the old and new systems concurrently until the new system is proved successful.

Quick Poll

Compare your answers to those of your colleagues or classmates.

1. Regarding documentation:
    - ❏ a. A nightmare. This would be my biggest failing.
    - ❏ b. I'm convinced. Not my favorite chore, but it's a necessity.
    - ❏ c. I see documentation as a way to make my mark, a way to show my boss that something is being accomplished.
2. About designing a system:
    - ❏ a. Too soon to know about this. For now, I feel hopelessly inadequate.

b. I have some dim idea that it could be done, but wouldn't know where to begin in a real-life situation.

c. Even though I have only minimal knowledge at this point, I can see myself planning a system some day.

3. Regarding a career as a systems analyst:

a. Not for me. I want to do something in which I can easily see results, not sit through endless meetings or worry about whether a client is unhappy.

b. Not my plan. I'll be on the other side of the desk as the client. But I'm glad I have learned enough to work effectively with an analyst.

c. Definitely a possibility. I like working with people but having a technical aspect too.

Discussion Questions

1. Which qualities of a systems analyst do you consider to be the most important?

2. Would the following most likely be good projects for acquisition by purchase, or outsourcing, or in-house development?

a. An inventory control system for a pizza franchise

b. A payroll system for a small retailer

c. A system to network and provide basic software offerings for 13 office personal computers

d. A system to draw airplane galley installation assembly diagrams for an airline manufacturer

e. A system to process market research data gathered for new toys to be produced by the country's largest toy manufacturer

f. A system to permit networked artists to collaborate by computer on artistic ventures

g. A system to manage patient appointments, dental records, and billing for a clinic with four dentists

h. A system to track traffic tickets issued by the state patrol and convey this information to the state drivers' licensing agency

i. A system to perform automated check-writing and expense tracking for a funeral home

j. A system to install a terminal in the field office of each franchisee, to be connected to the central headquarters of a truck rental company for the purpose of tracking truck locations

3. Should system evaluation be done by the analyst and the client organization or by an independent evaluating team?

Student Study Guide

Multiple Choice

1. Testing of each individual program or module is called
   a. program testing
   b. system testing
   c. volume testing
   d. unit testing

2. The preliminary investigation of a systems project is also called a(n)
   a. analysis survey
   b. feasibility study
   c. systems design
   d. evaluation

3. The people who will have contact with the system, such as employees and customers, are
   a. programmers
   b. users
   c. systems analysts
   d. clients

4. The SDLC is defined as a project involving
   a. two phases
   b. three phases
   c. four phases
   d. five phases

5. Phase one of a systems project involves
   a. a system survey
   b. a systems analysis
   c. data gathering
   d. questionnaires

6. The person who fills the role of change agent is the
   a. systems user
   b. administrator
   c. systems analyst
   d. client

7. The scope and true nature of the problem is determined during
   a. systems design
   b. systems development
   c. preliminary investigation
   d. systems analysis

8. A chart of positions and departments within an organization is
   a. a data flow diagram
   b. an organization chart
   c. a project management report
   d. a Gantt chart

9. Testing the system with large quantities of real data is called
   a. unit testing
   b. system testing
   c. parallel testing
   d. volume testing

10. In the course of a systems project, systems design
    a. follows systems analysis
    b. precedes systems analysis
    c. follows development
    d. is the fourth phase

11. Positioning of headings and columns for the report format, considered during systems design, might use
    a. a record layout
    b. a decision table
    c. an organization chart
    d. a printer spacing chart

12. Programming and testing are elements of
    a. systems analysis
    b. implementation
    c. systems development
    d. systems design
13. Data gathering and data analysis take place
    a. after the system survey
    b. during systems design
    c. after systems analysis
    d. during evaluation
14. The kind of interview where all questions are planned in advance is called
    a. preplanned
    b. observation
    c. structured
    d. unstructured
15. The entire new system is used by a portion of the users:
    a. direct conversion
    b. file conversion
    c. pilot conversion
    d. parallel conversion
16. A systems analyst would observe the flow of data and interrelations of people within an organization during
    a. detail design
    b. systems analysis
    c. preliminary design
    d. a system survey
17. Used to ensure that no alternative is overlooked during data analysis:
    a. data flow diagram
    b. Gantt chart
    c. organization chart
    d. decision table
18. The phase following detail design is
    a. preliminary investigation
    b. systems development
    c. implementation
    d. system conversion
19. Scheduling deadlines and milestones can be shown on a
    a. system survey
    b. prototype
    c. decision table
    d. Gantt chart
20. Turning an entire project over to an outside firm for development is called
    a. auditing
    b. preliminary investigation
    c. outsourcing
    d. prototyping
21. The person who requests study or work on a system is the
    a. client
    b. change agent
    c. analyst
    d. user
22. The data-gathering vehicle that permits high-volume anonymous answers:
    a. observation
    b. questionnaire
    c. unstructured interview
    d. structured interview
23. In the preliminary design phase, the analyst may prepare alternative
    a. candidates
    b. questionnaires
    c. organization charts
    d. decision tables
24. A data-gathering technique used with high-volume data:
    a. prototypes
    b. sampling
    c. data flow diagrams
    d. interviewing
25. A plan to trace data to its source is called
    a. an audit trail
    b. typing
    c. a structure
    d. volume testing

True/False

T F   1. Systems analysis is the process of developing a plan for an approved system.
T F   2. Users are people who will have contact with the system.
T F   3. A systems analyst normally performs both analysis and design.
T F   4. Documentation is the least important aspect of a systems project.
T F   5. A feasibility study needs to be conducted following data gathering.
T F   6. Questionnaires are usually a more expensive form of data gathering than are interviews.
T F   7. An organization chart shows the flow of data through an organization.
T F   8. A decision table can help ensure that no alternative is overlooked.
T F   9. In some cases it is possible to acquire a new system by purchasing it.
T F 10. Input requirements should be considered prior to considering output requirements.
T F 11. Problem definition includes the nature of the problem, its scope, and the objectives of the system.
T F 12. Prototyping tools include powerful high-level software.
T F 13. Project management software can be used to monitor the allocation of both people and resources.
T F 14. A systems flowchart is the same as a logic flowchart.
T F 15. A Gantt chart is a bar chart that depicts deadlines and milestones.
T F 16. A prototype is a complete nonworking model of the computer system.
T F 17. File conversion is one form of system conversion.
T F 18. Maintenance of the system should take only a short time if the previous work was done with care.
T F 19. Poor communication between analysts and users can result in a system that does not do what the user expected.
T F 20. As a data-gathering technique, interviewing is usually more expensive than questionnaires.

Fill-In

1. The process that evaluates a currently existing system to determine how it works and how it meets user needs: _____

2. List the three principal functions of a systems analyst.

   a. _____

   b. _____

   c. _____

3. The data analysis tool used to illustrate information flow within a system: _____

4. As related to data, the two major steps of the systems analysis phase:

   a. _____

   b. _____

5. The overall name for the five phases involved in developing a new project:

   _____

6. The person or organization that contracts to have a systems analysis done: _____

7. The files whose records represent transactions processed by online systems:

   _____

8. The type of interview that permits variation from planned questions: _____

9. Since a systems analyst brings change to an organization, the analyst is often referred to as

   _____

10. The by-product of understanding the system in the systems analysis phase: _____

11. In addition to questionnaires and interviews, name three sources of information for data gathering.

   a. _____

   b. _____

   c. _____

12. In data flow diagrams, the name for a repository of data: _____

13. Auditing and evaluation are part of this phase:

   _____

14. The most prolonged and expensive method of conversion: _____

15. Two other terms for the preliminary investigation:

   a. _____

   b. _____

16. Outsourcing may be considered in which SDLC phase? _____

17. Gathering a representative subset from a large volume of data is called _____

18. Alternative plans for a new system design are called

   _____

19. Programming should begin in this phase:

   _____

20. The word that describes an organized set of related components that accomplish a certain task:

   _____

21. Programmer testing of individual programs is called

   _____

22. It is possible to acquire a completed entire system for a fee; this is called _____

23. Schedule deadlines and milestones are shown on a

   _____

24. The monitoring and adjustment of the completed system is called _____

25. The type of system conversion in which the entire system is implemented on a certain group of users is called _____

26. The kind of interview in which all questions are planned in advance and not deviated from is called

   _____

27. A limited working system or part of a system is called a _____

28. The kind of testing in which an assessment is made of how programs work together is called

   _____

29. Temporarily joining the organization under analysis for the purpose of watching how things are done is called _____

30. The type of system conversion in which the system is implemented one step at a time is called

   _____

31. The participation of the user in each phase of the systems development life cycle is known generally

   as _____

32. The first of two subphases of design is called

   _____

33. The second phase of the systems development life cycle is called _____

34. The lines of authority in an organization are shown in a drawing called _____

35. The entire system is tested with real data in the testing phase called _____

36. An analyst who also does some programming usually has the title _____

37. The development of a system may be turned over to an outside firm; this is called

   _____

38. The type of system conversion in which the entire system is implemented immediately is called

   _____

39. The kind of software that allocates people and resources, monitors schedules, and produces status reports is called _____

40. The last phase of the systems development life cycle is called _____

Answers

Multiple Choice

1. d	6. c	11. d	16. b	21. a
2. b	7. c	12. c	17. d	22. b
3. b	8. b	13. a	18. b	23. a
4. d	9. d	14. c	19. d	24. b
5. a	10. a	15. c	20. c	25. a

True/False

1. F	6. F	11. T	16. F
2. T	7. F	12. T	17. F
3. T	8. T	13. T	18. F
4. F	9. T	14. F	19. T
5. F	10. F	15. T	20. T

Fill-In

1. systems analysis
2. a. coordination
   b. communication
   c. planning and design
3. data flow diagram
4. a. data gathering
   b. data analysis
5. systems development life cycle
6. the client
7. system journals
8. unstructured
9. change agent
10. system requirements
11. a. written documents
    b. observation
    c. sampling
12. file
13. implementation
14. parallel conversion
15. a. feasibility study
    b. system survey
16. design (preliminary design)
17. sampling
18. candidates
19. systems development
20. system
21. unit testing
22. acquisition by purchase
23. Gantt chart
24. maintenance
25. pilot conversion
26. structured
27. prototype
28. system testing
29. participant observation
30. phased conversion
31. user involvement
32. preliminary design
33. systems analysis
34. organization chart
35. volume testing
36. programmer/analyst
37. outsourcing
38. direct conversion
39. project management software
40. implementation

PLANET INTERNET

LIFE AND LIVING

As in every other category, the Internet has much to offer to enrich our daily lives. Let's begin with art.

Artworks. Begin on the ArtWeb site to see both original physical works—oil, watercolor, and so forth—or computer graphics artworks. Would you like to display your own artwork on the 'Net? Join other artists in the OTIS Project. Many graphics images are available for viewing and, with permission, perhaps downloading. The Lightscape Technologies site will be of particular interest to those interested in the use of light effects in computer graphics images. Finally, if you are interested in art as it applies to space, check out the NASA Cassini site, which includes art images, as shown here, of the Cassini mission, a multiyear project sending a two-story robotic spacecraft to Saturn.

A family affair. Check out the Kids' Web site, which has links to sites of interest to children so that parents and kids can explore together. The whole family will enjoy both CartooNet and the Electronic Zoo site. For a look at some animals in the wild, note the charming fellow shown here, found on the Wolf Adoption site.

Everyone can participate in the birthday site: Just input your name and birthday and it will show up on a list on your special day. If you

If you are curious about New York City, visit the charming Central Park site. If history is an interest, there is probably a site for any event or historic place you can think of; note the Colonial Williamsburg site. Finally, how would you like to send a postcard—on the 'Net, of course. The postcard site offers several attractive cards; you can write your own message and send it off to a fellow 'Net user.

Internet Exercises

1. **Structured exercise.** Begin with the AWL site with URL http://hepg.awl.com/ capron/planet/ and link to the United States home page. Click on your own home state to see what this site has to say about it.
2. **Freeform exercise.** Travel is just the thing to send you off in different directions worldwide. Begin with your favorite directory, click the travel menu, and link from site to glorious site.

mention an e-mail address, expect felicitations to roll in. Time to try a new mealtime experience? There are hundreds of cooking and recipe sites; just submit some favorite foods or ideas to a search engine.

The stay-at-home tourist. If you'd like to take an electronic field trip, then check the sights and sounds of the Fantastic Forest, or visit Virtual Antarctica, or perhaps go Around the World in 80 Clicks. Another must-see site is Sobek Mountain Travel, whether or not you enjoy trekking. It features fascinating locations and exquisite graphics. The United States of America site has a coast-to-coast map that can be clicked at a particular location to show more detailed information.

401

Mick Dalton pursued a business degree with the goal of a career in management. He was uncertain, however, about his career ambitions. He thought that someday he would like to be at the very top of an organization with, perhaps, an office with a stunning view. He thought it was more likely, however, that he would end up somewhere in the middle, reporting to the top bosses but with responsibilities for major activities below him. He assumed that his entry into management would be at the lowest rung on the ladder, in direct contact with the workers, supervising their operations and making sure they had what they needed to do the job.

As it happened, Mick did all these things, but not in the way he expected. While he was in college, he began a computer word processing service, typing up his classmates' term papers and résumés. He used part of his profits to buy a laser printer and desktop publishing software. Thus, he was able to produce professional-looking documents and was able to offer his services to local small businesses. Mick's business-on-the-side grew beyond his expectations; he decided to go into business for himself full-time after graduation. Mick's company eventually specialized in the production end of publishing periodicals and paperback books. As the company grew, Mick managed at all levels and, eventually, did indeed have a corner office overlooking the cityscape.

Whether managing your own company or someone else's—whether at the top, middle, or bottom level—the challenge is the same: to use available resources to get the job done on time, within budget, and to the satisfaction of all concerned. Let us begin with a discussion of how managers do this, then see how computer systems can help them.

Management Information Systems

Classic Models and New Approaches

> Classic Management Functions

Managers historically have had five main functions:

- **Planning**, or devising both short-range and long-range plans for the organization and setting goals to help achieve the plans
- **Organizing**, or deciding how to use resources, such as people and materials
- **Staffing**, or hiring and training workers
- **Directing**, or guiding employees to perform their work in a way that supports the organization's goals
- **Controlling**, or monitoring the organization's progress toward reaching its goals

All managers perform these functions as part of their jobs. The level of responsibility regarding these functions, however, varies with the level of the manager. The levels of management are traditionally represented as a pyramid, with the fewest managers at the top and the largest numbers at the lowest level (Figure 15-1). Often you will hear the terms *strategic, tactical,* and *operational* associated with high-level managers, middle-level managers, and low-level managers, respectively.

Whether the head of General Electric or of an electrical appliance store, a high-level manager must be concerned with the long-range view—the *strategic* level of management. For this manager, usually called an executive, the main focus is **planning.** Consider a survey showing that Americans want family vacations and want the flexibility and economy of a motor vehicle; however, they also want more space than the family car provides. To the president of a major auto company, this information may suggest further opportunities for expansion of the recreational vehicle line.

The middle-level manager of that same company must be able to take a somewhat different view because his or her main concern is the *tactical* level of management. The middle manager will prepare to carry out the

Figure 15-1 The management pyramid. (a) The classic view of management functions involves a pyramid featuring top managers handling strategic long-range planning, middle managers focusing on the tactical issues of organization and personnel, and low-level managers directing and controlling day-to-day operations. (b) The increasing use of networked personal computers in business is squeezing out middle- and low-level managers, thus flattening the pyramid.

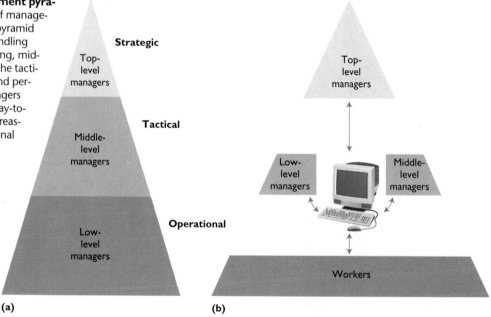

(a)   (b)

visions of the top-level managers, assembling the material and personnel resources to do the job. Note that these tasks focus on **organizing** and **staffing.** Suppose the public is inclined to buy more recreational vehicles. To a production vice president, this may mean organizing production lines using people with the right skills at the right wage and perhaps farming out portions of the assembly that can be done by less expensive, less skilled labor.

The low-level manager, usually known as a supervisor, is primarily concerned with the *operational* level of management. For the supervisor, the focus is on **directing** and **controlling.** Workers must be directed to perform the planned activities, and the supervisor must monitor progress closely. The supervisor—an assembly line supervisor in our recreational vehicle example—is involved in a number of issues: making sure that workers have the parts they need, checking employee attendance, maintaining quality control, handling complaints, keeping a close watch on the schedule, tracking costs, and much more.

To make decisions about planning, organizing, staffing, directing, and controlling, managers need data that is organized in a way that is useful for them. An effective management information system can provide it.

▶ MIS for Managers

A **management information system (MIS)** can be defined as a set of formal business systems designed to provide information for an organization. (Incidentally, you may hear the term *MIS system,* even though the *S* in the abbreviation stands for *system;* this is an accepted redundancy.) Whether or not such a system is called an MIS, every company has one. Even managers who make hunch-based decisions are operating with some sort of information system—one based on their experience. The kind of MIS we are concerned with here includes one or more computers as components. Information serves no purpose until it gets to its users. Timeliness is important, and the computer can act quickly to produce information.

The extent of a computerized MIS varies from company to company, but the most effective kinds are those that are integrated. An integrated MIS incorporates all five managerial functions—planning, organizing, staffing, directing, and controlling—throughout the company, from typing to top-executive forecasting. An integrated management computer system uses the computer to solve problems for an entire organization, instead of attacking them piecemeal. Although in many companies the complete integrated system is still only an idea, the functional aspects of MISs are expanding rapidly in many organizations.

The **MIS manager** runs the MIS department. This person's position has been called information resource manager, director of information services, chief information officer, and a variety of other titles. In any case, whoever serves in this capacity should be comfortable with both computer technology and the organization's business.

▶ The New Management Model

The traditional management pyramid that we discussed earlier means a very specific kind of communication. An executive has time to commu-

NEW DIRECTIONS

WORKING IN THE 21ST CENTURY

The approach of the millennium has inspired both deep thinkers and not-so-deep thinkers to contemplate our working lives in the next century. The ability to access information and services online will be a major factor. Here are some guesses about online future tripping:

- Using a computer and online services will be akin to using a phone. Everyone in or out of an office will know how.
- Since most workers will telecommute most of the time, work will be less central to people's lives. Work will become less of a place to go and more of a thing to do. Since most workers will be at home, the importance of family and community will increase.
- A telecommuting society means we will stop building skyscrapers to house office workers. However, some people may go to a "work center" just to hang out with other humans and not feel isolated.
- Large public companies will be replaced by hundreds of

smaller entrepreneurial companies that survive nicely by ordering supplies online, advertising their goods and services online, and selling directly to their customers via home computers.
- Workers will use their computers to access information and services related to accounting, the law, and medicine. Thus, since these services will

become less labor intensive, their prices to the consumer will drop significantly.
- Eventually, people working at home will use their online computer services for activities beyond their work—to bank, vote, send gifts, get advice, download entertainment, and chat with friends.

nicate with perhaps a handful of people. Each of these people can convey information to another five or six people below him or her. Information trickles down, layer by layer, either in meetings or more informally.

A Flattened Pyramid

Enter the computer network. Networks connect people to people, and people to data. Using e-mail, or perhaps groupware, information can be disseminated companywide as fast as fingers can fly over a computer keyboard. So much for passing along information through traditional hierarchical channels. The dispersion of information via the network has caused the traditional management pyramid to become flatter in structure and more physically distributed.

What are managers, so long the keepers of information, supposed to do now that, via the network, information is so freely available to so many workers? A good part of a manager's job, communicating above and below, has been replaced by the flow of information through the network. Many industries are finding that, to some extent, they can do without middle managers and have eliminated certain positions. Managers on all levels still have plenty to do, but they are doing it a bit differently from the ways of the past. Networks irrevocably alter the nature of managerial authority and work.

The Impact of Groupware

Consider the impact of groupware on worker interaction. As we discussed in Chapter 2, groupware permits information to be assembled in central databases. People working on a project contribute information to a database and can see and use information contributed by others.

The introduction of groupware can be a searing experience for some managers. Two reasons for this are changes in the way information is shared and changes in managerial authority. People acquire power in an organization by knowing things that others do not. Managers may feel threatened by groupware because they are not accustomed to unstructured information sharing. Studies have shown that groupware works best in organizations where there is already a fairly flexible corporate culture—that is, where an attitude of sharing and even egalitarianism already exists. Perhaps even more painful, managers may not enjoy being in the electronic spotlight when decisions that were once theirs alone are now fair game for comment and change by everyone involved. Furthermore, in contrast to organizations whose focal point is the manager, groupware supports organizations that are team-based and information-driven.

Consider another change from the old ways. Say a particular aspect of a project requires collaboration between two people, Jack and Jim, from different operational units under different management. The traditional way of doing business is for Jack to go to his manager and then for Jack's manager to talk to Jim's manager, who talks to Jim. Then the information flows in reverse, back to Jack. Up, across, down, and then back again. Now it is possible to accomplish the same communication using groupware. Information moves laterally, from worker to worker, saving a roundabout trip through the management maze.

As many managers have discovered, networks make leadership much harder. No longer able to look over their employees' shoulders, managers are learning to rely on other management techniques. They must first give careful attention to the selection and training of employees. Secondly, managers must set clear expectations for their employees. But most importantly, managers must use customer satisfaction as a measuring stick of employee performance in a networked environment.

Teamwork

The availability of networks and groupware coincides nicely with the concept of organizing employees into task-focused teams. Just as the manager is no longer the sole dispenser of wisdom and decisions, so the employee is no longer merely an individual in a static organization. Many companies are organizing their employees in teams. But a team has no permanence; work and people are organized around tasks. When a task is complete, the team is dispersed. When a new task is being tackled, a new team is assembled. Each team is composed of people whose skills are needed for the task at hand. In this kind of work environment, reorganization is a way of life.

Experts consider eight people an ideal team size. If a team gets much bigger than that, team members spend too much time communicating what is already inside their heads instead of applying that knowledge to their parts of the task. But what if the team is behind schedule? Imagine a status meeting in which it is revealed that a critical activity is behind schedule. The activity under scrutiny is to finalize product specifications for an electronic hoop, a toy that can be manipulated remotely and is expected to be a big hit for the upcoming holiday gift-buying season. This activity is critical because other activities down the line, including manufacturing and promotion, cannot begin until specifications are complete. The most common response to tardy projects is to add more people to the project, but this is exactly the wrong thing to do. If outsiders are belatedly added to an existing team, the project quickly comes to a halt in order to bring the new people up to speed. And, of course, from that moment forward, there are more people with whom one must communicate.

What is the proper solution? There is no ideal answer, other than to plan better in the first place, but most organizations find that the better part of wisdom is to rely on the commitment of the original team members. The good news, however, is that a properly composed team of an ideal size is less likely to get into trouble. Communication remains easy, and each member retains a strong sense of responsibility and participation while benefiting greatly from the contributions of teammates.

Top Managers and Computers

Since the early days of computing, managers at all levels have had computer support in the form of printed reports. In the past decade most managers, even the most resistant executives, have succumbed to the personal computer. Managers have found personal computer software useful for every aspect of their jobs, from something as simple as sending an e-mail message to complex chores such as designing a compensation package for a thousand employees. For top managers, executives who must have the vision to guide the entire company, sophisticated software is needed.

Decision Support Systems

Imagine yourself as an executive trying to deal with a constantly changing environment, having to consider changes in competition, in technology, in consumer habits, in government regulations, in union demands, and so on. How are you going to make decisions about those matters for which there are no precedents? In fact, making one-of-a-kind decisions—decisions that no one has had to make before—is the real test of a manager's mettle. In such a situation you would probably wish you could turn to someone and ask a few "what-if" questions (Figure 15-2).

"What if . . . ?" That is the question business people want answered, especially when considering new situations. A **decision support system (DSS)** is a computer system that supports managers in nonroutine

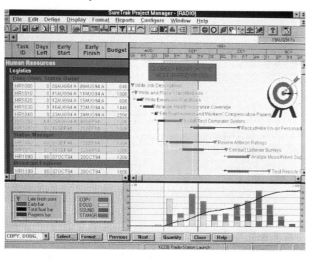

Figure 15-2 Making decisions with the help of a computer. Business people use computers to try out different scenarios without investing a great deal of time and money.

Getting Practical

YOUR ELECTRONIC AGENT

You have an important job and an activity-packed life. You long ago stopped traipsing from store to store shopping for particular goods or services; instead you use catalogs or the Yellow Pages and the telephone. A new camera? Flowers for a birthday? A Mexican restaurant? A vacation? The next logical step is to dispatch your own electronic agent to track down the best deal and, if you wish, purchase it for you.

An electronic agent, sometimes called a software agent, is a piece of software to which a person can delegate some degree of responsibility. The agent is given an order and goes shopping for you throughout the network. Suppose you have read some consumer articles and have decided that you want a camera weighing less than a pound with an automatic zoom lens for under $300.

You type in these instructions to your computer and let your software agent do the work.

While you go on with other tasks, the agent goes to a directory, finds camera stores, and then sifts through their camera inventories, looking for the required features and price. Eventually, the agent accumulates a list of acceptable choices, which is presented on your personal computer screen at your convenience. You can then choose which one, if any, to purchase. A variation on this option is available: You can give your agent advance authority to purchase a suitable camera with the best price, probably charging it to a credit card.

Someone eavesdropping on a discussion of agents might think that a real person was being described. The agent, of course, is just sophisticated software. Agent

software is available today. What is slow in coming, however, is businesses that are willing to pay to make their list of goods and services available to the network. It is a chicken-and-egg problem: Users will not flock to an online agency until many merchants and services are online, but the merchants and service providers will not sign up until there are many users.

Software agents are not limited to shopping. An agent is smarter than a standard search engine, partly because the agent indexes not the Web but the user. It knows its user's preferences and can, for example, find a list of appropriate restaurants in Phoenix for your next business trip. The list will include Mexican and Thai food (two of your favorites) but no fast food or cafeterias (anathema).

1 Type instructions to your electronic agent about a camera you want

2 Your agent finds the correct directory, in this case, camera stores

3 The agent checks the inventories of cameras listed by the camera stores

4 When you check back, the agent displays suitable options

decision-making tasks. The key ingredient of a decision support system is a modeling process. A **model** is a mathematical representation of a real-life system. A mathematical model can be computerized. Like any computer program, the model can use inputs to produce outputs. The inputs to a model are called **independent variables** because they can change; the outputs are called **dependent variables** because they depend on the inputs.

Consider this example. Suppose, as a manager, you have the task of deciding which property to purchase for one of your manufacturing plants. You have many factors to consider: the appraised value, asking price, interest rate, down payment required, and so on. These are all independent variables—the data that will be fed into the computer model of the purchase. The dependent variables, computed on the basis of the inputs, are the effect on your cash resources, long-term debt, and ability to make other investments. To increase complexity, we could add that the availability of workers and nearness to markets are also input factors. Increasing the complexity is appropriate, in fact, because decision support systems often work with problems that are more complex than any one individual can handle.

Using a computer model to reach a decision about a real-life situation is called **simulation.** It is a game of "let's pretend." You plan the independent variables—the inputs—and you examine how the model behaves based on the dependent variables—the outputs—it produces. If you wish, you can change the inputs and continue experimenting. This is a relatively inexpensive way to simulate business situations, and it is considerably faster than the real thing.

The decision-making process must be fast, so the DSS is interactive: The user is in direct communication with the computer system and can affect its activities. In addition, most DSSs cross departmental lines so that information can be pulled from the databases of a variety of sources, such as marketing and sales, accounting and finance, production and research and development. A manager trying to make a decision about developing a new product, for example, needs information from all of these sources.

A decision support system does not replace an MIS; instead, a DSS supplements an MIS. There are distinct differences between them. MIS emphasizes planned reports on a variety of subjects; DSS focuses on decision making. MIS is standard, scheduled, structured, and routine; DSS is quite unstructured and available on request. MIS is constrained by the organizational system; DSS is immediate and friendly.

Executive Support Systems

Top-level executives and decision makers face unique decision-making problems and pressures. An **executive support system (ESS)** is a decision support system especially made for senior-level executives. An executive support system is concerned with how decisions affect an entire organization. An ESS must take into consideration

- The overall vision or broad view of company goals
- Strategic long-term planning and objectives
- Organizational structure
- Staffing and labor relations
- Crisis management
- Strategic control and monitoring of overall operations

Executive decision making also requires access to outside information from competitors, federal authorities, trade groups, consultants, and news-gathering agencies, among others. A high degree of uncertainty and a future orientation are involved in most executive decisions. Successful ESS software must therefore be easy to use, flexible, and customizable.

Several commercial software packages are available for specific modeling purposes. The purpose might be marketing, sales, or advertising. Other packages that are more general provide rudimentary modeling but let you customize the model for different purposes—budgeting, planning, or risk analysis.

▶ Managing Personal Computers

Personal computers burst onto the business scene in the early 1980s with
little warning and less planning. The experience of the Rayer International Paper Company is typical. One day a personal computer appeared
on the desk of engineer Mike Burton—he had brought his in from
home. Then accountants Sandy Dean and Mike Molyneaux got a pair of
machines—they had squeezed the money for them out of the overhead
budget. Nobuko Locke, the personnel manager, got personal computers
for herself and her three assistants in the company's far-flung branch
offices. And so it went, with personal computers popping up all over the
company. Managers realized that the reason for runaway purchases was
that personal computers were so affordable: Most departments could
pay for them out of existing budgets, so the purchasers did not have to
ask anyone's permission.

Managers, at first, were tolerant. There were no provisions for managing the purchase or use of personal computers, and there certainly was
no rule against them. And it was soon apparent that these machines
were more than toys. Pioneer users had no trouble justifying their purchases—their increased productivity spoke for them. In addition to mas-
tering software for word processing, spreadsheets, and database access,
these users declared their independence from the MIS department (Figure 15.3).

Managers, however, were soon faced with several problems. The first
was that no one person was in charge of the headlong plunge into personal computers. The second problem was incompatibility—the new
computers came in an assortment of brands and models and did not
mesh well. Software that worked on one machine did not necessarily
work on another. Third, users were not as independent of the MIS

Figure 15-3 Personal computers. Managers must monitor the use of personal
computers in the workplace.

department as they had thought—they needed assistance in a variety of ways. In particular, they needed data that was in the hands of the MIS department. In addition, companies were soon past the stage of the initial enthusiasts; they wanted all kinds of workers to have personal computers, and those workers needed training. Furthermore, in just a few years, most companies networked their computers together, bringing a whole new set of responsibilities and problems. Finally, many companies had so many personal computers that they did not know how many, or where they were, or what software was on them. Many organizations solved these management problems in the following ways:

- They corrected the management problem by creating a new position called the personal computer manager, which often evolved to the network manager.
- They addressed the compatibility problem by establishing acquisition policies.
- They solved the assistance problem by creating information centers and providing a variety of training opportunities.
- They used software to locate, count, and inventory their personal computers.

Let us examine each of these solutions.

The Personal Computer Manager

The benefits of personal computers for the individual user have been clear almost from the beginning: increased productivity, worker enthusiasm, and easier access to information. But once personal computers move beyond entry status, standard corporate accountability becomes a factor. Large companies are spending millions of dollars on personal computers, and top-level managers want to know where all this money is going. Company auditors begin worrying about data security. The company legal department begins to worry about workers copying software illegally. Before long everyone is involved, and it is clear that someone must be placed in charge of personal computer use. That person is the **personal computer manager.**

There are four key areas that need the attention of this manager:

- **Technology overload.** The personal computer manager must maintain a clear vision of company goals so that users are not overwhelmed by the massive and conflicting claims of aggressive vendors plying their wares. Users engulfed by phrases like *network topologies* and *file gateways* or a jumble of acronyms can turn to the personal computer manager for guidance.
- **Cost control.** Many people who work with personal computers believe the initial costs are paid back rapidly, and they think that should satisfy managers who hound them about expenses. But the real costs entail training, support, hardware and software extras, and communications networks—much more than just the computer itself. The role of the personal computer manager includes monitoring all related expenses.
- **Data security and integrity.** Access to corporate data is a touchy issue. Many personal computer users find they want to download (or access) data from the corporate mainframe to their own machines,

MAKING THE RIGHT CONNECTIONS

REMOTE USERS

Many companies want their sales representatives out of the office, both to reduce office costs and to make the sales effort more effective. But these representatives must have adequate access to computer data. Offering remote users access to data residing in computers in the office frees them from having to carry around large amounts of data. Sales people using laptop computers can connect to the home office to download pricing information from the mainframe to the laptop and to upload order

entries from the field to the mainframe computer. The connection also manages electronic mail.

MIS managers have a variety of concerns about remote users and their access to information from the company's mainframe. The first concern is security. Remote users, at the least, should use a password when making connections. Training is a consistent problem because road warriors seldom come into the office for extended periods. Finally, MIS managers worry about equipment being lost or stolen.

and this presents an array of problems. Are they entitled to the data? Will they manipulate the data in new ways and then present it as the official version? Will they expect the MIS to take the data back after they have done who-knows-what with it? The answers to these perplexing questions are not always clear-cut, but at least the personal computer manager will be tuned in to the issues.

■ **Computer junkies.** What about employees who are feverish with the new power and freedom of the computer? When they are in school, these user-abusers are sometimes called hackers; on the job they are often called junkies because their fascination with the computer seems like an addiction. Unable to resist the allure of the machine, they overuse it and neglect their other work. Personal computer managers usually respond to this problem by setting down guidelines for computer use.

The person selected to be the personal computer manager is usually from the MIS area. Ideally, this person has a broad technical background, understands both the potential and limitations of personal computers, and is well known to a diverse group of users.

With the advent of networking, the personal computer manager is often the same person as the **network manager** or, if the network is a local area network, the **LAN manager.** The network manager must keep the network operational. The manager's basic task is to let network users share program and data files and resources such as printers. The network manager is responsible for installing all software on the network and making sure that existing software runs smoothly. The network manager also must make sure that backup copies are made of all files at regular intervals. In addition, the network must be kept free from viruses and other illegal software intrusions. The greatest challenge may be to make sure that the network has no unauthorized users.

Company managers often underestimate the amount of work it takes to keep even a small network going. In a large company an individual or even an entire team of people may be dedicated to this task. In a small company the network may be managed by someone who already has a full-time job at the company.

Personal Computer Acquisition

As we noted, workers initially purchased personal computers before any companywide or even officewide policies had been set. The resulting compatibility problems meant that they could not easily communicate or share data. Consider this example: A user's budgeting process calls for certain data that resides in the files of another worker's personal computer or perhaps involves figures output by the computer of a third person. If the software and machines these people use do not mesh, compatibility becomes a major problem.

In many companies MIS departments have now taken control of personal computer acquisition. The methods vary, but they often include establishing standards and restricting the number of vendors used. Most companies now have established standards for personal computers, for the software that will run on them, and for data communications. Commonly, users must stay within established standards so that they can tie into corporate resources. Some companies limit the number of vendors— sellers of hardware and software—from whom they allow purchases. Managers have discovered that they can prevent most user complaints about incompatibility, not to mention getting a volume discount, by allowing products from just a handful of vendors.

The Information Center

We mentioned the **information center** briefly in Chapter 2 as the place where workers can get help with software problems. In large organizations, the information center, often called by other names such as *support center,* offers help to users in several forms. The information center is devoted exclusively to giving users service. And best of all, user assistance is immediate, with little or no red tape.

Information center services often include the following:

- **Software selection.** The information center staff helps users determine which software packages suit their needs.
- **Data access.** If appropriate, the staff helps users get data from the large corporate computer systems for use on the users' computers.
- **Network access.** A staff typically offers information about using the network system, tells how to obtain passwords and authorization, disseminates security information, and probably offers regular classes on the Internet.
- **Training.** Education is a principal reason for an information center's existence. Classes are usually small, frequent, and on a variety of topics (Figure 15-4). The information center is not the only form of training, however; we will discuss training in more detail shortly.

■ **Technical assistance.** Information center staff members stand ready to assist in any way possible, short of actually doing the users' work for them. That help includes advising on company standards for hardware purchases, aiding in the selection and use of software, finding errors, helping submit formal requests to the MIS department, and so forth.

To be successful, the information center must be placed in an easily accessible location. The center should be equipped with personal computers and terminals, a stockpile of software packages, and perhaps a library. It should be staffed with people who have a technical background but whose explanations feature plain English. Their mandate is "the user comes first."

Dumping Technology on Workers

Any manager knows that simply "dumping" technology—hardware, software, networks, whatever—on workers in the hope of increased productivity would be a disaster. The first obvious approach is to provide training for the new technology, whatever it is.

Training: Pay Now or Pay Later   Organizations tend to be remiss about training. Years ago, vendors typically included training as part of the hardware or software package. Once training became a separate item with a separate price tag, organizations were more apt to think they could get along without it. Furthermore, although training was once needed for just a few technical workers, now training is needed for entire populations of workers companywide.

Those who do offer training too often rely on the one-shot teacher-in-the-classroom model. This traditional approach, however, does not work well. To begin with, unless the classes are off-site or attendance is rigor-

Figure 15-4 The information center. Classes are held at the information center to teach managers and other employees how to use the company's computers.

Looking Intently at the Screen

Suppose that you see an office worker with a furrowed brow, obviously involved in his work on the computer. But look more closely—is it a spreadsheet or a database inquiry on the screen? Why no, it is a game of solitaire. This fellow is goofing off at work.

Should he be playing solitaire on his personal computer at the office? Maybe. The game was included as an extra in Microsoft Windows, partly to promote friendliness to home users. Its popularity was rather a surprise, and not an especially pleasant one, to the companies whose employees are using Windows.

Some managers have adopted the attitude that a little relaxation with a computer game relieves stress, but many more have reacted negatively, prohibiting employees from playing games at the office. Some have gone so far as to remove all games from the company's personal computers.

ously enforced, participation may be sporadic because employees are much more concerned about the real work that has been abandoned on their desks. Furthermore, especially when new software is the topic, training lasting two days or two weeks, even hands-on in a computer-stocked classroom, yields minimal results.

Workers adopting new technology do need initial training, but they also need follow-up support. One approach that seems to work well is to cultivate home-grown gurus. When confronted with a computer problem, the first instinct of a baffled user is to consult a more knowledgeable friend or colleague. With this in mind, savvy companies, after the first round of training, ask for volunteers who would like to learn more. These users become the office gurus on that technology. Initially, they may not know a lot more than their colleagues, but they are usually a bit ahead and, by sheer numbers of consultations, accumulate more knowledge than other workers.

In-house support, such as an information center, can be a big factor in the success of new technology. The best guarantee that workers will absorb training, however, is prior motivation, achieved by getting them involved.

Involving the Workers   The catchphrase often used is *empowering the workers*. It is a variation on the systems analyst precept of user involvement. Rather than simply installing new technology and training the workers, begin with the workers—the people who will be using the technology. To put it another way, deal with the people at the same time as you deal with the technology.

Paine Webber, a stock brokerage, offers a model approach. Paine Webber wanted to upgrade its brokers' ten-year-old computer system to a network that would offer far more information access and control. The systems analyst began by surveying the attitudes of the 5000-plus brokers. He discovered that approximately one-third of the brokers felt the current system met their needs, another third thought they would like some improvements, and the final third thought that the current system was hopelessly outmoded.

The company's response was to build a dazzling new system with the old system built into it. Paine Webber unfolded the new system branch by branch, emphasizing not the wonders of technology but what the system could do for brokers. The instructors were not technical types but specially trained Paine Webber employees who already knew the brokerage business. This worked well for everyone, even those who were initially reluctant. Workers whose comfort level was the old system could begin with that version, but most of them gradually picked up the features of the new system.

Finally, regarding worker involvement, do not forget the generation gap. Employees who grew up playing video games have a built-in advantage over their elders, who may show the foot-dragging signs of a pre-computer upbringing. In fact, training experts recommend that big-time computerphobes loosen up by playing computer games. This way they will at least become comfortable with a mouse and with interactions that cause changes on the computer screen.

Computers at Work

GALLERY

Computers in a Variety of Settings

In this gallery we look at some of the ways in which workers put computers to use on the job. The photo that opens this gallery shows airline workers using a computer to track airplane gate assignments.

When people think of computers in the workplace, they probably envision a traditional office setting. Computers, however, are in all kinds of workplace settings, some of which are shown here.

1. This architect uses her computer in a traditional office setting.
2. This nurseryman carries his computer around the greenhouse to record growth progress and any problems.
3. Many hard-hat workers use computers both for information and to record work completed for billing purposes.
4. This worker is using his computer to monitor pipes in a ship.
5. Medical workers of all kinds use computers as essential components of their work. This lab technician records test results and uses software to make comparisons.
6. "Three Men and a Computer" would be a realistic movie title. Here, these marketers argue the success of strategies in different markets.
7. The owner of a bicycle shop sells and repairs bicycles and records absolutely everything—customers, bikes, repair records, and billing—on his computer.
8. The workings of this cement factory can be monitored by one person and a raft of computers.

Computers on the Go

Many workers need their computers on the job no matter where they are, so they simply take their computers with them.

9. Some workers catch up on work wherever they are, even on a bench in the park.

10. Computers and cappuccino—not an unusual combination these days.

11. These three business people have a quick conference over their computers at the airport.

12. Computers are used in all aspects of farming. Here, a farmer records crop planting information.

13. Some workers fearlessly use their laptop computers in public places, even if they do draw some attention.

14. This attorney takes his notebook computer with him to record the results of his research in the law library.

15. This marine biologist uses a laptop computer, wrapped to protect it from moisture, to record data she observes in various water-related environments.

16. It makes sense for these workers, the architect and the lead contractor, to have a computer handy on-site to access design and materials information and to record data.

9

10

11

12

4

GALLERY

13

16

14

15

Computer Graphics at Work

Computer graphics software lets designers choose from a wide range of colors and styles to create just the image they need, whether for advertising, magazine covers, tourism, or some other useful purpose.

17. Artist Stefano Maugeri renders a computer image of a trolley car to be used as a product illustration.

18. Artist Pamela Hobbes made this graphic to accompany a Kid Fare feature in the Chicago Tribune.

19. This stunning image was made by graphic artists to use as their own advertising logo.

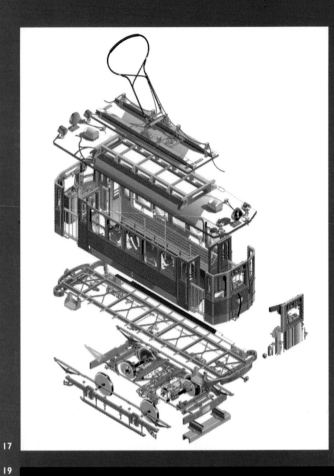

17

18

19

20. Artist Marc Yankus made this graphic to be used by AT&T in an advertisement that discussed technology and the environment, and 21. this image to be used as a cover for a math book.

22. Artist Diane Fenster made this illustration to accompany a magazine article comparing color monitors.

23. Artist Tom White made this graphic to accompany an magazine article about filling out tax forms.

THE COMPUTER DESIGN & ART EXHIBITION

20

21

22

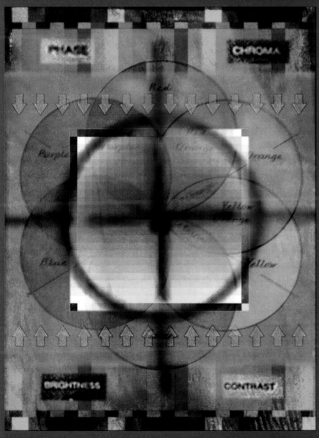

23

Robots at Work

When most people think of robots, they probably have in mind the typical humanoid-shaped automaton of classic science fiction movies. But robots of all shapes and sizes are performing a variety of serious tasks—without looking much like people.

24. A multiple exposure of a computer-controlled robot doing arc welding on the pipework of a car exhaust.

25. This robotic arm is used in manufacturing microchips on wafers.

26. This pharmaceutical robot arm can accurately prepare an order of medicine.

27. This robot is guarding art objects at the Los Angeles County Museum of Art. The robot's computer has detailed maps of the museum; it travels on three wheels, using an ultrasonic navigation system. Its detectors can give warnings of smoke, fire, and increased humidity or gases. It can also detect movement and warn of an intruder.

24
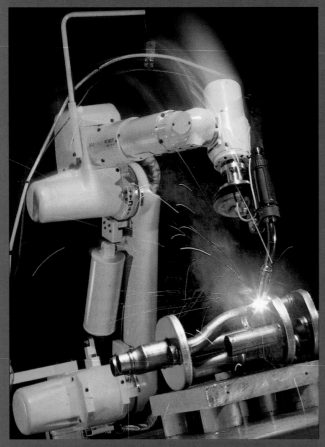

25
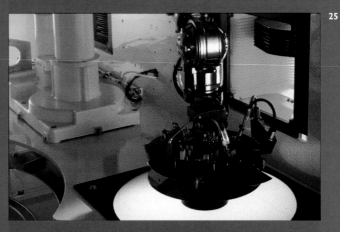

26
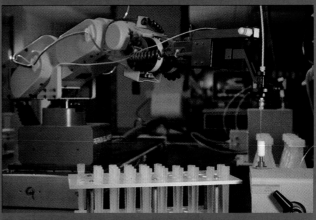

27

Do You Even Know Where Your PCs Are?

Many corporate administrators, when put to the test, are embarrassed to admit that they do not know where corporate personal computers are in use in the company; in fact, they do not even know how many there are. One manager, for example, was quite certain that the company had 600 personal computers and an average of 12 users per printer. The reality turned out to be quite different; there were 1100 computers and one printer per computer. To make matters even worse, managers have no idea what software is on the computers—Microsoft Excel or WordPerfect, or perhaps the latest incarnation of Doom.

This is a critical problem because administrators have no idea how to budget for their personal computers. Contrary to folklore, personal computers cost much more than their original modest price. The initial purchase price of a corporate personal computer accounts for only 10 percent of its lifetime cost. The rest is spent on troubleshooting, administration, software, and training. If the computers are hidden, then so are the costs of maintaining them. Clearly, administrators must confront the missing-computers problem.

Specialized computer services now offer a sort of lost-and-found for personal computers and related equipment. Corporate personal computers that are networked—and that means most of them—can be counted and interrogated by software set up on the network. The polling software not only counts computers but also determines their components and software.

Once companies get a handle on what they have, they can begin containing costs.

Leading Business into the Future

Who will manage businesses in the future? Someone once remarked, somewhat facetiously, that all top management—presidents, chief executive officers (CEOs), and so forth—should be drawn from the MIS ranks. After all, the argument goes, computers pervade the entire company, and people who work with computer systems can bring broad experience to the job. Today, most presidents and CEOs still come from legal, financial, or marketing backgrounds. But as the computer industry and its professionals mature, that pattern could change.

★ ★ ★ ★

There are challenges for managers at every level. In addition to the ordinary technological changes for which they can be somewhat prepared, they face technology on the cutting edge, the subject of the next chapter.

CHAPTER REVIEW

Summary and Key Terms

■ All managers have five main functions: **planning**, **organizing**, **staffing**, **directing**, and **controlling**. A management pyramid shows that top-level managers focus primarily on strategic functions, especially long-range planning; middle-level managers focus on the tactical, especially the organizing and staffing required to implement plans; and low-level managers are concerned mainly with operational functions, controlling schedules, costs, and quality as well as directing personnel.

■ A **management information system (MIS)** is a set of business systems designed to provide information for decision making. A computerized MIS is most effective if it is integrated.

■ The **MIS manager**, a person familiar with both computer technology and the organization's business, runs the MIS department.

■ The traditional management pyramid has been flattened by the dissemination and sharing of information over computer networks. The impact of groupware has removed exclusive manager access to information and has forced managers to share decision making. Some companies are organizing workers into teams around tasks.

■ A **decision support system (DSS)** is a computer system that supports managers in non-routine decision-making tasks. A DSS involves a **model**, a mathematical representation of a real-life situation. A computerized model allows a manager to try various "what-if" options by varying the inputs, or **independent variables**, to see how they affect the outputs, or **dependent variables**. The use of a computer model to reach a decision about a real-life situation is called **simulation**. Since the decision-making process must be fast, the DSS is interactive, allowing the user to communicate directly with the computer system and affect its activities.

■ An **executive support system (ESS)** is a decision support system for senior-level executives, who make decisions that affect an entire company.

■ When personal computers first became popular in the business world, most businesses did not have general policies regarding them, which led to several problems. Many businesses created the position of **personal computer manager** (later called the **network manager** or **LAN manager**) to ensure coordination of personal computers, established acquisition policies to solve the compatibility problem, established **information centers** to provide assistance to users, provided formal and informal training for users, and used software to monitor their existing personal computers.

Quick Poll

Compare your answers to those of your colleagues or classmates.

1. With the increasing pervasiveness of computers in the workplace,
   ❑ a. I envision the management pyramid flattening out to very few at the top—managers the workers would never see.
   ❑ b. I can imagine a time when a manager is needed merely to arrange people in teams and then the teams manage themselves.
   ❑ c. The role of the computer in management seems overblown. We still need managers to deal with everyday problems related to people, schedules, and plans.
2. Which, if any, of these jobs might appeal to you, assuming you had the background:
   ❑ a. Helping people in an information center

❏ b. Managing a network
❏ c. MIS manager
3. Regarding managing as a career:
   ❏ a. Middle managers continue to be replaced by computers—I'd get ulcers waiting for the ax.
   ❏ b. I like organizing and I like people, so I'd probably like managing.
   ❏ c. The only part that appeals to me is strategic planning; I don't want to worry about people problems.

Discussion Questions

1. Suppose a team of eight people in a construction firm is designing a new hospital. The team members, drawn from several departments, include two engineers, two architects, an electrician, a plumber, a graphic designer, and a planner. How and by whom might the classic management functions be carried out?
2. Describe a problem situation that could be simulated through a decision support system. Specify the input factors and the types of output.
3. What special pressures might be on a network manager?

Student Study Guide

True/False

T F   1. The information center typically offers users training and assistance.
T F   2. The function of the network manager is to help executives with decision support systems.
T F   3. Communication of information is most efficient through the traditional management pyramid.
T F   4. Decision support systems help managers in nonroutine decision-making tasks.
T F   5. A model is a mathematical representation of an artificial situation.
T F   6. Middle-level managers focus on planning.
T F   7. Inputs to a model are called independent variables.
T F   8. Groupware is usually focused on groups of executives.
T F   9. The use of personal computers by managers is declining.
T F 10. Simulation is using a model to predict real-life situations.
T F 11. Part of the reason for changes in the classic management model is the increased use of networked computers.
T F 12. A personal computer manager is concerned only with technical issues.
T F 13. The use of groupware encourages workers in different organizations to communicate laterally, as opposed to going through the traditional management hierarchy.
T F 14. The use of networked computers in the organization has made information more unavailable than ever to workers.
T F 15. The flattened management pyramid has significantly increased the need for more mid-level managers.

Answers

True/False

1. T	6. F	11. T
2. F	7. T	12. F
3. F	8. F	13. T
4. T	9. F	14. F
5. F	10. T	15. F

PLANET INTERNET

RESEARCH AND RESOURCES

Need information? Need it fast? Whether commonplace or rare, any information you may need is probably somewhere on the Internet.

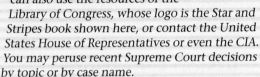

Government resources. The government had a head start and has made excellent use of the Internet. We have already mentioned the White House web site (in Chapter 1), but you can also use the resources of the Library of Congress, whose logo is the Star and Stripes book shown here, or contact the United States House of Representatives or even the CIA. You may peruse recent Supreme Court decisions by topic or by case name.

Although you may have little inclination to do so, you can access the Internal Revenue Service site to get forms or advice. The U.S. Census Bureau has an enormous amount of information that is useful to businesses and organizations large and small. The Smithsonian, whose identifying castle is shown here, has searchable historic information and a significant online photo collection. The National Archives houses the Declaration of Independence, the Constitution (indexed), and a wonderful set of historic posters, such as the woman rolling up her sleeves for the war effort shown here.

Information you can use. Consider bits of information you might need in any given week. A weather forecast for your travel destination? Every sort of weather information is available, for regions and individual cities. Buying a new or used car? Pricing information is just a computer away. Going camping? Check the National Parks Service for locations, entrance fees, and campground reservation information.

As you would expect, consumer information is available on the Internet on just about any topic. Further, the National Fraud Information Center post alerts to current scams. The Old Farmer's Almanac supplies crop information and, notably, weather predictions. Bartlett's Familiar Quotations lets you find that needed quote in a hurry. Some sites offer an entire comprehensive library online; others are devoted to information on fairly specific topics, such as the Sixties. Finally, would you just like a good book? Project Gutenberg makes books available online.

Reaching out. Nonprofit organizations such as the Internet Nonprofit Center, whose logo is shown here, use the 'Net to provide information to donors and volunteers. Impact Online helps people get involved with nonprofits nationwide. One advantage of a truly *world wide* web is the possibility of addressing worldwide issues. The site for Friends of the Earth, an environmental group, is in Britain.

Internet Exercises

1. **Structured exercise.** Begin with the AWL site with URL http://hepg.awl.com/capron/planet/, and enjoy the historic posters at the National Archives.
2. **Freeform exercise.** Pick one topic at the Smithsonian to explore in depth.

Joyce Lindsay worked as a credit consultant for Nordstrom, a chain of stores selling high-quality clothing. Joyce had developed significant expertise over a period of years. Consider this example. A customer comes to the store, selects a $300 coat, and hands her Nordstrom charge card to the sales clerk. However, the customer's credit limit is just $1000, and she has existing unpaid credit of $875. Should the customer be allowed to charge the coat anyway, or should the clerk adhere strictly to the credit limit? This ticklish question is turned over to Joyce, who, after quickly reviewing the customer's records, is able to grant the extra charge.

Although this seems like a system that works pretty well, Nordstrom recently converted the whole process to an expert system, a computer system in which the computer plays the role of expert. Why go to all that trouble and expense? Why not just stick with human experts? Well, there are problems with human experts. They are typi-cally expensive, subject to biases and emotions, and they may even be inconsistent. However, the biggest problem is that the expertise of one individual is not readily available to multiple users at the same time. Finally, there have been occasions when experts have resigned or retired, leaving the company in a state of crisis. The computer, however, is ever present and just as available as the telephone.

When the new expert system was being developed at Nordstrom, computer specialists approached Joyce to ask her how she made her decisions. Some experts cling to the notion that their decisions are based on instinct, some kind of gut reaction. Study always reveals, how-ever, that their "instincts" are based on a set of rules, possibly so embed-ded in their brains that the experts themselves are not even aware of it. Joyce was able to articulate most of her procedures to the computer spe-cialist. In the example just given, the purchaser's records showed that she consistently paid her bill on time, that her average monthly balance was usually low, and that she had a good job. These insights, along with many other rules, became part of the new expert system.

What about Joyce? Is she now out of a job? No. With the installa-tion of the computerized system, her role as expert has changed. She is now a consultant to the expert system, which needs constant updating and monitoring. Joyce has also been assigned some manage-ment responsibilities and, generally, has a more interesting job than she had before.

CHAPTER

16

The Cutting Edge

Expert Systems, Robotics, and Virtual Reality

The Artificial Intelligence Field

Artificial intelligence (AI) is a field of study that explores how computers can be used for tasks that require the human characteristics of intelligence, imagination, and intuition. Computer scientists sometimes prefer a looser definition, calling AI the study of how to make computers do things that—at the present time—people can do better. The phrase "at the present time" is significant because artificial intelligence is an evolving science: As soon as a problem is solved, it is moved off the artificial intelligence agenda. A good example is the game of chess, once considered a mighty AI challenge. But now that most computer chess programs can beat most human competitors, chess is no longer an object of study by scientists and thus no longer on the artificial intelligence agenda.

Today the term *artificial intelligence* encompasses several subsets of interests (Figure 16-1):

- **Problem solving.** This area of AI includes a spectrum of activities, from playing games to planning military strategy.
- **Natural languages.** This facet involves the study of the person/computer interface in unconstrained English language.
- **Expert systems.** These AI systems present the computer as an expert on some particular topic.
- **Robotics.** This field involves endowing computer-controlled machines with electronic capabilities for vision, speech, and touch.

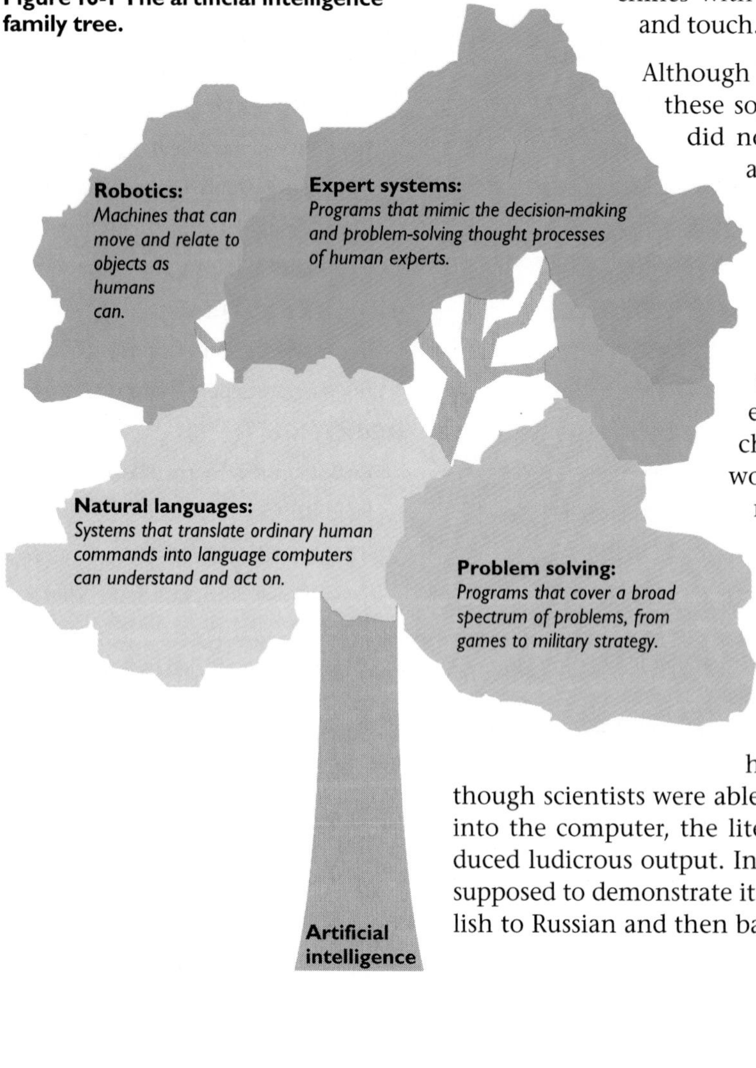

Although considerable progress has been made in these sophisticated fields of study, early successes did not come easily. Before examining current advances in these areas, let us pause to consider some early moments in the development of artificial intelligence.

Early Mishaps

In the early days of artificial intelligence, scientists thought that the computer would experience something like an electronic childhood, in which it would gobble up the world's libraries and then begin generating new wisdom. Few people talk like this today because the problem of simulating intelligence is far more complex than just stuffing facts into the computer. Facts are useless without the ability to interpret and learn from them.

An artificial intelligence failure on a grand scale was the attempt to translate human languages via the computer. Although scientists were able to pour vocabulary and rules of grammar into the computer, the literal word-for-word translations often produced ludicrous output. In one infamous example the computer was supposed to demonstrate its prowess by translating a phrase from English to Russian and then back to English. Despite the computer's best

Figure 16-1 The artificial intelligence family tree.

Robotics: Machines that can move and relate to objects as humans can.

Expert systems: Programs that mimic the decision-making and problem-solving thought processes of human experts.

Natural languages: Systems that translate ordinary human commands into language computers can understand and act on.

Problem solving: Programs that cover a broad spectrum of problems, from games to military strategy.

Artificial intelligence

MAKING THE RIGHT CONNECTIONS

REPORTS FROM THE BOTTOM OF THE OCEAN

An oceanographer needs to know what the water is like deep inside the ocean. The knowledge gleaned improves our understanding of how currents transport heat around the globe and, perhaps more importantly, our understanding of how climates are likely to change over time. One possibility for studying the ocean depths is to take a boat with a few dozen crew members and stick a thermometer into the ocean. But boats are slow and expensive, so very little data can be gathered this way.

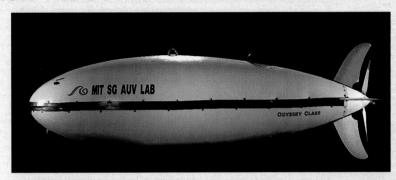

Enter Odyssey, the undersea robot, 8 feet long and weighing in at 50 pounds. Its innards, shown here, include two glass spheres that can withstand the pressure of miles of ocean water above it. Inside one sphere is the robot's computer and also a compass and pitch-and-roll sensors for navigation. The other sphere holds batteries to power the electronics and the motor. The motor itself and most of the sensors needed—sonars, camera, temperature and salinary sensors—come with their own pressure housings and can be arranged outside the spheres. An aerodynamically shaped outer plastic cover and rudders at the tail complete the picture.

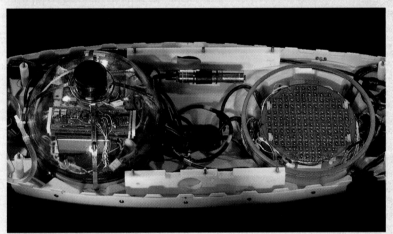

An early application of Odyssey was an experiment for the U.S. Navy off the North Slope of Alaska. Odyssey was dropped through a hole cut through the 6-foot-thick ice, swam around gathering data, and managed to find the hole again for retrieval. The Navy wanted to gather data on how ice breaks up, a poorly understood process that affects how the Earth responds to global warming.

But there is not just one Odyssey. The eventual plan is to have thousands of them, all cruising along the ocean depths gathering data. And what about communications? Several times a day, each will surface long enough to report its location and its current data via satellite.

efforts, the saying "The spirit is willing, but the flesh is weak" came back "The vodka is good, but the meat is spoiled."

An unfortunate result of this widely published experiment was the ridicule of artificial intelligence scientists, considered dreamers who could not accept the limitations of a machine. Funding for AI research disappeared, plunging the artificial intelligence community into a slump from which it did not recover until expert systems emerged in the 1980s. Nevertheless, a hardy band of scientists continued to explore artificial intelligence, focusing on how computers learn.

How Computers Learn

The study of artificial intelligence is predicated on the computer's ability to learn and to improve performance based on past errors. The two key elements of this process are called the knowledge base and the inference engine. A **knowledge base** is a set of facts and rules about those facts. An **inference engine** accesses, selects, and interprets a set of rules. The inference engine applies the rules to the facts to make up new facts—thus the computer has learned something new. Consider this simple example:

FACT: Amy is Ken's wife.
RULE: If X is Y's wife, then Y is X's husband.

The computer—the inference engine—can apply the rule to the fact and come up with a new fact: Ken is Amy's husband. Although the result of this simplistic example may seem of little value, it is indeed true that the computer now knows two facts instead of just one. Rules, of course, can be much more complex and facts more plentiful, yielding more sophisticated results. In fact, artificial intelligence software is capable of searching through long chains of related facts to reach a conclusion—a new fact.

Further explanation of the precise way in which computers learn is beyond the scope of this book. However, the learning discussion can be used as a springboard to the question that most people ask about artificial intelligence: Can a computer really think?

The Artificial Intelligence Debate

To imitate the functioning of the human mind, a machine with artificial intelligence would have to be able to examine a variety of facts, address multiple subjects, and devise a solution to a problem by comparing new facts to its existing storehouse of data from many fields. So far, artificial intelligence systems cannot match a person's ability to solve problems through original thought instead of by using familiar patterns as guides.

There are many arguments for and against crediting computers with the ability to think. Some say, for example, that computers cannot be considered intelligent because they do not compose like Beethoven or write like Shakespeare. The response is that neither do most ordinary human musicians or writers—you do not have to be a genius to be considered intelligent.

Look at it another way. Suppose you rack your brain over a problem and then—Aha!—the solution comes to you all at once. Now, how did you do that? You do not know, and nobody else knows either. A big part of human problem solving seems to be that jolt of recognition, that ability to see things suddenly as a whole. Experiments have shown that people rarely solve problems by using step-by-step logic, the very thing that computers do best. Most modern computers still plod through problems one step at a time. The human brain beats computers at "aha!" problem solving because it has millions of neurons working simultaneously.

Back to the basic question: Can a computer think or not? One possible answer: Who cares? If a machine can perform a task really well, does it matter whether it actually thinks? Still another answer is, Yes, machines will really think, but not as humans do. They lack the sensitivity, appreciation, and passion that are intrinsic to human thought.

Data Mining

Computer brainpower can also be brought to bear on stores of data through **data mining**, the process of extracting previously unknown information from existing data. You might think that once data has been gathered and made available, you could know everything about it, but this is not necessarily so.

The information stored in hundreds of thousands of records on disk can be tallied and summarized and perhaps even cross-referenced in some useful way by conventional computer programs. It is these traditional processes that produce the standard reports of business—bills and tax records and annual reports. But conventional processes are unlikely to discover the hidden information that might give a competitive edge. The possible hidden information is just the sort of thing that a thinking person might uncover if the amount of data was a manageable size. But no human can find nuances in massive data stores. Data mining, however, in a somewhat humanlike manner, may uncover data relationships and trends that are not readily apparent.

Companies are indeed using data mining techniques to sift through their databases, looking for unnoticed relationships. Wal-Mart, for example, does this every day to optimize inventories. At the end of the day, all the sales data from every store comes into a single computer that then interprets the data. The computer might notice, for example, that a lot of green sweaters have been selling in Boston and that, in fact, the supplies were depleted. The same green sweeter sold hardly at all in Phoenix. A human can figure out the reason: It is St. Patrick's Day and there are many Irish in Boston. For next St. Patrick's Day, the computer will order a larger supply of green sweaters for the Boston stores.

The Natural Language Factor

The language people use on a daily basis to write and speak is called a **natural language.** Natural languages are associated with artificial intelligence because humans can make the best use of artificial intelligence if they can communicate with computers in natural language. Furthermore, understanding natural language is a skill thought to require intelligence.

Some natural language words are easy to understand because they represent a definable item: *horse, chair, mountain*. Other words, however, are much too abstract to lend themselves to straightforward definitions: *justice, virtue, beauty*. But this kind of abstraction is just the beginning of the difficulty. Consider the word *hand* in these statements:

- Morgan had a hand in the robbery.
- Morgan had a hand in the cookie jar.
- Morgan is an old hand at chess.
- Morgan gave Sean a hand with his luggage.
- Morgan asked Marcia for her hand in marriage.
- All hands on deck!

As you can see, natural language abounds with ambiguities; the word *hand* has a different meaning in each statement. In contrast, sometimes statements that appear to be different really mean the same thing: "Alan sold Jim a book for five dollars" is equivalent to " Jim gave Alan five dollars in exchange for a book." It takes sophisticated software to unravel such statements and see them as equivalent.

Feeding computers the vocabulary and grammatical rules they need to know is a step in the right direction. However, as you saw earlier in the account of the language translation fiasco, true understanding requires more: Words must be taken in context. Humans start acquiring a context for words from the day they are born. Consider this statement:

Jack cried when Alice said she loved Bill. From our own context, several possible conclusions can be drawn: Jack is sad, Jack probably loves Alice, Jack probably thinks Alice doesn't love him, and so on. These conclusions may not be correct, but they are reasonable interpretations based on the context the reader supplies. On the other hand, it would *not* be reasonable to conclude from the statement that Jack is a carpenter or that Alice has a new refrigerator.

One of the most frustrating tasks for AI scientists is providing the computer with the sense of context that humans have. Scientists have attempted to do this in regard to specific subjects and found the task daunting. For example, a scientist who wrote software so that the computer could have a dialogue about restaurants had to feed the computer hundreds of facts that any small child would know, such as the fact that restaurants have food and that you are expected to pay for it.

▷ Expert Systems

An **expert system** is a software package used with an extensive set of organized data that presents the computer as an expert on a particular topic. For example, a computer could be an expert on where to drill oil wells, or on what stock purchase looks promising, or on how to cook soufflés. The user is the knowledge seeker, usually asking questions in a natural— that is, English-like—format. An expert system can respond to an inquiry about a problem with both an answer and an explanation of the answer. For example, an expert system specializing in stock purchases could be asked if stocks of the Milton Corporation are currently a good buy. A possible answer is no, with backup reasons such as a very high price/earnings ratio or a recent change in top management. The expert system works by figuring out what the question means and then matching it against the facts and rules that it "knows" (Figure 16-2). These facts and rules, which reside on disk, originally come from human experts.

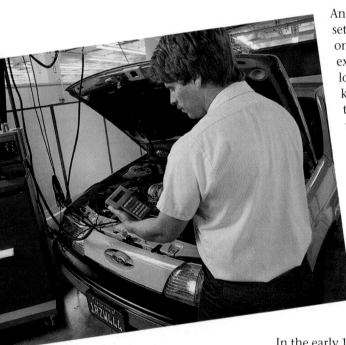

Figure 16-2 An expert system on the job. This expert system helps Ford mechanics track down and fix engine problems.

Expert Systems in Business

In the early 1980s expert systems began to make their way into commercial environments. Consider these examples:

- The Campbell Soup Company has an expert system nicknamed Aldo, for Aldo Cimino, the human expert who knows how to fix the company's cooking machines. Aldo was getting on in years and was being run ragged, flying from plant to plant whenever a cooker went on the blink. Besides, how would the company manage when he retired? Now Aldo's knowledge has been distilled into an expert system that can be used by workers in any location.
- Factory workers at the Boeing Company use an expert system to assemble electrical connectors for airplanes. In the old days workers had to hunt through 20,000 pages of cross-referenced specifications to find the right parts, tools, and techniques for the job—approxi-

mately 42 minutes per search. The expert system lets them do the same thing in about 5 minutes.

■ The United Airlines terminal at O'Hare Airport in Chicago handles 400 flights per day, which must be distributed among 50 gates. Complications include the limitations of jumbo jets, which do not maneuver easily into some gates. Furthermore, both the weather and heavy runway traffic can affect how quickly planes can get in and out. Airline employees, who used to track planes on a gigantic magnetic board, now keep track of gate positions with an expert system that takes all factors into account (Figure 16-3).

The cost of an expert system can usually be justified in situations where there are few experts but great demand for knowledge. It is also worthwhile to have a system that is not subject to human failings, such as fatigue.

Building an Expert System

Few organizations are capable of building an expert system from scratch. The sensible alternative is to buy an **expert system shell**, a software package that consists of the basic structure used to find answers to questions. It is up to the buyer to fill in the actual knowledge on the chosen subject. You could think of the expert system shell as an empty cup that becomes a new entity once it is filled—a cup of coffee, for instance, or a cup of sugar.

The most challenging task of building an expert system often is deciding who the appropriate expert is and then trying to pin down his or her knowledge. Experts often believe that much of their expertise is instinctive and thus find it difficult to articulate just why they do what they do. However, the expert is usually following a set of rules, even if the rules are only in his or her head. The person ferreting out the information, sometimes called a **knowledge engineer,** must have a keen eye and the skills of a diplomat.

Once the rules are uncovered, they are formed into a set of IF-THEN rules. For example, IF the customer has exceeded a credit limit by no more than 20 percent and has paid the monthly bill for six months, THEN extend further credit. After the system is translated into a computerized version, it is reviewed, changed, tested, and changed some more. This repetitive process can take months or even years. Finally, it is put into the same situations as the human expert would face, where it should give equal or better service but much more quickly.

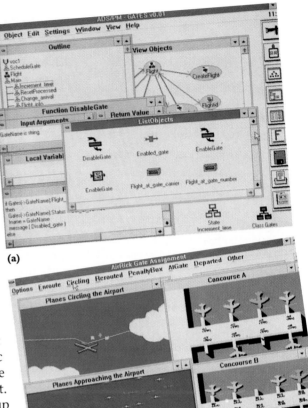

(a)

(b)

Figure 16-3 Airline scheduling program produced with the aid of an expert system. This system offers a graphical user interface to help solve a complex airport scheduling problem. (a) This screen illustrates the system's ability to display multiple views of objects and the relationships between them. (b) Various screen windows show planes circling the airport, the number of planes approaching the airport, gate information, and two concourses with planes at their gates.

▶ Robotics

Many people smile at the thought of robots, perhaps remembering the endearing C-3PO of *Star Wars* fame and its "personal" relationship with humans. But vendors have not made even a small dent in the personal robot market—the much-heralded domestic robots who wash windows have not yet become household staples. So where are the robots today? Mainly in factories.

Robot as Catcher

Catch this. This is one mean machine: It can catch a major-league fastball. The robot named WAM, for Whole Arm Manipulator, has a 3-foot appendage that reacts to what its very sensitive cameras see coming at it. But no one is trying to sign WAM to a major-league contract. In fact, WAM, developed at the Massachusetts Institute of Technology, will be used for precision manufacturing in hazardous environments.

Figure 16-4 Industrial robots.
(a) These standard robots are used in the auto industry to weld new cars. (b) This robot is not making breakfast. Hitachi uses the delicate egg, however, to demonstrate that its visual-tactile robot can handle fragile objects. The robot's sensors detect size, shape, and required pressure, attaining sensitivity almost equal to that of a human hand.

Robots in the Factory

Most robots are in factories, spray-painting and welding—and taking away jobs. The Census Bureau, after two centuries of counting people, has now branched out and today is counting robots as well. About 15,000 robots existed in 1985, a number that jumped to 50,000 just ten years later. What do robots do that merits all this attention?

A **robot** is a computer-controlled device that can physically manipulate its surroundings. There are a wide variety of sizes and shapes of robots, each designed with a particular use in mind. Often these uses are functions that would be tedious or even dangerous for a human to perform. The most common industrial robots sold today are mechanical devices with five or six directions of motion, so that they can rotate into proper position to perform their tasks (Figure 16-4).

Recently, **vision robots**, with the help of a TV-camera eye, have been taught to see in living color—that is, to recognize multicolored objects solely from their colors. This is a departure from the traditional approach, whereby robots recognize objects by their shapes (Figure 16-5), and from vision machines that "see" only a dominant color. For example, a robot in an experiment at the University of Rochester was able to pick out a box of Kellogg's Sugar Frosted Flakes from 70 other boxes. Among the anticipated benefits of such visual recognition skills is supermarket checkout. You cannot easily bar code a squash, but a robot might be trained to recognize it by its size, shape, and color.

Field Robots

Think of some of the places you would rather not be: inside a nuclear power plant, next to a suspected bomb, at the bottom of the sea, on the floor of a volcano, or in the middle of a chemical spill. But robots readily go to all those places. Furthermore, they go there to do some dangerous and dirty jobs. These days, **field robots**—robots "in the field"—inspect and repair nuclear power plants, dispose of bombs, inspect oil rigs used for undersea exploration, explore steaming volcanos, clean up chemical accidents, and even explore a battlefield in advance of soldiers. As an example, an undersea robot ventured into the icy waters off Finland and scanned the sunken ferry *Estonia*, sending back pictures of its weakened bow, thought to be a cause of the disaster. Newer undersea robots are being designed to swim like fish (Figure 16-6a). Going in another direc-

(a)

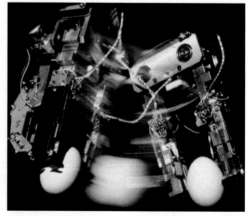

(b)

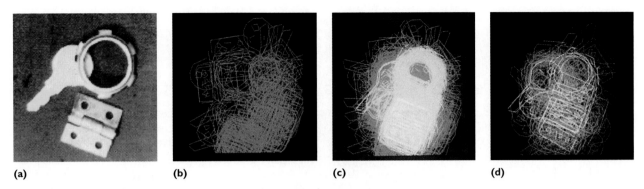

(a)   (b)   (c)   (d)

Figure 16-5 The seeing robot. Robots "see" by casting light beams on objects and matching their shapes to those of already "known" objects. In this machine-vision sequence, (a) the object is seen by the robot, (b) the object is matched to known shapes, (c) inappropriate shapes are eliminated, and (d) the object is recognized.

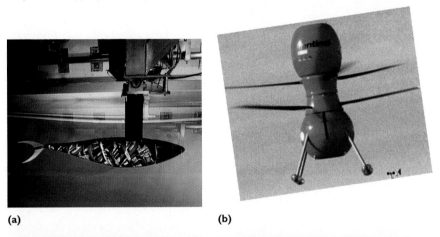

(a)   (b)

(c)

Figure 16-6 Field robots. (a) Nicknamed Robotuna, this undersea robot will, scientists hope, be able to map the ocean floor, track schools of real fish, or detect pollution—and then swim home with the data. (b) Can a robot really fly? Yes. Flying robots have both military and civilian uses. This Sentinel robot can soar up to 10,000 feet to spy on an enemy or to inspect high-voltage wires or to spot forest fires. (c) The robot called Spider checks gas tanks for cracks and sends computer images back to the ground, saving engineers from making a dangerous climb.

Getting Practical

ROBOTS COMING INTO OUR LIVES

If you think robots are not practical in your own life, think again. Like computers before them, robots will soon be everywhere. Here are some examples.

Fill it up. If filling your car's gas tank is not a favorite chore, you will be pleased to know that robots are taking over (see photo). Drivers pull up to a specially equipped station, swipe a plastic "tank card," and enter an identification number. The unit identifies the make and model of the auto, then guides the robotic arm to the car's fuel filler door. Once it is open, the robot then places the right grade and amount of gas in the tank and even replaces the cap.

My doctor the robot. If you have orthopedic surgery, you may find that a key player alongside the surgeon is a robot. For example, to make room for a hip implant, a robotic arm drills a long hole in a thigh bone. Robotic precision improves the implant, reduces pain after surgery, and speeds healing.

Lending a hand. Robots may soon be of significant use to the disabled. Researchers have already developed a robot for quadriplegics. The machine can respond to dozens of voice commands by answering the door, getting the mail, and even serving soup.

Road maintenance. In California, road signs may soon say "Robots at Work." Robots use lasers to spot cracks in the pavement and dispense the right amount of patch material. Soon robots will also be painting the road stripes.

Going bump in the night. Chip, the chunky errand boy on the night shift at Baltimore's Franklin Square Hospital, fetches medicine, late meals, medical records, and supplies. A robot, Chip finds his way using sensitive whiskers and touch pads to "feel." Nurses love him because he saves them from having to run all over the hospital.

tion, space researchers look forward to the day when "astrobots" can be stationed in orbit, ready to repair faulty satellites. Field robots may be equipped with wheels, tracks, legs, fins, or even wings (Figure 16-6b).

Field robots have largely been overshadowed by factory robots, mainly because until recently they have lacked the independence of their manufacturing counterparts, needing to be remotely controlled by human operators. Now, however, enough computer power can be packed into a field robot to enable it to make most decisions independently. Field robots need all the power they can get. Unlike factory robots, which are bolted to the ground and blindly do the same tasks over and over again, field robots must often contend with a highly unstructured environment, such as changing terrain and changing weather.

▶ Virtual Reality

The concept of **virtual reality**, sometimes called just **VR**, is to engage a user in a computer-created environment so that the user physically interacts with that environment. In fact, the user is so absorbed with the virtual reality interaction that the process is called **immersion.** Virtual reality alters perceptions partly by appealing to several senses at once—sight, hearing, and touch—and by presenting images that respond immediately to one's movements.

The visual part is made possible by sophisticated computers and optics that deliver to a user's eyes a three-dimensional scene in living color. The source of the scene is a database used by a powerful computer to display graphic images. The virtual reality system can sense a user's head and body movements through cables linked to the headset and glove worn by the user. That is, sensors on the user's body send signals to the computer, which then adjusts the scene viewed by the user. Thus, the user's body movements can cause interaction with the virtual (artificial) world the user sees, and the computer-generated world responds to those actions (Figure 16-7).

Travel Anywhere, but Stay Where You Are

At the University of North Carolina, computer scientists have developed a virtual reality program that lets a user walk through an art gallery. A user puts on a head-mounted display, which focuses the eyes on a screen and shuts out the rest of the world. If the user swivels his or her head to the right, pictures on the right wall come into view; similarly, the user can view any part of the gallery just by making head movements. This action/reaction presents realistic continuing changes to the user. Although actually standing in one place, the user feels as if he or she is moving and wants to stop short as a pedestal appears in the path ahead. It is as if the user is actually walking around inside the gallery.

In another example, scientists have taken data about Mars, sent back by space probes, and converted it to a virtual reality program. Information about hills, rocks, and ridges of the planet are used to create a Mars landscape that is projected on the user's head screen.

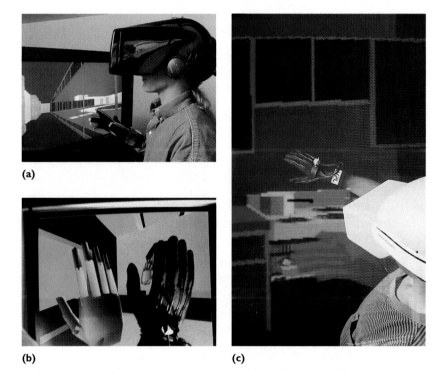

(a)

(b)

(c)

Figure 16-7 Virtual reality. (a) Users can "tour" a building by physically reacting—a turn of the head shows a different scene. (b) The data glove in the foreground has fiber-optic sensors to interact with a computer-generated world. (c) Virtual reality technology can be used to let people who are in wheelchairs design their own apartments.

NEW DIRECTIONS

FROM THE VIRTUAL TO THE REAL

Afraid of flying? We can help you with that, and you won't have to get near an airplane. Afraid of heights? We can give you the same fearful sensation without leaving the ground—and make you feel good about it. Need some expensive hands-on training? Now you can simulate it for half the price.

By donning a headset and using sensor controls, you can behave as if you were somewhere you are not. Trainers who help fearful flyers can let them simulate the identical experience, which is so real that sweaty palms are included. People who fear heights can "walk" a plank over a canyon, even lean-

ing daringly over the edge. Conventional treatment for phobias involves repeated exposure to experiences that cause anxiety. Virtual therapy saves time and money and has been shown to have a high success rate.

Training by virtual reality is being embraced by various segments of the community. Two important early users were doctors and pilots. But VR is moving to more generic audiences. The Oregon Research Institute, for example, is using virtual reality to help children learn to operate a motorized wheelchair (see photo). Not only does the training make them more self-sufficient, it gives them a sense of accomplishment.

While you personally may not yet be using virtual reality, it is emerging from the lab to various segments of society. Whether it someday joins the mainstream is yet to be seen.

The Promise of Virtual Reality

An embryonic technology such as virtual reality is filled with hype and promises. It is the practical commercial applications for real-world users that shows where this technology might lead. Here are some applications under development:

- Wearing head mounts, consumers can browse for products in a "virtual showroom." From a remote location, a consumer will be able to maneuver and view products along aisles in a warehouse.
- Similarly, from a convenient office perch a security guard can patrol corridors and offices in remote locations.
- Using virtual reality headsets and gloves, doctors and medical students will be able to experiment with new procedures on simulated patients rather than real ones.

Any new technology has its drawbacks. Some users experience "simulator sickness," even though they know the experience is not real. The developers of virtual reality are faced with daunting costs. Many hurdles remain in the areas of software, hardware, and even human behavior before virtual reality can reach its full potential.

★ ★ ★ ★

The immediate prospects for expert systems, robots, and virtual reality systems are growth and more growth. You can anticipate both increased sophistication and more diverse applications.

CHAPTER REVIEW

Summary and Key Terms

- **Artificial intelligence (AI)** is a field of study that explores how computers can be used for tasks that require the human characteristics of intelligence, imagination, and intuition. AI has also been described as the study of how to make computers do things that—at the present time—people can do better.

- Artificial intelligence is considered an umbrella term to encompass several subsets of interests, including problem solving, natural languages, expert systems, and robotics.

- In the early days of AI, scientists thought that it would be useful just to stuff facts into the computer; however, facts are useless without the ability to interpret and learn from them.

- An early attempt to translate human languages by providing a computer with vocabulary and rules of grammar was a failure because the computer could not distinguish the context of statements. This failure impeded the progress of artificial intelligence.

- The study of artificial intelligence is predicated on the computer's ability to learn and to improve performance based on past errors.

- A **knowledge base** is a set of facts and rules about those facts. An **inference engine** accesses, selects, and interprets a set of rules. The inference engine applies rules to the facts to make up new facts.

- People rarely solve problems using the step-by-step logic most computers use. The brain beats the computer at solving problems, because it has millions of neurons working simultaneously.

- **Data mining** is the process of extracting previously unknown information from existing data.

- **Natural languages** are associated with artificial intelligence because humans can make the best use of artificial intelligence if they can communicate with the computer in human language. Furthermore, understanding natural language is a skill thought to require intelligence. A key function of the AI study of natural languages is to develop a computer system that can resolve ambiguities.

- An **expert system** is a software package used with an extensive set of organized data that presents the computer as an expert on a specific topic. The expert system works by figuring out what the question means and then matching it against the facts and rules that it "knows."

- For years, expert systems were the exclusive property of the medical and scientific communities, but in the early 1980s they began to make their way into commercial environments.

- Some organizations choose to build their own expert systems to perform well-focused tasks that can easily be crystallized into rules, but few organizations are capable of building an expert system from scratch.

- Some users buy an **expert system shell,** a software package that consists of the basic structure used to find answers to questions. It is up to the buyer to fill in the actual knowledge on the chosen subject.

- The person working to extract information from the human expert is sometimes called a **knowledge engineer.**

- A **robot** is a computer-controlled device that can physically manipulate its surroundings. Most robots are in factories.

- **Vision robots** traditionally recognize objects by their shapes or else "see" a dominant color. But some robots can recognize multicolored objects solely from their colors.

■ **Field robots** inspect and repair nuclear power plants, dispose of bombs, inspect oil rigs for undersea exploration, put out oil well fires, clean up chemical accidents, and much more.

■ **Virtual reality**, sometimes called just **VR**, engages a user in a computer-created environment, so that the user physically interacts with the computer-produced three-dimensional scene. Since the user is so absorbed with the interaction, the process is called **immersion**.

Quick Poll

Compare your answers to those of your colleagues or classmates.

1. Can computers think?
   ❏ a. They do all sorts of jobs people once did. That's thinking at some level.
   ❏ b. Not really, because thinking includes reacting—with joy, sorrow, whatever.
   ❏ c. The discussion is pointless. Computers and humans are inherently different and will never "think" in equivalent ways.
2. About my own personal robot:
   ❏ a. It would not be of enough value to me to be bothered. Besides, with my luck, it would break.
   ❏ b. If it were advanced enough to do serious household chores, and if it were affordable, I'd be very interested.
   ❏ c. I would be very interested if I had some training and could experiment with the robot, altering its behavior.
3. Regarding virtual reality:
   ❏ a. It's great for kid games and fantasy movies, but not practical at this stage.
   ❏ b. It's a somewhat unformed technology but definitely promising.
   ❏ c. It has a few applications for architects and others but not for general use.

Discussion Questions

1. Describe the differences in the way humans and machines learn.
2. Is it possible to create an expert system for doing term papers? Why or why not?
3. What kind of jobs are threatened by robots? Consider some jobs you may wish to have, now or in the future. Are the workers who perform them likely to be replaced by robots?

Student Study Guide

True/False

T F   1. Artificial intelligence has always enjoyed wide respect from scientists and the government.
T F   2. *Artificial intelligence* is an umbrella term that covers many subjects.
T F   3. A knowledge base is a set of facts and rules about those facts.
T F   4. Early artificial intelligence scientists were called knowledge engineers.
T F   5. Early attempts to translate human language failed.
T F   6. An expert system is software.
T F   7. An expert system shell is used by the end-users of the expert system.
T F   8. Vision robots have sight capability that is significantly less than human capability.
T F   9. Field robots can do many tasks that are undesirable for humans.
T F 10. A knowledge engineer is a customer who uses an expert system.
T F 11. Using virtual reality, a user physically walks along hallways and from room to room.

T F 12. Most organizations that want expert systems do not attempt to build them from scratch.

T F 13. Using computers to mimic natural language is a relatively easy task for computer experts.

T F 14. Immersion refers to the environment of undersea robots.

T F 15. Computers generally solve problems in a step-by-step fashion.

T F 16. People always solve problems in a step-by-step fashion.

T F 17. An underlying assumption of artificial intelligence is that the computer can learn.

T F 18. Data mining means extracting previously unknown information from data files.

T F 19. An inference engine is the same as a knowledge base.

T F 20. Understanding natural language is a skill thought to require intelligence.

T F 21. At one time AI scientists were the subject of ridicule.

T F 22. In general, a given word in a natural language has a single meaning.

T F 23. Part of the need for data mining functions is related to a high volume of data.

T F 24. Most computer chess games can still be beaten by average human chess players.

T F 25. Most robots today are used in scientific experiments.

T F 26. Artificial intelligence is a subset of the field of expert systems.

T F 27. Some robots can swim, some robots can walk, and some robots can fly.

T F 28. Part of the difficulty with having a computer understand natural language is language ambiguities.

T F 29. The field of artificial intelligence has enjoyed broad support for several decades.

T F 30. Data mining involves both underground cables and underground storage.

Fill-In

1. The generic term for using computers for jobs requiring human characteristics: _____

2. The term for software that can be used to build an expert system: _____

3. The software that interprets facts and rules: _____

4. The kind of robot that can perform inspections and other dangerous tasks: _____

5. The person who extracts information from a human expert is called _____

6. When a person is totally involved in a VR experience, it is called _____

7. A device that can physically manipulate its surroundings is called _____

8. A set of facts and a set of rules about those facts is called _____

9. The language used by humans is called _____

10. The kind of robot that can distinguish objects by their shape or color: _____

Answers

True/False

1. F	6. T	11. F	16. F	21. T	26. F
2. T	7. F	12. T	17. T	22. F	27. T
3. T	8. T	13. F	18. T	23. T	28. T
4. F	9. T	14. F	19. F	24. F	29. F
5. T	10. F	15. T	20. T	25. F	30. F

Fill-In
1. artificial intelligence
2. expert system shell
3. inference engine
4. field robot
5. knowledge engineer
6. immersion
7. robot
8. knowledge base
9. natural language
10. vision robot

PLANET INTERNET

ENTERTAINMENT

Entertainment on the Internet falls into two categories. The first and largest category is *about* entertainment—sports, music, television, and movies. The second category includes the sites that offer online entertainment in and of themselves, notably games, children's sites, and especially humor.

Sports and more sports. You can follow any sport that captures your interest. The sport sites for the most popular sports—basketball, football, and baseball—compete with one another to offer the most complete account of scores, player statistics, schedules, standings, and even player injuries. ESPNet SportsZone is an example of a major sports presence on the Web; in fact it is a good example of a site that offers free access to much content but that charges a fee to access some of its popular services. Every manner of sport can be found on the Internet, from the Iditarod dog race in Alaska to the Tour de France cycling race in France.

Music, music, music. Everything you could possibly want to know about music is on the 'Net. Keep in mind that the multimedia capability of the Web means the potential for hearing as well as seeing the subject matter. The Rock and Roll Hall of Fame site has tourable exhibits and, among other things, a list of "500 songs that define rock and roll." Regardless of your taste—rock, classical, jazz, country, whatever—it's all on the 'Net.

The big guys. Conglomerates, especially those with an entertainment connection, are flocking to the Internet. As shown here, two such sites advertising their wares are Black Entertainment Television and MTV. If you prefer being a couch potato, the 'Net can serve your immediate needs with the site TV Tonight.

Online humor. The Internet has been a veritable hotbed of humor from the beginning. For a classic humor piece, see the purported news story of Microsoft acquiring the Vatican in exchange for stock. The Web's most famous cartoons are on the Doctor Fun site, where you can see a new cartoon each day and also check archives of previous cartoons. The Humor Archive is a good place to start for everything else.

Armchair entertainment. Ever wondered whether your phone number spells something interesting? For example, 929-2665 spells WAY-COOL. Stop by the Phonetic site to check yours out. If you like kitchen table games, the Games Domain site has every kind of game—board, card, and (of course) computer games.

Kids. There are many, many sites geared to entertaining children online. A popular site, as shown here, is Yeeeoww.

Go look. We have assembled a long list of entertainment links at the AWL site. Click and enjoy.

Internet Exercises

1. **Structured exercise.** Beginning with the AWL URL, http://hepg.awl.com/capron/planet/, go to the Phonetic site and get a new name for your telephone number. Hint: Give the two parts of your phone number separately; for 634-8366, for example, submit first 634 and then 8366.
2. **Freeform exercise.** Pick an interest, say music or sports, and compare offerings from the competing web sites.

Although the story of computers has deep roots, the most fascinating part—the history of personal computers—is quite recent. The beginning of this history turns on the personality of Ed Roberts the way a watch turns on a jewel. It began when his foundering company took a surprising turn.

Like other entrepreneurs before him, Ed Roberts had taken a big risk. He had already been burned once, and now he feared being burned again. The first time, in the early 1970s, he had borrowed heavily to produce microprocessor-based calculators, only to have the chip producers decide to build their own product and sell it for half the price of Ed's calculator.

Ed's new product was based on a microprocessor, too—the Intel 8080—but it was a *computer*. A little computer. The "big boys" at the established computer firms considered computers to be industrial products; who would want a small computer? Ed was not sure, but he found the idea so compelling that he decided to make the computer anyway. Besides, he was so far in

debt from the calculator fiasco that it did not seem to matter which project propelled him into bankruptcy. Ed's small computer and his company, MITS, were given a sharp boost by Les Solomon, who promised to feature the new machine on the cover of *Popular Electronics*. In Albuquerque, New Mexico, Ed worked frantically to meet the publication deadline, and he even tried to make the machine pretty, so it would look attractive on the cover (Figure A-1).

Making a good-looking small computer was not easy. This machine, named the Altair (after a heavenly *Star Trek* destination), looked like a flat box. In fact, it met the definition of a computer in only a minimal way: It had a central processing unit (on the chip), 256 characters (a paragraph!) of memory, and switches and lights on a front panel for input/output. No screen, no keyboard, no storage.

But the Altair was done on time for the January 1975 issue of *Popular Electronics,* and Roberts made plans to fly to New York to demonstrate the machine for Solomon. He sent the computer on ahead by railway

express. Ed got to New York, but the computer did not—the very first personal computer was lost! There was no time to build a new computer before the publishing deadline, so Roberts cooked up a phony version for the cover picture: an empty box with switches and lights on the front panel. He also placed an inch-high ad in the back of the magazine: "Get your own Altair kit for $397."

Ed was hoping for perhaps 200 orders. But the machine—that is, the box—fired imaginations across the country. Two thousand customers sent checks for $397 to an unknown Albuquerque, New Mexico, company. Overnight, the MITS Altair personal computer kit was a runaway success.

Ed Roberts was an important player in the history of personal computers. Unfortunately, he never made it in the big time; most observers agree that his business insight did not match his technical skills. But other entrepreneurs did make it. In this appendix we will glance briefly at the early years of computers and then examine more recent history.

History and Industry

The Continuing Story of the Computer Age

Figure A-1 The Altair. The term *personal computer* had not been coined yet, so Ed Roberts's small computer was called a "minicomputer" when it was featured on the cover of *Popular Electronics*.

▷ Babbage and the Countess

Born in England in 1791, Charles Babbage was an inventor and mathematician. When solving certain equations, he found the hand-done mathematical tables he used filled with errors. He decided that a machine could be built that would solve the equations better by calculating the differences between them. He set about making a demonstration model of what he called a **difference engine** (Figure A-2). The model was so well received that in about 1830 he enthusiastically began to build a full-scale working version, using a grant from the British government.

However, Babbage found that the smallest imperfections were enough to throw the machine out of whack. Babbage was viewed by his own colleagues as a man who was trying to manufacture a machine that was utterly ridiculous. Finally, after spending its money to no avail, the government withdrew financial support.

Despite this setback, Babbage was not discouraged. He conceived of another machine, christened the **analytical engine**, which he hoped would perform many kinds of calculations. Although it was never built in his time, a model was eventually put together by his son. It was not until 1991 that a working version of the analytical engine was built and put on public display in London. It embodied five key features of modern computers: an input device, a storage place to hold the number waiting to be processed, a processor, a control unit to direct the task to be performed and the sequence of calculations, and an output device.

If Babbage was the father of the computer, then Ada, the Countess of Lovelace, was the first computer programmer (Figure A-3). The daughter of English poet Lord Byron and of a mother who was a gifted mathematician, Ada helped develop the instructions for doing computations on the analytical engine. Lady Lovelace's contributions cannot be overvalued. She was able to see that Babbage's theoretical approach was workable, and her interest gave him encouragement. In addition, she published

Figure A-2 Charles Babbage's difference engine. Babbage's second difference engine was not completed in his lifetime. The one shown here was built in 1991 by the London Science Museum, according to Babbage's original design, in honor of Babbage's 200th birthday.

Figure A-3 Ada, the Countess of Lovelace. Augusta Ada Byron, as she was known before she became a countess, was Charles Babbage's colleague in his work on the analytical engine and has been called the world's first computer programmer.

a series of notes that eventually led others to accomplish what Babbage himself had been unable to do.

▷ Herman Hollerith: The Census Has Never Been the Same

The hand-done tabulation of the 1880 United States census took seven and a half years. A competition was held to find some way to speed the counting process of the 1890 United States census. Herman Hollerith's tabulating machine won the contest. As a result of the adoption of his system, an unofficial count of the 1890 population (62,622,250) was announced only six weeks after the census was taken.

The principal difference between Hollerith's and Babbage's machines was that Hollerith's machine used electrical rather than mechanical power (Figure A-4). Hollerith realized that his machine had considerable commercial potential. In 1896 he founded the successful Tabulating Machine Company, which, in 1924, merged with two other companies to form the International Business Machines Corporation—IBM.

▷ Watson of IBM

For more than 30 years, from 1924 to 1956, Thomas J. Watson Sr. ruled IBM with an iron grip. Cantankerous and autocratic, supersalesman Watson made IBM a dominant force in the business machines market, first as a supplier of calculators, then as a developer of computers.

Watson Smart? You Bet!

Just as computers were getting off the ground, Thomas J. Watson Sr. saw the best and brightest called to arms in World War II. But he did not just bid his employees a sad adieu. He paid them. Each and every one received one quarter of his or her annual salary, in twelve monthly installments. The checks continued to arrive throughout the duration of the war. Every month those former employees thought about IBM and the generosity of its founder.

The result? A very high percentage of those employees returned to IBM after the war. Watson got his brain trust back, virtually intact. The rest is history.

Figure A-4 Herman Hollerith's tabulating machine. This electrical tabulator and sorter was used to tabulate the 1890 census.

The Computer Museum

The Computer Museum in downtown Boston, Massachusetts, is the world's first museum devoted solely to computers and computing. The museum shows how computers have affected all aspects of life: science, business, education, art, and entertainment. Over half an acre of hands-on and historical exhibits chronicle the enormous changes in the size, capability, applications, and cost of computers over the past 40 years. Two minitheaters show computer classics as well as award-winning computer-animated films.

The Computer Museum Store offers a large selection of such unique items as state-of-the-art silicon chip jewelry and chocolate "chips," as well as books, posters, and cassettes.

Figure A-5 The ABC. John Atanasoff and his assistant, Clifford Berry, developed the first digital electronic computer.

IBM's entry into computers was sparked by a young Harvard professor of mathematics, Howard Aiken. In 1936, after reading Lady Lovelace's notes, Aiken began to think that a modern equivalent of the analytical engine could be constructed. Because IBM was already such a power in the business machines market, with ample money and resources, Aiken worked out a careful proposal and approached Thomas Watson. In one of those make-or-break decisions for which he was famous, Watson gave him $1 million. As a result, the Harvard Mark I was born.

The Start of the Modern Era

Nothing like the **Mark I** had ever been built before. It was 8 feet high and 55 feet long, made of streamlined steel and glass, and it emitted a sound during processing that one person said was "like listening to a roomful of old ladies knitting away with steel needles." Unveiled in 1944, the Mark I was never very efficient. But the enormous publicity it generated strengthened IBM's commitment to computer development. Meanwhile, technology had been proceeding elsewhere on separate tracks.

American military officials approached Dr. John Mauchly at the University of Pennsylvania and asked him to build a machine that would rapidly calculate trajectories for artillery and missiles. Mauchly and his student J. Presper Eckert relied on the work of Dr. John V. Atanasoff, a professor of physics at Iowa State University. During the late 1930s Atanasoff had spent time trying to build an electronic calculating device to help his students solve mathematical problems. He and an assistant, Clifford Berry, had succeeded in building the first digital computer that worked electronically; they called it the **ABC**, for **Atanasoff-Berry computer** (Figure A-5).

After Mauchly met with Atanasoff and Berry in 1941, he used the ABC as the basis for the next step in computer development. From this association ultimately came a lawsuit based on attempts to get patents for a commercial version of the machine Mauchly built. The suit was finally decided in 1974, when a federal court determined that Atanasoff had been the true originator of the ideas required to make an electronic digital computer actually work. (Some computer historians dispute this court decision.) Mauchly and Eckert were able to use the principles of the ABC to create the **ENIAC**, for **Electronic Numerical Integrator and Calculator**. The main significance of the ENIAC is that, as the first general-purpose computer, it was the forerunner of the UNIVAC I, the first computer sold on a commercial basis.

The Computer Age Begins

The remarkable thing about the computer age is that so much has happened in so short a time. We have leapfrogged through four generations of technology in about 40 years—a span of time whose events are within the memories of many people today. The first three computer "generations" are pinned to three technological developments: the vacuum tube, the transistor, and the integrated circuit. Each has drastically changed the nature of computers. We define the timing of each generation according to the beginning of commercial delivery of the hardware technology. Defining subsequent generations has become more complicated because the entire industry has become more complicated.

The First Generation, 1951–1958: The Vacuum Tube

The beginning of the commercial computer age can be dated to June 14, 1951. This was the date the first **UNIVAC—Universal Automatic Computer**—was delivered to a client, the U.S. Bureau of the Census, for use in tabulating the previous year's census. The date also marked the first time that a computer had been built for a business application rather than for military, scientific, or engineering use. The UNIVAC was really the ENIAC in disguise and was, in fact, built by Mauchly and Eckert, who in 1947 had formed their own corporation.

In the first generation, **vacuum tubes**—electronic tubes about the size of light bulbs—were used as the internal computer components (Figure A-6). However, because thousands of such tubes were required, they generated a great deal of heat, causing many problems in temperature regulation and climate control. In addition, although all the tubes had to be working simultaneously, they were subject to frequent burnout, and the people operating the computer often did not know whether the problem was in the programming or in the machine.

Another drawback was that the language used in programming was machine language, which uses numbers. (Present-day higher-level languages are more like English.) Using numbers alone made programming the computer difficult and time-consuming. The UNIVAC used **magnetic cores** to provide memory. These consisted of small, doughnut-shaped rings about the size of pinheads, which were strung like beads on intersecting thin wires (Figure A-7). To supplement primary storage, first-generation computers stored data on punched cards. In 1957 magnetic tape was introduced as a faster, more compact method of storing data.

The Second Generation, 1959–1964: The Transistor

Three Bell Lab scientists—J. Bardeen, H. W. Brattain, and W. Shockley—developed the **transistor**, a small device that transfers electronic signals across a resistor. (The name *transistor* began as a trademark concocted from *trans*fer plus re*sistor*.) The scientists later received the Nobel prize

Figure A-6 Vacuum tubes. Vacuum tubes were used in the first generation of computers.

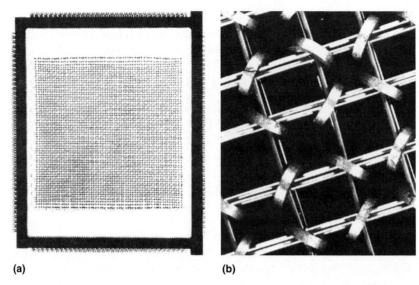

(a)   (b)

Figure A-7 Magnetic cores. (a) A 6- by 11-inch magnetic core memory. (b) Close-up of magnetic core memory. A few hundredths of an inch in diameter, each magnetic core was mounted on wires. When electricity passed through a wire on which a core was strung, the core could be magnetized as either on or off.

for their invention. The transistor revolutionized electronics in general and computers in particular. Transistors were much smaller than vacuum tubes, and they had numerous other advantages: They needed no warm-up time, consumed less energy, and were faster and more reliable.

During this generation another important development was the move from machine language to **assembly languages**, also called **symbolic languages**. Assembly languages use abbreviations for instructions (for example, L for LOAD) rather than numbers. This made programming less cumbersome.

After the development of symbolic languages came **high-level languages**, such as **FORTRAN** (1954) and **COBOL** (1959). Also, in 1962 the first removable disk pack was marketed. Disk storage supplemented magnetic tape systems and enabled users to have fast access to desired data.

Throughout this period computers were being used principally by business, university, and government organizations. They had not filtered down to the general public. The real part of the revolution was about to begin.

The Third Generation, 1965–1970: The Integrated Circuit

One of the most abundant elements in the earth's crust is silicon, a nonmetallic substance found in common beach sand as well as in practically all rocks and clay. The importance of this element to Santa Clara County, which is about 30 miles south of San Francisco, is responsible for the county's nickname: Silicon Valley. In 1965 Silicon Valley became the principal site for the manufacture of the so-called silicon chip: the integrated circuit.

An **integrated circuit (IC)** is a complete electronic circuit on a small chip of silicon. In 1965 integrated circuits began to replace transistors in computers. The resulting machines were called third-generation computers. Integrated circuits are made of silicon because it is a **semicon-**

ductor. That is, silicon is a crystalline substance that will conduct electric current when it has been "doped" with chemical impurities implanted in its lattice-like structure.

The chips were hailed as a generational breakthrough because they had desirable characteristics: reliability, compactness, and low cost. Mass production techniques have made possible the manufacture of inexpensive integrated circuits.

The beginning of the third generation was trumpeted by the IBM 360 series (named for 360 degrees—a full circle of service) in 1964. The System/360 family of computers, designed for both business and scientific use, came in several models and sizes. The "family of computers" concept made it possible for users to move to a more powerful machine without redoing the software that already worked on the current computer. The equipment housing was blue, leading to IBM's nickname, Big Blue.

The 360 series was launched with an all-out, massive marketing effort to make computers business tools—to get them into medium-size and smaller business and government operations where they had not been used before. Perhaps the most far-reaching contribution of the 360 series was IBM's decision to **unbundle** the software, that is, to sell the software separately from the hardware. This approach led to the creation of today's software industry.

Software became more sophisticated during this third generation. Several programs could run in the same time frame, sharing computer resources. This approach improved the efficiency of computer systems. Software systems were developed to support interactive processing, which used a terminal to put the user in direct contact with the computer. This kind of access caused the customer service industry to flourish, especially in areas such as reservations and credit checks.

The Fourth Generation, 1971–Present: The Microprocessor

Through the 1970s computers gained dramatically in speed, reliability, and storage capacity, but entry into the fourth generation was evolutionary rather than revolutionary. The fourth generation was, in fact, an extension of third-generation technology. That is, in the early part of the third generation, specialized chips were developed for computer memory and logic. Thus, all the ingredients were in place for the next technological development—the general-purpose processor-on-a-chip, otherwise known as the **microprocessor**, which became commercially available in 1971.

Nowhere is the pervasiveness of computer power more apparent than in the explosive growth in the use of the microprocessor. In addition to the common applications of digital watches, pocket calculators, and personal computers, you can expect to find microprocessors in virtually every machine in the home or business—cars, copy machines, television sets, bread-making machines, and so on. Computers today are 100 times smaller than those of the first generation, and a single chip is far more powerful than ENIAC.

The Fifth Generation: Onward

The term *fifth generation* was coined by the Japanese to describe the powerful, "intelligent" computers they wanted to build by the mid-1990s.

Better Late Than Never

For years, Gilbert Hyatt made a claim that most of his colleagues derided: He said he had invented the microprocessor, the circuitry at the heart of all computers and consumer electronics. To everyone's astonishment, however, the U.S. Patent Office in 1990 granted Hyatt a patent that made him the official inventor of the microprocessor.

Intel Corporation had long claimed credit for the invention, pointing to Ted Hoff, a former Intel engineer, as the inventor. However, Hyatt had filed for the patent on what he called the "microcomputer" back in 1970—beating Intel's first microprocessor, the 4004, which came out in 1971. Early on, Hyatt had solicited venture capitalists to support his new company to manufacture his invention. He claims that one of them leaked information to Intel.

Since receiving his patent, Hyatt has negotiated licensing agreements with a number of companies, making him an overnight multimillionaire.

APPLE-1
OPERATION
MANUAL

APPLE COMPUTER COMPANY
770 Welch Road
Palo Alto,   Calif. 94304

Figure A-8 Apple manual. Shown here is a collector's item: the very first manual for operation of an Apple computer. Unfortunately, the early manuals were a hodgepodge of circuit diagrams, software listings, and handwritten notes. They were hard to read and understand, enough to frighten away all but the most hardy souls.

Later the term evolved to encompass several research fields related to computer intelligence: artificial intelligence, expert systems, and natural language.

But the true focus of this ongoing fifth generation is connectivity, the massive industry effort to permit users to connect their computers to other computers. The concept of the information superhighway has captured the imaginations of both computer professionals and everyday computer users.

▶ The Story of Personal Computers

Personal computers are the machines you can "get closest to," whether you are an amateur or a professional. There is nothing quite like having your very own personal computer. Its history is very personal too, full of stories of success and failure and of individuals with whom we can readily identify.

Apple Leads the Way

As we noted in the beginning of this appendix, the very first personal computer was the MITS Altair, produced in 1975. But it was a gee-whiz machine, loaded with switches and dials but with no keyboard or screen. It took two teenagers, Steve Jobs and Steve Wozniak, to capture the imagination of the public with the first Apple computer. They built it in that time-honored place of inventors, a garage, using the $1300 proceeds from the sale of an old Volkswagen. Designed for home use, the Apple was the first to offer an easy-to-use keyboard and screen. Founded in 1977, Apple Computer was immediately and wildly successful. (Figure A-8 shows early documentation for the first commercial Apple computer.)

The first Apple computer, the Apple I, was not a commercial success. It was the Apple II that anchored the early years of the company. In fact, it was the combination of the Apple II and the spreadsheet software called VisiCalc that caught the attention of the business community and propelled personal computers into the workplace.

The IBM PC Standard

IBM announced its first personal computer in the summer of 1981. IBM captured the top market share in just 18 months, and even more important, its machine became the industry standard (Figure A-9). The IBM machine included innovations such as an 80-character screen line, a full upper- and lowercase keyboard, and the possibility of adding memory. IBM also provided internal expansion slots, so that peripheral equipment manufacturers could build accessories for the IBM PC. In addition, IBM provided hardware schematics and software listings to companies who wanted to build products in conjunction with the new PC. Many of the new products accelerated demand for the IBM machine. Even more important, many new companies sprang up just to support the IBM PC.

IBM made its computer from nonproprietary parts, opening the door for other manufacturers to do the same. Thus, other personal computer manufacturers emulated the IBM standard, producing IBM **clones**, copycat computers that can run software designed for IBM computers. Almost all the major personal computer manufacturers today—Compaq, Dell, Gateway, and many more—are IBM clones. In fact, clone computers

THE SOFTWARE ENTREPRENEURS

Ever thought you'd like to run your own show? Make your own product? Be in business for yourself? Entrepreneurs are a special breed. They are achievement oriented, like to take responsibility for decisions, and dislike routine work. They also have high levels of energy and a great deal of imagination. But perhaps the key is that they are willing to take risks.

Entrepreneurs often have still another quality—a more elusive one—that is close to charisma. This charisma is based on enthusiasm, and it allows them to lead people, form an organization, and give it momentum. Study these real-life entrepreneurs, noting their paths to glory and—sometimes—their falls.

Steve Jobs

Of the two Steves who formed Apple Computer, Steve Jobs was the true entrepreneur. Although they both were interested in electronics, Steve Wozniak was the technical genius, and he would have been happy to have been left alone to tinker. But Steve Jobs would not let him alone for a minute; he was always pushing and crusading. In fact, Wozniak had hooked up with an evangelist, and they made quite a pair.

When Apple was getting off the ground, Jobs wanted Wozniak to quit his job so that he could work full-time on the new venture. Wozniak refused. His partner begged and cried. Wozniak gave in. While Wozniak built Apple computers, Jobs was out hustling, finding the best marketing person, the best venture capitalist, and the best company president. This entrepreneurial spirit paid off in a spectacular way as Apple rose to the top of the list of personal computer companies.

Bill Gates

When Bill Gates was a teenager, he swore off computers for a year and, in his words, "tried to act normal." His parents, who wanted him to be a lawyer, must have been relieved when Bill gave up on computer foolishness and went off to Harvard in 1974. But Bill started spending weekends with his friend Paul Allen, dreaming about personal computers, which did not exist yet. When the MITS Altair, the first personal computer for sale, splashed on the market in January 1975, both Bill and Paul moved to Albuquerque to be near the action at MITS. But they showed a desire even then to chart their own course. Although they wrote software for MITS, they kept the rights to their work and formed their own company. It was called Microsoft.

When MITS failed, Gates and Allen moved their software company to their native Bellevue, Washington. They had 32 people in their employ in 1980 when IBM came to call. Gates recognized the big league when he saw it and put on a suit for the occasion. He was offered a plum: the chance to develop the operating system (a crucial set of software) for IBM's soon-to-be personal computer. Although he knew he was betting the whole company, Gates never hesitated to take the risk. He purchased an existing operating system, which he and his crew reworked to produce MS-DOS—Microsoft Disk Operating System. It was this product that sent Microsoft on its meteoric rise.

Mitch Kapor

Mitch Kapor did not start out on a direct path to computer fame and riches. In fact, he wandered extensively, working at jobs ranging from disk jockey to piano teacher to counselor. He had done some programming too, but did not like it much. In around 1978, however, he found he did like fooling around with personal computers. In fact, he had found his niche.

In 1983 Kapor introduced a software package called Lotus 1-2-3, and there had never been anything like it before. Lotus added the term *integrated package* (now called an office suite) to the vocabulary; the phrase described the software's identity as a combination spreadsheet, graphics, and database program. Kapor's product catapulted his company to the top of the list of independent software makers in just two years.

Figure A-9 The IBM PC. Launched in 1981, this early IBM PC rose to the top of the best-seller list in just 18 months.

now dominate the personal computer market, leaving IBM with a market share that is small when compared to its original success.

The Microsoft/Intel Standard

In the history of the computer industry, the spotlight has been on the fast-changing hardware. However, personal computer users now focus more on the tremendous variety of software. The dominant force in personal computer software is the Microsoft Corporation.

Microsoft supplied the operating system—the underlying software—for the original IBM personal computer. This software, called MS-DOS, was used by IBM and by the IBM clones, permitting tiny Microsoft to grow quickly. Microsoft eventually presented more sophisticated operating systems, notably Windows. The Windows operating system is used on computers powered by a microprocessor from the Intel Corporation; this potent combination, nicknamed *Wintel*, has become the dominant force in personal computer sales.

➤ The Internet Revolution

The word *revolution* is never far away when the discussion is about computers. But nothing in computer history has captured the attention of computer users as the Internet has. Even the acceptance of the personal computer pales in comparison. *Revolution* is truly an appropriate word.

Chapter 7 presented two critical points regarding the history of the Internet. The first is that the Internet was started as ARPANet, a network of equal computers that could survive a nuclear attack. Second, the Internet was made attractive to the average user by Dr. Tim Berners-Lee, who came up with the notion of links, and Marc Andreesen, who produced the first browser.

Unlike other parts of computer history, the Internet is well documented online. It makes sense to go to the source, rather than read an abbreviated version here. If you want to know more, submit words such as *Internet*, *history*, and *ARPANet* to a search engine, and several appropriate sites will be offered.

History is still being made in the computer industry, of course, and it is being made incredibly rapidly. A book cannot possibly pretend to describe all the very latest developments. Nevertheless, as we indicated earlier, the four areas of input, processing, output, and storage describe the basic components of a computer system, whatever its date.

CHAPTER REVIEW

Summary and Key Terms

■ Charles Babbage is called the father of the computer because of his invention of two computation machines. His **difference engine**, which could solve equations, led to another calculating machine, the **analytical engine**, which embodied the key parts of a computer system. Countess Ada Lovelace, who helped develop instructions for carrying out computations on Babbage's device, is often called the first programmer.

■ The first computer to use electrical power instead of mechanical power was Herman Hollerith's tabulating machine, which was used in the 1890 census in the United States. Hollerith founded a company that became the forerunner of International Business Machines Corporation (IBM).

■ Thomas J. Watson Sr. built IBM into a dominant force in the business machines market. He also gave Harvard professor Howard Aiken research funds with which to build an electromechanical computer, the **Mark I**, unveiled in 1944.

■ John V. Atanasoff, with assistant Clifford Berry, devised the first digital computer to work by electronic means, the **Atanasoff-Berry Computer (ABC).**

■ The **ENIAC (Electronic Numerical Integrator and Calculator),** developed by John Mauchly and J. Presper Eckert at the University of Pennsylvania in 1946, was the world's first general-purpose electronic computer.

■ The first computer generation began June 14, 1951, with the delivery of the **UNIVAC (Universal Automatic Computer)** to the U.S. Bureau of the Census. First-generation computers required thousands of **vacuum tubes**, electronic tubes about the size of light bulbs. The main form of memory was **magnetic core.**

■ Second-generation computers used **transistors**, which were small, needed no warm-up, consumed less energy, and were faster and more reliable. During the second generation, **assembly languages**, or **symbolic languages**, were developed. Later, **high-level languages**, such as **FORTRAN** and **COBOL**, were also developed.

■ The third generation featured the **integrated circuit (IC)**—a complete electronic circuit on a small chip of silicon. Silicon is a **semiconductor**, a substance that will conduct electric current when it has been "doped" with chemical impurities.

■ With the third generation, IBM announced the System/360 family of computers, which made it possible for users to move up to a more powerful machine without redoing the software that already worked on the current computer. IBM **unbundled** the software, that is, sold it separately from the hardware.

■ The fourth-generation **microprocessor**—a general-purpose processor-on-a-chip—grew out of the specialized memory and logic chips of the third generation.

■ The term *fifth generation,* coined by the Japanese, evolved to encompass artificial intelligence, expert systems, and natural language. But the true focus of the fifth generation is connectivity, permitting users to connect their computers to other computers.

■ The first personal computer, the MITS Altair, was produced in 1975. However, the first successful computer to include an easy-to-use keyboard and screen was offered by Apple Computer, founded by Steve Jobs and Steve Wozniak in 1977.

■ IBM entered the personal computer market in 1981 and captured the top market share in just 18 months. Other manufacturers produced IBM **clones**, copycat computers that can run software designed for IBM computers.

■ The worldwide leading software company is the Microsoft Corporation, which supplied the operating system for the original IBM personal computer and then went on to develop a variety of successful applications software.

This appendix offers beginning instruction in the language called **HTML**, which stands for **HyperText Markup Language.** It presents just enough information so that you can write a simple page for the Web.

We begin with some assumptions. The first is that you have studied the Internet, at least a little, and understand the meanings of the terms *World Wide Web, browser, server, Internet service provider, site, home page, hypertext, URL,* and *link*. If these terms are not familiar, please peruse Chapter 7, called *The Internet: A Resource for All of Us.* Other assumptions are that you have already seen several web sites and have linked from site to site.

HTML Primer

Writing Your Own Web Page

➤ Before You Start

Before you plunge into HTML code, you need to understand the requirements for writing, testing, and publishing a page on the Web. Further, it will be helpful to see where this appendix is headed.

Requirements

You need to have access to appropriate hardware and software.

Text editor. You need some software vehicle to use as a text editor, with which to write the HTML code for your web page. This can be a text editor such as Notepad that comes with Microsoft Windows, or perhaps a word processing program. Alternatively, there are HTML editors available for downloading from the Web. The software you use is not important as long as you can save the HTML file on disk as an ASCII text file.

Browser. You need a browser to test the HTML code and, later, to access the server. To use the browser to test your HTML file, you open the browser, but you need not actually make a connection to a server. That is, for testing purposes, at least at first, you can just use the browser, which understands HTML, on a personal computer or terminal.

Server. You will need to be connected to a server to test links to other sites. Once you have tested your page you will want it to publish it, that is, make it accessible to others on the Internet. You will need to send your files—the page HTML file and any files it may use, such as an image —to a server, where they will be stored on the server's disk. The page file will be given its own unique URL. There are several server possibilities, such as your college's computer, a web site such as GeoCities that offers free Web pages, or a local Internet service provider.

Where We Are Headed

HTML consists of a set of commands called **tags**; the tags tell the browser how to display the information provided. Many of them are quite simple. We will begin with just a few tags and then use them in a simple web page example. This way you can see right away how the HTML code and the resultant web page are related. We will expand that page a bit and incorporate other tags.

Next we will incorporate more tags as we write HTML code for a web page that is a résumé.

➤ The Basic Tags

We begin with the tags that define the overall form of an HTML document—file—and then move to tags that give basic structure to the way the page will appear. Then we will submit the first, if limited, HTML code to the browser to see how the resulting page looks (Table B-1).

Document Tags

Tags most often come in pairs, a beginning tag and an ending tag. The tag has a certain format: The command is enclosed in angle brackets, an

Table B-1 Some HTML Tags

Tag	Description
<HTML> . . . </HTML>	Mark start and end of an HTML file
<HEAD> . . . </HEAD>	Mark start and end of the HEAD section
<TITLE> . . . </TITLE>	Title for the page
<BODY> . . . </BODY>	Mark the start and end of the content of the page
<Hx> . . . </Hx>	Heading, where x is 1 through 6
<P> . . . </P>	Paragraph
 	Break to a new line
<EM> . . . </EM>	Emphasis
<STRONG> . . . </STRONG>	Strong emphasis
<I> . . . </I>	Italic
<B> . . . </B>	Boldface
<CENTER> . . . </CENTER>	Center text horizontally
<UL> . . . </UL>	Unordered list
<OL> . . . </OL>	Ordered list
<LI>	List item
<HR>	Horizontal rule
<IMG>	Image
<A> . . . </A>	Anchor; with attribute HREF provides a link

opening angle bracket (<) and a closing angle bracket (>). The very first tag of an HTML file, for example, must be <HTML>. Paired tags have another tag that looks almost like the first but has a forward slash (/) just before the command. The paired tags for the HTML command, which go at the beginning and end of an HTML file, are <HTML> and </HTML> (Figure B-1a).

Commands, by the way, are not case sensitive; they can be written in upper- or lowercase or some combination of the two. Many people prefer uppercase because the tags are then easier to spot when looking at an HTML file.

Immediately following the HTML command is the **head tag** pair, <HEAD> and </HEAD>, which enclose the HEAD section. The HEAD command encloses the TITLE command, which is written with the **title tag** pair, <TITLE> and </TITLE>. This command will cause a page title to be displayed at the very top of the browser window, above the browser control panel. After the HEAD section is the BODY section, enclosed by the **body tag** pair, <BODY> and </BODY>. All of the content of the page—headings, paragraphs, lists, images, and so forth—goes between the BODY tags.

Figure B-1a has a complete set of the tags just described, with lines drawn to show how the matching tag pairs are related. Notice that it is permissible for one set of tags to be completely enclosed within another set of tags; the two HEAD tags, for example, are enclosed between the two HTML tags. The enclosed tags are called **nested tags**. It is not permissible, however, for sets of tags to overlap (Figure B-1b).

The code you see in Figure B-1a is correct as it is. However, if you submitted it to a browser, the browser would produce only a blank page and the words *Test Title* at the top of the browser window. A blank page shows because there is not yet any content between the <BODY> and </BODY> tags. In the next section, we will add some content to the basic document structure in Figure B-1a.

Text Structure Tags

All tags discussed from this point forward belong between the two BODY tags described in the previous section.

Heading tags (not to be confused with the HEAD tag) come in pairs and produce six text sizes, largest to smallest, as follows: <H1> and </H1>, <H2> and </H2>, and so forth, through <H6> and </H6>. The text to be printed is placed between a pair of tags. Text to be printed very large would use a number 1 heading, for example, <H1>Theatre Schedule</H1>. The text generated by a number 6 heading, on the other hand, would be very small.

A paragraph of text is marked by the pair of **paragraph tags**, <P> and </P>. The browser inserts a blank line before the start of a paragraph. The text words within paragraph tags will be displayed by the browser with one space between any two adjacent words. You can, of course, use any kind of spacing when preparing an HTML file, to make it easy to read. Extra white space—blank spaces or lines—is simply ignored by the browser.

If you want a line break, that is, to end a line and begin a new one but not start a new paragraph, use the **line break tag**, <BR>. This is a single tag; it is not part of a pair. One more thing: A blank line follows a heading, so the only time you need to use the paragraph tag is when the paragraph follows another paragraph and you thus need to force a blank line.

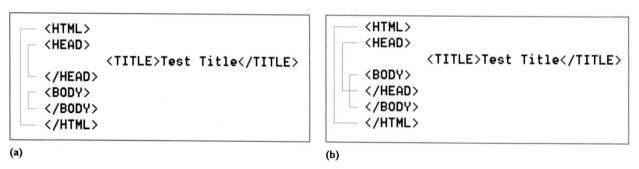

(a)   (b)

Figure B-1 Basic HTML document structures. (a) Lines have been drawn to mark pairs of tags. The <HTML> tag is used to define the document as containing HTML code. The <HEAD> tag defines the HEAD section, which contains the pair of <TITLE> tags that provide the title for the page. The entire content of the web page will be enclosed within the two <BODY> tags. (b) No, no, no. Overlapping tags are not permitted.

A First Example

Examine Figure B-2a, which shows the HTML code to describe a theater and mention its current plays. Note the file name at the top: Hayes.html. The first heading, a number 1 heading, will be the largest. The subheading will be of medium size, a number 3 heading. The first paragraph does not need paragraph tags because a blank line automatically follows the heading just above the paragraph. The second paragraph is marked with paragraph tags, so it will be set off with a blank line above it. The plays are listed within a paragraph, but they are forced by line breaks to appear on individual lines.

To test the HTML file, use the browser's Open command, and type in the exact path and name of the HTML file, as it is stored on disk. When the file is opened, the path and file name appear in the browser's Address

Figure B-2 HTML code and corresponding web page. (a) This HTML code was entered and saved as a text file using a text editor. (b) After the HTML file is opened by the browser, the HTML causes the browser to produce this page.

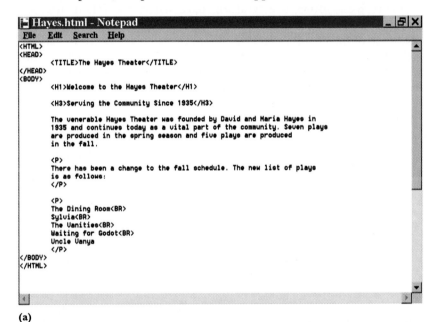

(a)

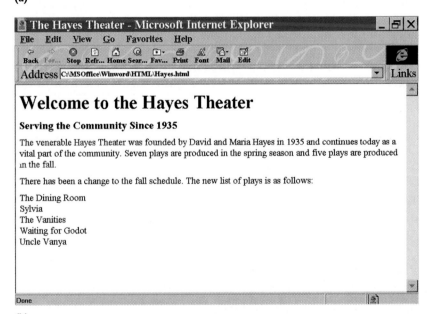

(b)

```
<UL>
<LI>Music Box, Maria Carey
<LI>Miracles, Kenny G
<LI>Superunknown, Soundgarden
<LI>Q's Jook Joint, Quincy Jones
<LI>Blue, LeAnn Rimes
<LI>Star Wars Trilogy, John Williams
</UL>
```
(a)

```
<OL>
<LI>Click on desired album.
<LI>Provide shipping address.
<LI>Select payment method.
<LI>Select shipping method.
<LI>Review order.
<LI>Confirm order.
</OL>
```
(b)

Figure B-3 Lists. (a) HTML code for an unordered list. A retail music site might list, in no particular order, albums on special that day. The browser will produce an indented, bulleted list of the albums. (b) HTML code for an ordered list. The same retail music site might present something like this list as the steps to be taken, in order, for purchasing an album; the browser will produce an indented, numbered list of the steps.

window at the top of the browser, and the browser's interpretation of the HTML—the web page—appears in the browser display window.

Figure B-2b shows the resulting page when the HTML text file Hayes.html is opened by the browser. Notice the title *The Hayes Theater* at the top of the browser window.

By the way, you may find on occasion that a displayed page is not what you thought the HTML code would produce. Whether this is due to an error or because you prefer a different outcome, you can simply return to the HTML file, make revisions, *remember to save the file,* and then reload–rerun–it through the browser. If the browser still has the same file path/name in its Address window, you need only click the address window and press *Enter* to make the page display again, presumably reflecting the changes you made to the HTML code.

Lists

A **list** is really a basic text structure, but it needs enough explanation to require its own section. The two kinds of lists used most often are unordered lists and ordered lists. An unordered list, also called a bulleted list, uses the **unordered list tag** pair, <UL> and </UL>, and produces an indented list with a browser-supplied character in front of it, probably a small circle or square. An ordered list uses the **ordered list tag** pair, <OL> and </OL>, and causes the browser to number the indented list items in order, usually 1., 2., and so forth. Whether unordered or ordered, each item in a list is preceded by a single **list item tag**, <LI> (Figure B-3).

The browser output in Figure B-2b shows several lines listing plays, an obvious candidate for a list. We will soon make this improvement to the page, along with some desirable style improvements described in the next section.

▶ Improving the Appearance of the Page

There are several things we can do to make a page more functional and more attractive. Although space prohibits listing all of them, we will mention some of the more common tags.

Style Tags

A popular option is style tags, logical and physical. Logical tags are related to the fact that different browsers are written by different people who have different ideas about how things should be done. In fact, you can submit the same HTML code to different browsers and see slightly different browser displays of the page. (This becomes more obvious with more complex pages.) **Logical style tags** leave it up to a browser to display text in its own way. The **emphasis tags**, <EM> and </EM>, with the text to be highlighted between them, will usually display italics. The **strong emphasis tag** pair, <STRONG> and </STRONG>, will likely display the text between the tags as boldface.

However, most people prefer to use **physical style tags**, which tell a browser exactly how to display the text. Physical style tags are easy to use, and they work with most browsers. Some commonly used physical tag pairs are the **italic tag** pair, <I> and </I>, and the **boldface tag** pair, <B> and </B>. Another popular style tag pair is the **center tag** pair. <CENTER> and </CENTER>. for horizontal centering.

Breaks Within the Page

A displayed page is not limited to the length of the screen; in fact, it has no length limits at all. Unless the person writing the code chooses to interfere, pages can go on in an uninterrupted fashion indefinitely. Most people, however, choose to divide the page into more manageable chunks. One way to do this is to use the single **horizontal rule tag**, <HR>, which places a narrow line across the page.

Enhancing the First Example

Returning to our first example, you can see some changes in the HTML code in Figure B-4a. From top to bottom, the first heading has been centered, the second heading has been centered and made italic, and the plays have been put in an unordered list and also made boldface. Notice that both the paragraph tags and the break tags were removed from the group of plays when it was made into a list. The new code has been saved (don't forget to save) and then submitted to the browser, which now shows the altered page in Figure B-4b.

▶ Adding Images

Few web sites offer only text. In fact, most are loaded with graphic images. But notice that sophisticated sites use graphics judiciously: They may be appropriate and attractive, but they are probably not enormous. This is because large graphics take too long to download, and visitors to the site get tired of waiting. But you certainly want images of some kind on your page, so we will cover the basics here.

The Résumé Example

The next HTML example will produce a résumé for a student majoring in computer science. He has written some web pages and is looking for a student internship at an Internet-related company. The HTML to create that page includes tags you already know and also image and link tags, the next two topics. You can preview the HTML for the résumé in Figure B-5a and see the résumé page in Figure B-5b.

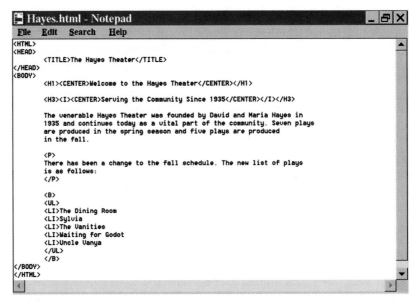

(a)

(b)

Figure B-4 Altered HTML code and changed page. (a) The original code from Figure B-2 has been changed to center the headings, make the second heading italic, and put the plays in a boldface unordered list. (b) The changed page.

Obtaining Images

There are several ways to obtain images to use on a web page. An easy way is to download them from a site that offers free images (Figure B-6). You could even pay for the use of images offered on various professional photography sites on the Web; as noted elsewhere, you cannot help yourself to copyrighted images. You can scan photographs or anything else on paper to a disk file or ask a copy center to perform this service for you. If you wish to create original graphics, several software packages are available for this purpose.

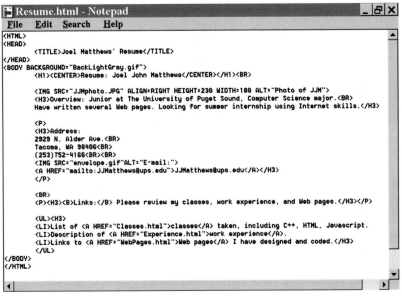

(a)

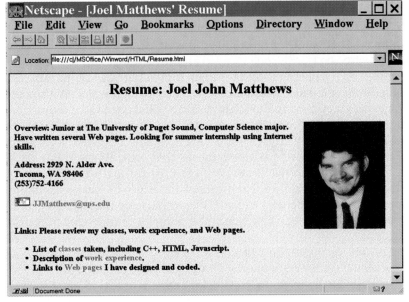

(b)

Figure B-5 HTML code and the resulting résumé page. (a) The HTML code includes image and link tags. (b) This first page of the résumé is deliberately short because it includes links to more detailed information, such as classes and work experience.

Image File Formats

The file formats most commonly used for images on the Internet are GIF (pronounced *jif*), for Graphic Interchange Format, and JPG (*j-peg*), for Joint Photographic Experts Group. These two formats are accepted by most browsers. The differences between the two formats and the situations that favor one over another are beyond the scope of this discussion. The photograph shown in Figure B-5b was scanned to JPG format.

Figure B-6 Images and icons. Thousands of images are available on the Web. The images shown here were downloaded from various web pages that offer them for free. The bars at the bottom are typical of those used by people who want more than plain horizontal rules.

The Image Tag

An image that is referenced right in the HTML code and whose file is loaded with the HTML code is called an **inline image**. An image can be included in a page by using the single **image tag**, <IMG>. But there is something new here: **attributes** associated with the tag. Within the image tag you must use the attribute SRC, which stands for *source*, that is, the location of the image to be used. The most efficient location for the graphic is in a nearby file; for testing purposes, it is easiest if the file is in the same directory—folder—as the file that contains the HTML code. (If an image in another location is used, its full path name must be stated.) Thus, unlike the text we used for pages in earlier examples, images are not embedded in the HTML code; only the reference to an image is in the code—the tag and the name of the file that holds the image.

The SRC attribute must be completely inside the image tag, and its associated file must be in quotes: <IMG SRC="JJMphoto.JPG">.

Another image attribute is ALT, for alternative text. Some browsers cannot view graphics, and some users (to save time) choose to turn off their browser's graphics capability. For these users, ALT includes text of your choosing that will be seen instead of the image. Note the alternative text for Joel John Matthew's photograph in Figure B-5a.

Image Sizing and Placement

How big should an image be? This could be an exact science, but often it is not. If you created a graphic using software, then you know its exact height and width in pixels (the dots that make up the image). If you do not have this information, you will probably have to do a little experimenting to see what looks right. HEIGHT and WIDTH are attributes of the <IMG> tag; you can see them used in Figure B-5a for JJMphoto.JPG. Most browsers will stretch the image to make it fit the height and width specified.

Placing an image may be easy or may take some experimenting. The <IMG> tag has an attribute called ALIGN, which lets you align the text with an adjacent image at the top (TOP), middle (MIDDLE), bottom (BOTTOM), or places in between. The default is that the text will be aligned with the bottom of the image. If you wanted to place an image so that the adjacent text runs next to the top of the image, you would use

```
<IMG SRC= "JJMphoto.JPG" ALIGN=TOP>
```

You can also set ALIGN to RIGHT (placing the image next to the right margin) or LEFT. Other <IMG> attributes that can help place an image are HSPACE and VSPACE, which force horizontal and vertical spacing, respectively.

➤ Adding Links

The power of the Internet is in links: You can link to any other site, and anyone else can link to yours. Further, links can be used to divide a page into more manageable pieces, with the first page linking to lower levels of information; those pages, in turn, can also link to lower levels. In the résumé example, for instance, instead of having one long page, we use an initial page, short and to the point, with links to other topics of interest: classes, work experience, and links to web pages (Figure B-5b).

The Anchor Tag

Links are accomplished by using the **anchor tag** pair, <A> and </A>. The key attribute of the anchor tag is HREF, which indicates a link destination. The anchor tag also includes the name of the word or words—the hypertext—that will be clicked to initiate the move to the new site. The format to link to another web page looks like this:

```
<A HREF="URL">Name</A>
```

Here, *URL* is replaced by the address of the page destination. *Name* refers to the highlighted word that you want the user to click on. An example:

```
<A HREF="http://www.kodak.com">Kodak</A>
```

This anchor links to the Kodak site, as indicated by its URL. On the page, a user would click the word *Kodak,* as indicated by the name after the URL.

In Figure B-5b, note that, in the bulleted list at the bottom, the words *classes, work experience,* and *Web pages* are highlighted in blue, indicating that they are links that can be clicked. Referring to the corresponding code in Figure B-5a, note that the anchor tags use those words as the names in the anchors. The URLs shown in those same code lines refer to files that are in the same directory as the HTML file for the original page. It is beyond our scope to show those files or their corresponding pages.

Final Touches to the Résumé

Two additions will be made to make Joel's résumé a more finished product. The first is rather necessary: If a potential employer found Joel's résumé on the Internet, the employer should be able to contact him via the Internet by using e-mail. The anchor tag and the HREF attribute can be used to reference the e-mail protocol as follows:

Color	Hexadecimal
Red	FF0000
Green	00FF00
Blue	0000FF
Black	000000
Dusty Rose	856363
Brass	B5A642
Cyan	00FFFF
Bronze	8C7723
Orange	FF7F00
Midnight Blue	2F2F4F
Neon Blue	4D4DFF
Violet	4F2F4F
Forest Green	238E23
Salmon	6F4242
Scarlet	8C1717
Khaki	9F9F5F
Pink	BC8F8F
Goldenrod	DBDB70
Yellow	FFFF00
Magenta	FF00FF
White	FFFFFF
Firebrick	8E2323
Cadet blue	5F9F9F
Silver	E6E8FA

Figure B-7 Background color digits.
Background colors are represented by six hexadecimal digits, two each for red, green, and blue, in that order. Other colors are possible by varying the two-digit numbers and how they are combined. Some samples are listed here, but you can experiment with any combination, using hexadecimal numbers from 00 (darkest) to FF (lightest). Full color charts, showing a swatch of color that matches a hexadecimal combination, can be found on several web sites. These numbers are used with the BGCOLOR attribute in the BODY tag; for example, BGCOLOR=#00FF00.

<A HREF="mailto:*e-mail address*">name</A>

As you can see in Figure B-5a, the e-mail address for Joel has been filled in as *JJMatthews@ups.edu;* he also uses the e-mail address as the name that will be printed on the page. We also used the <IMG> tag to sneak in a tiny letter icon just before the e-mail address.

One more thing. **Background** refers to the screen appearance behind the text and images. Rather than accepting a plain background, default white or gray in most browsers, we can take control and give a page a background with color or perhaps even texture. Backgrounds are added using an attribute of the <BODY> tag. One possibility is to use the attribute BGCOLOR with a six-digit hexadecimal code that signifies the desired background color, two digits each for red, green, and blue. For example, BGCOLOR=#FF0000 gives a red background. See Figure B-7 for other possibilities.

We chose instead to use the attribute BACKGROUND, which uses a graphic that is a small square that is **tiled** by the browser—spread down and across the screen to make a complete background (Figure B-8). In the résumé code, we told the browser to use a textured graphic file, Back-LightGray.gif, to create the tiled background. Note the <BODY> tag in Figure B-5a.

▶ Moving On

If you are serious about creating web sites, you need to know more about most of the topics touched on here. You also need to know about HTML topics that were not even mentioned: changing the size and color of text, making tables, producing forms, including animation and sound, and—most importantly—validating your code.

There are books that teach HTML in detail, with examples. In addition, many web sites offer all levels of HTML assistance. Another approach is to click the View Source option available on most browsers; this lets you see the HTML source code for whatever web page is currently in the browser display window. You may be able to learn something from the experts.

You may prefer to use software that lets you prepare web pages without worrying about the details of HTML commands. Check magazines and your local software store; new offerings come on the market regularly.

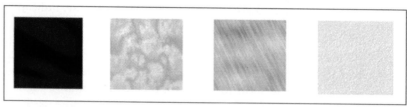

Figure B-8 Background graphics. These samples are graphics that can be tiled—moved across and down the screen—to fill in the complete background on a web page. Thousands of such samples can be found on the Web. The background should not interfere with text readability. The dark background, for example, would need a white text or some other light color. The background on the right is used in the résumé example, Figure B-5.

CHAPTER REVIEW

Summary and Key Terms

- The language called **HTML**, which stands for **HyperText Markup Language**, is used to write pages for the Web.
- Requirements for writing web pages are a text editor with which to write the HTML code for your web page; a browser to test the HTML code and, later, to access the server; and a server to test and publish the page.
- HTML consists of a set of **tags**, commands that perform specific functions.
- The **HTML tags** go at the beginning and end of an HTML file, the **head tags** enclose the page **title tags**, and the **body tags** enclose the content of the page.
- Tags enclosed within another set of tags are called **nested tags**.
- **Heading tags** print text in six sizes, **paragraph tags** enclose a paragraph of text, and the **line break tag** starts a new line.
- The two kinds of **lists** used most often are unordered lists and ordered lists. The **unordered list tags** produce an indented list with a browser-supplied character in front of each item, probably a small circle or square. The **ordered list tags** cause the browser to number the indented list items in order, usually 1., 2., and so forth. Each item in a list is preceded by a single **list item tag**.
- **Logical style tags** leave it up to the browser to highlight text in its own way. **Emphasis tags** will probably display italics, and **strong emphasis tags** will likely display the text as boldface. **Physical style tags** work with most browsers; some commonly used ones are the **italic tag**, the **boldface tag**, and the **center tag**. The **horizontal rule tag** places a narrow line across the page.
- For the foreseeable future, the standard file format for images on the Internet are GIF, for Graphic Interchange Format, and JPG, for Joint Photographic Experts Group.
- An image that is referenced right in the HTML code and whose file is loaded with the HTML code is called an **inline image**. An image can be included in a page by using the **image tag**, which offers several **attributes** within the tag, including SRC to define the location of the file, ALT to permit alternative text, HEIGHT and WIDTH for sizing, and ALIGN for placement.
- Links are accomplished by using the **anchor tag**. The key attribute is HREF, which indicates a link destination, an URL or a file name. The anchor tag also includes the name of the word or words—the hypertext—that will be clicked to initiate the move to the new site.
- **Background** refers to the screen appearance behind the text and images. Backgrounds are added using an attribute of the body tag. The attribute BGCOLOR uses a six-digit hexadecimal code that signifies the desired background color, two digits each for red, green, and blue. The attribute BACKGROUND uses a graphic that is a small square that is **tiled** by the browser—spread down and across the screen to make a complete background.

In Chapter 12 we described the five steps of the programming process in a general way. We noted that the first step, defining the problem, is related to the larger arena of systems analysis and design, a subject we examined in Chapter 14. The second step involves planning the solution, and the last three steps—coding, testing, and documenting the program—are done in the context of a particular programming language, such as BASIC.

This appendix will look more closely at the planning phase, detailing the steps to help you understand how to develop program logic. First you will be introduced to three different approaches to program planning—*flowcharting*, *structure charts*, and *pseudocode*—and examples of each. Normally, a programmer would use only one or two to reach a solution. We present all three here, side by side, so you can compare them.

Flowcharts, which present a map of a solution, were the primary planning device for many years. They were favored over other methods because logic is easier to follow with pictures than with words. But flowcharts have some drawbacks: They are not easy to change, and they tend to be too detailed. However, now flowcharts can be drawn and revised using flowcharting software.

A structure chart illustrates the structure of a program by depicting its parts as independent hierarchical modules. The resulting picture identifies a program's major functions at a high level, making it fairly easy to gain an overview quickly.

Pseudocode is easy to maintain. Since pseudocode is just words, it can be kept on a computer file and changed easily, using word processing or text editing. Although pseudocode is not a visual tool, it is nevertheless an effective vehicle for stating and following program logic. For these reasons, flowcharts have fallen out of favor and pseudocode has become popular. But flowcharts are often used as teaching devices, so we include them here.

In this appendix we will also examine another important topic: structured programming, an approach to programming that minimizes logic complexity. Let us begin with the pictures—flowcharts.

The Programming Process

Planning the Solution

▶ Flowcharts

A **flowchart** presents a visual map of a program. The flowchart uses arrows to represent the direction of the program flow and boxes and other shapes to display actions. Note that in this discussion we are talking about a **logic flowchart**, a flowchart that represents the flow of logic in a program. A logic flowchart is different from a **systems flowchart**, which shows the flow of data through an entire computer system. We examined systems flowcharts in Chapter 14.

We will use the ANSI flowchart symbols introduced in Chapter 12 (see Figure 12-1). Templates of ANSI symbols (Figure C-1) are available in many office-supply stores and college bookstores and are helpful in drawing flowcharts by hand. The most common symbols you will use represent process, decision, connector, start/stop, input/output, and direction of flow. Now let us use flowcharting to show just what programming is all about.

Figure C-2 shows how you might flowchart a program to find the sum of all numbers between 1 and 100. There are a number of things to observe about this flowchart.

First, the program uses two places in the computer's memory as storage locations, or places to keep intermediate results. In one location is a counter, which might be like a car odometer: Every time a mile passes, the counter counts it as a 1. In the other location the computer stores a sum—that is, a running total of the numbers counted. The sum location will eventually contain the sum of all numbers from 1 through 100: $1 + 2 + 3 + 4 + 5 + \ldots + 100$.

Second, as we start the program, we must **initialize** the counter and the sum. When you initialize you set the starting values of certain storage locations, usually as the program execution begins. We will initialize the sum to 0 and the counter to 1.

Third, note the looping. You add the counter to the sum and a 1 to the counter, and then you come to the decision diamond, which asks if the counter is greater than 100. If the answer is no, the computer loops back around and repeats the process. The decision box contains a **com-**

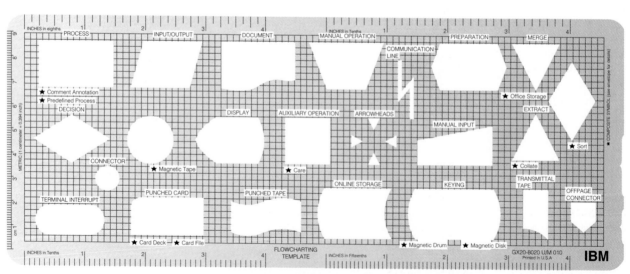

Figure C-1 A template containing standard ANSI flowcharting symbols.
Templates like this one are used as drawing aids.

pare operation; the computer compares two numbers and performs alternative operations based on the comparison. If the result of the comparison is yes, the computer produces the sum as output, as indicated by the print instruction.

A **loop**—also called an **iteration**—is the heart of computer programming. The beauty of the loop, which may be defined as the repetition of instructions under certain conditions, is that you, the programmer, have to describe certain instructions only once rather than describing them repeatedly. Once you have established the loop pattern and the conditions for concluding (exiting from) the loop, the computer continues looping and exits as it has been instructed to do. The loop is considered a powerful programming tool because the code is reusable; once written, it can be called upon many times. Notice also that the flowchart can be modified easily to sum the numbers from 1 through 1000 or 500 through 700 or some other variation. Now let us look at how structure charts are formed.

▶ Structure Charts

A **structure chart** graphically illustrates the structure of a program by showing independent hierarchical steps. This high-level picture identifies major functions that are the initial component parts of the structure chart. Each major component is then broken down into subcomponents, which are, in turn, broken down still further until sufficiently detailed components are shown. Since the components are pictured in hierarchical form, a drawing of this kind is also known as a **hierarchy chart**. A structure chart is easy to draw and easy to change, and it is often used to supplement or even to replace a logic flowchart.

An example of a structure chart is shown in Figure C-3. As the illustration shows, the top level of the structure chart gives the name of the program, Payroll process. The next level breaks the program down into its major functions: Read inputs, Compute pay, and Write outputs. One set of program statements performs each function. Each of these major functions is then subdivided further into smaller pieces. (We could break them down even further, but space does not permit it.)

The major functions are repeatedly subdivided into smaller pieces of manageable size. Each of these components is also, according to plan, as independent of the others as possible. For example, step 4.1, Write master, can be executed independently of any activity in step 4.3, Write paychecks.

We will use fairly small, concise structure charts in the examples in this appendix.

▶ Pseudocode

As you have learned, **pseudocode** is an English-like way of representing the solution to a problem. It is considered a "first draft" because the pseudocode eventually has to be translated into a programming language. Although pseudocode is like English and has some precision to it, it does not have the very definite precision of a programming language. Pseudocode cannot be executed by a computer. When using pseudocode to plan a program, you can concentrate on the logic and not worry

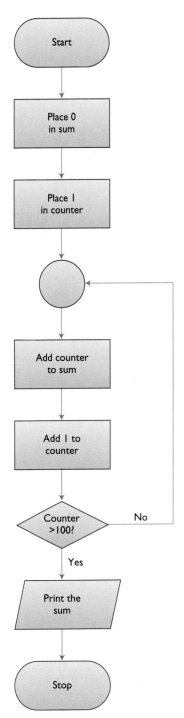

Figure C-2 A loop example. This flowchart uses a loop to find the sum of numbers from 1 through 100.

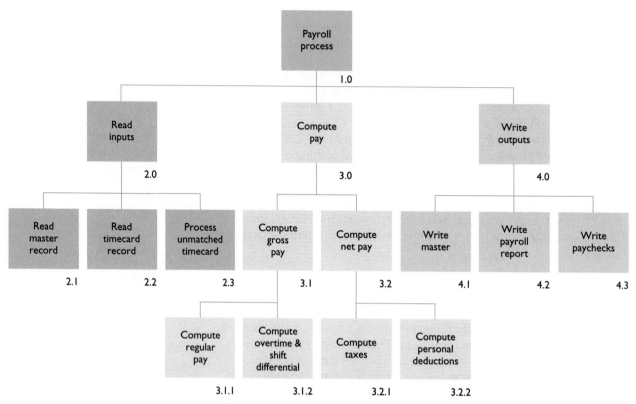

Figure C-3 A structure chart. The numbers outside the boxes refer to more detailed diagrams of these functions.

about the rules of a specific language. It is also easy to change pseudocode if you discover a flaw in your logic; once it is coded in a programming language, most people find that it is more difficult to change logic. Pseudocode can be translated into a variety of programming languages, such as Pascal or COBOL. It is helpful to introduce pseudocode in relation to flowcharting. Before doing so, however, let us consider structured programming.

▶ Structured Programming

Structured programming is a technique that emphasizes breaking a program into logical sections by using certain programming standards. Structured programming makes programs easier to write, check, read, and maintain. Here we will introduce some basic concepts of structure in this discussion of flowcharts, structure charts, and pseudocode. Note, however, that a programmer would use flowcharting, structure charts, or pseudocode to plan a solution. We present them together here so you can see how each method can be used to solve the same problem.

In a program, **control structures** control how the program executes. Structured programming uses a limited number of control structures to minimize the complexity of programs and thus to cut down on errors. There are three basic control structures in structured programming:

- Sequence
- Selection
- Iteration

These three are considered the basic building blocks of all program construction. You will see that we have used some of these structures already in Figure C-2.

Before we discuss each control structure in detail, it is important to note that each structure has only one **entry point** (the point where control is transferred to the structure) and one **exit point** (the point where control is transferred from the structure). This property makes structured programs easier to read and debug than unstructured programs.

Sequence

The **sequence control structure** is the most straightforward: One statement simply follows another in sequence. The left side of Figure C-4 shows the general format of a sequence control structure as it is used in flowcharting and in pseudocode. The right side of Figure C-4 shows an example of a sequence control structure: The two steps follow in sequence.

Selection

The **selection control structure** is used to make logical decisions. This control structure has two forms: IF-THEN-ELSE and IF-THEN. The IF-THEN-ELSE control structure works as follows: IF (a condition is true),

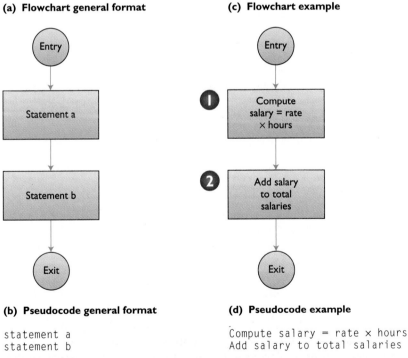

(a) Flowchart general format **(c) Flowchart example**

(b) Pseudocode general format
```
statement a
statement b
```

(d) Pseudocode example
```
Compute salary = rate × hours
Add salary to total salaries
```

Figure C-4 Sequence. (a and b) The general format of the sequence control structure. (c and d) An example of a sequence control structure. To compute the total of the movie extra's wages, ① determine the extra's salary for that week by multiplying the hourly rate times the number of hours worked that week. ② Add that extra's salary to the total of other extras to find the total.

THEN (do something), ELSE (do something different). For instance, IF the alarm clock goes off and it is a weekend morning, THEN just turn it off and go back to sleep, ELSE get up and go to work. Or, to use a more specific example, IF a student is a resident, THEN the fee equals number of credits times $450, ELSE fee is number of credits times $655. Figure C-5 shows the general format and an example of IF-THEN-ELSE in both a flowchart and in pseudocode.

IF-THEN is a special case of IF-THEN-ELSE. The IF-THEN selection is less complicated: IF the condition is true, THEN do something—but if it is not true, then do nothing. For example, IF the shift worked is shift 3, THEN add bonus of $50. Note that there will always be some action that results from using IF-THEN-ELSE; in contrast, IF-THEN may or may not produce action, depending on the condition. The IF-THEN variation is shown in Figure C-6.

(a) Flowchart general format

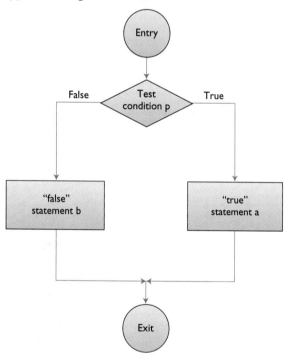

(c) Flowchart example

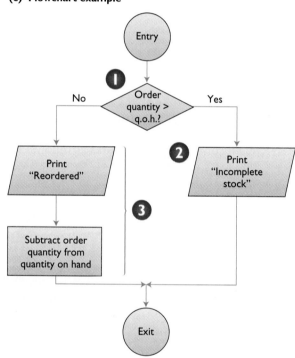

(b) Pseudocode general format

```
IF condition p THEN
    statement a
ELSE
    statement b
ENDIF
```

(d) Pseudocode example

```
IF order quantity > q.o.h. THEN
      Print "Incomplete Stock"
ELSE
        Print "Reordered"
        Subtract order quantity from q.o.h.
  ENDIF
```

Figure C-5 IF-THEN-ELSE. (a and b) The general format of the IF-THEN-ELSE control structure. There can be one or more statements for each of the two paths, True and False. (c and d) An example of an IF-THEN-ELSE control structure. A trucker orders tires at a truck-tire warehouse. IF ① the quantity of the tires ordered is greater than the quantity of the tires on hand (q.o.h.) THEN ② the computer prints "Incomplete stock," ELSE ③ it prints "Reordered" and subtracts the quantity ordered from the quantity on hand.

(a) Flowchart general format

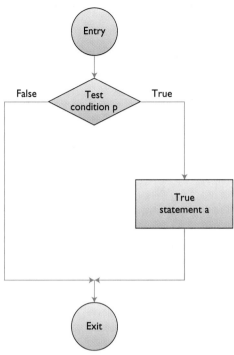

(c) Flowchart example

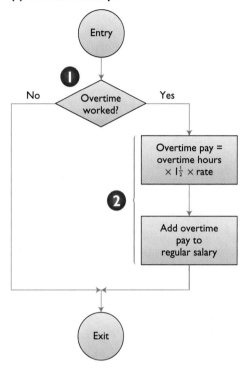

(b) Pseudocode general format

```
IF condition p THEN
   statement a
ENDIF
```

(d) Pseudocode example

```
IF overtime worked THEN
     Overtime pay = overtime hours × 1½ × rate
     Add overtime pay to regular salary
ENDIF
```

Figure C-6 IF-THEN. (a and b) The general format of the IF-THEN control structure, which is merely a special case of the IF-THEN-ELSE control structure. (c and d) An example of the IF-THEN control structure. IF ① a department store employee worked overtime THEN ② the program computes overtime pay by multiplying the overtime hours by 1½ times the hourly rate; the total is added to the employee's regular salary.

Iteration

The **iteration control structure** is a looping mechanism. The only necessary iteration structure is the DOWHILE structure, which is shown in Figure C-7. An additional form of iteration is called DOUNTIL; DOUNTIL is really just a combination of sequence and DOWHILE. Although DOUNTIL is not one of the three basic control structures, it is convenient to introduce the DOUNTIL structure now, and it is shown in Figure C-8.

When looping, you must give an instruction to stop the repetition at some point; otherwise, you could theoretically go on looping forever and never get to the end of the program. There is a basic rule of iteration, which is related to structured programming: *If you have several statements that need to be repeated, a decision about when to stop repeating has to be placed either at the beginning of all the loop statements or at the end of all the loop statements.*

If you put the loop-ending decision at the beginning, it is called a **leading decision**; if you put it at the end, it is called a **trailing decision**. The position of the decision constitutes the basic difference between DOWHILE and DOUNTIL. As Figure C-7 shows, DOWHILE tests at the beginning of the loop; the diamond-shaped decision box is the first action of the loop process. The DOUNTIL loop tests at the end, as you can see in Figure C-8. The DOUNTIL loop, by the way, guarantees that

(a) Flowchart general format

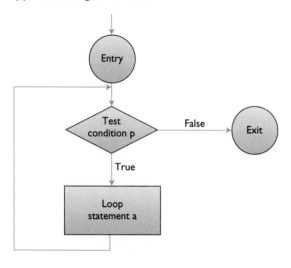

(c) Flowchart example

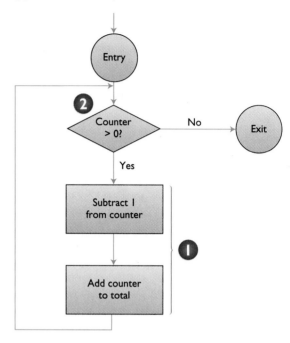

(b) Pseudocode general format

```
DOWHILE condition p
    statement a
ENDDO
```

Figure C-7 DOWHILE. (a and b) The general format of the DOWHILE control structure. (c and d) An example of the DOWHILE control structure. DO ① add counter to total and subtract 1 from counter WHILE ② counter is greater than 0.

(d) Pseudocode example

```
DOWHILE counter greater than zero
    ADD counter to total
    Subtract 1 from counter
ENDDO
```

the loop statements are executed at least once, because the loop statements are executed before you make any test about whether to get out. This guarantee is not necessarily desirable, depending on the program logic. Also note that the test condition of DOUNTIL must be false to continue the loop; this is an important difference from the DOWHILE loop.

These basic control structures may seem a bit complex in the beginning, but it is worth taking your time to learn them. In the long run they are the most efficient models for programming.

▶ Using Flowcharts, Structure Charts, and Pseudocode

Let us now consider four extended examples. In each example, solutions are shown in flowchart, structure chart, and pseudocode form. Keep in mind that normally you would select only one approach.

Example: Counting Salaries

Suppose you are the manager of a personnel agency that has 50 employees. You want to know how many people make over $30,000 a year, $20,000 to $30,000, and under $20,000.

Figure C-9 shows a solution to your problem. Let us go through the flowchart in Figure C-9a first. The circled numbers in the following text

(a) Flowchart general format

(c) Flowchart example

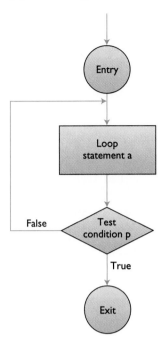

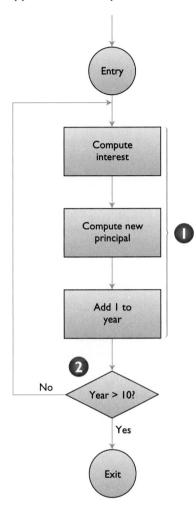

Figure C-8 DOUNTIL. (a and b) The general format of the DOUNTIL control structure. (c and d) Example of the DOUNTIL control structure. DO ① compute interest, compute new principal, and add the number 1 to year UNTIL ② the number of years is greater than 10.

(b) Pseudocode general format

```
DOUNTIL condition p
    statement a
ENDDO
```

(d) Pseudocode example

```
DOUNTIL year > 10
    Compute interest
    Compute new principal
    Add 1 to year
ENDDO
```

correspond to the circled numbers in the illustration. Use the structure chart and pseudocode in parts b and c of the figure for comparison.

① The program begins by initializing four counters to 0. The employee counter will keep track of the total number of employees in the company; the other counters—the high-salary counter, the medium-salary counter, and the low-salary counter—will count the numbers of employees in the salary categories.

② In the parallelogram-shaped input box, we indicate that the computer reads the salary at this point. A **Read** statement may be defined as code that brings something that is outside the computer into memory; to *read*, in other words, means to get. The Read statement causes the computer to get one employee's yearly salary; since the instruction is inside a loop, the computer will eventually get all salaries.

(a) Flowchart

(b) Structure Chart

(c) Pseudocode

```
set counters to ø
DOUNTIL employee counter = 50
   read a salary
   IF salary > 30,000 THEN
     add 1 to high-salary counter
   ELSE
     IF salary < 20,000 THEN
       add 1 to low-salary counter
     ELSE
       add 1 to medium-salary counter
     ENDIF
   ENDIF
   add 1 to employee counter
ENDDO
print out each counter
```

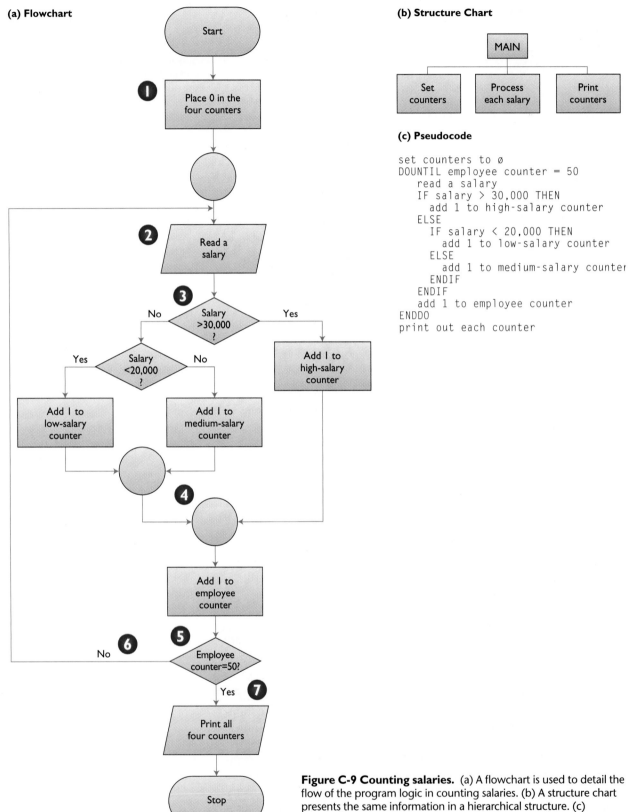

Figure C-9 Counting salaries. (a) A flowchart is used to detail the flow of the program logic in counting salaries. (b) A structure chart presents the same information in a hierarchical structure. (c) Pseudocode gets closer to the actual logic the program must follow.

③ The first of the diamond-shaped decision boxes is a test condition that can go either of two ways—Yes or No. Note that if the answer to the question "Salary > \$30,000?" is yes, then the computer will process this answer by adding 1 to the high-salary counter. If the answer is no, the computer will ask, "Salary < \$20,000?"—and so on. Notice that one control structure, the IF-THEN-ELSE for the 20,000 decision, is entirely inside the IF-THEN-ELSE for the 30,000 decision; this is easy to see from the indentations in the pseudocode.

④ For every decision box, no matter what decision is made, program control flows to a connector. And, as the flowchart shows, each decision box has its own connector. Note that, in this case, each connector is directly below the decision box to which it relates.

⑤ Whatever the kind of salary, the machine adds 1 (for the employee) to the employee counter, and a decision box then asks, "Employee counter = 50?" (the total number of employees in the company).

⑥ If the answer is no (employee counter does not equal 50), the computer makes a loop back to the first connector and goes through the process again. Note that this is a DOUNTIL loop because the decision box is at the end rather than at the beginning of the computing process (DO keep processing UNTIL employee counter equals 50).

⑦ When the answer is finally yes (employee counter does equal 50), the computer then goes to an output operation (a parallelogram) and prints the salary count for each of the three categories. The computing process then stops.

Review the flowchart and pseudocode and observe that every action is one of the three control structures we have been talking about: sequence, selection, or iteration.

Example: Checking Customer Credit Balances

In the example in this section, we will consider a flowchart that describes the process of checking a retail customer's credit balance (Figure C-10a). The structure chart (Figure C-10b) gives an overview. The pseudocode (Figure C-10c) provides another way to view the process. The file of customer records is kept on some computer-accessible medium, probably disk. This is a more true-to-life example than the previous salary example because, rather than a file with exactly 50 records, the file here contains an unknown number of records. The program has to work correctly no matter how many customers there are.

As store manager, you need to check the customer file and print out the record of any customer whose current balance exceeds the credit limit, so salesclerks will not ring up charge purchases for customers who have gone over their credit limits. (Recall that a record is a collection of related data items; a customer record would likely contain customer name, address, account number, and, as indicated, current balance and credit limit.) The interesting thing about this flowchart is that it contains the same input operation, "Read customer record," twice (see the parallelograms). We will see why this is necessary. Let us proceed through the flowchart:

① After reading the first customer record and proceeding through the connector, you have a decision box that asks, "Record received?" This is a test to see if you have run out of all customer records (which you probably would not have the first time through).

(a) Flowchart

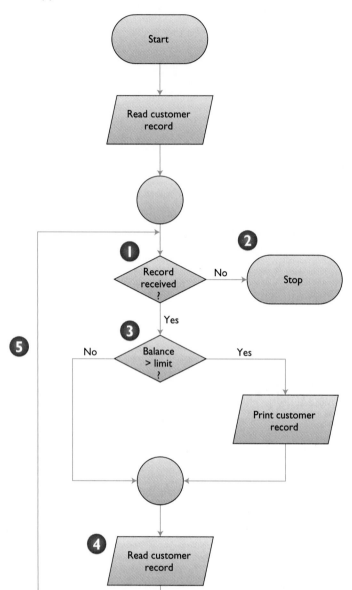

(b) Structure Chart

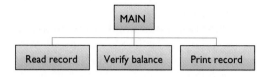

(c) Pseudocode

```
read record
DOWHILE there are more records
        IF balance > limit THEN
            print record
        ENDIF
        read record
ENDDO
```

Figure C-10 Checking a credit balance. (a) A flowchart details the program logic in checking a customer's credit balance. (b) The structure chart and (c) the pseudocode each show a different method of detailing the same procedures.

② If the answer is no (no record received), you have reached an **end of file**—meaning that no more records are in the file—and the process stops.

③ If the answer is yes (a record was received), the program proceeds to another decision box, which asks a question about the customer whose record you have just received: "Balance > limit?" This is an IF-THEN type of decision. If the answer is yes, then the customer is over the limit and, as planned, the computer prints the customer's record and moves on to the connector. If the answer is no, then the computer moves directly to the connector.

④ Now we come to the second Read statement, "Read customer record." Why are two such statements needed? Couldn't we just forget the second one and loop back to the first Read statement again? No.

The explanation lies in the rules of structure. As we stated, a loop requires a decision either at the beginning or at the end. If we omitted the second Read statement and looped back to the first Read statement, then the decision box to get us out of the loop ("Record received?") would be in the middle, not the beginning or the end of the loop. Why not put "Record received?" at the end? That strategy will not work either, because then the instructions would tell the computer to do the processing before the program had ascertained if there were a record to process.

In summary: The decision box cannot go at the end, and the rules say it cannot be in the middle; therefore, the decision must go at the beginning of the processing. Thus, the only way to read a second customer record after the computer has read the first one is to have the second Read statement where you see it. The first Read statement is sometimes called the **priming read.** This concept of the double Read may seem complicated at first, but it is very important. Reviewing the description of this flowchart may help.

⑤ Next, the program loops back to the connector and repeats the process. Incidentally, this is a DOWHILE loop because the decision box is at the beginning rather than at the end of the computing process (DO keep processing WHILE records continue to be received).

Note that, as before, each action in the program is either a sequence, a selection, or an iteration. In fact, since you have now seen two totally different examples—counting salaries and checking credit balances—you can begin to see how the control structures can be used for different applications. That is, the subject matter of the program may change, but the structured programming principles remain the same.

Example: Determining Shift Bonuses

Here is a description of the problem whose solution is represented in Figure C-11. The problem concerns awarding employees bonuses based on the shift worked. The example is a little more elaborate because it involves moving data—employee number, name, and bonus—to a report line to set it up before printing. As the figures show, a first-shift employee gets a bonus of 5 percent of regular pay, but employees who work the second or third shift get a 10 percent bonus. Also, the program counts the employees on the second or third shifts—that is, it performs one count for both shifts. If the shift is not 1, 2, or 3, then the program produces an error message.

Example: Computing Student Grades

Now let us translate a flowchart—and accompanying structure chart and pseudocode—into a program. You could type this program on a computer terminal connected to a mainframe or minicomputer, or key it directly into your personal computer. The keyed program is the programmer's source code, which we described in Chapter 12. The computer would deliver back to you on a screen the answers you seek. Figure C-12 shows the flowchart, structure chart, pseudocode, program, and output.

The program is written in QBasic, a programming language similar to English in many ways. So, even with no knowledge of QBasic, you can

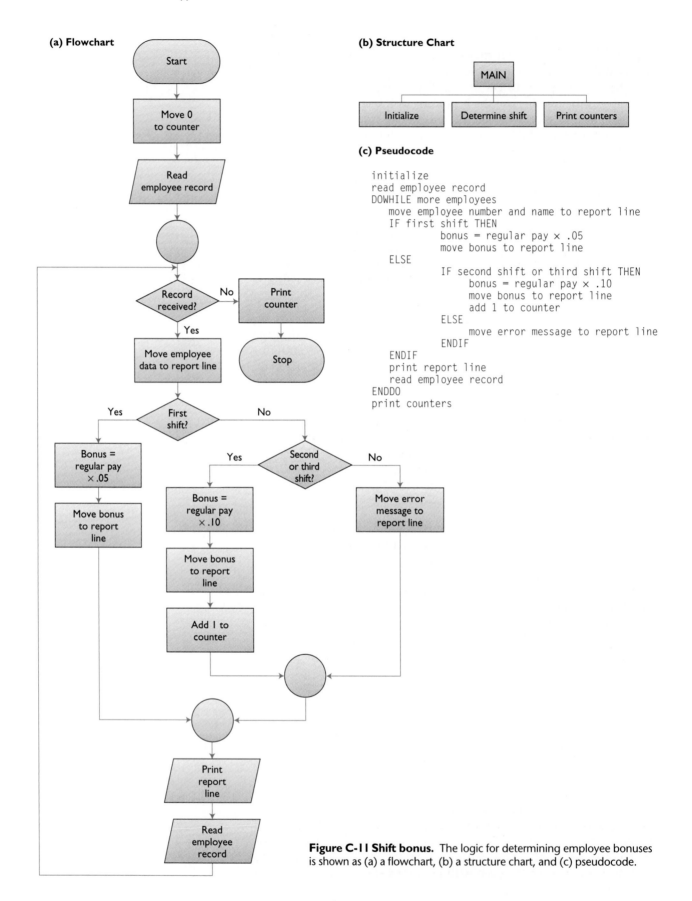

(a) Flowchart

(b) Structure Chart

(c) Pseudocode

```
initialize
read employee record
DOWHILE more employees
    move employee number and name to report line
    IF first shift THEN
            bonus = regular pay × .05
            move bonus to report line
    ELSE
            IF second shift or third shift THEN
                bonus = regular pay × .10
                move bonus to report line
                add 1 to counter
            ELSE
                move error message to report line
            ENDIF
    ENDIF
    print report line
    read employee record
ENDDO
print counters
```

Figure C-11 Shift bonus. The logic for determining employee bonuses is shown as (a) a flowchart, (b) a structure chart, and (c) pseudocode.

get a general understanding of the program. The numbers to the far left column of the QBasic program in Figure C-12d are not part of the program and are included only for reference in this discussion. If you were entering this program to the computer you would not include these numbers.

We will first talk generally about QBasic commands and then discuss the logic and program related to student grades in detail. In a program, lines that begin with an apostrophe (') are called remarks or comments. These lines contain notes that are useful to the programmer and possibly other programmers. Comment lines are intended to be a programmer convenience only; they are not executed by the computer (and hence are not included in a flowchart, structure chart, or pseudocode). Beginning program comments usually describe what the program is supposed to do and list the variable names. Variable names are symbolic names of locations in memory. As an alternative to an apostrophe, a comment line can begin with the word REM, which stands for remark.

A READ statement reads (gets) the data to be processed, as found in the DATA statements. A CLS statement clears the computer screen in preparation for expected program output. A PRINT statement tells the computer what message or data to output, in this case to the screen. The DO WHILE and LOOP statements together form a DOWHILE (leading decision) loop. By the way, QBasic will automatically change QBasic keywords such as READ or PRINT to uppercase, regardless of how you type them.

Our problem is, first, to compute the student grades (ranging from 0 through 100) for a group of students, and, second, to count the number of students whose computed points are less than 60. The grade points are based on student performance on two tests, a midterm exam, and a final exam, the scores of which have been weighted in a certain way. Note the comment lines in the program (Figure C-12d). Lines 1 through 23 describe the program, including the weights to assign to the test scores, and also list the program variable names. Line 24 is also a comment, noting that the following lines contain data to be processed. As we will soon see, lines 25 through 31 will be needed once we get to the READ statement in the program logic.

Now we will consider the logic and program for computing student grades in detail. The circled numbers in the text correspond to the circled numbers in the flowchart, but you may follow the pseudocode if you prefer. From this point forward, corresponding statement numbers from the program follow in parentheses.

① **Print headings** (program lines 34 through 41). This statement refers to the headings on the output report (skip ahead momentarily to Figure C-12e to see what they will look like). Line 34 issues a command to clear the screen. Line 35 produces a blank line (so the report will not hug the top of the screen), followed by line 35, which tabs over 10 spaces and then prints the overall heading, "Student Grade Report." The fact that the words to be printed are in quotes means they will be printed as they appear within the quotes. After printing another blank line (line 37) for attractive spacing, lines 38 and 39 print the three column headings. The commas between the words cause a move to a new column; thus, observing line 38, the three words Student, Student, and Total will appear in three different columns. Simi-

(a) Flowchart

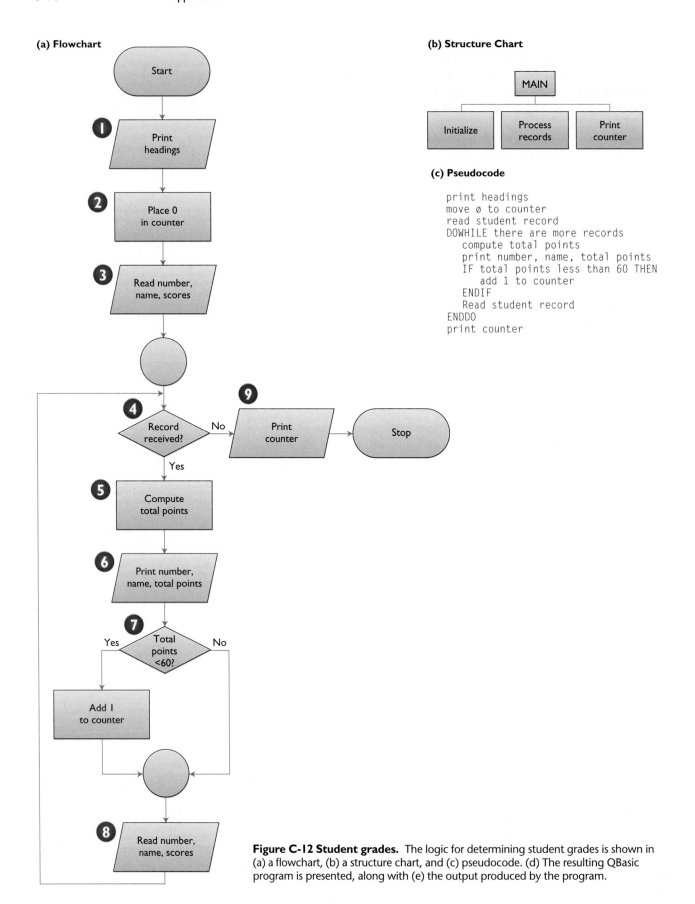

(b) Structure Chart

MAIN

Initialize | Process records | Print counter

(c) Pseudocode

```
print headings
move ø to counter
read student record
DOWHILE there are more records
   compute total points
   print number, name, total points
   IF total points less than 60 THEN
      add 1 to counter
   ENDIF
   Read student record
ENDDO
print counter
```

Figure C-12 Student grades. The logic for determining student grades is shown in (a) a flowchart, (b) a structure chart, and (c) pseudocode. (d) The resulting QBasic program is presented, along with (e) the output produced by the program.

larly, from line 39, the words Number, Name, and Points will appear in three columns, directly under the words from line 38.

② **Place 0 in counter** (line 42). This line is not a form of input; this line causes the initialization process that is required here, at the outset. The counter will count the number of students who score fewer than 60 points, as you will see later.

(d) QBasic program

```
1   '* **********************************************************************************
2   '* Program to Compute Student Points
3   '*
4   '* This program reads, for each student, student number, student name, and 4 test scores.
5   '* These scores are to be weighted as follows:
6   '* Test 1:         20 percent
7   '* Test 2:         20 percent
8   '* Midterm:        25 percent
9   '* Final:          35 percent
10  '* The program computes and prints the total points for each student and also counts the
11  '* number of students whose total points fall below 60.
12  '*
13  '* Variable Names:    Description:
14  '* Number             Student number
15  '* Name$              Student name
16  '* Score1             Score on test 1
17  '* Score2             Score on test 2
18  '* Score3             Score on midterm
19  '* Score4             Score on final
20  '* Total              Total points for a student
21  '* Count              Count of students with total points less than 60
22  '*
23  '* **********************************************************************************
24  '* Data to be processed
25  DATA 2164,Allen Schaab,60,64,73,78
26  DATA 2644,Martin Chan,80,78,85,90
27  DATA 3171,Christy Burner,91,95,90,88
28  DATA 5725,Craig Barnes,61,41,70,53
29  DATA 6994,Raoul Garcia,95,96,90,92
30  DATA 7001,Kay Mitchell,55,60,58,55
31  DATA 0,QUIT,0,0,0,0
32  '* **********************************************************************************
33  '* Program Initialization
34  CLS
35  PRINT
36  PRINT TAB(10); "Student Grade Report"
37  PRINT
38  PRINT "Student","Student","Total"
39  PRINT "Number","Name","Points"
40  PRINT
41  PRINT
42  Count=0
43  '*  Report Processing
44  READ Number, Name$, Score1, Score2, Score3, Score4
45  DO WHILE Name$<>"QUIT"
46          Total = .20*Score1 + .20*Score2 + .25*Score3 + .35*Score4
47          PRINT Number, Name$, Total
48          IF Total < 60 THEN Count = Count + 1
49          READ Number, Name$, Score1, Score2, Score3, Score4
50  LOOP
51  PRINT
52  PRINT TAB(5); "Number of students with total points < 60:";Count
53  END
```

(e) Output

Student Grade Report

Student Number	Student Name	Total Points
2164	Allen Schaab	70.4
2644	Martin Chan	84.4
3171	Christy Burner	90.5
5725	Craig Barnes	56.5
6994	Raoul Garcia	92.9
7001	Kay Mitchell	56.8

Number of students with total points < 60: 2

Figure C-12 Student grades (continued).

③ **Read number, name, scores** (line 44). This is the priming read. The input data to be used for the read statements begins at line 25. The READ in line 44 is the first read statement, so it will read the record with the first set of data: 2164 will be placed in Number, Allen Schaab in Name\$, and the four scores (60, 64, 73, and 78) placed in Score1 through Score4, respectively. Incidentally, the variable for name requires a \$ at the end because it will contain alphanumeric data.

④ **Record received?** (line 45). This is the beginning of the DOWHILE loop: DO process the loop WHILE a valid record is received. In QBasic this loop is initiated by DO WHILE and ended by LOOP. The decision box asks if a valid record was read. How will the computer know this? Because, in the program, an extra phony record was included at the end; the word QUIT indicates "end of file." (In line 45, <> means not equal.) If a valid record *is* received (any name other than QUIT) then the statements within the loop are executed for that record. The statements within the loop are lines 46 through 49.

⑤ **Compute total points** (line 46). The scores are weighted 20 percent for the first test, 20 percent for the second test, 25 percent for the midterm, and 35 percent for the final exam. The total of these weighted scores gives the course grade. In the program these percentages are documented in remark statements (lines 4 through 9). The formula that totals the scores and incorporates the weightings is stated in line 46. Here the expression .20*Score1 means 20 percent times the first test score (Score1). In QBasic the asterisk symbol (*) is used as the multiplication symbol.

⑥ **Print number, name, total points** (line 47). Student number, name, and total points are output in three columns.

⑦ **Total points < 60?** (line 48). This decision box is given as an IF-THEN statement. If a student has fewer than 60 points, 1 is added to Count.

⑧ **Read number, name, scores** (line 49). As is required by the rules of structure, we have here an instance of a repeated READ statement. The first time this statement is encountered, the data for Martin Chan will be read, the next time through the loop the data for Christy Burner, and so on. Eventually, of course, the data for QUIT will be encountered. This is the last statement within the loop, so the LOOP statement (line 50) causes transfer to the top of the loop, line 45, where the data just received is examined to see if it is a valid record. For each of the valid records, the loop statements will be executed and a line of output will be produced.

⑨ **Print counter** (lines 51, 52). When the program reaches the end of the file (because the name read is QUIT), the program drops out of the loop to the lines *below* the word LOOP. The program now prints a blank spacing line and then (line 52) prints the total number of students who have fewer than 60 points.

This chapter is useful to two types of audiences: students who expect to be users only and students who hope to be programmers. Students who will be users but not programmers can gain an appreciation of what it takes to plan a program. Even the simplest task can seem complex when expressed in step-by-step instructions. Those who will be programmers can understand that modern software is highly complex; they are unlikely to be bored.

CHAPTER REVIEW

Summary and Key Terms

- The planning phase of programming involves the steps necessary to help you understand how to develop program logic. Programmers and others can use flowcharting, structure charts, and pseudocode to plan a solution for a problem.

- **Flowcharts** are symbolic pictorial representations of step-by-step solutions to problems. They consist of arrows representing the direction a program takes and boxes and other symbols representing actions. A **logic flowchart** represents the flow of logic in a program; a **systems flowchart** shows the flow of data through an entire computer system.

- To **initialize** means to set the starting values of certain storage locations, usually as the program begins to execute.

- A **compare operation** occurs when the computer compares two numbers and performs alternative operations based on the comparison.

- A **loop**—also called an **iteration**—is defined as the repetition of instructions under certain conditions; once established, the loop is considered a powerful programming tool because the code is reusable.

- A **structure chart** graphically illustrates the structure of a program by showing independent hierarchical modules. It is also known as a **hierarchy chart.**

- **Pseudocode** is a way of representing the solution to a problem by using English to express the logic. It is considered a "first draft" for solving the problem because eventually it must be translated into a programming language.

- **Structured programming** is a technique that emphasizes breaking a program into logical sections by using certain universal programming standards. In more formal terms, structured programming is a set of programming techniques that includes a limited number of control structures, top-down design, and module independence.

- Structured programming uses **control structures** to handle execution. The **sequence control structure** involves one statement following another in sequence. A **selection control structure** can take one of two forms: IF-THEN-ELSE and IF-THEN. An **iteration control structure** is a looping mechanism that uses DOWHILE for **leading decisions** (at the beginning of the loop) and DOUNTIL for **trailing decisions** (at the end of the loop). Each structure has only one **entry point** (the point where control is transferred to the structure) and one **exit point** (the point where control is transferred from the structure). These characteristics make structured programs easier to read and debug than unstructured programs.

- A **Read** statement brings something that is outside the computer into memory; reading, in other words, means getting. The first Read statement is sometimes called the **priming read**. When you read to the **end of file**, there are no more records in the file, so the reading process stops.

Data can be represented in the computer in one of two basic ways: as **numeric data** or as **alphanumeric data.** The internal representation of alphanumeric data—letters, digits, special characters—was discussed in Chapter 3. Recall that alphanumeric data may be represented using various codes; ASCII is a common code. Alphanumeric data, even if all digits, cannot be used for arithmetic operations. Data used for arithmetic calculations must be stored numerically.

Data stored numerically can be represented as the binary equivalent of the decimal value with which we are familiar. That is, values such as 1050, 43218, and 3 that we input to the computer will be converted to the binary number system. In this appendix we shall study the binary number system (base 2) and two related systems, octal (base 8) and hexadecimal (base 16).

Number Systems

➤ Number Bases

A number base is a specific collection of symbols on which a number system can be built. The number base familiar to us is base 10, upon which the **decimal** number system is built. There are ten symbols—0 through 9—used in the decimal system.

Since society uses base 10, that is the number base most of us understand and can use easily. It would theoretically be possible, however, for all of us to learn to use a different number system. This number system could contain a different number of symbols and perhaps even symbols that are unfamiliar.

Base 2: The Binary Number System

Base 2 has exactly two symbols: 0 and 1. All numbers in the binary system must be formed using these two symbols. As you can see in column 2 of Table D-1, this means that numbers in the binary system become long quickly; the number 1000 in base 2 is equivalent to 8 in base 10. (When different number bases are being discussed, it is common practice to use the number base as a subscript. In this case we could say $1000_2 = 8_{10}$.) If you were to continue counting in base 2, you would soon see that the binary numbers were very long and unwieldy. The number 5000_{10} is equal to 10011100010000_2.

Table D-1 Number bases 10, 2, 8, 16: first values			
Base 10	**Base 2**	**Base 8**	**Base 16**
(Decimal)	(Binary)	(Octal)	(Hexadecimal)
0	0000	0	0
1	0001	1	1
2	0010	2	2
3	0011	3	3
4	0100	4	4
5	0101	5	5
6	0110	6	6
7	0111	7	7
8	1000	10	8
9	1001	11	9
10	1010	12	A
11	1011	13	B
12	1100	14	C
13	1101	15	D
14	1110	16	E
15	1111	17	F
16	10000	20	10

The size and sameness—all those zeros and ones—of binary numbers make them subject to frequent error when they are being manipulated by humans. To improve both convenience and accuracy, it is common to express the values represented by binary numbers in the more concise octal and hexadecimal number bases.

Base 8: The Octal Number System

The **octal** number system uses exactly eight symbols: 0, 1, 2, 3, 4, 5, 6, and 7. Base 8 is a convenient shorthand for base 2 numbers because 8 is a power of 2: $2^3 = 8$. As you will see when we discuss conversions, one octal digit is the equivalent of exactly three binary digits. The use of octal (or hexadecimal) as a shorthand for binary is common in printed output of main storage and, in some cases, in programming.

Look at the column of octal numbers in Table D-1. Notice that, since 7 is the last symbol in base 8, the following number is 10. In fact, we can count right through the next seven numbers in the usual manner, as long as we end with 17. Note, however, that 17_8 is pronounced "one-seven," not "seventeen." The octal number 17 is followed by 20 through 27, and so on. The last double-digit number is 77, which is followed by 100. Although it takes a little practice, you can see that it would be easy to learn to count in base 8. However, hexadecimal, or base 16, is not quite as easy.

Base 16: The Hexadecimal Number System

The **hexadecimal** number system uses exactly 16 symbols. As we have just seen, base 10 uses the familiar digits 0 through 9, and bases 2 and 8 use a subset of those symbols. Base 16, however, needs those ten symbols (0 through 9) and six more. The six additional symbols used in the hexadecimal number system are the letters A through F. So the base 16 symbols are: 0, 1, 2, 3, 4, 5, 6, 7, 8, 9, A, B, C, D, E, and F. It takes some adjusting to think of A or D as a digit instead of a letter. It also takes a little time to become accustomed to numbers such as 6A2F or even ACE. Both of these examples are legitimate numbers in hexadecimal.

As you become familiar with hexadecimal, consider the matter of counting. Counting sounds simple enough, but it can be confusing in an unfamiliar number base with new symbols. The process is the same as counting in base 10, but most of us learned to count when we were too young to think about the process itself. Quickly—what number follows 24CD? The answer is 24CE. We increased the rightmost digit by one—D to E—just as you would have in the more obvious case of 6142 to 6143. What is the number just before 1000_{16}? The answer is FFF_{16}; the last symbol (F) is a triple-digit number. Compare this with 999_{10}, which precedes 1000_{10}; 9 is the last symbol in base 10. As a familiarization exercise, try counting from 1 to 100 in base 16. Remember to use A through F as the second symbol in the teens, twenties, and so forth (... 27, 28, 29, 2A, 2B, 2C, 2D, 2E, 2F, 30, and so on).

► Conversions Between Number Bases

It is sometimes convenient to use a number in a base different from the base currently being used—that is, to change the number from one base

Table D-2 Summary conversion chart

From Base	To Base			
	2	8	16	10
2	—	Group binary digits by 3, convert	Group binary digits by 4, convert	Expand number and convert base 2 digits to base 10
8	Convert each octal digit to 3 binary digits	—	Convert to base 2, then to base 16	Expand number and convert base 8 digits to base 10
16	Convert each hexadecimal digit to 4 binary digits	Convert to base 2, then to base 8	—	Expand number and convert base 16 digits to base 10
10	Divide number repeatedly by 2; use remainders as answer	Divide number repeatedly by 8; use remainders as answer	Divide number repeatedly by 16; use remainders as answer	—

to another. Many programmers can nimbly convert a number from one base to another, among bases 10, 2, 8, and 16. We shall consider these conversion techniques now. Table D-2 summarizes the methods.

To Base 10 from Bases 2, 8, and 16

We present these conversions together because the technique is the same for all three.

Let us begin with the concept of positional notation. **Positional notation** means that the value of a digit in a number depends not only on its own intrinsic value but also on its location in the number. Given the number 2363, we know that the appearance of the digit 3 represents two different values, 300 and 3. Table D-3 shows the names of the relative positions.

Using these positional values, the number 2363 is understood to mean

$$
\begin{array}{r}
2000 \\
300 \\
60 \\
\underline{3} \\
2363
\end{array}
$$

This number can also be expressed as:

$$(2 \times 1000) + (3 \times 100) + (6 \times 10) + 3$$

We can express this expanded version of the number another way, using powers of 10. Note that $10^0 = 1$.

$$2363 = (2 \times 10^3) + (3 \times 10^2) + (6 \times 10^1) + (3 \times 10^0)$$

Once you understand the expanded notation, the rest is easy: You expand the number as we just did in base 10, but use the appropriate base of the number. For example, follow the steps to convert 61732_8 to base 10:

Digit	4th	3rd	2nd	1st (rightmost)
Table D-3 Digit positions				
Position	Thousand	Hundred	Ten	Unit

1. Expand the number, using 8 as the base:

$$61732 = (6 \times 8^4) + (1 \times 8^3) + (7 \times 8^2) + (3 \times 8^1) + (2 \times 8^0)$$

2. Complete the arithmetic:

$$61732 = (6 \times 4096) + (1 \times 512) + (7 \times 64) + (3 \times 8) + (2 \times 1)$$
$$= 24576 + 512 + 448 + 24 + 2$$

3. Answer: $61732_8 = 25562_{10}$

The same expand-and-convert technique can be used to convert from base 2 or base 16 to base 10. As you consider the following two examples, use Table D-1 to make the conversions. (For example, A in base 16 converts to 10 in base 10.)

Convert $C14A_{16}$ to base 10:

$$C14A_{16} = (12 \times 16^3) + (1 \times 16^2) + (4 \times 16^1) + (10 \times 16^0)$$
$$= (12 \times 4096) + (1 \times 256) + (4 \times 16) + (10 \times 1)$$
$$= 49482$$

So $C14A_{16} = 49482_{10}$.
Convert 100111_2 to base 10:

$$100111_2 = (1 \times 2^5) + (1 \times 2^2) + (1 \times 2^1) + (1 \times 2^0)$$
$$= 39$$

So $100111_2 = 39_{10}$.

From Base 10 to Bases 2, 8, and 16

These conversions use a simpler process but more complicated arithmetic. The process, often called the *remainder method*, is basically a series of repeated divisions by the number of the base to which you are converting. You begin by using the number to be converted as the dividend; succeeding dividends are the quotients of the previous division. The converted number is the combined remainders accumulated from the divisions. There are two points to remember:

1. Keep dividing until you reach a zero quotient.
2. Use the remainders in reverse order.

Consider converting 6954_{10} to base 8:

```
8|6954
8|869    2
8|108    5
8|13     4
8|1      5
 0       1
```

Placing the remainders backward, $6954_{10} = 15452_8$.

Now use the same technique to convert 4823_{10} to base 16:

```
16|4823
16|3017
16|18    13 (= D)
16|1     2
  0      1
```

The remainder 13 is equivalent to D in base 16. So $4823_{10} = 12D7_{16}$.

Convert 49_{10} to base 2:

```
2|49
2|24  1
2|12  0
2|6   0
2|3   0
2|1   1
 0    1
```

Again placing the remainders in reverse order, $49_{10} = 110001_2$.

To Base 2 from Bases 8 and 16

To convert a number to base 2 from base 8 or base 16, convert each digit separately to three or four binary digits, respectively. Use Table D-1 to make the conversion. Leading zeros—zeros added to the front of the number—may be needed in each grouping of digits to fill out each to three or four digits.

Convert 4732_8 to base 2, converting each octal digit to a set of three binary digits:

4	7	3	2
100	111	011	010

So $4732_8 = 100111011010_2$. Notice that leading zeros were sometimes needed to make three binary digits from an octal digit: for octal digit 3, 11 became 011 and, for octal digit 2, 10 became 010.

Now convert $A046B_{16}$ to base 2, this time converting each hexadecimal digit to four binary digits:

A	0	4	6	B
1010	0000	0100	0110	1011

Thus $A046B_{16} = 10100000010001101011_2$.

From Base 2 to Bases 8 and 16

To convert a number from base 2 to base 8 or base 16, group the binary digits from the right in groups of three or four, respectively. Again use Table D-1 to help you make the conversion to the new base.

Convert 111101001011_2 to base 8 and base 16:

In the base 8 conversion, group the digits three at a time, starting on the right:

111	101	001	011
7	5	1	3

So $111101001011_2 = 7513_8$.

For the conversion to base 16, group the digits four at a time, starting on the right:

1111   0100   1011
F   4   B

$111101001011_2 = F4B_{16}$.

Sometimes the number of digits in a binary number is not exactly divisible by 3 or 4. You may, for example, start grouping the digits three at a time and finish with one or two "extra" digits on the left side of the number. In this case just add as many zeros as you need to the front of the binary number.

Consider converting 1010_2 to base 8. By adding two zeros to the front of the number to make it 001010_2, we now have six digits, which can be conveniently grouped three at a time:

001   010
1   2

So $1010_2 = 12_8$.

Glossary

A

Access arm   A mechanical device that can access all the tracks of one cylinder in a disk storage unit.

Access time   The time needed to access data directly on disk, consisting of seek time, head switching, and rotational delay.

Accumulator   A register that collects the results of computations.

Acoustic coupler   A modem that connects to a telephone receiver rather than directly to a telephone line.

Acquisition by purchase   Buying an entire system for use by the organization, as opposed to designing a new system.

Active badge   A badge that, embedded with a computer chip, signals the wearer's location by sending out infrared signals, which are read by computers distributed throughout a building.

Active cell   The cell currently available for use in a spreadsheet. Also called the current cell.

Address   A number used to designate a location in memory.

Address register   A register used to help locate where instructions and data are stored in memory.

Alphanumeric data   Letters, digits, and special characters such as punctuation marks.

ALU   See *Arithmetic/logic unit.*

America Online (AOL)   A major online service that offers a variety of services.

Amplitude   The height of the carrier wave in analog transmission. Amplitude indicates the strength of the signal.

Amplitude modulation   A change of the amplitude of the carrier wave in analog data transmission to represent either the 0 bit or the 1 bit.

Analog transmission   The transmission of data as a continuous electrical signal in the form of a wave.

Analytical engine   A historically significant machine designed by Charles Babbage that embodied the key characteristics of modern computers.

Analytical graphics   Traditional line graphs, bar charts, and pie charts; used to illustrate and analyze data.

Anchor tag   In HTML, the command used to make a link. The key attribute of the anchor tag is HREF, which indicates a link destination. The anchor tag also includes the name of the word or words—the hypertext—that will be clicked to initiate the move to the new site.

ANSI   American National Standards Institute.

Antivirus   A computer program that stops the spread of a virus. Also called a vaccine.

AOL   See *America Online.*

Applet   A small program that can provide animation such as dancing icons and scrolling banners on a web site.

Applications software   Programs designed to perform specific tasks and functions, such as word processing.

Arithmetic/logic unit (ALU)   Part of the central processing unit, the electronic circuitry of the ALU executes all arithmetic and logical operations.

Arithmetic operations   Mathematical calculations that the ALU performs on data.

ARPANet   A network, established in 1969 by the Department of Defense, that eventually became the Internet.

Artificial intelligence   The field of study that explores computer involvement in tasks requiring intelligence, imagination, and intuition.

ASCII (American Standard Code for Information Interchange)   A coding scheme using 7-bit characters to represent data characters. A variation of the code, called ASCII-8, uses 8 bits per character.

Assembler program   A translator program used to convert assembly language programs to machine language.

Assembly language   A second-generation language that uses abbreviations for instructions, as opposed to only numbers. Also called symbolic language.

Asynchronous transmission   Data transmission in which data is sent in groups of bits, with each group of bits preceded by a start signal and ended with a stop signal. Also called start/stop transmission.

Atanasoff-Berry Computer (ABC)   The first electronic digital computer, designed by John V. Atanasoff and Clifford Berry, in the late 1930s.

ATM   See *Automated teller machine.*

Attribute   In object-oriented programming, a fact related to an object.

Audio-response unit   See *Voice synthesizer.*

Audit trail   A method of tracing data from the output back to the source documents.

Automated teller machine (ATM)   An input/output device connected to a computer used by bank customers for financial transactions.

Automatic recalculation   In a spreadsheet, when one value or calculation is changed, all values dependent on the changed item are automatically recalculated to reflect the change.

Automatic reformatting   In word processing, automatic adjustment of text to accommodate changes such as margin width.

Auxiliary storage   Another name for secondary storage, which is storage for data and programs. Auxiliary storage is most often on disk.

Axis   A reference line of a graph. The horizontal axis is the x-axis. The vertical axis is the y-axis.

B

Backbone   The major communication links that tie Internet servers across wide geographical areas.

Background   (1) In large computers, the memory area for running programs with low priorities. Contrast with *Foreground.* (2) On a web site, the screen appearance behind the text and images.

Backspace key   The key used to delete text characters to the left of the cursor.

Backup system   A method of storing data in more than one place to protect it from damage or loss.

Bandwidth   The number of frequencies that can fit on one communications line or link at the same time, or the capacity of the link.

Bar code   A standardized pattern of vertical marks that represents the Universal Product Code (UPC) that identifies a product.

Bar code reader   A stationary photoelectric scanner that inputs bar codes by means of reflected light.

Bar graph   A graph made up of filled-in columns or rows that represent the change of data over time.

BASIC (Beginner's All-purpose Symbolic Instruction Code)   A high-level programming language that is easy to learn and use. Originally for beginners , it is now also used in business and by personal computer users.

Batch processing   A data processing technique in which transactions are collected into groups, or batches, for processing.

Baud rate   The number of changes per second of a signal being used to transmit data.

Binary   Regarding number systems, the binary number system uses exactly two symbols, the digits 0 and 1.

Binary system   A system in which data is represented by combinations of 0s and 1s, which correspond to the two states off and on.

Biometrics   The science of measuring individual body characteristics; used in some security systems.

Bit   A binary digit.

Block copy command   In word processing, the command used to copy a block of text into a new location, leaving the text in its original location as well.

Block delete command   In word processing, the command used to erase a block of text.

Block move command   In word processing, the command used to remove a block of text from one location in a document and place it elsewhere.

Body tags   In HTML, a pair of tags that enclose the content of the page.

Boldface   Emphasizing text by printing characters in **darker** type than the surrounding text.

Bomb   An application that sabotages a computer by triggering damage—usually at a later date. Also called a logic bomb.

Boolean logic   Regarding search engines on the Internet, a mathematical system that can be used to narrow the search through the use of operators such as AND, OR, and NOT.

Booting   Loading the operating system into memory.

Bpi   See *Bytes per inch.*

Branch   In a flowchart, the connection leading from the decision to one of two possible responses. Also called a path.

Bridge   A device that recognizes and transmits messages to be sent to other similar networks.

Browser   Software used to access the Internet.

Bus or **bus line**   An electronic pathway for data travel among the parts of a computer. Also called a data bus.

Bus network   A network that has a single line to which each device is attached.

Business-quality graphics   See *Presentation graphics.*

Button   Clickable icons that represent menu choices or options.

Byte   Strings of bits (usually 8) used to represent one data character—a letter, digit, or special character.

Bytes per inch (bpi)   An expression of the amount (density) of data stored on magnetic tape.

C

C   A sophisticated programming language invented by Bell Labs in 1974.

C++   An object-oriented programming language; a version of C.

Cable modem   A fast communications link that uses coaxial television cables already in place without interrupting normal cable TV reception.

Cache   A relatively small amount of very fast memory that stores data and instructions that are used frequently, resulting in improved processing speeds.

CAD/CAM   See *Computer-aided design/computer-aided manufacturing.*

Candidates   In systems analysis and design, alternative plans offered in the preliminary design phase of a project.

Carrier sense multiple access with collision detection (CSMA/CD)   The line control method used by Ethernet. Each node has access to the communications line and can transmit if it hears no communication on the line. If two stations transmit simultaneously, they will wait and retry their transmissions.

Carrier wave   An analog signal used in the transmission of electric signals.

Cathode ray tube (CRT) The most common type of computer screen.

CD-R A technology that permits writing on optical disks.

CD-ROM See *Compact disk read-only memory.*

Cell The intersection of a row and a column in a spreadsheet. Entries in a spreadsheet are stored in individual cells.

Cell address In a spreadsheet, the column and row coordinates of a cell. Also called the cell reference.

Cell contents The label, value, formula, or function contained in a spreadsheet cell.

Cell reference In a spreadsheet, the column and row coordinates of a cell. Also called the cell address.

Centering Placing a line of text midway between the left and right margins.

Central processing unit (CPU) Electronic circuitry that executes stored program instructions. It consists of two parts: the control unit and the arithmetic/logic unit. The CPU processes raw data into meaningful, useful information.

Centralized Description of a computer system in which hardware, software, storage, and computer access is in one location. Contrast with *Decentralized.*

CERN The name of the site of the particle physics lab where Dr. Tim Berners-Lee worked when he invented the World Wide Web; sometimes called the birthplace of the Web.

CGA Color graphics adapter. An early color screen standard with 320x200 pixels.

Change agent The role of the systems analyst in overcoming resistance to change within an organization.

Character A letter, number, or special character such as $.

Characters per inch (cpi) An expression of the amount (density) of data stored on magnetic tape.

Chief information officer (CIO) Manager of an MIS department.

Circuit One or more conductors through which electricity flows.

CISC See *Complex instruction set computer.*

Class In object-oriented programming, an object class contains the characteristics that are unique to that class.

Client (1) An individual or organization contracting for systems analysis. (2) In a client/server network, a program on the personal computer that allows that node to communicate with the server.

Client/server A network setup that involves a server computer, which controls the network, and clients, other computers that access the network and its services. In particular, the server does some processing, sending the client only the portion of the file it needs or possibly just the processed results. Contrast with *File server.*

Clip art Illustrations already produced by professional artists for public use. Computerized clip art is stored on disk and can be used to enhance any kind of graph or document.

Clock A component of the CPU that produces pulses at a fixed rate to synchronize all computer operations.

Clone A personal computer that can run software designed for IBM personal computers.

CMOS See *Complementary metal oxide semiconductor.*

Coaxial cable Bundles of insulated wires within a shielded enclosure. Coaxial cable can be laid underground or undersea.

COBOL (COmmon Business-Oriented Language) An English-like programming language used primarily for business applications.

Cold site An environmentally suitable empty shell in which a company can install its own computer system.

Collaborative software See *Groupware.*

Collision The problem that occurs when two records have the same disk address.

Command A name that invokes the correct program or program segment.

Commercial software Software that is packaged and sold in stores. Also called packaged software.

Compact disk read-only memory (CD-ROM) Optical data storage technology using disk formats identical to audio compact disks.

Compare operation An operation in which the computer compares two data items and performs alternative operations based on the results of the comparison.

Compiler A translator that converts the symbolic statements of a high-level language into computer-executable machine language.

Complementary metal oxide semiconductor (CMOS) A semiconductor device that does not require a large amount of power to operate. The CMOS is often found in devices that require low power consumption, such as portable computers.

Complex instruction set computer (CISC) A CPU design that contains a large number of instructions of varying kinds, some of which are rarely used. Contrast with *Reduced instruction set computer.*

Computer A machine that accepts data (input) and processes it into useful information (output). A computer system requires four main aspects of data handling—input, processing, output, and storage.

Computer Fraud and Abuse Act A law passed by Congress in 1984 to fight computer crime.

Computer Information Systems (CIS) The department responsible for managing a company's computer resources. Also called Management Information Systems (MIS), Computing Services (CS), or Information Services.

Computer literacy The awareness and knowledge of, and the capacity to interact with, computers.

Computer Matching and Privacy Protection Act Legislation that prevents the government from comparing certain records in an attempt to find a match.

Computer operator A person who monitors and runs the computer equipment in a large system.

Computer programmer A person who designs, writes, tests, and implements programs.

Computer system A system that has a computer as one of its components.

Computer-aided design/computer-aided manufacturing (CAD/CAM) The use of computers to create two- and three-dimensional pictures of products to be manufactured.

Computing Services The department responsible for managing a company's computer resources. Also called Management Information Systems (MIS), Computer Information Systems (CIS), or Information Services.

Concurrently With reference to the execution of computer instructions, in the same time frame but not simultaneously. See also *Multiprogramming.*

Conditional replace A word processing function that asks the user whether to replace text each time the program finds a particular item.

Connector A symbol used in flowcharting to connect paths.

Consortium A joint venture to support a complete computer facility to be used in an emergency.

Continuous word system A speech recognition system that can understand sustained speech so that users can speak normally.

Control structure A pattern for controlling the flow of logic in a program. The three basic control structures are sequence, selection, and iteration.

Control unit The circuitry that directs and coordinates the entire computer system in executing stored program instructions. Part of the central processing unit.

Cookie An entry in a file stored on the user's hard drive that reflects activity on the Internet.

Coordinating In systems analysis, orchestrating the process of analyzing and planning a new system by pulling together the various individuals, schedules, and tasks that contribute to the analysis.

Copyrighted software Software that costs money and must not be copied without permission from the manufacturer.

CPU See *Central processing unit.*

CRT See *Cathode ray tube.*

CSMA/CD See *Carrier sense multiple access with collision detection.*

Current cell The cell currently available for use in a spreadsheet. Also called the active cell.

Current drive The disk drive currently being used by the computer system. Also called the default drive.

Cursor An indicator on the screen; it shows where the next user-computer interaction will be. Also called a pointer.

Cursor movement keys Keys on the computer keyboard that allow the user to move the cursor on the screen.

Custom software Software that is tailored to a specific user's needs.

Cut and paste In word processing and some other applications, moving a block of text by deleting it in one place (cut) and adding it in another (paste).

Cylinder A set of tracks on a magnetic disk, one from each platter, vertically aligned. These tracks can be accessed by one positioning of the access arm.

Cylinder method A method of organizing data on a magnetic disk. This method organizes data vertically, which minimizes seek time.

D

DASD See *Direct-access storage device.*

DAT See *Digital audio tape.*

Data Raw input to be processed by a computer.

Data communications The process of exchanging data over communications facilities.

Data communications systems Computer systems that transmit data over communications lines, such as public telephone lines or private network cables.

Data compression Making a large data file smaller by temporarily removing nonessential but space-hogging items such as tab marks and double-spacing.

Data Encryption Standard (DES) The standardized public key by which senders and receivers can scramble and unscramble messages sent over data communications equipment.

Data entry operator A person who keys data for computer processing.

Data flow diagram (DFD) A diagram that shows the flow of data through an organization.

Data item Data in a relational database table.

Data mining The process of extracting previously unknown information from existing data.

Data mirroring In RAID storage, a technique of duplicating data on a separate disk drive.

Data point Each dot or symbol on a line graph. Each data point represents a value.

Data striping In RAID storage, a technique of spreading data across several disks in the array.

Data transfer The transfer of data between memory and the place on the disk track—from memory to the track if writing, from the track to memory if reading.

Data transfer rate The speed with which data can be transferred to or from a disk and a computer.

Database An organized collection of related files stored together with minimum redundancy. Specific data items can be retrieved for various applications.

Database management system (DBMS) A set of programs that creates, manages, protects, and provides access to the database.

Date field   In a database file structure, a field that is used for dates.

DBMS   See *Database management system.*

Debugging   The process of detecting, locating, and correcting logic errors in a program.

Decentralized   Description of a computer system in which the computer and its storage devices are in one place but devices that access the computer are in other locations. Contrast with *Centralized.*

Decision box   The standard diamond-shaped box used in flowcharting; it indicates a decision.

Decision logic table   See *Decision table.*

Decision support system (DSS)   A computer system that supports managers in nonroutine decision-making tasks. A DSS involves a model, a mathematical representation of a real-life situation.

Decision table   A standard table of the logical decisions that must be made regarding potential conditions in a given system. Also called a decision logic table.

Default drive   The disk drive currently being used. Also called the current drive. This is the disk drive to which commands refer in the absence of any specified drive.

Default settings   The settings automatically used by a program unless the user specifies otherwise, thus overriding them.

Delete key   The key used to delete the text character at the cursor location or a text block that has been selected or marked.

Demodulation   The reconstruction of the original digital message after analog transmission.

Density   The amount of data stored on magnetic tape; expressed in number of characters per inch (cpi) or bytes per inch (bpi).

Dependent variable   Output of a computerized model, particularly a decision support system. Called dependent because it depends on the inputs.

DES   See *Data Encryption Standard.*

Desk-checking   A programming phase in which a programmer mentally checks the logic of a program to ensure that it is error-free and workable.

Desktop publishing   Using a personal computer, special software, and a laser printer to produce very high-quality documents that combine text and graphics.

Desktop publishing program   A software package for designing and producing professional-looking documents. Also called a page composition program or page makeup program.

Detail design   A systems design subphase in which the system is planned in detail, including the details of output, input, files and databases, processing, and controls and backup.

DFD   See *Data flow diagram.*

Diagnostics   Error messages provided by the compiler as it translates a program. Diagnostics inform the user of programming language syntax errors.

Difference engine   A historically significant machine designed by Charles Babbage to solve polynomial equations by calculating the successive differences between them. See also his other machine, *Analytical engine.*

Digital audio tape (DAT)   A high-capacity tape that records data using a method called helical scan recording, which places the data in diagonal bands that run across the tape rather than down its length.

Digital transmission   The transmission of data as distinct on or off pulses.

Digital video disk   A form of optical disk storage that has a double-layered surface and can be written on both sides, providing significant capacity. Also called DVD-ROM.

Digitizing tablet   A graphics input device that allows the user to create images. It has a special stylus that can be used to draw or trace images, which are then converted to digital data that can be processed by the computer.

Direct access   Immediate access to a record in secondary storage, usually on disk.

Direct conversion   A system conversion in which the user simply stops using the old system and starts using the new one.

Direct file organization   An arrangement of records so that each is individually accessible.

Direct file processing   Processing that allows the user to access a record directly by using a record key.

Direct-access storage device (DASD)   A storage device, usually disk, in which a record can be accessed directly.

Direct-connect modem   A modem connected directly to the telephone line.

Disaster recovery plan   Guidelines for restoring computer processing operations if they are halted by major damage or destruction.

Discrete word system   A speech recognition system limited to understanding isolated words.

Disk drive   A machine that allows data to be read from a disk or written on a disk.

Disk pack   A stack of magnetic disks assembled together.

Diskette   A single disk, made of flexible Mylar, on which data is recorded as magnetic spots. A diskette is usually 3½ inches in diameter, with a hard plastic jacket.

Displayed value   The calculated result of a formula or function in a spreadsheet cell.

Distributed data processing   A computer system in which processing is decentralized, with the computers and storage devices and access devices in dispersed locations.

Documentation   (1) Related to a program, a detailed written description of the programming cycle and specific facts about the program. (2) The instruction manual for packaged software. (3) In systems analysis and design, the written records of all phases of the systems development life cycle.

Domain   The name of the Internet service provider, as it appears in the Uniform Resource Locator.

Dot pitch   The amount of space between dots on a screen.

Download   In a networking environment, to receive data files from another computer, probably a larger computer or a host computer. Contrast with *Upload*.

DRAM   See *Dynamic random-access memory*.

DSS   See *Decision support system*.

DVD   See *Digital video disk*.

Dynamic random-access memory (DRAM)   Memory chips that are periodically regenerated, allowing the chips to retain the stored data. Contrast with *Static random-access memory*.

E

EDI   See *Electronic data interchange*.

EFT   See *Electronic fund transfer*.

EGA   Enhanced graphics adapter. A color screen standard with 640x350 pixels.

Electronic data interchange (EDI)   A set of standards by which companies can electronically exchange common business forms such as invoices and purchase orders.

Electronic fund transfer (EFT)   Paying for goods and services by transferring funds electronically.

Electronic mail (e-mail)   Sending messages from one terminal or computer to another.

Electronic software distribution   Downloading software from the originator's site to a user's site, presumably for a fee.

Electronic spreadsheet   A computerized worksheet used to organize data into rows and columns for analysis.

E-mail   See *Electronic mail*.

Encapsulation   In object-oriented programming, the containment of both data and its related instructions in the object.

Encryption   The process of encoding data to be transmitted via communications links, so that its contents are protected from unauthorized people.

End of file   The point in a program or module at which all records on a file have been read.

End-user   The person who buys and uses computer software or who has contact with computers.

ENIAC (Electronic Numerical Integrator and Computer)   The first general-purpose electronic computer, which was built by Dr. John Mauchly and J. Presper Eckert, Jr., and was first operational in 1946.

Equal-to condition (=)   A logical operation in which the computer compares two numbers to determine equality.

Erase head   The head in a magnetic tape unit that erases any data previously recorded on the tape before recording new data.

Ergonomics   The study of human factors related to computers.

ESS   See *Executive support system*.

Ethernet   A popular type of local area network that uses a bus topology.

E-time   The execution portion of the machine cycle; E-time includes the execute and store operations.

Event-driven   Refers to multiprogramming; programs share resources based on events that take place in the programs. One program is allowed to use a particular resource (such as the central processing unit) to complete a certain activity (event) before relinquishing the resource to another program.

Executive support system (ESS)   A decision support system for senior-level executives who make decisions that affect an entire company.

Expansion slots   The slots inside a computer that allow a user to insert additional circuit boards.

Expert shell   Software having the basic structure to find answers to questions that are part of an expert system; the questions themselves can be added by the user.

Expert system   Software that presents the computer as an expert on some topic.

Exploded pie chart   A pie chart with a "slice" that is separated from the rest of the chart.

External cache   Cache (very fast memory for frequently used data and instructions) on chips separate from the microprocessor.

Extranet   A network of two or more intranets.

F

Facsimile technology (fax)   The use of computer technology to send digitized graphics, charts, and text from one facsimile machine to another.

Fair Credit Reporting Act   Legislation that allows individuals access to their own credit records and gives them the right to challenge them.

Fax   See *Facsimile technology*.

Fax modem   A modem that allows the user to transmit and receive faxes without interrupting other applications programs, as well as performing the usual modem functions.

Feasibility study   The first phase of systems analysis, in which planners determine if and how a project should proceed. Also called a system survey or a preliminary investigation.

Federal Privacy Act   Legislation stipulating that government agencies cannot keep secret personnel files and that individuals can have access to all government files, as well as to those of private firms contracting with the government, that contain information about them.

Fiber optics   Technology that uses glass fibers that can transmit light as a communications link to send data.

Field   A set of related characters.

Field name   In a database, the unique name describing the data in a field.

Field robot A robot that is used on location for such tasks as inspecting nuclear plants, disposing of bombs, cleaning up chemical spills, and other chores that are undesirable for human intervention.

Field type In a database, a category describing a field and determined by the kind of data the field will accept. Common field types are character, numeric, date, and logical.

Field width In a database or spreadsheet, the maximum number of characters that can be contained in a field.

File (1) A repository of data. (2) A collection of related records. (3) In word processing, a document created on a computer.

File server A network relationship in which an entire file is sent to a node, which then does its own processing. Also, the network computer exclusively dedicated to making files available on a network. Contrast with *Client/server.*

File transfer protocol (FTP) Regarding the Internet, a set of rules for transferring files from one computer to another.

File transfer software In a network, software used to transfer files from one computer to another. See also *Download* and *Upload.*

Find command In word processing, the ability to locate certain text in the document. Also called the Search command.

Find-and-replace function A word processing function that finds and changes each instance of a repeated item.

Firewall A dedicated computer whose sole purpose is to talk to the outside world and decide who gains entry to a company's private network or intranet.

Flaming Sending insulting e-mail messages, often by large numbers of people in response to spamming.

Flash memory Nonvolatile memory chips.

Flatbed scanner A desktop scanner that scans a sheet of paper, thus using optical recognition to convert text or drawings into computer-recognizable form.

Flowchart The pictorial representation of an orderly step-by-step solution to a problem.

Font A complete set of characters in a particular size, typeface, weight, and style.

Font library A variety of type fonts stored on disk. Also called soft fonts.

Footer In word processing, the ability to place the same line, with possible variations such as page number, on the bottom of each page.

Footnote In word processing, the ability to make a reference in a text document to a note at the bottom of the page.

Foreground In large computers, an area in memory for programs that have a high priority. Contrast with *Background.*

Format (1) The process of preparing a disk to accept data. (2) The specifications that determine how a document or worksheet appears on the screen or printer.

Formula In a spreadsheet, an instruction placed in a cell to calculate a value.

FORTRAN (FORmula TRANslator) The first high-level programming language, introduced in 1954 by IBM; it is scientifically oriented.

Fourth-generation language A very high-level language. Also called a 4GL.

Frames The capability of some browsers to display pages of a site in separate sections, each of which may operate independently.

Freedom of Information Act Legislation that allows citizens access to personal data gathered by federal agencies.

Freeware Software that is free; said to be in the public domain.

Frequency The number of times an analog signal repeats during a specific time interval.

Frequency modulation The alteration of the carrier wave frequency to represent 0s and 1s.

Front-end processor A communications control unit designed to relieve the central computer of some communications tasks.

FTP See *File transfer protocol.*

Full justification In word processing, making both the left and right margins even.

Full-duplex transmission Data transmission in both directions at once.

Function A built-in spreadsheet formula.

Function keys Special keys programmed to execute commonly used commands; the commands vary according to the software being used.

G

Gantt chart A bar chart commonly used to depict schedule deadlines and milestones, especially in systems analysis and design.

Gateway A collection of hardware and software resources to connect two dissimilar networks, allowing computers in one network to communicate with those in the other.

GB See *Gigabyte.*

General-purpose register A register used for several functions, such as arithmetic and addressing purposes.

Gigabyte (GB) One billion bytes.

Gopher An Internet subsystem that lets a user find files through a series of narrowing menus.

Graphical user interface (GUI) An image-based computer interface in which the user sends directions to the operating system by selecting icons from a menu or manipulating icons on the screen by using a pointing device such as a mouse.

Graphics Pictures or graphs.

Graphics adapter board　A circuit board that enables a computer to display pictures or graphs as well as text. Also called a graphics card.

Graphics card　See *Graphics adapter board.*

Greater-than condition (>)　A comparison operation that determines whether one value is greater than another.

Groupware　Software that lets a group of people develop or track a project together, usually including electronic mail, networking, and database technology. Also called collaborative software.

GUI　See *Graphical user interface.*

H

Hacker　(1) An enthusiastic, largely self-taught computer user. (2) Currently, a person who gains access to computer systems illegally, usually from a personal computer.

Half-duplex transmission　Data transmission in either direction, but only one way at a time.

Halftone　In desktop publishing, a reproduction of a black-and-white photograph; it is made up of tiny dots.

Handheld scanner　A small scanner that can be passed over a sheet of paper, thus using optical recognition to convert text or drawings into computer-recognizable form.

Hard copy　Printed paper output.

Hard disk　A metal platter coated with magnetic oxide that can be magnetized to represent data. Hard disks are usually in a pack and are generally in a sealed module.

Hardware　The computer and its associated equipment.

Hashing　Applying a formula to a record key to yield a number that represents a disk address. Also called randomizing.

Head crash　The result of a read/write head touching a disk surface and causing all data to be destroyed.

Head switching　In reading or writing a disk, the activation of a particular read/write head over a particular track.

Head tags　In HTML, a pair of tags that enclose the page title tags.

Header　In word processing, the ability to place the same line, with possible variations such as page number, on the top of each page.

Heading tags　In HTML, tags that enclose headings to be printed; the tags permit the printing of headings in six different sizes.

Helical recording　Storing data on tape by placing it in tracks that run diagonally across the tape.

Hexadecimal　Regarding number systems, the hexadecimal number system uses exactly 16 symbols, the digits 0 through 9 and the letters *A* through *F.*

Hierarchy chart　See *Structure chart.*

High-level language　An English-like programming language that is easier to use than an older symbolic language.

Home page　The first page of a web site.

Host computer　The central computer in a network, to which other computers, and perhaps terminals, are attached.

Hot list　Regarding the Internet, a list of names and URLs of favorite sites.

Hot site　For use in an emergency, a fully equipped computer center with hardware, communications facilities, environmental controls, and security.

HTML　See *HyperText Markup Language.*

HTML tag　(1) Generally, in HTML, any tag; also called a command. (2) Specifically, in HTML, a pair of tags that must be placed at the beginning and end of an HTML file.

HTTP　See *HyperText Transfer Protocol.*

Hyperregion　On the World Wide Web, an icon or image that can be clicked to cause a link to another web site; furthermore, the cursor image changes when it rests on the hyperregion.

Hypertext　On the World Wide Web, text that can be clicked to cause a link to another web site; hypertext is usually distinguished by a different color and perhaps underlining; furthermore, the cursor image changes when it rests on the hypertext.

HyperText Markup Language (HTML)　A programming language used to write pages for the Web.

HyperText Transfer Protocol (HTTP)　A set of rules that provide the means of communicating on the World Wide Web by using links. Note the http at the beginning of each web address.

I

IC　See *Integrated circuit.*

Icon　A small picture on a computer screen; it represents a computer activity.

Image tag　In HTML, a command that permits an image to be included on a web site. Key attributes of the image tag are SRC to define the location of the file, ALT to permit alternative text, HEIGHT and WIDTH for sizing, and ALIGN for placement.

Imaging　Using a scanner to convert a drawing, photo, or document to an electronic version that can be stored and reproduced when needed. Once scanned, text documents may be processed by optical recognition software so that the text can be manipulated.

Immersion　Related to virtual reality. When a user is absorbed by virtual reality interaction, the process is said to be immersion.

Impact printer　A printer that forms characters by physically striking the paper.

Implementation　The phase of a systems analysis and design project that includes training, equipment con-

.

version, file conversion, system conversion, auditing, evaluation, and maintenance.

Indent In word processing, widening the margin for certain text.

Independent variable Input to a computerized model, particularly a decision support system. Called independent because it can change.

Indexed file organization The combination of sequential and direct file organization.

Indexed file processing A method of file organization that represents a compromise between sequential and direct methods. Indexed processing stores records in the file in sequential order, but the file also contains an index of keys; the address associated with the key is then used to locate the record on the disk.

Indexed processing See *Indexed file processing*.

Inference engine Related to the field of artificial intelligence, particularly how computers learn; a process that accesses, selects, and interprets a set of rules. The inference engine applies rules to the facts to make up new facts.

Information Input data that has been processed by the computer; data that is organized, meaningful, and useful.

Information center A company unit that offers employees computer and software training, help in getting data from other computer systems, and technical assistance.

Information Services The department responsible for managing a company's computer resources. Also called Management Information Systems (MIS), Computer Information Systems (CIS), or Computing Services.

Information utility A commercial consumer-oriented communications system, such as America Online or the Microsoft Network, that offers a variety of services, usually including access to the Internet.

Inheritance In object-oriented programming, the property meaning that an object in a subclass automatically possesses all the characteristics of the class to which it belongs.

Initialize To set the starting values of certain storage locations, often at the beginning of program execution.

Ink-jet printer A nonimpact printer that forms output text or images by spraying ink from jet nozzles onto the paper.

Inline image In HTML, an image that is referenced right in the HTML code and whose files is loaded with the HTML code.

Input Raw data that is put into the computer system for processing.

Input device A device that puts data in computer-understandable form and sends it to the processing unit.

Input requirements In systems design, the plan for input medium and content and forms design.

Instance In object-oriented programming, a specific occurrence of an object.

Instruction set The commands that a CPU understands and is capable of executing. Each type of CPU has a fixed group of these instructions, and each set usually differs from that understood by other CPUs.

Integrated circuit (IC) A complete electronic circuit on a small chip of silicon.

Integrated Services Digital Network (ISDN) A type of digital network that links computers and other devices in a single, very fast system.

Internal cache Cache (very fast memory for frequently used data and instructions) built into the design of the microprocessor. Contrast with *External cache*.

Internal font A font built into the read-only memory (a ROM chip) of a printer.

Internal modem A modem on a circuit board. An internal modem can be installed in a computer by the user.

Internal storage The electronic circuitry that temporarily holds data and program instructions needed by the CPU. Also called memory, main memory, primary memory, primary storage, and main storage.

Internet A public communications network once used primarily by businesses, governments, and academic institutions but now also used by individuals via various private access methods.

Internet service provider (ISP) An entity that offers, for a fee, a server computer and the software needed to access the Internet.

Interrupt In multiprogramming, a condition that temporarily suspends the execution of an individual program.

Interview In systems analysis, talking to anyone connected to an existing system for the purpose of data gathering.

Intranet A private Internet-like network internal to a certain company.

IP switches Internet protocol switches used to direct communications traffic among connected networks that have adopted the Internet protocol.

ISDN See *Integrated Services Digital Network*.

ISP See *Internet service provider*.

Italic Special emphasis given to words, especially in word processing, by *slanting* the type.

Iteration The repetition of program instructions under certain conditions. Also called a loop.

Iteration control structure A looping mechanism.

I-time The instruction portion of the machine cycle; I-time includes the fetch and decode operations.

J

Java A network-friendly programming language, derived from the C++ language, that allows software to run on many different platforms.

Joystick A graphics input device that allows fingertip control of figures on a CRT screen.

Justification In word processing, aligning text along the left or right margins, or both.

K

K or KB See *Kilobyte.*

Kerning In word processing or desktop publishing, adjusting the space between characters to create a more attractive or readable appearance.

Key A unique identifier for a record.

Key field In a database, a field that has been designated as a key can be used as the basis for a query of the database.

Keyboard A common computer input device similar to the keyboard of a typewriter.

Kilobyte (K or KB) 1024 bytes.

Knowledge base Related to the field of artificial intelligence, particularly how computers learn; a set of facts and rules about those facts.

Knowledge engineer Related to building an expert system, the person working to extract information from the human expert.

L

Label In a spreadsheet, data consisting of a string of text characters.

LAN See *Local area network.*

LAN manager A person designated to manage and run a computer network, particularly a local area network (LAN).

Laptop computer A small portable computer, usually somewhat larger than a notebook computer.

Laser printer A nonimpact printer that uses a light beam to transfer images to paper.

LCD See *Liquid crystal display.*

Leading In word processing or desktop publishing, the vertical spacing between lines of type.

Leading decision The loop-ending decision that occurs at the beginning of a DO-WHILE loop.

Less-than condition (<) A logical operation in which the computer compares values to determine whether one is less than another.

Librarian A person who catalogs processed computer disks and tapes and keeps them secure.

Light pen A graphics input device that allows the user to interact directly with the computer screen.

Line break tag In HTML, a tag that causes a break in the text.

Line graph A graph made by connecting data points with a line, particularly useful for showing trends over time.

Line spacing In word processing, the amount of space between lines of text in a document; single spacing and double spacing are common.

Link (1) A physical data communications medium. (2) On the World Wide Web, clickable text or image that can cause a change to a different web site.

Link/load phase A phase that takes the machine language object module and adds necessary prewritten programs to produce output called the load module; the load module is executable.

Liquid crystal display (LCD) The flat display screen found on some laptop computers.

List item tag In HTML, a tag that marks an item as part of a list.

Load module An executable version of a program.

Local area network (LAN) A network designed to share data and resources among several computers, usually personal computers in a limited geographical area, such as an office or a building. Contrast with *Wide area network.*

Logic chip A central processing unit on a chip, generally known as a microprocessor but called a logic chip when used for some special purpose, such as controlling some under-the-hood action in a car.

Logic error A flaw in the logic of a program.

Logic flowchart A flowchart that represents the flow of logic in a program.

Logical field In a database, a field used to keep track of true and false conditions.

Logical operations Comparing operations. The ALU is able to compare numbers, letters, or special characters and take alternative courses of action depending on the result of the comparison.

Logical style tags In HTML, commands that leave it up to the browser to highlight text in its own way. Emphasis tags will probably display italics, and strong emphasis tags will likely display the text as boldface. Contrast with *Physical style tags.*

Loop The repetition of program instructions under certain conditions. Also called iteration.

Lurking Reading messages in newsgroups without writing any.

M

Machine cycle The combination of I-time and E-time, the steps used by the central processing unit to execute instructions.

Machine language The lowest level of language; it represents data and instructions as 1s and 0s.

Magnetic core A small, flat doughnut-shaped piece of metal used as an early memory device.

Magnetic disk An oxide-coated disk on which data is recorded as magnetic spots.

Magnetic tape A magnetic medium with an iron-oxide coating that can be magnetized. Data is stored on the tape as extremely small magnetized spots.

Magnetic tape unit A data storage unit used to record data on and retrieve data from magnetic tape.

Magnetic-ink character recognition (MICR) A method of machine-reading characters made of magnetized particles. A common application is checks.

Magneto-optical (MO) A hybrid disk that has the high-volume capacity of an optical disk but can be written over like a magnetic disk. It uses both a laser beam and a magnet to properly align magnetically sensitive metallic crystals.

Mail merge Adding names and addresses, probably from a database, to a prepared document, such as a letter prepared using word processing.

Main memory The electronic circuitry that temporarily holds data and program instructions needed by the CPU. Also called memory, primary memory, primary storage, main storage, and internal storage.

Main storage The electronic circuitry that temporarily holds data and program instructions needed by the CPU. Also called memory, main memory, primary memory, primary storage, and internal storage.

Mainframe A large computer that has access to billions of characters of data and is capable of processing large amounts of data very quickly. Notably, mainframes are used by such data-heavy customers as banks, airlines, and large manufacturers.

MAN See *Metropolitan area network*.

Management information system (MIS) A set of formal business systems designed to provide information for an organization.

Management Information Systems A department that manages computer resources for an organization. Also called Computing Services or Information Services.

Margin In word processing, the unused space on the right and left sides of a document, and on the top and bottom of a document.

Mark In word processing, one marks a certain section of text, called a block, by using some sort of highlighting, usually reverse video. The text is usually selected in advance of some other command upon the text, such as Move.

Mark I An early computer built in 1944 by Harvard professor Howard Aiken.

Master file A semipermanent set of records.

MB See *Megabyte*.

Megabyte (MB) One million bytes. The unit often used to measure memory or storage capacity.

Megaflop One million floating-point operations per second. One measure of a computer's speed.

Megahertz (MHz) One million cycles per second. Used to express microprocessor speeds.

Memory The electronic circuitry that temporarily holds data and program instructions needed by the CPU. Also called main memory, primary memory, primary storage, main storage, and internal storage.

Memory management The process of allocating memory to programs and keeping the programs in memory separate from one another.

Memory protection In a multiprogramming system, the process of keeping a program from straying into other programs in memory.

Menu An on-screen list of choices.

Message In object-oriented programming, a command telling what—not how—something is to be done, which activates the object.

Method In object-oriented programming, instructions that tell the data what to do. Also called an operation.

Metropolitan area network (MAN) A network than spans a city.

MHz See *Megahertz*.

MICR See *Magnetic-ink character recognition*.

MICR inscriber A device that adds magnetic characters to a document, in particular, the amount of a check.

Microcomputer A relatively inexpensive type of computer, usually used by an individual in a home or office setting. Also called a personal computer.

Microprocessor A general-purpose central processing unit on a chip.

Microsecond One-millionth of a second.

Micro-to-mainframe link A connection between microcomputers and mainframe computers.

Microwave transmission Line-of-sight transmission of data signals through the atmosphere from relay station to relay station.

Millisecond One-thousandth of a second.

Minicomputer A computer with storage capacity and power less than a mainframe's but greater than a personal computer's.

MIPS Millions of instructions per second. A measure of how fast a central processing unit can process information.

MIS See *Management Information Systems*.

MIS manager A person, familiar with both computer technology and the organization's business, who runs the MIS department.

MITS Altair Generally considered the first personal computer, offered as a kit to computer hobbyists in 1975.

MMX See *Multimedia extension chip*.

Model (1) A type of database, each type representing a particular way of organizing data. The three database models are hierarchical, network, and relational. (2) In a DSS, an image of something that actually exists or a mathematical representation of a real-life system.

Modem Short for modulate/demodulate. A device that converts a digital signal to an analog signal or vice versa. Used to transfer data between computers over analog communications lines.

Modulation Using a modem, the process of converting a signal from digital to analog.

Monitor Hardware that features the computer's screen, includes housing for the screen's electronic components, and probably sits on a stand that tilts and swivels.

Monochrome   A computer screen that displays information in only one color, usually green, on a black background.

Monolithic   Refers to the inseparable nature of memory chip circuitry.

Mouse   A handheld computer input device whose rolling movement on a flat surface causes corresponding movement of the cursor on the screen. Also, a mouse button can be clicked to make selections from choices on the screen.

Motherboard   Inside the personal computer housing, a board that holds the main chips and circuitry of the computer hardware, including the central processing unit chip.

Motion Picture Experts Group (MPEG)   A set of widely accepted video standards.

MPEG   See *Motion Picture Experts Group.*

Multimedia   Software that typically presents information with text, illustrations, photos, narration, music, animation, and film clips—possible because the high-volume capacity of optical disks can accommodate photographs, film clips, and music. To use multimedia software, you must have the proper hardware: a CD-ROM drive, a sound card, and speakers. Multimedia also is offered on several Internet sites.

Multimedia extension chip (MMX)   A microprocessor that boosts a computer's ability to produce graphics, video, and sound by including many of the needed functions on the chip itself.

Multiprocessing   Using more than one central processing unit, a computer can run multiple programs simultaneously, each using its own processor.

Multiprogramming   A feature of large computer operating systems under which different programs from different users compete for the use of the central processing unit; these programs are said to run concurrently.

N

Nanosecond   One-billionth of a second.

Natural language   A programming language that resembles human language.

NC   See *Network computer.*

Nested tags   Tags enclosed within another set of tags.

Net box   See *Network computer.*

Net computer   See *Network computer.*

Netiquette   Appropriate behavior in network communications.

Network   A computer system that uses communications equipment to connect two or more computers and their resources.

Network computer   A computer used in conjunction with a television set to access the Internet. Also called a net computer or net box or Web TV.

Network interface card (NIC)   A circuit board that can be inserted into a slot inside a personal computer to allow it to send and receive messages on a local area network (LAN).

Network manager   A person designated to manage and run a computer network.

Network operating system (NOS)   An operating system designed to let computers on a network share resources such as hard disks and printers. A NOS supports resource sharing, data security, troubleshooting, and administrative control.

Newsgroup   An informal network of computers that allows the posting and reading of messages in groups that focus on specific topics. More formally called Usenet.

NIC   See *Network interface card.*

Node   A device, usually a personal computer, that is connected to a network.

Noise   Electrical interference that causes distortion when a signal is being transmitted.

Nonimpact printer   A printer that prints without striking the paper.

NOS   See *Network operating system.*

Notebook computer   A small portable computer.

O

Object   In object-oriented programming, a self-contained unit that contains both data and related facts and functions—the instructions to act on that data.

Object module   A machine language version of a program; it is produced by a compiler or assembler.

Object-oriented programming (OOP)   A programming approach that uses objects, self-contained units that contain both data and related facts and functions—the instructions to act on that data.

OCR   See *Optical character recognition.*

OCR-A   The standard typeface for characters to be input by optical character recognition.

Octal   Regarding number systems, the octal number system uses exactly eight symbols, digits 0 through 7.

Office automation   The use of technology to help achieve goals in an office. Often associated with data communications.

OMR   See *Optical mark recognition.*

Online   In a data communications environment, a direct connection from a terminal to a computer or from one computer to another.

Online service   A commercial consumer-oriented communications system, such as America Online or the Microsoft Network, that offers a variety of services, usually including access to the Internet. Also called an information utility.

OOP   See *Object-oriented programming.*

Operating environment   Software designed as a shell, an extra layer, for an operating system, so that the user does not have to memorize or look up commands.

Operating system A set of programs that lies between applications software and the computer hardware, through which a computer manages its own resources.

Operation In object-oriented programming, instructions that tell the data what to do. Also called a method.

Optical character recognition (OCR) A computer input method that uses a light source to read special characters and convert them to electrical signals to be sent to the computer.

Optical disk Storage technology that uses a laser beam to store large amounts of data at relatively low cost.

Optical mark recognition (OMR) A computer input method that uses a light source to recognize marks on paper and convert them to electrical signals to be sent to the computer.

Optical recognition system A category of computer input method that uses a light source to read optical marks, optical characters, handwritten characters, and bar codes and convert them to electrical signals to be sent to the computer.

Ordered list tags In HTML, a pair of tags enclosing a list of items that causes the browser to number the indented list items in order, usually 1., 2., and so forth.

Organization chart A hierarchical diagram depicting lines of authority within an organization, usually mentioning people by name and title.

Output Raw data that has been processed by the computer into usable information.

Output device A device, such as a printer, that makes processed information available for use.

Output requirements In systems design, the plan for output medium and content, types of reports needed, and forms design.

Outsourcing Assigning the design and management of a new or revised system to an outside firm, as opposed to developing such a system in-house.

P

Packaged software Software that is packaged and sold in stores. Also called commercial software.

Packet A portion of a message to be sent to another computer via data communications. Each packet is individually addressed, and the packets are reassembled into the original message once they reach their destination.

Page composition Adding type to a layout. In desktop publishing, the software may be called a page composition program.

Page composition program A software package for designing and producing professional-looking documents that combine text and graphics. Also called a page makeup program.

Page frame The space in main memory in which to place a page.

Page layout In publishing, the process of arranging text and graphics on a page.

Page makeup program A software package for designing and producing professional-looking documents that combine text and graphics. Also called a page composition program.

Page table The index-like table with which the operating system keeps track of page locations.

Pages Equal-size blocks into which a program is divided to be placed into corresponding noncontiguous memory spaces called page frames. See also *Page frame.*

Pagination In word processing, options for placing the page number in various locations on the document page.

Paging The process of dividing a program into equal-size pages, keeping program pages on disk, and calling them into memory as needed.

Pan To move the cursor across a spreadsheet or a database to force into view fields that do not fit on the initial screen.

Paragraph tags In HTML, tags that enclose a paragraph of text.

Parallel conversion A method of systems conversion in which the old and new systems are operated simultaneously until the users are satisfied that the new system performs to their standards; then the old system is dropped.

Parallel processing Using many processors, each with its own memory unit, that work at the same time to process data much more quickly than with the traditional single processor. Contrast with *Serial processing.*

Participant observation A form of observation in which the systems analyst temporarily joins the activities of the group.

Partition A separate memory area that can hold a program, used as part of a memory management technique that simply divides memory into separate areas. Also called a region.

Pascal A structured, high-level programming language named for Blaise Pascal, a seventeenth-century French mathematician.

Path In a flowchart, the connection leading from the decision box to one of two possible responses. Also called a branch.

PC card A credit-card-sized card that slides into a slot in the computer, most often a modem, in which a cable runs from the PC card to the phone jack in the wall. Originally known as PCMCIA cards, named for the Personal Computer Memory Card International Association.

PDA See *Personal digital assistant.*

Peer-to-peer network A network setup in which there is no controlling server computer; all computers on the network share programs and resources.

Pen-based computer A small portable computer that accepts handwritten input on a screen with a penlike stylus. Also called personal digital assistant.

Peripheral equipment All of the input, output, and secondary storage devices attached to a computer.

Personal computer   A relatively inexpensive type of computer, usually used by an individual in a home or office setting. Also called a microcomputer.

Personal computer manager   The manager in charge of personal computer use.

Personal digital assistant (PDA)   A small portable computer that is most often used to track appointments and other business information and that can accept handwritten input on a screen. Also called a pen-based computer.

Phase   (1) In data transmission, the relative position in time of one complete cycle of a carrier wave. (2) In systems analysis and design, a portion of the systems development life cycle (SDLC).

Phased conversion   A systems conversion method in which the new system is phased in gradually.

Physical style tags   In HTML, specific style commands, notably the italic tag, the boldface tag, and the center tag. Physical style tags work with most browsers. Contrast with *Logical style tags*.

Picosecond   One-trillionth of a second.

Pie chart   A pie-shaped graph used to compare values that represent parts of a whole.

Pilot conversion   A systems conversion method in which a designated group of users try the system first.

Pipelining   A processing arrangement whereby one instruction's actions—fetch, decode, execute, store—need not be complete before another instruction begins.

Pixel   A picture element on a computer display screen; a pixel is merely one dot in the display.

Platform   The hardware and software combination that comprises the basic functionality of a particular computer.

Plot area   The area in which a graph is drawn, that is, the area above the x-axis and to the right of the y-axis.

Plotter   A graphics output device that can draw hardcopy graphics output in the form of maps, bar charts, engineering drawings, and even two- or three-dimensional illustrations.

Plug-in   Software that can be added to a browser to enhance its functionality.

Point   A typographic measurement equaling approximately ½ inch.

Pointer   An indicator on a screen; it shows where the next user-computer interaction will be. Also called a cursor.

Point-of-sale (POS) terminal   A terminal used as a cash register in a retail setting. It may be programmable or connected to a central computer.

Polymorphism   In object-oriented programming, polymorphism means that when an individual object receives a message it knows how, using its own methods, to process the message in the appropriate way for that particular object.

Pop-up menu   A submenu that originates from a menu selection on the bottom of the screen.

POS terminal   See *Point-of-sale (POS) terminal*.

Positional notation   In dealing with number systems, the value of a digit in a number depends not only on its own intrinsic value but also on its location in the number. For example, the digit 2 has more value in the number 234 than in the number 762.

Preliminary design   The subphase of systems design in which the new system concept is developed.

Preliminary investigation   The first phase of the systems analysis and design life cycle, in which planners determine if and how a project should proceed. Also called a feasibility study or a system survey.

Presentation graphics   Sophisticated business graphics. Presentation graphics programs include a library of symbols and drawings called clip art. Also called a business-quality graphics program.

Primary memory   The electronic circuitry that temporarily holds data and program instructions needed by the CPU. Also called memory, primary storage, main storage, internal storage, and main memory.

Primary storage   The electronic circuitry that temporarily holds data and program instructions needed by the CPU. Also called memory, primary memory, main storage, internal storage, and main memory.

Priming read   The first read statement in a program.

Print preview   In word processing and some other applications, the ability to review one or more pages of a document on the screen as they will appear when printed.

Printer   A device for generating computer-produced output on paper.

Printer spacing chart   A chart used to determine and show a report format.

Process   (1) The computer action required to convert input to output. (2) An element in a data flow diagram that represents actions taken on data: comparing, checking, stamping, authorizing, filing, and so forth.

Process box   In flowcharting, a rectangular box that indicates an action to be taken.

Processor   The central processing unit (CPU) of a computer, a microprocessor.

Program   A set of step-by-step instructions that directs a computer to perform specific tasks and produce certain results. More generically called software.

Programmable read-only memory (PROM)   Chips that can be programmed with specialized tools called ROM burners.

Programmer/analyst   A person who performs systems analysis functions in addition to programming.

Programming language   A set of rules that can be used to tell a computer what operations to do. There are many different programming languages.

Project management software   Software that allocates people and resources, monitors schedules, and produces status reports.

PROM   See *Programmable read-only memory*.

Prompt　A signal that the computer or operating system is waiting for data or a command from the user.

Protocol　A set of rules for the exchange of data between a terminal and a computer or between two computers.

Prototype　A limited working system or subset of a system that is developed to test design concepts.

Pseudocode　An English-like way of representing the solution to a problem.

Public domain software　Software that is free and not copyrighted.

Pull-down menu　A menu of choices that appears, as a window shade is pulled down, when an initial menu choice is made.

Push technology　Software that automatically sends—pushes—information from the Internet to a user's personal computer. Also called webcasting.

Q

Query languages　A variation on fourth-generation languages that can be used to retrieve data from databases.

Questionnaire　In the data-gathering phase of systems analysis, a source of facts to be input as data.

Queues　Lists of programs on disk waiting to be run.

R

Ragged right margin　In word processing, the unjustified right margin of a document, or nonalignment of text at the right edge of a document.

RAID　See *Redundant array of inexpensive disks.*

RAM　See *Random-access memory.*

Random-access memory (RAM)　Memory that provides temporary storage for data and program instructions.

Randomizing　Applying a formula to a key to yield a number that represents a disk address. Also called hashing.

Range　A group of one or more cells, arranged in a rectangle, that a spreadsheet program treats as a unit.

Raster-scan technology　A video display technology. The back of the screen display has a phosphorous coating, which will glow whenever it is hit by a beam of electrons.

Read　To bring data outside the computer into memory.

Read-only memory (ROM)　Memory containing data and programs that can be read but not altered. Data remains in ROM after the power is turned off.

Read/write head　An electromagnet that reads the magnetized areas on magnetic media and converts them into the electrical pulses that are sent to the processor.

Real storage　That part of memory that temporarily holds part of a program pulled from virtual storage.

Real-time processing　Processing in which the results are available in time to affect the activity at hand.

Record　(1) A set of related fields. (2) In a database relation, one row.

Reduced instruction set computer (RISC)　A computer that offers only frequently used instructions. Since fewer instructions are offered, this is a factor in improving the computer's speed. Contrast with *Complex instruction set computer.*

Redundant array of inexpensive disks (RAID)　Secondary storage that uses several connected hard disks that act as a unit. Using multiple disks allows manufacturers to improve data security, access time, and data transfer rates.

Refresh　To maintain an image on a CRT screen by reforming the screen image at frequent intervals to avoid flicker. The frequency is called the scan rate; 60 times per second is usually adequate to retain a clear image.

Region　A separate memory area that can hold a program, used as part of a memory management technique that simply divides memory into separate areas. Also called a partition.

Register　A temporary storage area for instructions or data.

Relation　A table in a relational database model.

Relational database　A database in which the data is organized in a table format consisting of columns and rows.

Relational model　A database model that organizes data logically in tables.

Relational operator　An operator (such as <, >, or =) that allows a user to make comparisons and selections.

Removable hard disk cartridge　A supplemental hard disk, that, once filled, can be replaced with a fresh one.

Resolution　The clarity of a video display screen or printer output.

Resource allocation　The process of assigning resources to certain programs.

Response time　The time between a typed computer request and the response of the computer.

Retrovirus　A virus that is powerful enough to defeat or even delete antivirus software.

Reverse video　The feature that highlights on-screen text by switching the usual text and background colors.

Ring network　A "circle" of point-to-point connections between computers at local sites. A ring network does not contain a central host computer.

RISC　See *Reduced instruction set computer.*

Robot　A computer-controlled device that can physically manipulate its surroundings.

ROM　See *Read-only memory.*

ROM burner　A specialized device used to program progammable read-only memory (PROM) chips.

Rotational delay　For disk units, the time it takes for a record on a track to revolve under the read/write head.

Router A special computer that directs communications traffic when several networks are connected together.

S

Sampling In systems analysis, collecting a subset of data relevant to the system under study.

Sans serif A typeface that is clean, with no serif marks.

Satellite transmission Data transmission from earth station to earth station via communications satellites.

Scan rate The number of times a CRT screen is refreshed in a given time period. A scan rate of 60 times per second is usually adequate to retain a clear screen image.

Scanner A device that uses a light source to read text and images directly into the computer. Scanners can be of several varieties, notably handheld, sheetfeed, and desktop.

Screen A television-like output device that can display information.

Scrolling A feature that allows the user to move to and view any part of a document on the screen. Used especially in word processing, spreadsheets, and databases.

SDLC See *Systems development life cycle.*

Sealed module A disk drive containing the disks, access arms, and read/write heads sealed together.

Search command In word processing, the ability to locate certain text in the document. Also called the Find command.

Search engine Regarding the Internet, software that lets a user specify search terms that can be used to find web sites that include those terms.

Secondary storage Additional storage, often on disk, for data and programs. Secondary storage is separate from the CPU and memory. Also called auxiliary storage.

Sector method A method of organizing data on a disk in which each track is divided into sectors that hold a specific number of characters. Data on the track is accessed by referring to the surface number, track number, and sector number where the data is stored.

Security A system of safeguards designed to protect a computer system and data from deliberate or accidental damage or access by unauthorized persons.

Seek time The time required for an access arm to move into position over a particular track on a disk.

Select In word processing, to mark a certain section of text, called a block, by some sort of highlighting, usually reverse video. The text is usually selected in advance of some other command upon the text, such as Move.

Selection control structure A control structure used to make program logic decisions.

Semiconductor A crystalline substance that conducts electricity when it is "doped" with chemical impurities.

Semiconductor storage Data storage on a silicon chip.

Sequence control structure A control structure in which one statement follows another in sequence.

Sequential file organization The arrangement of records in ascending or descending order by a certain field called the key.

Sequential file processing Processing in which records are usually in order according to a key field.

Serial processing Processing in which a single processor can handle just one instruction at a time. Contrast with *Parallel processing.*

Serif Small marks added to the letters of a typeface; the marks are intended to increase readability of the typeface. Contrast with *Sans serif.*

Server (1) In a client/server network arrangement, the computer that controls and manages the network and its services; the server usually has hard disks that hold files needed by users on the network. (2) A computer used to access the Internet; it has special software that uses the Internet protocol.

Service program A prewritten program that performs routine file-handling tasks, such as file conversion and sort-merges. Also called a utility program.

Shareware Software that is given away free, although the maker hopes that satisfied users will voluntarily pay for it.

Sheetfeed scanner A scanner that uses a motorized roller to feed a sheet of paper across the scanning head, thus using optical recognition to convert text or drawings into computer-recognizable form.

Shell An operating environment layer that separates the operating system from the user.

SIMM See *Single in-line memory module.*

Simplex transmission Transmission of data in one direction only.

Simulation The use of a computer model, particularly a decision support system, to reach decisions about real-life situations.

Single in-line memory module (SIMM) A board containing memory chips that can be plugged into a computer expansion slot.

Sink In a data flow diagram, a destination for data going outside the system.

Site license A license permitting a customer to make multiple copies of a piece of software.

Smalltalk An object-oriented language that supports a particularly visual system.

Smart terminal A terminal that has some processing ability.

Social engineering A tongue-in-cheek term for con artist actions, specifically hackers persuading people to give away their passwords over the phone.

Soft copy Computer-produced output displayed on a screen.

Soft font A font that can be downloaded from the font library on disk with a personal computer to a printer.

Software Instructions that tell a computer what to do. Also called programs.

Software piracy The unauthorized copying of computer software.

SOHO Abbreviation for small office, home office, a designated group for which software is designed.

Source In a data flow diagram, an origin outside the system.

Source data automation The use of special equipment to collect input data as it is generated and send it directly to the computer.

Source document An instrument, usually paper, containing data to be prepared as input to a computer.

Source module A program as originally coded, before being translated into machine language.

Source program listing The printed version of a program as the programmer wrote it, usually produced as a byproduct of compilation.

Spamming Mass advertising on the Internet, usually done with software especially designed to send solicitations to users via e-mail.

Speech recognition Converting input data given as the spoken word to a form the computer can understand.

Speech recognition device A device that accepts the spoken word through a microphone and converts it into digital code that can be understood by a computer.

Speech synthesis The process of enabling machines to talk to people.

Spelling checker program A word processing program that checks the spelling of words in a document.

Spooling A process in which files to be printed are placed temporarily on disk.

Spreadsheet A worksheet divided into rows and columns that can be used to present and analyze business data.

SRAM See *Static random-access memory.*

Star network A network consisting of one or more computers connected to a central host computer.

Start/stop symbol An oval symbol used to indicate the beginning and end of a flowchart.

Start/stop transmission Asynchronous data transmission.

Static random-access memory (SRAM) A type of RAM that requires a continuous current to hold data. SRAM is usually faster but larger and more expensive than dynamic RAM. Contrast with *Dynamic random-access memory* (DRAM).

Storage register A register that temporarily holds data taken from or about to be sent to memory.

Structure chart A chart that illustrates the top-down design of a program and is often used to either supplement or replace a logic flowchart.

Structured interview In systems analysis, an interview in which only planned questions are used.

Structured programming A set of programming techniques that includes a limited number of control structures and certain programming standards.

Style In word processing, the way a typeface is printed—for example, in *italic.*

Submenu An additional set of options related to a prior menu selection.

Suite A bundle of basic software designed to work together.

Supercomputer The largest and most powerful category of computers.

Supervisor program An operating system program that controls the entire operating system and calls in other operating system programs from disk storage as needed.

Supply reel A reel that has tape with data on it or on which data will be recorded.

Surge protector A device that prevents electrical problems from affecting data files.

SVGA Super VGA. A superior screen standard with 800x600 pixels or 1024x768 pixels.

Symbolic address The meaningful name for a memory location. Instead of just a number, for example, a symbolic address should be something meaningful, such as NAME or SALARY.

Symbolic language A second-generation language that uses abbreviations for instructions. Also called assembly language.

Synchronous transmission Data transmission in which characters are transmitted together in a continuous stream.

Synonym The name for a record's disk address, produced by a hashing scheme, that is the same as a preexisting address for a different record.

Syntax The rules of a programming language.

Syntax errors Errors in the use of a programming language.

Synthesis by analysis Speech synthesis in which a device analyzes the input of an actual human voice, stores and processes the spoken sounds, and reproduces them as needed.

Synthesis by rule Speech synthesis in which a device applies linguistic rules to create an artificial spoken language.

System An organized set of related components established to perform a certain task.

System journal A file whose records represent real-time transactions.

System requirements A detailed list of the things a particular system must be able to do, based on the results of the systems analysis.

System survey The first phase of systems analysis, in which planners determine if and how a project should proceed. Also called a feasibility study or a preliminary investigation.

System testing A testing process in which the development team uses test data to determine whether programs work together satisfactorily.

Systems analysis   A phase of the systems development life cycle, involving studying an existing system to determine how it works and the ways in which it does or does not meet user needs, with an eye to improving the system.

Systems analyst   A person who plans and designs computer systems.

Systems design   A phase of the systems development life cycle, involving developing a plan for a new or revised system based on the results of the systems analysis phase.

Systems development   A phase of the systems development life cycle, whose activities include programming and testing.

Systems development life cycle (SDLC)   The multiphase process required for creating or revising a computer system.

Systems flowchart   A drawing that depicts the flow of data through some part of a computer system.

Systems software   All programs related to coordinating computer operations, including the operating system, programming language translators, and service programs.

T

Tab   In word processing, indenting the first line of a paragraph.

Tag   In HTML, a command that performs a specific function.

Take-up reel   A reel that always stays with the magnetic tape unit.

Tape drive   The drive on which reels of magnetic tape are mounted when their data is ready to be read to or written on by the computer system.

TCP/IP   See *Transmission Control Protocol/Internet Protocol.*

Telecommuting   Using telecommunications and computers at home as a substitute for working at an office outside the home.

Teleconferencing   A system of holding conferences by linking geographically dispersed people together through computer terminals or personal computers.

Teleprocessing   A system in which terminals are connected to the central computer via communications lines.

Template   (1) In desktop publishing, a predetermined page design that lets a user fill in text and art. (2) In a spreadsheet program, a worksheet that has already been designed for the solution of a specific type of problem, so that a user need only fill in the data.

Teraflop   One trillion floating-point operations per second. One measure of a computer's speed, especially as related to parallel processors.

Terminal   A device that consists of an input device (usually a keyboard), an output device (usually a screen), and a communications link to the computer.

Terminal emulation software   Data communications software that makes a personal computer act like a terminal, so that it can communicate with a larger computer.

Text block   A continuous section of text in a document that has been marked or selected.

Text editor   Software that is somewhat like a word processing program, used by programmers to create a program file.

Thesaurus program   With a word processing program, this program provides a list of synonyms and antonyms for a selected word in a document.

Tile   In reference to a screen background, spreading a pattern down and across the screen to make a complete background.

Time slice   In time-sharing, a period of time—a fraction of a second—during which the computer works on a user's tasks.

Time-driven   Time-sharing is said to be time-driven because each user is given a time slice in which the computer works on that user's tasks before moving on to another user's tasks.

Time-sharing   A special case of multiprogramming in which several people use one computer at the same time.

Title   The caption on a graph that summarizes the information in the graph.

Token passing   The protocol for controlling access to a Token Ring network. A special signal, or token, circulates from node to node, allowing the node that "captures" the token to transmit data.

Token Ring network   A network protocol that uses token passing to send data over the shared network cable. A computer that wants to send a message must capture the token before sending.

Top-level domain   Regarding the Internet, in a Uniform Resource Locator (URL), the last part of the domain name, representing the type of entity, such as organization or education or country.

Topology   The physical layout of a local area network.

Touch screen   A computer screen that accepts input data by letting the user point at the screen to select a choice. The finger touching the screen interrupts the light beams on the monitor's edge, pinpointing the selected screen location.

Track   On a magnetic disk, one of many data-holding concentric circles.

Trackball   A ball used as an input device; it can be hand-manipulated to cause a corresponding movement of the cursor on the screen. Trackballs are often built in on portable computers.

Trailing decision   The loop-ending decision that occurs at the end of a DO-UNTIL loop.

Transaction file   A file that contains all changes to be made to the master file: additions, deletions, and revisions.

Transaction processing   The technique of processing transactions one at a time, in the order in which they occur.

Transistor   A small device that transfers electrical signals across a resistor.

Translator   Software, typically a compiler, that converts a program into the machine language the computer can understand.

Transmission Control Protocol/Internet Protocol (TCP/IP)   A standardized protocol permitting different computers to communicate via the Internet.

Transparent   Computer activities of which a user is unaware even as they are talking place.

Transponder   A device in a communications satellite that receives a transmission from earth, amplifies the signal, changes the frequency, and retransmits the data to a receiving earth station. The transponder makes sure that the stronger outgoing signals do not interfere with the weaker incoming signals.

Trojan horse   An application that covertly places destructive instructions in the middle of a legitimate program but appears to do something useful.

Twisted pairs   Wires twisted together in an insulated cable. Twisted pairs are frequently used to transmit data over short distances. Also called wire pairs.

Type size   The size, in points, of a typeface.

U

Unbundle   To sell software separately from the hardware on which it will run.

Underlining   Emphasizing text by underscoring it.

Uniform Resource Locator (URL)   The unique address of a web page or other file on the Internet.

Unit testing   Testing an individual program by using test data.

UNIVAC I (Universal Automatic Computer I)   The first computer built for business purposes.

Universal Product Code (UPC)   A code number unique to a product. The UPC code is the bar code on the product's label.

Unordered list tags   In HTML, a pair of tags enclosing a list of items that produces an indented list with a browser-supplied character in front of each item, probably a small round circle or square.

Unstructured interview   In systems analysis, an interview in which questions are planned in advance, but the questionnaire can deviate from the plan.

UPC   See *Universal Product Code.*

Update   To keep files current by changing data as appropriate.

Updating in place   The ability to read, change, and return a record to its same place on the disk.

Upload   In a networking environment, to send a file from one computer to another, usually to a larger computer or a host computer. Contrast with *Download.*

URL   See *Uniform Resource Locator.*

Usenet   An informal network of computers that allows the posting and reading of messages in newsgroups that focus on specific topics. Also called newsgroups.

User   A person who uses computer software or has contact with computer systems.

User involvement   The involvement of users in the systems development life cycle.

User-friendly   A term to refer to software that is easy for a novice to use.

Utility program   A prewritten program that performs routine file-handling tasks, such as copying and sorting files. Also called a service program.

V

Vaccine   A computer program that stops the spread of a virus. Also called an antivirus.

Vacuum tube   An electronic tube used as a basic component in the first generation of computers.

Value   In a spreadsheet, data entered into a cell.

Variable   (1) On a graph, the items that the data points describe. (2) In a program, a name assigned to a memory location, whose contents can vary.

Vector   An arrow—a line with directional notation—used in a data flow diagram.

Vertical centering   In word processing, adjusting the top and bottom margins so that text is midway between the top and the bottom of the page.

Vertical market   A market consisting of a group of similar customers, such as dentists, who are likely to need similar software.

Vertical market software   Software for a group of similar customers, such as accountants or doctors.

Very high-level language   A fourth-generation language.

VGA   Video graphics array. A common screen standard with 640x480 pixels.

Video graphics   Computer-produced animated pictures.

Video Privacy Protection Act   Legislation that prohibits video vendors from revealing what videos their customers rent.

Videoconferencing   Computer conferencing combined with cameras and wall-size screens.

Virtual memory   See *Virtual storage.*

Virtual reality (VR)   A system in which a user is immersed in a computer-created environment, so that the user physically interacts with the computer-produced three-dimensional scene.

Virtual storage   A technique of memory management in which part of the application program is stored on disk and is brought into memory only as needed. The secondary storage holding the rest of the program is considered virtual storage.

Virus A set of illicit instructions that passes itself on to other programs with which it comes into contact.

Vision robot A robot that can recognize an object by its shape or color.

Voice input Using the spoken word as a means of entering data into a computer.

Voice mail A system in which a spoken message is digitized and stored in the recipient's voice mailbox. Later the recipient can dial the mailbox, and the system delivers the message in audio form.

Voice output device See *Voice synthesizer.*

Voice synthesizer A device that converts data in main storage to vocalized sounds understandable to humans. Also called an audio-response unit and voice output device.

Volatile Subject to loss when electricity is interrupted or turned off. Data in semiconductor storage is volatile.

Volume testing The testing of a program or a system by using real data in large amounts.

VR See *Virtual reality.*

W

Walkthrough A process in which a group of programmers—your peers—review your program and offer suggestions in a collegial way.

WAN See *Wide area network.*

Wand reader An input device that scans the special letters and numbers on price tags in retail stores and sends that input data to the computer. Often connected to a point-of-sale terminal in a retail store.

Web See *World Wide Web.*

Web site An individual location on the World Wide Web.

Web TV See *Network computer.*

Webcasting Software that automatically sends—pushes—information from the Internet to a user's personal computer. Also called push technology.

Weight In word processing or desktop publishing, the variation in the visual heaviness of a typeface; for example, words look much heavier when in **boldface** type.

"What-if" analysis The process of changing one or more spreadsheet values and observing the resulting calculated effect.

Wide area network (WAN) A network of geographically distant computers and terminals. Contrast with *Local area network.*

Wire pairs Wires twisted together in an insulated cable. Wire pairs are frequently used to transmit data over short distances. Also called twisted pairs.

Wireless Transmitting data over networks using infrared or radio wave transmissions instead of cables.

Word The number of bits that constitute a common unit of data, as defined by the computer system.

Word processing Computer-based creating, editing, formatting, storing, retrieving, and printing of a text document.

Word wrap A word processing feature that automatically starts a word at the left margin of the next line if there is not enough room for it on the line.

Worksheet Another name for an electronic spreadsheet, a computerized version of a manual spreadsheet.

Workstation A computer that combines the compactness of a desktop computer with power that almost equals that of a mainframe.

World Wide Web (the Web) An Internet subset of sites with text, images, and sounds; most web sites provide links to related topics.

WORM See *Write-once, read-many media.*

Worm A program that spreads and replicates over a network.

Write-once, read-many media (WORM) Media that can be written on only once; then they become read-only media.

X

x-axis The horizontal reference line of a graph, often representing units of time.

Y

y-axis The vertical reference line of a graph, usually representing values or amounts, such as dollars, staffing levels, or units sold.

Z

Zone recording Involves dividing a disk into zones to take advantage of the storage available on all tracks, by assigning more sectors to tracks in outer zones than to those in inner zones.

Credits

Frontispiece: Computer Illustration (c) Eric Yang.

Table of Contents
1: ©Steven Peters/TSI; 2: ©Telegraph Colour Library/FPG; 3: ©Mehau Kulyk/Photo Researchers; 5: ©Lightscapes/The Stock Market; 6: ©Bruce Ayers/TSI; 7: ©Bob Thomas/TSI; 8: ©Dick Luria/FPG; 10: ©William Westheimer/The Stock Market; 11: ©Stephen Simpson/FPG; 12: ©Jeff Zaruba/The Stock Market; 13: ©B. Chederros/Leo de Wys; 14: ©Larry Grant/FPG; 15: ©Vic Bider/TSI; 16: ©Telegraph Colour Library/FPG; 17: ©Ken Chernus/FPG; 18: ©Michael Rosenfeld/TSI; 19: ©Mason Morfit/FPG; 20: ©Dick Luria/FPG; 22: ©Michael Simpson/FPG; 23: Courtesy of Corel; 24: ©B. Busco/The Image Bank; 25: ©Weinberg/Clark/The Image Bank; 26: ©Joseph Drivas/The Image Bank; 27: ©Marc Yankus.

Introduction/Photo Essay
Fig.1:©Larry Grant/FPG;Fig. 2a:(c)Martin Rogers/TSI; Fig. 2b:©Andy Sacks/ TSI; Fig. 2c:©Howard Grey/TSI; Fig. 2d:©Jim Cummins/FPG; Fig. 3a:©Bruce Ayers/TSI; Fig. 3b:©Walter Hodges/TSI; Fig. 3c:©Ron Chapple/FPG; Fig. 3d:©Ron Chapple/FPG; Fig. 4:©Richard Kaylin/TSI; Fig. 5:Courtesy of Corel; Fig. 6:©Barros & Barros/The Image Bank; Fig. 7:Courtesy of Corel; Fig. 8:Courtesy of Levi Strauss & Co.; Fig. 9:©Tim Hazel/SPL/Photo Researchers; Fig.10:©Michael Simpson/FPG; Fig. 12a:©Arthur Tilly/FPG; Fig. 12b:©Stephen Simpson/FPG; Fig. 12c:©Andrew M. Levine/Photo Researchers; Fig.15:©Mehau Kulyk/SPL/Photo Researchers; Fig.16:©Hank Morgan/ Photo Researchers; Fig. 17:©Vladimir/Pcholkin/FPG; Fig. 18:©Erik Viktor/SPL/Photo Researchers; Fig. 19:Courtesy of Intergraph; Fig. 20:©Will & Deni McIntyre/Photo Researchers; Fig. 21:Courtesy of Corel Corporation.

Chapter 1
01.02 ©John Bagley; 01.03a:©Peter Steiner; 01.03b:©Shambroom/Photo Researchers; 01.04a:©The Stock Solution; 01.04b:Courtesy of Texas Instruments; 01.05a:©David R. Frazier/ Photo Researchers; 01.05b:©Damien Lovegrove/SPL/Photo Researchers; 01.08a:©Ed Kashi; 01.08b:Courtesy of IBM; 01.08c:(c)John Bagley; 01.08d:©Ed Taylor Studio/FPG; 01.09a:Courtesy of the Minnesota Supercomputer Center;

01.09b:Courtesy of the Minnesota Supercomputer Center; 01.10a:©Will & Deni McIntyre/Photo Researchers; 01.10b:©Mike Malyszko/FPG; 01.10c:©Tony Stone International; 01.11a:Courtesy of Pilot Corporation; 01.11b:Courtesy of Pilot Corporation; 01.MRC:Courtesy of the Century Plaza Suites Hotel; 01.GP:Courtesy of Kantek, Inc.; 01.MN.01:Courtesy of Connectix.

Chapter 2
02.02:©Neil Michael/Axiom; 02.03a:Courtesy of Knowledge Land; 02.03b:Courtesy of Knowledge Land; 02.03c:Courtesy of Knowledge Land; 02.05:Photo provided courtesy of Wired Magazine; 02.09.1:Courtesy of Lotus Development Corporation; 02.09.2:Courtesy of Lotus Development Corporation; 02.09.3:Courtesy of Lotus Development Corporation; 02.10:©Jeffery MacMillian; 02.MRC:(c)Greg Martin; 02.MN.01:©LLewellyn/ Uniphoto; 02.MN.02:Courtesy of Virgin Sound and Vision.

Chapter 3
03.09:Courtesy of Intel Corporation; 03.10:Courtesy of IBM; 03.11:Courtesy of Intel Corporation; 03.MRC:Courtesy of OnStar; 03.GP:©Tim Rue.
Planet Internet: All About Rio: Image reproduced with permission from ipanema.com.

Chapter 4
04.01a:Courtesy of Compaq Corporation; 04.01b:Courtesy of MacDonald's Corporation; 04.01c:Courtesy of IBM; 04.03a:©David Mallory Jones/Uniphoto; 04.03b:©David Biship/PhotoTake; 04.03d:Courtesy of Microsoft Corporation; 04.04a:©Vikki Hart/The Image Bank; 04.04b:Courtesy of Microsoft Corporation; 04.05:Courtesy of Cirque Corporation; 04.07a:Courtesy of Hewlett-Packard Company; 04.07b:Courtesy of Visioneer Communications, Inc.; 04.07c:Courtesy of Logitech, Inc.; 04.09a:Courtesy of Spectra Physics; 04.09b:Courtesy of McKesson Corporation; 04.11.1:Courtesy of IBM; 04.12:Courtesy of MidiLand; 04.13:©Hank Morgan/Photo Researchers; 04.14a:Courtesy of NEC Technologies; 04.14b:Courtesy of IBM; 04.14c:Courtesy of IBM; 04.15a:Courtesy of Hewlett-Packard Company; 04.16:Courtesy of Hewlett-Packard Company; 04.17a:Courtesy of Corel Corporation; 04.17b:Courtesy of Elscint Corporation; 4.17c:Courtesy of Corel Corporation;

04.19a–f:Stills from the video "Bonkers" used with permission from animators Eric Ritchey, Christina Li, Dave Byther, and Jason Baskett, animation faculty Profs. Kim Singhrs and Patrick Flynn, the Schools of Architecture, Electrical Engineering, and Computer Science at Washington State University, and Alias/Wavefront Technology for the donation of software used in production; 04.20a:©Hank Morgan/Science Source/Photo Researchers; 04.20b:©Berenguier/Jerrican/Photo Researchers; 04.21:©P. Goutier/The Image Works; 04.22:©Ed Kashi; 04.ND:©Telegraph Colour Library/FPG; 04.GP:Courtesy of Metatools, Inc.; 04.MN1:Courtesy of Florida State University; 04.MN2:Courtesy of Hyatt Corporation; 04.MN3:©Bob Thomas/TSI.
Planet Internet: Cartalk: http://www.cartalk.com; Doonsbury: Image ©1997 G.B. Trudeau, web page ©1997 Headland Digital Media.

Chapter 5
05.03a:©Frederick Bodin/Benjamin/Cummings; 05.03b:Courtesy of Kao Inforsystems Company; 05.04a:Courtesy of Ancodyne, Inc.; 05.04c:Courtesy of Seagate Technology Corporation; 05.05:Courtesy of Quantum Corporation; 05.06:Courtesy of Iomega Corporation; 05.10a:Courtesy of Pioneer Communications of America; 05.10b:Courtesy of NEC Technologies; 05.12:Courtesy of 3M Corporation.; 05.16a:©Lawrence Migdale/TSI; 05.MRC:©John Kelly/The Image Bank; 05.ND:©Telegraph Colour Library/FPG.
Planet Internet: PC Computing: Reprinted from PC/Computing. Copyright ©Ziff-Davis Publishing Co.; Jelly Belly: Used with permission of Herman Goelitz, Inc.; Snapple: Snapple is a registered trademark of Snapple Beverages Corporation; Cabodles Clip Art: http://www.Caboodles.com.

Chapter 6
06.01:Courtesy of Dell Corporation; 06.02.1:©Jose Louis Pelaes/The Stock Market; 06.05:Courtesy of Hayes Modem; 06.06:Courtesy of U.S Robotics; 06.11:©Hiroyuki Matsumoto/TSI; 06.16.1:Courtesy of IBM; 06.17:©John Turner/TSI; 06.18:Jim Cummins/FPG; 06.19:©Patti McConville/The Image Bank; 06.20a:©John Henley/The Stock Market; 6.20b:©Joe Cornish/TSI; 06.MRC:©Greg Pease/TSI; 06.ND:Courtesy of the Hyatt Hotel Corporation;

06.MN.01:Courtesy of Global Village Communications; 06.MN.03:Courtesy of Carnival Cruise Lines; 06.MN.04:©The Stock Market; 06.02.3:©Jose Pelaez/The Stock Market; 06.09d:©Rick Reinhard/FPG; 06.16.3:Courtesy of IBM; 06.20c:©HMS Images/The Image Bank; 06.20d:©Dan Bosler/TSI.
Planet Internet: Fashion Planet: Image reprinted with permission from Fashion Planet (www.fashion-planet.com); Price Waterhouse: Copyright 1997 ©Price Waterhouse World Firm, Ltd. All rights reserved.

Chapter 7
07.01:©Louis Psihoyos/ Matrix; 07.03:Courtesy of Netscape Communications; 07.ND:©Claudia Parks/The Stock Market; 07.GP:©Tom White Images. 07.08: Copyright 1997 Moore & Van Allen, PLLC, all rights reserved, used with permission; Kodak: Copyright © Eastman Kodak Company.

Chapter 8
08.03a:Courtesy of Eyedentify; 08.03b:Courtesy of Technology Recognition Systems; 08.MRC:©James Porto/FPG.
Planet Internet: Cyrano Love Letters: Used with permission. Copyright © 1997 Nando.net.

Chapter 9
09.09:Courtesy of Microsoft Corporation; 09.10:Joseph Maas/Paragon 3 09.14:©Adam Zakin/Benjamin/Cummings; 09.MRC:©Herbert Simms; 09.ND:Philadelphia Museum of Art/Corbis; 09.GP:Gary A. Conner/Photo Edit; 09.MN.01:Courtesy of Mindscape.
Planet Internet: World Wildlife: www.worldwildlife.org/action/home.htm developed in conjunction with NMP, Inc.; Cow-Boy: Used with permission from the Sega Corporation.

Chapter 10
Planet Internet: Tech City: www.computerworld.com/techcity/; Land Rover: www.LandRover.com developed in conjunction with Adjacency, Inc.; Kellogg: Copyright © 1997 Kelloggs Corporation.

Chapter 11
11.MRC:©Palmer/Kane /TSI; 11.ND:©Tom Draper Design/Seattle; 11.MN.01:©Mark Scott/FPG; 11.MN.02:©J.W. Burkey/TSI; 11.MN.03:©Romilly Lockyer/Image Bank; 11.PI:©Suzanne Opton.
Planet Internet: Amazon Books: Amazon.com site as of 8/15/97; reprinted with permission from Amazon.com.

Chapter 12
12.13:Courtesy of Microsoft Corporation; 12.ND:Photo provided courtesy of Hill & Knowlton, Inc.; 12.GP:©Tom White Images.

Chapter 13
13.05:Courtesy of Microsoft Corporation; 13.MRC:©Robert Visser/Greenpeace; 13.MN.01:©Matthew McVay/Stock Boston.
Planet Internet: Faces of Adoption: http://www.adopt.org; World Village: Copyright © 1997 Infomedia, Inc.

Chapter 14
14.MRC:(c) Ruven Afanador/Outline; 14.GP:©Tom White Images.

Chapter 15
15.02:Courtesy of Primavera; 15.03:©Peter Wiant; 15.MRC:© David Weintraub/Photo Researchers, Inc.; 15.ND:© Michael Simpson/FPG; 15.MN.01:Courtesy of Microsoft Corporation.
Planet Internet: Bartlett's Familiar Quotations: Reprinted with permission from Columbia University.

Chapter 16
16.02:©Ed Kashi/PhotoTake; 16.03a,b:Courtesy of AION Development Corporation; 16.04a:©Andy Sacks/TSI; 16.04b:Courtesy of Japan Airlines; 16.05a–d:Courtesy of Thinking Machines Corporation;16.06a:Courtesy of Dave Barrett/MIT; 6.06b:Courtesy of Control Data Corporation; 16.06c:©Fujiphotos/The Image Works; 16.07a:©P. Howell/Gamma-Liaison; 16.07b:Courtesy of VPL Research; 16.07c:Courtesy of David Sutton; 6.MRC:© Enrico Ferorelli; 16.ND:© Peter Chapman; 16.GP:Courtesy of BMW; 16.MN.01:© Hank Morgan/Rainbow; 16.MN.02:Courtesy of Superscape.
Planet Internet: MTV Copyright © 1997, MTV; Black Entertainment Television: Copyright 1997 Black Entertainment Television, Inc.

Visual Internet
Avalanche: Reprinted with permission from Avalanche Systems, Inc.; Iams: The Iams Company, makers of Eukanuba and Iams Foods; CandyStand and Oreo Hyper-Glyphics: Copyright © 1997 Nabisco, Inc. Developed by Skyworks Technologies, Inc.; Jazz: www.pobox.com/~onestopjazz; Andy's Garage: Andy's Garage Sale, Inc., a wholly owned subsidiary of Fingerhut Companies, Inc.; Warner Brothers: Copyright © 1997, Warner Brothers; Rollerblade: www.rollerblade.com developed in conjunction with Adjacency, Inc.

Buyer's Guide
Opener: Courtesy of Hewlett-Packard Company; page 3 top: Courtesy of Dell Corporation; bottom left: Courtesy of Princeton Graphic Systems; bottom right: Courtesy of MAG Innovision Systems; page 4 left: Courtesy of Gateway 2000; top right: Courtesy of IBM; middle: Courtesy of 3M Corporation; bottom: Courtesy of IBM; page 5 top left: courtesy of

IBM; right: Courtesy of Hewlett-Packard Company; bottom: Courtesy of Hewlett-Packard Company; page 6 top: Courtesy of Hewlett-Packard Company; bottom: Courtesy of IBM; page 7, 8: ©Neil Michael/Axiom.

Making Microchips Gallery
Opener: ©Manfred Kage/Peter Arnold, Inc.; 2: ©Geoff Tompkinson/SPL/Photo Researchers; 3: Courtesy of Precision Visuals International/SPL/Photo Researchers; 4: ©Robert Holmgren; 5: AT&T Archives; 6: Courtesy of IBM; 7: ©Ted Horowitz/The Stock Market; 8: Courtesy of TRW Inc.; 9: Courtesy of Micron Technology, Inc.; 10: ©Mel Lindstrom/TSI; 11: ©Andrew Syred/SPL/Photo Researchers; 12: AT&T Archives; 13, 14, 15: Courtesy of Hewlett-Packard Company; 16: ©Astrid & Hanns-Frieder Michler/SPL/Photo Researchers; 17: Courtesy of Advanced Micro Devices Inc.; 18: ©Mark Segal/TSI; 19: ©Telegraph Colour Library/FPG; 20: ©Rosenfeld Images Ltd./SPL/Photo Researchers; 21: ©Phil Matt/PhotoTake NYC.

Computers at Work Gallery
Opener: ©Arthur Meyerson; 1: ©Leo de Wys, Inc.; 2: ©Beck/The Stock Market; 3: ©Jay Freis/The Image Bank; 4: ©Mark Green/FPG; 5: ©Roger Tully/TSI; 6: ©Telegraph Colour Library/FPG; 7: ©Walter Hodges/TSI; 8: ©Charles Thatcher/TSI; 9: ©Mark Scott/FPG; 10: ©Howard Grey/TSI; 11: ©Dan Bosler/TSI; 12: ©Beck/The Stock Market; 13: Courtesy of IBM; 14: ©Lonnie Duka/TSI; 15: ©Jim Cummins/FPG; 16: ©Zigy Kaluzny/TSI; 17: Courtesy of Corel Corporation; 18: ©Pamela Hobbes; 19: Courtesy of Corel Corporation; 20: ©Diane Fenster; 21: Marc Yankus; 22: ©Marc Yankus; 23: ©Tom White; 24: ©Tom Tracy/TSI; 25: ©David Parker/600 Group/Science Source/Photo Researchers; 26: ©Index Stock Photo; 27: ©Hank Morgan/Science Source/Photo Researchers.

Computer Graphics Gallery
Opener: Bill Frymire; 1,2: Courtesy of Corel Corporation; 3: Image by John Stephens provided courtesy of Fractal Design Corporation; 4: ©Eric Yang; 5: Image by Judy York provided courtesy of Fractal Design Corporation; 6: Image by Marcia Broderick provided courtesy of Fractal Design Corporation; 7: Courtesy of Corel Corporation; 8: ©Diane Fenster; 9: Courtesy of Corel Corporation; 10: ©Wendy Grossman; 11: Courtesy of Corel Corporation; 12: ©Glenn Mitsui; 13: ©Bill Frymire; 14: Courtesy of Corel Corporation; 15: ©Nikita Beliaev; 16: ©Ian Armstrong; 17: ©Derek Owens; 18: ©Adrian Bauman; 19: ©Steve Gowers; 20: ©Rob Bolin; 21: ©Nathan O'Brien; 22: ©Ian Armstrong; 23–26: ©Katrin Eisman; 27: Courtesy of XAOS Corporation.

Index

controlling, as management function, 404, 405
control panel, in browsers, 199, 200
control structures, C-4–8, C-19
 iteration, C-7–8
 selection, C-5–6
 sequence, C-5
control unit, 70, 71, 87
cookies, 241, 244
COPY command (DOS), 350
copying, text blocks, 262, 271
copying and pasting, text blocks, 262
copyright issues
 Internet, 150, 151
 scanners, 102
 software, 45, 59
Corbis Publishing, 269
corrections, in word processing programs, 255
cost control, personal computer managers and, 412
cost reduction, computers and, 7
CPU. See central processing unit (CPU)
crash, head, 128, 149, 353
Cray supercomputers, 28
credit card fraud, 226
credit records, privacy of, 237–38
CRT. See cathode ray tube
CSMA/CD, 176, 187
Ctrl key, 98
current cells, in spreadsheet programs, 280, 293
cursors
 defined, 97, 117
 in word processing programs, 254
customer service, software for, 56
custom software, 42, 59
cutting and pasting, text blocks, 262, 271
CyberSuite, 25
cylinder method, of data organization, 133–34, 149

D

Dangerous Creatures, 45
data
 access plan, 141
 alphanumeric, D-0
 in databases, 308–9
 defined, 21
 ethics and, 116
 numeric, D-0
 organizing, 139–44
 processing, 144–48
data analysis, for systems analysis, 377–78
database management systems (DBMSs), 49–51, 59, 300–311
 defined, 300, 311
 entering data, 308–9
 field names, 307
 fields, 302
 field types, 307
 field widths, 307
 files, 302
 future of, 305
 key fields, 307
 models, 302
 operations, 309–10
 overview, 300–301

power of, 302–3
records, 302
relational, 302–3, 311
solving problems with, 304–6
transparency of, 303–4, 305
types of, 300
databases
 advantages of, 298, 301
 creating and using, 306–10
 defined, 140, 150, 300, 311
 file structure of, 306–8
 legal, 308
data communications, 23–25, 160–61, 186
 defined, 24, 160
 fraud, 226
 systems, 160–61, 186
data compression, 128, 149
data diddling, 226
Data Encryption Standard (DES), 240, 244
data entry operators, 58, 60
 in foreign countries, 96
data flow diagrams (DFDs), 377–78, 379, 394
 symbols in, 377
data gathering, for systems analysis, 376–77
data input, source data automation, 100–101
data integrity, personal computer managers and, 412–13
data items, 302, 311
data leakage, 226
data mining, 426–27, 435
data mirroring, 131, 149
data organization
 direct file processing, 142
 on hard disks, 131–34
 indexed file processing, 142–43
 methods, 142–43
 sequential file processing, 142
data points, in line graphs, 291, 293
data processing, 21, 144–48
 batch processing, 144–48
 transaction processing, 145–48
data redundancy, 301
data representation, 76–78
 binary system, 76–77
 coding systems, 77–78
data security, 232
datasheet view, in database management programs, 308
data stripping, 131, 149
data transfer, 144, 150
data transfer rate, 144, 150
data transmission, 164–67, 186
 analog, 164–65
 asynchronous, 166–67, 186
 combining methods of, 170–71
 digital, 164–65
 full-duplex, 167, 168, 186
 half-duplex, 167, 168, 186
 ISDN, 166–67, 186
 simplex, 167, 168, 186
 synchronous, 166–67, 186
data warehousing, 384
date fields, in databases, 307
dates, year 2000 problem, 320
DAT tape, 138, 150

DBMSs, See database management systems
debugging, in programming process, 323, 339
decentralized computer systems, 23–24, 33
decimal numbers, binary equivalents, 77
decision making, computers and, 6
decision support systems (DSSs), 409–10, 418
decision tables (decision logic tables), 378, 380, 394
decode, 74, 75
decoration, in spreadsheets, 283
default settings, 258
DEFRAG command, 358
DEL command (DOS), 350
Delete key
 making corrections with, 255
 uses of, 99
deleting, text blocks, 262, 271
demodulation, 165, 186
dependent variables, 409, 418
DES. See Data Encryption Standard
design view, in database management programs, 308
desk-checking, in programming process, 323, 339
desktop publishing, 263–69, 271
 defined, 263
 design, 265, 267
 fonts, 265–66
 halftones, 266–67
 kerning, 266
 leading, 266
 overview, 263–64
 publishing process, 264–67
 software, 48–49, 59, 267–68
detail design, in systems design, 379, 384–88
DFDs. See data flow diagrams
diagnostics, in programming process, 323, 339
difference engine, A-2, A-11
digital art, 269
digital audio tape (DAT), 138, 150
digital cameras, 109
digital transmission, 164–65, 186
digital video disks (DVD-ROM), 136, 150, 353
digitizing tablets, 114
DIR command (DOS), 350
direct-access storage device (DSAD), 142, 150
direct-connect modems, 165, 186
direct file processing, 141, 142, 150
directing, as management function, 404, 405
direction conversion, in system implementation, 391–92
disaster recovery plans, 231, 243
discrete word systems, 106, 117
disk drives, 22, 33, 128, 149
diskettes, 22, 33, 127–28
 advantages of, 127–28
 care of, 130
 components of, 128
 defined, 127, 149
disk packs, 128, 130
disk space, 130
 management, in Windows 98, 353

Mavis Beacon Teaches Typing, 254
medicine, computers and, 11
Meeting Meter, 53
meetings, costs of, 53
megabyte (MB), 77, 87, 131
megaflop, 83, 88
megahertz (MHz), 82, 88
memory
    addresses, 75–76
    background, 358
    components, 79–82
    defined, 19, 21, 33, 70, 72–73, 87
    foreground, 358
    locations, 75–76
    management, 358–60, 361
    protection, 359–60, 362
    RAM, 72, 80–82, 84, 88
    ROM, 72, 82, 84, 88
    semiconductor, 79–80
    sharing, 358–60
    virtual, 358–59
menus
    in browsers, 200, 216
    defined, 351
    pop-up, 351
    pull-down, 200, 216, 256–57, 270, 351
    in word processing programs, 256–57, 270
messages, in object-oriented programming, 337, 340
methods, in object-oriented programming, 335, 340
metropolitan area networks (MANs), 173, 187
MICR inscribers, 101, 102, 117
microcomputers. See personal computers
microphones, 23
microprocessors (microchips), 78, 87
    in automobiles, 73
    future technology, 85, 86
    history, A-7, A-11
    Intel, 84
    technological advances in, 78
Microsoft Access, 308
Microsoft Corporation, 351
    history, A-9, A-10, A-11
    Intellimouse, 97–98, 100
Microsoft Excel, 279
Microsoft Internet Explorer
    home page, 200
    in Windows 98, 353
Microsoft Network, 181–82
Microsoft Windows, 350–54, 361
    accessibility options, 354
    Windows 95, 352, 361
    Windows 98, 351, 352–53
    Windows CE, 353, 361
    Windows Explorer, 351
    Windows NT, 353–54, 361
    Wizards, 352, 353
micro-to-mainframe links, 173, 187
microwave transmission, 169, 170
milliseconds, 82
minicomputers, 29
MIPS, 83, 84, 88
MISs. See management information systems (MISs)
MIS managers, 405, 418
MITS Altair, A-0, A-2, A-8, A-9, A-11

MMX chip, 78, 88
models
    database management systems, 302
    in decision support systems, 409–10
    defined, 409
modems, 165–66, 186
    accessing the Internet with, 211
    acoustic coupler, 165, 186
    baud rate, 166
    cable, 211, 217
    data speeds, 165
    defined, 25, 33, 165
    direct-connect, 165, 186
    external, 165, 186
    internal, 165, 186
    in notebook and laptop computers, 166
    PC cards, 166, 186
    speed of, 162
    types of, 165–66
modulation, 165, 186
MO (magneto-optical) disks, 135, 149
monitors, 107–10, 118
    monochrome screens, 110, 118
monolithic chips, 80, 88
Moore's Law, 80
Mosaic, 197, 216
motherboards, 78, 79, 88
Motion Picture Experts Group. See MPEG
Motley Fool, 315
mouse, 20, 97–98, 100, 117
    trails feature, 110
mouse pointer, 97, 100, 117
mouse ring, 23
moving, text blocks, 261, 262, 271
MPEG, 136, 150
MS-DOS, 349–50, A-9, A-10
    commands, 349–50
multimedia, 136–38, 150
    applications, 137–38
    defined, 136
    disk requirements, 131
    hardware requirements, 136–37
    on the Internet, 139, 274–75
    plug-ins, 274–75
    sound output for, 112
multiprocessing, 356, 361
multiprogramming, 356–57, 361
    event-driven, 357
music
    on the Internet, 438
    output devices, 112

N

nanoseconds, 82, 83
natural languages, 326–27, 339, 424, 435
Nature Conservancy, 359
NCs. See net(work) computers
nested tags, B-4
netiquette, 214, 217
Netscape
    browser features, 201
    home page, 200
network cable, 174
net(work) computers (NCs) (net boxes), 31–32
network interface cards (NICs), 174, 187
network managers, 58, 60, 413–14, 418

network operating systems (NOSs), 354–55, 361
networks, 56, 160–88
    complexity of, 183–85
    components, 161–64
    computer commuting, 180–81
    data transmission, 164–67
    defined, 24, 161, 186
    design considerations, 162–64
    electronic data interchange, 179
    electronic fund transfers, 179
    electronic mail, 177
    facsimiles, 177–78
    file access, 162–63
    groupware, 178
    Internet, 182
    online services, 181–82
    operating systems, 354–55, 361
    privacy of employees on, 240
    protocols, 162
    teleconferencing, 178
    topologies, 162
    voice mail, 177
    wireless, 174
network topologies, 172, 173, 187
    bus, 172, 173, 187
    ring, 172, 173, 187
    star, 172, 173, 187
NewsCatcher, 172
newsgroups, 212–13, 217
    "adult," 213
    advertising in, 212–13
    lurking on, 212
    shorthand terminology, 212
    user behavior, 214–15
NICs. See network interface cards
nodes, in network topologies, 172, 187
noise, in communications links, 168, 169, 187
nonimpact printers, 110
nonvolatile RAM, 84
Nordstrom, 422
NOS. See network operating systems
notebook computers, 28, 30
    modems in, 166
Notes, 54
NOT operator, in Internet searches, 206
Nuclear macro virus, 234
number bases, D-2–7
    binary number system, 76–77, 87, D-2–3
    conversions between, D-3–7
    hexadecimal number system, D-3
    octal numbers system, D-3
number symbols, in spreadsheets, 282
numeric data, D-0
numeric fields, in databases, 307

O

objectives, of problems, 375, 394
object linking and embedding (OLE), 352, 361
object modules, 323, 339
object-oriented programming (OOP), 334–38, 340
    in business, 338
    languages, 337–38
    objects in, 334–37
objects
    activating, 337
    attributes, 335

walkthrough, in programming process, 323, 339
wand readers, 21, 33, 103, 117
WANs. *See* wide area networks (WANs)
Watson, Thomas J. Sr., A-3, A-11
Web. *See* World Wide Web
webcasting, 209–10, 217
WebCrawler, 207
webmasters, career potential, 221
web pages. *See also* home pages; HTML; Internet; World Wide Web
  adding images to, B-7-11
  adding links to, B-11–12
  appearance tags, B-6–7
  backgrounds for, B-12
  basic HTML tags, B-2–6
  frames in, 202, 204
  scrolling, 200
web sites. *See also* HTML; Internet; World Wide Web
  creating, 207–8, 217
  defined, 26
  hackers and, 224
  moving among, 204–5
  personal, 207–8
  rating systems, 208
  useless, 215
Web TV, 163
Well, The, 366
Western Governors University, 205
"what-if" analysis, in spreadsheets, 279, 293
wide area networks (WANs), 162, 172–73, 187

Windows (Microsoft). *See* Microsoft Windows
wireless keyboards, 23
wireless networks, 174
wire pairs, 168, 169
Wizards, in Windows 98, 352, 353
word processing, 252, 254–67, 270
  corrections in, 255
  creating, 254
  defined, 254
  desktop publishing, 263–69
  editing, 254
  features, 257–62
  find and replace, 260
  footnotes, 260
  formatting, 254, 257–59
  headers and footers, 261
  menus and buttons, 256–57
  overview, 254–56
  pagination, 260
  printing, 254
  print preview, 260
  retrieving, 254
  scrolling, 254–55
  search (find), 259
  spelling checkers, 262–63
  thesaurus programs, 262–63
  word wrap in, 255, 270
word processing software, 48–49, 56, 59
words (computer)
  defined, 77
  length of, 77
word wrap, in word processing programs, 255, 270
worksheets. *See also* spreadsheets
  defined, 279, 293

workstations, 29
World Wide Web, 26, 216. *See also* home pages; Internet; web pages; web sites
  business on, 209–11, 296–97
  copyright considerations, 150–51
  FAQs available on, 122–23
  history, 197–98
  multimedia plug-ins, 274–75
  privacy issues, 240–41
  resources on, 122–23
  searching, 201, 205–7
  site access restrictions, 344
  unusual sites, 248–49
WORM media, 135, 149
worms, 233, 244
Wozniak, Steve, A-8, A-9
write-once, read-many (WORM), media, 135, 149

X

x-axis, in line graphs, 290–91, 293

Y

Yahoo, 207
Yankee Doodle virus, 233
y-axis, in line graphs, 291, 293
year 2000 problem, 320

Z

zapping, 226
zone recording, 133